The
Business
Environment

Fourth Edition

The
Business
Environment

Fourth Edition

ADRIAN PALMER AND BOB HARTLEY

THE McGRAW-HILL COMPANIES

London · Burr Ridge IL · New York · St Louis · San Francisco · Auckland · Bogotá
Caracas · Lisbon · Madrid · Mexico · Milan · Montreal · New Delhi · Panama · Paris
San Juan · São Paulo · Singapore · Sydney · Tokyo · Toronto

The Business Environment
Adrian Palmer and Bob Hartley

Published by
McGraw-Hill Education
SHOPPENHANGERS ROA
MAIDENHEAD
BERKSHIRE SL6 2QL
Telephone: +44 (0) 1628 502 500
Fax: +44 (0) 1628 770 224
Website: http://www.mcgraw-hill.co.uk

British Library Cataloguing in Publication Data
A catalogue record for this book is available from the British Library

Library of Congress Cataloging in Publication Data
A catalogue record for this book is available from the Library of Congress

Editorial Director:	Melissa Rosati
Development Editor:	Caroline Howell
Editorial Assistant:	Nicola Wimpory
Senior Marketing Manager:	Petra Skyte
Senior Production Manager:	Max Elvey
New Media Developer:	Douglas Greenwood

Produced for McGraw-Hill by Steven Gardiner Ltd
Printed and bound by Ashford Colour Press Ltd, Gosport, Hants
Cover design by Hybert Design

ISBN 0 07 7097475

McGraw-Hill books are available at special quantity discounts.
Please contact the Corporate Sales Executive at the above address.

Brief Contents

Contents

3   Organizational objectives, growth and scale   70

The political environment   249

9   The legal environment   291

10   The international business environment   330

11   The social and demographic environment   378

Part 4 BRINGING IT TOGETHER: ENVIRONMENTAL ANALYSIS

13   The dynamic business environment: analysis and response   459

14   Case studies   492

Preface

Business organizations exist in an environment which is becoming increasingly complex and competitive. The firm in its business environment is similar to any living organism in the natural environment – survival and prosperity comes to those that are best able to adapt to their environment.

This book explores the complexity of forces that make up the business environment. It particularly aims to understand the impact of these forces on the activities of business organizations, and the nature of the decisions that organizations must take if they are to survive and prosper in a changing environment.

The book is structured in four parts. Part 1 provides contexts by analysing the general nature of the business environment. The key elements and forces in the environment are discussed within a systems framework.

In Part 2, we look inwardly at organizations to help us understand the internal factors that can facilitate or inhibit response to a changing external environment. A review is made of the different types of organizations which exist in the business environment, their objectives and internal processes. Part 2 concludes with a review of the increasingly important topic of the social responsibilities of business and the duties owed by business organizations to multiple stakeholder groups.

Part 3 switches the focus of attention to the external environment where we return to explore in more detail the environmental elements and forces introduced in Part 1. Dividing the business environment into a number of distinct areas inevitably involves some fairly arbitrary boundaries and the chapters in this part continually seek to provide links to other chapters. Part 3 begins with a discussion of the economic environment of business organizations, first at the microlevel of market competition and second at the macrolevel of national economic policy. Basic principles of micro- and macroeconomics are introduced. The political, legal, social and technological environments are explored in subsequent chapters. With increasing globalization of business, a chapter on firms' international environment brings together elements of the business environment in an international context.

Having explored individual elements of the business environment model introduced in Part 1, the final part returns to a more holistic perspective of the business environment. In this part we look at methods of analysing a complex environment and making decisions about future business strategy. Great attention is given to the role of information gathering, data analysis and the ways in which change can be implemented. Further integration of the business environment is provided through five case studies.

This fourth edition has itself responded to changes in the business environment with strengthened coverage of topics of contemporary concern. There is extensive coverage throughout the book of the impacts of electronic commerce. Social responsibility in marketing is given greater coverage at a time when the various stakeholders in organizations have ever-increasing expectations of their behaviour.

Learning throughout the book is supported in a number of ways. Each chapter contains a number of thought-provoking vignettes based on contemporary examples. In addition, each chapter has a mini case study with review questions and a further series of chapter review questions. Key terms are introduced and defined in a glossary. Suggestions are made for further reading and each chapter concludes with a list of websites which will allow the reader to pursue issues raised in the chapter. All of the websites listed in this book were freely accessible at the time of writing. The authors invite comments about any of the material contained in this book.

For this new edition we have updated the Online Learning Centre website, which contains the following additional material free of charge:

Accessible by students:

- Revision notes
- Extra question material with sample answers for exam revision
- Case studies with discussion questions
- Further reading and web links.

Accessible by lecturers only:

- Case Studies
- Extra essay style questions for teaching
- Lecturer's Manual
- PowerPoint lecture slides.

Visit the Online Learning Centre at www.mcgraw-hill.co.uk/textbooks/palmer

Adrian Palmer
mail@apalmer.com
www.apalmer.com

Bob Hartley
bob.hartley@northampton.ac.uk

The authors

Adrian Palmer is Professor of Services Marketing, University of Gloucestershire, Cheltenham, UK.

Bob Hartley is Head of Undergraduate Business Programmes, University College Northampton.

Specialist contributor to the Legal Environment: **Mary Mulholland** is Principal Lecturer in Law, De Montfort University, Leicester.

Publisher's Acknowledgements

We would like to thank the following university experts who took the time and effort to take part in the market research. They have added enormously to the development of this text.

Rishma Dattani – University of Wolverhampton
Alan Gully – Middlesex University, West London
Ian Harpe – Sheffield Hallam University
Linda Hesselman – University College London
Sarah Jenkins – University of Wales Cardiff
Lester Lloyd Reason – Anglia Polytechnic University
Steve Millard – Buckinghamshire Chilterns University College
A. E. Mitton – Manchester Metropolitan University
Lindsey Muir – Liverpool John Moores University
Tina Shadforth – Coventry University
Valerie Will – Paisley University

Chapter objectives identify the abilities and skills the student should be able to demonstrate after reading the chapter

chapter 1

What is the business environment?

CHAPTER OBJECTIVES

No company is an island, but exists in a sea of other organizations. Some of these organizations will be helpful to a company in meeting its objectives, while others will be out to compete with it. Some elements of the business environment will have direct and immediate impacts on an organization, while the effects of other elements may be more remote. Even within a company, one function can help or hinder the task of other functions.

The aim of this chapter is to review the nature of an organization's business environment and to understand the consequences for it of environmental change. The elements that make up an organization's micro-, macro- and internal environments are identified. After reading this chapter you should appreciate the complex interdependencies that exist in the business environment, and the growing importance of co-operative relationships between members of value chains.

Thinking around the subject boxes demonstrate examples and further explanations of key ideas in the chapter.

End of chapter Case Studies illustrate the issues covered in each chapter.

2.2.1 Sole trader or employee?

It can sometimes be difficult to decide whether a person is a self-employed sole trader or an employee of an organization. The distinction is an important one, because a trend during the 1990s was for large organizations to outsource many of their operations, often buying in services from apparently self-employed individuals. There can be many advantages in classifying an individual as self-employed rather than an employee. For the self-employed, tax advantages could result from being able to claim as legitimate business some expense items that are denied to the employee. The method of assessing income tax liability in arrears can favour an expanding small business. For the employer, designation as self-employed could save on National Insurance payments. It also relieves the employer of many

THINKING AROUND THE SUBJECT

What type of organization has won out in the battle to exploit the capabilities of the Internet? The early days of the Internet were dominated by stories of 'nerds' beavering away in a spare room at home to develop a website. This was a classic approach of the sole trader, which had previously seen low-cost, innovative individuals exploit new opportunities in mobile phone retailing and video rental, among many others. Free of any bureaucracy, entrepreneurial small sole traders could single mindedly pursue their dream of a 'new economy' in which any small business was able to communicate with the whole world from a humble makeshift office.

The small sole trader soon began to lose out in the competitive stakes, as big limited companies rapidly became the driving force in the Internet era. Buying their image on lumbering dinosaurs, the corporate giants adopted e-commerce, evolving their working practices and supply chains to gain substantial benefits. The advantages held by these established bricks-and-mortar companies over the upstart dotcom entrepreneurs included industry depth, a strong brand identity and customer trust. These established limited companies had good access to capital, and expertise in managing their existing businesses.

In a survey conducted in 2000, the consultant KPMG found that 75 per cent of European companies with turnover greater than £600 million had already used e-commerce to launch a new product or promote an existing one and 83 per cent expect to be using the Internet for business transactions within a year or two.

Meanwhile, what of the sole traders who were the pioneers of the Internet? Many of their business grew rapidly to establish a position in the marketplace, for example lastminute.com started on a very limited budget, but by 2001 had become a mainstream business with public limited company status. Other entrepreneurs could not keep up with the pace of competition and either sold out to larger, better resourced rivals (e.g. jungle.com sold out to the GUS group) or went into receivership through lack of funds (e.g. Boo.com).

With hindsight, could the respective roles of sole traders and large limited companies have been predicted? Was it only to be expected that sole traders would be the early innovators of a niche product, to be rapidly overtaken by larger companies when their markets became mainstream?

(1995) revealed the extent of small business owners' dissatisfaction with government regulations. More than 74 per cent of respondents complained about the burdens of VAT, which effectively makes businesses unpaid tax collectors for government. While larger firms may be able to afford a specialized accounting department, many small business owners are often left to to add the submission of VAT returns to their core tasks which they are expected to undertake personally. Government has hoped to stimulate the small business sector through requirements for certain government purchases to be put out to competitive bidding, but often the complexity of regulations governing competitive tenders have put many small businesses off of bidding. In the BCC survey, 71 per cent of managing directors of small businesses claimed that the requirement to complete government forms was costing them between 1 and 2 per cent of their turnover. Governments frequently declare that they are going to cut the red tape and bureaucracy which imposes burdens on small businesses. However, the historic reality has often been in the opposite direction. In Chapter 8 we will return to look at the work of the UK government's Better Regulation Task Force, which has sought to reduce the burden of government on business organizations.

CASE STUDY

TESCO STORES ADAPTS AS IT GROWS

Tesco Stores has grown to become a very profitable business and one of the UK's largest retailers. Today's Tesco is a long way from the humble barrow trading with which the business began, and an analysis of the company's growth illustrate the changes in form that Tesco has undergone in order to achieve its current market position.

The basis for the existing business of Tesco was founded shortly after the First World War when Jack Cohen left the flying corps with just £30 of capital available to him. His first taste of civilian entrepreneurship came with the decision to invest most of his £30 in the bulk purchase of tins of surplus war rations, which he proceeded to sell from a barrow in the street markets of London. As a sole trader, Jack Cohen needed the minimum of formality to get his business started. Furthermore, large capital investment was not required at a time when the typical retail unit was very small and selling through street markets was commonplace. The products which he sold were basic commodities which did not need large investment to create a distinctive and differentiated brand.

The name Tesco was first used by Cohen to differentiate the tea which he sold from that of his competitors. The name was derived by taking the first two letters of his own surname and prefixing it with the initials of the owner of the tea importing business from which he bought his tea – T. E. Stockwell. Cohen was buying the tea in bulk from the importer, repackaging it and selling it under a brand name.

Further growth came by developing sales to other market traders in addition to the sales he made to final consumers. He acted as a middleman, or wholesaler, operating from a small warehouse. Success came from being able to spot a good bargain and to fill his warehouse with cheap goods which he would resell to London street traders. Channels of distribution at this time tended to be based on a 'push' strategy in which entrepreneurs needed to actively sell products to the next stage in the chain of distribution.

Case Study Review questions follow each case study

Chapter Summaries and links to other chapters review and reinforce main topics covered in the chapter, and cross reference for further explanations and examples.

Chapter Review questions encourage students to assess and apply their knowledge of topics covered in the chapter.

Useful Websites are listed for further investigation and examples of relevant topics.

Key terms are grouped together at the end of each chapter so that you can review your understanding of new and important concepts defined throughout.

expectation. Legislation, while it was initially resisted by tour operators, has undoubtedly increased consumers' confidence in buying package holidays and lessened the chance of them buying a holiday from a rogue company, and thereby harming the reputation of the industry as a whole.

CASE STUDY Review Questions

1 What factors could explain the increasing amount of legislation which now faces tour operators?

2 Summarize the main consequences of the EU directive referred to above on the marketing of package holidays in the UK.

3 Is there still a role for voluntary codes of conduct in preference to legislation as a means of regulating the relationship between a tour operator and its customers?

CHAPTER Summary and links to other chapters

This chapter has noted the increasing effects that legislation is having on businesses. The principal sources of law have been identified. Statute law is becoming increasingly important, with more influence being felt from the EU. Legal processes and the remedies available to a firm's customers have been discussed. Voluntary codes of conduct are often seen as an alternative to law and offer firms lower cost and greater flexibility.

The discussion of business ethics in Chapter 5 relates closely to the legal environment. To many people, law is essentially a formalization of ethics, with statute law enacted by government (Chapter 8). The competition environment (Chapter 6) is increasingly influenced by legislation governing anticompetitive practices. We will see in Chapter 12 that legal protection for innovative new technologies is vital if expenditure on research and development is to be sustained. In addition to the aspects of law discussed in this chapter, legislation affects the status of organizations (Chapter 3), for example in the protection that is given to limited liability companies.

CHAPTER Review questions

1 Briefly identify the main ways in which the legal environment impacts on the activities of the sales and marketing functions of business organizations.

(Based on CIM Marketing Environment Examination)

2 Giving examples, evaluate the criticism that government legislation primarily impacts on those firms who can least afford to pay for it, mainly the small and the competitively vulnerable.

3 In the light of recent legislation in your own country, assess the extent to which the position of consumers compared to business has improved.

Finally, there is extensive coverage of the functions of pressure groups. The following references are useful for highlighting their relationship to business organizations.

Coxall, B. (2001) *Pressure Groups in British Politics*, Longman, Harlow.

Grant, W. (2000) *Pressure Groups and British Politics*, Palgrave, Basingstoke.

Useful websites

UK Government Gateway This is an important access point to UK government websites. Links are provided to many local and national government sites. http://www.open.gov.uk/

UK Parliament Provides information about the House of Commons and House of Lords including details of Committees, Acts, Bills, Elections, Members of Parliament and Publications. http://www.parliament.uk/

UK political parties Websites of the main UK political parties can be found at the following addresses:
Labour: http://www.labour.org.uk
Conservative: http://www.conservative-party.org.uk
Liberal Democrat: http://www.libdems.org.uk

Best Value in Local Government A forum for the UK local government (including police and fire) best value initiative. It will allow researchers and practitioners working with both pilot and non-pilot authorities to discuss how best value – economic, efficient and effective delivery of services – can be achieved. http://www.jbossell.co.uk/lists/best-value-in-local-government.html

EUsceptic.org A website providing links to various organizations sceptical of the European Union. http://www.eusceptic.org/

European Union online A useful entry point for information about the European Union. Provides information on the Parliament, the Council, the Commission, the Court of Justice, the Court of Auditors and other bodies of the European Union. http://europa.eu.int/index.en.htm

Fast Sheets on the European Union A comprehensive guide to how the European Community works, the Single Market, common policies, economic and monetary union and EU external relations. http://www.europarl.eu.int/factsheets/default.htm

Key terms

Act of parliament	Judiciary
Best value	Legislature
Cabinet	Lobbying
Charter Mark	Local government
Civil service	Non-departmental public bodies (NDPBs)
Directives	Parliamentary life cycle
European Commission	Political parties
European Council of Ministers	Pressure groups
European Court of Justice	Public private partnerships (PPPs)
European Economic Area (EEA)	QUANGOs
European Union (EU)	Regional government
Executive	Regulation
Ideology	Social exclusion
Judicial review	Task forces

Confederation of British Industry The CBI represents companies from all sectors of United Kingdom business and is the premier organization speaking for companies in the United Kingdom. Its website provides details of CBI surveys and discussion of topical economic issues. http://www.cbi.org.uk/home.html

Centre for Economic Performance The CEP was established by the Economic and Social Research Council. Based at the London School of Economics and Political Science, it is now one of the leading economic research centres in Europe and a world leader in economic research. Its website provides discussion on causes of countries' and firms economic performance. http://cep.lse.ac.uk

UK Treasury Home page of HM Treasury which includes analysis of recent government economic measures, revenue and expenditure analysis. http://www.hm-treasury.gov.uk/

European Central Bank Homepage of the ECB which provides European economic analysis. http://www.ecb.int/

Key terms

Accelerator effect	Interest rates
Borrowing	Invisibles
Business cycle	Macroeconomic analysis
Central bank	Models
Circular flow of income	Monetarism
Competitive cost advantage	Monetary Policy Committee
Confidence level	Multiplier
Deflation	Public sector net borrowing (PSNB)
Disposable income	Recession
Economic structure	Retail price index (RPI)
Exchange rate	Savings ratio
Fiscal policy	Turning point
Gross Domestic Product (GDP)	Unemployment
Inflation	Withdrawals
Injections	

Part 1
Contexts

1

What is the business environment?

CHAPTER OBJECTIVES

No company is an island, but exists in a sea of other organizations. Some of these organizations will be helpful to a company in meeting its objectives, while others will be out to compete with it. Some elements of the business environment will have direct and immediate impacts on an organization, while the effects of other elements may be more remote. Even within a company, one function can help or hinder the task of other functions.

The aim of this chapter is to review the nature of an organization's business environment and to understand the consequences for it of environmental change. The elements that make up an organization's micro-, macro- and internal environments are identified. After reading this chapter you should appreciate the complex interdependencies that exist in the business environment, and the growing importance of co-operative relationships between members of value chains.

1.1 SYSTEMS AND ENVIRONMENTS

In its most general sense, an environment can be defined as everything which surrounds a system. The environment of a central heating system, for example, comprises all of those phenomena which impact on the system's ability to operate effectively. The environment would therefore include such factors as the external air temperature, the insulation properties of the rooms being heated, the quality and consistency of fuel supplied, etc. A business organization can similarly be seen as a system, whose performance is influenced by a whole range of phenomena in its environment.

Business organizations exist to turn inputs from their environment (e.g. materials, labour and capital) into goods and services which customers in the environment seek to purchase. This transformation process adds value to the inputs, so that buyers are prepared to pay more to the business organization than the cost of resources that it has used up in the production process. This is the basis of a simple model of the organization in its environment illustrated in Figure 1.1. This transformation process within the organization cannot be seen as a steady state, because external environmental influences are continually shifting, so as to undermine the current balance within the system. Just as the central heating thermostat has to constantly react to ensure a balance between its inputs (the energy source) and its outputs (the required amount of heat), so too organizations must constantly ensure that the system continues to transform inputs into higher value outputs.

Of course, the organizations which form the centre of this transformation process take many shapes and forms, from a small sole trader through to a large multinational. The nature of the latter greatly affects the way in which it can adapt to its external environment. We will explore the great diversity of organizational types in the next chapter in the context of their ability to respond to environmental change.

Figure 1.1
The organization in its environment

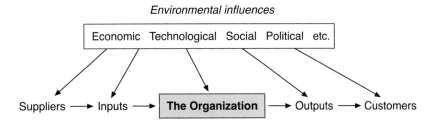

Figure 1.2
The principal elements of a business organization's environment

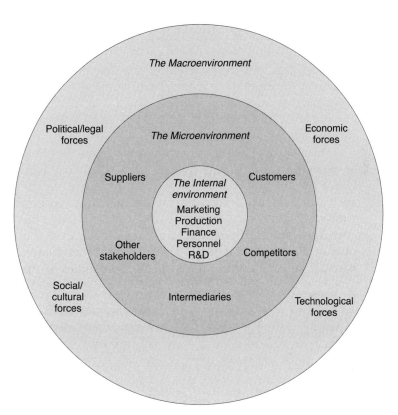

Throughout this book, we are going to disaggregate a business organization's environment into a number of components. For now, we will introduce three important elements of the business environment:

■ The microenvironment

■ The macroenvironment

■ The internal environment.

These are introduced schematically in Figure 1.2.

The external environment comprises all of those forces and events outside the organization that impinge on its activities. Some of these events impinge directly on the firm's activities – these can be described as forming an organization's *micro-environment*. Other events that are beyond the immediate environment nevertheless affect the organization and can be described as the *macroenvironment*. As well as looking to the outside world, managers must also take account of factors within other functions of their own firm. This is referred to as the *internal environment*.

The microenvironment of an organization includes suppliers and distributors. It may deal directly with some of these, while others exist with whom there is currently no direct contact, but could nevertheless influence its policies. Similarly, an organization's competitors could have a direct effect on its market position and form part of its microenvironment.

Beyond this immediate microenvironment is the macroenvironment which comprises a whole set of factors that can indirectly affect an organization's relationship to its markets. It may have no direct relationships with legislators as it does with suppliers, yet their actions in passing new legislation may have profound effects on the markets that the organization seeks to serve, as well as affecting its production costs. The macroenvironmental factors cover a wide range of nebulous phenomena. They represent general forces and pressures rather than institutions with which the organization relates.

Why should we study the business environment of organizations? History is full of examples of organizations that have failed to understand their operating environment, or simply failed to respond to change in the environment. The result has been a gradual decline in their profitability, and eventually they may cease to exist as a viable business unit. Theodore Levitt called this 'marketing myopia' and cited the example of railway companies who focused their vision on providing railway services, but failed to take account of the development of road transport (Levitt, 1960). Consider these more recent examples:

- The retailer Marks and Spencer assumed that its position was unassailable, but failed to take account of the great improvements in value being offered by its competitors. The result was that many of Marks and Spencer's loyal customers deserted it, leading to a sharp fall in profitability.

- The Shell oil company alienated many people with its proposal to dump the Brent Spar oil platform at sea, ignoring changing public attitudes towards the ecological environment in favour of its own technical analysis of the merits of dumping at sea.

- During the late 1990s, mobile phone companies made false assumptions about how people would continue to upgrade their mobile phones, resulting in over-enthusiastic demand forecasts and major cutbacks in the sector in 2001.

On the other hand, there have been many spectacular successes where organizations have spotted emerging trends in their business environment, and capitalized on these with new goods and services, or new ways of operating their business, in order to meet the new opportunities presented within the environment. Consider these examples:

- In the airline market, companies such as Ryanair and EasyJet spotted the opportunities represented by government deregulation and offered profitable low-cost 'no frills' air services, often aimed at people who would not previously have flown.

■ Many supermarkets and farmers have noted consumers' concern for the purity of the food which we eat, and this, combined with rising incomes, has led to the development of ranges of organic foods.

■ Many of the United Kingdom's pub owners have identified changing social behaviour, with less people using pubs as a regular venue primarily for beer drinking, but much greater dining out for social purposes. This has led breweries to increase their profits by reconfiguring their pubs as restaurants.

There is every indication that the pace of change in most organizations' business environments is speeding up, and it is therefore increasingly important for organizations to have in place systems for monitoring their environment and, just as importantly, for responding appropriately to such change. There is evidence that successful organizations are not so much those that deliver value to customers today, but those that understand how definitions of value are likely to change in the future. A company may have been very good at creating value through the typewriters that it made, but it may nevertheless have failed to deliver value into the future had it not understood the impact of information technology. In the eyes of customers, the company's traditional products would no longer represent good value when compared with the possibilities presented by the new technologies.

Of course, it is much more difficult to predict the future than to describe the past. A stark indication of the rewards of looking forwards rather than backwards is provided by an analyst who studied stock market performance. If a cumulative investment of $1 had been invested from 1900 on 1 January each year in the stock which had performed best in the previous year, and then reinvested the following year, the accumulated value in 2000 would have been just $250. However, if it had been invested each year in the stock which performed best in the year ahead, the accumulated value would be over $1 billion. Successful companies have often been those who understand their business environment and have invested in growth areas, while cutting back in areas which are most likely to go into decline. Being first to market when trends are changing can be much more profitable than simply reacting to a market trend. However, predicting future trends can be very difficult and can involve a lot of risk. The aim of this book is to provide frameworks for making well-informed judgements about the likely future state of the business environment, based on a sound analysis of emerging trends.

1.2   THE MICROENVIRONMENT

The microenvironment of an organization can best be understood as comprising all those other organizations and individuals who directly or indirectly affect the activities of the organization. The following key groups can be identified:

1   *Customers* are a crucial part of an organization's microenvironment. In a competitive environment, no customers means no business. An organization should be concerned about the changing requirements of its customers and should keep in touch with these changing needs by using an appropriate information gathering system. In an ideal world, an organization should

Figure 1.3
Plant growing has traditionally been associated primarily with the agricultural sector. However, Crocus.co.uk has shown how even such a basic agricultural activity can be transformed into a service. The company doesn't just grow and sell plants, but offers a complete service to the buyer which includes delivering and planting, as well as continuing to give advice about caring for the plant
(*Source*: Reproduced with permission of Crocus.co.uk)

We deliver it. We plant it.

We email advice on it.

It's a wonder we don't come round

and tuck it in at night.

At Crocus, our trained gardeners will deliver* weekends, mornings or until 8 in the evening. We'll plant for you if you like. And after a fond farewell, we'll even send your plants a regular email to make sure they're alright.

crocus.co.uk
GARDENERS BY NATURE

*Service only available in certain parts of the country.

know its customers so well that it is able to predict what they will require next, rather than wait until it is possibly too late and then follow.

2   *Suppliers* provide an organization with goods and services that are transformed by the organization into value-added products for customers. Very often, suppliers are crucial to an organization's marketing success. This is particularly true where factors of production are in short supply and the main constraint on an organization selling more of its product is the shortage of production resources. For example, following the Kobe earthquake in 1995, supplies of some types of computer chips became scarce, affecting computer assemblers' production schedules and consequently the range and prices of computers sold to the public. For companies operating in highly competitive markets where differentiation between products is minimal, obtaining supplies at the best possible price may be vital in order to be able to pass on cost savings in the form of lower prices charged to customers. Where reliability of delivery to customers is crucial, unreliable suppliers may thwart a manufacturer's marketing efforts.

3   *Intermediaries* often provide a valuable link between an organization and its customers. Large-scale manufacturing firms usually find it difficult to deal with each one of their final customers individually, so they choose instead to sell their products through intermediaries. The advantages of using intermediaries are discussed below. In some business sectors, access to effective intermediaries can be crucial for marketing success. For example, food manufacturers who do not get shelf space in the major supermarkets may find it difficult to achieve large volume sales.

4   *Other stakeholders* form an increasingly important part of an organization's microenvironment. In the case of customers, suppliers and intermediaries, an

---

THINKING AROUND THE SUBJECT

Can a company be a bad citizen, yet still be rated highly by customers? Research has suggested that consumers have clear ideas about which companies they trust and which they distrust. More importantly, it would appear that trust developed in different aspects of a company's environment feeds into how they are trusted as suppliers of goods and services. The message is clear – being a good citizen to all stakeholders is good for profitability.

The Consumers' Association carried out a survey of 1600 people in July 1998 and asked respondents to give detailed views on selected companies, covering issues of trust, corporate citizenship and corporate branding. Consumers were questioned on 12 aspects of trust, ranging from firms' honesty towards customers, how they treat staff, if their pricing is competitive and how truthful they are in advertising. The consistently high performing companies included Marks and Spencer, John Lewis and Boots, with Virgin, the Co-op and the BBC close behind. Sky television, British Airways and Ford were among the worst performers. It appeared that bad publicity on issues of employment relations and the natural environment fed through to customers. Issues such as the handling of a recent strike at British Airways seemed to have had a negative impact, while the Co-op and The Body Shop benefited from publicity about their environmental and ethical policies. The survey found a high correlation between a company's citizenship rating, customer satisfaction and loyalty.

organization has some form of contractual relationship (or may conceivably have, if it targets new customers, or changes suppliers or intermediaries). However, there is a wide range of other organizations and individuals in a firm's microenvironment which can directly affect its marketing effectiveness. These are sometimes referred to as the 'publics' of an organization and include pressure groups, government agencies and the local community. Society at large has rising expectations of organizations that are increasingly having to act in a socially responsible manner. A factory may, for example, be able to emit lawful amounts of pollution from its factory and doing so may have no direct consequence for the dealings it has with its customers, suppliers or intermediaries. However, the support of the affected publics may be crucial in the future, if, for example, the firm seeks planning permission to extend its plant. The social responsibility of organizations is an increasingly important subject which is considered in Chapter 5.

1.2.1   **Relationships between members of an organization's microenvironment**

A firm's microenvironment is distinguished from its macroenvironment by being comprised of actual individuals and organizations with whom the firm does business, or at least may potentially do business. This is sometimes described as the 'environmental set' of an organization, and an example of an environmental set for a car manufacturer is shown in Figure 1.4.

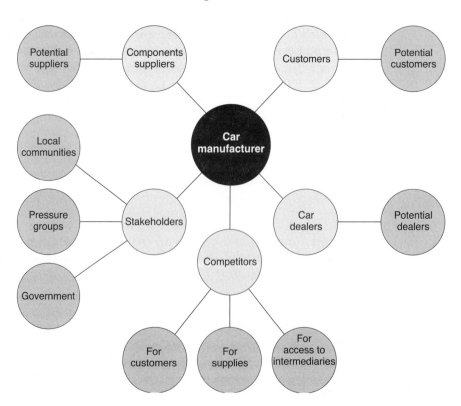

Figure 1.4
The 'environmental set' of a car manufacturer

The relationship between set members is likely to be complex and constantly changing. Change can take a number of forms, including:

- Shifts in the balance of power between members of the environment (e.g. retailers becoming more dominant relative to manufacturers)
- The emergence of new groups of potential customers
- Fringe pressure groups may come to represent mainstream opinions, in response to changes in social attitudes.

Understanding the relationship between members of an organization's environmental set is a crucial part of environmental analysis. Later in this chapter, shifts in relationships between buyers and sellers in a value chain will be reviewed. In later chapters, economic, political, social and technological forces will be reviewed in terms of their likely impacts on a firm's relationships with members of its environmental set.

1.3   THE MACROENVIRONMENT

While the microenvironment comprises individuals and organizations with whom a company interacts, the macroenvironment is more nebulous. It comprises general trends and forces that may not immediately affect the relationships that a company has with its customers, suppliers and intermediaries, but, sooner or later, macro-environmental change will alter the nature of these relationships. As an example, change in the population structure of a country does not immediately affect the way in which a company does business with its customers, but, over time, it may affect the numbers of young or elderly people who it is able to do business with.

Most analyses of the macroenvironment divide the environment into a number of areas. The principal headings, which form the basis for chapters of this text, are described below. It must, however, be remembered that the division of the macroenvironment into subject areas does not result in watertight compartments. The macroenvironment is complex and interdependent and these interdependencies will be brought out in later chapters. These are the headings for macroenvironmental analysis which are commonly used:

1.3.1   The economic environment

Businesses need to keep an eye on indications of a nation's prosperity. There are many indicators of a nation's economic health, of which two of the most common are measures of gross domestic product (GDP) and household disposable income. Many of these indicators tend to follow cyclical patterns related to a general economic cycle of expansion followed by contraction.

Throughout the economic cycle, the consumption of most goods and services tends to increase during the boom period and to decline during recessionary periods. The difficulty in forecasting the level of demand for a firm's products is therefore often quite closely linked to the difficulty of forecasting future economic prosperity. This difficulty is compounded by the problem of understanding the relationship between economic factors and the state of demand – most goods

In the late 1990s it became fashionable to talk about a 'new economy'. The environment of business organizations was to be changed forever in a brave new world in which 'new' Britain was ruled by 'new' labour, inhabited by 'new' man, who works in the 'new economy' and learns about the world through 'new' media. Electronic commerce would allow for almost infinite communication possibilities, breaking down international trade and cultural barriers in the process. Monopolies would be broken by the powerful forces of global competition facilitated by the Internet, and our neighbours would become not the person who lives next door, but a person anywhere in cyberspace who shares our interests and lifestyle. As the world entered the new millennium, it seemed that the business environment would never be the same again, or at least this is what many people thought.

Of course, many 'big ideas' have a habit of imploding and we need to ask whether any of the promises of the 'new world' have been delivered, or are ever likely to be. The idea that the 'new economy' had banished the economic cycle of prosperity and recession appeared to be dubious as the United States economy entered recession in 2001 after a prolonged period of expansion. Many questioned the myth of 'new man' as something which was more talked about in glossy magazines than experienced in everyday life.

Many of the 'new' world phenomena which helped to define the new economy soon began to lose their sparkle, leaving observers wondering whether there was really anything new. As an example, many commentators were excited by the prospects of new media advertising, and justified this by pointing to Procter and Gamble's decision to direct 80 per cent of its promotion budget to new media. But old media has a habit of fighting back hard, as witnessed by the huge amount of advertising by the new media owners themselves in traditional newspapers and television channels.

It soon became recognized that the 'new' economy is very dependent upon the 'old' economy. Electronic communication may be fine in theory as a means of improving global competition, but somebody still has to manufacture goods and deliver them, invariably using old economy methods.

Had the whole structure of the business environment changed, or was it simply transient details which had caused such excitement?

and services are positively related to total available income, but some, such as bus services and insolvency practitioners, are negatively related. Furthermore, while aggregate changes in spending power may indicate a likely increase for goods and services in general, the actual distribution of spending power among the population will influence the pattern of demand for specific products. In addition to measurable economic prosperity, the level of perceived wealth and confidence in the future can be an important determinant of demand for some high-value services.

An analysis of the economic environment will also indicate the level of competitor activity – an oversupply of products in a market sector normally results in a downward pressure on prices and profitability. Competition for resources could also affect the production costs of an organization, which in turn will affect its production possibilities and pricing decisions. Rising unemployment may put downward pressure on wage rates, favouring companies who offer a labour-intensive service.

1.3.2 **The political environment**

Politicians are instrumental in shaping the general nature of the external environment as well as being responsible for passing legislation that affects specific types of organization. At a national level, government is responsible for the nature of the economic environment (through its monetary and fiscal policy), the distribution of income and wealth between the public sector, the company sector and individuals and also between different groups of individuals. As the legislator, government passes laws that can affect market and production possibilities for individual firms, including the competitive framework within which firms operate.

The political environment includes supranational organizations that can directly or indirectly affect companies. These can be highly specific in their effects on an industry (e.g. the International Civil Aviation Organization is an international quasi-governmental body concerned with setting international standards in civil aviation) or they can be general multilateral agreements between governments (e.g. the World Trade Organization affects access to overseas markets for a number of industries).

1.3.3 **The social and cultural environment**

Attitudes to specific products change through time and at any one time between different groups. As an example, attitudes towards healthy living have changed from representing values held by a small fanatical minority to those that now represent mainstream cultural values. Businesses who monitored this emerging value system have been able to respond with a wide range of goods and services, such as fitness clubs and residential health breaks. The dominant cultural attitude towards the role of women has similarly changed, presenting many new challenges for marketers. The increased acceptability for young mothers to continue working has given rise to a large child and home care service sector. New challenges for businesses are posed by the diverse cultural traditions of ethnic minorities, as seen by the growth of travel agencies catering for families wishing to visit relatives or to go on religious pilgrimages.

1.3.4 **The demographic environment**

Changes in the size and age structure of the population are critical to many organizations, for predicting both the demand for its products and the availability of personnel required for production. Analysis of the demographic environment raises a number of important issues. Although the total population of most Western countries is stable, their composition is changing. Most countries are experiencing an increase in the proportion of elderly people.

Organizations have monitored this growth and responded with the development of residential homes, cruise holidays and financial portfolio management services aimed at meeting the needs of this growing group. At the other end of the age spectrum, the birth rate of most countries is cyclical. The decline in the birth rate in the United Kingdom in the late 1970s initially had a profound effect on those manufacturing and services companies providing for the very young, such as maternity wards in hospitals and kindergartens. Organizations that monitored the progress of this diminished cohort were prepared for the early 1990s when there were fewer teenagers requiring high schools or wanting to buy music from record shops. Companies who had relied in the early 1980s on the supply of teenage labour to provide a cheap input to their production process would have been prepared for the downturn in numbers by substituting the quantity of staff with quality and by mechanizing many jobs previously performed by this group.

Other aspects of the demographic environment that organizations need to monitor include the changing geographical distribution of the population (between different regions of the country and between urban and rural areas) and the changing composition of households (especially the growing number of single person households).

1.3.5   The technological environment

Businesses need to monitor technological developments and to understand their possible impact on four related business areas:

1   Technological development allows new goods and services to be offered to consumers – mobile telecommunications, karaoke bars and multimedia computers are recent examples.

2   New technology can allow existing products to be made more cheaply, thereby lowering their price and widening their markets. In this way, more efficient aircraft have allowed new markets for air travel to develop.

3   Technological development allows for new methods of distributing goods and services. Bank ATM machines allow many banking services to be made available at times and places that were previously not economically possible, while modern technology-based picking and scheduling systems allow home shopping services to be operated more efficiently than hitherto.

4   New opportunities for companies to communicate with their target customers have emerged. Many travel and financial services organizations have used information technology to develop databases to target potential customers and to maintain a dialogue with established customers.

1.3.6   The information environment

Information represents a bridge between the organization and its environment and is the means by which a picture of the changing environment is built up within the organization. Knowledge is one of the greatest assets of most organizations and its contribution to sustainable competitive advantage has been noted by many. In 1991, Ikujiro Nonaka began an article in the *Harvard Business Review* with a simple statement: 'In an economy where the only certainty is uncertainty, the one sure source of lasting competitive advantage is knowledge' (Nonaka, 1991). A firm's knowledge base is likely to include, among other things, an understanding of the precise needs of customers; how those needs are likely to change over time; how those needs are satisfied in terms of efficient and effective production systems and an understanding of competitors' activities.

Information about the current state of the environment is used as a starting point for planning future strategy, based on assumptions about how the environment will

The Internet is not just a tool that organizations can use to send messages to customers, suppliers and intermediaries. Monitoring chat groups and critical websites has become an important activity for organizations and their public relations agencies, anxious to spot any general shifts in attitudes, and specific comments which may harm the organization. News now crosses geographical frontiers quicker than a blink of the eye and corporate reputations can be savaged as disgruntled customers and shareholders swap comments on the World Wide Web. Thorns in the side of PR people include the McSpotlight site (www.mcspotlight.org) which carries information critical of McDonald's restaurants and the Boycott Shell site (www.essential.org/action/shell). Such sites can be created without the companies' knowledge, if they are not monitoring, and contributing to, the forums and chat rooms. And it can end up as a damaging mix of rumour and untruths.

Public relations agencies that have the technical expertise have set up monitoring services. One PR consultancy, Edelman, monitors the Internet, checking on 33 000 user groups and bulletin boards and regularly prepares web pages for its clients in anticipation of crises. These are then 'hidden' on the website, ready to be activated if needed.

Businesses have had to face up to the new realities of the Internet. Response times need to be immediate, with no specific deadlines that are typical of conventional published media. But at the same time, activists are changing the nature of the game which they have to deal with. When environmental activists staged a sit-in at Shell's London offices in 1999, the group broadcast the protest live to the Internet and e-mailed the press using a digital camera, laptop computer and mobile phone.

Quite aside from the battle of information technology is the fundamental question: why did a company allow itself to get into the position of exposing itself to criticism? Could this not have been foreseen? If there is little for people to campaign about, the dissident websites would probably lose much of their support.

change. It is also vital to monitor the implementation of an organization's corporate plans and to note the cause of any deviation from plan, and to identify whether these are caused by internal or external environmental factors. Information allows management to improve its strategic planning, tactical implementation of programmes and its monitoring and control. In turbulent environments, having access to timely and relevant information can give a firm a competitive advantage. This can be manifested, for example, in the ability to spot turning points in the business cycle ahead of competitors; to respond more rapidly to customers' changing preferences; and to adapt manufacturing schedules more closely to demand patterns, thereby avoiding a build up of stocks.

We will look in more detail at the ways in which information technology influences firms' business environment in Chapter 12, and will explore the implications of information for firms' responses to environmental change in Chapter 13.

1.4 VALUE CHAINS

It was noted at the beginning of this chapter that the purpose of organizations is to transform inputs bought from suppliers into outputs sold to customers. In carrying

Table 1.1   A value chain for ice cream

Value chain member	Functions performed
Farmer	Produces a basic commodity product – milk
Milk merchant	Adds value to the milk by arranging for it to be collected from the farm, checked for purity and made available to milk processors
Ice cream manufacturer	By processing the milk and adding other ingredients, turns raw milk into ice cream. Through promotion, creates a brand image
Wholesaler	Buys bulk stocks of ice creams and stores in warehouses close to customers
Retailer	Provides a facility for customers to buy ice cream at a place and a time that is convenient to them, rather than the manufacturer

out such a transformation, organizations add value to resources. In fact, the buyer of one firm's output may be another firm which treats the products purchased as inputs to its own production process. It in turn will add value to the resources and sell on its outputs to customers. This process can continue as goods and services pass though several organizations, gaining added value as they change hands. This is the basis of a value chain.

An illustration of the principles of a value chain can be made by considering the value-added transformation processes that occur in the process of making ice cream available to consumers. Table 1.1 shows who may be involved in the value-adding process and the value that is added at each stage.

The value of the raw milk contained in a block of ice cream may be no more than a couple of pennies, but the final product may be sold for over one pound. Customers are happy to pay one pound for a few pennies' worth of milk because it is transformed into a product that they value and it is made available at a time and place where they want it. In fact, on a hot sunny day at the beach, many buyers would be prepared to pay even more to a vendor who brings cold ice cream to them. Value – as defined by customers – has been added at each stage of the transformation process.

Who should be in the value chain? The ice cream manufacturer might decide that it can add value at the preceding and subsequent stages better than other people are capable of doing. It may, for example, decide to operate its own farms and produce its own milk, or sell its ice cream direct to the public. The crucial question to be asked is whether the company can add value more cost-effectively than other suppliers and intermediaries. In a value chain, it is only value in the eyes of customers that matters. If high value is attached to having ice cream easily available, then distributing it through a limited number of company-owned shops will not add much value to the product.

The process of expanding a firm's activities through the value chain is often referred to as vertical integration where ownership is established. Backward vertical integration occurs where a manufacturer buys back into its suppliers. Forward vertical integration occurs where it buys into its outlets. Many firms expand in both directions.

With service being used as an increasingly important basis for differentiation

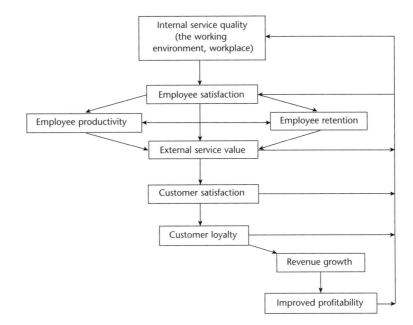

Figure 1.5
The service–
profit chain
(*Source*: Adapted from
Heskett *et al.* 1998)

between competing products, it is important that an organization looks not only outwardly at the value chain, but also inwardly at its own service profit chain. The concept of the service–profit chain is based on the idea that employee satisfaction and productivity feeds into customer satisfaction and loyalty, thereby improving profitability. Profitability in turn can help create a more productive and satisfying work environment (Figure 1.5).

Developments in information technology are offering new insights into the link between output quality and financial performance. Large multiple outlet service organizations are increasingly able to experiment with elements of service quality in test sites and to judge economic performance over time. A fast-food restaurant, for example may implement a new staff payment system or training programme in a number of 'experimental' sites and will be able to identify changes in perform- ance relative to other 'control' branches. Some service providers have disaggregated their information even further by linking service quality questionnaires to features of the service which a respondent actually received. In this way, individual employees or groups of employees can be linked to measures of quality. While information technology is opening up new possibilities for correlating data about inputs and perceived outcomes, the problem of analysing cross-sectional data remains. It is very difficult within a research framework to isolate all of the con- tributors to customers' perceptions of quality except those which the researcher is interested in.

1.4.1   **Intermediaries and channels of distribution**

The complexity of a firm's marketing environment can be seen in the pattern of intermediaries used to get goods and services from the producer to the consumer. Most large-scale manufacturing organizations cannot realistically hope to deal directly with each of the people who consume its products. Instead, they choose to deal through intermediaries, creating sets of interdependencies within their marketing environment.

A 'channel of distribution' comprises all those people and organizations involved in the process of transferring title to a product from the producer to the consumer. These are referred to as 'intermediaries'. Sometimes, products will be transferred directly from producer to final consumer – a factory selling specialized kitchen units directly to the public would fit into this category. Alternatively, the producer could sell its output through retailers or, if these are considered too numerous for the manufacturer to handle, it could deal with a wholesaler who in turn would sell to the retailer. Sometimes more than one wholesaler is involved in the process.

Intermediaries perform a number of functions:

1 They assist in the process of value creation, through undertaking any of the activities described below.

2 They make products locally available to consumers. Instead of customers having to travel to a central point of production, intermediaries assist in the task of making goods and services locally available at a time and a place that customers value.

3 They break down volumes from the very large quantities produced by the manufacturer to the small volumes required by the final customer.

4 In breaking down volume, intermediaries assist in the task of transferring ownership of goods and services. If the chocolate manufacturer Cadbury had to deal with each buyer of its products, its administrative and financial systems would be overwhelmed. It is much easier for it to deal with a small number of wholesalers who in turn deal with a larger number of retailers who sell the chocolate to millions of final customers.

5 Intermediaries provide valuable sales support at a local level, especially at the point of purchase. While manufacturers can advertise their products to the public nationally through the media, intermediaries can supplement this with valuable local promotional support.

6 Where a manufacturer is seeking to enter a market with which it is unfamiliar (e.g. a new overseas market), an intermediary can provide valuable insights into the proposed market.

7 Sometimes, intermediaries process goods and services as well as making them available to customers. Timber merchants, for example, cut timber to size for customers and car distributors carry out predelivery inspection of cars.

8 Customers often prefer to buy goods and services from intermediaries who offer a choice of competing products (Figure 1.6). Sometimes, customers may show greater loyalty to the intermediary than to the producer (e.g. many buyers of financial services may trust their broker of long standing to choose between competing policies on their behalf).

9 Goods and services often require after-sales support, such as carrying out warranty repairs on manufactured goods. Manufacturers often find this easier to undertake through intermediaries than doing it themselves.

Figure 1.6
In selling insurance intermediaries have a valuable role to perform in finding the best quotation for the client and providing after-sales service. NIG Skandia has built a successful business by working closely with insurance brokers and this advertisement from a recent campaign sought to redress the drift to direct sell insurers by stressing the advantages of using an intermediary.
(*Source*: Reproduced with permission of NIG Skandia)

DIRECT LINE CUSTOMERS COULD SAVE 20% BY TALKING TO AN INTERMEDIARY.

A recent survey of ex Direct Line car insurance customers now insuring with NIG Skandia, on the advice of their BROKERS & INDEPENDENT INTERMEDIARIES, showed on average they saved over 20% of the Direct Line price. If you are a Direct Line customer we suggest you call a broker or intermediary today to see how much money you could save.

This advertisement was sponsored by

NIG Skandia is one of the many insurance companies which sell their products through brokers and independent intermediaries who compare our rates with those of other insurers to offer you a policy which meets your needs on price, cover and service.

10 Intermediaries often share part of the risk of new products by agreeing to buy stock on a no-return basis before the product is launched.

These functions are of varying levels of importance in different markets. In some cases the manufacturer will be able to manage quite adequately without intermediaries and sell direct to its final consumers. The design of a channel of distribution is influenced by a number of factors:

1 *The type of product* For fast-moving consumer goods, customers will generally be unwilling to travel far to obtain a particular brand – an extensive network of outlets will be necessary. On the other hand, customers may be prepared to travel further to seek out higher value consumer durables.

2 *The nature of the product* Bulky and perishable products will be generally less capable of being handled by large numbers of intermediaries.

3 *The abilities of intermediaries* If the product is very specialized, it may be difficult to obtain intermediaries who can handle the product effectively. Ski tour operators have often sold their holidays direct to the public, claiming that travel agents have insufficient knowledge and training to effectively sell their holidays.

4 *The expectations of consumers* For some products, consumers expect to buy from an intermediary who offers a choice of products from a number of producers, as in the case of books and holidays. This could make direct selling of one company's products direct to the public more difficult. Consumers may, furthermore, have expectations about what constitutes an acceptable channel through which to buy a product. Attempts to sell cars and houses through supermarkets have failed partly for this reason.

In many markets, different channel structures can exist side by side. Commemorative porcelain products are frequently sold direct to the public by means of advertisements in magazines. Manufacturers of the same type of product can also be found selling them to retailers and indirectly to retailers through wholesalers. A company selling direct to consumers may find a niche product to sell or may present the offer to appeal to a particular segment that is more responsive to the idea of ordering by mail (e.g. individuals who are money rich/time poor, or segments of disabled housebound buyers). Where multiple channels are used simultaneously, companies must avoid alienating channel members who feel that they are facing unfair competition from other channels. For this reason, insurance brokers are often hostile to insurance companies who they act for when those companies choose to additionally sell their policies direct to the public.

Channel design is constantly adapting to changes in the business environment. A major change during the past two decades has occurred in the size of intermediaries. In many market sectors, multiple retail outlets have become dominant, often at the expense of the smaller business unit. Grocery retailing and DIY retailing are two areas where this has been particularly significant. The diversity of organizations involved in retailing can be appreciated by considering the following:

- In 1997, a total of 196 563 retailer businesses were recorded in the United Kingdom. Of these, 173 113 (or 88.1 per cent of the total) were single-outlet retailers (*Retail Pocket Book*, 1998).
- Large multiple retailers (those with more than 100 outlets) accounted for less than 1 per cent of all retail business organizations.
- Despite their small numbers, retailers with over 100 outlets have accounted for a disproportionately high proportion of total retail turnover (43 per cent in 1997).
- The greater efficiency of large multiples is evident from a comparison of the annual sales value per employee (£65 846 for single-outlet retailers compared to £77 734 in 1997 for large multiples).

Economies of scale in purchasing and promotion have been important causes of the increase in retailer concentration. Where retailers have become more concentrated and individually more powerful, there has been a tendency for them to deal directly with manufacturers, rather than to deal through wholesalers. The turnover of a large grocery supermarket can be more than that of a large wholesaler, leaving the latter to cater for the small and medium sized retailer.

1.4.2   **Push and pull channels of distribution**

The relative power of organizations in a channel of distribution has been changing. Before the advent of strong branding, a manufacturer would aggressively sell a product to a wholesaler who would buy and stock the product on what it considered to be the merits of the product. The wholesaler would in turn aggressively sell the product to retailers, who would buy on the basis of his or her experience and what he or she thought could be profitably sold to customers. This is known as a 'push' strategy of distribution. With the advent of branding, the manufacturer was able to cut out the uncertainty associated with the intermediaries by appealing to the final consumer directly through the medium of advertising. The final consumer would then go to a retailer and demand a specific brand rather than accept the generic brand that the retailer tried to push. Having demanded a specific brand from the retailer, the retailer will in turn order that brand from the wholesaler, who in turn will order from the manufacturer. This is known as a 'pull' strategy. In this situation, the intermediaries had become merely dispensers of presold goods. The two strategies are compared in Figure 1.7.

More recently, the growing strength of retailers has put them at the focal point of the channel of distribution. By building up their own strong brands, large retailers are increasingly able to exert pressure on manufacturers in terms of product specification, price and the level of promotional support to be given to the retailer. It is estimated that, in Britain, the four largest grocery retailers may account for over half of the sales of a typical manufacturer of fast-moving consumer goods. The dependency is not reciprocated, with very few retailers relying on one single supplier for more than 1 per cent of their supplies.

Figure 1.7
'Push' and 'pull' channels of distribution compared

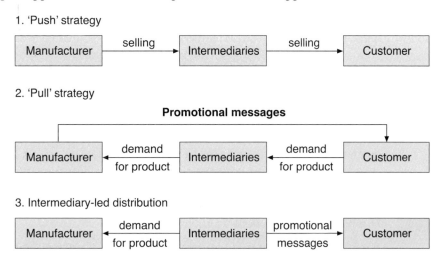

1. 'Push' strategy

Manufacturer → selling → Intermediaries → selling → Customer

2. 'Pull' strategy

Promotional messages

Manufacturer ← demand for product ← Intermediaries ← demand for product ← Customer

3. Intermediary-led distribution

Manufacturer ← demand for product — Intermediaries → promotional messages → Customer

Developments in channel structures

While large retailers have been consolidating their position, there has been recent growth in the number of specialist niche retailers. These have concentrated on such specialist niches as ties, fine cheeses, sportswear and bags. A number of environmental factors have contributed towards the development of these niche outlets. Greater affluence has resulted in consumers being able to express a desire for individualism which may be incompatible with a purchase from a large mainstream retailer. Although large retailers have often tried to enter niche markets, they may not have the flexibility of movement open to the smaller company.

Movement towards integrating the different stages of a channel of distribution has occurred in a number of ways. In its most simple form, integration can occur through agreement over operational matters – standardization of pallet sizes and packaging methods to suit the needs of manufacturer, wholesaler and retailer is one example. More recently, bar coding of products allows all intermediaries to process goods by a common standard much more efficiently. Sometimes, the agreement takes the form of a voluntary buying chain set up to act as a wholesaler on behalf of a group of retailers. Londis and Nisa are examples.

Channel integration could occur through common ownership of different stages in the channel of distribution – a manufacturer, for instance, buying its own retail outlets. Although this has occurred on a number of occasions during the past decade, the more common trend has been for companies to concentrate on the point of the value chain that they are best at doing. The retailer Asda, originally founded as a dairy to which retailing was later added, decided that its capital could be better employed in exploiting economies of scale in retailing rather than in operating dairies.

A very significant source of channel integration has come about through the development of franchising, which is discussed in more detail in Chapter 2.

Formats for intermediaries go through life cycles, just like any normal product. Forms of retailing are born and eventually decline in response to changes in the business environment. Full service retailing was the norm in the United Kingdom until the 1950s, but then went into decline with increasing real wage levels, to be replaced by the self-service store. With increasing car ownership and rising aspirations of consumers for greater choice, town centre supermarkets have been challenged by the larger out-of-town hypermarkets. The concept of the department store may be at a point of maturity, being challenged by the emergence of small niche outlets. Catalogue shops are a relatively recent innovation in the United Kingdom, resulting from the increasing cost of city centre floor space and have gained social acceptability as a method of shopping. Innovations in technology may allow further developments in the home shopping sector, allowing it to exploit the growing number of money-rich, time-poor households with access to the Internet. In areas such as financial services, companies are able to use information technology to target specific groups with sales offerings and achieve a sale with good after-sales service, without the need to deal through the traditional intermediary of the insurance broker.

The Internet environment

The Internet has emerged as a versatile tool in an organization's relationship with its business environment, combining a communication function with a distribution function. At its simplest, an organization's web page can simply give additional information about a company's products, for example many hotels have websites which give information about their location and the facilities available. The great strength of the Internet is to make promotional messages directly relevant to the user, so, for example, a train operator's website may give information relating to a specific journey that the user had enquired about. Beyond this, websites are increasingly being enabled to allow immediate fulfilment of a request, such as confirmation of a hotel booking or reservation of a plane ticket. The Internet has narrowed the gap between somebody receiving a message and being able to act upon it. The services sector has been at the leading edge of developments in electronic commerce, largely because it often does not have to cope with the problems of delivering tangible goods.

The Internet is extensively used for comparison shopping and a lot of research has gone into understanding which sites produce the best results in terms of moving an individual through the stages of purchase. A regularly updated site which contains information of direct relevance to a user and which is fast to download has become a minimum requirement for most users of the medium.

Similar to traditional promotional media, it can be difficult to make a company's website stand out in a crowded environment. With literally millions of communication messages seeking to find a web surfer, companies must develop a strategy for promoting their web presence. Without heavy promotion of a website address through conventional media, or paying for a 'hotlink' via a network navigator, a company's website may remain unseen in cyberspace. Many services companies have applied their website address to ancillary materials such as carrier bags, timetables and price lists, in much the same way as they would promote their telephone number. A lot of money has been spent by companies on advertisements in the traditional media drawing attention to their website. Buying access to target customers on the Internet has become an important activity, with portals such as Yahoo! charging for the use of banner advertisements on their popular websites. A number of companies, such as Doubleclick.com exist to collect information about individuals' usage patterns with a view to improving the targeting of advertisements through paid-for websites.

E-mail has also developed rapidly as a medium for communication. As a communication medium with customers, e-mail (and SMS text messaging) extends the profiling and interactivity features of direct mail. An accurate database of customers' preferences is essential if e-mail messages are not to be discarded as junk messages. The prospect of m-mail to individuals' mobile phones raises the prospect of a huge amount of low-cost messages being targeted at individuals, and senders of messages must ensure that their messages stand out from competitors and have immediate relevance to the recipient. Just as importantly for an organization, e-mail allows rapid internal communication between employees and members of its value chain who may be geographically quite dispersed. E-mail speeds up the process of gathering, sharing and disseminating information about the changing business environment.

Despite the enormous potential of the Internet to simplify communication between a company and its customers without recourse to intermediaries, problems of final delivery remain where tangible goods are involved. There are also many high-

Figure 1.8

The Internet has opened up a powerful distribution channel by which a company can communicate directly with each of its customers, providing rapid, low-cost distribution which need not involve intermediaries. The budget airline EasyJet has embraced the Internet and claims to be the 'Web's favourite airline'. During July 2000, 73 per cent of the airline's customers used the company's website for booking their tickets. The company is proud of the fact that it does not pay commission to intermediaries, and can pass on these savings in the form of low ticket prices.

(*Source*: Reproduced with permission of EasyJet Airline Company Ltd)

involvement goods where buyers feel more comfortable being able to see and feel the goods before they commit to a purchase. The failed Internet clothes retailer boo.com encountered the reality that most people would probably find it much easier and reassuring to try on clothes in a shop rather than relying on a computer image, thereby ensuring a continuing role for traditional high-street retailers.

1.5   BUYER–SELLER RELATIONSHIPS

The discussion of value chains earlier indicated that members of an organization's business environment are often being brought closer together to act co-operatively rather than in confrontation with each other. There is nothing new in the way that firms have sought to develop ongoing relationships with their customers and suppliers. In simple economies where production of goods and services took place on a small scale, it was possible for the owners of businesses to know each customer personally and to come to understand their individual characteristics. They could therefore adapt their product offer to the needs of individuals on the basis of knowledge gained during previous transactions and could suggest appropriate new product offers. They would also be able to form an opinion about customers' credit worthiness. Networks of relationships between buyers and sellers are still the norm in many Far Eastern countries and many Western exporters have found it difficult to break into these long-standing, closed networks.

With the growth in size of Western organizations, the personal contact that an organization can have with its customers has been diluted. Instead of being able to reassure customers on the basis of close relationships, organizations in many cases sought to provide this reassurance through the development of strong brands. Recent resurgence of interest in close buyer–seller relationships has occurred for a number of reasons:

1 In increasingly competitive markets, good products alone are insufficient to differentiate an organization's products from that of its competitors. For example, in the car sector, manufacturers traditionally differentiated their cars on the basis of superior design features such as styling, speed and reliability. Once most companies had reached a common standard of design,

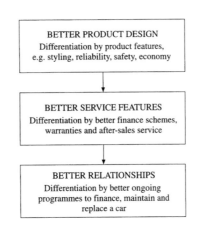

Figure 1.9
The business
environment of
car manufacturers
has changed from
one in which
marketing
activities
emphasize
differentiation
through tangible
design features,
to one where
differentiation is
based on the
quality of ongoing
buyer–seller
relationships

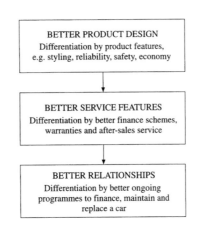

attention switched to differentiation through superior added-service facilities, such as warranties and finance. Once these service standards became the norm for the sector, many car manufacturers have sought to differentiate their cars on the basis of superior relationships. Therefore most major car manufacturers now offer customers complete packages which keep a car financed, insured, maintained and renewed after a specified period. Instead of a three-yearly one-off purchase of a new car, many customers enter an ongoing relationship with a car manufacturer and its dealers which gives the customer the support they need to keep their car on the road and to have it renewed when this falls due (Figure 1.9).

2   Developments in information technology have had dramatic effects in developing close buyer–seller relationships. The development of powerful user-friendly databases has allowed organizations to recreate in a computer what the individual small business owner knew in his or her head. Large businesses are therefore now able to tell very quickly the status of a particular customer, for example their previous ordering pattern, product preferences and profitability. Developments in information technology have also allowed companies to enter individual dialogues with their customers through direct mail and increasingly through electronic means. Increased production flexibility based on improved technology allows many manufacturers and service organizations to design unique products that meet the needs of individual customers, rather than broad groups of customers.

3   Just-in-time (JIT) production methods have become very widespread in Western countries, thanks to the lead given by Japanese manufacturing companies. It often makes sense for a manufacturer to keep its holdings of component parts down to an absolute minimum. This way, it ties up less capital, needs less storage space and suffers less risk of stocks becoming obsolete. Instead of keeping large stocks of components 'just in case' they are needed, manufacturers arrange for them to be delivered 'just in time' for them to be used in their production process. It is not uncommon to find car manufacturers receiving batches of components which within an hour are incorporated into a car. The JIT systems demand a lot of co-operation

between supplier and customer, which cannot easily be achieved if each transaction is to be individually bargained. Some form of ongoing relationship between the two is essential.

4 It has been commented that an emphasis on one-off transactions in which each transaction is bargained over is very much associated with a masculine business environment dominated by values of conquest and victory. In recent years, women have become much more important in the business environment, both as buyers and sellers. There is an extensive body of literature on differences in personality traits which exist between males and females. One important area of difference is in the way that males and females develop relationships with others, with masculine gender traits being characterized as aggressive and instrumental, while feminine traits are more commonly associated with showing empathy and resolving conflicts through reconciliation (Meyers-Levy and Sternthal 1991; Palmer and Bejou, 1995). Recent moves from warfare approaches to business exchange towards collaborative approaches may appear novel when judged by the stereotypical value systems of males, but may be considered normal by the value system of females. Although there is the possibility of role conflict, women as buyers and sellers are likely to bring values to commercial exchanges which are more relational than transactional.

Organizations use a number of strategies to develop co-operative buyer–seller relationships, including: recording information about buyers' preferences which allows their needs to be satisfied more effectively on future occasions; offering incentives to reward loyalty; and undertaking new product research with key customers.

Although there has been much recent interest in relationship marketing – for goods as well as for services – this has tended to emphasize the producer's perspective on a relationship. It can be argued that with increasing knowledge and confidence, consumers are increasingly happy to venture outside a long-term

In order to keep our records up to date please fill in all the following details and tick all relevant boxes. (Please use block capitals)

Are you the Travel Arranger? Yes ☐ No ☐
Are you the Traveller? Yes ☐ No ☐
What is the purpose of your Trip Business ☐ Leisure ☐

PLEASE FILL IN YOUR 3 MOST FREQUENT JOURNEYS AND TICK THE RELEVANT BOXES

UK DEPARTURE AIRPORT	DESTINATION AIRPORT	FREQUENCY	CLASS
1		☐ 1-5 TIMES ☐ 5-15 TIMES ☐ ABOVE 15	☐ ECONOMY ☐ BUSINESS ☐ FIRST CLASS
2		☐ 1-5 TIMES ☐ 5-15 TIMES ☐ ABOVE 15	☐ ECONOMY ☐ BUSINESS ☐ FIRST CLASS
3		☐ 1-5 TIMES ☐ 5-15 TIMES ☐ ABOVE 15	☐ ECONOMY ☐ BUSINESS ☐ FIRST CLASS

NAME: ______
POSITION: ______
COMPANY: ______
ADDRESS: HOME/WORK* ______
______ POSTCODE ______
TELEPHONE NO. ______
*PLEASE DELETE AS APPROPRIATE

OCCASIONALLY WE MAY PASS YOUR DETAILS ON TO OTHER COMPANIES IN THE TRAVEL INDUSTRY. PLEASE TICK THIS BOX IF YOU DO NOT WISH TO BE INCLUDED IN THESE MAILINGS ☐

Birmingham International Airport

Figure 1.10
Birmingham International Airport uses the opportunity of an information request to build up a profile of its customers. Through this simple device, it is able to build up a better picture of its environment in terms of key customer characteristics

(*Source*: Reproduced with permission of Birmingham International Airport Ltd)

Just because customers repeatedly come back to a company does not necessarily mean that they have a loyal relationship to a company. This point was made, tongue-in-cheek, during the continuing war of words between British Airways and Virgin Atlantic Airways. The latter had objected to BA's use of the advertising slogan 'The world's favourite airline'. Statistically, it was true that more passengers travelled internationally with British Airways than with any other airline, but surveys of airline users had consistently put Virgin ahead of BA in terms of perceived quality of service. Virgin's Richard Branson claimed that on BA's logic, the M25, London's notorious orbital motorway, could be described as the world's favourite motorway. Despite coming back to the motorway day after day, few motorists could claim to be loyal to it – they simply have no other choice.

The spat between BA and Virgin serves to underline the point that relationship marketing is about more than mere repetitious buying. True loyalty involves customers becoming an enthusiastic advocate of a company.

relationship with a service provider. This is reflected, for example, in the observation by the Consumers Association that nearly 20 per cent of the population had changed their bank account or credit card in a year, something which runs counter to earlier anecdotal observations that a relationship which individuals have with their bank is more enduring than the relationship with their spouse. With increased knowledge of financial services, consumers are more willing today to venture to another bank which offers them the best personal loan or the most attractive credit card. Also, a long-term relationship often begins with a good introductory discounts and a significant segment of many service markets is prepared to move its business regularly to the service provider which is offering the most favourable discount. The motorist who reviews his or her car insurance each year for example may not allow an insurance company to develop a long-term profitable relationship. In the case of many business-to-business services contracts, these may be reviewed regularly as a matter of course, as in the competitive tendering which is required for many government purchases of services. In such circumstances, it is often not possible to add value and higher prices to a long-term relationship.

1.6 THE INTERNAL ENVIRONMENT

Internally, the structure and politics of an organization affect the manner in which the organization responds to environmental change. We are probably all familiar with organizations which have failed to adapt to their environment and suffered as a result. Often, these failings can be traced back to shortcomings in the organization's internal structures and processes. When the Sainsbury's supermarket chain fell from its position as the leading UK grocery retailer in the mid-1990s, many commentators were quick to blame this on internal issues. It was widely reported that the Sainsbury family which controlled a majority of the company's shares had been too slow to delegate responsibilities to managers and had carried on acting as though it had an unassailable position. In effect, it had become like a great supertanker – marching along steadily but seemingly finding it difficult to change its direction.

The internal culture of an organization can greatly affect the way it responds to organizational change. In the case of Sainsbury's its culture was probably too much based on hierarchy and tradition which can be a weakness in a rapidly changing external environment. Organizational culture concerns the social and behavioural manifestation of a whole set of values which are shared by its members. Cultural values can be shared in a number of ways, including the way work is organized and experienced, how authority is exercised and delegated, how people are rewarded, organized and controlled and the roles and expectations of staff and managers.

In addition to its dominant culture, it is often possible to identify different subcultures within the same organization. Handy (1989) has argued that organizations tend to have elements of different cultures appropriate to the structure and circumstances of different operating units within their structure. We will explore the appropriateness of each of these for dealing with a turbulent external environment in Chapter 4.

Within many organizations, it has proved difficult to change cultural attitudes when the nature of an organization's business environment has significantly changed, leaving the established culture a liability in terms of managing change. As an example, the cultural values of UK clearing banks have for a long time continued to be dominated by prudence and caution when in some product areas such as insurance sales, a more aggressive approach to marketing management may be called for.

Many of the most successful commercial organizations, including the Virgin Group, Federal Express and McDonald's have attributed their success in part to the quality of leadership within their organizations. The results of poor leadership are evident in many failing companies, with numerous examples being found in both the public and private sectors. What is good leadership for one organization need not necessarily be so for another. Those operating in relatively stable environments may be best suited with a leadership style which places a lot of power in a hierarchical chain of command. In the United Kingdom, many banks until recently had leadership styles which have been drawn from models developed in the armed forces, evidenced by some managers having titles such as superintendent and inspector. Such rigid, hierarchical patterns of leadership may be less effective where the business environment is changing rapidly and a flexible response is called for (as has happened in the banking sector).

For many organizations, employees are the biggest item of cost and potentially the biggest cause of delay in responding rapidly to environmental change. Having the right staff in the right place at the right time can demand a lot of flexibility on the part of employees. Many organizations have sought to improve the effectiveness of their employees through a programme of 'internal marketing'. Internal marketing came to prominence during the 1980s and describes the application of marketing techniques to audiences within the organization. A central feature of internal marketing is to develop values in employees which are aligned with organizational values. That way, if change is required, employees are more likely to share in the threats and opportunities which environmental change presents, and to change their behaviour more enthusiastically.

Figure 1.11
British Airways recognizes in this advertisement that it cannot separate external marketing from internal human resource management. Its internal environment impacts directly on customers' perceptions of service quality.
(*Source*: Reproduced with permission of British Airways)

Thanks to everyone who works for British Airways, we've been voted 'Best Airline of the Year' for the 10th year running by the readers of Business Traveller Magazine.

BRITISH AIRWAYS
The world's favourite airline

Every organization can be considered to comprise an internal marketplace where diverse groups of employees engage in exchanges between each other. These internal exchanges include relationships between front line staff and the backroom staff, managers and the front-line staff, managers and the backroom staff, and, for large organizations, between the head office and each branch. It is not uncommon to find organizations where relationships between these different groups are characterized by distrust, lack of communication and even hostility. An organization that assigns marketing responsibilities to a narrow group of people, for example, may in fact create internal tensions which make it less effective at responding to changing consumer needs than one where marketing responsibilities in their widest sense are disseminated throughout the organization. Corporate plans cannot be developed and implemented without a sound understanding of the internal strengths and weaknesses of an organization. In Chapter 4 we will look in more detail at the effects of internal management structure on an organization's ability to respond to external environmental change.

There is a widely held view that if employees are not happy with their jobs, external customers will never be uppermost in their minds. Researchers have tended to agree that satisfied internal customers are a critical prerequisite to the satisfaction of external customers, especially within the services sector. This linkage is discussed further in Chapter 4.

COMPLACENCY ABOUT ENVIRONMENTAL CHANGE CAN BE THE BIGGEST ENEMY OF RETAILERS

'There's no need to ask the price – it's a penny' was the proud claim of Marks and Spencer a hundred years ago. From the start, it had developed a unique position in its market – an emphasis on low price, wide range and good quality. Over time, the M&S position was steadily developed, along with its profitability. By the early 1990s it looked unstoppable as a retailer, as it progressively expanded its product range from clothing to food, furnishings and financial services. A willing world seemed to be waiting for M&S to expand, and despite disappointing starts in the United States and Canada, it developed steadily throughout Europe and the Far East. Then, just like any star who has been put on a pedestal, the media began to savage the company. After a sudden drop in profits and sales during 1998, critics claimed that the company had lost its way. It appeared to be like a supertanker, ploughing straight ahead with a management that had become much less adaptable to change in its business environment than its nimbler competitors. Had it simply misread its business environment? Or had it become so complacent that it thought that the retail world still revolved around the mighty M&S?

M&S has often been held out as an example of how to manage effective relationships – with suppliers, employees and customers. The company worked closely on mutually supportive relationships with its manufacturers to ensure a continuous supply of high-quality products. It seemed that loyalty from dedicated manufacturers and its employees was feeding through into high levels of customer loyalty, with customers prepared to pay a price premium for the company's products. However, by the end of the 1990s it appeared that the relationships with key suppliers had become a weakness rather than a strength. The company's competitors had been taking advantage of the high value of sterling to buy opportunistically in world markets and to pass price savings on to customers. M&S's trusted network of domestic suppliers seemed to be a millstone round its neck. Could these relationships survive M&S's cost-saving attempts? Or did their existence prove the case of cynics who argue that relationships – contractual or informal – tie a company down and prevent it being opportunistic and exploiting new opportunities as they arise?

Many observers had commented on the fact that the company did not have a marketing department until 1998. Marketing, at least in terms of advertising the brand, had become so important to its competitors, but had never been high on M&S's agenda. According to Media Monitoring Services, M&S's total media spending between December 1997 and November 1998 was just £4.7 million, almost a drop in the ocean compared to the spending of Sainsbury's (£42.1 million); Tesco (£27.5 million); and Woolworths (£21.5 million). While other retailers had worked hard on building a brand image, M&S had relied on the quality of its stock to do the talking. The argument was that everyone knew what they were getting with M&S underwear or shirts – good quality at fair, but not cheap, prices. Similarly with food, M&S's offering was about quality rather than price. M&S believed its customers knew what the brand stood for and advertising was much less important than ensuring that it could obtain the right products at the right price. Was this enough in an increasingly competitive environment?

In 1998, M&S looked to marketing to help turn around its performance, describing its new marketing division for UK retail as 'a significant development in our retailing philosophy'. Many suspected that M&S's conversion to marketing had been encouraged by the example set by the star of modern retailing, Tesco, but that its reaction was too little and too late. There are many similarities between the problems facing M&S and those which Tesco faced a decade previously. In the early 1990s Tesco was a brand which looked like it had seen better days. The retailer's format was tired, its stores poorly laid out and the positioning of the company was still based on its founder's principle of 'pile it high and sell it cheap'. Its archrival, Sainsbury's, was regarded as the more upmarket store for the middle classes, who shopped for quality food in a more pleasant environment. Since then, Tesco had transformed its brand and its profitability. It realized that the trend in shopping was towards a more concerted focus on customer service and that store design, product quality and, crucially, its relationship with customers would be vital to success. Gaining a competitive edge was becoming even more important as saturation in the sector gave most people a choice of supermarkets which were within easy reach for their shopping. Tesco responded to the competitive challenge with more store assistants, new store designs, petrol stations, coffee shops, a new fascia, the Tesco Clubcard and 24-hour store opening. The list of Tesco's marketing initiatives seemed to be unstoppable, in an attempt to keep one step ahead of its competitors.

In contrast, M&S had failed to keep pace with customer service. In many issues of retail development, such as out-of-town shopping centres, Sunday opening and loyalty cards, it had lagged behind its main competitors. While it has stood still, the likes of Tesco and Sainsbury's appeared to have kept their eyes on environmental change and marched ahead until there was no longer much that felt exceptional about the M&S shopping experience. Analysts argued that M&S had failed to understand shoppers' behaviour and this had become evident in store layouts which did nothing to help shoppers bring clothing together to make outfits. In a typical M&S store, all jackets would be located in one area and all cardigans in another, for example. Its competitors had made much greater progress in bringing together co-ordinated sets of clothing which would encourage shoppers to spend more. Also, M&S has been criticized for making things difficult for customers by not accepting payment by major credit cards. Eventually it recognized that it had to adapt to what had become part of shoppers' expectations and belatedly began accepting all main credit cards.

In response to its current troubles, the newly created marketing department of M&S launched its first national campaign for retail towards the end of 1998. The ads followed an initial attempt at regional TV advertising earlier in the year, which the company was said to be very pleased with. The newly appointed chief executive claimed 'It's not that people don't like what we're selling, but that we haven't got the message across. There are an awful lot of people who love us for our knickers, but they don't love our home furnishings because they don't even know they are there.' Many critics thought the problems were much more deep-seated and blamed the store's problems on the fact that its autumn fashions were seen as dull and uninspiring and out of touch with consumers' preferences. Greater authority was pledged to the marketing department when it came to new product design.

In response to its pledge to listen to what its customers wanted, new designers were brought in to try to give the company's ranges more sparkle. The company even thought the previously unthinkable by proposing to stock manufacturers' own branded products, instead of relying entirely on M&S's own-label products. If customers wanted to obtain variety at M&S, the new thinking was that the company must adapt and offer it. Another area identified for development was direct marketing of fashion products – an area where the company had begun to lag behind its rivals who had developed interactive websites.

Serious questions remained about the company. How quickly could it change in response to its changed environment? The company had not been known for speedy decision making, so probably a major structural overhaul was essential before it could get down to the serious business of adapting to customers' changing needs. Also, there was a great danger of changing the company's position too far and too fast, thereby alienating its traditional customers without gaining sufficient new ones. As a warning of how not to change, M&S's rival Laura Ashley had repositioned itself so radically from its original format that it now failed to gain the support of any major group. M&S had itself tried to become more fashion conscious during the mid-1980s with similar effect, and had to make a hasty retreat to its traditional, more staid image.

(Based on 'Time for M&S to follow Tesco', *Marketing*, 28 January 1999)

CASE STUDY Review questions

1 Are the problems of M&S described in this case study a case of bad luck, or are they essentially a result of the company's failure to monitor and respond to environmental change?

2 There has been a lot of debate about whether the existence of a marketing department can actually be harmful to organizations because they can absolve everybody else from focusing on customers' needs. What then, do you make of M&S's decision to introduce a marketing department? Is this the most appropriate means of keeping abreast of environmental change, or should it have been doing more?

3 Have close relationships with its suppliers helped or hindered M&S's task of responding to change in its business environment?

CHAPTER Summary and links to other chapters

This chapter has reviewed the complex nature of an organization's business environment. The environment can be analysed at three levels: the microenvironment, comprising firms and individuals that an organization directly interacts with (or who directly affect its activities); the macroenvironment, comprising general forces that may eventually impact on the microenvironment; and the internal environment, comprising other functions within the organization.

This chapter has stressed the interrelatedness of all elements of the business environment. Although the social environment and technological environment are identified as separate elements, the two are closely linked (for example, technology has resulted in mass ownership of cars which has in turn affected social behaviour).

Subsequent chapters pay attention to each of the elements of the marketing environment, but the complexity of linkages must never be forgotten. The final chapter seeks to integrate these elements within dynamic analytic frameworks, which can be used to develop holistic forecasts of the future business environment.

Review questions

1 (a) Explain briefly what you understand by the 'environment' of a business.

(b) Prepare a list of recommendations which would aid a business to address change in its technical environment.

(Based on CIM Marketing Environment Examination)

2 Suppliers and intermediaries are important stakeholders in the microenvironment of the business.

(a) Explain the evolving role and functions of these stakeholders in the marketing-orientated business of the 1990s.

(b) With examples, comment on the growing importance of relationship marketing in this regard.

(Based on CIM Marketing Environment Examination)

3 Using a company of your choice, produce and justify an environmental set. You should include and rank at least five factors in your set.

(Based on CIM Marketing Environment Examination, June 1995)

References

Handy, C.B. (1989) *The Age of Unreason*, Harvard Business School Press, Boston, MA.

Heskett, J.L., W.E. Sasser and L.A. Schlesinger (1998) 'The service-profit chain: how leading companies link profit and growth to loyalty, satisfaction and value', *International Journal of Service Industry Management*, vol. 9, no. 3, pp. 145–76.

Levitt, T. (1960) 'Marketing myopia', *Harvard Business Review*, July–August, pp. 45–56.

Meyers-Levy, J. and B. Sternthal (1991) 'Gender differences in the use of message cues and judgements', *Journal of Marketing Research*, 28 (February), 84–96.

Nonaka, I. (1991) 'The knowledge-creating company', *Harvard Business Review*, vol. 69, no. 6, pp. 96–104.

Palmer, A. and D. Bejou (1995) 'The role of gender in the development of buyer–seller relationships', *International Journal of Bank Marketing*, vol. 13, no. 3, pp. 18–27.

Retail Pocket Book (1998) NTC/ACNielsen, Henley-on-Thames.

Selected further reading

A good starting point for understanding competitive advantage of firms and the role of value chains in achieving this is provided in Michael Porter's frequently cited book:

Porter, M.E. (1985) *Competitive Advantage: Creating and Sustaining Superior Performance*. Free Press, New York.

This has been brought up to date to take account of the World Wide Web in the following:

Porter, M.E. (2001) 'Strategy and the Internet', *Harvard Business Review*, March, vol. 79, pp 63–78.

For introductory reviews of the principles underlying the design of a channel of distribution, and discussion of contemporary issues, the following references are useful:

Betancourt, R. and D. Gautschi (1998) 'Distribution services and economic power in a channel', *Journal of Retailing*, Spring, vol. 74, no. 1, pp. 37(24).

Bowersox, D.J. (1992) *Strategic Marketing Channel Management*, McGraw-Hill, New York.

Christopher, M. (1997) *Marketing Logistics*, Butterworth-Heinemann, Oxford.

Rolnicki, K. (1998) *Managing Channels of Distribution*, Amacom.

Wren, B., J. Simpson and C. Paul (1998) 'Marketing channel relationships among small businesses', *International Small Business Journal*, July–September 1998, vol. 16, no. 4, p. 64(15).

There is now an extensive literature on the development of close buyer–seller relationships. A good summary of the principles can be found in the following three references:

Buttle, F. (ed.) (1996) *Relationship Marketing*, Paul Chapman London.

Gummesson, E. (1999) *Total Relationship Marketing*, Butterworth-Heinemann, Oxford.

Payne, A., M. Christopher, M. Clark and H. Peck (1998) *Relationship Marketing for Competitive Advantage*, Butterworth-Heinemann, Oxford.

A good analysis of networks between companies is provided in the following:

Cravens, D.W. and N.F. Piercy (1994) 'Relationship marketing and collaborative networks in service organizations', *International Journal of Services Management*, vol. 5, no. 5, pp. 39–53.

The importance of addressing the needs of all stakeholders in an organization is emphasized in the following:

Greenley, G. and G.R. Foxall (1997) 'Multiple stakeholder orientation in UK companies and the implications for performance', *Journal of Management Studies*, vol. 34, no. 2, pp. 259–84.

This chapter has provided a general overview of the components that make up the business environment. Suggestions for further reading on each of these components is given in later chapters.

Useful websites

Biz/Ed   Biz/ed is a business and economics resource for students, teachers and lecturers and includes news and case studies.   **http://www.bized.ac.uk**

Supply chain management discussion group   List for all aspects of purchasing and supply chain management, and interorganizational theory. The list supports the networking and collaborative activities of the International Purchasing & Supply Education & Research Association.   **http://www.jiscmail.ac.uk/lists/purchasing-supply-chain.html**

Newspaper websites   The quality daily newspapers have websites and these are a useful source of information about the business environment:

Financial Times: http://www.ft.com
Guardian: http://www.Guardian.co.uk
Sunday Times: http://www.the-sunday-times.co.uk
Telegraph: http://www.Telegraph.co.uk
The Times: http://www.the-times.co.uk

Key terms

Buyer–seller relationships	Microenvironment
Channels of distribution	Organizational culture
Environmental set	Stakeholders
Information environment	System
Intermediaries	Transformation process
Internal environment	Value chain
Macroenvironment	

Part 2
Looking inwardly at organizations

2

Types of business organizations

CHAPTER OBJECTIVES

The business environment comprises organizations of great variety in terms of their size, structure, ownership and legal status. All can have a role to play and it is not uncommon to find very different types of organizations operating alongside each other in the same business sector. The aim of this chapter is to explore the diversity of organizational types and the effects which organizational form and size have upon their responsiveness to environmental change.

2.1   ORGANIZATIONS AND THEIR ENVIRONMENT

Business organizations are extremely diverse in their form and functions, even within a single business sector. It is therefore difficult to define an 'ideal'. Instead, all organizational forms have advantages and disadvantages relative to the environment in which they operate and successful organizations capitalize on their advantages while recognizing their disadvantages. In a single business sector, there can be a role for both the one-person owner-managed business and the multinational organization. Both can adapt and find a role.

Analogies can be drawn between business organizations and their environment and the animal kingdom. In a natural habitat, the largest and most powerful animals can coexist with much smaller species. The smaller species can avoid becoming prey for the larger ones by being more agile or developing defences such as safe habitats which are inaccessible to their larger predators. Sometimes, a symbiotic relationship can develop between the two. In a bid to survive, animals soon learn which sources of food are easily obtainable and abandon those that are either inedible or face competition from more powerful animals. In Darwinian terms, the fittest survive, and an ecosystem allows for co-existence of living organisms, which have adapted in their own way to the challenges of their environment. As in the business environment, macroenvironmental change can affect the relationships between species, as, for example, has occurred with deforestation and the use of intensive farming methods.

Just as any study of the animal world may begin by examining the characteristics of the participants, so an analysis of the business environment could begin by looking at the characteristics of the organizations that make it up. Businesses need to understand the diversity of organizational types for a number of reasons.

1. Different types of organizations will be able to address their customers, suppliers and employees in different ways. Lack of resources could, for example, inhibit the development of expensive new products by a small business. Sometimes, the objectives of an organization – either formal or informal – will influence what it is able to offer the public.

2. As sellers of materials to companies involved in further manufacture, a company should understand how the buying behaviour of different kinds of organizations varies. A small business is likely to buy equipment in a different way to a large public sector organization.

3. We should be interested in the structure of business units at the macro-economic level. Many economists have argued that a thriving small-business sector is essential for an expanding economy and that the effect of domination by large organizations may be to reduce competition and innovation. We should therefore be interested in the rate of new business creation and trends in the composition of business units.

2.1.1   Classification of business organizations

There are many approaches to classifying organizations that would satisfy the interests identified above. Organizations are commonly classified according to their:

■ Size (e.g. turnover, assets, employees, geographical coverage)

■ Ownership (e.g. public, private, co-operative)

■ Legal form (e.g. sole trader, limited company)

■ Industry sector.

A good starting point for classifying businesses is to look at their legal form. A business's legal form is often closely related to its size, objectives, the level of resources it has available for marketing, and for new product development (the issues of organizational size and objectives are considered in more detail in the next chapter).

This chapter will firstly consider private sector organizations, which range from the small owner-managed sole trader to the very large public limited company. It will then review the diverse range of publicly owned organizations which operate as businesses. A third, and growing, group of organizations cannot be neatly categorized into private or public sector and include non-departmental public bodies (NDPBs) (often referred to as *QUANGOs*, quasi-autonomous non-governmental organizations) and charities. To put the diversity of organizations into context, Figure 2.1 illustrates the types of organizations that will be described in this chapter.

2.2   THE SOLE TRADER

The most basic level of business organization is provided by the sole trader. In fact, the concept of a separate legal form does not apply to this type of organization, for

Figure 2.1
A classification of organizational types

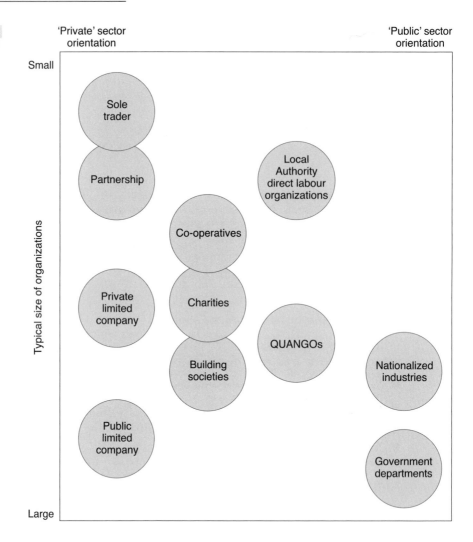

'Private' sector orientation

'Public' sector orientation

Small

Typical size of organizations

Sole trader

Partnership

Local Authority direct labour organizations

Co-operatives

Private limited company

Charities

QUANGOs

Building societies

Nationalized industries

Public limited company

Government departments

Large

the business and the individual are considered to be legally indistinguishable. An individual carries on business in his or her own name, with the result that the individual assumes all the rights and duties of the business. It follows that if the business is sued for breach of contract, this amounts to suing the individual. If the business does not have the resources to meet any claim, the claim must be met out of the private resources of the individual.

Becoming a sole trader requires the minimum of formality and for this reason it can be difficult to tell how many are being created or are in existence at any one time. The most commonly used indication is provided by VAT registrations, although this does not give a complete picture as businesses with a turnover of less than £52 000 (2000–01) do not need to register. Maintaining a business as a sole trader requires a minimum of formality – for example, there is no obligation to file annual accounts, other than for the assessment of the individual's personal tax liability.

It has been estimated that about 80 per cent of all businesses in the United Kingdom are sole traders, although they account for only a small proportion of gross domestic product. In some sectors of the economy they are a very popular business form and dominate sectors such as newsagents, window cleaners and hair-dressers. Sole traders can grow by taking on additional employees. There is no legal limit on the number of employees that a sole trader may have and there are many examples of sole traders employing over 100 people. At the other extreme, it is sometimes difficult to describe just when a sole trader business unit comes into existence, with many sole traders operating on a part-time basis – some 'moonlighting' without the knowledge of the tax authorities. Estimates of the annual value of this so-called 'black economy' are as high as £200 million per annum.

We should recognize a number of important characteristics of a sole trader. Firstly, it tends to have limited capital resources. Risk capital is generally only provided by the sole proprietor or close personal backers and additional loan capital is often only made available against security of the individual's assets. In the field of new product development, this type of business has very often made discoveries, but has been unable to see new products through to production and launch on account of a lack of funds. If a new product does make it into a competitive market, this type of business may face competition in price, promotional effort or product offering from larger and better resourced firms. The larger firm is likely to have greater resources to mount a campaign to see off a newer competitor.

Being relatively small, the sole trader may suffer by not being able to exploit the economies of scale available to larger firms. On the other hand, many sole traders aim for those sectors where economies of scale are either unimportant or non-existent, for example painting and decorating, hairdressing and outside catering. In many personal services, smallness and the personal touch, plus the fact that many small businesses do not need to charge their customers VAT, can be a strong selling point.

The small sole trader could find that it is too small to justify having its own expertise in many areas. Many do not have specialists to look after the accounting or advertising functions, for example. Furthermore, the goals and policies of the business can become totally dominated by the owner of the business. Although goals can be pursued determinedly and single-mindedly, the sole trader presents a narrower view than may be offered by a larger board of directors. The goals of a sole trader may appear very irrational to an outsider, where many individuals may be happy to continue uneconomic ventures on emotional grounds alone. Many very small caterers, for example, may be financially better off drawing unemployment benefit, but being a sole trader may satisfy wider goals of status or the pursuit of a leisure interest.

Many sole traders fail after only a short time, often because of the lack of management skills of an individual who may well be an expert in his or her own field of specialization. Others continue until they reach a point where lack of expertise and financial resources impose a constraint on growth. At this point, many sole traders consider going into partnership with another individual, or setting up a company with limited liability.

2.2.1 ## Sole trader or employee?

It can sometimes be difficult to decide whether a person is a self-employed sole trader or an employee of an organization. The distinction is an important one, because a trend during the 1990s was for large organizations to outsource many of their operations, often buying in services from apparently self-employed individuals. There can be many advantages in classifying an individual as self-employed rather than an employee. For the self-employed, tax advantages could result from being able to claim as legitimate business some expense items that are denied to the employee. The method of assessing income tax liability in arrears can favour an expanding small business. For the employer, designation as self-employed could save on National Insurance payments. It also relieves the employer of many

---

THINKING AROUND THE SUBJECT

What type of organization has won out in the battle to exploit the capabilities of the Internet? The early days of the Internet were dominated by stories of 'nerds' beavering away in a spare room at home to develop a website. This was a classic approach of the sole trader, which had previously seen low-cost, innovative individuals exploit new opportunities in mobile phone retailing and video rental, among many others. Free of any bureaucracy, entrepreneurial small sole traders could single mindedly pursue their dream of a 'new economy' in which any small business was able to communicate with the whole world from a humble makeshift office.

The small sole trader soon began to lose out in the competitive stakes, as big limited companies rapidly became the driving force in the Internet era. Belying their image as lumbering dinosaurs, the corporate giants adopted e-commerce, evolving their working practices and supply chains to gain substantial benefits. The advantages held by these established bricks-and-mortar companies over the upstart dot.com entrepreneurs included industry depth, a strong brand identity and customer trust. These established limited companies had good access to capital, and expertise in managing their existing businesses.

In a survey conducted in 2000, the consultant KPMG found that 75 per cent of European companies with turnovers greater than £500 million had already used e-commerce to launch a new product or promote an existing one and 83 per cent expect to be using the Internet for business transactions within a year or two.

Meanwhile, what of the sole traders who were the pioneers of the Internet? Many of their businesses grew rapidly to establish a position in the marketplace, for example lastminute.com started on a very limited budget, but by 2001 had become a mainstream business with public limited company status. Other entrepreneurs could not keep up with the pace of competition and either sold out to larger, better resourced rivals (e.g. jungle.com sold out to the GUS group) or went into receivership through lack of funds (e.g. Boo.com).

With hindsight, could the respective roles of sole traders and large limited companies have been predicted? Was it only to be expected that sole traders would be the early innovators of a niche product, to be rapidly overtaken by larger companies when their markets became mainstream?

duties that are imposed in respect of employees but not subcontractors, such as entitlement to sick pay, notice periods and maternity leave.

The problem of distinction is particularly great in the construction sector and for service sectors (such as market research) which employ large numbers of part-time workers. The courts would decide the matter, among other things, on the basis of the degree of control that the employer has over the employee and their level of integration within the organization. If the employer is able to specify the manner in which a task is to be carried out, and assumes most of the risk in a transaction, then an employment relationship generally exists. If, however, the required end result is specified but the manner in which it is achieved is left up to the individual, who also bears the cost of any budget overrun, then it is most likely that a contract for services will exist, in other words, self-employment.

2.3	PARTNERSHIPS

Two or more persons in partnership can combine their resources and expertise to form what could be a more efficient business unit. The Partnership Act 1890 defines a partnership as 'the relation which subsists between persons carrying on a business with a view to profit'. Partnerships can range from two builders joining together to a very large accountancy or solicitors' practice with hundreds of partners.

Partnerships are generally formed by contract between the parties, although, where this is not done, the Partnership Act 1890 governs relationships between the partners. Among the main items in a Partnership Agreement will be terms specifying:

1 The amount of capital subscribed by each partner

2 The basis on which profits will be determined and allocated between partners and the management responsibilities of each partner – some partners may join as 'sleeping partners' and take no active part in the management of the business

3 The basis for allocating salaries to each partner and for drawing personal advances against entitlement to profits

4 Procedures for dissolving the partnership and distributing the assets of the business between members.

Despite this internal agreement between partners, partnerships in England and Wales have not had their own legal personality. As a consequence, the partners incur unlimited personal liability for the debts of the business. Furthermore, each partner is jointly liable for the debts incurred by all partners in the course of business. An added complication of a partnership is that the withdrawal of any one partner, either voluntarily or upon death or bankruptcy, causes the automatic termination of the partnership. A new partnership will come into being, as it would if an additional partner was admitted to the partnership.

Because of the lack of protection afforded to partners, this form of organization tends to be relatively uncommon, except for some groups of professional people, where business risks are low and for whom professional codes of practice may prevent the formation of limited companies. To overcome the problem of limited liability, the Limited Liability Partnerships Act 2000 created a new form of partnership with limited liability. The Act extends limited liability to partnerships in specified circumstances and is likely to be popular with professional partnerships of accountants, solicitors, dentists and opticians.

2.4   LIMITED COMPANIES

It was recognized in the nineteenth century that industrial development would be impeded if investors in business always ran the risk of losing their personal assets to cover the debts of a business over which very often they had no day-to-day control. At the same time, the size of business units had become larger, causing the idea of a partnership to become strained. The need for a trading company to have a separate legal personality from that of its owners was recognized from the Middle Ages, when companies were incorporated by Royal Charter. From the seventeenth century, organizations could additionally be incorporated by Act of Parliament. Both methods of incorporating a company were expensive and cumbersome, and a simpler method was required to cope with the rapid expansion of business enterprises that were fuelling the Industrial Revolution. The response to this need was the Joint Stock Companies Act 1844, which enabled a company to be incorporated as a separate legal identity by the registration of a Memorandum of Association and payment of certain fees. The present law governing the registration of companies is contained in the Companies Act 1985. Today, the vast majority of trading within the United Kingdom is undertaken by limited companies. The legislation of most countries allows for organizations to be created that have a separate legal personality from their owners. In this way, separate legal identity is signified in the United States by the title 'Incorporated' after a company's name, by 'Sociétié Anomie' in France, 'Gmbh' in Germany and 'Sdn. Bhd.' in Malaysia.

When a limited company is created under UK legislation, it is required to produce a Memorandum and Articles of Association. The Memorandum regulates the relationships of the company with the outside world while the Articles of Association regulate the internal administration of the company. Most limited companies are registered as private limited companies, indicated in company names by the designation 'Limited'. However, some larger companies choose to register as Public Limited Companies (PLCs) and face tougher regulatory requirements. These are described later in this chapter.

2.4.1   The Memorandum of Association

This is a statement about the company's relations with the outside world and includes a number of important provisions:

1   The first item to be considered is the name of the company. If it is a Private Limited Company, the name must end with the word 'Limited' (or its Welsh

equivalent 'Cyf' for companies registered in Wales). A number of restrictions exist on the company's choice of name – for example, the name must not cause confusion with an existing company or suggest a connection with royalty. The trading name will very often be quite different from the registered name, in which case the company is required to display the name and address of its owner at its business premises, on its business stationery and to customers and suppliers on request.

2   The second important element of the memorandum is a statement as to whether the liability of its members is limited, and if so what the limit of liability will be in the event of the company being wound up with unpaid debts. The majority of companies are limited by shares. Members' liability to contribute to the assets of the company is limited to the amount – if any – that is unpaid on their shares. An alternative is for companies to be limited by guarantee. In these companies, the liability of each member to make up for any shortfall in assets in the event of the company being wound up is limited to the value of his or her guarantee. This type of company is comparatively rare, being found mainly among non-profit-making organizations, such as professional and trade associations. A further, less common type of company occurs where the Memorandum specifies unlimited liability of members. Because the members of such companies have unlimited liability for the company's debts, they are liable to lose their personal assets – a problem that gave rise to the limited liability company in the first place. There has, however, been an increase in the number of unlimited companies since 1967 because the Companies Act of that year exempted them from filing their accounts with the Registrar of Companies, and hence publicizing their financial affairs.

3   The third important element of the Memorandum is the objects clause. This is particularly important because it specifies the scope within which the company can exercise its separate legal personality. There are two principal consequences of having an objects clause. Firstly, the clause protects investors who can learn from it the purposes for which their money is to be used. Secondly, it protects individuals dealing with the company, who can discover the extent of the company's powers. Any act that the company performs beyond its powers is deemed to be *ultra vires* and therefore void. Therefore, even where the directors of a company are in agreement with a contract which is beyond its powers, the contract itself would be void. The principle of *ultra vires* was amended by the Companies Act 1985, section 35, so that any person who enters into a contract with a company which is outside its objects, but which is sanctioned by the directors of the company, will be able to enforce it against the company, providing that he or she did not know that the contract was beyond the company's powers. In practice, it is common for companies to contain an objects clause that is drafted in a deliberately broad manner, allowing considerable freedom for the directors to move away from their traditional business area.

2.4.2 The Articles of Association

While the Memorandum regulates the relationships of the company with the outside world, the Articles of Association regulate the internal administration of the company, the relations between the company and its members and between the members themselves. The articles cover such matters as the issue and transfer of shares, the rights of shareholders, meetings of members, the appointment of directors and procedures for producing and auditing accounts.

Companies seeking to expand by acquiring a company may be held back by the target company's Articles of Association. The Articles may, for instance, restrict ownership of shares by any one person to a fixed percentage of the total, as has been the case in many newly privatized companies. Different shares may attract different voting rights, so that, despite acquiring a majority of shares, the acquiring company is not able to acquire effective control of the company. As an example, the Forte Hotel Group (subsequently acquired by the Granada group) owned a majority of the shares in the Savoy Hotel Group, which it sought to exercise control over. However, most of the shares that it held carried no voting rights and it did not hold a majority of the voting shares. It was therefore frustrated in its efforts to influence the Savoy Group's policy.

2.4.3 Company administration

A company acts through its directors who are persons chosen by shareholders to conduct and manage the company's affairs. The number of directors and their powers are detailed in the Articles of Association and, so long as they do not exceed these powers, shareholders cannot normally interfere in their conduct of the company's business. The Articles will normally give one director additional powers to act as managing director, enabling him or her to make decisions without reference to the full board of directors.

Every company must have a secretary on whom Companies Acts have placed a number of duties and responsibilities, such as filing reports and accounts with the Registrar of Companies. The secretary is the chief administrative officer of the company, usually chosen by the directors.

2.4.4 Shareholders

The shareholders own the company and in theory exercise control over it. A number of factors limit the actual control that shareholders exercise over their companies. It was mentioned earlier that the Articles of a company might discriminate between groups of shareholders by giving differential voting rights. Even where shareholders have full voting rights, the vast majority of shareholders typically are either unable or insufficiently interested to attend company meetings, and are happy to leave company management to the directors, so long as the dividend paid to them is satisfactory. In the case of pension funds and other institutional holders of shares in a company, their concern may be mainly with the stability of the financial returns from the business. In most large organizations, private investors are in a distinct minority in terms of the value of shares owned. There has been a tendency in recent years for individual shareholders to use their privileged position to raise issues of social concern at companies' annual shareholders' meetings. For example, small shareholders have used meetings of water companies as a platform to protest about poor levels of service and excessive directors' salaries. In 2001 the annual shareholders' meeting of the BP oil company was presented with a number of motions by individual shareholders disgruntled with the company's environmental policy and involvement in Tibet. Shareholders' revolts can have widespread public relations implications for companies.

2.4.5   ### Company reports and accounts

A company provides information about itself when it is set up through its Memorandum and Articles of Association. To provide further protection for investors and people with whom the company may deal, companies are required to provide subsequent information.

An important document that must be produced annually is the annual report. Every company having a share capital must make a return in the prescribed form to the Registrar of Companies, stating what has happened to its capital during the previous year, for example by describing the number of shares allotted and the cash received for them. The return must be accompanied by a copy of the audited balance sheet in the prescribed form, supported by a profit and loss account that gives a true and fair representation of the year's transactions. Like the Memorandum and Articles of Association, these documents are available for public inspection, with the exception of unlimited companies, which do not have to file annual accounts. Also, most small companies need only file an abridged balance sheet and do not need to submit a profit and loss account.

As well as providing the annual report and accounts, the directors of a company are under a duty to keep proper books of account and details of assets and liabilities.

2.4.6   ### Liquidation and receivership

Most limited companies are created with a view to continuous operation into the foreseeable future (although, sometimes, companies are set up with an expectation that they should cease to exist once their principal objective has been achieved). The process of breaking up a business is referred to as liquidation. Voluntary liquidation may be initiated by members (for example where the main shareholder wishes to retire and liquidation is financially more attractive than selling the business as a going concern). Alternatively, a limited company may be liquidated (or wound up) by a court under section 122 of the Insolvency Act 1986. The first stage of an involuntary liquidation is generally the appointment of a receiver who has authority, which overrides the directors of the company. An individual or company who has an unmet claim against a company can apply to a court for it to be placed in receivership. Most receivers initially seek to turn round a failing business by consolidating its strengths and cutting out activities that brought about failure in the first place, allowing the company to be sold as a going concern. The proceeds of such a sale are used towards repaying the company's creditors, and, if there is a sufficient surplus, the shareholders of the company. However, many directors who have lost their businesses claim that receivers are too eager to liquidate assets and unwilling to take any risks that may eventually allow both creditors and shareholders to be paid off. The Insolvency Act 1986 allows a period of 'administration' during which a company can seek to put its finances into order with its creditors, without immediate resort to receivership. Section 5.8 of the Act defines the circumstances in which an administration order may be made by a court.

Receivership affects organizations small and large and prolonged periods of receivership can leave staff and customers very uncertain about the future. Notable receiverships in recent years have included the International Leisure Group and the Bank of Credit and Commerce International. The Finelist Group is an example of a smaller company that went into receivership, and in this case the receivers successfully sold a number of the company's car component supplies businesses shortly after the receivership in 2000.

2.4.7 Public limited companies

The Companies Act 1985 recognized that existing companies legislation did not sufficiently distinguish between the small owner-managed limited company and the large multinational firm. Thus the concept of the public limited company – abbreviated to PLC – came about. The basic principles of separate legal personality are similar for both private and public limited companies, but the Companies Act 1985 confers a number of additional duties and benefits on public limited companies.

The difference is partly one of scale – a PLC must have a minimum share capital of £50 000 compared to the £100 of the private limited company. It must have at least two directors instead of the minimum of one for the private company. Before a public limited company can start trading, or borrow money, it must obtain a 'business certificate' from the Registrar of Companies, confirming that it has met all legal requirements in relation to its share capital.

Against these additional obstacles of the public limited company is the major advantage that it can offer its shares and debentures to the public, something that is illegal for a private company, where shares are more commonly taken up by friends, business associates and family. As a private limited company grows, it may have exhausted all existing sources of equity capital, and 'going public' is one way of attracting capital from a wider audience. During periods of economic prosperity, there has been a trend for many groups of managers to buy out their businesses, initially setting up a private limited company with a private placement of shares. In order to attract new capital, and often to allow existing shareholders to sell their holding more easily, these businesses have often been reregistered as public companies.

There are a number of additional strengths and weaknesses to PLC status which can be noted. Many companies highlight PLC status in promotional material in order to give potential customers a greater degree of confidence in the company. Another major strength is the greater potential ability to fund major new product developments. Against this, the PLC is much more open to public examination, especially from the financial community. Management may develop business plans that will achieve a long-term payback, bringing it into conflict with possibly short-term objectives of City financial institutions. Indeed, a number of companies have recognized this problem of PLC status and reverted to private status by buying back shares from the public – the Virgin Group for example converted back to a private limited company after a few years as a PLC.

Larger limited companies can sometimes be described as multinational companies. They have operations in many countries, although subsidiaries would

---

THINKING AROUND THE COMPANY

Raising capital on the stock markets may be easy for a public limited company when times are good, but interest can soon dry up when investors' confidence sags. The year 2000 had been very good for flotations, with records broken in terms of the number and value of issues. In that year a total of 138 companies joined the official list of the London Stock Exchange, raising a total of £10.6 billion. If the Alternative Investment Market is included the total number of flotations was 299.

Despite perceptions that 2000's crop of flotations was mainly attributable to the new rush of dot.com companies, they still only represented about half of all new flotations, with 49 companies joining the high-tech Techmark Index being balanced by 39 'traditional' companies which included EasyJet and the broker Collis Stewart.

Spectacular early gains from many floats soon reversed into equally spectacular losses as the dot.com bubble boomed and burst. The 'stags', who took early profits, reaped the biggest gains, leaving more loyal investors to bear the pain as their share values suffered. For a company seeking to raise additional capital, picking the height of the market can make an enormous difference to the amount

they actually receive. Lastminute.com got its timing just about right, hitting the market at about the peak of dot.com mania. High-profile investors such as Louis Vuitton's Bernard Arnault, actress Joanna Lumley, celebrity chef Gordon Ramsey and Lord Rothermere, publisher of the *Daily Mail*, reflected public confidence that their investments could only grow in value and were ready to throw money into the sector.

One year later sentiment had changed significantly and companies found investors much more reluctant to provide capital not just for dot.com companies, but for new flotations overall. One sign of the times was the flotation of part of Orange PLC in February 2001. The owners of Orange – France Telecom – were forced to reduce the offer price prior to flotation, and even then the shares fell by 15 per cent within the first week of trading. Despite the bleak outlook for the telecoms sector at the time, the Orange share offer was oversubscribed by members of the general public. Were investors slow to learn the lessons of the recent past? Could companies such as France Telecom afford to hold out until market sentiment had changed and their share offers would be able to command a premium?

usually be registered locally in each country of operation. A multinational company based overseas may register a subsidiary in the United Kingdom as a private limited company in which it holds 100 per cent of the shares. UK-based companies which are holding companies for overseas subsidiaries are most likely to be registered as public limited companies.

Today, although public limited companies are in a numerical minority, they account for a substantial proportion of the equity of the limited company sector and cover a wide range of industries which typically operate at a large scale – for example banking, car manufacture and property development.

2.4.8 ### Advantages and disadvantages of limited companies

To summarize, comparisons between sole traders and partnerships on the one hand and limited companies on the other, can be made at a number of levels. Firstly, formation of a limited company is relatively formal and time consuming – for a sole trader there is the minimum of formality in establishing a business. The added formality continues with the requirement to produce an annual return and set of accounts. On the other hand, limited company status affords much greater protection to the entrepreneur in the event of the business getting into financial difficulty. Raising additional funds would usually be easier for a limited company, although personal guarantees may still be required to cover loans to the company. Additional funding which limited company status makes possible, especially public limited company status, allows organizations to embark on more ambitious expansion plans. While a sole trader may concentrate on small niche markets, a limited company may be in a better position to tackle mainstream mass markets.

2.5 ## COMMERCIAL AND QUASI-COMMERCIAL ORGANIZATIONS OPERATING IN THE PUBLIC SECTOR

Government has traditionally been involved in providing goods and services that cannot be sensibly provided by market forces – for example defence, education and basic health services. Government involvement has, however, developed beyond providing these public services to providing goods and services that could also be provided by private sector organizations.

Public sector organizations take a number of forms, embracing government departments and agencies, local government, nationalized industries and all other undertakings in which central or local government has a controlling interest. Here we will focus on those public sector organizations that supply goods and services to consumers. Those government organizations that are primarily policy making in nature will be considered in more detail in Chapter 8 dealing with the political environment. In between those branches of government responsible for providing goods and services and those responsible for policy are an increasing number that are involved in both. For example, many public services such as National Health

Service Trusts are increasingly selling services at a profit, although this is not their primary function and represents a small part of their total turnover.

2.5.1   State-owned enterprises

Goods and services provided on a commercial basis have often been provided through state-owned enterprises, often referred to as nationalized industries. Most countries have a state-owned industry sector and the size of the sector generally reflects the political ideology of a nation. The United States has traditionally had very few government-owned business organizations, France has taken nationalization to sectors such as banking which many would consider a prerogative of the private sector, while the United Kingdom has seen a once large state-owned industry sector shrink with changes in political ideology. The UK state-owned industries accounted for less than 1 per cent of GD Product in 1999, having fallen from 9 per cent in 1979.

Governments first became involved in industry for largely pragmatic reasons. Thus in 1913, a key shareholding in the Anglo-Iranian Oil Company – the precursor of British Petroleum – was acquired by the British government to ensure oil supplies to the Royal Navy. During the interwar years, the Central Electricity Generating Board, the British Broadcasting Corporation and the London Passenger Transport Board were created to fill gaps that the private sector had not been capable of filling. Whereas the reasons for the creation of these early nationalized industries were largely pragmatic, the early postwar period saw a large number of nationalized industries created for increasingly ideological reasons. During the Labour government of the early postwar years, the state acquired control of the coal, electricity, gas, iron and steel industries and most inland transport. Some industries returned to the private sector during the Conservative government of the 1950s, while others were added by subsequent Labour governments.

The 1980s and 1990s have seen a great demise in the role of nationalized industry, not just in the United Kingdom but throughout the world. Postwar Europe may have needed centralized planning and allocation of resources to facilitate the reconstruction effort, but the mood had been changed by the relatively affluent, consumer-oriented years of the 1980s. The view went around that governments were bad managers of commercial businesses and that private sector organizations were much more capable of giving good value to consumers. In the rush to sell off state-owned industries, privatization was often confused with deregulation. Simply transferring a nationalized industry to the private sector could easily create a private monopoly which was unresponsive to consumers' needs. Consequently, most privatization has been accompanied by measures to deregulate sectors of the economy. Where this has been impractical, government intervention has been retained in the form of regulation of prices and service standards.

Governments have chosen a number of methods to transfer state-owned industries to the private sector. The most common have been:

1 *Sale of shares to the public*   Before shares in a state-owned organization can be sold to the public, a private sector limited company with a shareholding must

be formed. Initially, all of the new company's shares are owned by the government, and privatization subsequently involves selling these shares to the public. For large privatizations, shares may be targeted at international investors in order to secure the substantial amounts of share capital sought. Sale to the general public has been undertaken where it would be considered politically unacceptable to exclude small investors from the benefits of privatization.

2 *Trade sale* Smaller state-owned industries have often be easily sold to other private sector companies as a complete entity. This happened, for example, in the sale of the then state-owned Rover Group to British Aerospace. Sometimes, parts of nationalized industries have been broken away for sale to private buyers (e.g. the shipping and hotel operations of British Rail were separated from the parent organization for sale to the private sector, long before the rail privatization of the 1990s). The administrative costs of this method of disposal are relatively low, but governments are open to allegations that they sold off a private sector asset too cheaply to favoured buyers.

3 *Management/employee buy-out* This is often a popular option for people-intensive businesses which financial institutions may have difficulty in deciding on a value, especially in industries with a history of poor industrial relations. It was used as a method of disposing of the National Freight Corporation and parts of the National Bus Company.

4 *Franchising/subcontracting* Sometimes, it may be politically unacceptable, or just impractical to dispose of government assets into the private sector. Instead, the government may retain ownership of the assets, but pay a contractor to provide services using those assets. Contracts would usually include an incentive for the contractor, so that as their performance rises, the payment that they receive increases. In the United Kingdom, much of the management of the motorway network and Royal Navy dockyards is now in the hands of private sector consortia who receive bonus-related payments in return for work undertaken.

Prior to their privatization, many state-owned organizations have been restructured to make them more attractive to potential buyers. This has typically involved writing off large amounts of debt and offering generous redundancy payments to workers who would not therefore become a liability to a new owner. In doing this, Conservative governments have been accused of providing subsidies for private buyers, although, very often, such action has been essential to provide a buyer with a competitive business proposition.

While governments may be committed to reducing the role of state-owned industries, it has proved difficult to sell many of them for a variety of practical and ideological reasons. In the case of the Post Office, ideological objections have been raised at the prospect of the Royal Mail letter delivery monopoly being owned by a private sector company. This has not, however, prevented the Post Office from being reorganized along business lines, with private limited companies being formed for the main business units, one of which – Girobank – was sold off to

As a state-run enterprise, British Railways had for a long time been derided as a bad joke. Most rail passengers would be able to recount stories of late and cancelled trains, tasteless sandwiches from the buffet car and equipment that was well past its sell-by date. Fares were perceived to be very expensive.

The railways came into public ownership because they had ceased to make profits for their private owners in the 1920s and 1930s. They became starved of new investment and this was seen as a major hindrance for the postwar Labour government's national reconstruction plans. It is true that the great modernization plan of the postwar period did see a lot of new investment in the railways, for example new signalling and the replacement of steam trains with diesel and electric trains. Unfortunately, much of this investment was not customer-focused and customers increasingly voted with their wallets by going elsewhere. Passengers deserted in large numbers to the private car, coach services and, to an increasing extent, domestic air services. Freight customers found the cost, speed and reliability of road haulage gaining an edge over the railways. To the Conservative government of the 1990s, British Railways was suffering from a lack of entrepreneurship which could be overcome by replacing public sector employees and finance with new ideas and new capital brought in from the private sector.

Critics argued that rail privatization would be a privatization too far, and there was much debate about the best way that it could be achieved. British Railways was eventually spilt up into a large number of separate businesses. Ownership and maintenance of the track passed to Railtrack whose shares were offered to the public. Railtrack in turn subcontracted much of its maintenance work to other private companies. Train operation was sold off to 26 franchised companies, who leased trains from three privatized rolling stock companies. All of these are regulated by the Office of the Rail Regulator (Ofrail).

It did not take long for the critics of privatization to argue that the railways were now in worse shape than they ever were under state ownership. Even after allowing for early teething difficulties, there was often a suspicion that when things went wrong, companies simply passed the blame to one another. Train operators accused Railtrack if a train was late and Railtrack may have blamed a train operator for causing a blockage on its lines. This fragmentation was felt most seriously where accidents occurred and it was difficult to pin down responsibility. Worryingly, it seemed that the service quality improvements sought from privatization had actually gone into reverse. During 1998, a survey found that only 71.3 per cent of Virgin trains on its London–Glasgow route arrived on time or within 10 minutes of the scheduled time. Great Western and Great North Eastern Trains did not fare much better at 83.5 per cent and 88 per cent respectively, down on their preprivatization levels of reliability. Astonishingly, an international comparison found the Pakistan Railways route from Lahore to Karachi achieving 88 per cent reliability. Even the steam-hauled trains operating from Accra to Kumasi in Ghana beat Virgin's reliability, at 85 per cent. Critics of privatization argued that private companies were too concerned with cutting costs in order to meet their shareholders' expectations. Cost cutting and poor communications between companies was highlighted following a number of serious rail crashes, such as those which occurred near to London's Paddington station in 1999 and at

Hatfield in 2000. With most companies only having franchises of around seven years, cost reduction rather than investment was seen as the best way of improving profitability. At the same time as service quality was evidently deteriorating, the cost to the exchequer of supporting train services had actually increased. During 1998, private railway companies received £1.8 billion from the government, more than four times the £446 million support that British Rail received in 1990. In the first five years of privatization, private train operators were expected to receive £15 billion in operating subsidies, about double in real terms what British Railways had received in the last five years of state ownership.

Has rail privatization been a success? With railways being a long-term business, it may take some time to tell whether the investment necessary to run a reliable and efficient railway will yield benefits. Supporters of privatization point to a number of new initiatives introduced by the private companies, such as more flexible pricing, investment in improved station buildings and improved facilities for business class passengers. But could it be that much of the improvement, such as new train liveries and staff uniforms, is superficial while the fabric of the railway continues to suffer under-investment?

the Alliance and Leicester Building Society while another – the parcel delivery service – was restructured to act more like one of the private parcel companies with which it is having to compete in an increasingly competitive market.

It is also possible that attitudes towards privatization may be turning and after a decade of operation, it is now possible to see their problems as well as benefits. Very few people would advocate turning back the clock in sectors such as telecommunications where privatization and deregulation have been associated with rapidly falling prices and improving service standards. However, it is more doubtful whether privatization of the bus or water supply industries has been entirely beneficial. Customers of newly privatized train companies have pointed out that punctuality fell sharply in the years immediately after privatization, while public subsidies more than doubled. The complex relationships between companies in the rail industry have led many people to suggest that gaps in safety coverage exist, and that the centralized 'command and control' approach of the former state-owned British Rail offered a safer railway at a lower cost.

Table 2.1 gives a list of UK privatizations of state-owned industries. This is not a complete list. In some cases, the sale of shares was phased in over a number of periods.

The importance of a customer orientation within public corporations has been influenced by the nature of the market in which they operate. Following the late 1940s nationalizations, marketing was seen in many of the nationalized industries as being secondary to production. The relative unimportance of marketing was often associated with some degree of monopoly power granted to the industry. In these circumstances, public corporations could afford to ignore marketing. However, as production of the basic industries caught up with demand and the economy became more deregulated during the 1980s, consumers increasingly had choice between suppliers offered to them. For example, the deregulation of the

Table 2.1   UK privatizations

Organization	Date of privatization	Method of privatization
British Aerospace	1981	Public sale of shares
National Freight Corporation	1982	Employee/managment buy-out
British Telecom	1984	Public sale of shares
Jaguar	1984	Public sale of shares
Sealink	1984	Trade sale
British Gas	1986	Public sale of shares
British Petroleum	1986	Public sale of shares
BA Helicopters	1986	Trade sale
National Bus Company	1986–91	Trade sales/management buy-outs
British Airports Authority	1987	Public sale of shares
British Airways	1987	Public sale of shares
Rolls-Royce	1987	Public sale of shares
Leyland Bus Company	1987	Trade sale
British Steel	1988	Public sale of shares
Rover Group	1988	Trade sale
Regional Water Companies	1989	Public sale of shares
Regional Electricity Companies	1990	Public sale of shares
Powergen/National Power	1991	Public sale of shares
Scottish Electricity Companies	1991	Public sale of shares
British Coal	1994	Trade sale
British Rail	1994–97	Public sale of shares/trade sales

coach industry in 1981 and the growth in private car ownership placed increasing competitive pressure on British Rail, and hence an increasing importance for the organization to become customer oriented. British Rail was increasingly set profit objectives rather than poorly specified social objectives.

What could be seen as either a strength or a weakness for the state-owned industries has been finance for investment and new product development. Investment comes from government – either directly or through guarantees on loans from the private sector. Profits earned have not necessarily been ploughed back into the business. The public sector has since the 1930s been seen as one instrument for regulating the economy, cutting back or increasing investment to suit the needs of the national economy rather than the needs of the particular market that the corporation is addressing. As well as limiting the amount of investment funds available, government involvement has also been accused of delay caused by the time which it has taken to scrutinize and approve a proposal. By the time approval had been granted, the investment could be too late to meet changed market conditions.

State-owned industries are perceived as an instrument of government, and although theoretically they may have an independent constitution government is frequently accused of exercising covert pressure in order to achieve political favour. Fuel prices, rail fares and telephone charges have all at some time been subject to these allegations, which make life for managers in nationalized industries more difficult because of their confused objectives.

Britain is widely credited with having taken the lead in privatizing state-owned industries, and many countries have followed. The European Union (EU) has taken actions to reduce the anticompetitive consequences of having large subsidized public sector organizations distorting markets. This has been particularly true in the case of airlines, where many European countries have continued to support loss-making state-owned carriers. As an example, the EU Transport Commissioner has acted on objections from a number of European private sector airlines to reduce the amount of funding which the French government could give to Air France in its attempts to restructure.

2.5.2 **Local authority enterprise**

In addition to providing basic services such as roads, education, housing and social services, local authorities have a number of roles in providing marketable goods and services in competitive markets. For a long time, local authorities have operated bus services and leisure facilities, among others. Initially they were set up for a variety of reasons – sometimes to provide a valuable public service, at other times to help stimulate economic development or to earn a profit to supplement the local authority's income. Sometimes, where a project was too large for one authority and benefited many neighbouring authorities, a joint board would be formed between the authorities. This sometimes happened with local authority controlled airports, for example East Midlands Airport was formed by a joint board comprising Leicester, Derby, Nottingham, Derbyshire and Nottinghamshire authorities.

Increasingly, UK local authorities are being forced to turn their trading activities into businesslike units, separately accountable from the rest of the local authority's activities. In the case of local authority bus and airport operations, the Local Government Act 1988 required local authorities to create limited companies into which their assets are placed. Like any limited company, local authority owned companies are required to appoint a board of directors and to produce an annual profit and loss statement. By creating a company structure, it becomes easier to introduce private capital or, indeed, to sell off the business in its entirety to the private sector. This has occurred in the case of a large number of local authority bus companies and smaller airports.

Even where separate business units have not been created, local authority services are being exposed to increasing levels of competition. Operations in such areas as highway maintenance, refuse collection and street cleaning must now be assessed to ensure that they offer the 'best value' to the local authority. Local authorities have appointed Best Value units to monitor their activities against competitive benchmarks, and where necessary put the provision of services out to competitive tender. Where a private sector company takes over the provision of services for a local authority and takes on its employees, the new employer will generally take on responsibilities for accrued rights to redundancy payments, among other things. Best value requirements are discussed further in Chapter 8.

In other non-commercial local authority services, clients are being offered greater choice. With the advent of locally managed foundation schools, the governing bodies of schools are adopting – if somewhat grudgingly – a marketing orientation to ensure that the service they are offering is considered better than neighbouring schools that pupils would have the choice of attending. Only by attracting clients can they ensure funding for their school.

2.5.3

Private sector and public sector organizations compared

Although public sector organizations cover a wide range of services operating in diverse environments, a few generalizations can be made about the ways in which their business activities differ from those practised by the private sector:

- The aim of most private sector organizations is to earn profits for their owners. By contrast to these quantifiable objectives, public sector organizations operate with relatively diverse and unquantified objectives. For example a museum may have qualitative scholarly objectives in addition to relatively quantifiable objectives, such as maximizing revenue or the number of visitors.

- The private sector is usually able to monitor the results of its marketing activity, as the benefits are usually internal to the organization. By contrast, many of the aims that public sector organizations seek to achieve are external and a profit and loss statement sometimes cannot be produced in the way that is possible with a private sector organization operating to narrow internal financial goals.

- The degree of discretion given to a private sector manager is usually greater than that given to a counterpart in the public sector. The checks and balances imposed on many of the latter reflects the fact that their organizations are accountable to a wider constituency of interests than the typical private sector organization.

- Many of the marketing mix elements that private sector organizations can tailor to meet the needs of specific groups of users are often not open to public sector organizations. For non-traded public services, price – if it is used at all – is a reflection of centrally determined social values rather than the value placed on a service by consumers.

- Public sector organizations are frequently involved in supplying publicly beneficial services where it can be difficult to identify just who the customer is. Should the customer of a school be regarded as the student, their parents or society as a whole which is investing in a trained workforce of tomorrow?

- Just as the users of some public services may have no choice in who supplies their service, so, too, the suppliers may have no choice in who they can provide services to. Within the public sector, organizations may be constrained by statute from providing services beyond specified groups of users. On the other hand, some public sector organizations may be required by law to supply a service to specific groups, even though a market-led decision may lead them not to supply.

NON-DEPARTMENTAL PUBLIC BODIES

There are many types of organizations that do not fit neatly into the private or public sectors. Non-departmental public bodies (NDPBs) is the title given to a type of organization which has traditionally been referred to as a *QUANGO*. The NDPBs have been around in their modern form since before the Second World War and semi-independent public bodies of one sort or another have been part of British governance for two hundred years. They are used to carry out a variety of trading and policy formulation roles. We will return to their policy role in Chapter 8 and briefly note here the reasons why they have become an important type of business orientated organization. The following are the most important characteristics of NDPBs:

- They provide services that are considered politically inappropriate for private companies to provide.

- The assets of the organization are vested in a body whose constitution is determined by government and cannot be changed without its approval.

- Management of an NDPB is generally by political appointees rather than directly elected representatives.

- In theory, NDPBs operate at 'arm's length' from government and are free from day-to-day political interference.

- NDPBs have structures and processes that resemble private sector organizations in terms of their speed and flexibility.

- NDPBs are generally relatively small organizations compared to the larger bureaucracies, from which they were separated. Because of their autonomous nature, NDPBs may be financially more accountable than a department within a large government departmental structure. However, many would argue that they are generally much less politically accountable where vital public services are concerned.

- Decisions can generally be made much more speedily by a self-governing organization compared to a large government department where approval must first be obtained from several layers of a hierarchy.

The following are examples of NDPBs that have been created recently in Britain:

- Housing Associations, which now own and maintain much of the housing stock previously owned by local authorities.

- In many areas, organizations with the characteristics of NDPBs have been created to market areas as tourism destinations.

- Regional Development Agencies, which have been given, among other things, a remit to encourage inward investment to their areas.

In all of the above examples, bodies are motivated to satisfy the needs of their 'users' more effectively, as users usually have some element of choice. If a local tourist board is ineffective in attracting tourists to its area, it may lose local tourism expenditure to nearby areas whose boards have been more effective.

In practice, the business activities of NDPBs are often highly constrained. Many continue to depend upon central or local government for a large part of their income, which is protected from competition. Managers cannot act with as much freedom as their equivalents in the private sector, because the public and local media often take a keen interest in vital public services and are ready to voice their opposition about the activities of a non-elected body responsible for essential services. Another issue that has not been significantly put to the test is what happens to an NDPB if it fails to attract clients and therefore funding. Government would generally not allow such bodies to 'go out of business' in a way that a private sector organization can go into receivership. Instead, the tendency has been for the assets of a failing NDPB (such as a local tourist board) to be handed over to another body whose management has proved itself to be more capable of meeting clients' needs efficiently and effectively.

2.7   OTHER TYPES OF ORGANIZATION

2.7.1   Co-operative societies

Co-operatives can be divided into two basic types according to who owns them: consumer co-operatives and producer co-operatives.

Consumer co-operative societies date back to the mid-nineteenth century when their aims were to provide cheap, unadulterated food for their members and to share profits among members rather than hand them over to outside shareholders. The number of co-operative societies grew during the last half of the nineteenth century but has declined during recent years as a result of mergers, so that there were 46 retail societies in 1998. Nevertheless, co-operative societies collectively remain the fifth largest retailer in the United Kingdom.

Each co-operative society is registered under the Industrial and Provident Societies Acts, and not the Companies Acts, and has its own legal personality, very much as a private limited company. The main contrast between the two comes in the form of control of the society – an individual can become a member of a co-operative by buying one share and is entitled to one vote. Further shares can be purchased, but the member still only has one vote, unlike the private limited company where voting power is generally based on the number of shares held. The appeal of a shop owned by customers has declined of late, as customers have been attracted by competing companies offering lower prices and/ or better service. So the co-operative movement has responded by taking on many of the values of the private sector, for example through the abolition of 'dividend' payments and advertising low prices for all. However, the movement has tried to capitalize on its customer ownership by appealing to customers on the basis of its social responsibility. Promotion of co-operative retail stores has often sought to stress their 'green' credentials, while the Co-operative Bank has stressed that it does not lend for unethical purposes.

Producer co-operatives are formed where suppliers feel they can produce and sell their output more effectively by pooling their resources, for example by sharing manufacturing equipment and jointly selling output. Producer co-operatives are popular among groups of farmers, allowing individual farmers to market their produce more effectively than they could achieve individually. An example is Milk Marque, a dairy farmers' co-operative that has taken over many of the functions of the UK government's Milk Marketing Board. For the marketing of a producer co-operative to be successful, members need to share a sense of vision and have clear leadership. Where this is lacking, many producer co-operatives may be successful in buying products for their members at a discount, but less successful at marketing their output. Co-operative societies remain important in the agriculture and fishing sectors, where 1099 were recorded in 1994.

Producer co-operatives may fall foul of legislation to protect the competitiveness of markets where collectively the producers account for a high proportion of sales in the market. However, as most producer co-operatives tend to be quite local in their membership, there is usually the possibility of competition from producers located in other areas.

2.7.2   Charities and voluntary organizations

The aims of this group of organizations can be quite complex. Meeting a good cause, such as famine relief or cancer research, is clearly very important. However, these organizations often also set trading objectives, as where charities run shops to raise funds. Often, the way in which such businesses are run is just as important as the funds generated. For example, Dr Barnados runs coffee shops where providing training for disadvantaged staff is seen to be as important as providing a fast service for customers or maximizing the profits of the outlet.

In the United Kingdom, charities that are registered with the Registrar of Charities are given numerous benefits by the government, such as tax concessions (although recent changes in legislation have introduced stricter controls over their activities in order to reduce abuses of their status). Where a charity has substantial trading activities, it is usual for these to be undertaken by a separately registered limited company, which then hands over its profits to the charity.

In some respects, charities have become more like conventional trading organizations, for example in their increasingly sophisticated use of direct marketing techniques. However, in other respects they can act very differently to private and public sector organizations. Customers may show a loyalty to the charity's cause, which goes beyond any rational economic explanation. Employees often work for no monetary reward, providing a dedicated and low-cost workforce, which can help the organization achieve its objectives.

2.7.3   Building societies

Building societies are governed by the Building Societies Acts, which have evolved over time to reflect their changing role. They were for some time seen as being

Figure 2.2

Public limited companies have grown in number in recent years and added a number of former building societies whose members voted for conversion. Although PLC status does give numerous benefits over mutual status, there are also many benefits of remaining mutual. The Coventry Building Society has stressed the benefits of remaining mutual, arguing that it is achieving high levels of customer satisfaction and a financial performance which matches PLCs and returns the benefits to members

(*Source*: Reproduced with permission of the Coventry Building Society)

almost monopoly providers of money for house purchase, with strict regulations on the powers of societies in terms of their sources of funds and the uses for which loans could be advanced. With the liberalization of the home mortgage market, building societies now have wider powers of lending and borrowing and face much greater competition. As a result of this, societies have had to embrace marketing activities more fully. The Building Societies Act 1986 further allowed building societies the possibility of converting to public limited company status, eliminating the remaining controls imposed by the Building Society Acts (Figure 2.2).

2.7.4   **Franchise organizations**

Franchising refers to trading relationships between companies (see Figure 2.3). In terms of their legal status, the companies themselves could be any one of the types previously described. The franchisor (who owns the franchise brand name) is more likely to be a public or private limited company, while the franchisee (who buys the right to use the franchise from the franchisor) is more likely to be a sole trader, partnership or private limited company. The franchisor and franchisee have legally separate identities, but the nature of the franchise agreement can make them very interdependent.

Franchising is a rapidly growing type of business relationship and the British Franchise Association estimates that by the end of the 1990s, it accounted for over 20 per cent of retail sales in the United Kingdom. Franchising offers a ready-made

Figure 2.3
The elements of
franchising

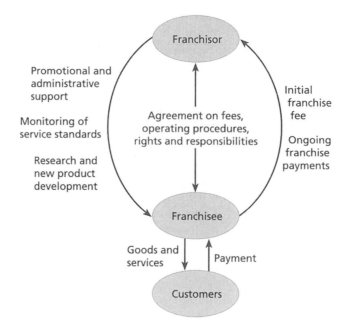

business opportunity for the entrepreneur who has capital but does not want the risk associated with setting up a completely new business afresh. A good franchise operation will have a proven business format and would already be well established in its market. The franchisee would be required to pay an initial capital sum for the right to use the name of the franchisor. This may sometimes seem high, but represents a relatively less risky investment than starting a completely new business. It has been estimated that whereas about 90 per cent of all new businesses fail within three years of starting up, 90 per cent of all franchisees survive beyond this period (British Franchise Association, 2001).

As well as the initial capital sum, a franchise agreement will usually include provisions for the franchisee to purchase stock from the franchisor and to pass on a percentage of turnover or profit. The franchisor undertakes to provide general marketing and administrative back-up for the franchisees.

Public services are increasingly being delivered by franchized organizations in order to capitalize on the motivation of smaller scale franchisees which was described above. Public sector franchises can take a number of forms:

1. The right to operate a vital public service can be sold to a franchisee who, in turn, has the right to charge users of the facility. The franchisee will normally be required to maintain the facility to a required standard and to obtain government approval of prices to be charged. In the United Kingdom, the government has offered private organizations franchises to operate vital road links, including the Dartford river crossing and Severn Bridge. In the case of the latter, an Anglo-French consortium acquired the right to collect tolls from users of the bridge and in return agreed to carry out routine maintenance work on it and to build a second river crossing.

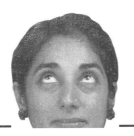

YOU HAVE THE HEAD FOR BUSINESS...

...WE HAVE THE HAT THAT FITS

As the clear brand leader in the Print-on-Demand market, we are seeking our next generation of franchisees to rapidly develop established centres. If you are capable of developing local business to exceed £1 million turnover, contact us to arrange a serious discussion on **0345 626748**

Major towns & cities available.

■ DIGITAL DESIGN PRINT COPY

www.prontaprint.com

Quote Ref: FT06/01

2 Government can sell the exclusive right for private organizations to operate a private service which is of public importance. In 2000, the UK government auctioned licences which would allow companies to offer 'third generation' mobile phone services. The government raised £22 billion from the sale of these licences and stipulated conditions under which mobile phone services would be provided by the successful bidders. Private sector radio and television broadcasting is operated on a franchise basis where the government invites bids from private companies for exclusive rights to broadcast in specified areas and/or times.

3 Where a socially necessary but economically unviable service is provided in a market-mediated environment, government can subsidize provision of the service by means of a franchise. An example of this can be seen in the way subsidies are paid by government to privatized train companies in order to support train services. The award of franchises followed competitive tendering.

4   Even though a public service is not market mediated at the point of delivery, production methods may nevertheless be market mediated and part of the production function may be provided through a franchise agreement. Such an arrangement can have benefits for customers where the franchisee is rewarded partly on the basis of feedback from users. A recent application of this type of franchise can be found in the field of higher education.

5   In the United Kingdom, possibly the longest established public sector franchise is seen in the Post Office. In addition to government-owned 'Crown' post offices, 'sub' post offices have traditionally been operated on a franchise basis in smaller towns. Franchises have been taken up by a variety of small shops and newsagents and generally offer a more limited range of postal office services compared to Crown offices.

2.8   'VIRTUAL' ORGANIZATIONS

The term 'virtual' organization has been widely used in recent years, and although it does not represent a particular legal basis for an organization, it is nevertheless useful to examine its characteristics.

The virtual organization refers to a network of independent companies, suppliers, customers, even one-time rivals linked by information technology to share skills, cost, and access to one another's markets and resources. The network can comprise any combination of legal form, for example multinational airlines may co-operate through virtual organizations to procure engineering resources, while more locally, many small businesses co-operate to promote tourism destinations. A characteristic of virtual organizations is that they may have no central office or internal hierarchy. Electronic commerce has facilitated their development. Hale and Whitlam (1997) define as 'virtual' any organization that is continually evolving, redefining and reinventing itself for practical business purposes. The aim of such organizations is to deliver services through structures and processes that are fast, flexible and flat. Virtual organizations can use computer-mediated communication to become more flexible and responsive than traditional business structures. They can allow small businesses to collaborate with minimal bureaucracy and can create value cost effectively. By drawing together essentially freelance individuals, virtual organizations can benefit from an inherent responsiveness to change in the business environment.

PROMOTING INWARD TOURISM: AN ORGANIZATIONAL CHALLENGE FOR LOCAL AUTHORITIES

The tourism sector provides evidence of a wide range of types of organization. A typical tourist desti-nation is likely to include many guesthouses, small hotels and restaurants operated by sole traders. Many of these have grown to become partnerships or limited companies. In addition to small busi-nesses, the tourism sector also has many much larger public limited companies, for example the large hotel and fast-food chains which can be found in most tourist destinations. But there is also a major role for government organizations. Much of the tourism infrastructure in the form of roads, car parks and signposting is provided by local and national government. In many countries local bus services are provided by government-owned operating companies.

Many tourist destinations remain dominated by small-scale organizations, but how can these col-lectively market the destination where they are located? It is, after all, quite likely that most tourists will need to be attracted to the destination before a small hotel or guest house has any hope of attracting that tourist to their particular business. There have therefore been many attempts to collectively market tourism destinations. By pooling resources, firms acting collectively can potentially achieve awareness and market growth levels that would not have been possible had individual firms acted alone in addressing their own localized markets with relatively unsophisticated marketing activities.

Private sector organizations have traditionally been good at attracting customers to their own facilities such as hotels and amusement parks. Local authorities have increasingly been taking an active role in promoting inward tourism to their areas, largely on account of their role in local economic development. The tourism product being marketed is a combination of elements from both the private and public sectors – the former responsible for tourist attractions operating to narrow com-mercial criteria, while the latter has responsibility for infrastructure and planning policies which affect tourism. In view of the external benefits inherent in area tourism promotion, the local authorities also play a large role in promoting the benefits of its area. But how can local authorities with traditional bureaucratic cultures match the entrepreneurial skills of the private sector? Moreover, how do they avoid duplicating the efforts of the private sector they are helping to promote? The solution adopted in many tourist seeking areas is co-operation between all parties involved in tourism. In many areas, public–private sector partnerships have been created.

Tourism marketing management poses a number of problems for local authorities. Many of the facilities which impinge on tourists' enjoyment of an area – such as car parking, cleanliness, planning and conservation policies – have traditionally operated in a bureaucratic planning culture rather than a marketing culture. In marketing an area, local authorities are constrained by bureau-cratic culture and political pressure to meet the needs of its own residents as well as those of potential visitors. But against this, the visitors who the local authority is seeking to attract are becoming increasingly selective in the face of competition from many areas – in short, local authorities have had to become very customer centred in their attempts to attract visitors.

In an attempt to combine the need for centrally administered marketing of an area with the dynamism of the private sector, local collaborative marketing ventures have become common in this field. Examples include the Birmingham Visitor and Convention Bureau and the Greater Glasgow and Clyde Valley Tourist Board. Co-operative tourism marketing organizations typically comprise district and county councils, urban development corporations, local landowners, hotel owners and operators of tourism attractions. Each partner contributes funds to support items of expenditure which in their own right might not yield a return, but result in more tourist spending across the area as a whole. Most of these organizations have been incorporated as formal limited companies, providing an organizational structure which is separately accountable and is attractive to private sector partners.

The creation of tourism development companies has brought the dynamism of private sector type organizations to a framework in which strategic marketing decisions and action programmes can be developed. Examples of successful collaboration include the development of conference centres which bring together private sector conference and hotel developers, transport operators and local authorities. A local authority's objectives (such as creating employment or eliminating eyesores) can often be achieved more effectively by delivering its services – such as signposting, car park provision and land-use planning – within the framework of a marketing strategy developed jointly with the private sector.

The development of electronic commerce now offers new opportunities for collaboratively marketing tourism destinations. There is the potential to create 'virtual co-operation', whereby potential tourists can browse through websites of individual facilities at a destination and develop a coherent picture of the destination experience on offer. The creative linking of websites facilitates the profiling of enquiries in a way that allows potential tourists to develop their own package of experiences from a visit to a destination.

CASE STUDY Review questions

1 Contrast the objectives of public and private sector organizations which are involved in tourism.

2 Summarize the benefits of collaboration between public and private sector organizations in the tourism sector.

3 What do you understand by 'external benefits' of tourism promotion?

CHAPTER Summary and links to other chapters

There are numerous ways of classifying business organizations. Classification based on legal status is useful because this is often related to other factors such as size, the ability to raise fresh capital and the level of constraints imposed on marketing managers. Private sector organizations range from the informality of the sole trader to the formality of the public limited company. In between is a diverse range of organizations, each of which has its role in the business environment. Some of these differences will become apparent in Chapter 6 which reviews competition within markets. While small sole traders may be associated with perfectly competitive markets, the reality of most markets is of domination by a small number of public limited companies. There is also diversity within public sector organizations, although this group as a whole has tended to diminish in relative importance in most Western countries. Chapter 8 continues the discussion of organizational structures within the public sector by focusing on government bodies that are policy making rather than operational. The following chapter will discuss how organizations grow. This chapter has laid the ground by suggesting that there are differences in organizations' inherent abilities to grow.

CHAPTER   Review questions

1   (a)   Identify the main strengths of two of the following types of business enterprise:

- Sole trader
- Partnership
- Limited company
- Plc

and assess the extent to which the strengths of one form are weaknesses of the other.

(b)   Prepare two slides for a business presentation comparing the ability of the two forms of enterprise to cope with a changing environment.

(Based on CIM Marketing Environment Examination)

2   In what ways are the marketing efforts of a sole trader and a limited company of similar size likely to differ?

3   For what reasons might a manufacturer of fitted kitchens seek PLC status? What are the advantages and disadvantages of this course of action?

4   Why have governments found it difficult to privatize state-owned postal services? Suggest methods by which private sector marketing principles can be applied to state-owned postal services.

5   Critically assess the benefits to the public of turning branches of the National Health Service into self-governing trusts.

6   Why have franchise organizations become so important in the United Kingdom?

References

British Franchise Association (2001) *The British Franchise Association Annual Survey of Franchising*, BFA, London.
Hale, R. and P. Whitlam (1997) *Towards the Virtual Organization*, McGraw-Hill, Maidenhead.

Selected further reading

A useful starting point for further reading is one of a number of books discussing the purpose of organizations and their role in society:

Bagnall, G. (1992) 'Legal Aspects of Business Start-up', SLS Legal Publications, Belfast.
Cyert, R. and J. March (1992) *A Behavioural Theory of the Firm*, 2nd edn, Blackwell, Oxford.
Handy, C. (1993) *Understanding Organizations*, 4th edn, Penguin, London.

For a review of current statistics on the composition of business units, the following sources are useful:

Department of Trade and Industry, *SME Statistics*, The Stationery Office, London.
Office for National Statistics, *Annual Abstract of Statistics*, The Stationery Office, London.

To gain a further insight into the financing of business organizations and the role of shareholders, the following is useful:

Davis, E.W. (1994) *Finance and the Firm: An Introduction to Corporate Finance*, 2nd edn, Oxford University Press, Oxford.

The following provides a useful background on franchising:

British Franchise Association, *The British Franchise Association Annual Survey of Franchising*, BFA, London.

The nature of public sector organizations has changed considerably in recent years and the following provide an overview of this change:

Farnham, D. and S. Horton (1996) *Managing the New Public Services*, 2nd edn, Macmillan, Basingstoke.
Lawton, A. (1994) *Organization and Management in the Public Sector*, 2nd edn, Pitman, London.

This chapter has noted the recent growth in QUANGOs and these are discussed in the following:

Milne, K. (1997) 'Opening a can of Quangos', *New Statesman*, 27 March, vol. 126, no. 4327, p. 24.
Mulgan, G. (1994) 'Democratic dismissal, competition and contestability among the quangos', *Oxford Review of Economic Policy*, October, vol. 10, no. 3, pp. 51–60.

Charities are becoming increasingly involved in business activities and their distinctive characteristics are discussed in the following:

Sargeant, A. (1999) *Marketing Management for Non-Profit Organizations*, Oxford University Press, Oxford.

For a review of 'virtual' organizations, the following are useful sources:

Barnatt, C. (1997) 'Virtual Organization in the Small Business Sector: The Case of Cavendish Management Resources', *International Small Business Journal*, vol. 15, no. 4, pp. 36–47.
Davidow, W.H. and M.S. Malone (1992) *The Virtual Corporation*, Harper Collins, New York.

Useful websites

British Franchise Association   Useful resources relating to the role of franchising.
http://www.british-franchise.org/menu.html

Building Societies Association   The Building Societies Association is the trade association for the United Kingdom's building societies. This site provides useful resources relating to the role of building societies.
http://www.bsa.org.uk/

Business Bureau   A commercial site offering an overview of the legislation with particular relevance to small business creation and management.   **http://www.businessbureau-uk.co.uk/law/law.html**

Confederation of British Industry   The CBI is the premier organization speaking for companies in the United Kingdom. Its website provides details of CBI surveys and discussion of topical issues affecting business organizations.   **http://www.cbi.org.uk/home.html**

Co-operative Society links   This site provides links to co-operative societies throughout the world.
http://www.jlp86.freeserve.co.uk/pages/links.html

Virtual Society Research Programme   An ESRC funded programme at Oxford University into the impacts of virtual electronic relationships.   **http://www.virtualsociety.org.uk**

Key terms

Building societies	Privatization
Charities	Public limited company
Co-operative society	QUANGO
Flotation	Receivership
Franchising	Share capital
Limited company	Shareholders
Liquidation	Sole trader
Nationalized industry	Stock exchange
Non-departmental public body	Virtual organization
Partnership	

3

Organizational objectives, growth and scale

CHAPTER OBJECTIVES

In the previous chapter we saw that business organizations take a variety of forms, and this is reflected in a diversity of organizational objectives. Like most living organisms, business organizations have an almost inherent tendency to grow. Growth satisfies a wide range of interests, including those of shareholders, directors, employees and government agencies. The first aim of this chapter is to explore the nature of organizational objectives and reasons for organizational growth. Growth can go beyond a point where diseconomies of scale set in, and this chapter explores the constraints on growth and reasons behind the recent resurgence in small businesses. The chapter reviews strategies (formal and informal) that organizations use to pursue growth. Raising finance to fund growth can be a critical issue and rapid growth which is overreliant on loan capital can prove very risky. The merits of organic growth and growth by acquisition are discussed in this chapter.

THE OBJECTIVES OF ORGANIZATIONS

All organizations exist to pursue objectives of one description or another. It is important to understand the nature of organizational goals as these will affect – among other things – the way the organization makes purchases, sets prices or pursues a market share strategy. Whether somebody is selling to or competing with another organization, a study of the organization's objectives will help to understand how it is likely to act.

Very broadly, organizational goals can be classified into a number of categories:

1. Those that aim to make a profit for their owners
2. Those that aim to maximize benefit to society
3. Those that aim to maximize benefits to their members.

Of course, many organizations combine these objectives, as in the case of the trading activities of charities which aim to make the maximum profits which can, in turn, benefit disadvantaged groups in society. In the following section we will look in detail at more specific objectives of business organizations.

Profit maximization

It is often assumed that business organizations will always try to maximize their profits, through a combination of maximizing revenue and minimizing costs. It is often thought that the pursuit of profit maximization is the unifying characteristic of all private sector business organizations and, indeed, economic theory is very much based on the notion of the profit maximizing firm.

However, simple models of profit maximization are open to question, even if it is recognized for the moment that profit may be of only marginal relevance to organizations that exist largely for their members' or society's benefit. These are some of the more important limitations on profit maximizing theories:

1   The profit maximizing objective must be qualified by a time dimension. A firm pursuing a short-term profit maximizing objective may act very differently to one that seeks to maximize long-term profit. This may be reflected in a differing emphasis on research and development, new product development and market development strategies. Whether an organization is able to pursue long-term profit maximizing objectives will be influenced by the nature of the environment in which it operates. It has frequently been suggested that the financial environment of the United Kingdom and the emphasis on short-term results has caused UK organizations to pursue much more short-term profit goals than organizations in, for example, Japan, where the nature of organizational funding has allowed a longer time for projects to achieve profits. Similarly, an organization operating in a relatively regulated environment – such as patented medicines – will be in a stronger position to plan for long-term profit maximization than one that is operating in a relatively unpredictable and competitive market.

2   A second major criticism of the dominance of profit maximization as a business objective is that maximization is not observed to occur in practice. In most organizations, there is a separation of ownership from management where the managers of the company have little or no stake in the ownership of the company. Managers may be inclined to pursue policies more in line with their own self-interests, so long as they make sufficient profit to keep their shareholders happy. Instead of pursuing maximum profits, the managers of the company may pursue a policy of maximizing sales turnover, subject to achieving a *satisfactory* level of profits.

3   In practice, it can be very difficult to quantify the relationship between production costs, selling prices, sales volumes and profit. Managers may have inadequate knowledge about these linkages with which to pursue profit maximization effectively.

3.1.2   Market share maximization

Market share maximization may coincide with profit maximization, in cases where there is a close correlation between market share and return on investment. It has been suggested that this occurs in many sectors, such as UK grocery retailing. There are other instances, however, where there is a less straightforward relationship between market share and profitability. For example, in the UK retail travel agency sector, both the market leader and small specialist retailers have achieved reasonable returns on investment, but many medium-sized firms have faced below average returns.

There are circumstances and reasons why a firm may pursue a policy of maximizing market share independently of a short-term profit maximizing objective. Domination of a particular market may give stability and security to the organization. This might be regarded as a more attractive option for the management than maximizing profits. Building market share may itself be seen as a short-term strategy to achieve longer term profits, given that there may be a relationship between the two.

Pursuing a market share growth objective may influence a number of aspects of a firm's business activities, for example it may cut prices and increase promotional expenditure, accepting short-term losses in order to drive its main rivals out of business, leaving it relatively free to exploit its market.

3.1.3 Corporate growth

As an organization grows, so too does the power and responsibility of individual managers. In terms of salaries and career development, a growth strategy may appear very attractive to these people, not only for their own self-advancement, but also as an aid to attracting and retaining a high calibre of staff, attracted by the prospects of career development. However, such enthusiasm for growth could lead the owners of the business to pursue diversification into possibly unknown and unprofitable areas. As an example, the fashion retailer Next which is now very successful, earlier came very close to bankruptcy when it expanded too rapidly into relatively unknown activities such as the operation of convenience stores and travel agencies. Shareholders are often happy to back the management and

---

THINKING AROUND THE SUBJECT

Should a company 'stick to its knitting' and do what it is good at, or search continually for new products and new markets? Countless companies have reported disastrous results after growing into areas they knew very little about. Many UK clearing banks diversified into estate agency, but regretted the move later. W H Smith went through bad years in the mid-1990s when the newsagent's diversification into DIY retailing and television, among other things, failed to work. The airport operator BAA diversified into hotels, but soon realized that it made more sense to concentrate on its airport operations and leave hotels to expert operators in the field.

But isn't growth into new markets essential for companies, especially those facing static or declining markets? One of the United Kingdom's leading grocery retailers, Asda, would not be where it is today had not the

Associated Dairy company taken a risk and set up a retailing operation. The security services company Securicor knew that it was taking a risk when it invested in a joint venture with British Telecom to create the successful Cellnet mobile phone network. And a small company called WPP (the initials standing for Wire Plastic Products) took huge risks on its way to becoming the owner of one of the world's leading advertising agencies, J Walter Thompson.

It is fine with hindsight to criticize a firm's decisions about which direction its corporate growth should take. But in an uncertain world, risks have to be taken. A sound analysis of a company's strengths and weaknesses and of its external environment certainly helps, but successful growth also depends upon an element of luck.

take risks when times are good, but may benefit in the longer term by being more cautious and critical of its management's recommendations.

Satisficing

Given that the managers of a business are probably not going to benefit directly from increased profits, the argument has been advanced that managers aim for *satisfactory* rather than *maximum* possible profits. Provided that sufficient profit is made to keep shareholders happy, managers may pursue activities that satisfy their own individual needs, such as better company cars for themselves, or may pursue business activities that give them a relatively easy life or add to their ego. To achieve these diverse individual objectives, part of the organization's profit that could be paid out to shareholders is diverted and used to pay for managerial satisfaction. The extent to which satisficing represents an important business objective can be debated. It can be argued that in relatively competitive markets, competitive pressures do not allow companies to add the costs of these management diversions to their selling prices. If they did, they would eventually go out of business in favour of companies whose shareholders exercised greater control over the costs of their managers. Only in stable and less competitive markets can these implied additional costs be borne by adding to prices.

There has been a growing tendency for the owners of a business to give senior managers of the business contracts of employment that are related to profit performance. While this may lessen the extent of the apparent conflict of objectives for management, a trade-off may still have to be made where, for example, a decision is required on whether to spend more money on better company cars for managers. Should they spend the money and get all of the benefit for themselves, or save costs in order to increase profits, of which they will receive only a share?

Satisficing behaviour can have a number of implications for a company's operations. Buying behaviour in any organization is likely to be complex, but companies that are satisficing are likely to attach greater importance to the intangible decision factors such as ease of order, familiarity with a sales representative and the level of status attached to a particular purchase, rather than the more objective factors such as price and quality. There may be a tendency to recruit staff on a more informal basis, with the implication that recruitment is driven by a desire to be surrounded by like-minded people, rather than the type of employee who is most effective at maximizing income from customers.

Survival

For many organizations, the objective of maximizing profit is a luxury for management and shareholders alike – the overriding problem is simply to stay in business. Many businesses have had to close not because of poor profitability – their long-term profit potential may have been very good – but because they ran out of short-term cash flow. Without a source of finance to pay for current expenses, a longer term profit maximizing objective cannot be achieved. Cash-flow problems could come about for a number of reasons, such as unexpected increases in costs, a fall in revenue resulting from unexpected competitive pressure or a seasonal pattern of activity that is different to that which was predicted. Survival as a business objective can influence business decisions in a number of ways. Pricing decisions may reflect the need to liquidate stock regardless of the mark-up or contribution to profit. This was evident during the Gulf War when many airlines were brought close to bankruptcy by the combination of falling volume of passenger business and increased fuel prices. In order to survive what many airlines thought would be a temporary blip, many offered very low fares just to keep cash flowing in order to cover their overheads. The need to survive can also affect an organizations' promotional activities. An advertising campaign to build up long-term brand loyalty may be sacrificed to a cheaper sales promotion campaign which has a shorter payback period. In order to survive, a firm may impose a 'freeze' on new staff recruitment and capital investment. The company may hope that this will be sufficient to overcome the short-term problem, but it may be creating longer term problems by weakening the ability of the company to meet customers' needs effectively and profitably.

3.1.6   Loss making

A company may be part of a group that needs a loss maker to set off against other companies in the group who are making profits that are heavily taxed by the Inland Revenue. Situations can arise where a subsidiary company makes a component that is used by another member of the group and although that subsidiary may make a loss, it may be more tax efficient for the company as a whole to continue making a loss rather than buy in the product at a cheaper price from an outside organization.

3.1.7   Personal objectives

Many businesses, especially smaller ones, appear to be pursuing objectives that have no economic rationality. They do not pursue maximum profits, and indeed may be quite happy making no profits at all. They may have no desire to grow and may be in no immediate danger of failure. Many small businesses are created to satisfy a variety of personal objectives. This was illustrated by the results of a survey undertaken by National Westminster Bank into the reasons why individuals set up their own business. It was claimed by 31 per cent of respondents that their main reason was a desire for independence, while only 26 per cent saw an opportunity to make money as the primary motivation. About 15 per cent were tempted into setting up their own business because they had been made redundant. Many new business owners also sought to combine a business with a hobby activity, a desire to remain active and the opportunity for friendly encounters with customers.

Many small businesses are set up by individuals using a capital lump sum which they have received (such as an inheritance or a redundancy payment). Many people in such circumstances have used their lump sum to invest in what are perceived as relatively pleasant and enjoyable businesses such as antique shops, tea-rooms and restaurants. Many fail in a competitive environment where personal objectives cannot be achieved without undue economic sacrifice (e.g. it has been estimated that over 80 per cent of all new restaurants fail within two years of opening).

However, many others continue to provide goods and services for an acceptable sacrifice from the owners in a marketplace where profit-motivated companies would be unable to meet their objectives. This may partly explain the domination of UK antique shops by small-business owner-managers and the absence of large chains of profit-motivated businesses.

3.1.8 Social objectives of commercial organizations

Occasionally, commercial organizations have overt social objectives of one form or another, usually alongside a financial objective, for example a requirement that the organization must at least break even. Charities such as Oxfam, while having clear objectives in maximizing their revenue, also state their objectives in terms of which groups they seek to benefit. Where they engage in trading activities (such as Oxfam shops), their social objectives may result in buying supplies from disadvantaged groups, even though this may not be the most commercially profitable.

Historically, many owners of commercial companies have adopted social objectives. For example, Quakers such as Cadbury and Rowntree sought to maximize the moral welfare of their workforce. In modern times, the Body Shop has an objective of not supporting experiments on animals, an objective that pervades many aspects of the company's business activities, including new product development and promotion. Even organizations which for the most part are pursuing profit objectives may pursue social objectives in some small areas of activity, as where an organization runs a sports or social club for its employees at a loss. The social responsibility of organizations, and the views of critics who are cynical about firms' social objectives, are discussed further in Chapter 5.

3.1.9 Maximizing benefits to consumers

An overriding objective of a marketing-oriented organization is to maximize consumer satisfaction. However, this has to be qualified by a second objective that requires the organization to meet its financial objectives. In the case of consumer co-operatives, maximizing the benefits to their customers has had significance beyond the normal marketing concept of maximizing consumer satisfaction. The co-operative movement was originally conceived to eliminate the role of the outside shareholder, allowing profits to be passed back to customers through a dividend which is related to a customer's spending rather than their shareholding. Any action that maximized the returns to the business by definition maximized the benefits to consumers.

The importance of consumer co-operatives has declined since the 1950s for a number of reasons. Consumer co-operatives could appear very attractive to consumers at a time when firms were essentially production oriented and when the demand for goods exceeded their supply. With the reversal of this situation, other retailers with greater organizational flexibility and a more overt marketing orientation have attracted custom by offering additional services to customers, often associated with lower prices.

During the 1990s, building societies had been to promote the fact that they did not have any shareholders to satisfy, and could therefore pass on savings to members. This led some building societies, such as Nationwide, to argue that they offered consistently lower mortgage rates than those societies that converted to public limited company status and who must therefore meet the profit expectations of shareholders.

3.1.10 Maximizing public benefits

In many government and charity organizations, it is difficult to talk about the concept of profit or revenue maximization. Instead, the organization is given an objective of maximizing specified aspects of public benefit, or 'externalities', subject to keeping within a resource constraint. Public sector hospitals are increasingly embracing the philosophy of marketing, but it is recognized that it would be inappropriate for them to be given a strictly financial set of objectives. Instead, they might be given the objective of maximizing the number of operations of a particular kind within a resource constraint. Similarly, a charity campaigning for improved road safety may set an objective of maximizing awareness of its cause among important opinion formers.

There is frequently a gap between the publicly stated objectives of a public sector organization and the interpretation and implementation of these objectives by the staff concerned. As in a private sector organization, management in the public sector could promote secondary objectives that add to their own individual status and security, rather than maximizing the public benefit. A manager of a hospital may pursue an objective of maximizing the use of high technology because this may be perceived as enhancing his or her career, even though the public benefit could be maximized more efficiently with simpler technology. Charities have sometimes been accused of becoming self-perpetuating bureaucracies, anxious to protect their organization, rather than being driven primarily by a passion for the cause that they promote.

In recent years, more pressure has been placed on public services such as education and defence to operate according to business criteria. As suppliers of services, public sector organizations are increasingly being set quantified objectives that reflect the needs of their clients. Improved research methods to find out more about client needs and more effective communication of their offering to clients have been part of this process towards a greater business orientation. Many public services have themselves become major consumers of services as peripheral activities such as cleaning and catering have been subcontracted out. This has resulted in the growth of a market-oriented service sector. Very often, the management and staff previously providing an ancillary service within a public sector organization have bought out the operation from their employer and now have to sell the service back to the authority. Their objectives have changed from a vague notion of maximizing public benefit to one of maximizing their own profit.

3.1.11 Complexity of objectives

A number of possible objectives for organizations have been suggested above. In practice, an organization is likely to be pursuing multiple objectives at any one time. Furthermore, objectives are likely to change through time. Trying to identify the objectives that are influencing the behaviour of an organization can present a number of practical problems.

The first place to look for a statement of an organization's objectives might be its Memorandum and Articles of Association. In the UK, this statement is required by the Companies Acts for all limited companies and includes an objects clause. In practice, companies frequently draw up their objects clause in a way that is so wide that the company can do almost anything.

A more up-to-date statement of objectives may be found in the annual report and accounts which limited companies must produce annually and submit to Companies House where they are available for public inspection. The report includes a Directors' report which may give an indication of the goals that the company is working towards. Many companies publish a mission statement, which gives a broad statement of the anticipated future direction that its business will take. We will return to the subject of mission statements in the following chapter.

Beyond this, the true objectives may be difficult for an outsider to determine. Indeed, clearly stating objectives in too much detail may put a firm at a commercial disadvantage when competitors adapt their behaviour accordingly. Even insiders may have difficulty identifying objectives.

3.2   THE GROWTH OF ORGANIZATIONS

It was noted earlier that organizations, like most living organisms, have an almost inherent tendency to grow. In this section, the reasons for growth and the options for growth that are open to business organizations are explored.

3.2.1   Reasons for growth

An organization can grow in size for a number of reasons:

1   The markets in which the organization operates may be growing, making growth in output relatively easy to achieve. In addition, in a rapidly growing market, if an organization were to maintain a constant output, its market share would be falling. Growth may be considered not so much a luxury as a necessity if it is to maintain its position in the market place. This could be particularly important for industries where economies of scale are an important consideration.

2   A critical mass may exist for the size of firms in a market, below which they are at a competitive disadvantage. For example, a retail grocery chain which is aiming for a broad market segment will need to achieve a sufficiently large size in order to obtain bulk discounts from suppliers which can in turn be passed on in lower prices to customers. Size could also give economies of scale in many other activities such as advertising, distribution and administration. Many new businesses may include in their business plan an objective to achieve a specified critical mass within a given time period.

3 An overt policy of growth is often pursued by organizations in an attempt to stimulate staff morale. A growing organization is likely to be in a strong position to recruit and retain a high calibre of staff.

4 In addition to the formal goals of growth, management may in practice pursue objectives that result in growth. Higher rates of growth can bring greater status and promotion prospects to managers of an organization, even if a more appropriate long-term strategy may indicate a slower rate of growth.

5 Some organizations may grow by acquiring competitors in order to limit the amount of competition in a market where this is considered to be wasteful competition. Many local bus operators in the UK have acquired routes from their competitors for this purpose, although the Competition Commission may impose conditions on such takeovers where there is a serious threat to the public interest. We will return to this subject in Chapter 6.

3.3.2 Organizational life cycles

It is common to talk about products going through a life cycle from launch, through growth and maturity to eventual decline. Many have suggested that organizations also go through a similar type of life cycle. There is evidence that an organization's goals may change over time. It has been argued by Grenier (1972) that periods of steady evolutionary growth are followed by periods of revolutionary development. Periods of crisis exist between states of stability (Hudson, 1995). A number of factors trigger the different stages in the life cycle of an organization. These can be external threats and opportunities (for example, the emergence of a powerful competitor or the availability of new technology), or the emergence of internal strengths and weaknesses (for example the appointment of a proactive manager or retirement of senior figures).

Within the private commercial sector, new enterprises have been associated with a missionary zeal, prompted by the need to survive in a fiercely competitive environment. Over time, an enterprise can establish a niche for itself, allowing it greater control over its markets (Sasser *et al.* 1978). This is an invitation for satisficing behaviour by managers, where personal social goals may achieve greater prominence relative to formal corporate goals (Cyert and March, 1963; Krabuanrat and Phelps, 1998).

One analysis of services organizations by Sasser *et al.* (1978) identified a number of stages in the life cycles of organizations:

■ *Stage 1 Entrepreneurial* In this stage, an individual identifies a market need and offers a product to a small number of people, usually operating from one location. While most entrepreneurs stay at this stage, some begin to think about growth, often entailing a move to larger and/or additional sites.

■ *Stage 2 Multisite rationalization* In this stage, the successful entrepreneur starts to add to the limited number of facilities. It is during this stage that the skills required for being a multisite operator begin to be developed. By the end of this stage, the organization gains a certain degree of stability at a level of critical mass. At this stage, franchising starts to be considered.

- *Stage 3 Growth* Here the company's concept has become accepted as a profitable business idea. The company is now actively expanding through the purchase of competitors, franchising/licensing the concept, developing new company-operated facilities or a combination of the three. Growth is not only influenced by the founder's desire to succeed but also from the pressures placed upon the company by the financial community.

- *Stage 4 Maturity* The number of new outlets declines and revenues of individual facilities stabilize and in some cases decline. This tends to be caused by a combination of four factors: changing demographics within the firm's market, changing needs and tastes of consumers, increased competition and 'cannibalization' of older products by firms' newer products.

- *Stage 5 Decline/regeneration* Firms can become complacent, and unless new products are developed or new markets found, decline and deterioration soon follows.

By identifying a company's position in the life cycle, the major objectives, decisions, problems and organizational transitions needed for the future can be anticipated. Thus firms can plan for necessary changes rather than react to a set of conditions that could have been predicted earlier.

3.2.3   Types of organizational growth

Growth of organizations can be analysed in terms of:

1 The object of the growth, which can be defined in terms of the development of new markets and/or new products

2 Organizational issues about how the growth is achieved.

The first of these issues can be analysed with the help of growth option matrices. For the second, two basic growth patterns for organizations can be identified – organic growth and growth by acquisition – although many organizations grow by a combination of the two processes.

3.2.4   Product/market expansion

An organization's growth can conceptually be analysed in terms of two key development dimensions: markets and products. This conceptualization forms the basis of the product/market expansion grid proposed by Ansoff (1957). Products and markets are each analysed in terms of their degree of novelty to an organization and growth strategies identified in terms of these two dimensions. In this way, four types of growth strategy can be identified.

The four growth options are associated with differing sets of problems and opportunities for organizations. These relate to the level of resources required to implement a particular strategy and the level of risk associated with each. It follows, therefore, that what might be a feasible growth strategy for one organization may not be for another. The characteristics of the four strategies are described below:

1   *Market penetration strategies* This type of strategy focuses growth on the existing product range by encouraging higher levels of take-up among the existing target markets. In this way a specialist tour operator in a growing sector of the holiday market could – all other things being equal – grows naturally, simply by maintaining its current business strategy. If it wanted to accelerate this growth, it could do this firstly by seeking to sell more holidays to its existing customer base and secondly by attracting customers from its direct competitors. If the market was in fact in decline, the company could only grow by attracting customers from its competitors through more aggressive marketing policies and/or cost reduction programmes. A market penetration strategy offers the least level of risk to an organization – it is familiar with both its products and its customers.

2   *Market development strategies* This type of strategy builds upon the existing product range that an organization has established, but seeks to find new groups of customers for them. In this way a specialist regional ski tour operator that has saturated its current market might seek to expand its sales to new geographical regions or aim its marketing effort at attracting custom from groups beyond its current age/income groups. While the organization may be familiar with the operational aspects of the product that it is providing, it faces risks resulting from possibly poor knowledge of different buyer behaviour patterns in the markets which it seeks to enter. As an example of the potential problems associated with this strategy, many UK retailers have sought to offer their UK shop formats in overseas markets only to find that those features that attracted customers in the United Kingdom failed to do so overseas.

3   *Product development strategies*   As an alternative to selling existing products into new markets, an organization may choose to develop new products for its existing customers. For example, a ski tour operator may have built up a good understanding of the holiday needs of a particular market segment, such as the 18–35-year-old affluent aspiring segment, and then seeks to offer a wider range of services to them than simply skiing holidays. It might offer summer activity holidays in addition. While the company minimizes the risk associated with the uncertainty of new markets, it faces risk resulting from lack of knowledge about its new product area. Often a feature of this growth strategy is collaboration with a product specialist who helps the organization produce the service, leaving it free to market it effectively to its customers. A department store wishing to add a coffee shop to its service offering may not have the skills and resources within its organization to run such a facility effectively, but may subcontract an outside catering specialist, leaving it free to determine the overall policy that should be adopted.

4   *Diversification strategies* Here, an organization expands by developing new products for new markets. Diversification can take a number of forms. The company could stay within the same general product/market area, but diversify into a new point of the distribution chain. For example, an airline that sets up its own travel agency moves into a type of service provision that is

Figure 3.1
An application of
Ansoff's growth
matrix to a hotel
operator

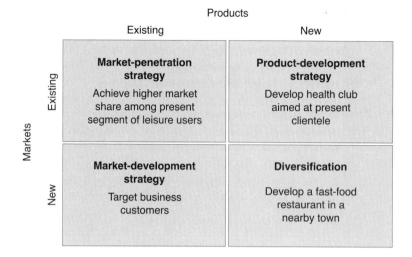

Figure 3.1 An application of Ansoff's growth matrix to a hotel operator

new to the organization, as well as dealing directly with a segment of the market with which it had previously probably had few sales transactions. Alternatively, the airline might diversify into completely unrelated service areas aimed at completely different groups of customers – by purchasing a golf course or car dealership, for example. Because the company is moving into both unknown markets and unknown product areas, this form of growth carries the greatest level of risk. Diversification may, however, help to manage the long-term risk of the organization by reducing dependency on a narrow product/market area.

An illustration of the framework, with reference to the specific options open to a seaside holiday hotel, is shown in Figure 3.1.

In practice, most growth that occurs is a combination of product development and market development. In very competitive markets, organizations would probably have to slightly adapt their products if they are to become attractive to a new market segment. For the leisure hotel seeking to capture new business customers, it may not be enough to simply promote existing facilities; in order to meet business peoples' needs, it might have to offer refurbished facilities to make them more acceptable to business customers and offer new facilities (e.g. the facility for visitors to pay by account).

3.2.5   Organic growth

Organic growth is considered to be the more natural pattern of growth for an organization. The initial investment by the organization results in profits, an established customer base and a well-established technical, personnel and financial structure. This provides a foundation for future growth. In this sense, success breeds success, for the rate of the organization's growth is influenced by the extent to which it has succeeded in building up internally the means for future expansion. All aspects of the organization can be said to evolve gradually. For example, the accounting and finance function may initially be under the day-to-day control of one person, but as the organization expands, so it becomes necessary to develop specialist areas within accounting, each with its own section head.

An organization may grow organically by tackling one market segment at a time, using the resources, knowledge and market awareness it has gained in order to tackle further segments. A firm may grow organically into new segments in a number of ways. Many retail chains have grown organically by developing one region before moving on to another – Sainsbury's grew organically from its southern base towards the northern regions, while Asda grew organically from its

How does a company expand in a rapidly growing market when its owners take great pride in not borrowing beyond their means? Birmingham based Hi-Tech Selection is a recruitment agency that specializes in obtaining staff for the IT sector. It began life in a small way with a telephone, a card filing system and an overdraft of £1000. During the 1990s it grew gradually so that by 1998 it employed 14 staff and had an annual turnover of £1 million. This was a good example of organic growth, with the company doing everything gradually, for example using old computer equipment until it could afford a new system and only taking on new staff when they could be justified. New office accommodation was purchased, but only when the company had accumulated sufficient funds to pay for the deposit. But this gradualist approach prevented the company exploiting opportunities in the rapidly developing IT recruitment sector, estimated in 1998 to be growing at 30 per cent a year. The big growth was in the contract employment market, where the agency pays temporary staff directly, then bills the company to whom they are subcontracted. Because companies pay the agency in arrears, this type of work demands a level of working capital which was beyond Hi-Tech. Another major growth area was mainland Europe where the IT recruitment industry was still in its infancy.

How could the company break out of its cautious financial approach to fund its growth? Organic growth alone would be insufficient to exploit the opportunities becoming available, but it would be relatively risk free and leave the founders in control of their business. Raising fresh equity through a venture capital company would lessen this control. One option that the company adopted early on was to factor its invoices with the Royal Bank of Scotland. The bank paid 65 per cent of the value of the company's sales to customers upfront, then took a percentage fee when the invoice was eventually paid.

Should the company speed up its growth beyond that which could be achieved organically? Although the immediate prospects looked good, the market for IT recruitment services is inherently unstable. Millennium bug scares may have kept the company busy during 1999, and conversion to the euro may have offered hope for the future, but the company was just as prone to a downturn from the dot.com crash which occurred towards the end of 2000. The company must be able to downsize just as rapidly as it can grow to meet changes in the market. Many growing small companies have found to their cost that rising overheads can lose them the competitive advantage that they once had as market-challenging small businesses.

northern base towards the south. Other organizations have grown organically by aiming a basically similar product at new segments of the market – as Thomson Holidays has done in developing slightly differentiated holidays aimed at the youth and elderly markets.

Where new market opportunities suddenly appear, an organization may not have the specialized resources that would allow it to grow organically. Within the financial services sector, a study by Ennew *et al.* (1992) found that many of the assets of companies, such as specialized staff and distribution networks, were quite specific to their existing markets and could not easily be adapted to exploit new markets. Growth by acquisition was in many cases considered to be a better method of expansion.

3.2.6 Growth by acquisition

The rate of organic growth is constrained by a number of factors, for example the rate at which the market that an organization serves is growing. An organization seeking to grow organically in a slowly developing sector such as food manufacture will find organic growth more difficult than an organization serving a rapidly growing sector such as on-line computer information services. In some cases, organic growth is difficult because of a scarcity of resources (e.g. prime locations for retail sites), and growth by acquiring other companies is the easiest way of acquiring those resources. Also, companies with relatively high capital requirements will find organic growth relatively difficult.

Growth by acquisition may appear attractive to organizations where organic growth is difficult. In some cases it may be almost essential in order to achieve a critical mass which may be necessary for survival. The DIY retail sector in the United Kingdom is one where chains have needed to achieve a critical size in order to exploit economies in buying, distribution and promotion. Small chains have not been able to grow organically at a sufficient rate to achieve a critical mass, resulting in their take-over or merger to form larger chains. Sainsbury's, former owners of the Homebase chain of DIY outlets, sought to challenge the market leader B&Q. Organic growth would have involved considerable expenditure in new sites in a sector that was becoming saturated. Instead it sought to achieve economies of scale by acquiring its competitor Texas Homecare. Texas had itself grown by acquiring a number of smaller chains, such as Unit Sales. During 2001, the Homebase chain was sold by Sainsbury's, mindful of the fact that it had not achieved the economies of scale to compete with the market leader.

A major problem for firms seeking to grow within the service sector by acquisition lies in the fact that often the main assets being acquired are the skills and knowledge of the acquired organization's employees. Unlike physical assets, key personnel may disappear following the acquisition, reducing the earning ability of the business. Worse still, key staff could defect to the acquiring company's competitors. During the consolidation of the dot.com sector which occurred during 2000–01, there is evidence that a lot of the acquiring firms' investments in their acquisitions were lost when key personnel left with their list of contacts and specialized knowledge.

Growth by acquisition may occur where an organization sees its existing market sector contracting and it seeks to diversify into other areas. The time and risk associated with starting a new venture in an alien market sector may be considered too great – acquiring an established business could be less risky, allowing access to an established client base and technical skills.

It was noted earlier that growth in itself might be seen as good for developing staff morale in allowing career progression. The organization may formally encourage growth by acquisition for this very reason, while staff may have informal objectives directed towards this end. Acquiring new subsidiaries could satisfy this objective for a company that is operating in otherwise static markets.

Growth by acquisition can take a number of forms. The simplest form is the agreed take-over whereby one firm agrees to purchase the majority of the share capital of another company. Payment can be in the form of cash or shares in the acquiring company, or some combination of the two. A take-over can be mutually beneficial where one company has a sound customer base, but lacks the financial resources to achieve a critical mass, while the other has the finance but needs a larger customer base. Many take-overs occur where the founder of a business is seeking to retire and to liquidate the value of the business.

While the majority of take-overs are mutually agreed, circumstances often arise where a take-over is contested. This particularly affects public companies whose shares can be bought and sold openly. Typically a cash-rich firm would identify another company that it recognizes as underperforming because of poor management. Its argument for a take-over is based on the appeal of its proven management style being applied to the underperforming assets of the target company, increasing the profitability of the latter's assets. Disputed take-overs can become very bitter affairs, with each side trying to prove its own performance while denigrating that of the other party. The battle is often made even more vitriolic because of contrasting cultural styles. For the target company, exposure of its management style and practices may be a new and unwelcome event, and represents a desire to remain independent.

During a contested take-over bid, the marketing strategy of both target and bidding companies can be significantly affected during the short term. To prove the ability of the existing management, the target company's marketing programmes may focus on boosting short-term market share, possibly at the expense of long-term brand building. Communication programmes can become aimed at the financial community as much as the final consumer, for example by amending adverts for branded products to include the corporate name, thereby associating the company with a much broader portfolio of brands than may have been appreciated by members of the financial community. New product launches may be brought ahead of the ideal launch date in order to impress the financial community. Contested take-overs can also have a serious effect on staff, and many key employees may fear instability in the future and leave for more secure positions.

For public companies, the Stock Exchange imposes strict rules about how a take-over bid may be conducted, covered by the City Code on Take-overs and Mergers and monitored by the Panel on Take-overs. An acquiring company cannot simply quietly acquire shares in a company until it has achieved a majority shareholding.

It must declare its holding once it has reached a 10 per cent holding and must make a formal take-over offer once it has acquired 30 per cent. The offer document itself is tightly prescribed in terms of the information that it must contain.

3.2.7   Mergers

A merger is a variation on a take-over where two existing companies agree to set up one new company which issues shares to the shareholders of each of the existing companies in agreed proportions and in exchange for existing shareholdings. Many agreed take-overs show characteristics of a merger and it is difficult to strictly distinguish between the two. Mergers can range in scale from two local solicitors merging their practices, through to multinational mergers characterized by the merger that took place in 2001 between AOL and Time Warner. An important reason for a merger is to allow greater cross-selling opportunities between the two companies' sets of customers and to allow for more efficient sharing of resources. The benefits of a merger can be particularly great where two merging companies have complementary resources. In the case of the AOL–Time Warner merger, AOL gained access to Time Warner's archive of film and published material, while Time Warner gained new channels of distribution for this archive.

As with take-overs, proposed mergers often fail because of cultural differences between the companies involved. During 1998, a proposal to merge Glaxo Wellcome with Smith Klein Beecham to create the world's largest pharmaceutical company is reported to have failed because of disagreements among the boards of the two companies about how they would divide their responsibilities after the merger.

Mergers, like take-overs, also run the risk of being blocked by regulatory authorities on the grounds that they may restrict the extent of competition in a market. This is considered further in Chapter 6.

3.2.8   Joint ventures

Diversification into new business areas can be risky, even for a cash-rich business. It may lack the management skills necessary in the market that it seeks to enter, while the barriers to entry may present an unacceptably high level of risk to the company. One way forward is to set up a joint venture where companies with complementary skills and financial resources join together. A new limited company is usually formed with shares allocated between the member companies and agreement made on where the financial and human resources are to come from. There are many examples of joint ventures to be found in new high-technology, high-capital sectors such as telecommunications and broadcasting. The Iridium satellite-based, mobile telephone service required such large amounts of capital that providing it was beyond the financial means and risk acceptability of any one company. A number of telecommunications and technology companies therefore shared in the development of Iridium. Sometimes regulatory requirements may favour a joint venture rather than direct market entry. Although British Telecom could probably have succeeded by itself in launching a mobile telephone service in the United Kingdom, fear by regulatory agencies of market domination initially limited the company to membership of the Cellnet joint venture with Securicor.

A joint venture is commonly used where a company seeks to enter an overseas market by matching its technical and financial resources with the local market knowledge of a company based in the target market. For example, when British Telecom sought to enter the Dutch telephone market, it entered a joint venture with Dutch Railways to jointly develop the Telfort phone service.

Where joint ventures are a success, the partners often seek to liquidate their investment by 'floating' the joint venture as a public limited company in its own right.

3.2.9

Management buy-outs

Management buy-outs (and the related format of a 'buy-in') have become popular in recent years. A buy-out is an autonomous company which is created by the management and/or employees of an organization buying part or all of the business of their former employers. Funding a buy-out often leaves the company highly geared, with the management putting in relatively little of their own equity capital relative to the loan capital provided by a merchant bank. Such buy-outs often involve very complex financing, with the merchant bank seeking a route by which its minority shareholding can be liquidated by flotation very quickly after-wards, or assets of the newly formed business sold off to repay the loans. This method of financing growth can be very attractive at a time of an expanding economy and relatively low interest rates, but high gearing has spelt difficulty for many new buy-outs when the state of the economy turned out to be below expecta-tion and interest rates rose above the level that had been budgeted for. Companies could not defer payment of interest on loans in the way that they could defer paying a dividend to the risk-taking shareholders. Sometimes, the finances of the business had to be restructured, usually to the detriment of the shareholders, as occurred in the case of the MFI furniture group (an earlier buy-out from the Asda group) during the early 1990s. Nevertheless, some management buy-outs have proved spectacularly successful for the small number of directors who bought shares in them. Managers who bought the Porterbrook train leasing company from British Rail and sold it two years later in 1997 to Stagecoach PLC, saw an initial investment of under £100 000 turned into shares which were sold for over £5 million.

3.2.10

Horizontal and vertical integration

Amalgamations between firms can take the form of horizontal integration, vertical integration or diversification. *Horizontal* integration occurs where firms involved in the same stage of manufacture of a product amalgamate to achieve greater economies of scale and – subject to Competition Commission approval – to reduce the level of wasteful competition in a market. The consolidation which occurred in the UK brewing industry during the late 1990s, when the number of

Figure 3.2
Possible growth
patterns for a
brewery

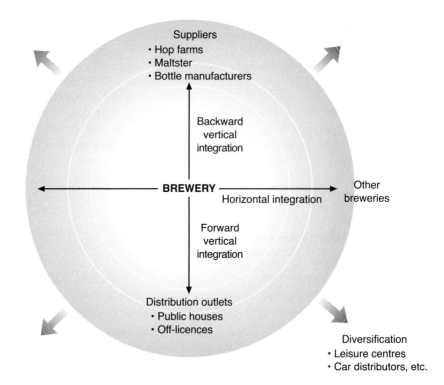

mass-production brewers was drastically cut though mergers, fell into this category. It is increasingly being recognized that growth through horizontal integration can pose serious problems for the competitiveness of a market, which may be good for producers, but may limit the choice and/or raise prices for consumers. We will return in Chapter 6 to review the regulatory constraints on this type of growth.

Vertical integration occurs where a company acquires either its suppliers (backward integration) or its distributors (forward integration). Tour operators integrating backwards have ensured provision of aircraft capacity by acquiring or setting up their own airline, while others have integrated forwards by acquiring travel agents. Diversification occurs where firms acquire another firm operating in unrelated business areas, the main purpose of the acquisition often being to spread risk through a balanced portfolio of activities. Figure 3.2 applies this framework of analysis to possible growth patterns for a brewery.

3..2.11   Globalization

Markets are becoming increasingly globalized, forcing firms in many sectors to see their market not just as the domestic economy, but the whole world. Many industry sectors have witnessed a series of mergers as companies grow in order to achieve economies of scale. In the case of volume car manufacturers, this has resulted in a shrinking number of manufacturers, but those that remain now incorporate a number of brands. Ford, for example, now owns Volvo, Land Rover and Jaguar, while Chrysler and Daimler Benz merged in 2000 to form a new multinational organization. There are major economies of scale open to car manufacturers. Companies operating at a large scale are able to maintain a cost-effective position at the leading edge of design through investment in research and development the cost of which can be spread over a large volume of output. The Volkswagen group, for example, is able to spread the enormous development costs of a new car 'platform' over three quite distinct brands – Volkswagen, Audi and Skoda. If each of these brands had to undertake their own development work, their cars would lose competitive advantage to a company which was able to spread development costs over larger volume.

By expanding overseas, a company that has developed a strong brand can stretch the coverage of that brand. By developing in a foreign market, the company will start with the advantage that some visitors from its domestic market will already understand what the brand stands for. Similarly, for residents of the new market, many may have already become familiar with the brand during visits to the manufacturer's home market. In short, there are economies of scale in promoting a brand in multiple markets simultaneously.

A company may find itself forced to expand into overseas markets because of saturation of its domestic market. Saturation can come about where a product reaches the maturity stage of its life cycle in the domestic market, while being at a much earlier stage of the cycle in less developed foreign markets. The market for cigarettes may be mature in most Western markets, but China represents a new growth opportunity for western companies.

International markets are becoming increasingly homogenized. The car industry serves as a good example of one where distinctive national preferences have diminished, and companies are able to manufacture one product, with only minor adaptations to make it suitable for the whole world. Instead of talking about market segments defined by national boundaries, companies operating at a global scale increasingly talk about cross-national segments of socio-economic and lifestyle groups.

We will return to look at issues of globalization in more detail in Chapter 10.

3.3   SOURCES OF FINANCE FOR GROWTH

As far as the private sector is concerned, there are two basic methods of financing growth. On the one hand, companies can raise risk capital (often referred to as *equity* capital) from shareholders for which a relatively high rate of return will be required. To supplement this, companies use a second and relatively less expensive form of *loan* finance. This must be repaid regardless of the fortunes of the company. The relationship between the two is referred to as *gearing* – a company which has a high amount of loan finance relative to equity capital is said to be highly geared. An optimum balance exists between the two types of finance, although this varies between different industry sectors.

3.3.1   Methods of raising equity capital

One method by which a sole trader or partnership can raise fresh capital is by forming a private limited company and selling shares in the company. For a private limited company, the sale of shares cannot be advertised to the public, so they have to be placed privately. For smaller companies, blocks of shares are often sold to relations or business associates. New opportunities to gain access to equity share capital have been provided through a relatively new type of intermediary – the venture capital company. These intermediaries develop an understanding of the opportunities for investment in smaller private companies and provide the link – and often also the management support – through which investment from cash-rich individuals and organizations such as pension funds is provided.

To gain access to significant amounts of new equity capital from a much wider financial community, a private company may 'go public' by forming a public limited company. Becoming a public company requires a special resolution to be passed by the shareholders and the Articles of Association to be amended to take out those restrictions that apply to a private company (previously discussed in Chapter 2).

To acquire a full listing on the Stock Exchange, a considerable amount of time and money must be spent to meet the requirements of the Stock Exchange Council. These essentially aim to ensure that anybody considering buying shares in the company is adequately informed about the record, current position and future prospects of the company. A detailed prospectus, including five years' trading figures, with audited accounts must be produced. The actual sale of shares can take place in a number of ways, the most important of which are:

■ An Offer for Sale to the general public, where a specified number of shares is offered at a fixed price, usually underwritten to guarantee the share income to the company. This tends to be an expensive method of raising equity capital
■ Sale by Tender which involves selling the shares to the highest bidders
■ Placement with financial institutions without the formality of a public offer for sale.

The cost of raising fresh equity through a share issue can be considerable, reflecting the work of the accountants, bankers, solicitors and underwriters involved. For a typical small share sale valued at £10 million, between 5 and 10 per cent would be lost in issuing expenses.

Obtaining access to equity capital through the stock market can be very expensive for smaller companies who can be caught in a dilemma. Small, rapidly growing businesses in fast-growing sectors such as biotechnology may need fresh capital to sustain their growth. However, until they have achieved successful operation for a number of years, they cannot seek funding to bring about that growth. The stock markets in many countries have recognized this dilemma by creating secondary markets for companies which fall short of the high standards normally imposed on companies dealing on the main market. At the same time, such secondary stock markets provide opportunities for investors who are more willing to take a speculative risk in a company that could produce a spectacular return, or could just as easily prove to be a complete failure.

In the United Kingdom, an alternative to obtaining a full listing on the Stock Exchange is to seek one on the Alternative Investment Market (AIM). This is much

Small businesses often reach a point where they need more capital if they are to expand. The dot.com boom of 2000 produced many small businesses which had been started in the owners' garages or spare rooms, but soon grew to the point where additional capital became essential in order to sustain growth. But raising additional equity capital can reduce the control which the owners have in their businesses, and cut their share of future profits. Hindsight can be great in deciding when a small business should go to the market to raise additional capital, or indeed to sell out completely to a larger organization which has the resources to exploit the full potential of the company. Some had a lucky break and went to the market at just the right time, raising capital for the company, cash for themselves and still retaining some degree of control. Among the winners were Brent Hoberman and Martha Lane Fox, founders of lastminute.com. The company floated on the London Stock Exchange in March 2000 at the peak of dot.com mania. Shares which floated at £3.70 shortly after flotation were down to less than 60p a year later, reducing the value of the company from £140 million to less than £20 million.

Somebody who did less well was Dave Stanworth, who may be quite typical of the new generation of dot.com entrepreneurs in terms of his background. He left school with no qualifications and worked casually in a series of jobs as, among other things, a bricklayer and a bookie. In his spare time he played with the Internet and eventually developed a website called Games Domain. By 1997, it was clear that his venture would need more resources than he had available. He had tried to raise money from venture capitalists, but at this time the hysteria of dot.com frenzy had not yet taken off and he found few backers. Stanworth decided that the best option for him would be to sell out to a better-resourced organization and take a smaller equity stake in the larger organization. In 1997 he sold the business to Attitude Network in return for an equity stake in Attitude. Attitude was itself taken over by theglobe.com, a larger company which was able to raise additional capital through its listing on the US NASDAQ market (a market which is more open to high-risk, start-up companies, similar to the UK's Alternative Investment Market). At the peak of the dot.com boom, theglobe.com shares peaked at $39.47 and Stanworth's personal stake in the company was valued at more than $3 million. This rags to riches story soon turned to rags again, because just one year later during the 'dot.bomb' period, theglobe.com's shares fell from their peak of $39.47 to just 31 cents, cutting the value of Stanworth's holding to just $25 000. The company had joined the so-called '90 per cent club' – those companies whose shares had fallen to more than 90 per cent of their peak value. In this, the company was not alone, as the club included such notable names as QXL.com and Interactive Investor International.

Despite the turnaround in fortunes of the dot.com sector, it seemed that many entrepreneurs were unwilling to give up with their dream. While many accountants and bankers might have abandoned the sector for the safety of more traditional sectors, many 'nerds' were determined to exploit the potential of the Internet, with or without the help of fickle capital markets.

less costly to companies seeking to raise fresh finance. The Alternative Investment Market is a higher risk to investors as the information companies are required to submit is lower. However, each company must warn potential investors of their risks and must have a nominated adviser approved by the Stock Exchange. The role of the adviser is central to AIM, as the stock market does not look at companies' prospectuses. Advisers are required to confirm to the Exchange that the directors of a company have been guided on their responsibilities and obligations in respect of the AIM rules and that the rules have been obeyed. Advisers can be fined for poor performance. The stock markets of many countries have developed similar schemes to promote small, relatively high-risk business ventures (e.g. France's Nouveau Marche).

An alternative method of raising fresh equity capital for an established business is to call on existing shareholders to subscribe for additional shares. This is known as a *rights* issue and shareholders are given the right to purchase additional shares at a specified price in proportion to their existing shareholding. Where a company is in financial difficulty with excessive debt, it may renegotiate with its creditors to turn some of its loans into equity capital. Shares are then given to creditors in return for cancelling part of the loans outstanding to them. This happened with the financially beleaguered Eurotunnel company, whose shareholders saw the value of their shares fall as new shares were created to pay off debts rather than to invest in new revenue-generating assets.

3.3.2   Retained earnings

Free enterprise idealists would argue that a company's profits should be entirely distributed to its shareholders so that they can decide how they should be re-invested. In practice, companies tend to retain a proportion of profits for reinvestment within the business, encouraged by tax advantages. The amount distributed to shareholders in the form of a dividend tends to be kept at a stable level, meeting a norm for that particular industry and the expectations of shareholders. While retained earnings may seem an easy source of finance for a company, there is a danger that if it does not achieve an adequate internal return on these retained earnings, it may become the subject of a take-over bid from another company that considers that it could manage the capital of the business more effectively.

3.3.3   Loan capital

For the small business, loans for expansion may be obtained from family and friends. However, when loan requirements exceed the capabilities of these sources, commercial loans are sought and some form of security against the loan will usually be required. In many cases, the directors of a limited company will have to pledge their personal possessions as security for the company's loans, despite the separate legal identity of the company.

Debentures are loans to a company carrying interest at a fixed rate and are generally repayable on a specified date. Debenture holders receive priority over shareholders for annual income payments and when the assets of the business are liquidated. Some – called mortgage debentures – are backed by a particular fixed asset belonging to the company as security, while others are secured by a floating charge on the company's assets in general. In the event of default on payment, the lender has the right to take over the security offered and sell it in order to repay the outstanding loan. A company may also have unsecured loan stock. Lenders of this stock are in the same position as trade creditors in ranking for repayment in the event of liquidation, although still ahead of shareholders.

3.3.4   Other sources of finance

Shares and debentures provide long-term finance for long-term growth. In the short term, the survival of many companies is influenced by being able to collect money due to them as quickly as possible. Some companies resort to 'factoring' by selling a debt they are owed to a finance company and receiving payment, less a premium, immediately. On the other hand, firms seek to delay paying their debts to suppliers for as long as possible, thereby providing an additional source of short-term finance. Small companies often complain about having to wait for payment from large companies who use smaller businesses as a source of finance for their own operations. Although there are a number of initiatives to 'name and shame' slow payers (for example a list of poor payers is published by the Federation of Small Businesses), some business owners may be so dependent on a customer that they would not wish to stop doing further business with a slow payer.

3.4   ORGANIZATIONAL SCALE

There is continuing debate about whether there is an 'ideal' size for business organizations. In fact, there are advantages and disadvantages of large firms and they can be found coexisting with much smaller firms in most sectors. This section reviews recent debate about the benefits of large organizations against small business units.

3.4.1   Economies of scale

In many sectors, large organizations have advantages over smaller ones. These are some of their principal advantages:

1. In some industries there are significant economies of scale in production processes. This is particularly true of industries where fixed costs of production are a high proportion of total costs. Therefore sectors such as car manufacture and banking allow large organizations to spread the high cost of capital equipment over a greater number of units of output, thereby pursuing what Porter (1980) described as a cost leadership strategy. In sectors that use high technology, or that require highly trained labour skills, a learning curve effect may be apparent (also called a *cost experience curve*). By operating at a larger scale than its competitors, a firm can benefit more from the learning curve and thereby achieve lower unit costs. While this may be true of some industries,

others face only a very low critical output at which significant economies of scale occur – plumbing and hairdressing, for example. For organizations in these sectors, cost leadership would be a difficult strategy as many rival firms would also be able to achieve maximum cost efficiency.

2 As well as being more efficient at turning inputs into outputs, larger firms may be able to acquire their inputs on more advantageous terms in the first place. One reason for the success of large-scale retailers is the much greater bargaining power they have over suppliers, compared to smaller retailers. Often, smaller organizations have joined together in voluntary buying chains in order to increase their bargaining power with suppliers. Many farmers' co-operatives realize that a group of farmers can collectively achieve lower prices from suppliers than one farmer negotiating alone. As well as being able to bring greater bargaining power to negotiations with suppliers, buying on a large scale can give savings in the logistical costs of transferring goods from supplier to buyer.

3 Large-scale production can allow for *economies of scope*, by allowing a wider range of goods and services to be offered. This can take the form of additional design features which could not be included if production was on a small scale (e.g. small manufacturers of food products may not be able to afford as much on designing eye-catching packaging as their larger competitors) or additional services that a firm is able to offer (large building societies may, for example, be able to offer a much more comprehensive range of investment services than their smaller competitors).

4 A company's promotion effort can be much more efficient where it is aimed at a large-volume national (or even international) market, rather than a purely local one. National television and press advertising may be an efficient medium for a large-scale national company, which gives it a promotional advantage over smaller scale local producers who must rely on various local and regional media.

5 Investors generally prefer companies that have a proven track record of stability. By being able to diversify into a number of different products and market segments, companies are able to offer this stability, resulting in 'blue chip' companies being able to obtain equity and loan capital at a lower cost than smaller companies.

6 With relationship marketing becoming an important part of many organizations' strategies, the ability to cross-sell related goods and services becomes crucial. By operating at a larger scale with a broad portfolio of products, cross-selling can be facilitated.

3.4.2   **Limits to growth**

Most organizations pursue growth to a greater or lesser degree. However, there are limits to how far and how fast a company can grow. Growth by acquisition – being relatively risky – can reveal limits beyond which a company cannot sustain growth.

Growth by acquisition is commonly associated with high borrowings resulting in a high level of gearing. The use of relatively cheap debt capital may be attractive while the company is profitable, but can leave the company dangerously exposed when conditions deteriorate. Faced with a fixed charge for interest, the organization may be forced to liquidate some of its assets by disposing of subsidiaries, to raise cash to meet its interest payments. Many Internet companies that grew rapidly during the late 1990s found themselves unable to service debt repayments when the sector faced severe problems in 2000. Organizations that grew organically at a slower rate without reliance on such a high level of borrowed capital survived the subsequent recession better.

The ability of the management structure of a company to respond to growth sets a further limit. Many companies have benefited by having a dynamic personality leading during a period of rapid growth, only to find that a large organization needs a much broader management base once it passes a critical size. Organizations such as Next and Amstrad have suffered where the management structure has not grown to meet the needs of a very different type of organization. If a company does not restructure itself as it grows, diseconomies of scale may set in.

Legislative constraints are increasingly limiting the ability of firms to grow. In industry sectors where there are significant economies of scale in production, and competition takes place at a global level, there is often a great logic behind the motivation to merge and grow. However, the need to compete from a position of strength needs to be balanced against regulators' increasing concerns that the competitiveness of markets should be maintained. It can be difficult for regulators to define this balance with government policy objectives often pulling in different directions. Most countries have laws to prevent one firm dominating a market or having undue influence over it and the EU is playing an increasingly important role in this respect. We will return to the subject of legislation governing anti-competitive situations in Chapter 6.

3.4.3 De-mergers

Conglomerates sometimes reach a size and diversity that produce more problems than opportunities for the group as a whole. A number of conglomerates have therefore split themselves up in a reversal to the process of merging, sometimes referred to as *de-merging*. The initial cause of a de-merger is often the recognition that shareholders' total share value would increase if they had shares in two or more separate businesses rather than the one conglomerate holding company. Stock markets often have difficulty placing a value on the shares of highly diversified companies, and many de-mergers have seen the combined value of the de-merged companies' shares very quickly exceed the previous price of the shares of the former holding company. This was true in the de-mergers of Racal and Vodafone, ICI and Zenecca, and Granada Media and Compass Catering.

The move to a de-merger may be strengthened by conflicts of interest within a conglomerate. A third party buyer from a conglomerate may fear that purchases from one member company would prejudice the confidentially in other areas of its business. This was one reason raised in the de-merger of AT&T into three separate operating units responsible for telecommunications operations, equipment and information services. A rival telecommunications operator may have been suspicious about buying its equipment from a conglomerate whose telecommunication division was its arch rival. De-merging of activities sometimes follows an investigation by the Competition Commission and may be a condition of a merger between two companies proceeding.

3.4.4 ### The resurgence of small business

The term *small business* (or SME, standing for *small and medium-sized enterprise*) is difficult to define. In an industry such as car manufacture, a firm with 100 employees would be considered very small, whereas among solicitors, a practice of that size would be considered large. The term small business is therefore a relative one, based typically on some measure of numbers of employees or capital employed. Within the European Union, the Eurostat definition of small companies is often used:

Microorganizations:	0–9 employees
Small organizations:	10–99 employees
Medium-sized organizations:	100–499 employees
Large organizations:	500+ employees

Despite the tendency of firms to grow, there has been renewed interest in the role of small businesses within the economy. It is suggested that many of Britain's competitors, such as emerging Far Eastern economies, have attributed their growth to a strong small business sector. During recent years, developed economies have seen a significant increase in the number of small businesses, especially in the expanding services sector.

In the United Kingdom, the Department of Trade and Industry's Small and Medium Size Enterprise statistics highlight a number of features of the small business sector:

1 There has been a significant growth in the number of small firms, up from around 2.4 million in 1980 to 3.7 million in 1997.

2 Of these 3.7 million businesses, over 2.7 million were 'size class zero' businesses, those made up of sole traders or partners without any employees.

3 Small- and medium-sized businesses accounted for 99 per cent of all businesses, 45 per cent of non-government employment and 40 per cent of turnover (excluding the finance sector). By contrast, the 7000 largest businesses accounted for 43 per cent of non-government employment and 46 per cent of turnover.

4 In 1997, at least 99 per cent of businesses in all sectors except electricity, gas and water supply and mining were SMEs.

5 Although the number of small firms is increasing, large numbers of firms also go out of business. For example, in 1994, although there was a net increase of

24 000 small firms, this represented 446 000 new start-ups, less 422 000 closures.

Advocates of small business argue that they are important to the economy for a number of reasons:

1. They generally offer much greater adaptability than larger firms. With less bureaucracy and fewer channels of communications, decisions can be taken rapidly. A larger organization may be burdened with constraints which tend to slow the decision-making process, such as the need to negotiate new working practices with trade union representatives or the need to obtain board of directors' approval for major decisions. As organizations grow, there is an inherent tendency for them to become more risk averse by building in systems of control which make them slower to adapt to changes in their business environment.

2. It is also argued that small businesses tend to be good innovators. This comes about through greater adaptability, especially where large amounts of capital are not required. This is often true of the service sector where typical low-cost innovations have included video film rental services and home delivery fast-food services. Small firms can also be good innovators where they operate in markets dominated by a small number of larger companies and the only way in which a small business can gain entry to the market is to develop an innovatory product aimed at a small niche. The soap powder market in Britain is dominated by a small number of large producers, yet it was a relatively small company that identified a niche for environmentally friendly powders and introduced innovatory products to the market.

3. Most large firms started off as very small businesses, so it is important to the health of the economy that there is a continuing supply of growing companies to replace those larger firms that die.

The change in the structure and organization of industry and commerce, the growing emphasis on specialized services and the application of new technology have tended to encourage small business. Flexible manufacturing systems are increasingly able to allow a business to function at a much lower level of output than previously. An example is in printing, where new production processes have allowed entrepreneurs to undertake small print runs on relatively inexpensive machinery. The success of the small printer has been further encouraged by the proliferation of small business users of printed material requiring small print runs and a rapid turn-round of work. The tendency for large companies to subcontract functions such as cleaning and catering in order to concentrate on their core business has also given new opportunities to the small business sector.

It is not only small entrepreneurs who have been creating new small businesses, for larger organizations have also recognized their value and have tried to replicate them at a distance from their own structure. Many large manufacturing organizations operating in mature markets have created autonomous new small business units to serve rapidly developing or specialist niche markets, free of the bureaucratic culture of the parent organization. Local authorities were required by the

Local Government Act 1988 to set up their own direct labour organizations which are effectively small units operating under the umbrella of the authority, albeit subject to rules and regulations specified in the Act. In the education sector, many universities have established small research companies at arm's length from the universities' organizational structures.

While small business has certainly seen a resurgence in recent years, it should also be recognized that they have a very high failure rate. Conclusive evidence of the failure rate of small businesses is difficult to obtain, especially in view of the problem of identifying new businesses that do not need to register in the first place. However, one indication of the failure rates comes from an analysis of VAT (value added tax) registrations, which shows that during the 1990s, only about one-third of businesses set up 10 years previously were still registered. More detailed evidence was provided by the results of a survey undertaken by Warwick University in 1995 (Cressy and Storey, 1995). It found that less then 20 per cent of new small businesses survive more than six years, a poorer record than indicated by VAT returns, which exclude very small firms. The research suggested that it was the very small firms that had the shortest lives, and described the characteristics of the small firm entrepreneur most likely to succeed. Businesses started by 50–55 year-olds were found to be twice as likely to survive as those begun by people in their twenties, for example. Also significant were the number of proprietors, and whether they had a specific qualification and work experience in the same sector.

3.4.5   Government and small business

Governments in many countries have been keen to support small businesses. They have pointed to the successful small-business-led economies of the Far East and sought to emulate their growth through the creation of a strong domestic small business sector. The presence of large numbers of small businesses in a market is also useful for increasing the competitiveness of markets, thereby achieving government objectives of a more flexible economy and lower inflation.

Such motivations partly explain some of the concessions that governments have made to the small business sector. These include a lower 20 per cent rate of corporation tax for firms with annual profits of less than £300 000 p.a. and a lower rate of 10 per cent for company profits of £10 000 or less (2000–01), allowing companies to re-invest more of their profits. Small firms with a turnover of less than £52 000 p.a. (2000/01) are exempt from the need to charge VAT and have been freed from a wide range of duties that apply to larger companies, especially those relating to employment rights. To encourage the development of new businesses, many supportive innovations have been launched by central government, including various training schemes sponsored by Regional Development Agencies.

Small business owners are often sceptical about governments' support for them, pointing out that government legislation often imposes disproportionate burdens on them. Cynics might argue that governments have seen the encouragement of small business as a simple means of getting unemployed people off the list of the unemployed. A survey of small businesses by the British Chambers of Commerce

(1995) revealed the extent of small business owners' dissatisfaction with government regulations. More than 74 per cent of respondents complained about the burdens of VAT, which effectively makes businesses unpaid tax collectors for government. While larger firms may be able to afford a specialized accounting department, many small business owners are often left to add the submission of VAT returns to their core tasks which they are expected to undertake personally. Government has hoped to stimulate the small business sector through requirements for certain government purchases to be put out to competitive bidding, but often the complexity of regulations governing competitive tenders have put many small businesses off of bidding. In the BCC survey, 71 per cent of managing directors of small businesses claimed that the requirement to complete government forms was costing them between 1 and 2 per cent of their turnover. Governments frequently declare that they are going to cut the red tape and bureaucracy which imposes burdens on small businesses. However, the historic reality has often been in the opposite direction. In Chapter 8 we will return to look at the work of the UK government's Better Regulation Task Force, which has sought to reduce the burden of government on business organizations.

CASE STUDY

TESCO STORES ADAPTS AS IT GROWS

Tesco Stores has grown to become a very profitable business and one of the UK's largest retailers. Today's Tesco is a long way from the humble barrow trading with which the business began, and an analysis of the company's growth illustrates the changes in form that Tesco has undergone in order to achieve its current market position.

The basis for the existing business of Tesco was founded shortly after the First World War when Jack Cohen left the flying corps with just £30 of capital available to him. His first taste of civilian entrepreneurship came with the decision to invest most of his £30 in the bulk purchase of tins of surplus war rations, which he proceeded to sell from a barrow in the street markets of London. As a sole trader, Jack Cohen needed the minimum of formality to get his business started. Furthermore, large capital investment was not required at a time when the typical retail unit was very small and selling through street markets was commonplace. The products which he sold were basic commodities which did not need large investment to create a distinctive and differentiated brand.

The name Tesco was first used by Cohen to differentiate the tea which he sold from that of his competitors. The name was derived by taking the first two letters of his own surname and prefixing it with the initials of the owner of the tea importing business from which he bought his tea – T. E. Stockwell. Cohen was buying the tea in bulk from the importer, repackaging it and selling it under a brand name.

Further growth came by developing sales to other market traders in addition to the sales he made to final consumers. He acted as a middleman, or wholesaler, operating from a small warehouse. Success came from being able to spot a good bargain and to fill his warehouse with cheap goods which he would resell to London street traders. Channels of distribution at this time tended to be based on a 'push' strategy in which entrepreneurs needed to actively sell products to the next stage in the chain of distribution.

It became clear to Cohen that he was capable of selling considerably more stock and making more profit if he had more outlets. In 1930 he therefore opened his first shop in an arcade in Tooting, south London. To do this and run his wholesale business would have been stretching the financial and managerial abilities of his sole trader status. He therefore decided to take on a partner – Sam Freeman – to buy and run the Tooting shop. The following year he formed another separate partnership with a nephew Jack Vanger to open a second shop in Chatham, followed by a third partnership to run a shop in London.

In 1932, Cohen formed two private limited companies to run his two core businesses. Tesco Stores Ltd ran the retail business and by 1938 had grown to a chain of 100 shops. Growth had been fuelled by attracting private equity capital and using retained profits. The second company – J. E. Cohen Ltd – was created to run the growing wholesale business.

Backward vertical integration occurred when Cohen became involved in businesses which supplied the wholesale and retail trade. In 1942 Railway Nurseries (Cheshunt) Ltd was set up by buying farmland to supply Tesco with fresh vegetables. A couple of years later, Goldhanger Fruit Farms Ltd in Essex was created to supply Tesco with fresh and canned fruits, as well as supplying other retailers.

Numerous private companies now existed to run the Tesco businesses and in 1947 these were brought together in one holding company – Tesco Stores (Holdings) Ltd. The holding company held the share capital of the subsidiary companies which had been built up over the previous years. To provide additional equity capital for future growth, the holding company became a public company in December 1947 by offering 250 000 shares of 5p nominal value at 75p each to the general public. The money provided by the share issue was used to develop larger stores, in particular the new style of self-service store which was modelled on the American example and which proved increasingly successful for Tesco. The company had developed its own brands in a number of product areas such as tea and dairy products, but still relied on selling other manufacturers' products at lower prices than competing retailers. After the Second World War, the role of the retailer was changing as manufacturers sought to develop strong brands and to promote the benefits of their brands direct to the public. The power of the retailer to influence the decision of the customer was being reduced with the development of mass media aimed at the final consumer, particularly following the introduction of commercial television in the mid-1950s. Distribution strategies were changing from push to pull. Tesco aimed to make branded goods available to consumers at the lowest possible price – the company's motto became 'pile it high and sell it cheap'. The main constraint on offering lower prices was the existence of Resale Price Maintenance which allowed manufacturers to control the price at which its products were sold to the public by retailers. The abolition of Resale Price Maintenance in 1964 was to be extremely beneficial to Tesco's business strategy in which low prices were seen as a key element of its marketing. Further shares were sold during the 1950s and 1960s, allowing the company to expand rapidly and to open supermarkets in most towns throughout Britain. A major rights issue in January 1991 raised £572 million from existing shareholders to fund further expansion and to reduce the level of gearing. As the company's core business of selling groceries and household goods approached saturation, the company diversified into related areas such as the sale of petrol and the creation of in-store coffee shops.

The bulk of Tesco's growth has been organic in nature – as management abilities and financial reserves were built up, they were used to develop more stores and to enter different stages of the distribution process. On occasions, however, growth has come about by acquisition, for example the acquisition of the Yorkshire-based Hillards group in 1987, the Scottish chain William Low in 1994 and the Irish chain Stewarts in 1997. The last two acquisitions allowed Tesco to expand rapidly in regions where it was poorly represented at the time. With saturation in the UK grocery market approaching, Tesco has sought to diversify internationally, for example by acquisition of the Lotus chain in Thailand and the creation of new outlets in Hungary.

By 1997, Tesco PLC had overtaken Sainsbury's for the distinction of being the largest grocery retailer in the UK, owning over 500 stores, employing a total of over 130 000 staff and selling 20 000 lines, of which about 3000 were own-brand products. Market traders such as Jack Cohen's original business still exist alongside Tesco, and in reaching its present position, it is possible to observe a number of changes which Tesco has had to go through. In order to grow, Tesco had to offer some unique advantage over its competitors. In the early days this was based on low price, and this price orientation was emphasized as late as 1977 when Tesco initiated a price-cutting war among the major supermarkets. More recently, Tesco has sought to differentiate itself by offering a better quality of service. Most new development of the 1980s and 1990s was focused on large out-of-town super- stores offering a wide choice of products with easy car parking facilities. When markets here approached saturation, the company developed its city centre 'Metro' stores. As it has grown, Tesco has been able to achieve greater economies of scale in distribution and promotion. It has also used size to exert greater power in the chain of distribution and to achieve competitive pricing. In the year 2000–01, the company became the first UK grocery retailer to report annual profits in excess of £1 billion, although its great market strength led many to suspect that it might be abusing its market power to pay very low prices to its suppliers, especially within the struggling UK agriculture sector. Others would argue that financial success came from the company's sheer efficiency and ability to meet customers' needs better than its competitors.

CASE STUDY Review Questions

1 Identify the diversity of legal forms that Tesco has adopted at different stages of its development.

2 Summarize the strategies that have been used to bring about growth.

3 In what ways has the company's marketing adapted to changes in its business environment?

CHAPTER Summary and links to other chapters

Organizations pursue diverse objectives, some formal and others informally held by managers. Most organizations have a tendency to grow thereby satisfying the needs of a wide range of internal and external interests. It has been noted that certain types of organizations, such as public limited companies, have the ability to grow faster than others where availability of external finance imposes a constraint on growth (Chapter 2). This chapter has discussed various growth strategies, noting that growth that is too rapid or too dependent on loan capital can be highly risky. For most organiza- tions, the sustainability of growth is highly dependent on the state of the national or international economic environment (see Chapter 7).

A large organization is able to achieve numerous advantages over a smaller one, including the ability to invest in new technologies (Chapter 12) and exploitation of overseas markets (Chapter 10). In principle, large organizations should be better able to invest in comprehensive information systems (Chapter 12), although it must be remembered that size in itself can create barriers between customers and decision-makers. This chapter concluded by exploring the reasons behind the recent resurgence in small business units. The ability to keep in touch with customers and to react to changes in the marketing environment were noted as important advantages. Increasing concern about the possible harmful effects for consumers of market domination by large organizations is discussed further in Chapter 6.

CHAPTER   Review questions

1   (a)   Prepare a short report outlining the main reasons why businesses of different sizes exist.

   (b)   Are there any relationships between the size of the business and the market in which it operates?

   (Based on CIM Marketing Environment examination)

2   What problems for the marketing management of a furniture manufacturer might arise from rapid growth?

3   In what ways have the objectives of newly privatized industries changed compared to those of the state-owned organizations that they replaced?

4   What are the problems and opportunities for marketing management arising from a policy of growth through diversification?

5   Explain the resurgence of interest in the small business sector.

6   Choose one industry sector with which you are familiar and examine how small and large firms have found roles in which they can coexist with each other.

References

Ansoff, H.I. (1957) 'Strategies for diversification', *Harvard Business Review*, September–October, vol. 25, no. 5, pp. 113–24.

British Chambers of Commerce (1995) *Small Firms Survey: Regulation*, BCC, London.

Cressy, R. and D. Storey (1995) 'Small and Medium Sized Enterprises', Warwick University Business School, Warwick.

Cyert, R.M. and J.G. March (1963) *A Behavioural Theory of the Firm*, Prentice-Hall, Englewood Cliffs, NJ.

DTI (1995) *Small Firms in Britain 1995*, Department of Trade and Industry, London.

Ennew, C., P. Wong and M. Wright (1992) 'Organisational Structures and the Boundaries of the Firm: Acquisitions and Divestments in Financial Services', *The Services Industries Journal*, vol. 12, no. 4, pp. 478–97.

Grenier, L.E. (1972) 'Evolution and Revolution', *Harvard Business Review*, July–August, pp. 37–46.

Hudson, M. (1995) *Managing Without Profit: The Art of Managing Third Sector Organizations*, Penguin Books, Harmondsworth.

Krabuanrat, K. and R. Phelps (1998) 'Heuristics and rationality in strategic decision making: an exploratory study', *Journal of Business Research*, vol. 41, no. 1, January, pp. 83–93.

Porter, M. (1980) *Competitive Strategy: Techniques for Analyzing Industries and Competitors*, Free Press, New York.

Sasser, W.E., R.P. Olsen and D.D. Wyckoff (1978) *Management of Service Operations: Texts, Cases, Readings*, Allyn and Bacon, Boston, MA.

Selected further reading

Numerous authors have sought to prescribe strategies for successful, profitable growth. The following are classic contributions to the field:

Ansoff, H.I. (1957) 'Strategies for diversification', *Harvard Business Review*, September–October, vol. 25, no. 5, pp. 113–24.

Levitt, T. (1960) 'Marketing myopia', *Harvard Business Review*, July–August, vol. 28, pp. 140–171.

Porter, M. (1980) *Competitive Strategy: Techniques for Analyzing Industries and Competitors*, Free Press, New York.

Mergers and acquisitions often generate a lot of press coverage when they are contested and a lot can be learnt by following coverage of such a contested take-over in the *Financial Times*. For a general review of the subject, the following references are useful:

Gaughan, P. (ed.) (1999) *Mergers, Acquisitions, and Corporate Restructuring*, Wiley, Chichester.

Harvard Business Review (ed.), 'Harvard Business Review on Mergers & Acquisitions, 2001'.

Voss, B. (1998) 'Mergers, acquisitions and alliances', *Journal of Business Strategy*, vol. 19, no. 5, pp. 51–55.

Finance for organizational growth can be a complex topic, but the following references provide a useful insight:

Atrill, P. (1998) *Financial Management for Non-Specialists,* Prentice-Hall, Hemel Hempstead.

McLaney, E. (2000) *Business Finance*, 5th edn, Prentice-Hall, Hemel Hempstead.

Van Horne, J. (1997) *Financial Management and Policy*, 11th edn, Prentice-Hall, Hemel Hempstead.

The following provides a useful set of readings on multinational businesses:

Hood, N. and S. Young (eds) (1999) The Globalization of Multinational Enterprise Activity and Economic Development, Palgrave, Basingstoke.

For a review of the role of small businesses and the reasons for their recent resurgence, the following are useful:

Burns, P. and J. Dewhurst (1996) *Small Business and Entrepreneurship*, 2nd edn, Macmillan, Basingstoke.

Bygrave, B. (1998) 'Building an enterprise economy; lessons from the US', *Business Strategy Review*, vol. 9, no. 2, pp. 11–18.

Keasey, K. and R. Watson (1993) *Small Firm Management*, Blackwell, Oxford.

Westhead, P. and S. Birley (1995) 'Employment growth in new independent owner managed firms in Great Britain', *International Small Business Journal*, April–June, vol. 13, no. 3, pp. 11–35.

Williams, S. (2000) *Lloyds TSB Small Business Guide*, 14th edn, Penguin, Harmondsworth.

Useful websites

Business Bureau   A Small Business Information resource offering help, advice and guidance for new and expanding businesses.   **http://www.businessbureau-uk.co.uk**

Small Business discussion forum   The aim of this list is to act as a forum for academic discussion relating to small business issues. It is essentially interdisciplinary in nature although the emphasis is placed on the analysis of small-scale enterprise rather than prescriptive or how-to-do-it approaches.
http://www.jiscmail.ac.uk/lists/small-business-issues.html

Key terms

Acquisitions	Joint ventures
Cash flow	Management buyout
Charities	Mergers
Companies Acts	Mission statement
Consolidation	Organic growth
Co-operatives	Organizational life cycle
Debentures	Organizational objectives
Directors	Profit maximization
Diseconomies of scale	Prospectus
Diversification	Rights Issue
Economies of Scale	Satisficing
Equity capital	Small business
Externalities	SMEs
Factoring	Social objectives
Flotation	Stock Exchange
Globalization	Take-overs
Horizontal integration	Vertical integration

4

The internal environment

CHAPTER OBJECTIVES

Much of this book is concerned with the external environmental forces that impinge on an organization's activities. But we must also recognize that the ability of the organization to respond to challenges and opportunities in its external environment is often very dependent on its internal environment. A new development in technology, for example, may present an organization with a major opportunity, but if it has a poorly motivated staff, or if its management structures and processes are ineffective, the opportunity may pass it by.

The aim of this chapter is to look at a number of aspects of the internal environment which revolve around the people within the organization. We will begin by looking at how it organizes itself in terms of its structures. Related to this are processes which can help or hinder the task of responding to environmental change. Following this, we will take a more microlevel look at how organizations manage their human resources, so that they have a highly motivated workforce which has the flexibility to respond to environmental change.

For many small businesses, it is often quite possible for one individual person to perform all of the main tasks which are necessary to operate their business as a going concern. The task of keeping accounts, seeking new orders and recruiting new staff are typically undertaken by the small business owners, in addition to their main role in producing the goods and services that customers buy. In larger organizations, giving such a wide range of tasks to one individual does not make much sense. The arguments of 'scientific management' would point to the advantages of groups of individuals specializing in doing one function very well, rather than being a 'jack of all trades' and doing all functions only moderately well. So large organizations have evolved with sales functions that can sell better than its competitors, production people who are more productive and accounts people who are more cost-effective.

In the process of specialization of functions, it is possible that as many problems are created as are solved. In addition to the benefits of economies of scale and specialization, problems of integrating the different organizational functions arise. The case of an organization's 'left hand' not knowing what its 'right hand' is doing is sadly all too familiar.

An organization operating in a fiercely competitive environment would typically attach great importance to its marketing department as a means of producing a focused marketing strategy by which it can gain competitive advantage over its competitors. By contrast, an organization operating in a relatively stable environment is more likely to allow strategic decisions to be taken by personnel who are not marketing strategists – for example, pricing decisions may be taken by accountants with less need to understand the marketing implications of price decisions.

In many instances, the main factor governing the success of an organization is its access to key resources and technologies. It is not surprising therefore to find the research and development function being the most important function within it. Responsibilities given to each of the different functions within an organization vary from one company to another, reflecting the competitive nature of their business environments and also their traditions and organizational inertia.

In a competitive business environment, a guiding influence on organizational design should be the end-customer for whom the organization is creating value. In a truly customer-focused organization, marketing responsibilities cannot be confined to something called a marketing department. In the words of Drucker (1973): 'Marketing is so basic that it cannot be considered to be a separate function. It is the whole business seen from the point of view of its final result, that is, from the customer's point of view.'

In competitive business environments, customers are at the centre of all of an organization's activities. The customer is not simply the concern of the marketing department, but also all of the production and administrative personnel whose actions may directly or indirectly have an impact on the goods and services bought by customers. In a typical organization, the activities of a number of functional departments have direct and indirect impacts on customers:

- Personnel plans can have a crucial bearing on marketing plans. The selection, training motivation and control of staff cannot be considered in isolation from marketing objectives and strategies. Possible conflict between the personnel and marketing functions may arise where, for example, marketing demands highly trained and motivated staff, but the personnel function pursues a policy which places cost reduction above all else.

- Production managers may have a different outlook compared to marketing managers. A marketing manager may seek to respond as closely as possible to customers' needs, only to find opposition from production managers who argue that a service of the required standard cannot be achieved. A marketing manager of a railway operating company may seek to segment markets with fares tailored to meet the needs of small groups of customers, only to encounter hostility from operations managers who are responsible for actually issuing and checking travel tickets on a day-to-day basis and who may have misgivings about the confusion which finely segmented fares might cause.

- The actions of finance managers frequently have direct or indirect impact on marketing plans. Ultimately, finance managers assume responsibility for the allocation of funds which are needed to implement a marketing plan. At a more operational level, finance managers' actions in respect of the level of credit offered to customers or towards stockholdings can also significantly affect the quality of service and the volume of customers which the organization is able to serve.

All these departments should 'think customer' and work together to satisfy customer needs and expectations. There is argument as to what authority the traditional marketing-department should have in bringing about this customer orientation. In a truly mature marketing-oriented company, marketing is an implicit part of everybody's job. In such a scenario, marketing becomes responsible for a narrow range of specialist functions such as advertising and marketing research. Responsibility for the relationship between the organization and its customers is spread more diffusely throughout the organization. Gummesson (1999) uses the term 'part time marketer' to describe staff working in service organizations who may not have any direct line management responsibility for marketing, but whose activities may indirectly impinge on the quality of service received by customers.

It has been argued that the introduction of a marketing department as the principal interface between an organization and its competitive environment can bring problems as well as benefits. In a survey of 219 executives representing public and private sector services organizations in Sweden, Gronroos (1982) tested the idea that a separate marketing department may widen the gap between marketing and operations staff. This idea was put to a sample drawn from marketing as well as other functional positions using a Likert-type scale with five points ranging from agreeing strongly to disagreeing strongly. The results indicated that respondents in a wide range of service organizations considered there to be dangers in the creation of a marketing department – an average of 66 per cent agreed with the notion, with higher than average agreement being found among non-marketing executives and those working in the hotel, restaurant, professional services and insurance sectors.

4.2   BASES FOR ORGANIZING A COMMERCIAL ORGANIZATION

Four basic approaches to allocating management responsibilities within an organization can be identified, although in practice most organizations use a combination of approaches. The four approaches which will be discussed below are:

- Management by functions performed
- Management by geographical area covered
- Management of products or groups of products
- Management by groups of customers served.

4.2.1   Organization based on functional responsibilities

A traditional and common way of allocating responsibilities within an organization is to do so on the basis of identifiable functions. In most commercial organizations, a number of core functions can be identified, the most typical being operations, marketing, personnel and finance. The exact title of these functions may vary between organizations, for example personnel is often referred to as the human resources function. In larger organizations, these functions are further subdivided into areas of specialist responsibility, for example the marketing function would typically be divided into functions covering advertising, sales, marketing research and customer services, etc. The nature of an organization's environment will influence the relative size and importance of each of its functional areas of management. The precise division of the functional responsibilities will depend upon the nature of an organization. Buying and merchandising are likely to be an important feature in a retailing company, while research and development will be an important function for a technology-based on.

The main advantage of allocating responsibilities by functions is that it allows individuals and groups of individuals to develop expertise in their functional area. Personnel managers can become expert in the latest employment legislation, or be familiar with latest thinking on recruitment policies. This expertise may not be developed if personnel management responsibilities were dispersed throughout the organization. A further advantage of functional approaches to management lies in their administrative simplicity. Clearly defined hierarchical structures can allow for rapid identification of lines of authority and responsibility.

Against these advantages, division of responsibilities solely on the basis of functions can have disadvantages. Most seriously, there can be a tendency for corporate goals to become secondary to functional managers' much narrower functional goals. Functions should be seen as a means to an end (usually defined in terms of corporate profitability) and should not come to be seen as ends in their own right. It is not uncommon to find destructive rivalry between functional specialists for their share of budgets.

THINKING AROUND THE SUBJECT

How is the marketing manager seen within organizations? One message of this book is that in increasingly competitive markets, marketing can be fundamental to success, which should be reflected in its status within an organization. But this does not stop many companies looking suspiciously on their marketing managers. They have been described as the wideboys of British business – never in the office, always over budget and not properly accountable. A survey undertaken in 1998 by the Chartered Institute of Marketing highlighted the apparent problem when it found that 80 per cent of senior managers claimed there was a cultural prejudice in their companies against marketing managers. Although 38 per cent named marketing as the most important factor in business success, marketing managers appeared to be under-represented on companies' boards of directors. While 51 per cent of companies had a marketer on the board, finance directors were represented on 88 per cent of boards. Relatively few chief executives have a background in marketing. The marketing department is often the first to feel the effects of recession.

Is this apparent prejudice within organizations against marketing justified? Have marketers concentrated too much on short-term gimmicks and too little on long-term strategy? Or have marketers simply failed to promote their own reputations within the organizations where they work? And is this apparent anti-marketing mentality a peculiarly British phenomenon where marketing and selling are often viewed with suspicion?

4.2.2   Management by product type

Multioutput organizations frequently appoint a product manager to manage a particular product or group of products. This form of organization does not replace the functional organization, but provides an additional layer of management which coordinates the functions' activities. The product manager's role includes a number of key tasks:

- Developing a long-range and competitive strategy for a product or group of products
- Preparing a budgeted annual plan
- Working with internal and external functional specialists to develop and implement programmes, for example in relation to advertising and sales promotion
- Monitoring the product's performance and changes occurring in its business environment
- Identifying new opportunities and initiating product improvements to meet changing market needs.

A product management organization structure offers a number of advantages:

- The product offering benefits from an integrated cost-effective approach to planning. This particularly benefits minor products, which might otherwise be neglected.
- The product manager can in theory react more quickly to changes in the product's business environment than would be the case if no one had specific responsibility for the product. Within a bank, a mortgage manager is able to devote a lot of time and expertise to monitoring trends in the mortgage market and can become a focal point for initiating and seeing through change when this is required because of environmental change.
- Control within this type of organization can be exercised by linking product managers' salaries to performance.

Against this, product management structures are associated with a number of problems.

- The most serious problem occurs in the common situation where a product manager is given a lot of responsibility for ensuring that objectives are met, but relatively little control over resource inputs which they have at their disposal. Product managers typically must rely on persuasion to get the co-operation of marketing, operations and other functional specialist departments. Sometimes this can result in conflict, for example where a product manager seeks to position a service in one direction, while the advertising manager seeks to position it in another in order to meet broader promotional objectives.
- Confusion can arise in the minds of staff within an organization as to whom they are accountable to for their day-to-day actions. Staff involved in selling insurance policies in a branch bank, for example, may become confused at

The conventional wisdom is that product managers in organizations should work together to put their customers' needs above internal management demarcations. But could there sometimes be an ethical case against too much sharing of information by product managers?

Consider the case of merchant banks which offer investment management and capital raising services. In a proposed take-over bid, it is often necessary for those involved in raising the capital required by a client to work very discreetly for fear of prematurely raising the share price of the target company. If this information were available to those staff working in investment management, it would give them an unfair advantage over the market generally, allowing them to build up a shareholding in the

target company ahead of the announcement of a take-over bid. Merchant banks have sought to build 'Chinese walls' around their operations where this risk is present and the adoption of a functional marketing management structure allows greater effective separation of functions. Numerous other service industries can be identified where similar ethical problems can be lessened by the adoption of a product management structure – accountants selling both auditing services and management consultancy services to a company may be tempted to gain business in the latter area at the expense of integrity in the former. How do large diversified firms convince their customers that information given in confidence to one section of the organization will not be used against them in another section?

possibly conflicting messages from an operations manager and a product manager.

■ Product management structures can lead to larger numbers of people being employed, resulting in a higher cost structure which may put the organization at a competitive disadvantage in price sensitive markets.

■ Research has suggested that the existence of the optimal product management form is rare and that it is typically associated with an unwillingness of senior management to delegate authority to product managers. While the product management form may be appropriate for a diversified conglomerate, it may be inappropriate for complex multioutput organizations where many functions and products are closely interdependent, allowing very little freedom of action for individual product managers.

4.2.3 Market management organization

Many organizations provide goods and services to a diverse range of customers who have widely varying needs. As an example, a cross-channel ferry operator provides the basically similar service of transport for private car drivers, coach operators and freight operators, among others. However, the specific needs of each group of users vary significantly. A coach operator is likely to attach different importance compared with a road haulier to service attributes such as flexibility, ease of reservations, the type of accommodation provided, etc. In such situations, market managers can be appointed to oversee the development of particular markets, in much the same way as a product manager oversees particular products. Instead of being given specific financial targets for their products, market managers are usually given growth or market share targets. The main advantage of this form of organization is that it allows management efforts to be focused on meeting the needs of distinct and identified groups of customers – something which should be at the heart of all truly marketing-oriented organizations. Market managers can keep a close eye on their market sector and should be in a strong position to respond to environmental change. It is also likely that innovative goods and services are more likely to emerge within this structure than where an organization's response is confined within traditional product management boundaries. Market management structures are also arguably more conducive to the important task of developing relationships with customers, especially for business-to-business services. Where an organization has a number of very important customers, it is common to find the appointment of key account managers to handle relationships with those clients in order to exploit marketing opportunities which are of mutual benefit to both.

Many of the disadvantages of the product management organization are also shared by market-based structures. There can again be a conflict between responsibility and authority, and this form of structure can also become expensive to operate.

4.2.4   Organization based on geographical responsibilities

Organizations providing goods and services to national or international markets frequently organize many of their functions on a geographical basis. This particularly applies to the sales function, although it could also include geographically designated responsibilities for new product development (e.g. a retailer with regional management structures responsible for new store opening) and some local responsibility for promotion.

In most organizations with some form of regional structure, a delicate balance has to be maintained between the responsibilities of the headquarters and the branches. Some delegation of responsibilities to regional branch managers can be vital to secure speedy and effective response to purely local issues. This is especially true of delegated responsibility in overseas markets where headquarters management may have little idea of the cultural factors which affect the dynamics of a distant overseas market. On the other hand, too much delegation can result in inconsistencies in the way that a global brand is developed and promoted.

4.2.5   Integrated approaches

Overall, the management structure of an organization must allow for a flexible and adaptable response to customers' needs within a changing environment, while aiming to reduce the level of confusion, ambiguity and cost inherent in some structures. The differences in organizational structures described above, and their

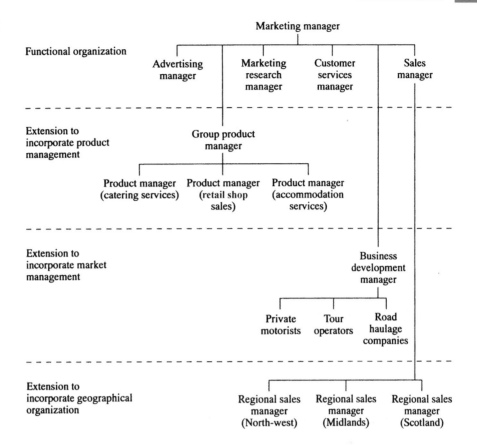

Figure 4.1
Alternative forms
of marketing
department
organization
structure showing
typical
applications to a
ferry operator

Functional organization — Marketing manager — Advertising manager — Marketing research manager — Customer services manager — Sales manager

Extension to incorporate product management — Group product manager — Product manager (catering services) — Product manager (retail shop sales) — Product manager (accommodation services)

Extension to incorporate market management — Business development manager — Private motorists — Tour operators — Road haulage companies

Extension to incorporate geographical organization — Regional sales manager (North-west) — Regional sales manager (Midlands) — Regional sales manager (Scotland)

typical application to the marketing operations of a car ferry operator are illustrated in Figure 4.1. The great diversity of organizational structures highlights the fact that there is not one unique structure which is appropriate to all firms, even within the same industry sector. Indeed, most organizational structures exhibit characteristics of all four basic approaches discussed above.

The problem of how to bring people together in an organization to act collectively, while also being able to place responsibility on an individual is one which continues to generate considerable discussion. We will now consider two ideas which seek to integrate these approaches. The first, the matrix approach to management, is essentially about creating a flexible organization based on a combination of the design characteristics discussed above. The second approach – often referred to as business process reengineering – starts the process of organizational design with a clean sheet of paper and develops structures and processes which are most appropriate for the environment in which an organization operates.

4.2.6   Matrix approach to management

Organizations which produce many different products for many different markets may experience difficulties if they adopt a purely product- or market-based

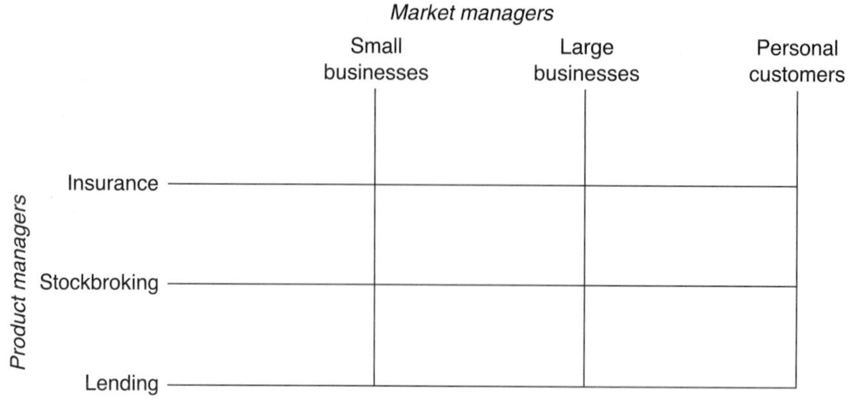

Figure 4.2
**Matrix
organization
structure applied
to a financial
services
organization**

Market managers

	Small businesses	Large businesses	Personal customers

Product managers

Insurance

Stockbroking

Lending

structure. If a product management structure is adopted, product managers would require detailed knowledge of very diverse markets. Likewise, in a market management structure, market managers would require detailed knowledge of possibly very diverse product ranges. The essence of a matrix type of organization is to allow individuals to concentrate on a functional, product, market or geographical specialization and to bring them together in taskforce teams to solve problems taking an organizational view rather than their own narrow specialist view. Product managers can concentrate on excellence in production, while market managers focus on meeting consumer needs without any preference for a particular product (see Figure 4.2). An example of matrix structures can be found in many vehicle distributors where market managers can be appointed to identify and formulate a market strategy in respect of the distinct needs of private customers and contract hire customers among others, as well as being appointed to manage key customers. Market managers work alongside product managers who can develop specialized activities such as servicing, bodywork repairs and vehicle hire which are made available to final customers through the market managers.

The most important advantages of matrix structures are that they can allow organizations to respond rapidly to environmental change. Short-term project teams can be assembled and disbanded at short notice to meet changed needs. Project teams can bring together a wide variety of disciplines and can be used to evaluate new services before full-scale development is undertaken. A bank exploring the possibility of developing a banking system linked to customers' mobile phones might establish a team drawn from staff involved in marketing to personal customers and staff responsible for technology-based research and development. The former may include market researchers and the latter computer development engineers.

The flexibility of matrix structures can be increased by bringing temporary workers into the structure on a contract basis as and when needed. During the 1990s there was a trend for many organizations to lay off significant numbers of workers – including management – and to buy these back when needed. As well as cutting fixed costs, such 'modular' or 'virtual' organizations have the potential to respond very rapidly to environmental change.

Where matrix structures exist, great motivation can be present in effectively managed teams. Against this, matrix-type structures can be associated with problems. Most serious is the confused lines of authority which may result. Staff may not be clear about which superior he or she is responsible to for a particular aspect of their duties, resulting in possible stress and demotivation. Where a matrix structure is introduced into an organization with a history and culture of functional specialization, it can be very difficult to implement effectively. Staff may be reluctant to act outside a role which they have traditionally defined narrowly and guarded jealously. Finally, matrix structures invariably result in more managers being employed within an organization. At best this can result in a costly addition to the salary bill. At worst, the existence of additional managers can also slow down decision-making processes where the managers show a reluctance to act outside a narrow functional role.

4.2.7 Business process reengineering

Most management change within organizations occurs incrementally. The result of this is often a compromised organization structure which is unduly influenced by historic factors which are of no continuing relevance. Vested interests within an organization frequently result in an organization which is production rather than customer focused.

The underlying principle of business process reengineering is to design an organization around key value adding activities. Essentially, reengineering is about *radically* redesigning the *processes* by which an organization does business in order that it can achieve major savings in cost, or improvements in output, or both. Seen as a model, the organization which is most effective is the one which adds most value (as defined by customers) for the least cost.

Business process reengineering focuses on operational aspects of a business, rather than its strategy and starts the design of processes and structures with a clean sheet of paper. This is in contrast to most organizational change which starts with an analysis of the existing structure and attempts to tinker with it. Reengineering starts by asking: 'If we were a new company, how would we organize ourselves?' It follows that reengineering can stand for a total sudden change, inevitably challenging vested interests within an organization who are comfortable within their own departmental boundary.

To be effective, reengineering needs to be led by strong individuals who have authority to oversee implementation from beginning to end. They will need a lot of clout because fear, resistance and cynicism will inevitably slow the task down. At first sight though, this approach to reorganization would appear to be in conflict with the principles of Total Quality Management and other participative schemes that stress employee involvement in change. In fact, reengineering only works effectively if it takes place in an environment of continuous improvement based on TQM principles. Successful companies therefore seek to involve their employees in the detail of implementation, even if the radical nature of the agenda is not negotiable.

The activities of the American telecommunications company GTE has provided a model for business process reengineering which has been copied by many companies within the sector throughout Europe. The starting point was the company's belief that its customers wanted one central point of contact who could be responsible for seeing an enquiry through, whether the enquiry was to fix a faulty phone, question a bill, sign up for additional services or any combination of services offered by the company. The company wanted to avoid the all too common situation where customers were bounced from one office to another, and sometimes disappeared in cracks which were on the boundary between departmental responsibilities.

An early change involved examining the work of repair clerks, who had traditionally taken down information from a customer, filled out a report card and sent it on to other employees who would check out the problem and fix it. GTE wanted the whole process to happen while the customer was still on the line –

something that was currently happening just once for every 200 calls. The first step in reengineering was to move testing and switching equipment to the desks of the repair clerks who were renamed 'front-end technicians'. The aim was to increase the proportion of calls that the clerks could pass on without further referral.

The second step was to link the repair service with sales and billing. To do this, GTE gave its telephone operators new computer software linked to databases that allowed them to handle almost any problem a customer may have.

The results of this reengineering? After two years, the company claimed to have raised its customer satisfaction levels and improved productivity by 20–30 per cent, although the costs in terms of staff training and redundancies were high. Sceptics of business process reengineering were more doubtful. Hadn't telecommunications firms been doing this kind of internal change for a long time, and wasn't the current change merely a result of new technology and increasingly competitive markets?

4.3 IMPROVING ORGANIZATIONAL EFFECTIVENESS

We are probably all familiar with organizations which have failed to adapt to their environment and suffered as a result. Often, these failings can be traced back to shortcomings in the organization's internal structures and processes. When the Sainsbury's supermarket chain fell from its position as the leading UK grocery retailer in the mid-1990s, many commentators were quick to blame this on internal issues. It was widely claimed that the Sainsbury family which controlled a majority of the company's shares had been too slow to delegate responsibilities to managers and had carried on acting as though it had an unassailable position. In effect, it had become like a great supertanker – sailing along steadily but finding it difficult to change its direction.

Numerous studies have sought to identify those factors within organizations which result in an organization being able to address environmental change

Figure 4.3
The 7 'S's
approach to
improving
internal
organizational
effectiveness

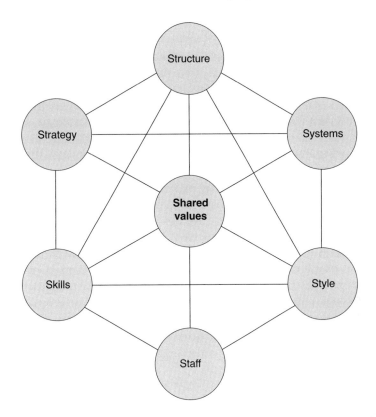

more effectively. The McKinsey 7S framework developed by Peters and Waterman (1982) identified seven essential elements for a successful business, based on a study of the most successful American companies (Figure 4.3). The elements are broken down into the hardware (Strategy, Structure and Systems) and the software (Skills, Staff, Styles and Shared values). Formalized strategies, structures and systems on their own were not considered to be sufficient to bring about success – these could only be operationalized with appropriate intangible 'software'.

Where the main pressure on an organization is the need to respond to changing customer requirements, a number of methods can be used to develop a more responsive marketing orientation within an organization:

■ The appointment of senior management who have a good understanding of the philosophies and practices of marketing.

■ The introduction of in-house educational programmes which aim to train non-marketing employees to empathize with customers' expectations.

■ The introduction of outside consultants who can apply their previous experience of introducing a marketing culture to an organization from an impartial perspective.

■ A commonly used method of making management think in marketing terms is to install a formal market-oriented planning system. This can have the effect of forcing managers to work through a list of market-related headings, such as an analysis of the competitive environment and identification of market opportunities when developing their annual plans.

There has been debate about the relationship between strategy and the organizational structure within which such strategy is developed and implemented. The traditional view is that structures adapt to fit the chosen strategy, although more recent thought has focused on the idea that strategy is very much dependent upon the structure adopted by an organization. An approach suggested by Giles (1988) is a structured iterative planning process which works by creating a cross-functional team of managers for the purpose of designing a marketing plan for a market or market segment selected by top management for attention. The managers' initial view of their target market is challenged and refined through a focused marketing audit which requires continual iteration, forcing participants to go backwards and forwards through the process. The resulting marketing plan is likely to represent a high degree of commitment and ownership by those involved in creating it. The attraction of this type of approach is that it challenges managers to design better ways of addressing their markets by allowing things to be said which in a conventional planning process may be politically unacceptable. The marketing problem defines the agenda, rather than having it determined by the structure and political ideology of the organization. The process is designed to bring about marketing-led strategic change within the organization (Piercy 1997).

4.4 ORGANIZATIONAL CULTURE

Organizational culture concerns the social and behavioural manifestation of a whole set of values which are shared by members of the organization and can be defined as 'some underlying structure of meaning that persists over time, constraining people's perception, interpretation and behaviour' (Jelinek *et al.*, 1983). Cultures can be quite enduring, as where new employees soon become aware of the distinctive ways that the organization does things. Cultural values can be shared in a number of ways, including:

- The way work is organized and experienced
- How authority is exercised and delegated
- How people are rewarded, organized and controlled
- The values and work orientation of staff
- The degree of formalization, standardization and control within the organization
- The value placed on structured processes of planning, analysis and control rather than instinct and gut feeling, etc.
- How much initiative, risk taking, scope for individuality and expression is given
- Rules and expectations about such things as informality in interpersonal relations, dress, personal eccentricity, etc.

■ Status accorded to senior members of the organization or particular functions

■ Expectations for team working or success on the basis of individual efforts.

There are often many visible manifestations of these deep-seated cultural values, including the type of buildings occupied by the organization and the image projected in its publicity and public relations.

An organization's culture may be quite imperceptible, indeed people who have belonged to it for a long time may not be aware of any alternative way of doing things. Elements of the culture may be questioned where individual or group expectations do not correspond to the behaviours associated with the prevailing values of those who uphold 'the culture'. Central command and control cultures within an organization may become increasingly questioned at a time when other social institutions are embracing more democratic cultures.

Handy (1989) identified four types of organizational culture:

1 The power culture is found mainly in smaller organizations where power and influence stem from a single central source, through which all decisions, communication and control are channelled. Because there is no rigid structure within the organization, it is theoretically capable of adapting to change very rapidly, although its actual success in adapting is dependent on the abilities of the central power source.

2 The role culture is characterized by a formal, functional organization structure in which there is relatively little freedom and creativity in decision making. Such organizations are more likely to be production oriented and can have difficulty responding to new market opportunities.

3 The task culture is concerned primarily with getting a given task done. Importance is therefore attached to those individuals who have the skill or knowledge to accomplish a particular task. Organizations with a task-oriented culture are potentially very flexible, changing constantly as new tasks arise. Innovation and creativity are highly prized for their own sake.

4 The person culture is characterized by organizations which are centred on serving the interests of individuals within them. It is a relatively rare form of culture in any business organizations, but can characterize campaigning pressure groups.

As individual organizations develop, it is essential that the dominant culture adapts. While a small business may quite successfully embrace a centralized power culture, continued growth may cause this culture to become a liability. Similarly, the privatization of public utilities calls for a transformation from a bureaucratic role culture to a task-oriented culture.

Within many organizations, it has proved difficult to change cultural attitudes when the nature of an organization's business environment has significantly changed, rendering the established culture a liability in terms of strategic management. As an example, the cultural values of UK clearing banks have for a long time continued to be dominated by prudence and caution when in some product areas,

Many organizations have developed a culture of putting their employees first. This at first might sound contradictory to the marketing philosophy which puts customers at the centre of a firm's thinking, but there are many examples of companies who have made this proud claim and achieved credible results. The American South Western Airlines has frequently been cited as an advocate of this approach, and has expanded rapidly and profitably. The airline has argued that employees are such a major part of its service offer and that if they are not happy it is unlikely that the airline's customers will be happy. Being a relatively new airline with no history of poor industrial relations undoubtedly helps employees to identify with the company's mission. Having staff incentive schemes which encourage employees to perform to their best in a highly competitive market also helps. But can this approach work in all situations? If employees do not share a company's mission, management's attempts to put employees first may not be reciprocated in the form of employees' enthusiastic contribution to the business. And if there is very little external competition to spur them on, captive customers may come second best by a long way.

In reality, it is difficult to talk about a culture in which employees come first, if by implication customers come second. They should both be seen as part of a virtuous circle in which attention given to one reinforces attention given to the other.

such as insurance sales, a more aggressive approach to marketing management is called for.

4.5 THE FLEXIBLE ORGANIZATION

We have seen how management structures can help or hinder the task of responding to organizational change at a strategic level. We will now consider how organizations can be made more flexible to environmental change at a more short-term or operational level. To continue the analogy with a central heating system and its environment (introduced in Chapter 1), we will now move from looking at how the system adapts to long-term climatic change, to how it copes with day-to-day changes in weather.

For many organizations, employees are the biggest item of cost and potentially the biggest cause of bottlenecks in responding rapidly to environmental change, especially within the services sector. Having the right staff in the right place at the right time can demand a lot of flexibility on the part of employees. Too often, customers are delayed because, although staff are available, they are not trained to perform the task which currently needs performing urgently. At other times, employees may go about a backroom task oblivious of the fact that delays are occurring elsewhere. Worse still, employees could have a negative attitude towards their job, and see a customer's problem as nothing to do with them and take no interest in finding staff who may be able to help. Many service industries have been notorious in the past for rigid demarcation between jobs which were organization-focused rather than customer-focused. In Britain, train drivers and guards for a long while existed as two separate groups which were not able to stand in for the other. With privatization and increased competition for rail franchises, this mindset has been changed, so that employees who are trained in one area can substitute in the other, if required.

To improve their flexibility, many organizations have sought to develop multiple skills among their employees so that they can be switched between tasks at short notice. Within the hotel sector, for example, it is quite usual to find staff multiskilled in reception duties, food and beverage service and room service. If staff shortages occur within one area, staff can be rapidly transferred from less urgent tasks where there may be sufficient staff coverage anyway. An effective multitasking strategy must be backed up by adequate training so that employees can effectively perform all the functions that are expected of them.

Flexibility in working also applies to the rostering of employees' duties. Where patterns of demand are unpredictable, it is useful to have a pool of suitably trained staff who can be called up at short notice. Many service providers therefore operate 'standby' or 'callout' rotas, where staff are expected to be available to go into work at short notice.

A flexible workforce sounds attractive in principle, but there are some drawbacks. Training in multiple skills would appear to be against the principles of scientific management, wherein employees specialize in one task and perform this as efficiently as possible. Multiple-skill training represents an investment for firms, and in industry sectors with high turnover, such as the hospitality sector, the benefits of this training may be short lived. Recruiting staff may become more expensive, with staff capable of performing numerous tasks able to command higher salaries than somebody whose background only allows them to perform a narrower range of tasks. Finally, there is also the problem that requiring staff to work flexible hours may make their working conditions less attractive than a job where they had certainty over the days and times that they will be working. Expecting excessive flexibility may be contrary to the principles of internal marketing (discussed later in this chapter), exacerbating problems where there is a shortage of skilled staff. Companies have to compete with other employers for the best staff and if a job is perceived as offering too much uncertainty, staff may prefer to work elsewhere where working conditions are more predictable.

Flexibility within an organization can be achieved by segmenting the workforce into core and peripheral components. Core workers have greater job security and have defined career opportunities within an internal labour market. In return for this job security, core workers may have to accept what Atkinson (1984) terms 'functional flexibility' whereby they become responsible for a variety of job tasks. The work output of this group is intensified, but in order for this to be successful, employees require effective training and motivation which in turn has to be sustained by effective participation methods.

Peripheral employees, on the other hand, have lesser job security and limited career opportunity. In terms of Atkinson's prescription they are 'numerically flexible', while financial flexibility is brought about through the process of 'distancing'. In this situation a firm may utilize the services and skills of specialist labour

The conventional wisdom is that services organizations need highly flexible employment practices so that they can effectively and efficiently meet customers' varying demands when and where they occur. But how far should a company go in pursuit of flexibility? Stories abound of companies who pay young people very low wages and provide very insecure employment. In the UK, the Burger King chain attracted a lot of bad publicity in 1996 when it was alleged to have paid some of its part-time staff wages which amounted to little more than £1 per hour and gave little notice of when they would be required to work. To some, this sounded like exploitation, which subsequent minimum wage legislation has sought to overcome. To others, young people were at least being given an opportunity to work and customers benefited by lower prices. But apart from the ethics of such practices is the question whether too much flexibility makes good business sense. If staff can be laid off at very short notice, will they show such concern to customers as an employee who has more secure employment? Or will the insecurity keep employees on their toes to perform well at all times? Can flexibility be applied to complex organizational processes, or is it realistically limited to jobs which have been highly industrialized and deskilled?

but acquire it through a commercial contract as distinct from an employment contract. This process is referred to as subcontracting. The principal characteristics of the flexible firm are illustrated in Figure 4.4.

As a strategic tool, the model of the flexible firm has important implications for organizations which operate in an unstable environment. However, critics of the concept have suggested that the strategic role attributed to the flexibility model is often illusory, with many organizations introducing 'flexibility' in very much an opportunistic manner. It has been noted that the opportunities for introducing this model of flexibility are greater in the UK than in most other EU countries, where stricter rules on staff layoffs apply.

4.6   LEADERSHIP

Many of the most successful commercial organizations, including the Virgin Group, Federal Express and McDonald's attribute their success in part to the quality of leadership within their organizations. The results of poor leadership are evident in many failing organizations, especially within the public sector.

What is good leadership for one organization need not necessarily be so for another. Organizations operating in relatively stable environments may be best suited with a leadership style which places a lot of power in a hierarchical chain of command. In the UK, many banks until recently had leadership styles which have been drawn from models developed in the armed forces, evidenced by some managers having titles such as superintendent and inspector. Such rigid, hierarchical patterns of leadership may be less effective where the business environment

Figure 4.4
Components of the flexible firm

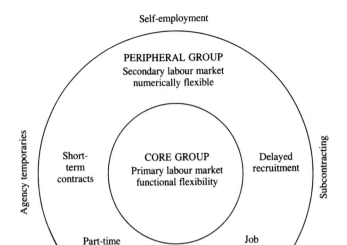

EXTERNAL LABOUR SOURCES

Self-employment

PERIPHERAL GROUP
Secondary labour market
numerically flexible

CORE GROUP
Primary labour market
functional flexibility

Short-term contracts

Delayed recruitment

Agency temporaries

Subcontracting

Part-time employees

Job sharing

Increased outsourcing

is changing rapidly and a flexible response is called for (as has happened in the banking sector). The literature has developed two typologies of leadership – transactional and transformational – which broadly correspond respectively with the control and empowerment approaches described later in this chapter.

What makes a good leader of people? And are leaders born, or can individuals acquire the skills of leadership? On the latter point there is little doubt that development is possible, and successful companies have invested heavily in leadership development programmes. As for what makes a successful leader of organizations, there have been many suggestions of desirable characteristics, including:

■ Setting clear expectations of staff

■ Recognizing excellence appropriately and facilitating staff in overcoming their weaknesses

■ Leading by example

■ Being able to empathize with employees

■ Showing adaptability to changing circumstances.

In too many companies, bad leadership is characterized by:

■ 'Management by confusion' in which expectations of staff are ambiguously stated and management actions are guided by a secretive 'hidden agenda'

■ Reward systems which are not based on performance and are perceived as being unfair

Beginning with a small shop in Dundalk in 1960, the Irish grocery retailer SuperQuinn has grown to a successful chain of 12 shops and 7 shopping centres employing over 2000 people throughout Ireland. A large part of this success has been attributed to the leadership style of the company's founder, Feargal Quinn, and the emphasis on linking employees' activities to excellence in service quality. But what makes such leadership style distinctive?

An important principle is that managers should lead by example and never lose contact with the most important person in the organization – the customer. It is the task of a leader to set the tone for customer-focused excellence. To prevent managers losing sight of customers' needs, Quinn uses every opportunity to move them closer to customers, including locating their offices not in a comfortable room upstairs, but in the middle of the sales floor.

Managers regularly take part in customer panels where customers talk about their expectations and perceptions of SuperQuinn. Subcontracting this task entirely to a market research agency is seen as alien to the leadership culture of the company. The company requires its managers to spend periods doing routine front-line jobs (such as packing customers' bags), a practice which has become commonplace in many successful services organizations. This keeps managers close to the customer and improves their ability to empathize with junior employees.

Does this leadership style work? Given the company's level of growth, profits and rate of repeat business, it must be doing something right, contradicting much of the scientific management theories that management is a specialist task which can be separated from routine dealings with customers and employees.

- The deliberate or inadvertent creation of an 'us and them' attitude
- Failing to understand the aspirations of employees
- Failing to take the initiative where environmental change calls for adaptation.

4.7   DEFINING THE ORGANIZATIONAL MISSION

A corporate mission statement is a means of reminding everybody within the organization of its essential purpose. Drucker (1973) identified a number of basic questions which management should ask when it perceives itself drifting along with no clear purpose, and which form the basis of a corporate mission statement:

- What is our business?
- Who is the customer?
- What is value to the customer?
- What will our business be?
- What should our business be?

By forcing management to focus on the essential nature of the business which

Figure 4.5
Example of a mission statement – British Gas plc
(Reproduced with permission of British Gas Trading Ltd)

Statement of Purpose
We aim to be ...
a world class energy company and the leading international gas business
by ...
▶ running a professional gas business providing safe, secure and reliable supplies
▶ actively developing an international business in exploration and production of oil and gas
▶ making strategic investments in other energy-related projects and business world wide
▶ satisfying our customers wishes for excellent quality of service and outstanding value
▶ constantly and energetically seeking to improve quality and productivity in all we do
▶ caring for the environment
▶ maintaining a high quality workforce with equal opportunities for all
▶ cultivating good relations with customers, employees, suppliers, shareholders and the communities we serve and thereby improving returns to our shareholders

British Gas

they are in and the nature of customer needs which they seek to satisfy, the problem of 'marketing myopia' advanced by Levitt (1960) can be avoided. Levitt argued that in order to avoid a narrow, short-sighted view of its business, managers should define their business in terms of the needs that they fulfil rather than the products they produce. In the classic example, railway operators had lost their way because they defined their service output in terms of the technology of tracked vehicles, rather than in terms of the core benefit of movement which they provided. Accountants learnt the lesson of this myopic example by redefining their central purpose away from a narrow preoccupation with providing 'accounting services' to a much broader mission statement which spoke about providing 'business solutions'. More recently, many freight transport companies have defined their mission in terms of managing customers' complete logistical needs.

In the services sector, where the interface between the consumer and production personnel is often critical, communication of the values contained within the mission statement assumes great importance. The statement is frequently repeated by organizations in staff newsletters and in notices at their place of work. An example of a mission statement which is widely communicated to the workforce – as well as to customers – is provided by British Gas (see Figure 4.5).

The nature of an organization's mission statement is a reflection of a number of factors:

■ The organization's ownership, which can lead to marked contrasts in the mission statements of public sector, private sector and charity organizations.

■ The previous history of the organization, in particular any distinct competencies which it has acquired or images which it has created in the eyes of potential customers.

■ Environmental factors, in particular, the major opportunities and threats which are likely to face the organization in the foreseeable future.

THINKING AROUND THE SUBJECT

Is a mission statement a valuable guiding principle for all of a firm's employees, or just more management fudge? Part of the distinctive Marks and Spencer culture which pervades all its workers is based on its efforts at disseminating its mission statement. This is conveyed to all employees through various means – notices displayed at critical points around its stores, items in staff newsletters and training programmes among others. Human resource management policies have worked to make employees highly receptive to the company's mission statement and frequent repetition in key places serves to reinforce employees' commitment. As a result, most of the organization's employees are knowledgeable about – and work towards achieving – the following mission:

■ To offer customers a selective range of high-quality well-designed and attractive merchandise at reasonable prices.

■ To encourage suppliers to use the most modern and efficient techniques of production and quality control dictated by the latest discoveries in science and technology.

■ With the co-operation of suppliers, to ensure the highest standards of quality control.

■ To plan the expansion of stores for the better display of a widening range of goods for the convenience of our customers.

■ To simplify operating procedures so that business is carried on in the most efficient manner.

■ To foster good human relations with customers, suppliers and staff.

If Marks and Spencer has used its mission statement effectively, the question needs to be asked why they are often ridiculed or sniggered at by employees in other companies? Are the mission statements too unrealistic? Or has the company communicated them inappropriately and failed to get employees to share their values?

■ Resources available – without resources available for their accomplishment, a mission statement has little meaning.

Missions define in general terms the direction in which an organization seeks to move. They contain no quantifiable information which allows them to be operationalized. For this to happen, objectives need to be set.

4.8   CREATING INVOLVEMENT BY EMPLOYEES

It can be difficult for an organization to respond to environmental change if it does not have the confidence of its employees, for whom change may be viewed with suspicion. While it is probably unrealistic to say that a happy workforce necessarily results in an organization which is more effective at embracing change, there are many things that it can do to secure the active participation of its employees in change. We will now review some key elements of the employment relationship which can facilitate this.

4.8.1**Motivating employees**

Motivation concerns the choices which employees make between alternative forms of behaviour in order that they as employees attain their own personal goals. The task of management is to equate the individual's personal goals with those of the employing organization – that is, getting employees morally involved with the service which they help to produce. This in turn requires employees to consent to the management of their work activity. Maslow (1943) argued that motivation is based on individuals' desire to satisfy various levels of need. These levels range from the need to realize potential and self-development down to the satisfaction of basic needs such as hunger, thirst and sex. Rewards for reaching goals can be tangible, for example money, or intangible (e.g. commendations or awards which add to status or self-esteem). An organization has to bring about congruence between its own goals and those of its employees. This is the basis for designing an appropriate motivation package. Within the UK tourist attractions sector, a comparison can be made between many commercial operations (e.g. Alton Towers and Warwick Castle) where financial incentives are an important motivator and the National Trust, which attracts many unpaid volunteers, motivated by a desire to share in the preservation of historic buildings.

4.8.2 **Consent**

The term 'consent' covers a variety of management-led initiatives and strategies which seek to give it authority without actively emphasizing its coercive power. In the United Kingdom during the 20th century there have been various forms of employee participation and involvement designed to aid management in the generation of consent. Such initiatives include scientific management, industrial management, the human relations approach, welfare, paternalism, professionalized and proceduralized personnel management, and more recently Human Resource Management (HRM). Each initiative has its own prescription for the generation of consent.

Scientific management approaches seek co-operation between employer and employee in terms of the division of labour, whereby individual employees work in predefined ways as directed by management. Advocates of scientific management see mutual benefits for the employee and employer. For the former, specializing in one work activity would give the opportunity to earn more, especially through piece rates pay systems, while management would benefit through greater work control and higher productivity. What Taylor, the leading advocate of scientific management, did not expect was the hostility of employees to what is often described as the process of deskilling. Many attempts have been made to deskill jobs in accordance with the scientific management prescription. However, it is necessary to balance the benefits of specialization and improved efficiency against employees' sense of alienation from their job which occurs where they are involved in only a very small part of a production process.

Paternalism is often associated with Quaker employers such as Cadbury or Rowntree who attempted to show that they were interested in their workforce at home as well as at work. Within the services sector, many retail employers such as Marks and Spencer have taken a paternalistic attitude towards their employees by providing such benefits as on-site welfare services or temporary accommodation for their employees. This and other benefits, such as subsidized social clubs are designed to encourage employee identification with the company, and therefore loyalty, which legitimizes managerial authority and hence consent to it.

In contrast to the economically based consent strategies of scientific management, the *human relations* approach looks at man as a social animal. Mayo in his study of General Electric in the United States argued that productivity was unrelated to work organization and economic rewards as suggested by scientific management. Mayo emphasized the importance of atmosphere and social attitudes, group feelings and the sense of identification which employees had. He suggested that the separation of employees which scientific management had created prevented them from experiencing a sense of identification and involvement which is essential for all humans. Hence one solution was to design group structures into production processes. Such processes were thought to assist in the generation of employees' loyalty to their organization via the work group. Mayo's work is similar in focus to that of Herzberg and Maslow. Maslow suggested that humans have psychological needs as well as economic needs. Only when the psychological needs have been catered for do the economic needs come into play. To Herzberg, humans have lower and higher order needs. The former are the basic economic needs of food and shelter whereas the latter are more psychologically based in terms of recognition and contribution to the group and organization.

All of the management initiatives and strategies described in this section are in part efforts to generate employee consent to management authority without management exercising its authority via coercion. Where this consent is obtained, employees can be motivated by some form of participation in the organization. Such participation gives the employee a small stake in the organization, be it financial or in the form of discretionary control over the performance of their work function.

4.8.3 Participation

An employee's participation in an organization may be limited to purely economic matters – payment is received in return for work performed. Alternatively, participation may manifest itself through more qualitative measures such as employee involvement in decision making through quality circles or team briefings. The process of creating involvement can take the form of devolution of some areas of traditional personnel activity to line management in order that the employees actually doing the work and those responsible for managing particular sections feel that they are somehow involved in it together. This can apply, for example to selecting, recruiting and appraising employees within a work group.

Communication

Internal communication between management and employees is usually most notable when it is absent. Rumours about revised working arrangements, reductions in the workforce and changes to the terms of employment often circulate around companies, breeding a feeling of distrust by employees in their management. Some managers may take a conscious decision to give employees as little information as possible, perhaps on the basis that knowledge is power. There are sometimes good strategic reasons for not disseminating information to employees (for example business strategy may be a closely guarded secret in order to keep competitors guessing). However, in too many organizations information is unnecessarily withheld from employees, creating a feeling of an underclass in terms of access to information. Such practices do not help to generate consent and involvement by employees.

In good-practice organizations, information can be communicated through a number of channels. The staff newsletter is a well-tried medium, but in many instances these are seen as being too little, too late and with inadequate discussion of the issues involved. Many organizations use team briefings to cascade information down through an organization and to communicate back upwards again. The Internet is developing new possibilities for communicating information to a company's employees and allows much greater personalization to the specific needs of individual employees. External advertising should regard the internal labour force as a secondary target market. The appearance of advertisements on television can have the effect of inspiring confidence of employees in their management and pride in their company.

Strategies to increase employees' involvement

The methods which an organization uses to encourage involvement among its employees are likely to be influenced by the type of person it employs and the extent to which their jobs present opportunities to exercise autonomy (that is, the extent to which employees are able to control their own work processes) and discretion (the degree of independent thinking they can exercise in performing their work).

This section considers various strategies to increase employees' involvement. In practice, organizations are most likely to be concerned with securing greater employee involvement by making individual employee objectives more congruent to those of the whole organization. This type of involvement may be available to all employees, but the extent to which their participation is real and effective may well depend on where they are positioned in the employment hierarchy, that is, whether they are within the core or the peripheral groups of workers. Increased participation is brought about by a combination of consultation and communication methods, and team briefings.

- 'Open door' policies encourage employees to air their grievances and to make suggestions directly to their superiors. The aim of this approach is to make management accessible and 'employee friendly'. To be effective, the human relations approach would require employees to feel that they do in fact have a real say in managerial matters. As a consequence, management must appear to be open and interested in employee relations. It is likely that this approach to managerial style and strategy will emphasize open management through some of the methods described below.

- Team briefings are a system of communication within the organization where a leader of a group provides group members (up to about 20) with management derived information. The rationale behind briefing is to encourage commitment to and identification with the organization. Team briefings are particularly useful in times of organizational change, although they can be held regularly to cover such items as competitive progress, changes in policy and points of future action. Ideally, they should result in information 'cascading' down through an organization. The difference between briefing and Quality Circles (see below) centres on their respective contents. Briefing sessions are likely to be more general and relate to the whole organization, whereas Quality Circles relate to the specific work activity of a particular group of employees. Any general points of satisfaction or dissatisfaction can be aired in briefings and then taken up in specific Quality Circles.

- Quality Circles (QCs) are small groups of employees who meet together with a supervisor or group leader in an attempt to discuss their work in terms of production quality and service delivery. The QC's often work within a Total Quality Management approach. To be successful, the QC leader has to be willing to listen to and act upon issues raised by QC members. This is essential if the QC is to be sustained. Circle members must feel their participation is real and effective, therefore the communication process within the QC must be two way. If Quality Circles appear to become only a routinized listening session, members may consider it to be just another form of managerial control.

- Total Quality Management (TQM) policies rest upon the generation of an organizational mission or philosophy which encourages all employees and functional areas to regard themselves as providers and customers of other departments. The central idea behind TQM is the generation among all staff of a greater awareness of customer needs, the aim of which is to improve quality and or reduce production or internal transaction costs. Employees are encouraged to act outside of what they may see as a narrowly defined role, to appreciate the impact which their actions will have on the total service perceptions of the organization's customers.

- The pattern of ownership of an organization can influence the level of consent and participation. Where the workforce owns a significant share of a business, there should in principle be less cause for 'us and them' attitudes to develop between management and the workforce. For this reason, many labour-intensive service organizations have significant worker shareholders and there is evidence that such companies can out-perform more conventionally owned organizations.

Many services firms proudly promote the fact that they are owned by their employees. But do they deliver better service quality to customers? Research undertaken by Dolan and Brierley (1992) in the bus sector showed how two companies – People's Provincial of Fareham and Derbyshire-based Chesterfield Transport – had capitalized on their worker ownership to perform better than their more conventionally owned rivals.

To the employees, a financial investment in the two companies studied proved attractive. Over a period of five years, the value of employees' investments in People's Provincial more than doubled, while with Chesterfield Transport it increased by over fourfold within two years. Like many employee buy-outs of larger government-owned organizations, take-over bids were attracted from larger predators, boosting the value of employees' shareholdings.

The research highlighted four important benefits which had resulted from worker ownership:

■ Traditional hierarchies were broken down, which gave much greater operational flexibility to the companies (for example, inspectors and management would accept it as normal to change their duties and drive buses when the need arose). This was particularly important as the uneven pattern of demand required great flexibility.

■ Costs were held down because staff recognized that they would benefit directly from the resulting increase in profits. Similarly, staff became more willing to pass on ideas about ways in which services could be improved or costs saved.

■ Absenteeism was reduced, as was the need for formal disciplinary measures to be taken. Employees could see the need for a high level of service performance and were able to share in the resulting benefits.

■ All workers had access to financial information, resulting in a more constructive approach to negotiations on work schedules and pay, for example.

The authors concluded that employee ownership – by increasing the level of participation – can give companies a competitive advantage in services industries where flexibility in production and commitment to high standards of service quality are important. But the question remains why so many employee-owned bus companies in the United Kingdom have sold out to larger predators. Is a one-off cash bonus to employee shareholders more important than involvement in the ownership of their company? And do customers notice any difference once a large company takes over?

4.9   TRAINING AND DEVELOPMENT

Training refers to the acquisition of specific knowledge and skills which enable employees to perform their job effectively. The focus of staff training is the job. In contrast to this, staff development concerns activities which are directed to the future needs of the employee, which may themselves be derived from the future needs of the organization. As an example, workers may need to become familiar with personal computers, electronic mail and other aspects of information technology which as yet are not elements within their own specific job requirements.

Training is essential if any process of change is to be actively consented to by the workforce. Initially this may be merely an awareness-training programme whereby the process of change is communicated to the workforce as a precursor to the actual changes. It may involve making employees aware of the competitive market pressures which the organization faces and how the organization proposes to address them. This initial process may also involve giving employees the opportunity to make their views known and to air any concerns they might have. This can help to generate some involvement in the process of change and could itself be the precursor to an effective participation forum.

A practical problem facing many organizations that allocate large budgets to staff training is that many other organizations in their sector may spend very little, relying on staff being poached from the company doing the training. This occurs, for example, within the banking sector where many building societies have set up cheque account operations using the skills of staff attracted from the 'big four' UK banks. The problem also occurs in many construction-related industries and in the car repair business. While the ease with which an organization can lose trained staff may be one reason to explain UK companies' generally low level of spending on training and development, a number of policies can be adopted to maximize the benefits of such expenditure to the organization. Training and development should be linked to the generation of loyalty by employees. Where such efforts to increase moral involvement are insufficient to retain trained staff, an organization may seek to tie an individual to it by seeking reimbursement of any expenditure if the employee leaves the organization within a specified time period. Reimbursement is most likely to be sought in the case of expenditure aimed at developing the general abilities of an individual as opposed to their ability to perform a functional and organizational specific task.

Another mechanism which can assist an organization in its goals of recruiting and retaining staff is a clearly defined career progression pathway. Career progression refers to a mechanism which enables employees to visualize how their working life might develop within a particular organization. Clearly defined expectations of what an individual employee should be able to achieve within an organization and clear statements of promotion criteria can assist the employee in this regard. Additionally, the creation and use of an internal labour market, for instance through counselling and the dissemination of job vacancy details, are vital. An organization can introduce vertical job ladders or age- or tenure-based remuneration and promotion programmes to assist in the retention of core employees.

During periods of scarcity among the skilled labour force, offers of defined career paths may become essential if the right calibre of staff are to be recruited and retained. As an example, many retailers which had previously operated relatively casual employment policies introduced career structures for the first time during the tight labour market of the late 1980s. Conversely, during the following period of recession it became very difficult for employers to maintain their promises with a consequent demotivational effect on staff. In this way, the demise of profitability in UK branch banking in the 1990s brought about considerable disillusionment among core bank employees who saw their career progression prospects made considerably more difficult than they had expected, despite good work performance on their part.

REWARDING STAFF

The process of staff recruitment and more crucially the retention of staff, is directly influenced by the quality of reward on offer. The central purpose of a reward system is to improve the standard of staff performance by giving employees something which they consider to be of value in return for good performance. What employees consider to be a good reward is influenced by the nature of the motivators which drive each individual. For this reason, one standardized reward system is unlikely to achieve maximum motivation among a large and diverse workforce.

Rewards to employees can be divided into two categories – non-monetary and monetary. Non-monetary rewards cover a wide range of benefits, some of which will be a formal part of the reward system, for example subsidized housing or sports facilities and public recognition for work achievement (as where staff are given diplomas signifying their level of achievement). At other times, non-monetary rewards could be informal and represent something of a hidden agenda for management. In this way, a loyal, long-standing restaurant waiter may be rewarded by being given a relatively easy schedule of work, allowing unpopular Saturday nights to be removed from their duty rota.

Monetary rewards are a more direct method of improving the performance of employees and are a more formal element of human resource management policy. In the absence of more informal and unquantifiable benefits, monetary rewards can form the principal motivator for employees. A number of methods are commonly used by organizations to reward employees financially:

■ Basic hourly wages are used to reward large numbers of secondary, or non-core employees. These reflect inputs rather than outputs.

■ A fixed salary is more commonly paid to the core workers of an organization. Sometimes the fixed salary is related to length of service – for example many public sector service workers in the United Kingdom receive automatic annual increments not related to performance. As well as being administratively simple, a fixed salary avoids the problems of trying to assess individuals' eligibility for bonuses, which can be especially difficult where employees work in teams. A fixed salary can be useful to a firm where long-term development of relationships with customers is important and staff are evaluated qualitatively for their ability in this respect rather than quantitatively on the basis of short-term sales achievements. Many financial services companies have adopted fixed salaries to avoid possible unethical conduct by employees who may be tempted to sell commission-based services to customers whose needs have not been properly assessed.

- A fixed annual salary plus a variable commission is commonly paid to service personnel who are actively involved in selling, as a direct reward for their efforts.

- Performance related pay (PRP) is assuming increasing importance within organizations. The PRP systems seek to link some percentage of an employee's pay directly to their work performance. In some ways PRP represents a movement towards the individualization of pay. A key element in any PRP system is the appraisal of individual employees' performance. For some workers, outputs can be quantified relatively easily, for example the level of new accounts opened forms part of most bank managers' performance related pay. More qualitative aspects of job performance are much more difficult to appraise, for example the quality of advice given by doctors or dentists. Qualitative assessment raises problems about which dimensions of job performance are to be considered important in the exercise and who is to undertake the appraisal. If appraisal is not handled sensitively, it could be viewed by employees with suspicion as a means of rewarding some individuals according to a hidden agenda. However, some form of performance related pay is generally of great use to organizations. It can allow greater management control and enable management to quickly identify good or bad performers. If handled appropriately, it can also assist in the generation of consent and moral involvement, because employees will have a direct interest in their own performance.

- Profit-sharing schemes can operate as a supplement to the basic wage or salary and can assist in the generation of employee loyalty through greater commitment. Employees can be made members of a trust fund set up by their employer where a percentage of profits are held in trust on behalf of employees, subject to agreed eligibility criteria. Profit-sharing schemes have the advantage of encouraging staff involvement in their organization. Such schemes do, however, have a major disadvantage where despite employees' most committed efforts, profits fall due to some external factor such as an economic recession. There is also debate about whether profit sharing really does act as a motivator to better performance in large companies, or merely becomes part of basic pay expectations. In the United Kingdom, examples of profit-sharing schemes have been set up by Tesco, British Gas and Sainsbury's.

- In many services organizations, an important element of the financial reward is derived from outside the formal contract of employment. This in particular refers to the practice of tipping by customers in return for good service. The acknowledgement of tipping by employers puts greater pressure on front-line service staff to perform well and in principle puts the burden of appraisal on the consumer of a service directly. It also reduces the level of basic wage expected by employees. While customers from some countries – such as the United States – readily accept the principle of tipping, others – including the British – are more ambivalent. In the public sector, attempts at tipping are often viewed as a form of bribery.

CONTROLLING AND EMPOWERING STAFF

It follows from the previous discussion of management theories that there are two basic approaches to managing people. On the one hand, staff can be supervised closely and corrective action taken where they fail to perform to standard. On the other hand, staff can be made responsible for controlling their own actions. The latter is often referred to as 'empowering' employees. The problem of control is particularly great in people-intensive service industries where it is usually not possible to remove the results of poor personnel performance before their effects are felt by customers. While the effects of a poorly performing car worker can be concealed from customers by checking his or her tangible output, the inseparability of the service production/consumption process makes quality control in the services sector difficult to achieve.

Should an organization's employees be closely controlled, or should they be empowered to act in the best way they see fit? The degree of empowerment given to employees, or the control exercised over them depends on the nature of their operating environment. For highly standardized, homogeneous goods and services, employees can be controlled by mechanistic means such as rules and regulations. For high-contact, highly variable services, high levels of empowerment may be more appropriate.

Empowerment essentially involves giving employees discretion over the way they carry out their tasks. One of the underlying assumptions of those advocating empowerment is that employees' values will be in line with those of the organization. Berry (1995: 208) noted that empowerment is essentially a state of mind. An employee with an empowered state of mind should experience feelings of: (1) control over how their job is performed; (2) awareness of the context in which the job is performed; (3) accountability for their work output; (4) shared responsibility for unit and organizational performance; and (5) equity in the rewards based on individual and collective performance. Discussion of empowerment frequently stresses the need to share information, so that employees understand the context in which they work. Empowered employees need to be rewarded in a timely fashion and their initiatives, triumphs and achievements acknowledged. Empowerment also implies a culture which encourages employees to experiment with new ideas and can tolerate them making mistakes and learning from them. Such a culture would be more in line with the image of the 'Learning Organization' (Garvin, 1993). Organizations must be prepared to allow employees the freedom to act and to make decisions based on their own judgement. If an employee is empowered, then that employee must be able to decide how best to deal with the needs of customers and should be accountable and responsible to deal with problems of customer complaints and operational difficulties caused.

Attitudinal changes in employees resulting from empowerment include increased job satisfaction and reduced role stress. A consequence of increased job satisfaction is greater enthusiasm for their job, which can be reflected in increased levels of involvement. Behaviourally, empowerment can lead to quicker response by employees to the needs of customers, as less time is wasted in referring customers' requests to line managers. In situations where customer needs are highly variable, or the nature of demand is highly volatile, empowerment can facilitate rapid response to environmental change.

Advocates of tighter control mechanisms point to the disadvantages of empowerment. One of the consequences of empowerment is that it increases the scope of employees' jobs, requiring employees to be properly trained to cope with the wider range of tasks which they are expected to undertake. It also impacts on recruitment as it is necessary to ensure that employees recruited have the requisite attitudinal characteristics and skills to cope with empowerment. Hartline and Ferrell (1996) found that while empowered employees gained confidence in their abilities, they also experienced increased frustration and ambiguity through role conflict. Additionally, because empowered workers are expected to have a broader range of skills and to perform a greater number of tasks, they are likely to be more expensive to employ because of their ability to command higher rates of pay.

Even with highly empowered employees, some form of control system is necessary. Control systems are closely related to reward systems in that pay can be used to control performance – for example, bonuses forfeited in the event of performance falling below a specified standard. In addition, warnings or ultimately dismissal form part of a control system. In an ideal organization which has well-developed strategies to increase employees' involvement, this by itself should lead to considerable self-control or informal control from their peer group. Where such policies are less well developed, three principal types of control are used – simple, technical and bureaucratic controls.

- Simple controls are typified by direct personal supervision of personnel – for example a head waiter can maintain a constant watch over junior waiters and directly influence performance when this deviates from standard.

- Technical controls can be built into the service production process in order to monitor individuals' performances – for example, a supermarket checkout can measure the speed of individual operators and control action (e.g. training or redeployment) taken in respect of those shown to be falling below standard.

- Bureaucratic controls require employees to document their performance, for example the completion of work sheets by a service engineer of visits made and jobs completed. Control action can be initiated in respect of employees who on paper appear to be underperforming.

In addition to these internal controls, the relationship which many front-line service personnel develop with their customers allows customers to exercise a degree of informal control. College lecturers teaching a class would in most cases wish to avoid the hostility from their class which might result from consistently delivering a poor standard of performance – in other words, the class can exercise a type of informal control.

4.12   INTERNAL MARKETING

Many organizations have sought to improve their internal effectiveness through a programme of 'internal marketing'. Internal marketing came to prominence during the 1980s and describes the application of marketing techniques to audiences within the organization. An early definition of internal marketing provided by Berry (1980) was:

> ... the means of applying the philosophy and practices of marketing to people who serve the external customers so that (i) the best possible people can be employed and retained, and (ii) they will do the best possible work.

The term *internal marketing* is relatively new and best practice reflects much of what has been part of organizations' human resource management strategy. In an attempt to clarify the concept of internal marketing Varey and Lewis (1999) have conceptualized a number of its important dimensions:

- *Internal marketing as a metaphor*   Organization jobs and employment conditions are 'products' to be marketed and managers should think like a marketer when dealing with people. However, it is the employer who is both buyer and consumer in the employment relationship, rather than the employee.

- *Internal marketing as a philosophy*   Managers may hold a conviction that Human Resource Management requires 'marketing-like' activities. However, this does not address employees' divergent needs and interests which may themselves be quite different from those of the organization. This is especially the case if the 'marketing' activities are actually promotional advertising and selling of management requirements. Employees may merely be seen as the manipulatable subject of managerial programmes.

- *Internal marketing as a set of techniques*   Human resource management may adopt market research, segmentation and promotional techniques in order to inform and persuade employees. But internal marketing as the manipulation of the '4Ps' imposes management's point of view on employees and cannot be said to be employee (customer) centred. Therefore, it is employees who must change their needs or must understand the position of the employer as they respond to the market.

- *Internal marketing as an approach*   There is an explicit symbolic dimension to human resource management practices, such as employee involvement and participation, and statements about the role of employees within the organization. These are used to bring about indirect control of employees. Nevertheless, the symbolism of internal marketing may reveal many contradictions. For example, individualism contradicts team working, and the service culture as defined by management may contradict attitudes towards employee flexibility and responsibility. The complexities of managing people and their actions and knowledge may be reduced to mere 'techniques' of symbolic communication.

Much debate surrounds just how internal marketing fits within traditional human resource management structures and processes. Hales (1994), for example, is critical of the 'managerialist' perspective on internal marketing and of the literature on internal marketing as an approach to human resource management. Viewed as an activity in isolation, internal marketing is unlikely to succeed. For that to happen, the full support of top management is required.

4.12.1   Internal exchange relationships

Every organization can be considered to be a marketplace consisting of a diverse group of employees who engage in exchanges between each other (Foreman and Money, 1995). In order to have their needs met, employees are often dependent upon internal services provided by other departments or individuals within their organization. These internal exchanges include relationships between front-line staff and the backroom staff, managers and the front-line staff, managers and the backroom staff, and for large organizations, between the head office and each branch. In the most general sense, employees have been seen by some as 'consumers' of services provided by their employer, such as a pleasant working environment, provision of a pension scheme and good facilities for performing their tasks.

Increasingly, organizations are asking internal service departments, such as information technology, human resources, accounting and media services, to be more accountable. In a growing number of instances, organizations have out-sourced the services traditionally provided by such internal departments, resulting in extended 'network' or 'virtual' organizations. This has resulted in employees effectively trading services with other employees within their organization.

This view of different internal suppliers and customers, some of which deal directly within the service delivery process and some which provide support services to the service delivery process, appears to be closely related to the concept of the value chain (Porter, 1985). A modified value chain in terms of internal suppliers is shown in Figure 4.7.

This idea of a value chain and internal trading of services is closely related to the idea developed in the Total Quality Management literature of 'Next operation as a customer' (NOAC) (Denton, 1990). NOAC is based on the idea that each group within an organization should treat the recipients of their output as an internal customer and strive to provide high quality outputs for them (e.g. Lukas and Maignan, 1996). Through this approach, quality will be built into the service delivered to the final customer.

There are, however, problems in drawing analogies between internal and external markets for goods and services. External customers can usually take their business elsewhere if they are not satisfied with the service provided, while internal customers may be required to use a designated service unit within their organization. Consequently, the internal customer is frequently a *captive* customer (Albrecht, 1990). Employees as customers may be tied to employment contracts with little short-term prospect of 'buying' employment elsewhere.

There is a widely held view that if employees are not happy with their jobs, external customers will never be uppermost in their minds. Researchers have tended to agree that satisfied internal customers are a critical prerequisite to the

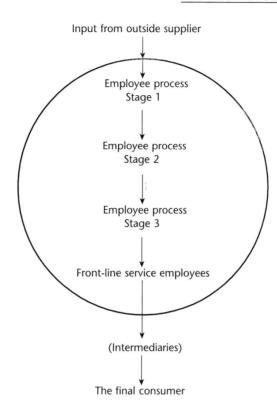

Figure 4.7
A modified value chain for internally produced services

Input from outside supplier

Employee process
Stage 1

Employee process
Stage 2

Employee process
Stage 3

Front-line service employees

(Intermediaries)

The final consumer

satisfaction of external customers. From an internal marketing perspective, many researchers have argued that by satisfying the needs of their internal customers, firms enhance their ability to satisfy the needs of their external customers. Nevertheless, many have recognized the three-way fight between the firm, the contact personnel and the customer. Delivering goods and services is thus a 'compromise between partially conflicting parties' (Bateson, 1989). To give an example, it may sound like a good idea to give employees longer rest breaks because this satisfies their needs as internal 'customers'. But longer rest breaks may result in greater waiting time for external customers as fewer staff are now available to serve them. A fine balance has to be drawn and there is no conclusive proof that in all situations happier employees necessarily result in happier external customers and a more profitable service operation.

4.13   INDUSTRIAL RELATIONS

As we saw in Chapter 2, commercial organizations range from small family businesses to large multinational organizations, covering external environments which range from protected and regulated to highly competitive. In reflection of this diversity, there is great variety in the manner in which managements negotiate employment conditions with their workforces. For organizations employing large numbers of staff, much of the employment relationship has traditionally been conducted collectively between the employer and groups of employees.

The essential features of collective bargaining are threefold.

■ Firstly, a collective bargaining system recognizes trade unions with whom management negotiates on substantive issues such as pay and procedural issues, e.g. discipline and redundancy. Collective bargaining formally recognizes the presence, within the organization of an outside body – the trade union.

■ Secondly, the pluralist approach to the employment relationship emphasizes a divergence of interests between the employer and employees. This divergence is considered best settled via a process of compromise and negotiation.

■ Thirdly, a recognition that industrial action of some type, for example overtime bans, 'go slows' and strikes might be used in order to pursue employee interests. This third feature of collective bargaining is overexaggerated by the media, some academics and politicians. As an element in collective bargaining, it only becomes a consideration if the first two elements have failed. Nevertheless, many sectors such as railways and car manufacturing have periodically suffered bad disruption as a result of failures in collective bargaining. Because services cannot be stored, the effects of disruption can be felt by customers immediately.

Efforts to stress a closer identification with business objectives through increasing individual's level of involvement at work do not sit easily with the presence of an outside body which stresses the significance of collective action. Organizations which do not feel secure with trades unions are likely to attempt to marginalize their impact through their derecognition and the creation of organization-specific employee relations policies described below. Many organizations have moved on from the traditional view of industrial relations to the situation where they speak of 'Employee Relations'. Marchington and Parker (1990) identified three reasons for the use of the term 'Employee Relations'.

1 The term has become fashionable and appears to be less adversarial than industrial relations. Thus, there has been growth in the use of the term, although slippage in the use of the word occurs in some cases without any change in behaviour.

2 It is increasingly used by personnel managers to describe the part of their work which is concerned with the regulation of relations between employer and employees. The internal regulation of this relationship is seen in many organizations to supersede any external regulation, through collective bargaining and/or trade union membership. This can be the case even though trade union membership still exists in a particular organization.

3 Employee relations focuses on that aspect of managerial activity which is concerned with fostering an identification with the employing organization and its business aims. It therefore concerns itself with direct relations between employees and management – that is, independently of any collective representation by trades unions.

Many not-for-profit sector services such as museums and leisure services are increasingly being given clearly defined business objectives which make it much more difficult for officers to continue doing what they like doing rather than what the public they serve wants. A commercial orientation has been most rapidly adopted by those public sector services which provide marketable goods and services, such as swimming pools and municipal bus services. It is much more difficult to adopt a marketing orientation where the public sector is a monopoly provider of a statutory service.

The degree of discretion given to a public sector manager is usually less than that given to a counterpart in the private sector. It could be argued that statutorily determined standards affect public sector organizations to a greater extent than the private sector – for example, the provision of educational facilities is constrained by the need to adhere to the national curriculum. Even where a local authority has a significant area of discretion, the checks and balances imposed on many public sector managers reflects the fact that local authorities are accountable to a wider constituency of interests than the typical private sector organization.

Managers within the private sector are usually able to monitor the results of their activity as the benefits are usually internal to the organization. By contrast, many of the aims which not-for-profit organizations seek to achieve are external and a profit and loss statement or balance sheet cannot be produced in the way which is possible with a private sector organization operating to narrow internal financial goals.

CASE STUDY

FROM 'PATIENTS' TO 'CONSUMERS': THE EFFECTS OF CHANGE IN THE EXTERNAL ENVIRONMENT ON THE INTERNAL ENVIRONMENT OF GENERAL PRACTITIONERS

The business environment of general practitioners in the United Kingdom has gone through a succession of changes during the 1990s. Indeed, before the 1980s, few people would even have described the environment of a GP as a 'business' environment. Gone are the days when doctors such as the legendary radio character Doctor Finlay could carry on practising regardless of anything but their narrowly defined professional code of practice. Today the world of GPs is encroached upon from numerous directions – from elements of the political environment which seek greater accountability of doctors' actions; from the social environment, where 'patients' have become 'consumers', along with ever-rising expectations of their general practitioners. The legal environment has posed new challenges for doctors, as the rights of patients have increased relative to those of the doctor. At the same time, doctors working for the National Health Service have been set a widening range of targets, the achievement of which influence the funding they receive. The cosy small practice of Doctor Finlay has become even more of a myth as doctors' surgeries have grown bigger, justifying the appointment of specialist practice managers. As a sign of the times, commercial organizations such as Boots the Chemist have moved into the world of general practitioners by opening walk-in surgeries in busy places.

Doctors in the United Kingdom have largely followed a few basic principles when it comes to getting paid. They negotiate a level of fees for services to be provided, in return for which they expect to perform their duties to the best of their abilities and in accordance with their code of conduct. Doctors employed by the National Health Service (NHS), as well as self-employed general practitioners have negotiated with the NHS by focusing on the costs of providing their services and the idea of a fair rate of pay for highly qualified staff. Performance related pay has not yet appeared to any significant extent on doctors' pay agenda in the United Kingdom, although there are pressures to introduce it. However, it is becoming increasingly common in the United States, demonstrating some of the benefits – as well as problems – of evaluating performance within the personal services sector.

In the United States, a large share of doctors' services are bought by Health Maintenance Organizations (HMOs) which in turn obtain their funding from employers' health insurance payments. The HMOs vary in the way they pay contracting doctors, but traditionally it has been either on the basis of a fixed fee per patient per year or a fee per visit. Doctors would typically expect to have 5000 patients on their lists – a single HMO may account for half of these. US Healthcare Inc is one of a growing number of HMOs which has introduced an incentive scheme into the way it pays its doctors. Each year, it carries out a questionnaire survey of its subscribing members to see how they like their doctors and links doctors' payments to these results, a bonus payment of 15 per cent being typical.

Among the questions that the company uses in its questionnaire for assessing doctors' performance are:

■ How easy is it to make appointments for checkups?

■ How long is the waiting time in a doctor's surgery?

■ How much personal concern does the doctor show?

■ How readily can patients follow up test results?

■ Would doctors recommend their doctor to others?

In addition, the company monitors the percentage of each doctor's patients who transfer to another doctor during the course of the year.

Incentive pay schemes for doctors are gaining popularity, spurred by a belief that they may help upgrade the quality of medical care provided by HMOs and other managed care programmes. However, a number of questions have been raised about the legitimacy of this approach. Sceptics do not like the idea of basing incentives on patients' sense of 'quality', arguing that patients rely too much on fringe issues such as a receptionist's attitude or a doctor's punctuality. The sceptics would prefer to see assessment based on more sophisticated studies of illnesses, treatments and patient outcomes, something which is much more difficult to evaluate. Another problem often raised is that individual doctors' incentive payments can disrupt their ability to work together in a collegial way. The Harvard Community Health Plan typified organizations which introduced and then withdrew incentive schemes following arguments between doctors about the size of their respective bonuses.

Another group of sceptics argue that where incentive payment schemes have been introduced for doctors, they have had only a short-term effect in changing doctors' behaviour.

Paying doctors partly on the basis of the quality of their service is in its early stages in the United States and many advocates of incentive payment schemes hope that current shortcomings can be remedied by more sophisticated measuring systems in the future. What happens there today will doubtless be observed by the United Kingdom's NHS as it moves towards a more competitive internal market environment.

CASE STUDY Review Questions

1 What are the benefits of attempting to measure the performance of doctors? If you were a manager for an organization which provides funding for doctors, how would you like to see doctors appraised?

2 What part do you think ethics play in determining doctors' performance? Do you think doctors' performance assessment is really within the domain of business management?

3 Other professional groups, e.g. lawyers, engineers and architects should perhaps institute performance appraisals. If you were a business manager of an organization representing one of these professional groups, how would you evaluate members' professional performance? What marketing benefits would you see from carrying out routine appraisals? What resistance would you expect to encounter in implementing an appraisal system?

CHAPTER Summary and links to other chapters

An organization's internal environment comprises its structures and processes, which are influenced by the dominant culture of the organization. The effectiveness of these structures and processes can help or hinder the task of responding to environmental change. Strong leadership can provide a focused effort at marshalling the resources of an organization to meet the challenges and opportunities posed by the external environment. Employees usually make up a critical element of the internal environment and this chapter has discussed methods by which organizations seek to gain the moral involvement of employees to share the challenges and opportunities of external change.

Noticeable differences in the internal environment are often present in different types of organization (Chapter 2), with the culture of a typical sole trader being very different to that of a public limited company or a charity organization. Differences are likely to occur where a company operates in overseas countries (Chapter 10). Growth (Chapter 3) has often formed a central cultural value. Its opposite – contraction – can be difficult to manage. The treatment of employees is often considered to be an important element of an organization's social responsibility (Chapter 5). The political and legal environments have had major impacts on the nature of the internal environment, for example with respect to employees' rights (Chapters 8 and 9). The development of new technologies (Chapter 12) has changed the nature of many jobs and improved internal communications.

CHAPTER Review questions

1 Discuss the ways in which improvements in the internal environment of organizations can lead to more effective responsiveness to changes in the external environment.

2 Do you agree with the notion that having a marketing department can actually be a barrier to the successful development of a marketing orientation? Give examples.

3 'Mission statements are the result of senior managers undertaking management development courses. They may have the language, but mission statements are invariably ignored by the very people who they are aimed at'. Is this a fair statement?

4 Every now and again management gurus develop new ideas for managing organizations, such as business process reengineering. Is there too much hype in such prescriptions?

5 Discuss the ways in which a fast-food restaurant can increase the level of participation among its staff.

6 What are the main differences in implementing a market-oriented management structure within the public as opposed to the private service sector?

References

Albrecht, K. (1990) *Service Within*, Dow Jones-Irwin, Homewood, IL.

Atkinson, J. 1984) 'Manpower strategies for flexible organizations', *Personnel Management*, August.

Bateson, J.E.G. (1989) *Managing Services Marketing – Text and Readings*, 2nd edn, Dryden Press, Fort Worth, TX.

Berry, L.L. (1980) 'Services marketing is different', *Business*, May–June, vol. 30, no. 3, pp. 24–29.

Berry, L.L. (1995) 'Relationship marketing of services – growing interest, emerging perspectives', *Journal of the Academy of Marketing Science*, vol. 23, no. 4, pp. 236–45.

Denton, D.K. (1990) 'Customer focused management', *HR Magazine*, August, pp. 62–67.

Dolan, P. and I. Brierley (1992) *A Tale of Two Bus Companies*, Partnership Research, London.

Drucker, P.F. (1973) *Management: Tasks, Responsibilities and Practices*, Harper & Row, New York.

Foreman, S. and A. Money (1995) 'Internal marketing: concepts, measurement and application', *Journal of Marketing Management*, vol. 11, no. 8, pp. 755–768.

Garvin, D.A. (1993) 'Building a learning organization', *Harvard Business Review*, July–August, pp. 78–91.

Giles, W. (1988) 'Marketing planning for maximum growth', in M.J. Thomas (ed.), *The Marketing Handbook*, Gower Press, Aldershot.

Gronroos, C. (1982) *Strategic Management and Marketing in the Service Sector*, Swedish School of Economics and Business Administration, Helsingfors.

Gummesson, E. (1999) *Total Relationship Marketing*, Butterworth Heinemann, Oxford.

Hales, C. (1994) 'Internal marketing as an approach to human resource management: a new perspective or a metaphor too far?', *Human Resource Management Journal*, vol. 5, no. 1, pp. 50–71.

Handy, C.B. (1989) *The Age of Unreason*, Harvard Business School Press, Boston, MA.

Hartline, M.D. and O.C. Ferrell (1996) 'The management of customer contact service employees: an empirical investigation', *Journal of Marketing*, October, vol. 60, pp. 52–70.

Jelinek, M., L. Smirich and P. Hirsch (1983) 'Introduction: a code of many colours', *Administrative Science Quarterly*, vol. 28, p. 337.

Levitt, T. (1960) 'Marketing myopia', *Harvard Business Review*, July–August, pp. 45–56.

Lukas, B.A. and I. Maignan (1996) 'Striving for quality: the key role of internal and external customers', *Journal of Market Focused Management*, vol. 1, pp. 175–97.

Marchington, M. and P. Parker (1990) *Changing Patterns of Employee Relations*, Harvester Wheatsheaf, London.

Maslow, A. (1943) 'A theory of human motivation', *Psychological Review*, vol. 50, no. 4, pp. 370–396.

Peters, T.J. and R.H. Waterman (1982) *In Search of Excellence: Lessons from America's Best Run Companies*, Harper & Row, New York.

Piercy, N. (1997) *Market-led Strategic Change*, Butterworth-Heinemann, Oxford.

Porter, M.E. (1985) *Competitive Strategy: Techniques for Analyzing Industries and Competitors*, Free Press, New York.

Varey, R.J. and B.R. Lewis (1999) 'A broadened conception of internal marketing', *European Journal of Marketing*, vol. 33, no. 9/10, pp. 926–944.

Selected further reading

This chapter has discussed very briefly some of the basic principles of human resource management as they apply to service organizations. For a fuller discussion of these principles, the following text is recommended

Beardwell, I. and L. Holden (2000) *Human Resource Management Textbook*, Prentice-Hall, Hemel Hempstead.

The following provides a useful summary of the literature on control vs. empowerment of employees:

Rafiq, M. and P.K. Ahmed (1998) 'A customer-oriented framework for empowering service employees', *Journal of Services Marketing*, vol. 12, no. 5, pp. 379–393.

The issue of organizational culture is well covered in the following:

Hofstede, G. (1991) *Culture and Organizations*, McGraw-Hill, Maidenhead.

Leppard, J. and M. McDonald (1991) 'Marketing planning and corporate culture: a conceptual framework which examines management attitudes in the context of marketing planning', *Journal of Marketing Management*, vol. 7, pp. 213–235.

Mullins, L. (1998) *Management and Organizational Behaviour*, 5th edn, Prentice-Hall, Hemel Hempstead.

Stapley, L.F. (1996) *The Personality of the Organization: A Psycho-dynamic Explanation of Culture*, Free Association Books, London.

The following provide insights to the importance of leadership style within an organization:

Landsberg, M. (2000) *The Tools of Leadership*, HarperCollins, London.

Maccoby, M. (2000) 'Narcissistic leaders', *Harvard Business Review*, vol. 78, pp. 69–74.

Internal marketing often passes under a number of names, and the following are useful introductions to the topic:

Varey, R.J. and B.R. Lewis (1999) 'A broadened conception of internal marketing', *European Journal of Marketing*, vol. 33, no. 9/10, pp. 926–944.

Piercy, N. and N. Morgan (1990) 'Internal marketing: the missing half of the marketing programme', *Long Range Planning*, vol. 8, no. 1, pp. 4–6.

Forman, S.K. and A.H. Money (1995) 'Internal marketing: concepts, measurement and application', *Journal of Marketing Management*, vol. 11, no. 8, pp. 755–768.

Useful websites

Chartered Institute of Personnel and Development   Website of the UK association which represents human resource management professionals.   **http://www.ipd.co.uk/**

General HRM Links   Nottingham Trent University's page provides useful links to various HRM websites.   **http://www.nbs.ntu.ac.uk/depts/hrm/hrm_link.htm**

Institute of Directors   Website of the organization representing leaders of UK industry, which aims to improve the quality of leadership through the Institute's professional development programme. **http://www.iod.co.uk/**

International Labour Organization (ILO)   This website provides information on employment statistics and practices throughout the world.   **http://www.ilo.org**

The Future of Work   Series of working papers provided by University of Leeds that touch on the impact of the Internet on patterns of work.   **http://www.leeds.ac.uk/esrcfutureofwork/output/papers.html**

Key terms

Control	Leadership
Employee involvement	Matrix organization structures
Empowerment	Mission statement
Flexible workforce	Motivation
Functional organization	Organizational culture
Human resource management (HRM)	Organizational effectiveness
Incentives	Staff development
Industrial relations	Training
Internal marketing	

5

The social responsibility of organizations

CHAPTER OBJECTIVES

Commercial organizations survive by making an adequate level of profits for their shareholders. In order to achieve this, the organization must respond to the needs of customers who provide it with its revenue. However, while customers are crucial to profitability, they are not the only group whose needs it is necessary to satisfy in order to ensure survival. In Chapter 1 we briefly reviewed other organizations in the micro- and macroenvironments which can have an impact on a company. The aim of this chapter is to take a more detailed look at the various stakeholder groups which may have no direct relationship with an organization, but which can nevertheless have an impact on its activities. Good corporate governance and ethical practices may not secure further sales to customers in the short term, but may be crucial for survival in the longer term. After studying this chapter you should have an awareness of the need for social responsibility by commercial organizations.

INTRODUCTION

'The customer is king' is a traditional business maxim and according to this, every-thing that a company does should be geared towards satisfying the needs of its customers. But should commercial organizations also have responsibilities to the public at large? The question is becoming increasingly important, as commercial organizations have never before been subjected to such a critical gaze from those who are quick to identify the harmful side-effects of their activities.

There are philosophical and pragmatic reasons why organizations should act in a socially responsible manner. Philosophically, models of a responsible society would have companies doing their bit to contribute towards a just and fair society, alongside the contributions of other institutions such as the family and the church. More pragmatically, commercial organizations need to take account of society's values because if they don't, they may end up isolated from the values of the customers they seek to attract. In increasingly discriminating markets, buyers may opt for the more socially responsible company. Acting in an antisocial way may have a long-term cost for a company and ultimately not serve the needs of those customers who prefer to deal with one that is socially acceptable. Antisocial behaviour by companies may also attract the attention of regulatory bodies who have the power to add to a company's production costs, or to make it impossible to satisfy customer demand in the first place.

This chapter begins by identifying the key stakeholders in organizations which it should have a responsibility towards. It then explores the complex moral and practical issues behind the concept of social responsibility by business.

5.2   THE STAKEHOLDERS OF ORGANIZATIONS

It is common to describe stakeholders as those organizations and individuals who may not necessarily have any direct dealings with a company, but who are nevertheless affected by its actions. In turn, a company can be significantly affected by the actions of its stakeholders.

The following principal stakeholders in business organizations can be identified (Figure 5.1):

Customers   There is an argument that the customer is *not* always right in the goods and services they choose to buy from a company. Customers may sometimes not be aware of their true needs or may have these needs manipulated by exploitative companies. Taking a long-term and broad perspective, companies should have a duty to provide goods and services which satisfy these longer term and broader needs rather than their immediately felt needs. There have been many examples where the long-term interests of customers have been ignored by companies. Increasingly, legislation is recognizing that the customer is *not* always right and companies have a duty to consider the long-term interests of customers as stakeholders. This has been very clearly seen in the mis-selling of pensions in the United Kingdom during the 1980s. Private pension companies knew that many members of occupational pension schemes would have undoubtedly been better off remaining in their scheme, rather than making alternative private pension arrangements. Nevertheless, many employees were tempted by short-term incentives to leave

Figure 5.1
A stakeholder approach to business organizations

their employers' schemes and to take out private pensions, leaving them financially worse off over the longer term. Regulatory authorities have recognized the wider interests of customers by requiring the pensions companies to provide compensation to customers who were sold a pension which was inappropriate to their long-term needs.

There are many more examples of situations where customers are probably not right and their long-term interests have been neglected by companies, including:

■ Tobacco companies who fail to impress upon customers the long-term harmful effects of buying and consuming their cigarettes

■ Manufacturers of milk for babies who should make mothers aware of the significant long-term health benefits to children of using breast milk rather than manufactured milk products

■ Car manufacturers who add expensive stereo equipment to cars as standard equipment, but relegate vital safety equipment to the status of optional extras.

In each of these cases, most people might agree that, objectively, buyers are being persuaded to make a choice against their own long-term self-interest. But on what moral grounds can society say that consumers' choices in these situations are wrong? According to some individuals' sense of priorities, an expensive hi-fi system may indeed be considered to offer a higher level of personal benefit than an airbag.

Customers as individual consumers usually fail to evaluate the external costs that they cause other consumers collectively to incur. External costs can take many forms, such as:

■ Congestion which one car driver causes to other drivers

■ The pollution suffered by residents living near waste tips caused by disposing of fast-food packaging

■ Noise nuisance suffered by people living near a noisy nightclub.

In each case, market mechanisms have failed to make buyers of a good or service pay for the external social costs that they have forced on others. Organizations that think strategically would recognize that socially unacceptable levels of external costs might bring pressure for legislation which results in higher costs or prohibition of an activity completely. For the organization, this will have the effect of raising selling prices to customers or making impossible the provision of goods and services demanded by customers.

Employees   It used to be thought that customers were not concerned about how their goods were made, just so long as the final product lived up to their expectations. This may just have been true for some manufactured goods, but probably never was for services where production processes are highly visible. Today, increasingly large segments of the population take into account the ethics of a firm's employment practices when evaluating alternative products. If all other things are equal, a firm that has a reputation for ruthlessly exploiting its employees, or not recognizing the legitimate rights of trade unions may be denigrated in the minds of many buyers. For this reason, some companies, such as Marks and Spencer, have gone to great lengths to challenge allegations made about the employment practices of their overseas suppliers.

Firms often go way beyond satisfying the basic legal requirements of employees. For some businesses, getting an adequate supply of competent workers is the main constraint on growth and it would be in their interest to promote good employment practices. This is true of many high-tech industries. In order to encourage staff retention, in particular of women returning to work after having children, companies have offered attractive packages of benefits, such as working hours which fit around school holidays and sponsoring events which promote a caring image.

Can going beyond legal requirement for employees ever be considered altruistic rather than just good business? Quaker companies such as Cadburys have been associated with a tradition of paternalism towards their staff. But could such altruism be essentially seen as an investment by the organization, which will have a payback in terms of better motivated staff?

Local Communities   Market-led companies often try to be seen as a 'good neighbour' in their local community. Such companies can enhance their image through the use of charitable contributions, sponsorship of local events and being seen to support the local environment. Again, this may be interpreted either as part of a firm's genuine concern for its local community or as a more cynical and pragmatic attempt to buy favour where its own interests are at stake. If a metal manufacturer installs improved noise installation, is it doing it to genuinely improve the lives of local residents or merely attempting to forestall prohibition action taken by the local authority?

Government   The demands of government agencies often take precedence over the needs of a company's customers. Government has a number of roles to play as stakeholder in commercial organizations:

- Commercial organizations provide governments with taxation revenue, so a healthy business sector is in the interests of the government.

- Governments are increasingly expecting business organizations to take over many responsibilities from the public sector, for example with regard to the payment of sickness and maternity benefits to employees.

- It is through business organizations that governments achieve many of their economic and social objectives, for example with respect to regional economic development and skills training.

As a regulator which impacts on many aspects of business activity, companies often go to great lengths in seeking favourable responses from such agencies. In the case of many UK private sector utility providers, promotional effort is often aimed more at regulatory bodies than final consumers. In the case of the water industry, promoting greater use of water to final consumers is unlikely to have any significant impact on a water utility company, but influencing the disposition of the

Office of Water Regulation, which sets price limits and required service standards, can have a major impact.

Intermediaries   Companies must not ignore the wholesalers, retailers and agents who may be crucial interfaces between themselves and their final consumers. These intermediaries may share many of the same concerns as customers and need re-assurance about the company's capabilities as a supplier who is capable of working with intermediaries to supply goods and services in an ethical manner. Many companies have suffered because they failed to take adequate account of the needs of their intermediaries (for example, Body Shop and McDonald's have faced occasional protests from their franchisees where they felt threatened by a business strategy which was perceived as being against their own interests).

Suppliers   Suppliers can sometimes be critical to business success. This often occurs where vital inputs are in scarce supply or it is critical that supplies are delivered to a company on time and in good condition. The way in which an organization places orders for its inputs can have a significant effect on suppliers. Does a company favour domestic companies rather than possibly lower priced overseas producers? (Marks and Spencer has traditionally prided itself on buying the vast majority of its merchandise from UK producers, so a few eyes were turned when it announced in 1998 that it was to source a greater proportion from lower cost overseas producers and to terminate relationships with some of its UK-based suppliers.) Does it divide its orders between a large number of small suppliers, or place the bulk of its custom with a small handful of preferred suppliers? Does it favour new businesses, or businesses representing minority interests when it places its orders?

Taking into account the needs of suppliers is again a combination of shrewd business sense and good ethical practice.

The financial community   This includes financial institutions that have supported, are currently supporting or who may support the organization in the future. Shareholders – both private and institutional – form an important element of this community and must be reassured that the organization is going to achieve its stated objectives. Many company expansion schemes have failed because the company did not adequately consider the needs and expectations of potential investors.

5.3   THE SOCIETAL MARKETING CONCEPT

Some marketers have argued that marketing cannot claim to be a discipline if it is unwilling to investigate systematically issues of social welfare and the impacts of market-based distribution systems (e.g. Anderson, 1982). The existence of external costs and benefits and the presence of multiple stakeholders in an organization serve to emphasize this point. External costs occur where a company causes another person or company to incur costs for which the latter cannot claim reimbursement from the former.

Supporters of the societal marketing concept point to a change of heart by companies who attach importance not just to satisfying their customers' needs, but the needs of society as a whole. However, a distinction should be made between social philanthropy and the societal marketing concept. There have always been companies who have given to good causes quite independently of their marketing strategy.

Rising consumer incomes have resulted in the growing importance of the augmented elements of a purchase. The external benefits provided by consumer purchases are becoming a larger element of the total product offering that consumers use to judge competing products in increasingly competitive markets. Fragmentation of consumer markets has resulted from growing diversity in the needs that consumers seek to satisfy. To most people, goods and services no longer have to provide for the most basic level of physiological or social needs.

According to Maslow, when individuals' basic physiological and social needs are satisfied, higher order needs become motivators which influence their buying behaviour. In these circumstances, consumers seek to satisfy a relatively intangible inner need for peace of mind, which may come about through knowledge that their purchase is helping to change the world in a way which they consider desirable. Fifty years ago, a packet of washing powder would have largely satisfied a need to produce tangible cleanliness. With most of the population being able to afford cleaning powders which could produce this effect, emphasis moved to promoting washing powder on the basis of satisfying social needs. So one brand was differentiated from another by signifying greater care for the family or was seen to produce results which were visible and valued by peer groups. Today, manufacturers of washing powder recognize that a significant segment seeks to buy more than the packet of washing powder – it seeks also to buy a chance to change the world by reducing ecological damage caused by washing powders containing high levels of harmful phosphates (Figure 5.2).

Possible examples of societal marketing approaches adopted by firms include:

■ Designing products which minimize ecological damage (e.g. using recycled paper for burger containers, rather than styrene)

■ Supporting charitable causes (e.g. newspapers and supermarkets giving tokens with which schools can buy books)

■ Promoting the fact that a company recruits heavily among disadvantaged groups in society such as the disabled.

Critics of the societal marketing concept see it as short-term and cynical manipulation by a company of its principal stakeholders. Others have pointed out that there is not necessarily any incompatibility between traditional marketing objectives and societal objectives. For example, Arbratt and Sacks (1988) give the reminder that the societal marketing concept does not involve a company in foregoing its long-term profitability and survival objectives.

Figure 5.2
Maslow's
hierarchy of
needs can be
used to illustrate
how changing
levels of needs
have influenced
the dominant
factors
influencing the
purchase of
washing powder

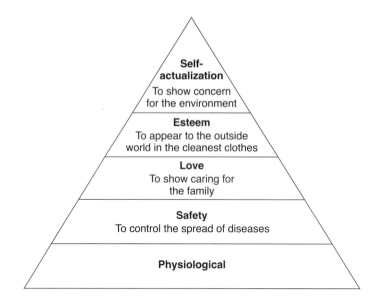

Criticisms of the societal marketing concept can take two forms; philosophical and pragmatic:

■ At a philosophical level, it has been argued by the followers of Milton Friedman that firms should concentrate on doing what they are best at – making profits for their owners. The idea of social responsibility by firms has been criticized as it would allow business organizations to become too dominant in society. By this argument, any attempt by firms to contribute to social causes is a form of taxation on the customers of their businesses. It would be better for firms to leave such money in the hands of their customers, so that customers themselves can decide what worthy causes they wish to support. Alternatively, donations to social causes should be handled by government which is democratically accountable, unlike business firms. There is particular strength in this argument where benefits are provided by private sector organizations who have considerable monopoly power, such as utility companies. It may be too simplistic to say that customers voluntarily buy a company's products and therefore consent to the payment of social contributions. In reality, many markets are uncompetitive and customers may have very little choice.

■ More pragmatically, companies often support social causes because it is a cheap way of gaining attention and a unique selling proposition. In a market in which product offers are all broadly similar and with saturation advertising, sponsorship of a social cause may allow a company to develop a unique identity for its products. Critics of the societal marketing concept argue that most external benefits provided under the guise of societal marketing are in fact rapidly internalized by their provider. As examples, litter bins sponsored by a fast-food restaurant, the provision of recycling points by supermarkets and donations to animal charities are not altruism, but simply a new way of buying awareness of a company and liking of it, using values which are currently fashionable.

THINKING AROUND THE SUBJECT

Large retailers have been fighting to make moral as well as financial capital from their marketing. Tesco's decision to extend its computers for schools promotion (whereby customers were rewarded with vouchers which could be used to buy computer equipment for schools), showed that 'social' promotions can be highly beneficial to a retailer. Tesco saw a dual benefit from the scheme: a perception that the company cares about the community, and a build-up in sales as parents are encouraged to shop at Tesco to benefit their local school. Numerous companies have gone along the route of social promotions. All argue that their initiatives are not altruism, but good business practice. But questions remain to be asked. Why do customers prefer to pay a few extra pennies for their groceries to a 'social' retailer, rather than giving their money directly to a good cause? Does social marketing give too much power to business?

Governments have recently sought to pass on responsibility for many aspects of social provision (e.g. sponsorship of the arts). Is there a danger in expecting the commercial sector to undertake such a role? Commercial organizations tend to be very selective in which sections of society they support. Firms have a habit of supporting causes which have popular appeal (for example animal charities and equipment for schools), but may fail to protect minorities in society who command very little public prestige. For example, very few commercial organizations support activities in the fields of mental illness or freedom for political prisoners. It can be argued that responsibilities for such causes cannot be given up by the public sector and handed to private sector organizations.

Collectively, consumers represent roughly the same group as the electorate. Electors have always expected government to act in the best public interest, otherwise – in the extreme – the government will not be re-elected. Consumers are developing similar expectations towards the suppliers of private sector goods. If they do not feel the company is acting in the public interest, their goods will not be purchased. In taking on this role, some have suggested that private sector companies are becoming more important than governments in setting the agenda for ecological reform. There are examples of where this has happened, such as the development of organically grown vegetables and the replacement of CFCs in aerosols. These initiatives originated primarily with the private sector rather than the government.

5.4   ECOLOGICAL RESPONSIBILITY

Issues affecting our natural ecology have captured the public imagination in recent years. The destruction of tropical rain forests and the depletion of the ozone layer leading to global warming have serious implications for our quality of life, not necessarily today, but for future generations. Business is often seen as being in

Figure 5.3

In a market which is dominated by basically similar service offers, an ethical positioning may give a business a competitive advantage in the eyes of some customers. Many people would regard the major UK supermarkets as being essentially similar in their service offer, but in this advertisement Sainsbury's is seeking to promote its ethical credentials

(*Source*: Reproduced with permission of Sainsbury's Supermarkets Ltd)

conflict with the need to protect the natural ecology. It is very easy for critics of business to point to cases where greed and mismanagement have created long-lasting or permanent ecological damage. Have the rain forests been destroyed partly by our greed for more hardwood furniture? More locally, is our impatience for getting to our destination quickly the reason why many natural habitats have been lost to new road developments?

There is argument about whether ecological problems are *actually* getting worse, or whether our perceptions and expectations are changing. Charles Dickens's description of Victorian London painted a grim picture of heavy manufacturing industry causing widespread pollution and using up natural resources in a manner which today would be considered quite profligate. Objectively, any comparison with industry today will probably leave the impression that environmental issues are lessening in their technical importance. Supporters of this view will point to the relatively clean air which we enjoy today, compared to the smogs which previously descended upon industrial areas, often for very lengthy periods. When salmon were caught in the River Thames in the 1990s for the first recorded time in over 50 years, it would be easy to gain the impression that the ecological environment was improving. Set against this is the worry that the actions we are taking today could be storing up major ecological problems for the future. A lot of ecological change – such as the depletion of the ozone layer over Antarctica – is happening at a much faster rate than previously and there is no certainty about the magnitude and effects of subsequent global warming.

A market-led company cannot ignore threats to the natural ecology. Commercial organizations' concern with the ecological environment has resulted from two principal factors:

1 There has been growing pressure on natural resources, including those that directly or indirectly are used in firms' production processes. This is evidenced by the extinction of species of animals and depletion of hardwood timber resources. As a result of overuse of physical resources, many industry sectors, such as North Sea fishing, have faced severe constraints on their production possibilities.

2 The general public has become increasingly aware of ecological issues and, more importantly, has shown a greater willingness and ability to spend money to alleviate the problems associated with ecologically harmful practices.

At a macroenvironmental level, support for the ecological environment has sometimes been seen as a 'luxury' which societies cannot afford as they struggle to satisfy the essentials of life. As these necessities are satisfied, individuals, and society collectively, can move on to satisfy higher order needs to protect what are seen as aesthetic benefits such as fresh air and a rich flora and fauna. The idea of environmentalism being a luxury is supported by the observation that countries with the strongest environmental movements, such as the United States and Germany, tend also to be the richest economically. Many poorer countries tolerate poor environmental conditions in order to gain a competitive cost advantage over their more regulated Western competitors.

Assessing ecological impacts

It can be difficult for an organization to know just what is meant by the idea of being friendly to the ecological environment. Consumers may be confounded by alternative arguments about the consequences of their purchase decisions, with goods which were once considered to be environmentally 'friendly' suddenly becoming seen as enemies of the environment as knowledge and prejudice changes. The following are recent examples which show how it can be difficult to evaluate the ecological credentials of a product:

- Recycling of old newspapers has traditionally been thought of as a 'good' thing, but recent thinking has suggested that there are greater environmental benefits from burning them and planting new trees to grow fresh materials, rather than using energy to transport and recycle used paper.

- In the 1980s, diesel was seen as a relatively clean fuel because it produced less greenhouse gases and diesel engines were more efficient than petrol engines. By the 1990s, particulates released into the environment by diesel engines had become linked with increasing levels of asthma and the environmental credentials of diesel were downgraded.

- Similarly, some of the shine was taken off of unleaded petrol when studies began showing that an additive of unleaded petrol – benzine – was carcinogenic.

- Both the supporters and opponents of proposals to build bypasses around towns use environmental arguments to support their arguments. Opponents argue that a new road in itself will create more road traffic which is environmentally harmful, while supporters argue that environmental impacts will be lessened by moving traffic out of town where it causes less harm.

Most members of the public are not experts on the technical aspects of ecological impacts of business activities. They may therefore be easily persuaded by the most compellingly promoted argument, regardless of the technical merit of the case. Very often, a firm may have a technically sound case, but fail to win the hearts and minds of consumers who seem intent on believing the opposite argument that is in accordance with their own prejudices. This was seen clearly in debate about how to decommission Shell's Brent Spar oil platform. Government and the scientific community appeared to agree that environmental risks would be minimized by dumping the platform in deep water. Considerable risks would result from breaking it up on land, removing toxic materials and dumping the remains in landfill sites. Despite the backing that Shell received from the UK government and members of the scientific community, the public sympathy was with Greenpeace, which mounted a campaign against Shell. The public appeared to trust Greenpeace rather than a multinational oil company. Damage to the marine environment was easier for the public to conceptualize and become emotional about, compared to unrecognized risks on land which would occur 'somewhere else'. A highly effective campaign promoted Shell as the villain of the piece, causing great harm to Shell's reputation. Because of this, Shell was forced to back down and settle for dismantling its platform on land.

One of the United Kingdom's leading tour operators – British Airways Holidays – has drawn up a 'green list' of environmentally friendly hotels in the Caribbean. In a survey among its customers, more than half said they would choose an airline or tour operator which took into account environmental issues. British Airways decided to follow a number of German tour operators by using a survey of 100 hotels carried out by the International Hotels Environment Initiative (IHEI) and the Caribbean Hotel Association. Thirteen hotels which were identified as having the best environmental practices, achieving at least a 75 per cent 'pass rate' in key areas, were given an eco-logo in British Airways brochure. British Airways may be following public sentiment, but will its eco-friendly labels significantly influence buyers' choices? How large is the segment that would actually be prepared to pay a higher price for an environmentally friendly hotel, rather than simply saying it would? Might this approach work for up-market holiday destinations such as the Caribbean, but be largely irrelevant to the more price-sensitive market for holidays in Spain?

Is a firm's pursuit of more consumption by consumers fundamentally opposed to ecological interests? Taken to its logical extreme, consumption of the vast majority of goods and services can result in some form of ecological harm. For example, the most environmentally friendly means of transport is to avoid the need for transport in the first place. The most environmentally friendly holiday is for an individual to stay at home. Individuals with a true concern for preserving their ecological environment would choose to reduce their consumption of goods and services in total. At the moment, such attitudes are held by only a small minority in Western societies, but the development of a widespread anticonsumption mentality would have major implications for business organizations.

5.4.2 How business can capitalize on 'green consumerism'

The green consumer movement can present businesses with opportunities as well as problems. Proactive companies have capitalized on ecological issues by reducing their costs and/or improving their organizational image. These are some examples of how firms have adapted to the green movement:

■ Many markets are characterized by segments which are prepared to pay a premium price for a product that has been produced in an ecologically sound manner. Some retailers, such as Body Shop, have developed valuable niches on this basis. What starts off as a 'deep green' niche soon expands into a larger 'pale green' segment of customers who prefer ecologically sound products, but are unwilling to pay such a high price premium.

■ Being 'green' may actually save a company money. Often, changing existing environmentally harmful practices primarily involves overcoming traditional mind sets about how things should be done (e.g. using recyclable shipping materials may involve overcoming traditional one-way supply chain logistics).

THINKING AROUND THE SUBJECT

Tourism is often seen as a clean industry, but marketers in the travel and tourism sector are having to address increasing concern about the environmental damage caused by tourism. Every year, 120 million glossy brochures are produced, of which an estimated 38 million are thrown away without being used. In resorts, the development of tourism frequently produces problems of waste and sewage disposal, while local residents find themselves competing for scarce water supplies. British travellers may worry about the damage that tourism causes to the environment, but recent surveys have shown that one in ten of them prefers to holiday in unspoilt or environmentally sensitive areas. Green Flag International, a non-profit-making organization, has been set up to promote conservation and to persuade tour operators that being 'green' can actually save them money. Among other things, it advocates using small, privately run guest houses and hotels, shops and public transport, and employing local people as guides. Hotels are advised on saving water and electricity, for example by not changing room towels every day. The organization also seeks to educate tourists to evaluate the environmental impact of their visit before booking a holiday and urges tour operators to include in their brochures a statement of their environmental policies. Why do so few people who claim to be green still seek out the cheapest package holiday, regardless of its ecological impacts? And if being green does not always cost money, why do so many tour operators seem set in their ways?

- In Western, developed economies, legislation to enforce environmentally sensitive methods of production is increasing. A company which adopts environmentally sensitive production methods ahead of compulsion can gain experience to competitive advantage ahead of other companies

5.5   BUSINESS ETHICS

Ethics is essentially about the definition of what is right and wrong. However, a difficulty occurs in trying to agree just what is right and wrong. No two people have precisely the same opinions, so critics would argue that ethical considerations are of little interest to business. It can also be difficult to distinguish between ethics and legality, for example it may not be strictly illegal to exploit the gullibility of children in advertisements, but it may nevertheless be unethical.

Culture has a great effect in defining ethics and what is considered unethical in one society may be considered perfectly acceptable in another. In Western societies, ethical considerations confront commercial organizations on many occasions. For example:

- A drug company may advertise a product and provide information which is technically correct, but omit to provide vital information about side-effects associated with using the product. Should a company be required to spell out the possible problems of using its products, as well as the benefits?

- A dentist is short of money and diagnoses spurious problems which call for unnecessary remedial treatment. How does he reconcile his need to maximize his earning potential with the need to provide what is best for his patient?

- In order to secure a major new construction contract, a salesperson must entertain the client's buying manager with a weekend all-expenses paid holiday. Should this be considered ethical business practice in Britain? Or in South America?

It is suggested that society is becoming increasingly concerned about the ethical values adopted by its commercial organizations. With expanding media availability and an increasingly intelligent audience, it is getting easier to expose examples of unethical business practice. Moreover, many television audiences appear to enjoy watching programmes which reveal alleged unethical practices of household name companies. To give one example, the media has on a number of occasions focused attention on alleged exploitative employment practices of suppliers used by some of the biggest brand names in sportswear.

Firms are responding to increasing levels of ethical awareness by trying to put their own house in order. These are some examples of how firms have gone about the task:

- Many companies have identified segments of their market who are prepared to pay a premium price in order to buy a product which has been produced in an ethical manner or from a company that has adopted ethical practices. Many personal investors are concerned not just about the return that they will get, but the way in which that return will be achieved. This explains the increasing popularity of ethical investment funds that avoid investing in companies which are considered to be of a socially dubious nature. In the food sector, many consumers would consider the treatment of cattle grown for meat to be inhuman and unethical and would be happy to buy from a supplier who they knew acted ethically in the manner in which the cattle were raised and slaughtered. Many with particularly strong convictions may refuse to buy meat at all.

- Greater attention to training can make clear to staff just what is expected of them, for example that it is unethical (and in the long term commercially damaging) for a pensions company's salespeople to try to sell a policy to a person which really does not suit their needs. Training may emphasize the need to spend a lot of time finding out just what the true needs of the customer are.

- More effective control and reward systems can help to reduce unethical practices within an organization. For example, salespeople employed by a financial services company on a commission only basis are more likely to try to sell a policy to a customer regardless of the customer's needs compared to a salaried employee who can take a longer term view of the relationship between the company and its clients.

THINKING AROUND THE SUBJECT

The 1980s and 1990s saw a great growth in investment funds which claimed to invest only in businesses which are run ethically. Many investors preferred to know that their investment was not just benefiting themselves, but society as a whole. It was also claimed that a good ethical investment fund need perform no worse than one run without explicit ethical considerations. By 1998 there were over 30 ethical investment funds in the UK. However, a report by the Social Affairs Unit was scornful of ethical investment, because ethics is about judgements on what people do with products. It cited the example of funds' refusal to invest in the nuclear industry, which implied that the industry was totally bad, despite the valuable role which nuclear radiation plays in medicine. Similarly, it is very much an individual judgement whether nuclear electricity generation is good or bad. So what is the role of ethical investment trusts? Ethics is very much about statements of what is right and wrong, and these vary between individuals, between cultures, and they change through time. Can an investment trust ever be said to represent the views of a society as a whole?

There are many documented cases to show that acting ethically need not conflict with a company's profit objectives, and indeed can add to profitability. For example, good safety standards and employment policies can improve productivity. In the United Kingdom, the DIY retailer B&Q has reduced discrimination against older workers by employing predominantly older people in some of its stores. It is claimed that these stores have become the firm's most profitable.

5.6 **CORPORATE GOVERNANCE**

The media is taking a great interest in major companies whose internal style of governance appears to be inconsistent with their role as a trusted market-led organization. Recent examples of poor corporate governance have included numerous cases of so called 'fat cat' directors paying themselves large salary increases while worsening the employment conditions of their lower paid employees.

In the United Kingdom, a number of attempts to develop blueprints for corporate governance have been developed (e.g. those by the Cadbury and Greenbury committees). 'Good practice' in corporate governance is increasingly being defined in terms of:

■ Having in place internal control systems which prevent the type of abuse of directors' power which occurred in the former Maxwell group of companies

■ Having an appropriate structure for the board of directors which combines full-time executive directors with non-executive directors brought in from outside

■ Striking a balance when remunerating senior directors and employees between the reassurance of a long-term salary and performance for results

■ Recognizing employees as increasingly important stakeholders in organizations;

THINKING AROUND THE SUBJECT

'Handcuffs courtesy of Yale' could be the future as British police forces recruit marketing officers and embrace the practices of sponsorship. Since 1994, British police forces have been able to raise up to one per cent of their overall budget through sponsorship. Initiatives so far have included police vehicles being sponsored by car manufacturers and insurance companies being called in as sponsors for antiburglary and crime prevention crackdowns. But the head of public relations for West Yorkshire Police conceded that this would not mean police officers walking around with McDonald's logos on their uniforms. Nevertheless, the sponsoring of vital public services does raise ethical issues. What would happen if a sponsor was itself being investigated of a suspected criminal act? Are there some essential public services which should be driven solely by social policy needs and not by market forces?

there have been many initiatives, such as 'Investors in People' to promote the training and development of an organization's workforce.

Good corporate governance is culturally conditioned and what may constitute bad governance in one culture may be accepted as normal in others, reflecting economic, political, social and legal traditions in each country. Despite convergence, differences still predominate, for example in attitudes towards the disclosure of directors' salaries.

CASE STUDY

SMOKING MAY BE BAD, BUT TOBACCO COMPANIES' PROFITS HAVE LOOKED GOOD

After the arms industry, the tobacco industry must be one of the most politically incorrect business sectors. Yet during the late 1990s tobacco companies in the United Kingdom appeared to be very popular with the Stock Market, outperforming the FTSE all-share index by 36 per cent during 1998.

Tobacco companies now place less emphasis on fighting the health lobby, and no longer pretend that tobacco is anything other than harmful. But fortunately for the tobacco firms, nicotine is an addictive drug. Although cigarette consumption has declined in most developed countries, one person in four still smokes. Moreover, among some groups, especially young women, the rate of smoking has shown some increase in recent years. Tobacco companies also benefit from periods of economic recession. While job cuts may be bad news for most consumer goods and services companies, it has historically also been linked to an increase in smoking.

The tobacco companies have survived many years of attempts to control tobacco sales throughout Europe, but a planned EU directive banning all tobacco advertising would make it increasingly difficult for tobacco companies to get new brands established. As a result, the big three UK companies, BAT, Gallagher and Imperial Tobacco looked at strengthening their brands with promotional campaigns and joint ventures. BAT linked up with the Ministry of Sound nightclub to push its Lucky Strike brand, while Gallagher tried to promote the Benson and Hedges name through a branded coffee. One industry expert expected to see an army of cigarette girls pushing cigarettes in pubs and corner shops, thereby getting round controls on advertising.

While the costs of promoting cigarettes in Europe have been increasing, tobacco companies have been keen to exploit overseas markets where measures to protect the public are less tough. In the countries of eastern Europe, the companies have pushed their products, hoping to capitalize on the hunger for Western brands. Gallagher has a plant in Kazakhstan and has heavily promoted its Sovereign brand in the former Soviet Union. The biggest opportunities for Western tobacco companies, however, are in China which is the world's biggest market in terms of volume. The Chinese smoke 1.7 trillion cigarettes a year, making the British market of just 77 billion look quite small. State-owned brands such as Pagoda dominate the market with an estimated 98 per cent market share. With import duties of 240 per cent, most foreign cigarettes enter the Chinese market through unauthorized channels, including those smuggled by the Chinese army. Greater trade liberalization will inevitably give freer access to the Chinese market for Western tobacco companies. These will undoubtedly pay significant levels of taxes to the authorities, so a financially strained government may be unwilling to reduce tobacco consumption too much, especially when smoking is so pervasive through the population.

CASE STUDY   Review questions

1 What measures could or should governments take to bring about a significant reduction in smoking?

2 What factors could explain a booming share price at the same time as Europeans' attitudes towards smoking are becoming more hostile?

3 How would you defend a Western tobacco company in its attempts to develop the Chinese market for cigarettes?

CHAPTER   Summary and key links to other chapters

In a mature business environment, organizations must think beyond their own customers to society as a whole. There are good philosophical and pragmatic reasons why firms should act in a socially responsible manner. At a time of increasing competition in many markets, good social credentials can act as a differentiator in the eyes of increasingly sophisticated buyers. Although social responsibility by firms can achieve long-term paybacks, there can still be doubt about what is the most responsible course of action. Discussion about ecological issues and ethics is often muddied by lack of agreement on what is right and wrong.

The following key linkages to other chapters should be noted. Ethics is founded upon what a society considers right and wrong, and social values are constantly changing (Chapter 11), reflected in legislation by governments (Chapters 8 and 9). Fierce competition within a market and a high degree of price sensitivity by buyers can encourage firms to engage in unethical practices (Chapter 6). New technologies are continually posing new challenges and opportunities for organizations in their efforts to act responsibly (Chapter 12). Expectations of responsibility by firms can differ markedly between countries (Chapter 10). Internally, ethical practice is closely linked to human resource management practices (Chapter 4).

CHAPTER   Review questions

1 Giving examples, explain what is meant by the term environmental lobbies. Provide a resumé of the tactics you would advise a high profile company to use in managing relations with special interest groups.

(Based on CIM Marketing Environment examination)

2 (a) Identify *two* stakeholder groups and briefly assess the nature and terms of their stake in the organization.

(b) Prepare a brief for your marketing director outlining the concept of social responsibility and indicating how this might be applied to your customers and how it might be of overall benefit.

(Based on CIM Marketing Environment December examination)

3 For what reasons might a fast-food restaurant company choose to adopt the societal marketing concept? By adopting the concept, is it really changing the way it does business?

4 Is it possible to define an ethical code of conduct which is applicable in all countries? How should a multinational company attempt to define a global ethical code of conduct?

5 What is meant by good corporate governance, and why has the topic become an important issue in many countries?

6 What should be the response of businesses to pressure groups' claims that their activities are causing ecological damage?

References

Anderson, P. (1982) Marketing, Strategic Planning and Theory, *Journal of Marketing*, Spring, pp. 15–26.
Arbratt, R. and D. Sacks (1988) 'Perceptions of the societal marketing concept', *European Journal of Marketing*, vol. 22, pp. 25–33.

Suggested further reading

For a general review of 'environmentalism', the following references provide a useful overview of the issues involved:

Bromley, D. (ed.) (1995) *The Handbook of Environmental Economics*, Blackwell, Oxford.
Cairncross, F. (1991) *Costing the Earth*, Harvard Business School Press, Boston, MA.
Pepper, D. (1996) *Modern Environmentalism*, Taylor and Francis, London.

The general discussion on environmental issues can be followed up with a discussion on the impact of such issues on business organizations:

Howard, E. and P. Bansal (1997) *Business and the Natural Environment*, Butterworth-Heinemann, Oxford.

Roberts, J.A. and D.R. Bacon (1997) 'Exploring the subtle relationship between environmental concern and ecologically conscious behaviour', *Journal of Business Research*, vol. 40, no. 1, pp. 79–89.

Welford, R. (1995) *Environmental Strategy and Sustainable Development: The Corporate Challenge for the Twenty-first Century*, Routledge, London.

The following provides an interesting insight into the arguments for action against organizations that are considered to be environmentally unfriendly:

Seel, B., M. Paterson and B. Doherty (2000) *Direct Action in British Environmentalism*, Taylor and Francis, London.

Responses by business to environmental issues are covered in the following:

Arason-Correa, J.A. (1998) 'Strategic proactivity and firm approach to the natural environment', *Academy of Management Journal*, October, vol. 41, no 5, pp. 556–567.

Dutton, G. (1996) 'Green Partnerships', *Management Review*, vol. 85, no. 1, pp. 24–28.

Fineman, S. and K. Clarke (1996) 'Green stakeholders: industry interpretations and response', *Journal of Management Studies*, vol. 33, no. 6, pp. 80–105.

Freeman, R.E., J. Pierce and R. Dodd (2000) *Environmentalism and the New Logic of Business*, Oxford University Press, Oxford.

Menon, A. and A. Menon (1997) 'Environmental marketing strategy: the emergence of corporate environmentalism as a marketing strategy', *Journal of Marketing*, vol. 61, no. 1, January, 51–67.

Peattie, K. (1995) *Environmental Marketing Management: Meeting the Green Challenge*, Pitman, London.

For a discussion of business ethics and good corporate governance, the following references are useful:

Cottrill, K. (1996) 'Global codes of conduct', *Journal of Business Strategy*, May–June, vol. 17, no. 3, pp. 55–59.

Davies, P. (ed.) (1997) *Current Issues in Business Ethics*, Routledge, London.

Donaldson, T. (ed.) (1995) *Case Studies in Business Ethics*, Prentice-Hall, Hemel Hempstead.

Epstein, E.M. (1998) 'Business ethics and corporate social policy: reflections on an intellectual journey, 1964–1996, and beyond', *Business and Society*, March, vol. 37, no. 1, pp. 7–39.

Hoffman, M. and R.E. Frederick (eds) (1995) *Business Ethics: Readings and Cases in Corporate Morality*, 3rd edn, McGraw-Hill, New York.

Robin, D.P. and E.E. Reidenbach (1987) 'Social responsibility, ethics and marketing strategy: closing the gap between concept and application, *Journal of Marketing*, January, vol. 51, pp. 44–58.

Schlegelmilch, B.B. (1998) *Marketing Ethics: An International Perspective*, International Thomson Business Press, London.

Solomon, R.C. (1992) *Ethics and Excellence*, Oxford University Press, Oxford.

Weiss, J.W. (1998) *Business Ethics: A Stakeholder and Issues Management Approach*, 2nd edn, Dryden, Fort Worth, TX.

The following reader provides insights to issues of corporate governance:

Harvard Business Review, (2000) *Harvard Business Review on Corporate Governance*, Harvard Business School Press, Boston, MA.

Useful websites

Business ethics discussion group   The purpose of this list is to facilitate debate and discussion between members of the academic, research and business communities who are interested in the systematic study or practical investigation of the ethical issues facing business and industry.
http://www.jiscmail.ac.uk/lists/business-ethics.html

MIT Technology, Business and Environment programme   MIT's Technology, Business and Environment site provides discussion and links to other sites concerning the links between business excellence and the environment.   **http://web.mit.edu/ctpid/www/tbe.html**

Greenpeace   Home page of Greenpeace.   **http://greenpeace.org**

Friends of the Earth   Home page of Friends of the Earth UK.   **http://www.foe.co.uk**

The Environment Council   This independent UK charity brings together people from all sectors of business, non-governmental organizations, government and the community to develop long-term solutions to environmental issues.   **http://www.the-environment-council.org.uk/**

Governance   Governance is an international monthly newsletter on issues of corporate governance, boardroom performance and shareholder activism. It provides analysis of key events, publications and reports on corporate governance issues.   **http://www.governance-news.com/index.htm**

Key terms

Corporate governance	Green marketing
Ecological impacts	Societal marketing
Ethics	Stakeholders
External costs	

Part 3
Elements of the external business environment

6

The competition environment

CHAPTER OBJECTIVES

Organizations must compete for customers and resources, including personnel, equipment and financial resources. The abundance of resources relative to those who want to buy them determines the competitiveness of a market. Organizations are living in an increasingly competitive business environment. Yet there is significant variation in the level of competition that occurs in different markets. The aim of this chapter is to gain a greater understanding of the dynamics of competition and how it impacts on an organization's activities. This chapter begins by exploring the concept of market structure and notes the range of structures from perfect competition to pure monopoly. The principles of perfect competition are studied as a basic building block for understanding market competitiveness. Highly competitive markets are presumed to favour the interests of consumers by putting downward pressure on prices. In practice, most companies supplying goods and services to a market seek to avoid head-on competition by differentiating their products and developing strong brands that buyers come to trust. This chapter reviews the steps taken by government agencies to counter abuse of monopoly power.

INTRODUCTION TO THE COMPETITION ENVIRONMENT

Competition is a crucial fact of life to most organizations operating in a commercial environment. Competition usually arises when companies seek to attract customers from rival companies by offering better products and/or lower prices. Competition can also arise in the acquisition of resources, and where these are scarce relative to the demand for them, rival buyers will bid up their price. However, competition in customer and resource markets can be complex and a full understanding of each market is needed if the effects of competition on an organization are to be fully appreciated. This chapter begins by reviewing the fundamentals of competitive markets which are characterized by 'perfect competition' (sometimes referred to as 'atomistic competition'). In fact, perfect competition is the exception rather than the norm and most markets have imperfections which allow some organizations in the market to have undue influence over it. It is because of these imperfections that governments have intervened, believing that, in general, competitive markets are better for consumers.

Economists define markets in terms of the interaction between two groups:

■ Those seeking to buy products

■ Those seeking to sell them.

Economists distinguish between those economic influences that operate at the level of the individual firm and those that relate to the economy as a whole. The study of an organization and its customers/suppliers in isolation from the rest of the economy is generally referred to as *microeconomic* analysis. In this type of analysis, the national economy is assumed to be stable. However, this assumption is rarely true, so economists seek to understand the workings of the economy and, from this, the effects of changes in the national (and international) economy on individual organizations. This is generally referred to as *macroeconomic* analysis.

This chapter is concerned primarily with microeconomic influences as they affect the decisions made by individual firms, for example with regard to their pricing and production levels. The following chapter will return to macroeconomic analysis.

6.1.1   Market structure

The market conditions facing suppliers of goods and services vary considerably. Customers of water supply companies may feel they are being exploited with high prices and poor service levels by companies who know that their customers have little choice of supplier. On the other hand, customers are constantly wooed by numerous insurance companies who are all trying to sell basically similar products in a market that provides consumers with a lot of choice. Differences in the characteristics and composition of buyers and sellers define the structure of a market.

The term market structure is used to describe:

■ The number of buyers and sellers operating in a market.

■ The extent to which the market is concentrated in the hands of a small number of buyers and/or sellers.

■ The degree of collusion or competition between buyers and/or sellers.

An understanding of market structure is important to businesses, not only to understand the consequences of their own actions but also the behaviour of other firms operating in a market. Market structures range from the theoretical extremes of perfect competition and pure monopoly. In practice, examples of the extremes are rare and most analysis therefore focuses on levels of market imperfection between the two extremes (Figure 6.1).

Figure 6.1
A continuum of market structures

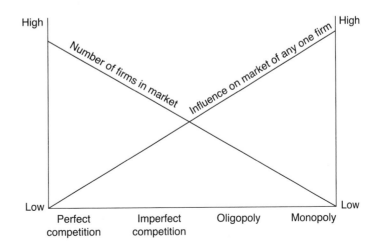

PERFECT COMPETITION

This is the simplest type of market structure to understand and corresponds very much with most people's ideas of what a very competitive market should be like. Government policy makers often pursue a vision of perfect competition as the ideal market structure. Although perfectly competitive markets in their theoretical extreme are rarely found in practice, a sound understanding of the way they work is essential for understanding competitive market pressures in general.

Perfectly competitive markets are attributed these principal characteristics:

1   There are a large number of small producers supplying to the market, each with similar cost structures and each producing an identical product.

2   There are also a large number of buyers in the market, each responsible for purchasing only a small percentage of total output.

3   Both buyers and sellers are free to enter or leave the market, that is there are no barriers to entry or exit.

4   In a perfectly competitive market, there is a ready supply of information for buyers and sellers about market conditions.

Some markets come close to having these characteristics, for example:

- Wholesale fruit and vegetable markets
- The 'spot' market for oil products
- Stock markets where shares are bought and sold (Figure 6.2).

THINKING AROUND THE SUBJECT

The term 'Confusion pricing' has often been used to describe the pricing practices of firms operating in the mobile phone, electricity, gas and mortgage sectors, to name but a few. Even some companies have been heard to use the term, off the record. In an ideal world, we would all be able to evaluate the options open to us and make a rational choice from the available options. We might still appear to act irrationally by placing a high value on a service feature which somebody else would regard as being quite frivolous. But how do you go about the task of evaluation when there is enormous choice and service providers appear to go out of their way to confuse buyers? Many buyers of mobile phone services have been overwhelmed at the choices available to them – in the UK, four basic networks, dozens of different tariffs for each network and hundreds of different handsets. One professor of mathematics calculated that it would take a UK buyer over a year to evaluate the costs and benefits of all permutations of networks, tariffs and handsets. To many people, the tariff plans offered by the phone companies seem unbelievably complex, with an array of peak/off-peak price plans, 'free' inclusive minutes and discounts for loyalty. Is such an approach to pricing compatible with theories of competitive markets, which assumes a ready availability of information? Will buyers' comparison sites, such as www.buy.co.uk and www.ofgem.gov.uk reduce the confusion or simply add to it?

Figure 6.2
Stock markets come close to satisfying the requirements of perfect competition, with large numbers of people buying and selling shares, resulting in daily movement in share prices

Treas 6pc 2028	114.06	-0.07	129.51	113.15
War Ln 3½%	66.54	-0.11	78.64	66.02
Trs 2½% IL 2009	214.11	-0.48	220.39	211.28

BANKS -0.97%

Abbey Nat	1245	+7	1315	960
Allnce & Leic	817	-13	855	649
Alld Irish	803½	-½	857¾	622½
Bk of Ireind	700	-¼	713¾	510½
Bk of Scot	803	-29	869½	598½
Barclays	2180	-31	2345	1836
Bradfd & Bngly	311	-4	338	262
Egg	158½	+1½	166	116½
Halifax	822		848	609
HSBC	842½	+5½	1094	776
Lloyds TSB	711½	+5	776	600
Northern Rock	578	-7	602½	424
Ryl Bk Sct	1567	-81	1775	1309
Stan Chart	911	-241	129½	758

BUILDING +1.48%

Abbey	230	-2½	260
Aggregate Ind	90*	-¼	
AMEC	505*		

Greene Kng	638½	+1	668½	52
Nichols	124½	+½	134	10:
Regent Inns	177½		204½	1:
Scot&New	557½	+4½	574	4:
SFI	237½	+13½	294½	17:
SA Breweries	543*	+2	566½	4:
Wetherspn	367½	-½	422	33:
Whitbread	677*	+16	699	54:
Wolv&Dud	481*	+1	486	4:
Yates Group	173	-3½	226½	12:
Young Br NV	600*		675	4:

ELECTRONICS

Alba	327½
Amstrad	5:
Blick	
Chemring	
Chloride	
Converr	
Datrr	

In reality, very few markets fully meet the economists' criteria for perfect competition and even those markets described above have imperfections (e.g. wholesale fruit and vegetable markets are increasingly influenced by the practice of large retailers contracting directly with growers).

Perfect competition implies that firms are price *takers* in that competitive market forces alone determine the price at which they can sell their products. If a firm cannot produce its goods or services as efficiently as its competitors, it will lose profits and eventually go out of business. Customers are protected from exploitive high prices, because as long as selling a product remains profitable, companies will be tempted into the market to satisfy customers' requirements, thereby putting downward pressure on prices. Eventually, competition between firms will result in excessive profits being eliminated so that an equilibrium is achieved where loss-making firms have left the market and the market is not sufficiently attractive to bring new firms into it.

Probably the most important reason for studying perfect competition is that it focuses attention on the basic building blocks of competition: demand, supply and price determination.

6.2.1 Demand

Demand refers to the quantity of a product that consumers are willing and able to buy at a specific price over a given period of time. In economic analysis, demand is

Figure 6.3
A demand curve
for medium-fat
cheddar cheese

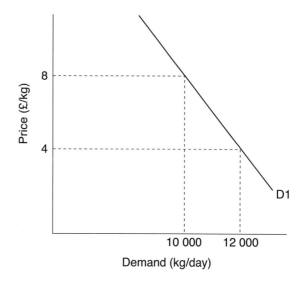

measured not simply in terms of what people would like to buy – after all, most people would probably want to buy expensive holidays and cars. Instead, demand refers to how many people are actually *able and willing* to buy a product at a given price and given a set of assumptions about the product and the environment in which it is being offered. Demand is also expressed in terms of a specified time period, for example so many units per day.

In general, as the price of a product falls, so the demand (as defined above) can be expected to rise. Likewise, as the price rises, demand could be expected to fall. This relationship can be plotted on a simple graph. In Figure 6.3, a demand curve for medium-fat cheddar cheese is shown by the line D1. This relates, for any given price shown on the vertical axis, the volume of demand, which is shown on the horizontal axis. Therefore, at a price of £8.00 per kg, demand is 10 000 units per period within a given area, while at a price of £4.00, the demand has risen to 12 000 units.

It is important to note that the demand curve drawn here refers to total market demand from all consumers and is not simply measuring demand for one producer's output. The importance of this distinction will become clear later, as the implication of this is that firms have to make their price decisions based on overall market conditions.

The demand curve D1 is based on a number of assumptions. These include, for example, assumptions that the price of substitutes for cheese will not change or that consumers will not suddenly take a dislike to cheddar cheese. Demand curve D1 measures the relationship between price and market demand for one given set of assumptions. When these assumptions change, a new demand curve is needed to explain a new relationship between price and quantity demanded.

In Figure 6.4, two sets of fresh assumptions have been made and new demand curves D2 and D3 drawn, based on these new sets of assumptions. For new demand curve D2, more cheese is demanded for any given price level (or, alternatively, this can be restated in terms of any given number of consumers demanding cheese

Figure 6.4
Alternative
demand curves
for cheese, based
on differing
assumptions

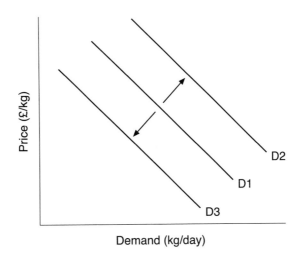

Figure 6.4 Alternative demand curves for cheese, based on differing assumptions

being prepared to pay a higher price). There are a number of possible causes of the shift of the demand curve from D1 to D2:

1. Consumers could have become wealthier, leading them to demand more of all goods, including cheese.

2. The price of substitutes for cheddar cheese (e.g. meat or other types of cheese) could have increased, thereby increasing demand for cheese.

3. Demand for complementary goods (such as savoury biscuits) may increase, thereby leading to an increase in demand for cheese.

4. Consumer preferences may change. This may occur, for example, if cheddar cheese is found to have health-promoting benefits.

5. An advertising campaign for cheddar cheese may increase demand for cheese at any given price.

Similarly, a number of possible reasons can be put forward to explain the shift from demand curve D1 to D3, where for any given price level, less is demanded:

1. Consumers could have become poorer, leading them to demand fewer of all goods, including cheese.

2. The price of substitutes for cheddar cheese (e.g. meat or other types of cheese) could have decreased, thereby making the substitutes appear more attractive and reducing demand for cheese.

3. Demand for complementary products may fall.

4. Cheddar cheese may become associated with health hazards, leading to less demand at any given price (Figure 6.5).

5. An advertising campaign for substitute products may shift demand away from cheddar cheese.

The demand curves shown in Figures 6.3 and 6.4 have both been straight, but this is a simplification of reality. In fact, demand curves would usually be curved,

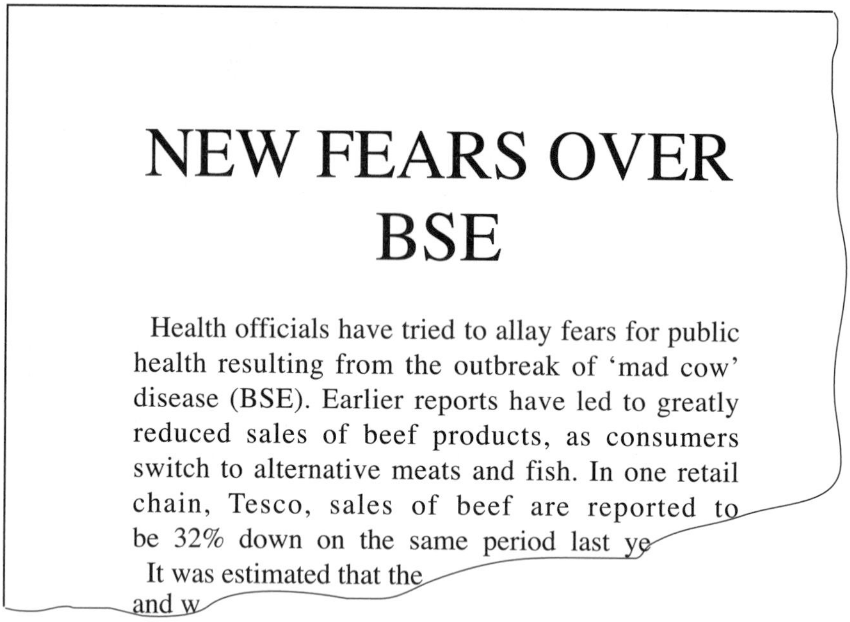

Figure 6.5
News headlines
such as this one
relating to the
BSE food scare
could have been
expected to shift
the demand curve
for a wide range
of meat-related
products. While
part of this shift
may be only short
term, some meat
eaters may not
have resumed
buying meat,
resulting in a
long-term shift in
the demand curve

NEW FEARS OVER BSE

Health officials have tried to allay fears for public health resulting from the outbreak of 'mad cow' disease (BSE). Earlier reports have led to greatly reduced sales of beef products, as consumers switch to alternative meats and fish. In one retail chain, Tesco, sales of beef are reported to be 32% down on the same period last ye

It was estimated that the
and w

indicating that the relationship between price and volume is not constant for all price points. There may additionally be significant discontinuities at certain price points, as where buyers in a market have psychological price barriers, above or below which their behaviour changes. In many markets, the difference between £10.00 and £9.99 may be crucial in overcoming buyers' attitudes that predispose them to regard anything over £10 as being unaffordable and anything below it as a bargain.

Actually collecting information with which to plot a demand curve poses theoretical and practical problems. The main problem relates to the cross-sectional nature of a demand curve, that is it purports to measure the volume of demand across the ranges of price possibilities. However, this kind of information can often only be built up by a longitudinal study of the relationship between prices and volume over time. There is always the possibility that, over time, the assumptions on which demand is based have changed, in which case it is difficult to distinguish between a movement along a demand curve and a shift to a new demand curve. It is, however, sometimes possible for firms to conduct controlled cross-sectional experiments where a different price is charged in different regions and the effects on volume recorded. To be sure that this is accurately measuring the demand curve, there must be no extraneous factors in regions (such as differences in household incomes) that could partly explain differences in price/volume relationships.

The demand curves shown in Figures 6.3 and 6.4 slope downwards, indicating the intuitive fact that as price rises, demand falls and vice versa. While this is intuitively plausible, it is not always the case. Sometimes, the demand curve slopes upwards, indicating that as the price of a product goes up, buyers are able and willing to buy more of the product. Classic examples of this phenomenon occur where a product becomes increasingly desirable as more people consume it.

A telephone network which has only one subscriber will be of little use to the first customer who will be unable to use a telephone to call anyone else. However, as more customers are connected, the value of the telephone network becomes greater to each individual who is correspondingly willing to pay a higher price. This phenomenon helps to explain why large international airports can charge more for aircraft to land than smaller regional airports. As the number of possible aircraft connections increases, airlines' willingness to pay high prices for landing slots increases.

Upward-sloping demand curves can also be observed for some products sold for their 'snob' value. Examples include some designer label clothes where high price alone can add to a product's social status. Upward-sloping demand curves can be observed over short time periods where a 'bandwagon' effect can be created by rapidly rising or falling prices, for example, in stock markets the very fact that share prices are rising may lead many people to invest in shares.

Supply

Supply is defined as the amount of a product that producers are willing and able to make available to the market at a given price over a particular period of time. Like demand, it is important to note that at different prices there will be different levels of supply, reflecting the willingness and/or ability of producers to supply a product as prices change.

A simple supply curve for medium-fat cheddar cheese is shown in Figure 6.6. The supply curve slopes upwards from left to right, indicating the intuitively plausible fact that as market prices rise, more suppliers will be attracted to supply to the market. Conversely, as prices fall, marginal producers (such as those who operate relatively inefficiently) will drop out of the market, reducing the daily supply available.

It is again important to distinguish movements along a supply curve from shifts to a new supply curve. The supply curve S1 is based on a number of assumptions about the relationship between price and volume supplied. If these assumptions are

Figure 6.6
A supply curve for cheese

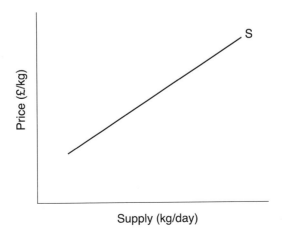

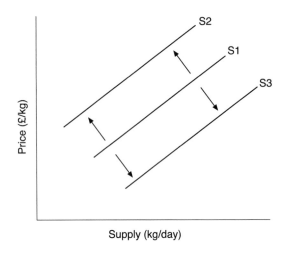

Figure 6.7
Alternative supply curves for cheese, based on differing assumptions

broken, a new supply curve based on the new set of assumptions needs to be drawn. In Figure 6.7, two new supply curves, S2 and S3, are shown. S2 indicates a situation where, for any given price level, total supply to the market is reduced. This could come about for a number of reasons, including:

1. Production methods could become more expensive, for example because of more stringent health and safety regulations. Therefore, for any given price level, fewer firms will be willing to supply to the market as they will no longer be able to cover their costs.

2. Extraneous factors (such as abnormally bad weather) could result in producers having difficulty in getting their produce to market.

3. Governments may impose additional taxes on suppliers (e.g. extending the scope of property taxes to cover agricultural property).

The new supply curve S3 indicates a situation where, for any given price level, total supply to the market is increased. This could come about for a number of reasons, including:

1. Changes in production technology, which result in cheddar cheese being produced more efficiently and therefore suppliers being prepared to supply more cheese at any given price (or, looked at another way, for any given volume supplied, suppliers are prepared to accept a lower price).

2. Extraneous factors (such as favourable weather conditions) could result in a glut of produce which must be sold and the market is therefore flooded with the additional supply.

3. Governments may give a subsidy for each kilogram of cheese produced by suppliers, thereby increasing their willingness to supply to the market.

6.2.3   Price determination

An examination of the demand and supply graphs indicates that they share common axes. In both cases the vertical axis refers to the price at which the

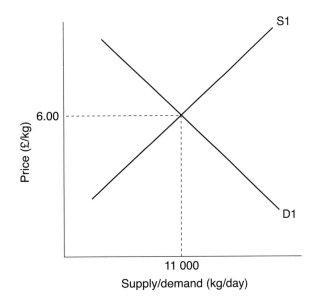

Figure 6.8
Supply and
demand for
cheese, showing
the equilibrium
market price

product might change hands, while the horizontal axis refers to the quantity changing hands.

It is possible to redraw the original demand and supply lines (D1 and S1) on a single graph (Figure 6.8). The supply curve indicates that the lower the price, the less cheese will be supplied to the market. Yet at these lower prices, customers are willing and able to buy a lot of cheese – more than the suppliers collectively are willing or able to supply. By following the supply curve upwards, it can be observed that suppliers are happy to supply more cheese, but at these high prices, there are few willing buyers. Therefore, at these high prices supply and demand are again out of balance.

Between the two extremes there will be a price where the interest of the two groups will coincide. This balancing of supply and demand is the foundation of the theory of market price, which holds that in any free market there is an 'equilibrium price' that matches the quantity that consumers are willing and able to buy (i.e. demand) with the quantity that producers are willing and able to produce (i.e. supply).

In perfectly competitive markets, the process of achieving equilibrium happens automatically without any external regulatory intervention. Perfectly competitive markets do not need any complicated and centralized system for bringing demand and supply into balance, something that is difficult to achieve in a centrally planned economy, such as those which used to predominate in Eastern Europe.

In Figure 6.8, supply and demand are brought precisely into balance at a price of £6.00. This is the equilibrium price and, at this price, 11 000 kg of cheese per day will be bought and sold in the market. If a company wants to sell its cheese in the market, it can only do so at this price. In theory, if it charged a penny more, it would get no business because everybody else in the market is cheaper. If it sells at a penny less, it will be swamped with demand, probably selling at a price that is below its production costs.

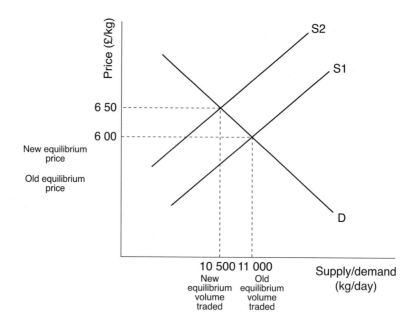

Figure 6.9
A shift in the
supply curve for
cheese, showing
the new
equilibrium
market price

It is important to remember that in a perfectly competitive market, individual firms are price takers. The market alone determines the 'going rate' for their product. Changes in the equilibrium market price come about for two principal reasons:

1 Assumptions about suppliers' ability or willingness to supply change, resulting in a shift to a new supply curve.

2 Assumptions about buyers' ability or willingness to buy change, resulting in a shift to a new demand curve.

The effects of shifts in supply are illustrated in Figure 6.9. From an equilibrium price of £6.00 and volume of 11 000 kg, the supply curve has shifted to S2 (perhaps in response to the imposition of a new tax on production). Assuming that demand conditions remain unchanged, the new point of intersection between the demand and supply lines occurs at a price of £7.50 and a volume of 10 500 kg. This is the new equilibrium price. A similar analysis can be carried out on the effects of a shift in the demand curve, but where the supply curve remains constant.

New equilibrium prices and trade volumes can be found at the intersection of the supply and demand curves. In practice, both the supply and demand curves may be changing at the same time.

The speed with which a new equilibrium price is established is dependent upon how efficiently a market is working. In pure commodity markets where products are instantly perishable, rapid adjustments in price are possible. Where speculators are allowed to store goods, or large buyers and sellers are able to unduly influence a market, adjustment may be slower. The extent of changes in price and volume traded is also dependent on the elasticities of demand and supply, which are considered in the following sections.

6.2.4 Elasticity of demand

Elasticity of demand refers to the extent to which demand changes in relation to a change in price or some other variable such as income. What is important here is to compare the proportionate (or percentage) change in demand with the proportionate (or percentage) change in the other variable, over any given period of time.

The most commonly used measure of elasticity of demand is price elasticity of demand. Information on this is useful to business organizations to allow them to predict what will happen to the volume of sales in response to a change in price. This section is concerned with the responsiveness of a whole market to changes in price. It will be recalled that in a perfectly competitive market, firms must take their selling price from the market, so the only elasticity that is of interest to them is the elasticity of the market as a whole.

Price elasticity of demand refers to the ratio of the percentage change in demand to the percentage change in price. In other words, it seeks to measure how the sales of a product respond to a change in its price. This can be expressed as a simple formula:

$$\text{Price elasticity of demand} = \frac{\text{Change in demand (\%)}}{\text{Change in price (\%)}}$$

Where demand is relatively unresponsive to price changes, demand is said to be inelastic with respect to price. Where demand is highly responsive to even a small price charge, demand is described as being elastic with respect to price.

Two demand curves are shown in Figure 6.10. D2 is more elastic than D1, as indicated by the greater effect on volume of a change in price, compared with the effects of a similar price change with D1.

A number of factors influence the price elasticity of demand for a particular product. The most important is the availability of substitutes. Where these are readily available, buyers are likely to switch between alternative products in

Figure 6.10
A comparison of a relatively inelastic demand function (D1) with a relatively elastic one (D2)

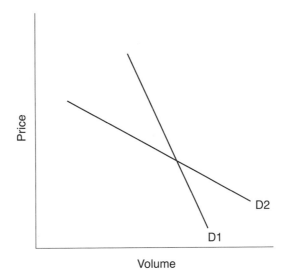

Figure 6.11
Airlines such as
Ryanair have
identified a
market for low-
cost air travel,
indicating a high
price elasticity of
demand. As
prices have been
reduced, sales of
tickets by so
called low-cost,
no-frills airlines
have increased
considerably
(Reproduced with
permission of Ryanair)

What is there in common between the haggling over prices which takes place in many eastern markets, and modern direct marketing techniques? At first sight the two would appear to be worlds apart, but in fact they can both be processes by which the seller seeks to establish the maximum amount that a buyer is prepared to pay. In the eastern bazaar, the seller will learn that some buyers are more price sensitive than others, resulting in each transaction being uniquely priced. This is exactly what modern direct marketing firms often seek to achieve, except that they have a mass of information on each customer to initiate a price or a level of purchase incentive. And if this price is too high, the company might try again with a lower price or better incentive, knowing what the likely reaction of a particular market segment will be to the lower price. Credit-card companies, mortgage lenders and banks have used such techniques and are becoming increasingly sophisticated in their use. Can a centralized database do a better job than one-to-one haggling in a marketplace? And what about the new generation of web-based auction sites, such as eBay and QXL? Can these hope to match supply and demand in a virtual auction as effectively as traditional auctioneers have done in front of a crowd of bidders? Or is the virtual auction another example of the Internet helping to restore the competitiveness of markets?

response to price changes. The absolute value of a product and its importance to a buyer can also influence its elasticity. For example, if infrequently purchased boxes of matches increased in price by 10 per cent from 10p to 11p, buyers would probably not cut back on their purchases. However, if the price of television sets increased by the same percentage amount from £300 to £330, many buyers may pull out of the market.

For any measure of elasticity, it is important to consider the time period over which it is being measured. In general, products are much more inelastic to changes in price over the short term, when possibilities for substitution may be few. However, over the longer term, new possibilities for substitution may appear. This explains why petrol is very inelastic over the short term, but much more so over the long term. Faced with a sudden increase in petrol prices (as happened following the Gulf War) motorists have little choice other than paying the increased price. However, over the longer term, they can reduce their purchases of petrol by buying more fuel-efficient cars, rearranging their pattern of life so that they do not need to travel as much, or by sharing cars.

Further measures of elasticity of demand can be made by considering the responsiveness of demand to changes in the assumptions on which the demand curve is based. The most important of these is income elasticity of demand, which measures the responsiveness of demand to changes in buyers' combined incomes and can be expressed in the following way:

$$\text{Income elasticity of demand} = \frac{\text{Change in demand (\%)}}{\text{Change in income (\%)}}$$

In general, as a population's income rises, the demand for particular products rises, giving rise to a positive income elasticity of demand. Where there is a particularly strong increase in demand in response to an increase in incomes (or vice versa), a product can be said to have a high income elasticity of demand. This is true of luxuries such as long-haul air holidays and fitted kitchens, whose sales have increased during times of general economic prosperity, but declined during recessionary periods. On the other hand, there are some goods and services whose demand goes down as incomes increase. These are referred to as *inferior goods* and examples in most Western countries include local bus services and household coal.

It is useful for business organizations to understand income elasticity of demand in order to plan a response to anticipated changes in aggregate income. If, for example, a general rise in consumer income looks likely to reduce the sales of a product that has a negative income elasticity, a business may seek to shift its resources to making products with a positive income elasticity. In trying to plan for the future, businesses rely on their own historical information about sales/income relationships, and also government and private forecasts about current and future levels and distribution of income.

A third measure of demand elasticity to note is a product's cross-price elasticity of demand. This refers to the percentage change in demand for product A when the price of product B changes. Where products are very close substitutes, this may be a very important measure to understand consumer demand. For example, the price of butter can have a significant effect on demand for margarine.

It is possible to identify numerous other *ad hoc* measures of elasticity of demand. Firms may be interested in the responsiveness of demand to changes in some measure of the quality of their product. For example, a railway operator may be interested in the effects on demand of improvements in service reliability or a bus operator may be interested in establishing the percentage increase in passenger demand resulting from a given percentage increase in frequency of a bus route.

6.2.5   **Elasticity of supply**

The concept of elasticity can also be applied to supply, so as to measure the responsiveness of supply to changes in price. Elasticity of supply is measured by the formula:

$$\text{Elasticity of supply} = \frac{\text{Change in supply (\%)}}{\text{Change in price (\%)}}$$

If suppliers are relatively unresponsive to an increase in the price of a product, the product is described as being inelastic with respect to price. If producers increase production substantially as prices rise, the product is said to be elastic.

As with price elasticity of demand, time is crucial in determining the elasticity of supply. Over the short term, it may be very difficult for firms to increase supply, making it very inelastic with respect to price. In the case of markets for agricultural products, elasticity is determined by the growing cycle and new supply may only be forthcoming in time for the next season. For many manufacturing processes,

Sometimes, a company is just not able to respond to changes in market price by supplying more of the product which has become popular. The market for organic vegetables during the late 1990s illustrates this point. A combination of rising incomes, greater awareness of health issues and a stream of food safety scares had led to rapid growth in demand for organic produce throughout Europe. But how can farmers grow organically on land which has been saturated by decades of artificial fertilizers? The Soil Association, which operates a widely recognized accreditation scheme for organic produce, required that farmland should be free of artificial fertilizer for at least five years before any crops grown on it could be described as organic. So despite the rapid growth in demand and the price premiums that customers were prepared to pay, retailers found it difficult to satisfy demand. Furthermore, with a difficult and intermittent supply, could retailers risk their brand name by being seen as an unreliable supplier of second rate produce? Marks and Spencer launched a range of organic vegetables in 1997, only to withdraw them soon afterwards, blaming the difficulty on obtaining regular and reliable supplies.

supplies can eventually be increased by investing in new productive capacity and taking on additional workers. Over the longer term, supply is more elastic.

6.2.6   Limitations of the theory of perfect competition

Although government policy makers often view perfectly competitive markets as an ideal to aim towards, the automatic balancing of supply and demand at an equilibrium price, as described above, is seldom achieved in practice. These are some of the more important reasons why perfect competition is rarely achieved in practice:

1   Where economies of scale are achievable in an industry sector, it is always possible for firms to grow larger and more efficient, and thereby be able to exercise undue influence in a market. In general, perfect competition only applies where production techniques are simple and opportunities for economies of scale are few.

2   Markets are often dominated by large buyers who are able to exercise influence over the market. The domestic market for many specialized defence products may be competitive in terms of a large number of suppliers, but demand for their products is dominated by one government buying agency.

3   It can be naive to assume that high prices and profits in a sector will attract new entrants, while losses will cause the least efficient to leave. In practice, there may be a whole range of barriers to entry which could cover the need to obtain licences for production, the availability of trained staff and access to distribution outlets. Also, there are sometimes barriers to exit where firms are locked into long-term supply contracts or where it would be very expensive to lay off resources such as labour.

To what extent do buyers of goods and services shop around and compare prices when choosing between competing products? Do they even have any idea of a baseline price for a category of product? The BT Business Price Perception Survey suggests that even business buyers – who are sometimes thought to act with greater economic rationality than private buyers – are often wide of the mark when it comes to understanding prices. In its 1997 annual survey, it found knowledge of telephone prices to be particularly bad, probably reflecting the plethora of price plans which have emerged in recent years. Respondents gave the average price of a five minute peak national call as £2.15, whereas in fact it was only 44p. Another sector with confusing price structures is railways. Here, respondents estimated the price of a second-class return ticket from London to Edinburgh at £54, compared to the actual price of £64. By contrast to the wide variations in service price estimates, respondents were quite accurate in their assessment of the price of a pint of beer. The average estimate of £1.73 for a pint of lager was just 2p off the true average. What does this imply for companies' pricing policies? The assumption of perfect competition that buyers have complete knowledge of prices is becoming increasingly invalid. Many companies have segmented their markets by offering differentiated product offers for different segments at different prices. Sometimes this process of price discrimination can be taken too far so that it leaves buyers confused. Is there sometimes a case for adopting an 'Everyday Low Price' approach by offering a limited number of prices for a given product, something which has been adopted by many of the new low-cost, no-frills airlines? And what of intelligent search engines which are now available on the Internet? Will these make it easier for us to shop around and gain a better understanding of comparative prices?

4   A presumption of perfectly competitive markets is that buyers and sellers have complete information about market conditions. In fact, this is often far from the truth. On the simple point of making price comparisons, much research has been undertaken to show that buyers often have little knowledge of the going rate price for a particular category of product. For example, the use of bar-code scanning equipment by retailers has resulted in many products no longer carrying a price label, weakening customers' retained knowledge of prices. Sometimes, as in the case of telephone call tariffs or credit card interest charges, prices are very difficult to comprehend.

In Chapter 13 we will look at dynamic models of competitive market forces. In this respect, Michael Porter identified five forces which contribute to competition within a market: the power of suppliers, the power of buyers, the threat of new entrants, the threat of substitute products and the intensity of rivalry between competing firms. It should be stressed again that so far in this chapter we have merely looked at the basic building blocks by which we begin to understand competition within markets.

MONOPOLISTIC MARKETS

At the opposite end of the scale to perfect competition lies pure monopoly. In its purest extreme, monopoly in a market occurs where there is only one supplier to the market, perhaps because of regulatory, technical or economic barriers to entry which potential competing suppliers would face. Literally speaking, a monopoly means that one person or organization has complete control over the resources of a market. However, this rarely occurs in practice. Even in the former centrally planned economies of Eastern Europe, there have often been active 'shadow' markets which have existed alongside official monopoly suppliers. Sometimes, monopoly control over supply comes about through a group of suppliers acting in collusion together in a 'cartel'. As with the pure monopoly, companies would join a cartel in order to try to protect themselves from the harsh consequences (for suppliers) of competition. Probably the best example of a cartel is OPEC (oil producing exporting countries) which during the 1970s and 1980s had significant monopoly power over world oil price and output decisions.

Government definition of a monopoly is less rigorous than pure economic definitions. In the United Kingdom, two types of monopoly can occur:

1 A *scale* monopoly occurs where one firm controls 25 per cent of the value of a market.

2 A *complex* monopoly occurs where a number of firms in a market together account for over 25 per cent of the value of the market and their actions have the effect of limiting competition.

It can, however, be difficult to define just what is meant by 'the market'. While in Britain there may be just a few companies who between them have a near monopoly in the supply of bananas, when looked at in the context of the fruit market more generally, monopoly power diminishes. Also, is it most appropriate to confine attention to the UK market or to include overseas markets in a definition of monopoly? A firm may have a dominant market position at home, but may face severe competition in its overseas markets. In fact, the European Union now takes a Europe-wide perspective for assessing monopoly power for many products which can only sensibly be marketed Europe-wide. Therefore, although BAe Systems (formerly British Aerospace) has a dominant position in a number of its UK markets, when seen in a European context, it does in fact face severe competitive pressure.

Effects on prices and output of monopoly

A monopolist can determine the market price for its product and can be described as a 'price maker' rather than a 'price taker'. Where there are few substitutes for a product and where demand is inelastic, a monopolist may be able to get away with continually increasing prices in order to increase its profits.

In a pure monopoly market, consumers would face prices that are higher than would have occurred in a perfectly competitive market. Furthermore, because prices are higher, a downward sloping demand curve would indicate that output would be lower than in a competitive market. It is therefore commonly held that monopolies are against the public interest by leading to higher prices and lower output. Although there are occasionally circumstances where monopoly yields greater public benefit than free competition (discussed later in this chapter), the general policy of governments towards monopoly has been to restrict their power.

6.3.2 Implications of monopoly power for a firm's marketing activities

In a pure monopoly, a firm's output decisions would be influenced by the elasticity of demand for its products. So long as demand remained elastic, it could continue raising prices and thereby its total revenue. While a firm may have monopoly power over some of its users, it may face competition if it wishes to attract new segments of users. It may therefore resort to differential pricing when targeting the two groups. As an example, train operating companies have considerable monopoly power over commuters who need to use their trains to arrive at work in central London by 9.00 a.m. on weekdays. For such commuters, the alternatives of travelling to work by bus or car may be very unattractive. However, leisure travellers wishing to go shopping in London at off-peak times may be much more price sensitive. Their journey is optional to begin with and their flexibility with respect to their time of travel is greater. For them, the car or bus provides a realistic alternative. As a result, train operators offer a range of price incentives aimed at off-peak leisure markets, while charging full fare for its peak-period commuters.

Organizations that think strategically will be reluctant to fully exploit their monopoly power. By charging high prices in the short term, a monopolist could give signals to companies in related product fields to develop substitutes that would eventually provide effective competition. Blatant abuse of monopoly power could also result in a referral to the regulatory authorities (see below).

6.4 IMPERFECT COMPETITION

Perfectly competitive markets may be ideal for consumers because they have a tendency to minimize prices and maximize outputs. However, lower prices are not attractive to suppliers, because, for any given level of output, lower prices mean lower revenue and therefore lower profit. It is not surprising therefore that firms seek to limit the workings of perfectly competitive markets. It could be argued that most firms would like to be in the position of a monopolist and able to control the price level and output of their market. This is an unrealistic aim for most firms, but, in practice, firms can create imperfections in markets that give them limited monopoly power over their customers.

One of the assumptions of perfect competition is that products offered in a particular market are identical. An entrepreneur can seek to avoid head-on competition with its competitors by trying to sell something that is just a little bit different compared to its competitors. Therefore, in a market for fresh vegetables, a vegetable trader may try to get away from the fiercely competitive market for generic fresh vegetables, for which the price is determined by the market, by slightly differentiating its product. These are some possible differentiation strategies in respect of the sale of potatoes that it could pursue:

- The trader might concentrate on selling specially selected potatoes, for example ones that are particularly suited to baking.
- A delivery service might be provided for customers.
- The potatoes could be packed in materials that prevent them being bruised.
- The trader might offer a no-quibble money-back guarantee for people who buy potatoes that turn out to be bad.
- The potatoes could be baked and offered with a range of fillings.
- The potatoes might be processed into tinned or dried potatoes.
- As a result of any of the above actions, the trader could develop a distinct brand identity for the potatoes, so that buyers do not ask just for potatoes, but for 'Brand X' potatoes by name.

In the example above, the trader has taken steps to turn a basic commodity product into something that is quite distinctive, so it has immediately cut down the number of direct competitors that it faces. In fact, if its product really was unique, it would have no direct competition; in other words, it would be a monopoly supplier of a unique product. However, it must not be forgotten that although the way the trader has presented the potatoes may be unique, they are still broadly similar to the potatoes that everybody else is selling. The trader therefore still faces indirect competition, including competition from other foods such as rice and pasta which provide a substitute for potatoes.

If a trader has successfully differentiated its product, it is no longer strictly a price taker from the market. It may be able to charge 10p a kilogram more than the

---

THINKING AROUND THE SUBJECT

When is a white T-shirt more than just a T-shirt? The answer is when it has a desirable brand name emblazoned on it. This route to product differentiation can be highly profitable as consumers are prepared to pay hefty price premiums for brands that are currently in vogue. CDR International, a brand protection consultant, carried out research in 1998 to assess just how desirable some of our favourite brand names are. When shown a white T-shirt, consumers said they would, on average, pay a premium of 33 per cent if it carried a designer label. This premium was even higher (at 37 per cent) for those in the 16–35 age group, or in the C1 socio-economic group (who would be prepared to pay 42 per cent more). Protecting a brand name against illegal counterfeiting is always a challenge, and over half of respondents in CRD's survey claimed that they would be happy to buy good counterfeits. Which brands were considered the most desirable by carrying the highest price premium? The top brand was Nike, followed by Calvin Klein, Rolex, Adidas and Levi Strauss.

going rate for its selected and packaged potatoes, if customers think that the higher price is good value for a better product. It will be able to experiment to see just how much more buyers are prepared to pay for its differentiated product.

6.4.1   The role of brands

The process of branding is at the heart of organizations' efforts to remove themselves from fierce competition between generic products. Summarizing previous research, Doyle (1989) described brand building as the only way for a firm to build a stable, long-term demand at profitable margins. Through adding value that will attract customers, firms are able to provide a base for expansion and product development and to protect themselves against the strength of intermediaries and competitors. There has been much evidence linking high levels of advertising expenditure to support strong brands with high returns on capital and high market share (Buzzell and Gale, 1987) (Figure 6.12).

Branding simplifies the decision-making process by providing buyers with a sense of security and consistency which distinguishes a brand from a generic commodity. There have been many conceptualizations of the unique positioning attributes of a brand. These usually distinguish between tangible dimensions that can be objectively measured (such as taste, shape, reliability) and the subjective values that can only be defined in the minds of consumers (such as the perceived personality of a brand). With increasing affluence, the non-functional expectations of brands have assumed increasing importance. A number of dimensions of a brand's emotional appeal have been identified, including trust, liking and sophistication and it has been shown that products with a high level of subjective emotional appeal are associated with a high level of customer involvement (Laurent and Kapferer, 1985). This has been demonstrated, for example, in the preference shown for branded beer compared to a functionally identical generic beer. As consumers buy products, they learn to appreciate their added value and begin to form a relationship with them. For example, as Pitcher (1985) observed, there are many companies selling petrol and credit cards, but individual companies such as Shell and American Express have created brands with which customers develop a relationship and guide their choice in a market dominated by otherwise generic products.

The traditional role of branding has been to differentiate products, but brands have been increasingly applied to organizational images too. This has occurred particularly with services where the intangibility of the product causes the credentials of the provider to be an important choice criterion.

In recent years there has been a growth in the number of 'own label' or 'private label' products sold by retailers. The suggestion that the growth of generic products is challenging traditional product branding strategy can be partly explained by a shift in buyers' brand allegiance, away from those of manufacturers and towards those of intermediaries. Through continued investment, retailers have developed products that have comparable functional qualities to manufacturers' branded products. In many cases, retailers' own label products have developed a sufficiently

Figure 6.12
Toblerone has removed
itself from the fierce
competition for chocolate by
developing a distinctive
brand. By developing a
unique identity and
maintaining high quality
standards, the brand
commands a premium price
among those chocolate
buyers who value its
distinctive attributes

THINKING AROUND THE SUBJECT

How do people choose a taxi? In London, the famous black taxis are highly regulated in terms of the standards of drivers, the vehicle itself and prices charged. Drivers must pass a 'knowledge' test before being allowed to operate, and cannot refuse to carry a passenger, except in clearly specified situations. Few people would bother spending much effort in selecting one cab from another – they have been reduced to a commodity whose consistent standards and fares are rigorously maintained by the licensing body, the Public Carriage Office.

Contrast this with the situation in towns where regulations are minimal and buyers may have little idea about the integrity of the car that they are getting into or the reliability of its driver. This is the classic opportunity for the development of brands which help to differentiate one company's taxis from another's and simplify buyers' choice process. It is open to individual operators to develop a brand which is associated with reliability, safety and courteousness. Often, operators are allowed to set their own prices to reflect the strength of their brand. Next time a customer seeks a taxi, he or she may know which taxi companies to avoid and which to go for out of preference.

Debate has taken place between those who would like to see a free market in taxis and those who see regulation as vital to the public interest. What is the experience in your area? Of what value are brands in guiding the choices of taxi users?

strong brand reputation that they can command a price premium over other manufacturers' branded products.

Many have argued that both the functional and emotional dimensions of brands have been facing growing challenges. Research has suggested that consumers are becoming increasingly critical of the messages of brand-building advertising, especially those aimed at creating abstract brand personalities. It is also claimed that consumers are becoming increasingly confident, ready to experiment and to trust their own judgement and less tolerant of products that do not contribute to their own values. The functional qualities of brands have come under pressure from increasing levels of consumer legislation. Characteristics such as purity, reliability and durability may have traditionally added value to a brand, but these are increasingly enshrined in legislation and therefore less capable of being used to differentiate one product from another.

6.4.2   Imperfect competition and elasticity of demand

The analysis of price decisions for firms in a competitive market indicated that, for any one firm, price is given by the market. An individual firm cannot increase profits by stimulating demand through lower prices, nor would it gain any benefit by seeking to raise its prices. This changes in an imperfectly competitive market where a firm acquires a degree of monopoly power over its customers. Each firm now has a demand curve for its own unique product.

Firms face a downward sloping demand curve for each of their products, indicating that, as prices fall, demand increases and vice versa. In fact, a number of demand curves describing a firm's market can be described, ranging from the general to the specific brand. For example, in the market for breakfast cereals, the demand curve for cereals in general may be fairly inelastic, on the basis that people will always want to buy breakfast cereals of some description (Figure 6.13). Demand for one particular type of cereal, such as corn flakes, will be slightly more elastic as

Figure 6.13
A comparison of elasticities of demand for breakfast cereals at different levels of product specificity

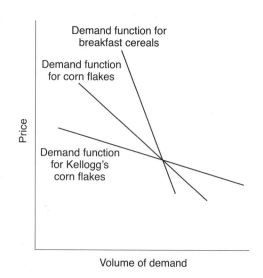

Table 6.1   Effects of elasticity of demand and price changes on total revenue

Price elasticity of demand	Price change	Revenue effect
High	+	−
(elastic demand)	−	+
Low	+	+
(inelastic demand)	−	−

people may be attracted to corn flakes from other cereals such as porridge oats on the basis of their relative price. Price becomes more elastic still when a particular brand of cereals is considered. To many people, Kellogg's corn flakes can be easily substituted with other brands of corn flakes, so if a price differential between brands developed, switching may occur. By lowering its price, a firm may be able to increase its sales, but what is important to firms is that they increase their total revenue (and, thereby, profits). Whether this happens depends upon the elasticity of demand for the product in question.

Total revenue is a function of total sales multiplied by the selling price per unit. Table 6.1 summarizes the effects on total revenue of changes in price, given alternative assumptions about elasticity.

<table>
<tr><td>6.4.3</td></tr>
</table>

Oligopoly

One step on from imperfect competition is a market structure often referred to as *oligopoly*. It lies somewhere between imperfect competition and pure monopoly. An oligopoly market is one that is dominated by a small number of sellers who provide a large share of the total market output. The crucial point about oligopoly markets is that all suppliers in the market are interdependent. One company cannot take price or output decisions without considering the specific possible responses of other companies.

Oligopoly is a particularly important market structure in industries where economies of scale are significant. They are typical of oil refining and distribution, pharmaceuticals, car manufacturing and detergents. Customers of oligopoly organizations may not immediately appreciate that the products they are buying come from an oligopolist as such firms often operate with a variety of brand names (the detergent manufacturers Unilever and Procter and Gamble between them have over 50 apparently competing detergent products on sale in the United Kingdom).

Oligopolists generally understand their relationship to one another and there is often a reluctance to 'rock the boat' by upsetting the established order. One firm is often acknowledged as the price leader and firms wait for their actions before adjusting their prices. In the UK car market, it has often been suggested that other manufacturers wait for Ford to adjust its prices before making their own price decisions. It has been suggested that firms may not match upward price movements, in the hope of gaining extra sales, but they would match downward

Americans are devoted to the idea that air travel is cheap following deregulation of the domestic market for air travel in the 1970s. But are low prices in fact a myth? And is it really a competitive market? The theory of airline deregulation in the United States was irresistible. Any United States airline would be allowed to operate on any route, setting its fares as it liked. New airlines soon appeared and initially held down fares through competitive pressures. However, the major carriers have since acquired such a dominant position that US air fares rose on average 20 per cent during 1997. What went wrong? The established airlines had managed to control 'slots' at the principal hub airports, making it difficult for new entrants to obtain slots. Many of the larger airlines also resorted to predatory pricing to keep away newcomers. This involves offering low fares on routes and at times that are competitive with other airlines, but charging higher fares where it has an effective monopoly. The lesson from US airline deregulation is that price competition may be expected in theory, but there are many reasons why it does not happen in practice. Even anti-interventionist governments recognize the need to intervene in order to maintain the competitiveness of a market.

price changes for fear of losing market share. Price wars between oligopolists can be very expensive to participants, so there is a tendency to find alternative ways to compete for customers, such as free gifts, coupons, added value offers and sponsorship activities.

Oligopolists have often been accused of collusion and creating barriers to entry for newcomers (such as signing exclusive distribution rights with key retailers). It has therefore been suggested that an oligopoly market structure is against the public interest. Against this argument, the public interest may benefit from economies of scale that allows products to be made at a lower unit cost than would be achievable by smaller scale companies. Furthermore, while oligopolists may have a cosy market in their home country, they may face severe competition as an outsider in overseas markets. The benefits of scale in their domestic market can give them the resources and low unit costs with which to tackle an overseas market, thereby helping a country's balance of trade and creating additional employment.

At a local level, it has frequently been suspected that groups of building contractors, school bus contractors, solicitors and estate agents covertly agree not to rock the boat by agreeing to conform to guidelines for pricing and tendering. The existence of trade and professional associations may provide a legitimate cover for such relationships and understandings to develop. In societies where business life is closely intermingled with social standing, the temptation to conform may be strengthened, and studies of eastern trading systems have highlighted this influence (Fock and Woo, 1998; Tsang, 1998). Some evidence of this can be seen in the extensive network of co-operative *keiretsu* and relationships among Japanese distributors that has led selling prices to consumers to be higher than in comparable overseas markets (Klinedinst and Sato, 1994; Goldman, 1991).

| 6.5 | **COMPETITION POLICY** |

The vision of competitive markets that bring maximum benefit to consumers is often not achieved. The imperfections described above can be summarized as resulting from:

1 The presence of large firms that are able to exert undue influence over participants in a market, for example through scale economies.

2 Collusion between sellers (and sometimes buyers) which has the effect of restricting price competition and the availability of products.

3 Barriers to market entry and restraints on trade which may prevent a company moving into a market (e.g. a manufacturer may prevent a retailer from selling competing manufacturers' products).

4 Rigidity in resource input markets which prevent supply moving to markets of strong demand (e.g. labour inflexibility may prevent a company from exploiting markets that have high levels of profitability).

Because of the presumed superiority of competitive markets, the law of most developed countries has been used to try to remove market imperfections where these are deemed to be against the public interest. This section initially considers the common law of England as a method by which anticompetitive practices have been curbed. More significantly, a growing body of legislation based on statute law is now available to governments and organizations seeking to curb anticompetitive practices.

| 6.5.1 | **Common law approaches to improving market competitiveness** |

Common law evolves over time on the basis of case judgments which set a precedent for subsequent cases to follow (see Chapter 9). There is case law that holds that agreements between parties that have the effect of restraining free trade are unlawful. Sometimes, it may appear to be sensible for a business person to make a contract with another company by which he or she agrees to limit the parties with whom they can trade in the future. In return for an exclusivity clause, the business person may receive preferential treatment from the other party. Such agreements have often been referred to as *solus agreements* and have been frequently used, for example in contracts between oil companies and petrol station owners. Such an agreement normally contains a tying covenant by which the station owner agrees, in return for a rebate on the price, to sell only the supplier's brand of petrol, a compulsory trading covenant that obliges the garage owner to keep the garage open at reasonable hours and a continuity covenant that requires him or her, if the business is sold, to obtain the acceptance of the agreement by the purchaser. In one important case, a garage owner had two garages and a solus agreement in respect of each, one for $4\frac{1}{2}$ years and the other for 21 years. The garage owner felt that the actions of the oil company were threatening his profits and sought to obtain his petrol from a cheaper source, in defiance of his agreement. The case came before the House of Lords which held that the essence of the solus agreements was to unreasonably restrict the garage proprietor's freedom of trading.

It is important to note the word 'reasonable'. In deciding whether the agreement between the oil company and petrol station owner was reasonable and therefore valid, the Law Lords stressed the importance of taking into account the public interest and held the $4\frac{1}{2}$ year agreement reasonable but the 21 year agreement too long and therefore unreasonable and invalid. The petrol station owner was therefore free to buy his fuel from another source, regardless of the agreement.

The 'public interest' is important in deciding whether a restrictive agreement is reasonable or not. The courts may feel that by tying a company to a supplier for 21 years, effective competition in a market is reduced, thereby resulting in higher prices for everybody.

While the case of the petrol station dated from the 1960s, more recent examples have been reported of firms seeking to rely on the common law to break free from a restrictive agreement. In the United Kingdom, tenants of pubs often sign agreements with breweries that prevent them buying much of their beer from third parties, in return for which the brewery may provide a tenancy agreement and other support for the tenant. A number of tenants have approached the courts to have clauses restricting their rights to make third party purchases of beer set aside, on the grounds that they have the effect of unreasonably restricting trade. To independent brewers seeking new outlets for their beer, it is important that such restraints on trade are removed to allow them access to the market.

A claim of restraint of trade can also be made against a company buying a business that restricts the future business activity of the person from whom they have bought the business. An individual who has set up a successful business may often be tempted by a take-over bid from another company. The acquiring company may be keen to grow so that it can achieve economies of scale, or it may simply want access to the target company's customers. Whatever the reason for the take-over, the acquiring company will often seek a clause restricting the seller of the business from going straight back into the marketplace and setting up another business which is in competition with the one that it has just sold. The owners of such businesses are usually required to agree to a clause that limits their rights to set up another estate agency business in competition with that of the acquiring company. Again, any clause has to be 'reasonable'. A clause prohibiting the seller of a business from setting up an estate agency chain within a 25 mile radius of its base for a period of three years from the date of sale would almost certainly be considered reasonable. A clause prohibiting the seller from entering into any form of business anywhere in the country within 10 years would almost certainly be deemed to be unreasonable. If a clause in an agreement is deemed by a court to be unreasonable, it may remove it from the contract. It can, however, be difficult to know what a court will consider to be 'reasonable' in the circumstances of a particular case.

6.5.2   Statutory intervention to create competitive markets

As the economy has become more complex, common law has proved inadequate on its own to preserve the competitiveness of markets. Common law has therefore been supplemented by statutory legislation, that is laws passed by government as an act of policy. One outcome of statutory intervention has been the creation of a regulatory infrastructure, which in the United Kingdom includes the Office of Fair Trading, the Competition Commission and regulatory bodies to control specific industries. However, much of the current regulatory framework in the United Kingdom is based on the requirements of Articles 85 and 86 of the Treaty of Rome.

6.5.3 **Articles 85 and 86 of the Treaty of Rome**

Article 85 of the Treaty of Rome prohibits agreements between organizations and arrangements between organizations that affect trade between member states of the European Union and in general prohibits anticompetitive practices, such as price fixing, market sharing and limitations on production. However, Article 85(3) provides for exemptions where restrictions on competition may be deemed to be in the public interest.

Article 86 prohibits the abuse of a dominant market position within the European Union in so far as it may affect trade between member states; the fact that a business has a monopoly position is not in itself prohibited.

The European Commission – which oversees implementation of Articles 85 and 86 – can prohibit mergers where the combined turnover exceeds €200 million or where the company will have over 25 per cent of a national market and the merger will have an adverse effect on competition.

The European Commission is playing an increasingly important role in the policing of competition in the United Kingdom. Among recent examples, it intervened to impose conditions in the proposed alliance between British Airways and American Airlines, which would have widespread implications for competition on air routes between Europe and the United States. In 1998, following a seven-year investigation of the sugar market, it fined British Sugar £28 million and Tate and Lyle £5 million for abusing the 90 per cent market share they had between them in order to keep prices artificially high.

The requirement contained in Articles 85 and 86 of the Treaty of Rome that competition shall not be distorted implies the existence in the market of *workable competition*. This can be interpreted as the degree of competition necessary to ensure the observance of the basic requirements and attainment of the objectives of the Treaty, in particular the creation of a single market achieving conditions similar to those of a domestic market. Workable competition reflects an economic pragmatism. *Perfect* competition where producers respond instantly and inevitably to consumer demand and where the efficient allocation of resources is ensured, is in practice an illusion. *Workable* competition is concerned to achieve the most efficient resource allocation available, given the constraints of a modern economy where consumer choice cannot be perfectly expressed (Weatherill, 1996).

The EU often has difficulty in reconciling the need for firms to operate globally at a large scale, and the resultant domination of the EU market by that firm. Proposed mergers between European airlines (e.g. a proposed merger between British Airways and the Dutch airline KLM) have raised the issue of whether it was justifiable to sacrifice competition on a small number of domestic routes in order to give an enlarged, efficient carrier a chance of taking on American carriers who were already operating at a large scale.

6.5.4   UK competition legislation

Domestic legislation is used to control anticompetitive practices where their effects are confined within national boundaries. In the United Kingdom, the 1998 Competition Act reformed and strengthened competition law by prohibiting anti-competitive behaviour. The Act introduced two basic prohibitions: a prohibition of anticompetitive agreements, based closely on Article 85 of the Treaty of Rome; and a prohibition of abuse of a dominant position in a market, based closely on Article 86 of the Treaty of Rome. The Act prohibits agreements which have the aim or effect of preventing, restricting or distorting competition in the United Kingdom. Since anticompetitive behaviour between companies may occur without a clearly delineated agreement, the prohibition covers not only agreements by associations of companies, but also covert practices.

A number of agencies have responsibility for preserving the competitiveness of markets in the United Kingdom, the most important being:

- The Director General for Fair Trading
- The Competition Commission
- Public utility regulators.

In addition, a number of other organizations are active either in using legislation to protect the competitiveness of markets or by drawing attention to abuses in monopoly power. At a local level, trading standards departments have powers to prosecute companies using misleading prices, among other things. Consumer champions who can draw attention to anticompetitive practices include Citizens Advice Bureaux, Ombudsmen and the media (discussed in more detail in Chapter 9).

6.5.5   The Office of Fair Trading

The UK Office of Fair Trading (OFT) is headed by the Director General of Fair Trading and has a general duty to keep under review commercial activities in the United Kingdom. On the advice of the OFT, the President of the Board of Trade may make an order to prohibit harmful consumer trade practices, infringement of which is a criminal offence. Trading standards departments of local authorities can report persistent offenders to the OFT which may prosecute in serious cases. It may also refer a case to the Competition Commission.

6.5.6   The Competition Commission

The Competition Commission (previously known as the Monopolies and Mergers Commission) has no power to initiate its own investigations. Instead, it responds to referrals which can be made by the following bodies:

- The Secretary of State for Trade
- The Director General of Fair Trading
- Public utility regulators
- The Independent Television Commission.

An investigation by the Competition Commission is normally completed within three months. The Commission only has power to make recommendations to the referring body. It is up to the latter whether the recommendations should be implemented. In the case of existing or potential monopolistic situations, the Commission can recommend divestment of assets or other action to reduce the undesirable elements of monopoly power.

6.5.7   **Evaluating claims of anticompetitive practices**

A fine balance often exists between the co-operation among firms which leads to lower prices/better products for consumers, and co-operation which leads to collusion and a reduction in consumer choice. There is diversity in interpretation of the notion of the 'public interest', which may be explained partly by cultural/ political factors, and developments in our understanding of the consequences of market imperfection. It is evident, for example, that contemporary interpretations of anticompetitive practices differ significantly between Japanese and European systems of government regulation.

Regulatory bodies are increasingly recognizing that co-operative relationships between companies can become anticompetitive. The following examples give an indication of recent thinking in the UK:

- A ruling by the Monopolies and Mergers Commission (the predecessor of the Competition Commission) into the UK impulse ice-cream market illustrates how a long-standing agreement aimed at delivering value to each party can be held to be anticompetitive. Bird's Eye Wall's had a 70 per cent market share of the UK impulse ice-cream market, and employed a series of tactics to defend its market domination, some of which attracted criticism for being anticompetitive. An MMC report published by the Department of Trade and Industry in July 1998 ruled that, on matters of distribution, Wall's had created ties through 'freezer exclusivity' agreements in an anticompetitive manner. In essence, freezer exclusivity as practised by Wall's involved supplying retailers with branded freezer units rent-free on condition that they were used to display only Wall's products. Nestlé, owner of the Lyons Maid brand, operated a similar system, although it had a much lower level of market penetration. For retailers, the offer of free equipment and the going rate of mark-up on ice cream sold might have appeared attractive. But this had the effect of creating a barrier to entry for market challengers such as Mars, for whom the established suppliers' exclusivity contracts provided a barrier through a time bond (because freezer contracts were typically provided over a period of several years); an economic bond (through cancellation clauses) and a psychological bond (through the reluctance of many small businesses to become involved in change).

■ Further evidence of manufacturers' attempts to use relationships to restrict competition was provided by EU allegations that Coca-Cola had been unfairly creating exclusive deals with retailers by offering incentives not to stock rival brands (Mazur, 1999). In 1999, European Union competition officials investigated Coca-Cola operations in Germany, Austria and Denmark, as well as three bottlers of the soft drink, to consider whether the company had been abusing its relationships with distributors.

■ Structural ties within a distribution channel have played an important role in the car sector, but these have been increasingly questioned by regulatory authorities. The UK car market is characterized by close control by car manufacturers of their local dealers. Ties are created through loans given by manufacturers to develop dealers' premises, extensive training by manufacturers of dealers' staff and service blueprints which prescribe the dealers' operations and limit their choice of supplier. Such close relationships have been allowed to continue under dispensation from the European Commission until 2003, justified, among other reasons by the relative ease with which vehicle safety recalls can be organized and spare parts made available. However, the closeness of the relationships between car manufacturers and their dealers which exist in the UK have been cited as a contributory factor to high comparative prices being charged for cars in the UK. The continued dispensation for this agreement illustrates the dynamic nature of the interpretation of the benefits of cooperation. The dispensation resulted partly from a political compromise and

---

THINKING AROUND THE SUBJECT

A typical bottle of perfume may cost only pennies to make, but can end up selling for £20–30 in UK stores. Inevitably, consumer groups have cried foul, accusing perfume companies of fixing prices. The companies' critics have pointed to the low prices charged for identical products in overseas markets where buyers are more price sensitive and the companies cannot sustain high prices. They also point to the refusal of the companies to supply perfumes to discount stores such as Tesco and Asda, who are pledged to lower the prices charged to consumers. This all sounds like a very anti-competitive situation that the Office of Fair Trading should seek to eradicate. But in fact, the OFT investigated the perfume sector in 1997 and amazed some of its critics by giving the perfume companies a clean bill of

health. Restricting sales to discount chains could be justified because such shops do not have trained staff to give advice about the company's products. More importantly, the OFT recognized that price often adds to the perceived value of a perfume. If a perfume became known for being low in price, the cachet associated with wearing it would be lost. People like to flaunt the fact that they have an expensive perfume.

Undaunted, discount retailers sought to obtain supplies of perfumes from the grey market in countries overseas where price levels are generally lower. Who is right? Should we be able to buy low price designer fragrances from the retailer that is prepared to obtain the best price? Or will the low-price in the long run destroy the value of the item that we seek?

the complexity of linking co-operation to public benefits. The reluctance of regulatory authorities to extend this dispensation may be a reflection of the growing political power of consumer interests relative to that of manufacturers.

■ In February 2001, a report by the OFT uncovered evidence of anticompetitive behaviour and price fixing within the legal, accountancy and architectural professions. The OFT made recommendations to end a variety of restrictive practices within the professions, for example the Bar rule which prevented members of the general public briefing barristers directly without going through a solicitor first.

6.5.8   ### Control on price representations

One of the assumptions of a perfectly competitive market is that participants in it have complete information about competing goods and services. In reality, buyers may find it very difficult to judge between competing suppliers because prices are disclosed in a deceptive or non-comparable manner. Legislation, such as the Consumer Protection Act 1987, makes it illegal for a company to give misleading statements about the price of goods or services. This not only helps to protect consumers from exploitation, but also helps to preserve the competitiveness of a market. Consumer protection legislation is considered in more detail in Chapter 9.

6.5.9   ### Regulation of public utilities

During the 1980s, the privatization of many UK public sector utilities resulted in the creation of new private sector monopoly companies, including those providing gas, water, telephones and electricity. The United Kingdom led the way in privatizing public utilities and many other countries have now followed its example.

To protect the users of these services from exploitation, the government response has been twofold:

1. Firstly, government has sought to increase competition, in the hope that the invisible forces of competition will bring about lower prices and greater consumer choice. In this way, the electricity generating industry was divided into a number of competing private suppliers (National Power, Powergen, Nuclear Electric, Scottish Power and Scottish Hydro), while conditions were made easier for new generators to enter the market. The problem here is that there may be very real barriers to entry in markets where the capital cost of getting started can be very high. For many of the newly privatized monopolies, effective competition proved to be an unrealistic possibility. It has not been possible, for example, to develop a competitive market for domestic water supply.

2. Where competition alone has not been sufficient to protect the consumer's interest, government has created a series of regulatory bodies which can determine the level and structure of charges made by these utilities. The regulatory bodies can determine the pattern of competition within a sector by influencing relationships between competitors and easing barriers to entry.

These are some of the more significant regulatory bodies in the United Kingdom:

Oftel – regulates the telecommunications sector
Ofgem – regulates the gas and electricity sectors
Ofwat – regulates the water supply sector.

In general, private sector companies operating in monopoly utility markets require a licence from their regulator to do so. The regulator takes a view as to what constitutes the public interest when reviewing operators' licences to trade. Prices charged, standards of service and speed of service are all factors that the regulator can insist the companies implement if they are to carry on trading. Unresolved issues can be referred from a regulator to the Competition Commission.

In utility markets where competition is absent, regulators have to balance what is desirable from the public's point of view with the companies' need to make profits, which will in turn provide new capital for investment in improvements. Over the long term, favouring consumers with short-term price constraints may result in lower investment in a sector, leading to supply shortages. Regulators are trying to combine market forces with a degree of centralized planning and there have been concerns about the difficulties of achieving this.

6.5.10   **Control of government monopolies**

Although the UK government has gone a long way in privatizing and deregulating markets that were previously the preserve of state organizations, there are still many services that cannot be sensibly privatized or deregulated. It is difficult, for example, to privatize roads or to expose consumers to serious competition for road space. It would be almost impossible to deregulate social services or the police force. It used to be thought that because the government actually provided the service, the public interest was thereby automatically protected. Government and the public were considered one and the same thing. However, with an increasingly consumerist society, it has become clear that what government thinks is good for the public is not necessarily what the public actually wants. Therefore, where it is impractical to privatize publicly provided services, government has taken a number of measures to try to protect consumers from exploitation. These are some of the methods that have been used:

1   *Arm's length organizations*   It was noted in Chapter 3 that agencies (such as QUANGOs) at 'arm's length' from government have grown in numbers in recent years. With these types of organizations, managers are given clearly defined targets which are intended to reflect the interests of the users of the service, rather than just the narrower interests of government.

2   *Market testing*   Sometimes, local and central government tests the market to see whether part of the work of a department can be subcontracted to an outside organization, or whether internal production represents 'best value'. Even some specialized services, such as accounting, architectural and legal services, have been put out to market tender. It is sometimes argued that a clear producer–buyer division makes it much easier for the body providing

TABLE 1 – *Potential savings (**standard rate** electricity)*

Payment Method ▶	Standard Credit			Direct Debit			Prepayment		
Electricity Usage ▶	Small	Medium	Large	Small	Medium	Large	Small	Medium	Large
Bill with Powergen	£136	£236	£336	£125	£226	£326	£144	£244	£345
Amerada / Amerada.co.uk	3-4	11-14	18-25	1-6	16-21	30-36	(38)	(58)	(77)
Atlantic Electric and Gas	7	24	41	7	24	41	(7)	(7)	(7)
British Gas	(1)	15	32	(1)	15	32	0	5	10
Eastern Energy	3	5	7	3	5	8	(7)	(8)	(7)
Energy Supplies UK	2	2	2	5	10	15	(30)	(43)	(56)
London Electricity / SWEB	7	12	17	0-7	8-12	16-17	(41)-(79)	(62)-(113)	(83)-(147)
Northern Electric & Gas	6	18	30	6	18	30	(16)	(20)	(25)
Norweb Energi	(1)	9	18	(6)	6	18	(7)	(7)	(7)
npower	8	26	44	2	22	42	(47)	(37)	(28)
Scottish and Southern	14	15	17	7	13	19	(22)	(29)	(37)
ScottishPower	2	18	34	1	21	42	(7)	(7)	(7)
Seeboard Energy	0	9	18	(2)	7	16	(7)	(7)	(7)
Swalec	14	15	17	7	13	19	(7)	(7)	(7)
Utility Link	(4)	18	40	(15)	8	30	(18)	2	22
Yorkshire Electricity	(6)	2	10	(2)	6	15	(29)	(21)	(12)

SAVINGS (£)

TABLE 2 – *Potential savings (**Economy 7** electricity)*

Bill with Powergen	£193	£333	£473	£182	£322	£462	£201	£341	£481
Amerada / Amerada.co.uk	4-7	4-6	4	1-4	4-5	5-7	(41)	(70)	(99)
Atlantic Electric and Gas	18	33	49	18	33	49	(7)	(7)	(7)
British Gas	(2)	13	28	(2)	13	28	3	10	17
Eastern Energy	3	4	7	3	5	7	(7)	(8)	(7)
Energy Supplies UK	4	5	5	2	4	5	(33)	(49)	(65)
London Electricity / SWEB	6	10	14	1-6	9-10	17	(37)-(88)	(53)-(127)	(69)-(167)
Northern Electric & Gas	13	14	14	13	14	14	(13)	(15)	(17)
Norweb Energi	5	9	14	5	11	16	(7)	(7)	(7)
npower	6	9	11	1	8	15	(36)	(33)	(31)
Scottish and Southern	17	21	24	12	21	30	(19)	(27)	(34)
Scottish Power	(9)	(4)	1	(8)	(1)	6	(40)	(35)	(31)
Seeboard Energy	(6)	(12)	(17)	(8)	(14)	(20)	(19)	(28)	(37)
Swalec	17	21	24	12	21	30	(7)	(7)	(7)
Utility Link	3	28	52	(7)	17	42	(12)	9	31
Yorkshire Electricity	(1)	9	19	3	13	23	(24)	(14)	(4)

SAVINGS (£)

The small print The saving figures are based on the assumption that you are currently a customer of Powergen. Bill calculations are based on annual consumptions of 1,650kWh (small), 3,300kWh (medium) and 4,950kWh (large) for standard rate electricity, and 3,300kWh (small) 6,600kWh (medium) and 9,900kWh (large) for Economy 7 electricity. Economy 7 bills assume 55% night time usage. The calculated bills of each company are compared with those of Powergen to work out your possible savings. All prices shown include VAT.

Figure 6.14

Better information about prices may help to improve the competitiveness of markets. Within the gas and electricity supply sectors, the UK government has been concerned that relatively few private customers have switched their supplier, possibly because of confusion about the true cost of competing companies' supplies. To try to overcome this, the regulatory body Ofgem operates the site, www.ofgem.gov.uk which aims to give visitors to the site a fair comparison of companies which are licensed to supply gas and electricity

(*Source*: Reproduced with permission of Ofgem)

money for a service to exercise control over standards of performance and to create a market at the point of production, even if not at the point of consumption. For example, a local authority producing its own refuse collection services has to balance the needs of consumers with its need for good industrial relations, etc. By contracting out the service, the authority can concentrate single-mindedly on ensuring that the contractor is performing to the agreed standard.

3 *Customers' Charters* These have become popular as a method of providing consumers of public services with standards of service which government organizations are expected to meet. They have been introduced to protect-health service patients and parents of school children, among others, against

poor service provided by a public sector monopoly organization. Cynics have dismissed them as government hype which conceals underlying expenditure cuts and unnecessarily raises consumers' expectations. However, by setting out standards of performance, a charter gives a clear message to the management and employees of a state organization about the standards that users expect of them.

CASE STUDY

RAIL SECTOR ADAPTS TO NEW COMPETITIVE ENVIRONMENT

The business environment of train services in Britain during the past 30 years has changed from a government monopoly to one in which numerous private sector companies compete, in theory at least. As the structure of the rail sector has changed from a centrally planned public service to a competitive private sector industry, new forms of pricing have emerged.

The political environment has had an important effect on the operation and pricing of train services. Before the 1960s, railways were seen as essentially a public service and fares were charged on a seemingly equitable basis which was related to production costs. Fares were charged strictly on a cost per mile basis, with a distinction between first and second class, and a system of cheap day returns which existed largely through tradition. From the 1960s, the state-owned monopoly British Rail moved away from social objectives with the introduction of business objectives. With this came a recognition that pricing must be used to maximize revenue rather than to provide social equality. However, government intervention occasionally came into conflict with British Rail's business objectives. As an example, it was instructed to curtail fare increases during the 1980s as part of the government's anti-inflation policy and again in the autumn of 1991 it was instructed to reduce some proposed Inter City fare increases on account of the poor quality of service on some routes.

The privatization of British Railways in the mid-1990s through the sale of franchises to 23 operating companies led to further developments in pricing. Recognizing the importance of maintaining an integrated passenger network, the government appointed a regulator of rail services with powers to specify fares charged for a range of types of ticket and to ensure that through tickets are still available for journeys which involve more than one rail company. However, the newly privatized companies exploited opportunities to offer new types of tickets targeted at different segments of the population. Virgin Railways used the experience of its airline to promote book-ahead tickets which offered bargain prices to fill off-peak capacity. At the same time, signs of genuine price competition between rival rail operators began to appear. Segments of the London–Scotland market were contested by Great North Eastern Railway and Virgin, while Chiltern Railways sought to appeal to the price sensitivity of travellers from Birmingham to London.

Yet despite the expectation that markets would become more competitive following privatization, many cynics have argued that little has changed since the days of British Rail. Competition between railways for passengers' business has only occurred in limited numbers of areas, while the regulator Ofrail retains substantial control over pricing and standards of service.

One constant theme in the development of railway pricing has been the proliferation of fares between any two points. For a return journey from Leicester to London, no fewer than 23 different fares were available in 2001. A number of market segments have been identified and a distinctive marketing mix has been developed for each. The business traveller typically has a need for the flexibility of travelling at any time of the day and because an employer is often picking up the bill, this segment tends to be relatively insensitive to the price charged. Some segments of the business market demand higher standards of quality and are prepared to pay a price of £73.00 for an executive package which includes 'first-class' accommodation and additional services such as meals and car parking. Leisure segments are on the whole more price sensitive and prepared to accept a lower level of flexibility. Those who are able to book their ticket one week in advance can pay just £18.

A keen eye is kept on the competition in determining prices. Students are more likely than business travellers to accept the coach as an alternative and therefore the Leicester to London student rail fare of £15.20 is pitched against the equivalent student coach fare of £11.75, the higher rail fare being justified on the basis of a superior service offering. For the business traveller, the comparison is with the cost of running a car, parking in London, and more importantly, the cost of an employed person's time. Against these costs, the executive fare of £73.00 is probably good value. For the family market, the most serious competition is presented by the family car, so a family discount railcard allows the family as a unit to travel for the price of little more than two adults.

The underlying cost of a train journey is difficult to determine as a basis for pricing. Fixed costs have to be paid by train operating companies to Railtrack for the use of the track and terminals. In addition, trains and staff represent a fixed cost, although many companies have sought to make these more flexible. Companies recognize that trains operating in the morning and afternoon peak periods cost more to operate as fixed costs of vehicles used solely for the peak period cannot be spread over other off-peak periods. The underlying costs of running commuter trains has been publicly cited by train operating companies as the reason for increasing season ticket charges by greater than the rate of inflation during recent years, although the fact that commuters often have no realistic alternative means of transport may have also been an important consideration in raising prices.

CASE STUDY Review questions

1 Should governments intervene to regulate rail fares?

2 Evaluate the financial benefits to rail operators of offering reduced fares to students.

3 Are train fares too expensive?

CHAPTER Summary and links to other chapters

This chapter has reviewed the variety of market structures that exist, and the effect market structure has on a firm's pricing and product decisions. Perfectly competitive markets are presumed to favour consumers, but can limit the revenues of profit-seeking firms. In their purest extreme, this market structure is unusual. Product differentiation is a means by which a firm can avoid head-on competition and can be strengthened with the development of distinctive brands and the application of new tech-nologies to develop new products (Chapter 12). The trend towards globalization of business (Chapter 10) is having the effects of making markets more competitive. This chapter has taken a microeconomic perspective on pricing and competition. Pricing is also affected by macroeconomic factors and these are discussed in Chapter 7. Public policy usually seeks control of anticompetitive practices and the legal framework for controlling such practices is discussed further in Chapter 9.

CHAPTER Review questions

1 In the context of market structure analysis, what are the options available to firms in a highly competitive market to improve profitability? (12 marks)

Select one of the options and discuss it, making clear how lasting the profit improvement is likely to be in the long run. (8 marks)

(Based on CIM Marketing Environment Examination)

2 Identify the impact and discuss the likely marketing response to two of the following environmen-tal changes affecting a major oil refining and distributing company:

- The introduction of a carbon tax
- A breakthrough in cost-effective solar power stations
- A well-financed new entrant entering its main market
- Teleconferencing and telecommunications growing rapidly
- Cut-price supermarket petrol sales expanding significantly.

(Based on CIM Marketing Environment Examination question)

3 You have been asked by your marketing director to provide a brief report analysing the profit-ability of your industry.

(a) Selecting an industry of your choice, identify the key elements of its structure and summarize the forces that determine its long run profitability. (12 marks)

(b) Append with your recommendations a note on the strategies a company could adopt in order to maintain or improve profitability. (8 marks)

(Based on CIM Marketing Environment Examination question)

4 (a) Show, using diagrams, what would happen to the market price of compact discs if a new technological development suddenly allowed CDs to be produced at a much lower cost than previously.

(b) What factors might cause the demand curve for CDs to shift upwards?

5 In a medium-sized English town, one bus company recently agreed to buy the operations of another operator, giving the acquiring company over 80 per cent of the local market for scheduled bus services. In view of a possible referral of the take-over by the Office of Fair Trading to the Competition Commission, assess the advantages and disadvantages to the public of the existence of a local monopoly.

6 Summarize the problems facing the government in its attempts to control the price of public water supply.

References

Buzzell, R.D. and Gale, B.M. (1987) *The PIMS Principle*, Free Press, New York.

Doyle, P. (1989) 'Building successful brands: The strategic options', *Journal of Marketing Management*, vol. 5, no. 1, pp. 77–95.

Fock, H. and Woo, K. (1998) 'The China market: strategic implications of Quanxi', *Business Strategy Review*, vol. 7, no. 4, pp. 33–43.

Goldman, A. (1991) 'Japan's distribution system: institutional structure, internal political economy, and moderniza- tion, *Journal of Retailing*, vol. 67, no. 2, pp. 154–183.

Klinedinst, M. and Sato, H. (1994) 'The Japanese co-operative sector', *Journal of Economic Issues*, vol. 28, no. 2, pp. 509–517.

Laurent, G. and Kapferer, J.-N. (1985) 'Measuring consumer involvement profiles', *Journal of Marketing Research*, February, vol. 22, pp. 41–53.

Mazur, L. (1999) 'Watchdogs bite back at abuse by monopolies', *Marketing*, 29 July, p. 16.

Pitcher, A. (1985) 'The role of branding in international advertising', *International Journal of Advertising*, vol. 4, no. 3, pp. 241–246.

Tsang, W.K. (1998) 'Can Quanxi be a source of sustained competitive advantage for doing business in China', *The Academy of Management Executive*, vol. 12, no. 2, pp. 64–74.

Weatherill, S. (1996) *Cases and Materials on EC Law*, 3rd edn, Blackstone Press, London.

Selected further reading

This chapter has provided only a very brief overview of the principles of economics as they affect pricing. For a fuller discussion, one of the following texts is useful:

Grant, S.J. (2000) *Stanlake's Introductory Economics*, 7th edn, Longman, Harlow.

Lipsey, R.G. and Chrystal, K.A. (1999) *Principles of Economics*, 9th edn, Oxford University Press, Oxford.

The following provides a more applied approach to price determination:

Hanna, N. and Dodge, R. (1997) *Pricing*, Macmillan, Basingstoke.

The following article examines the impacts of the Internet on price awareness and levels of competition within a market:

Sinha, I. (2000) 'Cost transparency: the net's real threat to prices and brands', *Harvard Business Review*, March, vol. 78, no. 2, pp. 43–47.

There is now extensive literature on the benefits of brand building and how it adds value to consumers:

Aaker, D. (1996) *Building Strong Brands*, Free Press, New York.

Aaker, D.A. and Joachimsthaler, E. (1999) The lure of global branding', *Harvard Business Review*, November– December, vol. 77, pp. 137–142.

Chernatony, L. de and McDonald, M. (1998) *Creating Powerful Brands*, Butterworth-Heinemann, Oxford.

Gardiner, P. and Quintin, S. (1998) 'Building brands using direct marketing: a case study', *Marketing Intelligence and Planning*, January–February, vol. 16, no. 1, pp. 6–12.

Competition policy and law is reviewed in the following references:

Cini, M. and McGowan, L. (1997) *Competition Policy in the European Union*, Macmillan, Basingstoke.

Dosi, G., Teece, D. and Chytry, J. (1997) *Technology, Organization and Competitiveness*, Oxford University Press, Oxford.

Furse, M. (2000) *Competition Law of the UK & EC*, Blackstone, London.

Helm, D. and Jenkinson, T. (1997) *Competition in Regulated Industries*, Clarendon Press, Oxford.

Korah, V. (1997) *Cases and Materials on EC Competition Law*, Hart, Oxford.

Useful websites

DTI: Building the knowledge driven economy   Background paper relating to the government's White Paper 'Our Competitive Future: Building the Knowledge Driven Economy'. The paper covers issues of knowledge as a means towards competitive advantage.   **http://www.dti.gov.uk/comp/competitive/an.reprt.htm**

Competition Commission   Home page of the UK Competition Commission, providing links to previous cases investigated by the Commission.   **http://www.competition-commission.gov.uk/**

Key terms

Anticompetitive practices	Markets
Brands	Monopoly
Competition Commission	Oligopoly
Demand	Perfect competition
Elasticity of Demand	Price determination
Elasticity of Supply	Regulation
Imperfect competition	Supply
Market structure	

chapter

7

The national economic environment

CHAPTER OBJECTIVES

Few organizations can avoid being affected by the state of their macroeconomic environment. Such factors as the amount of money in consumers' pockets, the interest rate that businesses have to pay on loans and the value of the exchange rate all affect business organizations to a lesser or greater degree. The aim of this chapter is to understand the nature of the national economy – or macroeconomic environment – in which organizations operate. Special attention is given to the reading of economic indicators, which can help organizations to anticipate and react rapidly to a change in the economic environment. Business cycles are an important fact of life and this chapter reviews how governments seek to manage them and business organizations prepare for them.

7.1 MACROECONOMIC ANALYSIS

In the previous chapter, microeconomic analysis of a firm's competitive environment made a number of assumptions about the broader economic environment in which the firm operates. In the analysis of supply and demand in any given market, changes in household incomes or government taxation were treated as an uncontrollable external factor to which a market responded. For most businesses, a sound understanding of this broader economic environment is just as important as understanding short-term and narrow relationships between the price of a firm's products and demand for them.

An analysis of companies' financial results has often indicated that business people attribute their current success or failure to the state of the economy. For example, a retail store that has just reported record profit levels may put this down to a very high level of consumer confidence, while a factory that has just laid off workers may blame a continuing economic recession for its low level of activity. Few business people can afford to ignore the state of the economy because it affects the willingness and ability of customers to buy their products. It can also affect the price and availability of its inputs. The shop that reported record profits may have read economic indicators correctly and prepared for an upturn in consumer spending by buying in more stocks or taking on more sales assistants.

This chapter is concerned with what has often been described as *macroeconomic* analysis. Although the workings of the economy at a national level are the focus of this chapter, it must be remembered that even national economies form part of a larger international economic environment. Issues of international economic analysis will be returned to in Chapter 10.

This chapter begins by analysing the structure of the national economy and the interdependence of the elements within this structure. The national economy is a complex system the functioning of which is influenced by a range of planned and unplanned forces. While unplanned forces (such as turbulence in the world economic system) can have significant impacts on the national economic system, organizations are particularly keen to understand the planned interventions of governments, who seek to influence the economy for a variety of social and political reasons.

7.2   THE STRUCTURE OF THE ECONOMY

Most analyses of national economies divide the productive sectors into three categories:

1. The primary sector which is concerned with the extraction and production of basic raw materials from agriculture, mining and oil exploration, etc.
2. The secondary sector which transforms the output of the primary sector into products that consumers can use (e.g. manufacturing, construction, raw material processing, etc.)
3. The services sector.

Comparisons can be drawn between the three sectors described above and value chains described in Chapter 1. In general, these three sectors add progressively higher levels of value to a product.

A further division in the economy occurs between the productive sector and the consumption sector. Intervening as both a producer and a consumer, government provides a third element of an economy. The relationship between producers and consumers is the basis for models of the circular flow of income, discussed later in this chapter.

7.2.1   Measures of economic structure

The relative importance of the three productive sectors described above has been changing. Evidence of this change is usually recorded by reference to three key statistics:

1. The share of gross domestic product (GDP) which each sector accounts for.
2. The proportion of the labour force employed in the sector.
3. The contribution of the sector to a nation's balance of payments.

A key trend in Britain, like most developed economies, has been the gradual decline in importance of the primary and manufacturing sectors, and the growth in the services sector. The extent of the change in the UK economy, when measured by shifts in GDP and employment, is indicated in Table 7.1.

While the statistics in Table 7.1 appear to show a number of clear trends, the figures need to be treated with a little caution for a number of reasons:

1. Fluctuations in the value of GDP for the primary sector often have little to do with changes in activity levels, but instead reflect changes in world commodity

Table 7.1 Composition of the UK productive sector					
	1969	1979	1989	1995	1999
Primary					
Share of GDP (%)	4.3	6.7	4.2	2.7	3.4
Workforce (%)	3.6	3.0	2.1	1.4	1.7
Secondary					
Share of GDP (%)	42.0	36.7	34.5	30.1	26.1
Workforce (%)	46.8	38.5	28.9	18.3	20.0
Services					
Share of GDP (%)	53.0	56.5	61.3	67.2	70.5
Workforce (%)	49.3	58.5	69.0	76.5	78.3

Source: Compiled from *Economic Trends, Employment Gazette.*

levels. Oil represents a major part of the UK's primary sector output, but the value of oil produced has fluctuated from the very high levels of the early 1980s to the very low levels of the 1990s, largely reflecting changes in oil prices.

2   The level of accuracy with which statistics have been recorded has been questioned, especially for the services sector. The system of Standard Industrial Classifications (SICs) for a long while did not disaggregate the service sector in the same level of detail as the other two sectors.

3   Part of the apparent growth in the services sector may reflect the method by which statistics are collected, rather than indicating an increase in overall service level activity. Output and employment is recorded according to the dominant business of an organization. Within many primary and secondary sector organizations, many people are employed producing service-type activities, such as cleaning, catering, transport and distribution. Where a cook is employed by a manufacturing company, output and employment is attributed to the manufacturing sector. However, a common occurrence during recent years has been for manufacturing industry to contract out many of these service activities to external contractors. Where such contracts are performed by contract catering, office cleaning or transport companies, the output becomes attributable to the service sector, making the service sector look larger, even though no additional services have been produced – they have merely been switched from internally produced to externally produced.

Nevertheless, the figures clearly indicate a number of significant trends in the economy:

1   The primary sector in the United Kingdom, like in most developed economies, has been contracting in relative importance. There are supply- and demand-

side explanations of this trend. On the supply side, many basic agricultural and extractive processes have been mechanized, resulting in them using fewer employees and thereby consuming a lower proportion of GDP. Many primary industries have declined as suppliers have been unable to compete with low-cost producers in countries that are able to exploit poor employment working conditions. On the demand side, rising levels of affluence have led consumers to demand increasingly refined products. In this way, consumers have moved from buying raw potatoes (essentially a product of the primary sector) to buying processed potatoes (e.g. prepared ready meals) which involve greater inputs from the secondary sector. With further affluence, potatoes have been sold with added involvement of the service sector (e.g. eating cooked potatoes in a restaurant).

2 Output of the secondary sector in the United Kingdom fell from 42 per cent of GDP in 1969 to 26 per cent in 1999, reflecting the poor performance of manufacturing industry. This can again be partly explained by efficiency gains by the sector, requiring fewer resources to be used, but more worryingly by competition from overseas. The emergence of newly industrialized nations with a good manufacturing infrastructure and low employment costs, rigidities in the UK labour market, declining research and development budgets relative to overseas competitors and the effects of exchange rate policy have all contributed to this decline.

3 In respect of its share of GDP, the services sector saw almost continuous growth during the period 1969–99, with banking, finance, insurance, business services, leasing and communications being particularly prominent. In 1999, the services sector accounted for 70 per cent of GDP, up from 53 per cent in 1969.

7.2.2 Towards a service economy?

Today, there is little doubt that the services sector has become a dominant force in developed economies, accounting for about three-quarters of all employment in the United States, United Kingdom, Canada and Australia. Between 1980 and 1992, it is reported that the EU created almost 1.3 million new jobs per year in the services sectors – twice the average for the rest of the economy (Eurostat, 1995).

The United Kingdom, like many developed economies, has traditionally run a balance of trade deficit in manufactured goods (i.e. imports exceed exports), but has made up for this with a surplus in 'invisible' service 'exports'. In 1999, while the United Kingdom's visible balance was in deficit by £26.7 billion, there was an invisible surplus of £11.5 billion.

During periods of recession in the manufacturing sector, the service sector has been seen by many as the salvation of the economy. Many politicians have been keen to promote the service sector as a source of new employment to make up for the diminishing level of employment within the primary and secondary sectors. A common argument has been that the United Kingdom no longer has a competitive cost advantage in the production of many types of goods and therefore these sectors of the economy should be allowed to decline and greater attention paid to those service sectors that showed greater competitive advantage. The logic of this argument can be pushed too far, in particular:

- A large part of the growth in the service sector during the 1980s and 1990s reflected the buoyancy of the primary and secondary sectors during that period. As manufacturing industry increases its level of activity, the demand for many business-to-business services such as accountancy, legal services and business travel increases. During periods of recession in the manufacturing sectors, the decline in manufacturing output has had an impact on the services sector, evidenced, for example, through lower demand for business loans and export credits.

- The assumption that the United Kingdom has a competitive cost advantage in the production of services needs to be examined closely. In the same way that many sectors of UK manufacturing industry lost their competitive advantage to developing nations during the 1960s and 1970s, there is evidence that the once unquestioned supremacy in certain service sectors is being challenged. Financial services markets which achieved prominence in London when the United Kingdom was the world's most important trading nation are increasingly following world trade to its new centres such as Frankfurt. High levels of training in some of Britain's competitor nations have allowed those countries to firstly develop their own indigenous services and then to develop them for export. Banking services which were once a net import of Japan are now exported throughout the world.

- Over-reliance on the service sector could pose strategic problems for the United Kingdom. A diverse economic base allows a national economy to be more resilient to changes in world trading conditions.

7.2.3   International comparisons

There appears to be a high level of correlation between the level of economic development in an economy (as expressed by its GDP per capita) and the strength of its services sector. It is debatable whether a strong services sector leads to economic growth or is a result of that economic growth. The debate can be partly resolved by dividing services into those that are used up in final consumption and those that provide inputs to further business processes (see below).

The International Labour Office's *Year Book of Labour Statistics* (ILO, 1997) illustrates the magnitude of these differences in 1995 (or the most recent year for which figures were available at that date). The more highly developed economies were associated with high percentages of workers employed in the services sector, for example the United States (75 per cent), Canada (75 per cent), Australia (74 per cent), the United Kingdom (70 per cent) and Switzerland (69 per cent). Western countries that are considered to be less developed have proportionately fewer employed in their services sector, for example Spain (59 per cent), Portugal (53 per cent), Ireland (53 per cent) and Greece (49 per cent). The lowest levels of services employment are found in the less developed countries, for example Mexico (29 per cent), Bangladesh (28 per cent) and Ethiopia (9 per cent).

7.2.4 — Consumer, producer and government sectors

Consumer goods and services are provided for individuals who use up those goods and services for their own enjoyment or benefit. No further economic benefit results from the consumption of the product. In this way, the services of a hairdresser can be defined as consumer services. On the other hand, producer goods and services are those that are provided to other businesses in order that those businesses can produce something else of economic benefit. In this way, a road haulage company sells services to its industrial customers in order that they can add value to the goods that they produce, by allowing their goods to be made available at the point of demand.

The essential difference between production and final consumption sectors is that the former creates wealth while the latter consumes it. Traditionally, economic analysis has labelled these as *firms* and *households* respectively. The discussion later in this chapter will indicate problems that may arise where an apparently prosperous household sector is not backed by an equally active production sector.

There has been continuing debate about the role of government in the national economy which has led to shifts in the proportion of GDP accounted for by the public sector. During the 1980s, the UK government regarded the public sector as a burden on the country and set about dismantling much of the state's involvement in the economy. Privatization of public corporations and the encouragement of private pensions were just two manifestations of this. By the mid-1990s, the proportion of UK government expenditure as a proportion of total GDP appeared to have stabilized in the range 38–42 per cent, with increasing social security spending offsetting much of the reduction in expenditure accounted for by state-owned industries. Figure 7.1 illustrates the cyclical nature of public spending and taxation as a proportion of UK GDP.

Governments do not always take such a 'hands-off' approach. The economies of Eastern Europe have in the past been dominated by central planning in which the government determined the lion's share of income and expenditure in the

Figure 7.1
Trends in UK government taxation and spending as a proportion of GDP 1978–2000
(*Source:* Based on *Annual Abstract of Statistics*)

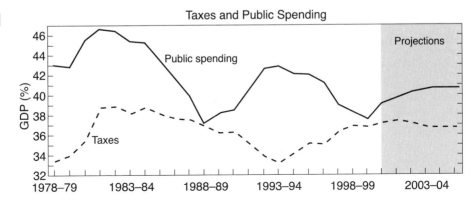

economy. Even in Britain shortly after the Second World War, the government assumed a very major role in the economy, with the nationalization of many essential industries.

Organizations need to keep their eyes on political developments which shift the balance of resources between public and private sectors. A company that is involved in the marketing of health service products, for example, will be very interested in the government's view about the respective roles to be played by the private sector and the National Health Service.

7.3   THE CIRCULAR FLOW OF INCOME

Households, firms and government are highly interdependent and the level of wealth created in an economy is influenced by the interaction between these elements. To understand the workings of a national economy, it is useful to begin by developing a simple model of a closed economy comprising just two sectors – firms and households – which circulate money between each other.

The simplest model of a circular flow of income involves a number of assumptions:

- Households earn all their income from supplying their labour to firms.

- Firms earn all their income from supplying goods and services to households.

- There is no external trade.

- All income earned is spent (i.e. households and firms do not retain savings).

In this simple model, the income of households is exactly equal to the expenditure of firms and vice versa. It follows that any change in income from employment is directly related to changes in expenditure by consumers. Similarly, any change in sales of goods and services by firms is dependent upon employment. In this simplified economy, income, output, spending and employment are all interrelated (Figure 7.2). Of course, this simplified model of the economy is almost impossible

Figure 7.2
The circular flow of income based on a simplified model of a national economy

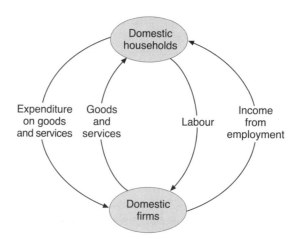

to achieve in practice, because most economies are affected by factors that upset this stable equilibrium pattern of income and expenditure.

Instability in this static model can come about for two principal reasons: additional money can be injected into the circular flow, while money currently circulating can be withdrawn. Injections have the effect of increasing the volume and speed of circulation of money within this flow, while withdrawals have the opposite effects.

Withdrawals can take a number of forms:

- Savings by households which occur when income is received by them but not returned to firms.

- Government taxation which removes income received by households and prevents them from returning it to firms in the form of expenditure on goods and services. Taxation of businesses diverts part of their expenditure from being returned to households.

- Spending on imported goods and services by households means that this money is not received by firms, who cannot subsequently return it to households in the form of wages.

The opposite of withdrawals are injections, and these go some way to counterbalancing the effects described above in the following ways:

- Firms may earn income by selling goods to overseas buyers. This represents an additional source of income which is passed on to households.

- Purchases by firms of capital equipment which represents investment as opposed to current expenditure.

- Instead of reducing the flow of income in an economy through taxation, governments can add to it by spending on goods and services.

A revised model of the circular flow of income, incorporating these modifications, is shown in Figure 7.3. This modified model of the economy still involves a number of fairly unrealistic assumptions (e.g. that consumers do not borrow money). In addition, it is unrealistic to assume that households only earn income from employment activity. They also receive it from returns on investments, property rentals and self-employment. However, it serves to stress the interdependence of the different sectors of the economy and the fact that, through this interdependence, changes in behaviour by one group can result in significant changes in economic performance as a whole. Of particular interest to government policy makers and businesses alike is the effect on total economic activity of changing just one element in the circular flow. This is commonly referred to as the *multiplier effect* (described below).

7.3.1   **The Phillips machine model of the economy**

In an attempt to demonstrate the workings of the economy, the Phillips machine model draws on the principles of fluid dynamics. The basic principle of the model is

Figure 7.3
A modified
circular flow of
income
incorporating
injections and
withdrawals

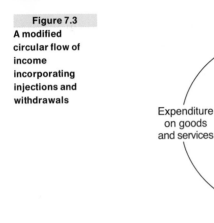

Figure 7.4
The Phillips
machine model of
how the national
economy works

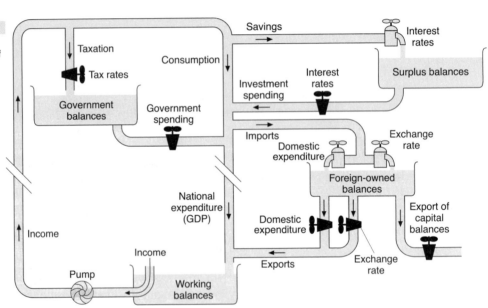

that water circulates around the machine's tubes in an analogous way to money circulating around the economy (Figure 7.4).

One starting point for the machine is to consider the holding tank which contains the total amount of money available for transactions. The fuller the tank, the greater the amount of money that flows into the neighbouring chamber as incomes. These are then pumped to the top of the machine from where they cascade down through the machine's central chambers. Some of this is taken out of the flow as government taxation, while additional money re-enters the flow as government expenditure. Further amounts are drawn off as some households choose to save some of their incomes. These savings flow into a tank holding households' surplus balances, some of which are used to finance spending on investment, which re-enters the main flow later. The higher the level of surplus balances available for investment, the lower the interest rate and the greater the amount of new investment. Interest rates can be held constant by drawing some of the surplus funds into a spare tank at the back of the machine. The main flow now comprises consumers' spending, some of which goes on imports, thereby building up foreigners' holdings of sterling in another tank, thereby lowering the value of sterling. The fuller the tank, and therefore the lower the exchange rate, the greater the flow out of the pipe at the bottom which comprises exports. The exchange rate can be held constant by diverting foreign-held sterling into another tank at the back.

The main flow now represents total national expenditure, which equals total national income. It falls back into the bottom tank from which it started, thereby topping up balances available for transactions. The flow throughout the system can be modified by inserting partial blockages at strategic points. The resulting flows move pens which record the impact on key variables such as domestic expenditure and exports.

7.3.2   The multiplier effect

The multiplier effect can be compared to the effects of throwing a stone into a pond of water. The impact of the stone with the water will cause an initial wave to be formed, but beyond this will be waves of ever-decreasing strength. The strength of these ripples will lessen with increasing distance from the site of original impact and with the passage of time. Similarly, injecting money into the circular flow of income will have an initial impact on households and businesses directly affected by the injection, but will also be indirectly felt by households and firms throughout the economy.

The multiplier effect can be illustrated by considering the effects of a major capital investment by private sector firms or by government. The firm making the initial investment spends money buying in supplies from outside (including labour) and these outside suppliers in turn purchase more inputs. The multiplier effect of this initial expenditure can result in the total increase in household incomes being much greater than the original expenditure. A good example of the multiplier effect at work in the United Kingdom is provided by the Millennium Dome project at Greenwich, opened in 2000. An important reason for the government supporting this project was the desire to regenerate an economically depressed part of London. Government expenditure initially created employment during the construction of the Dome and from new operations within the Dome itself. This expenditure then rippled out to other business sectors, such as hotels and transport. The level of activity generated additional demand for local manufacturing industry, for example visitors require food that may be produced locally, the producers of which may in turn require additional building materials and services to increase production facilities.

The extent of the multiplier effects of initial expenditure is influenced by a number of factors. Crucial is the extent to which recipients of this initial investment recirculate it back into the national economy. If large parts of it are saved by households or used to buy imported goods (whether by firms or by households), the multiplier effects to an economy will be reduced. In general, income that is received by individuals who have a high propensity to spend each additional pound on basic necessities is likely to generate greater multiplier benefits than the same money received by higher income households who have a greater propensity to save it or to spend it on imported luxuries. The implications of this for government macroeconomic policy will be considered later.

The multiplier effect can be used to analyse the effects of withdrawals from the circular flow as well as injections. Therefore, if firms spend less on wages, household income will fall as a direct result, leading indirectly to lower spending by households with other domestic firms. These firms will in turn pay less to households in wages, leading to a further reduction in spending with firms, and so on.

Multiplier effects can be studied at a local as well as a national level. Government capital expenditure is often made with a view to stimulating areas of severe unemployment (as in the case of the Millennium Dome and grants given by Regional Development Agencies to support private sector investment in Tyneside). However, whether the local economy is helped will depend upon how much subsequent expenditure is retained within the area. In one study of the regional multiplier effects of siting a call centre for British Airways in a deprived part of Tyneside, it was found that a high proportion of the staff employed commuted in from other, more prosperous areas, thereby limiting the multiplier benefits to the deprived area.

As well as examining the general macroeconomic effects of spending by firms on household income and vice versa, multiplier analysis can also be used to assess the impact of economic activity in one business sector upon other business sectors. Many economies suffer because vital economic infrastructure remains undeveloped, preventing productivity gains in other sectors. The availability of transport and distribution services has often had the effect of stimulating economic development at local and national levels, for example following the improvement of rail or road services. The absence of these basic services can have a crippling effect on the development of the primary and manufacturing sectors – one reason for Russian agriculture not having been fully exploited has been the ineffective distribution system available to food producers.

One approach to understanding the contribution of one business sector to other sectors of the economy is to analyse input–output tables of production and data on labour and capital inputs. In one study (Wood, 1987) these were used to estimate the effects that productivity improvements in all of the direct and indirect supply sectors had on the productivity levels of all other sectors. Thus, some apparently high productivity sectors (such as chemicals) were shown to be held back by the low productivity of some of their inputs. On the other hand, efficiency improvements in some services such as transport and distribution were shown to have had widespread beneficial effects on the productivity contribution of other sectors.

7.3.3   The accelerator effect

Changes in the demand for consumer goods can lead, through an accelerator effect, to a more pronounced change in the demand for capital goods. This phenomenon

Figure 7.5
The accelerator effect on new aircraft orders of changes in passenger demand

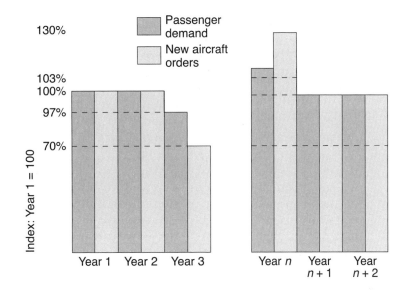

is known as the *accelerator effect*. A small increase in consumer demand can lead to a sudden large increase in demand for plant and machinery with which to satisfy that demand. When consumer demand falls by a small amount, demand for plant and machinery falls by a correspondingly larger amount.

The accelerator effect is best illustrated by reference to an example (Figure 7.5) based on consumers' demand for air travel and airlines' demands for new aircraft. In this simplified example, an airline operates a fleet of 100 aircraft and during periods of stable passenger demand buys 10 new aircraft each year and retires 10 older aircraft, retaining a stable fleet size of 100 aircraft. Then, some extraneous factor (e.g. a decline in the world economy) may cause the airline's passenger demand to fall by 3 per cent p.a. The airline responds to this by reducing its capacity by 3 per cent to 97 aircraft (assuming that it can reschedule its aircraft so that it is able to accommodate all of its remaining passengers). The easiest way to achieve this is by reducing its annual order for aircraft from 10 to 7. If it continued to retire its 10 oldest aircraft, this would have the effect of reducing its fleet size to 97, in line with the new level of customer demand. What is of importance here is that while consumer demand has gone down by just 3 per cent, the demand facing the aircraft manufacturer has gone down by 30 per cent (from 10 aircraft a year to 7). If passenger demand settles down at its new level, the airline will have no need to cut its fleet any further, so will revert to buying 10 new aircraft a year and selling 10 old ones. If passenger demand picks up once more, the airline may seek to increase its capacity by ordering not 10 aircraft, but, say, 13.

7.3.4   **Inflation**

It should be apparent that multiplier effects are associated with injections to the circular flow of income, causing more money to chase a fixed volume of goods and services available for consumption. This leads to the classic case of *demand pull inflation*, when excessive demand for goods and services relative to their supply results in an increase in their market price level. Demand pull inflation can result from an increase in the availability of credit, excessive spending by government and tax cuts that increase consumers' disposable incomes, so allowing them to buy more goods and services.

An alternative cause of inflation is referred to as *cost push inflation*. On the supply side, increases in production costs (such as higher wage costs, rising raw material costs, higher overheads, additional costs of health and safety legislation) may push up the price at which companies are prepared to supply their goods to the market, unless they are offset by increases in productivity.

An inflationary spiral can be created where higher wages in an economy result in greater spending power, leading to demand pull inflation. The resulting higher cost of consumer goods leads workers to seek wage increases to keep them ahead of inflation, but these increases in wage costs add a further twist to cost-plus inflation, and so on. Because markets are seldom perfectly competitive and therefore unable to correct for inflation, governments are keen to intervene to prevent inflationary processes building up in an economy (see below).

7.3.5   Complex models of the economy

The simple model of the economy presented above is based on many assumptions which need to be better understood if model making is to make a useful contribution to policy making. It is important for governments to have a reasonably accurate model of how the economy works so that predictions can be made about the effects of government policy. A model should be able to answer such questions as:

■ What will happen to unemployment if government capital expenditure is increased by 10 per cent?

■ What will happen to inflation if income tax is cut by 2p in the pound?

■ What will be the net effect on government revenue if it grants tax concessions to firms investing in new capital equipment?

Companies supplying goods and services also take a keen interest in models of the economy, typically seeking to answer questions such as:

■ What effect will a cut in income tax have on demand for new car purchases by private consumers?

■ How will company buyers of office equipment respond to reductions in taxation on company profits?

■ Will the annual budget create a feeling of confidence by consumers which is sufficiently strong for them to make major household purchases?

Developing a model of the economy is very different from developing a model in the natural sciences. In the latter case, it is often possible to develop closed models where all factors that can affect a system of interrelated elements are identifiable and can be measured. Predicting behaviour for any component of the model is therefore possible based on knowledge about all other components. In the case of economic models, the system of interrelated components is open rather than closed. This means that not only is it difficult to measure components, it can be difficult to identify what elements to include as being of significance to a national economy. For example, few models accurately predicted that a sudden rise in oil prices by OPEC producers would have a major effect on national economies throughout the world. Furthermore, it is very difficult to develop relationships between variables that remain constant through time. Whereas the relationship between molecules in a chemistry model may be universally true, given a set of environmental conditions, such universal truths are seldom found in economic modelling. This has a lot to do with the importance of attitudes of firms and consumers which change through time for reasons that may not become clear until after the event. For example, a 2 per cent cut in income tax may have achieved significant increases in consumer expenditure on one occasion, but resulted in higher levels of savings or debt repayment on another occasion. The first time round, factors as ephemeral as good weather and a national success in an international football championship could have created a 'feel good' factor which was absent the following time round.

7.4 THE BUSINESS CYCLE

From the discussion in the previous sections, it should become quite apparent that national economies are seldom in a stable state. The situation where injections exactly equal withdrawals can be described as a special case, with the normal state of affairs being for one of these to exceed the other. An excess of injections will result in economic activity increasing, while the opposite will happen if withdrawals exceed injections. This leads to the concept of the business cycle which describes the fluctuating level of activity in an economy. Most developed economies go through cycles that have been described as:

- Recession–prosperity
- Expansion–contraction
- Stop–go and
- 'Boom and bust'

Figure 7.6 shows the pattern of the business cycle for the United Kingdom, as measured by fluctuations in the most commonly used indicator of economic activity – the gross domestic product (described below).

7.4.1 Measuring economic activity

Gross domestic product (GDP) is just one indicator of the business cycle. In fact, there are many indicators of economic activity that may move at slightly different times to each other. Some 'leading' indicators may be used as early warning signs of an approaching economic recession, with other indicators – if not corrected by

Figure 7.6
Annual rate of
change of UK
gross domestic
product
(*Source:* Based on
Annual Abstracts of
Statistics)

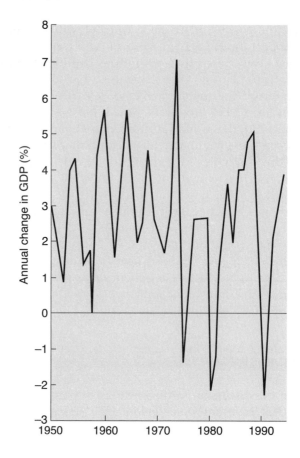

government intervention – following a similar trend in due course. Some of the more commonly used indicators of the business cycle are described below.

Gross domestic product   This index measures the total value of goods and services produced within the economy and can be used to compare economic performance over time and to compare performance between countries. In a typical year, the economies of Western Europe countries may expand by 2–3 per cent p.a., although this has reached 4–5 per cent in boom years, while GDP has actually fallen during recessionary periods. Until their financial difficulties of the late 1990s, many 'tiger' economies of the Far East had sustained growth rates of GDP in the order of 5–8 per cent p.a. One derivative of this index is a figure for GDP per capita. Therefore, if GDP is going up by 2 per cent a year and the population is constant, it means that, on average, everybody is 2 per cent better off. Whether this is true in reality, of course, depends not only on how the additional income is distributed but also on an individual's definition of being better off (GDP takes no account of 'quality of life').

Unemployment rates   Because of the profound social and economic implications of high levels of unemployment, governments normally monitor changes in unemployment levels closely. Unemployment tends to rise as the economy enters a general economic recession and falls as it enters a period of recovery. Unemployment occurs where firms are unable to sell their output and seek to scale back their workforce, either by laying off existing workers or not recruiting new ones. This results in less spending by the growing number of unemployed people, thereby exacerbating firms' sales difficulties. Actually measuring trends in unemployment over time can be difficult, as definitions used by governments frequently change. Cynics would say that this is done to hide the true level of unemployment, for example by excluding people who are on job training schemes.

Output levels   The output of firms is an important indicator of the business cycle, and is closely watched because of its effects on employment and the multiplier effects of firms producing less and therefore spending less with their suppliers. In the United Kingdom, the government's *Business Monitor* publishes regular indicators of outputs for different sectors. Another widely quoted source of data on output is the Confederation of British Industry (CBI) which publishes monthly and quarterly surveys on industry's output, investment and stock levels. This provides a good indication of changes in different sectors of the economy and possible future business trends. In addition to these widely used and formalized methods of measuring output, a number of *ad hoc* approaches have been used, which it is claimed give early indicators of an economic recovery or downturn. Examples include:

- Sales of first-class tickets by train operating companies, where a fall in sales is often an early indication of firms cutting back expenditure ahead of major cuts in output.

- The number of commercial vehicles crossing the Severn Bridge between England and Wales has been correlated with output of the manufacturing sector in general.

- Sales of Ford Transit vans have been associated with a revival in fortunes by the small business sector and rising sales of heavy trucks with growing confidence by firms to invest in capital equipment.

Average earnings   Unemployment figures record the extreme case of workers who have no employment. However, underemployment can affect the national economy just as importantly as unemployment as workers are put on short-time working or lose opportunities for overtime working. Conversely, average earnings may rise significantly during the early years of a boom as firms increase overtime working and bid up wage rates in an attempt to take on staff with key skills.

Disposable income   Average disposable income refers to the income that individuals have available to spend after taxation. It follows that as taxes rise, disposable income falls. A further indicator of household wealth is discretionary income, which is a measure of disposable income less expenditure on the necessities of life, such as mortgage payments. Discretionary income can be significantly affected by sudden changes in the cost of mortgages and other items of expenditure, such as travel costs, which form a large component of household budgets.

Consumer spending   Trends in consumer spending may diverge from trends in discretionary income on account of changes in consumers' propensity to borrow or save. When consumer spending runs ahead of discretionary income, this can be explained by an increase in borrowing. Conversely, spending may fall faster than discretionary income, indicating that consumers are repaying debts and/or not borrowing additional money. There are numerous indicators of consumer spending, including the government's Family Expenditure Survey. More up-to-date information is supplied by the Credit Card Research Group (CCRG), an organization representing the main UK credit card issuers. After making a number of assumptions about changing card-using habits, CCRG is able to monitor changes in the volume of consumer spending using credit cards. It is also able to monitor consumer borrowing using credit cards and net repayments of credit card debts.

Savings ratio   The savings ratio refers to the proportion of individuals' income that is saved rather than spent. Saving/borrowing levels are influenced by a number of factors, including the distribution of income in society (poorer people tend to save less, therefore any redistribution of income to this group would have the effect of reducing net savings) and consumers' level of confidence about the future (see below). During periods of high consumer confidence, savings ratios tend to fall as consumer borrowing rises. This was true of the expansionary period of the late 1980s when the proportion of household income saved reached a low point of 2.8 per cent. During the recessionary years of the mid- to late 1990s, savings ratios increased sharply, reaching a high point of 12 per cent in 1996 before gradually falling again to 3.5 per cent in the more prosperous year of 2000. Businesses look to a fall in savings ratios as an early indicator of increasing consumer confidence.

Confidence levels   Private individuals and businesses may have a high level of income and savings, but there is no guarantee that they will spend that money or take on new debt in making purchases of expensive items. They may only be happy about making major spending decisions if they feel confident about the future. Higher confidence may result, for example, from consumers feeling that they are not likely to be made unemployed, that their pay is going to keep up with inflation and that the value of their assets is not going to fall. A number of confidence indices are now published, for example by chambers of commerce and the CBI, covering both private consumers and businesses. The organization GfK publishes a monthly Consumer Confidence Barometer for the European Commission.

Inflation rate   Inflation refers to the rate at which prices of goods and services in an economy are rising. A commonly used general indicator of inflation in the United Kingdom is the retail prices index (RPI) which is based on information collected about the prices of goods and services consumed by an average household. This is a commonly used 'headline' rate of inflation which is frequently used by employees as a basis for wage negotiations and is used by the UK government for adjusting the value of a number of social security benefits. The RPI may be too general to be of relevance to the spending patterns of certain individuals or organizations, so there are numerous alternative indices covering specific sectors. Many building societies, for example, produce indices of house price inflation, while specialized indices are available for new car purchases and construction costs, among others. The government publishes a monthly producer prices index which measures changes in the prices of goods bought by manufacturing firms. A rise in this indicator can signal later increases in the RPI when the components are incorporated into finished goods bought by households. Inflation affects different groups of consumers with different effects. During a period of falling interest rates and fuel prices, a home-owning, car-using household may experience negative inflation, leaving it with greater discretionary income. At the same time, the cost of public transport and rented housing may be increasing, leaving groups dependent on public transport and paying rents to a housing association facing a high level of inflation, thereby leaving less discretionary income.

Interest rates Interest rates represent the price that borrowers have to pay to a lender for the privilege of using its money for a specified period of time. Interest rates tend to follow a cyclical pattern which is partly a reflection of the level of activity in the economy. During periods of recession, the supply of funds typically exceeds demand for them (caused, for example, by consumers being reluctant to spend, thereby building up their savings, and by the unwillingness of consumers and firms to borrow to pay for major expenditure items). In these circumstances, interest rates have a tendency to fall. During a period of economic prosperity, the opposite holds true, and interest rates have a tendency to rise. Rates are also influenced by government intervention, as governments have frequently used them as a tool of economic management. In general, low interest rates are seen as desirable because they reduce the cost of firms' borrowings and increase consumers' level of discretionary income through lower mortgage costs. However, during periods of unhealthily excessive demand in the economy, governments use high interest rates to try to dampen down demand from firms and consumers.

Overseas trade figures The monthly overseas trade figures indicate the difference between a country's imports and exports. A lot of attention is given to the 'current account' which measures overseas transactions in goods and services but not capital (discussed further in Chapter 10). In general, a current account surplus is considered good for an economy, suggesting that an economy's production sector is internationally competitive. A detailed analysis of overseas trade figures indicates trends that can often be related to the business cycle and can be used to predict future levels of activity in the economy. At the height of a boom cycle, imports of manufactured goods may rise much faster than corresponding exports, possibly suggesting unsustainable levels of household consumption. Rising imports of capital equipment may give an indication that firms are ready to invest in additional domestic productive capacity following the end of a period of recession.

Throughout much of the 1990s, growth of the US economy seemed almost unstoppable. Was this the dawn of the New Economy in which governments manage to manipulate economies so effectively that the historical pattern of 'boom and bust' became a thing of the past? Sadly, towards the end of 2000, the US economy came back to earth.

What causes such long and sustained booms, such as the US economy had just enjoyed? Can we learn anything from previous booms that might help us to understand future business cycles?

The economic historian Angus Maddison undertook an analysis of the world economy over the past millennium and noted just three periods of rapid advance in incomes per head. The first occurred from 1950–73, when average global real incomes per head rose at a compound annual rate of 2.9 per cent. The other two periods were 1973–98 and 1870–1913. In the last two periods, average real incomes per head rose at a compound average annual rate of 1.3 per cent.

Interestingly, these periods of prolonged economic boom appeared to have three things in common:

1 Each of these periods was associated with a process of rapid international economic integration, with trade and global capital flows growing faster than world output. For example between 1973 and 1988, world exports rose from 10.5 per cent of world GDP to 17.2 per cent.

2 All three periods were associated with significant catching up by laggard economies with world leading economies. Between 1870 and 1913, the catching up was by Western Europe, the United States and some former European colonies, on the United Kingdom; between 1950 and 1973, it was by Western Europe, Japan and a few small east Asian countries, on the United States; and between 1973 and 1998, it was by much of the rest of Asia (including China), again on the United States. It was noted that the bigger the gap between the laggards and the leaders, the faster the rate of convergence has been.

3 The final feature of these periods has been a historically unprecedented rate of technological advance, generating rising real incomes per head in the world's most advanced economies.

The declining costs of transport and communications undoubtedly lie behind much of the development of the global economy over the last several centuries. The Internet should be seen as just the latest innovation which continues a long historical sequence.

But what about the future? Over the past couple of decades, the world's two most populous countries, China and India, with 2.25 billion people between them – (or just under 40 per cent of the total world population) – have been growing faster than both the world as a whole and its economic leaders. Should this lead us to believe that economic growth will continue? Can the rate of technological advance be sustained? Between 1973 and 1995, the rate of US growth in labour productivity per hour fell to just under 1.5 per cent a year, from 3 per cent between 1950 and 1973. Even with the development of the Internet, are rates of growth in productivity sustainable? Looking ahead, what new scientific and technological advances are likely to sustain a continued growth in productivity?

Exchange rates   The exchange rate is the price of one currency in terms of another (e.g. an exchange rate of £1 = $1.55 means that £1 costs 1.55 dollars). A number of factors influence the level of a country's exchange rate, but as an economic indicator the rate is often seen as an indication of the willingness of overseas traders and investors to hold that country's currency. Falling rates of exchange against other currencies may be interpreted as overseas investors losing their confidence in an economy or its government, leading them to sell their currency holdings and thereby depressing its price. The theory of exchange rate determination and the implications for business are discussed in more detail in Chapter 10.

7.4.2   **Tracking the business cycle**

It is easy to plot business cycles with hindsight. However, businesses are much more interested in predicting the cyclical pattern in the immediate and medium-term future. If the economy is at the bottom of an economic recession, that is the ideal time for firms to begin investing in new productive capacity. In this case, accurate timing of new investment can have two important benefits:

1   Firms will be able to cope with demand as soon as the economy picks up. At the end of previous economic recessions, demand has often initially outstripped the restricted supply, leading many domestic firms and consumers to buy from overseas. Firms have often only invested in new capacity once overseas competitors have built up market share, and possibly created some long-term customer loyalty, too.

2   At the bottom of the business cycle, resource inputs tend to be relatively cheap. This particularly affects wage costs and the price of basic raw materials such as building materials. Good timing can allow a firm to create new capacity at a much lower cost than it would incur if it waited until it was well into the upturn, when rising demand would push up resource costs.

Analysing turning points in the business cycle has therefore become crucial to marketers. To miss an upturn at the bottom of the recession can result in a firm missing out on opportunities when the recovery comes to fruition. On the other hand, reacting to a false signal can leave a firm with expensive excess stocks and capacity on its hands. A similar problem of excess capacity can result when a firm fails to spot the downturn at the top of the business cycle.

It is extremely difficult to identify a turning point at the time when it is happening. Following the recession of the early 1990s, there were a number of false predictions of an upturn, some politically inspired by governments keen to encourage a 'feel-good' factor ahead of an election. There was a widespread feeling in 1994 that the UK economy had reached a turning point and many companies began investing in new stock and capacity in expectation of this upturn. When the predicted revival in domestic consumer expenditure failed to transpire, companies in product fields as diverse as cars, fashion clothing and electrical goods were forced to sell off surplus stocks at low prices.

Getting out of a trough in the business cycle is very dependent upon the confidence of firms and individuals about the future. Cynics may argue that governments are acting in a politically opportunistic way by talking about the onset of recovery. However, if the government cannot exude any confidence for the future, there is less likelihood of firms and individuals being prepared to invest their resources for the future.

Firms try to react to turning points as closely as possible in a number of ways:

■ Companies that are highly dependent on the business cycle frequently subscribe to the services of firms that have developed complex models of the economy and are able to make predictions about future economic performance. Some of these models (such as those developed by major firms of stockbrokers) are general in their application and based on models of the economy used by government policy makers in the Treasury. Specialized models seek to predict demand for more narrowly defined sectors, such as construction.

■ Companies can be guided by key lead indicators which have historically been a precursor of a change in activity levels for the business sector. For a company manufacturing heavy trucks, the level of attendance at major truck trade

What happens to consumers' spending patterns in the shops when recession sets in? The more expensive retailers insist that quality shines through in hard times, while discount retailers say that they will win business from more expensive competitors. The out-of-town shopping centres may claim that they are a natural destination for bargain hunters and will attract families who are watching their pennies. By contrast, their high street rivals say that cash-strapped families will be spending in dribs and drabs and will make the occasional shopping trip to town but will not have enough discretionary income to justify a visit to an out-of-town centre.

Amidst this hype and speculation, a survey by HSBC bank identified furniture, cars and DIY goods as the first casualties of a downturn. HSBC estimated that for every 1 per cent drop in consumer spending, sales of vehicles would drop by 4.64 per cent; furniture and electrical goods by 1.87 per cent; and DIY sales by 1.61 per cent. The sectors most protected are utilities which should suffer only a 0.32 per cent fall for every 1 per cent drop in spending; newspapers and books (0.32 per cent) and food (0.36 per cent). This is borne out in the financial performance of retailers during the recession of the early 1990s, when companies such as Harveys Furnishings, Dixons and Wickes DIY all suffered falls in profit, while Boots and W H Smith's profits actually rose.

Despite the analysis of spending patterns during previous recessions, doubts often remain that things will be the same next time around. Could DIY stores actually benefit as people trade down from paying people to do their maintenance and building work for them? And what about food? Could people actually increase their spending, as they substitute premium ready prepared meals or more expensive eating out at restaurants?

exhibitions could indicate the number of buyers who are at the initial stages in the buying process for new trucks.

■ Instead of placing all their hopes in accurate forecasts of the economy, companies can place greater emphasis on ensuring that they are able to respond to economic change very rapidly when it occurs. At the bottom of the cycle, this can be facilitated by developing flexible production methods, for example by retaining a list of trained part-time staff who can be called on at short notice, or having facilities to acquire excess capacity from collaborating firms overseas at very short notice. At the top of the cycle, the use of short-term contracts of employment can help a company to downsize rapidly at minimum cost. The development of 'efficient customer response' systems seeks to simplify supply chains so that orders can be fulfilled rapidly without the need to carry large stockholdings.

7.5   MACROECONOMIC POLICY

The national economy has been presented as a complex system of interrelated component parts. To free market purists, the system should be self-correcting and need no intervention from governments. In reality, national economies are not closed entities and equilibrium in the circular flow can be put out of balance for a number of reasons, such as:

■ Increasing levels of competition in the domestic market from overseas firms who have gained a cost advantage.

■ Changes in a country's ratio of workers to non-workers (e.g. the young and elderly).

■ Investment in new technology which may replace firms' expenditure on domestic wages with payments for capital and interest to overseas companies.

Most Western governments have accepted that the social consequences of free market solutions to economic management are unacceptable and they therefore intervene to manage the economy to a greater or lesser extent.

7.5.1   Policy objectives

This section begins by reviewing the objectives governments seek to achieve in their management of the national economy.

Maintaining employment   However unemployment is defined, its existence represents a waste of resources in an economy. Individuals who have the ability and willingness to work are unable to do so because there is no demand from employers for their skills. Workers' services are highly perishable in that, unlike stocks of goods, they cannot be accumulated for use when the economy picks up. Time spent by workers unemployed is an economic resource that is lost for ever. Most developed economies recognize that unemployed people must receive at least the basic means of sustenance, so governments provide unemployment benefit. Rising unemployment increases government expenditure. As well as representing a wasted economic resource, unemployment has been associated with widespread social problems, including crime, alcoholism and drug abuse. High levels of unemployment can create a divided society, with unemployed people feeling cut off from the values of society while those in employment perceive many unemployed as being lazy or unwilling to work.

In general, governments of all political persuasions seek to keep unemployment levels low, in order to avoid the social and economic problems described above. However, many suspect that governments with right-wing sympathies are more likely to tolerate unemployment on the grounds that a certain amount of unemployment can bring discipline to a labour market which could otherwise give too much economic bargaining power to workers. An excess of labour supply over demand would result in wages paid to workers falling, at least in a free market. This may itself be seen as a desirable policy objective by lowering prices for consumers and increasing firms' competitiveness in international markets.

In their attempts to reduce unemployment, governments must recognize three different types of unemployment which each require different solutions:

1   Structural unemployment occurs where jobs are lost by firms whose goods or services are no longer in demand. This could come about through changing fashions and tastes (e.g. unemployment caused by the closure of many traditional UK seaside hotels); because of competition from overseas (for example, many jobs in the textile, ship building and coal mining industries have been lost to lower-cost overseas suppliers); or a combination of these factors. Where a local or national economy is very dependent upon one business sector and workers' skills are quite specific to that sector, the effects of structural employment can be quite severe, as can be seen in the former ship building areas of Tyneside or coal mining areas of South Wales. Governments have tackled structural employment with economic assistance to provide retraining for unemployed workers and Regional Assistance Grants to attract new employers to areas of high unemployment.

2   Cyclical unemployment is associated with the business cycle and is caused by a general fall in demand, which may itself be a consequence of lower spending levels by firms. Some business sectors, such as building and construction, are particularly prone to cyclical patterns of demand, and hence cyclical unemployment. The long-term cure for cyclical employment is a pick-up in demand in the economy, which governments can influence through their macroeconomic policy.

3   Technological unemployment occurs where jobs are replaced by machines and has had widespread implications in many industrial sectors such as car manufacture, banking and agriculture. Governments have to accept this cause of unemployment, as failure to modernize will inevitably result in an industry losing out to more efficient competition. For this reason, attempts to subsidize jobs in declining low-technology industries are normally doomed as overseas competitors gain market share, and eventually lead to job losses which are

greater than they would have been had technology issues been addressed earlier. Where a low-technology sector is supported by import controls, consumers will be forced to pay higher prices than would otherwise be necessary. Where the goods or services in question are necessities of life, consumers' discretionary income will effectively fall, leading to lower demand for goods and services elsewhere in the economy. Although technological unemployment may be very painful to the individuals directly involved, the increasing use of technology usually has the effect of making necessities cheaper, thereby allowing consumers to demand new goods and services. One manifestation of this has been the growth in services jobs, as consumers switch part of their expenditure away from food and clothing (which have fallen in price in real terms) towards eating out and other leisure pursuits.

Stable prices Rapidly rising or falling prices can be economically, socially and politically damaging to governments. Rapidly rising prices (inflation) can cause the following problems:

- For businesses, it becomes difficult to plan ahead when selling prices and the cost of inputs in the future are not known. In many businesses, companies are expected to provide fixed prices for goods and services which will be made and delivered in the future at unknown cost levels.

- Governments find budgeting difficult during periods of high inflation. Although many government revenues rise with inflation (e.g. value added tax), this may still leave an overall shortfall caused by higher costs of employing government workers and higher contract costs for new capital projects.

- Inflation can be socially divisive as those on fixed incomes (e.g. state pensioners) fall behind those individuals who are able to negotiate wage increases to compensate for inflation. Inflation also discriminates between individuals who own different types of assets. While some physical assets such as housing may keep up with inflation, financial assets may be eroded by inflation rates that exceed the rate of interest paid. In effect, borrowers may be subsidized by lenders.

- High levels of inflation can put exporters at a competitive disadvantage. If the inflation level of the United Kingdom is higher than competing countries, UK firms' goods will become more expensive to export, while the goods from a low-inflation country will be much more attractive to buyers in the United Kingdom, all other things being equal. This will have an adverse effect on UK producers and on the country's overseas balance of trade (assuming that there is no compensating change in exchange rates).

High levels of inflation can create uncertainty in the business environment, making firms reluctant to enter into long-term commitments. Failure to invest or reinvest can be ultimately damaging for the individual firm as well as the economy as a whole.

This is not to say that completely stable prices (i.e. a zero rate of inflation) is necessarily good for a national economy. A moderate level of price inflation encourages individuals and firms to invest in stocks, knowing that their assets will increase in value. A moderate level of inflation also facilitates the task of realigning prices by firms. A price reduction can be achieved simply by holding prices constant during a period of price inflation. Where price inflation causes uncertainty for firms purchasing raw materials, this uncertainty can often be overcome by purchasing on the 'futures' market. Such markets exist for a diverse range of commodities such as oil, grain and metals and allow a company to pay a fixed price for goods delivered at a specified time in the future, irrespective of whether the market price for that commodity has risen or fallen in the meantime.

The opposite of inflation is deflation, and this too can result in social, economic and political problems:

■ Individuals and firms who own assets whose value is depreciating perceive that they have become poorer and adjust their spending patterns accordingly. In Britain during the early 1990s, many individuals saw their most important asset – their house – falling in value as part of a general fall in property prices. In extreme cases, individuals felt 'locked' into their house as they had borrowed more to buy it than the house was currently worth. They therefore had difficulty trading up to a larger house, thereby possibly also creating demand for home-related items such as fitted kitchens. More generally, falling property prices undermined consumers' confidence, in sharp contrast to the 1980s when rising house prices created a 'feel good' factor, fuelling spending across a range of business sectors.

■ Individuals and firms will be reluctant to invest in major items of capital expenditure if they feel that, by waiting a little longer, they could have obtained those assets at a lower price.

■ Deflation can become just as socially divisive as inflation. Falling house prices can lead many people who followed government and social pressures to buy their house rather than renting to feel that they have lost out for their efforts.

Economic growth   Growth is a goal shared by businesses and governments alike. It was suggested in Chapter 3 that businesses like to grow, for various reasons. Similarly, governments generally pursue growth in gross domestic product for many reasons:

■ A growing economy allows for steadily rising standards of living, when measured by conventional economic indicators. In most Western economies, this is indicated by increased spending on goods and services that are considered luxuries. Without underlying growth in GDP, increases in consumer spending will be short lived.

■ For governments, growth results in higher levels of income through taxes on incomes, sales and profits. This income allows government to pursue socially and politically desirable infrastructure spending, such as the construction of new hospitals or road improvements.

■ A growing economy creates a 'feel good' factor in which individuals feel confident about being able to obtain employment and subsequently feel confident about making major purchases.

Economic growth in itself may not necessarily leave a society feeling better off, as economic well-being does not necessarily correspond to quality of life. There is growing debate about whether some of the consequences of economic growth, such as increased levels of pollution and traffic congestion, really leave individuals feeling better off. There is also the issue of how the results of economic growth are shared out between members of a society.

Distribution of wealth Governments overtly and covertly have objectives relating to the distribution of economic wealth between different groups in society. In the United Kingdom, the trend since the Second World War has been for a gradual convergence in the prosperity of all groups, as the very rich have been hit by high levels of income, capital gains and inheritance taxes, while the poorer groups in society have benefited from increasing levels of social security payments. During periods of Labour administrations, the tendency has been for taxes on the rich to increase, tilting the distribution of wealth in favour of poorer groups. However, the period of the Conservative governments in the 1980s saw this process put into reverse as high income groups benefited from the abolition of higher rates of income tax and the liberalization of inheritance taxes. At the same time, many social security benefits were withdrawn or reduced in scope or amount, leaving many lower or middle income groups worse off. The post-1997 Labour government has tended to reverse this trend, for example by introducing a statutory minimum wage and increasing a number of benefits paid to disadvantaged groups.

The effects of government policy objectives on the distribution of income can have profound implications for organizations' marketing activities. During most of the post-Second World War years, the tendency was for mid-market segments to grow significantly. In the car sector, this was associated with the success of mid-range cars such as the Ford Escort and Mondeo. During periods of Labour administration, the sale of luxury cars had tended to suffer. The boom of the late 1980s and mid-1990s saw the rapid rise in income of the top groups in society, resulting in a significant growth in luxury car sales. Manufacturers such as BMW, Mercedes Benz and Jaguar benefited from this trend. At the same time, the worsening of the fortunes of many lower income groups partly explained the growth in very low-priced basic cars such as those manufactured by Lada, Skoda and FSO.

Stable exchange rate A stable value of sterling in terms of other major currencies is useful to businesses which are thereby able to accurately predict the future cost of raw materials bought overseas and the sterling value they will receive for goods and services sold overseas. Stable exchange rates can also help consumers, for example in budgeting for overseas holidays. It is, however, debatable just what the 'right' exchange rate is that governments should seek to maintain (this is discussed further in Chapter 10).

An important contributor to maintaining a stable exchange rate is the maintenance of the balance of payments. Governments avoid large trade deficits, which

The Future Foundation reported in 2001 that there is likely to be a significant growth in the wealth of the richest 20 per cent of the UK population. It predicted that the wealth of this group would increase by 50 per cent during the period 2000–05, largely made up of 'sixties generation' people who are typically individual-istic and liberal minded. Individuals with readily disposable assets (excluding houses and pension policies) of more than £50 000 are expected to exceed five million by 2005, and have been dubbed the 'mass affluent'. Typical members of this group are retired professionals, married but with no dependent children, and who inherited property from parents, and received windfalls from privatized utilities and building society conversions. They are also likely to have a substantial occupational pension.

For businesses, the attractions of such a group are enormous and many financial services companies, for example, have targeted this group with products that meet their needs. For governments, the emergence of this mass-affluent group raises a number of issues. Should policy seek to reduce the imbalances which are inherent in a society where some people have a good pension, and others don't? Should this group be excluded from means-tested benefits, simply because they have saved for their retirement whereas others have either chosen, or not been able to save for theirs? Should this group be expected to provide its own healthcare, or should the state continue to provide a service for all, regardless of wealth?

can have the effect of lowering the exchange rate. From a business perspective, balance of trade surpluses tend to benefit the economy through the creation of jobs, additional economic growth and a general feeling of business confidence. Surpluses created from overseas trade can be used to finance overseas lending and investment, which in turn generate higher levels of earnings from overseas in future years.

Government borrowing   Government borrowing represents the difference between what it receives in any given year from taxation and trading sources and what it needs in order to finance its expenditure programmes. The difference is often referred to as public sector net borrowing (PSNB). The level of PSNB is partly influenced by political considerations, with right-wing free market advocates favouring a reduced role for the government, reflected in a low level of net borrowing. Advocates of intervention are happier to see the PSNB rise. Government borrowing tends to rise during periods of economic recession and fall during periods of boom. This can be explained by income (especially from income and profits taxes) rising relative to expenditure during a boom and expen-diture (especially on social security benefits) rising relative to income during a recession. Taxes and public spending tend to be quite cyclical, reflecting political ideology and the state of the national and international economy and trends were discussed earlier (see Figure 7.1). Figure 7.7 shows a breakdown of total government budgeted income and expenditure by category for the year 2001–02.

Figure 7.7

A comparison of UK government total revenues and expenditure for 2001–02

(*Source*: Based on Treasury Budget Statement, 2001)

Income

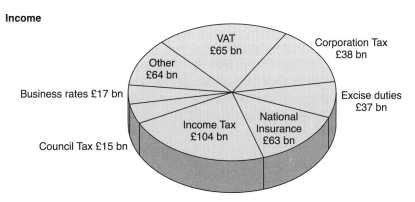

Total receipts £398 bn

Expenditure

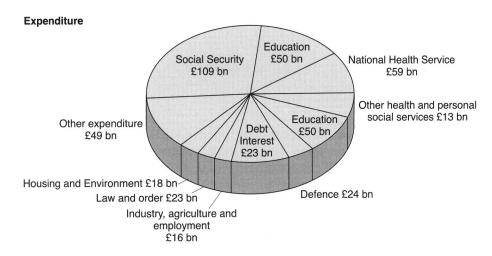

Total expenditure £394 bn

7.5.2 Government management of the economy

From government policy objectives come strategies by which these policy objectives can be achieved. This is an area where it can be possible to line up a dozen economists and get a dozen different answers to the same problem. Sometimes, political ideology can lead to the strategy being considered to be just as important as the policy objectives with supporters of alternative strategies showing very strong allegiance to them.

In trying to reconcile multiple objectives, governments invariably face a dilemma in reconciling all of them simultaneously. Of the three principal economic objectives (maintaining employment, controlling inflation and economic growth), satisfying objectives for any two invariably causes problems with the third (see Figure 7.8). It is therefore common for governments to shift their emphasis between policy objectives for political and pragmatic reasons. However, many surveys of business leaders have suggested that what they consider important above all else is *stability* in government policy. If the

Figure 7.8
Problems in
reconciling
conflicting
economic policy
objectives

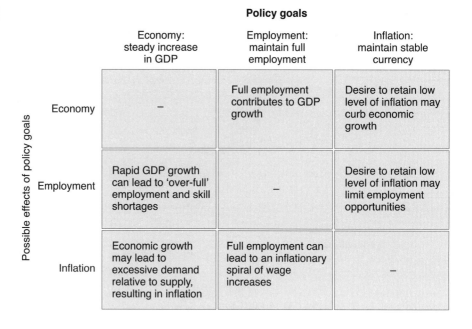

| | **Policy goals** | | |
Possible effects of policy goals	Economy: steady increase in GDP	Employment: maintain full employment	Inflation: maintain stable currency
Economy	–	Full employment contributes to GDP growth	Desire to retain low level of inflation may curb economic growth
Employment	Rapid GDP growth can lead to 'over-full' employment and skill shortages	–	Desire to retain low level of inflation may limit employment opportunities
Inflation	Economic growth may lead to excessive demand relative to supply, resulting in inflation	Full employment can lead to an inflationary spiral of wage increases	–

government continually changes the economic goal posts, or its economic strategy, businesses' own planning processes can be put into confusion.

Sometimes, policy can be implemented in pursuit of one objective, only for adverse side-effects to appear leading to policy being directed to solving this second problem. During much of the 1990s, UK governments put the reduction in inflation as the top economic policy priority and achieved this through high interest rates and a strong value of sterling, among other things. However, high interest rates and a strong pound created recessionary conditions, signified by falling demand, rising unemployment and reduced levels of investment. Resolving these problems then became a priority for government policy.

Two commonly used approaches to economic management can be classified under the headings of:

1. Fiscal policy, which concentrates on stimulating the economy through changes in government income and expenditure

2. Monetary policy, which influences the circular flow of income by changes in the supply of money and interest rates.

Fiscal policy Government is a major element of the circular flow of income, both as tax collector and as a source of expenditure for goods and services and payments to households. Increases in government spending have the effect of injecting additional income into the circular flow and, through the multiplier effect, thereby increasing the demand for goods and services. Reductions in government spending have the opposite effect. Changes in taxation can similarly affect the circular flow of income (e.g. a cut in income tax effectively injects more money into the economy).

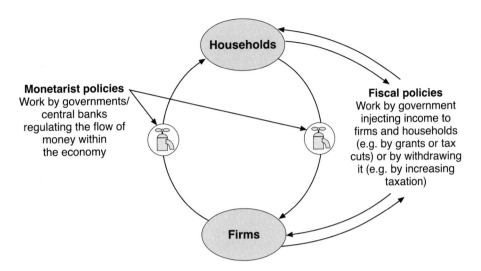

Figure 7.9
**The monetarist
and fiscal
approaches to
management of
the economy**

The use of fiscal measures to regulate the economy achieved prominence with the economist John Maynard Keynes, whose followers are generally referred to as *Keynsians*. Keynes developed his ideas as a means of overcoming the high levels of unemployment and falling commodity prices which were associated with the Great Depression of the 1930s. Conventional economics had failed to return resource markets to equilibrium, largely because of rigidities that had built up in markets. Instead, Keynes advocated the use of fiscal policy to increase the level of aggregate demand within the economy. Through a multiplier effect, spending by workers employed on government 'pump-priming' projects would filter through to private sector suppliers, who would in turn employ further workers, thereby eventually eradicating unemployment. If the economy showed signs of becoming too active, with scarcity in resource markets and rising price levels, suppression of demand through fiscal actions would have the effect of reducing inflationary pressures (Figure 7.9).

In the 1930s, fiscal measures were considered quite revolutionary and resulted in such projects as the electrification of railways and the construction of the National Grid being undertaken not just for the end result, but also for the multiplier benefits of carrying out the construction tasks. More recently, road building and government-funded construction in general have been used as a regulator of the economy, on account of their high employment content and low levels of initial 'leakage' to imported supplies.

Critics of fiscal policy have argued that fiscal intervention is a very clumsy way of trying to return the economy to equilibrium and a method that achieves temporary rather than permanent solutions to underlying economic problems. Keynsian policies call for bureaucratic civil servants to make quasi-commercial decisions, which they are generally ill equipped to do. There is much evidence of failed fiscal policy at a local level where government grants and tax incentives have been given to attract industry to depressed areas, only for those industries to close down after a few years (e.g. car factories built in Northern Ireland, Merseyside and Glasgow with government grants and tax concessions have often proved to be commercial failures). Critics of fiscal policy look to monetarist policies as an alternative.

Monetary policy   By contrast, the monetarist approach uses changes in the volume of money supply to influence aggregate demand in the economy. Monetarism achieved prominence with the work of Milton Friedman and found favour in the United Kingdom with the Conservative government of the early 1980s. The basic proposition of monetarism is that government need only regulate the supply of money in order to influence the circular flow of income. From this, adjustments in the economy happen automatically by market forces without the need for intervention by government in the running of business organizations (Figure 7.9). If government wishes to suppress demand in the economy, it would do this by restricting the volume of money in circulation in the economy (e.g. by raising interest rates or restricting the availability of credit). It would do the opposite if it wished to stimulate the economy.

Monetarism appeals to free market purists because of the limited government hands-on intervention that is required. However, governments have found it politically unacceptable to pursue monetarist policies to their logical conclusion. Suppressing demand by controlling the availability of money alone could result in unacceptably high levels of interest rates.

THINKING AROUND THE SUBJECT

During 1998, it appeared that the world economy was heading into recession, triggered by events such as the collapse of many Far Eastern economies. In the UK, manufacturers had complained bitterly about high interest rates, which had the effect of keeping the value of the pound high, which in turn harmed exports. In October 1998, the Bank of England announced a one per cent cut in the base rate, the largest single cut for many years. The Bank had clearly realized that high interest rates had done their job in controlling inflation, but now the greatest danger was of depressed demand in the economy leading to a recession. It might have been expected that this cut in interest rates would have sent a positive sign to businesses who should have been enthusiastic that the very thing they had been campaigning for, lower interest rates, had come a step closer. Usually, a cut in interest rates sent stock markets climbing. This time, after initial euphoria, reality set in as business leaders guessed that the Bank had made such a large cut out of desperation. What did it know that had caused it to take this action? Were there even worse signs that economic recession was just around the corner? After an initial rally, the stock market fell and companies continued to cut back their capacity. Was a generation of managers becoming much more sophisticated at reading economic signals? And what did this mean for the ability of traditional fiscal approaches to control the economy?

7.5.3   Limitations of government intervention in the national economy

At a practical level, critics of both monetarist and fiscal approaches to economic management have pointed to their failure to significantly influence the long-term performance of an economy. More recently, the fundamental concept of government intervention has been challenged in an emerging body of theoretical and empirical research which is commonly referred to as *rational expectations theory*. Proponents of the theory claim that it is too simplistic to regard government economic intervention in terms of simple stimulus-response models. It is naive, for example, to assume that private companies will take an increase in government capital spending as a cue to increase their own productive capacity. Instead, firms rationally assess the likely consequences of government intervention. Therefore an increase in government capital expenditure may lead to an expectation of eventually higher interest rates and inflation. Faced with this rational expectation, firms may decide to cut back their own expenditure, fearing the consequences for their own business of high inflation and interest rates. This is the opposite of the government's intended response. The theory of rational expectations holds that business people have become astute at interpreting economic signals and, because of this, government's ability to manage the national economy is significantly reduced.

7.5.4   The central bank

A nation's central bank plays an important role in the management of the national economy. In the United Kingdom, the Bank of England acts as a lender of last resort and has responsibility for regulating the volume of currency in circulation within the economy. Through its market operations, it intervenes to influence the exchange rate for sterling. The Bank of England also has a supervisory role in respect of privately owned banks within the United Kingdom.

Countries differ in the extent to which powers of the central bank are separated from government. In the United States and Germany, for example, granting the central bank a quasi-autonomous status and allowing it freedom to make decisions on monetary policy has for a long time been regarded as a means of guaranteeing prudent management of the money supply against political intervention for possibly short-term opportunistic objectives. Against this, the argument is put forward that central banks should be politically accountable and should be influenced by the social and political implications of their actions and not just the more narrowly defined monetary ones. In the United Kingdom, the Bank of England has traditionally been influenced by the Treasury arm of government. However, the incoming Labour government in 1997 decided to give autonomy to much of the Bank's activity through a newly formed Monetary Policy Committee (MPC), made up of a panel of eight economics experts, plus the Governor of the Bank of England who acts as Chair. The new committee is free to set interest rates at a level which it considers prudent and in the best interests of the country. Opinion remains divided on the relative merits of a politically influenced central bank and one that is above narrow political interests. While there is evidence that the MPC has acted with integrity, many business leaders have accused it of being dominated by academics and financiers who are unable to empathize with the problems faced by businesses. Employers' pressure groups, such as the CBI, feel less able to put pressure on the MPC than they previously could on Treasury ministers.

Throughout the EU, the development of a single currency is placing much greater power over monetary policy in the hands of the central bank of the European Central Bank. The power of Euro-zone member states to determine their own interest rates and monetary policy is handed over to the central bank which also handles member states' currency reserves. The subject of the single European currency is discussed further in Chapter 10.

CASE STUDY

LOTTERY FEVER LINKED TO CHANGES IN NATIONAL ECONOMY

For many years, UK government policy had been cautious towards gambling, viewing it as a bad influence in society which needed to be controlled by legislation. By the early 1990s, popular mood had been changing, helped not least by the sight of major national lotteries in other countries of Europe and the United States. A 1992 White Paper on lotteries eventually led to the licensing of the United Kingdom's first National Lottery by the government's newly created Office of National Lottery (Oflot). Within a year of its launch in 1994, observers were suggesting that the lottery was having a significant effect on the national economy as a whole.

From the beginning, the licensed lottery operator Camelot (owned by a consortium of Cadbury Schweppes, De La Rue, GTech and ICL) found forecasting demand for lottery tickets to be very difficult. The only evidence which could be drawn on was large national lotteries overseas (where differing cultural attitudes may have limited extrapolation to the United Kingdom) and smaller local lotteries in the United Kingdom which had much smaller prizes than those anticipated by Camelot (and therefore did not create any major publicity impact). Although the UK gaming market (covering activities from football pools to casinos) was then currently worth an estimated £15 billion a year, the question remained how much National Lottery income would be derived from customers switching from other forms of gambling, and how much would be switched from completely different forms of consumer expenditure.

In the event, weekly sales of lottery tickets shortly after launch were about £60 million, slightly ahead of forecast. This increased significantly with the launch of 'Instant' scratch cards, which achieved annual sales of around £1 billion a year. Within six months of launch, research had shown that 25 million people (out of an eligible total of 44 million) played the National Lottery every week. The Wednesday and Saturday afternoon queues at Lottery retailers seemed to have become a ritual for many, hoping that their 1 in 14 million chance of winning the jackpot prize would come good.

Before long, critics of the National Lottery were pointing to its harmful side-effects, in addition to the religious groups who had traditionally seen gambling as immoral. The most vociferous critics were companies involved in other gambling activities, with attendance at bingo halls and participation in football pools significantly down. The National Lottery was directly blamed for the Littlewoods Pools company's decision to lay off about 10 per cent of its workforce shortly after its launch.

Beyond this, many more companies from consumer goods and services sectors blamed the National Lottery for diverting consumer expenditure away from their products. Research had shown that previous non-gamblers had been drawn to the National Lottery and the average weekly stake money of about £2.50 was causing diversion of expenditure from other consumer goods and services. It effectively represented a withdrawal from the circular flow of income and was blamed for prolonging an economic recession at a time when consumer confidence and expenditure remained low. Worse still, research showed quite clearly that the most important purchasers of lottery tickets were people from relatively low income groups. This group's purchases of lottery tickets was particularly harmful as people with low incomes have a higher propensity to spend their money rather than to save it. Whereas a high income person may buy lottery tickets using money which would otherwise have been saved, lower income groups are more likely to divert expenditure from other products. Total national income could be further reduced by a multiplier effect.

Although the initial effect of the Lottery was to take money out of the circular flow of income, over the longer term, the distribution of its income had potential to stimulate the economy. Income from the National Lottery is distributed in a number of ways. For each £1 lottery ticket, 50p is returned to the public in the form of prizes. The large size of the top prizes (up to £17.8 million) has given individuals income beyond a level which they could realistically immediately return to the domestic circular flow of income. Faced with such large prize winnings, much has been saved, or in many cases invested in overseas assets.

For the remainder of the £1 lottery stake, 12p is taken by the Treasury, representing a further withdrawal. The lottery operator and retailers each take 5p, leaving 28p to be given to good causes (sports, arts, charities, the National Heritage and the Millennium Fund). The distribution of money to good causes may go some way to generating more positive multiplier effects. In addition to numerous grants to local organizations (for example grants to sports clubs to renew their facilities), a number of much larger grants have been given by the five grant-giving bodies. Many grants were given for projects to mark the Millennium (e.g. a £7 million grant for the restoration of the waterfront at Portsmouth). The Millennium Commission (which administers grants by the Millennium Fund) insisted, like the other grant giving bodies, that all payments should go towards new capital projects, rather than being used to fund current expenditure.

What was initially seen by many as little more than a game has had significant redistributive effects on the national economy. Millions of people have diverted expenditure from routine goods and services; a few new millionaires have been created and grants paid for out of prize money have created multiplier benefits in the areas where they are used.

CASE STUDY Review questions

1 Does the National Lottery benefit the national economy overall?

2 What would be the effect on the national economy of replacing a small number of very large weekly prizes with a large number of relatively small ones?

3 What would you expect to be the overall effect of the National Lottery on charity organizations?

CHAPTER   Summary and links to other chapters

This chapter has reviewed the structure of national economies and the flow of income between different elements of the economy. Producers, consumers and government are interrelated in the circular flow of income. Business cycles occur because the speed of the circular flow of income temporarily increases or decreases. Although governments seek to limit the magnitude of the business cycle, the cycle can pose problems (and opportunities) for business organizations. The rate at which an organization can grow can be constrained by the rate at which the national economy is growing (Chapter 3). This chapter has reviewed economic indicators that companies can read in order to better understand and predict the environment in which they operate. A good information system (Chapter 12) should be able to analyse leading indicators of the economy rapidly and effectively.

The state of the economic environment is very much influenced by politicians and the interaction between the economic and political environments is developed further in Chapter 8. This chapter has recognized that the national economic environment is part of the international economic environment and international economic issues are returned to in Chapter 10.

CHAPTER   Review questions

1   'Economic policy is the product of the conflicting desires of governments for price stability and full employment stability.' Discuss this statement in the context of your government's economic policies.

(Based on CIM Marketing Environment examination question)

2   What would be the marketing implications of your current government's current economic policies?

(Based on CIM Marketing Environment examination question).

3   During 1997, the UK government announced that it would fund the creation of a new university campus in a deprived part of Belfast. What multiplier benefits are likely to be associated with this project?

4   Identify some of the consequences for a UK vehicle manufacturer of a UK inflation rate of 5 per cent p.a., compared to a European Union average of 2 per cent.

5   Contrast the effects of 'tight' fiscal and 'tight' monetary policies on the construction sector.

6   In the context of 'rational expectations' theory, what evidence could you suggest to indicate that business people 'see through' the short-term implications of government economic policies?

References

Eurostat (1995) *Europe in Figures*, 4th edn, Official Publications of the European Communities, Luxembourg.
International Labour Office (1997) *Year Book of Labour Statistics*, Geneva.

Wood, P.A. (1987) 'Producer Services and Economic Change, Some Canadian Evidence, in *Technological Change and Economic Policy*, K. Chapman and G. Humphreys, eds, Blackwell, Oxford.

Selected further reading

Macroeconomics can be a complex subject and this chapter has only reviewed the key elements of the macro-economic system. For a fuller discussion of the subject, the following references are useful:

Artis, M.J. (ed.) (1996) *Prest and Coppock's The U.K. Economy: A Manual of Applied Economics*, 14th edn, Oxford University Press, Oxford.

Burda, M. and Wyplosz, C. (1997) *Macroeconomics: A European Text*, Oxford University Press, Oxford.

Curwen, P. (1997) *Understanding the UK Economy*, 4th edn, Macmillan, Basingstoke.

Griffiths, A. and Wall, S. (eds) (2001) *Applied Economics: An Introductory Course*, 9th edn, Prentice-Hall, Hemel Hempstead.

Kay, J. (1997) *The Business of Economics*, Oxford University Press, Oxford.

For a review of UK economy, the following statistical data is published regularly by the Office for National Statistics:

Economic Trends: A monthly compendium of economic data which gives convenient access from one source to a range of economic indicators.

UK National Accounts (*The Blue Book*): the principal annual publication for national account statistics, covering value added by industry, the personal sector, companies, public corporations, central and local government. Published annually.

For a discussion of business cycles and how to interpret them, the following provides good coverage:

Hildebrand, G. (1992) *Business Cycle Indicators: A Complete Guide to Interpreting the Key Economic Indicators*, Probus, Chicago, IL.

Mullineux, A., Dickinson, D. and Peng, W. (1993) *Business Cycles: Theory and Evidence*, Blackwell, Oxford.

Ploeg, F. van der (ed.) (1994) *Handbook of International Macroeconomics*, Blackwell, Oxford.

Zarnowitz, V. (1998) 'Has the Business Cycle been abolished?', *Business Economics*, vol. 33, no. 4, pp. 39–46.

Can governments realistically expect to change the pattern of expenditure within the economy? The following reference reviews rational expectations theory:

Miller, P.J. (ed.) (1994) *The Rational Expectations Revolution: Readings from the Front Line*, MIT Press, Cambridge, MA.

Useful websites

Institute of Economic Affairs   The IEA aim is to explain free-market ideas to the public, including politicians, students, journalists, businessmen, academics and anyone interested in public policy.
http://www.iea.org.uk/

Institute for Fiscal Studies   IFS is an independent research organization which aims to provide high-quality economic analysis of public policy. The IFS home page provides links to analysis of topical economic issues, government Budgets, IFS surveys and other online economics and social sciences resources.
http://www1.ifs.org.uk

Business Cycle Indicators   The Conference Board is a not-for-profit, non-advocacy organization business research and membership organization with 2800 companies and other enterprises in 63 counties. It provides timely research on management practices and economic trends and is a frequently quoted private source of business information.   **http://www.tcb-indicators.org/**

Confederation of British Industry   The CBI represents companies from all sectors of United Kingdom business and is the premier organization speaking for companies in the United Kingdom. Its website provides details of CBI surveys and discussion of topical economic issues.   **http://www.cbi.org.uk/home.html**

Centre for Economic Performance   The CEP was established by the Economic and Social Research Council. Based at the London School of Economics and Political Science, it is now one of the leading academic research centres in Europe and a world leader in economic research. Its website provides discussion on causes of countries' and firms economic performance.   **http://cep.lse.ac.uk**

UK Treasury   Home page of HM Treasury which includes analysis of recent government economic measures, revenue and expenditure analysis.   **http://www.hm-treasury.gov.uk/**

European Central Bank   Homepage of the ECB which provides European economic analysis. **http://www.ecb.int/**

Key terms

Accelerator effect	Interest rates
Borrowing	Invisibles
Business cycle	Macroeconomic analysis
Central bank	Models
Circular flow of income	Monetarism
Competitive cost advantage	Monetary Policy Committee
Confidence level	Multiplier
Deflation	Public sector net borrowing (PSNB)
Disposable income	Recession
Economic structure	Retail price index (RPI)
Exchange rate	Savings ratio
Fiscal policy	Turning point
Gross Domestic Product (GDP)	Unemployment
Inflation	Withdrawals
Injections	

8

The political environment

CHAPTER OBJECTIVES

Political developments at local, national and, increasingly, the European level, can affect the framework in which goods and services are produced and sold. Issues such as macroeconomic policy, the distribution of income and regulation versus deregulation are essentially the result of political decisions. Business organizations cannot afford to ignore developments in their political environment and must respond appropriately to change. The aim of this chapter is to explore the nature of the political environment in which organizations operate and to provide an overview of the two-way influence between business organizations and government. In the wider context of the political environment it also discusses the role of pressure groups in the political process. After reading this chapter you should be able to appreciate the impacts of government on business organizations' activities.

All aspects of an organization's business environment are interrelated to some extent, and this is especially true of the political environment. Interlinkages occur in many ways, for example:

1 Political decisions inevitably affect the economic environment, for example in the proportion of GDP accounted for by the state and the distribution of income between different groups in society (Chapter 7).

2 Political decisions also influence the social and cultural environment of a country (Chapter 11). For example, governments create legislation, which can have the effect of encouraging families to care for their elderly relatives or allowing shops to open on Sundays. In short, the actions of politicians are both a reflection of the social and cultural environment of a country and also help to shape it.

3 Politicians can influence the pace at which new technologies appear and are adopted, for example through tax concessions on research and development activity (Chapter 12).

The political environment is one of the less predictable elements in an organization's business environment. Although politicians issue manifestos and other policy statements, these have to be seen against the pragmatic need of governments to modify their policies during their period in office. Change in the political environment can result from a variety of internal and external pressures. The fact that democratic governments have to seek re-election every few years has contributed towards a cyclical political environment. Turbulence in the political environment can be seen by considering some of the major swings that have occurred in the political environment in the United Kingdom since the Second World War:

■ During the late 1940s the political environment stressed heavy government intervention in all aspects of the economy, including ownership of a substantial share of productive capacity.

■ During the 1950s there was a much more restrained hands-off approach in which many of the previously nationalized industries were deregulated and sold off.

■ During the 1960s and 1970s the political environment oscillated in moderation between more and less government involvement in the ways businesses are run.

■ The 1980s saw a significant change in the political environment, with the wholesale withdrawal of government from ownership and regulation of large areas of business activity.

■ During the 1990s political commentators detected a shift away from the radicalism of the 1980s to more middle of the road policies based on a social market economy.

■ With the election of a New Labour government in 1997, there has been a gradual retreat from the free-market idealism of previous Conservative governments.

8.1.1   **The importance of monitoring the political environment**

It is important for organizations to monitor their political environment, because change in this environment can impact on business strategy and operations in a number of ways:

1   At the most general level, the stability of the political system affects the attractiveness of a particular national market. While radical change rarely results from political upheaval in most Western countries, the instability of governments in many less developed countries leads to uncertainty about the economic and legislative framework in which goods and services will be provided.

2   At a national level, governments pass legislation that directly affects the relationship between the firm and its customers, relationships between itself and its suppliers and between itself and other firms and individuals. Sometimes legislation has a direct effect on the organization, for example a law giving consumers rights against the seller of faulty goods. At other times, the effect is less direct, as where changes in legislation concerning anticompetitive practices alter an organization's relative competitive advantage in a market.

3   As employers, governments see business organizations as an important vehicle for social reform through legislation which affects employment relationships. During the last 30 years, organizations have been affected by a wide range of employment legislation, affecting, among other things, discrimination against disadvantaged groups, minimum wages and more stringent health and safety requirements.

4 The government is additionally responsible for protecting the public interest at large, imposing further constraints on the activities of firms, for example where the government lays down design standards for cars to protect the public against pollution or road safety risks.

5 The economic environment is influenced by the actions of government. It is responsible for formulating policies that can influence the rate of growth in the economy and hence the total amount of spending power. It is also a political decision as to how this spending power should be distributed between different groups of consumers and between the public and private sectors.

6 Government at both a central and local level is itself a major consumer of goods and services, accounting for about 40 per cent of the United Kingdom's gross domestic product in the late 1990s (refer back to Figure 7.1).

7 Government policies can influence the dominant social and cultural values of a country, although there can be argument about which is the cause and which is the effect. For example, UK government policies of the 1980s emphasized wealth creation as an end in itself and these policies also had the effect of generating a feeling of confidence among consumers. This can be directly linked to an increase in consumer spending at a higher rate than earnings growth, and a renewed enthusiasm for purchasing items of ostentatious consumption.

It should be remembered that organizations have to not only monitor the political environment – they also contribute to it. This can happen where organizations feel threatened by change and lobby government to intervene to pass legislation that will protect their interests. Indeed, many people have argued that large multinational organizations can have more power than a host government. This is especially true of many smaller and less developed countries, where a multi-national's decision to invest/divest in the country can force government policy changes. The role of lobbying and pressure groups will be discussed later in this chapter.

To understand the nature of the political environment more fully and its impact on organizations, it is necessary to examine the different aspects of government. Government influence on businesses in the United Kingdom can be divided into the following categories:

■ Central government

■ Local government

■ European Union (EU) government

■ Supranational government.

8.2   CENTRAL GOVERNMENT

The government system of most Western countries can be divided into four separate functions. The United Kingdom is quite typical in dividing functions of

Figure 8.1
The progress of
legislation
through
Parliament

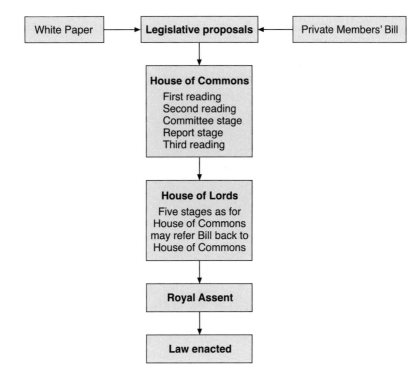

government between the legislature, the executive, the civil service and the judiciary. These collectively provide sovereign government within the United Kingdom, although as will be seen later, this sovereignty is increasingly being subjected to the authority of the EU.

8.2.1   Parliament

Parliament provides the supreme legislative authority in the United Kingdom and comprises the Queen, the House of Commons and the House of Lords. The House of Commons is the most important part of the legislature as previous legislation has curtailed the authority in Parliament of the monarch and the House of Lords. It is useful to be aware of the procedures for enacting new legislation so that the influences on the legislative process can be fully understood (Figure 8.1).

New legislation starts life as a Bill and passes through parliamentary processes to the point where it becomes an Act of Parliament. Most Bills that subsequently become law are government sponsored and often start life following discussion between government departments and interested parties. On some occasions, these discussions may lead to the setting up of a Committee of Enquiry or (less frequently) a Royal Commission which reports to the government. The findings of such a committee can be accepted, rejected or amended by the government which puts forward ideas for discussion in a green paper. Following initial discussion, the government would submit definite proposals for legislation in the form of a White Paper. A Parliamentary Bill would then be drafted, incorporating some of the comments that the government has received in response to the publication of the White Paper. The Bill is then formally introduced to Parliament by a first reading in the House of Commons at which a date is set for the main debate at a second reading. A vote is taken at each reading, and if it is a government bill, it will invariably pass at each stage. If it passes the second reading, the Bill will be sent to a Standing Committee for a discussion of the details. The Committee will in due course report back to the full House of Commons and there will be a final debate where amendments are considered, some of which originate from the Committee and some from members of the House of Commons in general. The Bill then passes to the House of Lords and goes through a similar five stages. The Lords may delay or amend a Bill, although the Commons may subsequently use the Parliament Act to force the Bill through. Finally, the Bill goes to the monarch to receive the Royal Assent, upon which it becomes an Act of Parliament.

This basic model can be changed in a number of ways. First, in response to a newly perceived problem, the government could introduce a Bill with very few clauses and with the agreement of party managers could cut short the consultation stages, speed up the passage of the Bill through its various stages and provide Royal Assent within a matter of days, instead of the months that it could typically take. This has occurred, for example, in the case of a one clause Bill to prohibit trade in human organs, a measure that had received all-party support. A second variation on the basic model is provided by Private Members' Bills. Most Bills start life with government backing. However, backbench Members of Parliament can introduce their own Bills, although the opportunities for doing this are limited and if they do not subsequently receive government backing, their chances of passing all stages of the Parliamentary process are significantly reduced.

In the chapter on the legal environment (Chapter 9), it is noted that law derives from two principal sources – statute law and case law. Case law evolves gradually and is determined by judges who aim to be impartial and free from any sectional interest. The ability of organizations to influence change in this aspect of the law is therefore very limited. However, this cannot be said of statute law passed by Parliament. The lobbying of Members of Parliament has become an increasingly important activity, brought about by individuals and pressure groups to try to protect their interests where new legislation is proposed which may affect them. Typical of tasks for which professional lobbyists have been employed in recent years are:

- A major campaign by tobacco companies against a Bill which would have limited their ability to sponsor sporting events

- The insurance industry lobbied hard against a clause in a Finance Bill which introduced a new Insurance Premium Tax on insurance policies

- The British Roads Federation regularly lobbies for greater expenditure on roads, and seizes opportunities presented by relevant new Bills to include provisions which are more supportive of increased expenditure on roads

- Each year, prior to the Chancellor of the Exchequer's annual Budget speech (which forms the basis of a Finance Act), considerable lobbying is undertaken

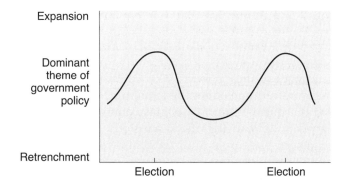

Figure 8.2
The political life cycle

by vested interests that appeal for more public spending to be directed to their cause and/or less taxation to be imposed on it.

If organizations are to succeed in influencing their political environment, they need to identify the critical points in the passage of a Bill at which pressure can be applied and the critical members who should form the focus of lobbying (for example the members of the Committee to whom the Bill is sent for detailed examination). As we will see later, much legislation which passes through the UK parliament is enacting EU legislation. At this stage it may be too late for lobbyists to achieve significant change in the overall policy underlying the Bill, although it may still be possible to amend details of its implementation.

Political parties typically make bold promises in their election manifestos. If elected, they may promptly enact legislation that formed the flagship of their campaign. However, after a honeymoon period, governments must set to work addressing structural issues in the economy which will take some time to make good. This may involve painful economic measures in the short term, but the payoff is improved economic performance in a few years' time. With a five-year election cycle for Parliament in the United Kingdom, it is often claimed that voters have short memories and will forget austere economic conditions of two or three years ago. What matters at election time is the appearance that economic conditions are getting better. Therefore, government economic planning may try to achieve falling unemployment, stable prices and a consumer boom just ahead of a general election. This may itself lead to structural problems which must be sorted out after the election, leading to a repeat of this cyclical process (see Figure 8.2). The existence of the political cycle frequently impacts on the economic environment, with periods of increased expenditure just before an election and reduced expenditure shortly after. Organizations may acknowledge this cycle by gearing up for a boom in sales just ahead of a general election.

8.2.2   The executive

Parliament comprises elected representatives whose decisions, in theory, are carried out by the executive arm of government. In practice, the executive plays a very important role in formulating policies which parliament then debates and invariably accepts. In the United Kingdom, the principal elements of the executive comprise the Cabinet and Ministers of State.

The Cabinet

The main executive element of central government is made up of the Prime Minister and Cabinet, who determine policy and who are responsible for the consequences of their policies. The Cabinet is headed by the Prime Minister who has many powers, including the appointment and dismissal of Ministers and determining the membership of Cabinet committees, chairing the Cabinet and setting its agenda, summarizing the discussions of the Cabinet and sending directives to ministers. The Prime Minister is also responsible for a variety of government and non-government appointments and can determine the timing of a general election. Many have argued that Britain is moving towards a system of presidential government by the Prime Minister, given the considerable powers at his or her disposal. There are, however, a number of constraints on the power of the Prime Minister, such as the need to keep the loyalty of the Cabinet and the agreement of Parliament, which may be difficult when the governing party has only a small majority in the House of Commons.

In practice, the Prime Minister is particularly dependent upon the support of a small inner cabinet of senior colleagues for advice and assistance in carrying policy through the party. In addition to this small inner cabinet surrounding him or her, recent years have seen the development of a small group of outside advisers on whose loyalty the Prime Minister can totally rely. Some are likely to be party members sitting in Parliament, while others may be party loyalists who belong to the business or academic community. There have been occasions when it has appeared that the Prime Minister's advisers were having a greater influence on policy than their Cabinet colleagues.

The ideological background of the Prime Minister and the composition of the government may give some indication of the direction of government policy. On government attitudes towards issues such as competition policy and personal taxation, organizations should study the composition of the government to try to predict future policy.

Ministers of State

The government of the country is divided between a number of different departments of state (see Figure 8.3). Each department is headed by a Minister or Secretary of State who is a political appointee, usually a member of the House of Commons. They are assisted in their tasks by junior ministers. The portfolio of responsibilities of a department frequently changes when a new government comes into being. Ministers are often given delegated authority by Parliament, as where an Act may allow charges to be made for certain health services, but the Minister has the delegated power to decide the actual level of the charges.

The civil service

The civil service is the secretariat responsible for implementing government policy. In the United Kingdom, civil servants are paid officials who do not change when

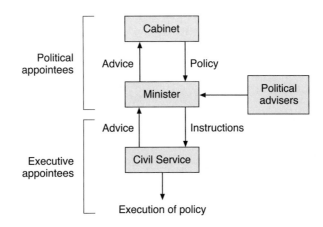

Figure 8.3
The UK government system of departmental administration: a simplified diagram

the government changes, adding a degree of continuity to government (although in some countries such as the United States, it is customary for senior officials to be political appointees and therefore replaced following a change of government). Although legally, civil servants are servants of the Crown, they are technically employed by a separate government department and are responsible to a Minister. Each department is generally headed by a Permanent Secretary, responsible to the Public Accounts Committee of Parliament. The Permanent Secretary is a professional administrator who gives advice to his or her Minister, the latter being a political appointee who generally lacks expertise in the work of the department.

The fact that civil servants are relatively expert in their areas and generally remain in their posts for much longer than their Minister gives them great power. A delicate relationship develops between the Permanent Secretary and the Minister, based on sometimes conflicting goals. The Minister may view an issue in terms of broader political opportunities while the civil servant may be more concerned about his or her status and career prospects resulting from a change affecting his or her department.

The nature of the career civil servant is changing with the emergence of non-departmental public bodies (NDPBs) to take over many of the activities of civil service departments (see below). In theory, these new executive agencies should be much freer of ministerial control, meeting longer term performance standards with less day-to-day ministerial intervention as to how this should be achieved.

Organizations seeking to influence government policy must recognize the power that civil servants have in advising their Minister, especially on the details of proposed legislation. Civil servants are usually involved in consultation exercises, for example on the details of proposed food regulations. In some countries, business may seek to influence the policy-making process at this stage through overt or covert bribery. This is not a feature of most mature democracies such as the United Kingdom, and business seeks to exert influence in a more mutually co-operative manner. Civil servants require information on the background to policy and need to understand its possible implications. A close dialogue between the business community and civil servants can increase the chances of civil servants' policy recommendations being based on a sound understanding of business needs, rather than ignorance.

The United Kingdom's system of government has often been held out as an example of good governance. Politicians decided policy and if the electorate did not like their policies, they could be thrown out of office at the next election. Civil servants were the loyal servants of politicians who got on and implemented their masters' policies. Because the electorate could not throw out a civil servant directly, ministers took responsibility for the actions of their civil servants. Carefully honed sets of procedures and codes of conduct were developed which made the UK civil service an example to the world of professionalism.

What then are we to make of recent developments which would appear to blur the distinction between elected politicians and an appointed civil service? The 1990s saw a big growth in policy advisers who report to the Prime Minister or other senior ministers, but who are still technically civil servants. These special advisers are overtly chosen by Ministers on the basis of their political views, breaking the tradition of neutrality within the civil service. They have often been given the label of 'spin doctor' for the way in which they represent the views of their Minister. Do these advisers debase the whole principle of a politically neutral civil service? Are they one step towards the development of a presidential style of government on the American model? Are spin doctors merely providing a substitute for substantive actions by the politicians? Against this, isn't good government all about strong leadership? Could these special advisers be beneficial in the way that they cut through the delaying tactics of the civil service machinery in their efforts to see the politically accountable executive's wishes implemented?

The blurred distinction between functions does not end with special policy advisers. Governments have been increasingly enthusiastic about the use of 'task forces' to implement policy in such areas as education, housing and environmental protection. These typically draw membership from a wide range of interests, including business organizations, but they are invariably political appointments and not democratically accountable in the way that a civil servant is accountable to his or her Minister. Are the possible benefits for strong government worth the possible price of less accountability to the electorate?

8.2.6 The judiciary

Most democratic systems of government provide a number of checks and balances against the abuse of executive power. The judiciary is independent of government and judges in the United Kingdom are answerable to the Crown and not to politicians. Through the court system, citizens can have some redress against a legislature, executive or civil service that acts beyond its authority. If complainants believe that they have suffered because a government minister did not follow statutory consultation procedures, they may apply to the courts for a judicial review of the case. A court may order that ministers reconsider the matter by following statutory procedures.

Business organizations have become increasingly willing to use the courts to challenge allegedly incorrect government procedures which have put them at a disadvantage. The proliferation of industry sector regulators in the UK has created many opportunities for aggrieved business organizations to challenge the processes of the regulator. As an example, the UK National Lottery regulator Oflot was challenged in the High Court during 2000 by Camelot – the existing Lottery franchise holder – when it alleged that it had been procedurally incorrect in the manner that it granted a new franchise to the rival People's Lottery. The Court instructed the regulator to reconsider its decision.

8.2.7 'Joined-up government'

Central government can at times seem an amorphous mass of departments, each not appearing to know what the other one is doing. There have been many documented cases where different government departments have taken completely opposing policy directions, thereby cancelling each other out. In a notable example, one government agency was giving grants to farmers to drain land for cultivation, at the same time as another was giving grants to create marshlands out of farmland.

The UK government sought to overcome such problems with the publication in March 1999 of a White Paper on Modernizing Government. As a result of this, a government task force asked groups of public sector volunteers, called *Integrated-Service Teams*, to put themselves in the position of a member of the public experiencing one of a number of major life events, such as leaving school, becoming unemployed, changing address, having a baby or retiring. Team members contacted the relevant departments and agencies direct, and their research gave insights into the problems resulting from the way services are organized, and what might be done to improve things. The study found, for example, that people had to give the same information more than once to different – or even the same – organizations: for example Housing Benefit and Income Support forms both ask for very similar information.

Having identified the problems, Service Action Teams (SATs) were created to look into particular life episodes that caused most problems in dealing with multiple departments and agencies. Early evidence of the move to joined-up government was seen in the trial integration of previously separate agencies dealing with finding employment and the payment of unemployment benefits.

Creating 'joined-up' thinking is never easy, even within profit-oriented private sector organizations. In seeking to achieve integration within government, the administration must balance the need to share responsibilities with the need to hold manageable sized units accountable for their actions.

8.2.8 Impacts of government on business operations

Very few governments, whether free market or interventionist, would claim to have made life more difficult for businesses to operate. Yet a frequent complaint of many businesses, especially small-business owners, is that government expects them to do too much administration on behalf of the government. Despite frequent high-profile government campaigns against red tape, the volume of regulation continues to have a major impact on the costs of business organizations. While large organizations may be able to afford specialists to handle administrative

Table 8.1   Estimated costs to UK businesses of compliance with selected regulations

Regulation	Date introduced	Estimated cost to business (£)
Working time directive	1999	7.65 bn
National minimum wage	1999	3.07 bn
Working families tax credit	2000	240 m
Requirement to provide stakeholder pensions	2001	200 m
Requirement to provide parental leave	1999	72 m
Part-time workers directive	2000	54 m
Entitlement to additional maternity leave	1999	39 m

Note: Figures show estimated annual administrative and financial costs to UK businesses, calculated in 2001.

Source: Adapted from British Chambers of Commerce *Burdens Barometer.*

matters and can spread the cost over large volumes of output, government regulation can hit small businesses very hard. Consider some of the following examples of regulations that have added to the costs of business organizations in recent years:

- Value added tax (VAT) effectively makes most business organizations tax collectors on behalf of government and small-business owners must become familiar with complex sets of regulations.

- Legislation to give additional rights to employees bears down particularly heavily on small businesses. Granting maternity rights to new mothers may be easily absorbed by large organizations, but a small business may experience great difficulties when one person who represents a large and critical part of the workforce decides to exercise their rights.

- The mounting volume of consumer protection and health and safety legislation has a particularly big impact on small businesses which do not generally have the expertise to readily assimilate the provisions of new regulations.

A number of attempts have been made to quantify the costs to business organizations of government regulation. Table 8.1 shows costs which have been calculated by the British Chambers of Commerce to be a direct result of some recent UK government regulations.

It appeared to many that even the introduction of the Internet – which was supposed to simplify many administrative tasks, led to new government-imposed burdens on businesses. Worried at the prospect of organized crime using the Internet, the government passed the controversial Regulation of Investigatory Powers (RIP) Act. This was bitterly contested by business for its provisions enabling the interception of e-mails and electronic correspondence.

The incoming New Labour government of 1997 set out – as with many previous governments – on a mission to reduce unnecessary regulation, by creating the Better Regulation Task Force. The task force has produced a number of recommendations to government about ways in which the administrative burden could be reduced, but in reaching its recommendations it has to balance efficiency improvements against the often opposing need for greater protection of individuals which regulations provide.

The work of the task force can be seen in its impact on regulation governing the use of electronic signatures over the Internet. While the RIP was viewed as interventionist and heavy-handed, the Electronic Communications Act, passed in 2000, has been broadly accepted as positive and light of touch. The Act allows companies and individuals to use electronic signatures to conduct their business, and accredits organizations providing encryption services. Industry welcomed the move as it will enable companies to take advantage of technology to speed up their legal transactions. Moreover, the government listened to industry and the Better Regulation Task Force and adopted a hands-off solution to regulation saying it would not intervene in accreditation if the industry came up with an effective self-regulation system before 2005.

8.2.9 Charter Marks

Charter Mark is a UK government award scheme which aims to recognize and encourage excellence in public service. It also plays a powerful role as a quality improvement tool focusing on customer service and service delivery. Unlike many quality management tools adopted by the private sector (which essentially focus on production processes), the Charter Mark is unique among quality schemes in the way it concentrates on results – the service the customer actually receives. Achieving the Charter Mark standard is an indication that a government department or agency has put its 'customers' first.

All public sector organizations that deal directly with the public are eligible to apply for a Charter Mark. The scheme is also extended to voluntary organizations providing a service to the public and receiving at least 10 per cent of their income from public sector funds. Government subcontractors can apply as long as they provide a service to the public, which is provided elsewhere by another public sector organization.

Applying for a Charter Mark involves three key stages. First, an organization measures its service against 10 Charter Mark criteria and makes an application. Second, the application is subject to expert scrutiny, including a visit by an assessor. Thirdly, based on the evidence provided, the organization receives detailed feedback on how to improve service further. If the 10 criteria are met, the Charter Mark is awarded.

A wide range of government organizations have been successful in applying for a Charter Mark, including branches of the Benefits Agency and Courts services and local HGV testing stations.

8.3 POLITICAL IDEOLOGIES

It was noted earlier that political ideologies in the United Kingdom have changed through a series of cycles during the period following the Second World War. It is important to consider the issue of dominant political ideologies, as they can have such a major impact on the business environment. At one extreme, the ideology of the immediate postwar Labour government placed great importance on the role of the state, and this resulted in many private sector organizations being taken into state ownership. The political ideology of the incoming Conservative government in 1979 was very different on this and many other issues. As a consequence of this shift, large parts of state control of business were dismantled and nationalized industries sold off. For business organizations, understanding shifts in dominant ideologies can be crucial to understanding the future nature of their business environment. Two important and recurring ideological issues which affect business organizations are the distribution of wealth between different groups in society and the role of the state versus the private sector in delivering goods and services. Political parties represent the gathering of individuals who share a political ideology.

8.3.1   Political parties

Most members of parliament belong to a political party. In general, the views of members of political parties cross a range of policy issues, so they can be distinguished from single-interest groups such as the Campaign for Nuclear Disarmament. The existence of political parties makes the management of parliamentary business more efficient, because party leaders can generally be assured of the support of their members when passing new legislation. Parties also provide a hierarchical organization through which MPs can become junior ministers and eventually take a place in the executive.

From the perspective of the electorate, belonging to a political party identifies an individual candidate with a known set of values. There is a lot of evidence that when voting for a member of parliament, a substantial proportion of voters are guided primarily by the party affiliation of a candidate, rather than the personal views and characteristics of the candidate.

Political parties represent an ideological point of view, although it has been noted that in recent years the ideological gap between the main UK parties has been reducing. Some cynics suggested that the incoming New Labour government in 1997 shared many of the values of the previous Conservative government and was far removed from the ideological zeal with which the 1945 Labour government took office. The main parties have tended to converge on a relatively moderate ideology, leaving extreme parties such as the National Front and Socialist Workers Party to pursue more radical agendas. Of course, the prevalence of an ideology represents shifts in the value of society as a whole. The radical free market stance of the incoming Conservative government of 1979 found a ready reception by an electorate who had come to see the shortcomings of the previous Labour government which was seen by many as being too restrictive and closely aligned with the inflexible attitudes of the trade unions. The fact that extreme ideologies have not found great recent support in the UK, and the fact that the difference between the two main parties has been narrowed, is a reflection of relatively moderate political values held by the population as a whole.

Because political parties represent a diverse range of views, it is not surprising that party leaders often find it difficult to gain the unanimous support of all members on all issues. In the United Kingdom, members of the main political parties are divided on issues such as the level of involvement with the European Union, defence expenditure and educational policy. Nevertheless, a political party stands for a broad statement of ideological values which its members can identify with. In the United Kingdom, the Conservative party has traditionally been identified with such core values as the self-reliance of individuals, less rather than more government and the role of law and order. The Labour party, by contrast, has traditionally stood for state intervention where market failure has occurred, protection of the weak in society from the strong and efforts to reduce inequalities in wealth. The Liberal Democrat party has traditionally appealed to people who believe in open democratic government in a market economy with government intervention where market mechanisms have produced inequalities or inefficiencies.

The Conservative party has traditionally been seen as the party of business and the Labour party as the party of organized labour. This has been true as far as the funding of the parties goes, with the Conservative party receiving sizeable donations from business organizations while many Labour MPs are sponsored by trade unions (although the number of donations by business to New Labour has increased in recent years). In general, the free market enterprise values of the Conservative party would appear to favour the interests of businesses, while the socialist values of the Labour party would appear to be against business interests. Historically, business has been worried at the prospect of a Labour government, as witnessed by the fall in stock market prices which has often followed a Labour party election victory. However, the United Kingdom, like many Western countries, has seen increasing levels of convergence between parties which makes business leaders very uncertain about just what makes a party's policies distinctive. For example, the UK Labour party has traditionally been opposed to privatization of public utilities, but the New Labour government elected in 1997 had no plans to renationalize previously privatized companies, and indeed proposed privatizing London Underground and the air navigation services. As political parties have targeted the crucial middle ground 'floating voter', their underlying ideologies have become increasingly indistinguishable.

The UK political environment has traditionally been dominated at a national level by two major parties. By contrast, many other European countries have a long tradition of multiple parties which represent different shades of opinion and each send small numbers of members to their legislative body. The result is often that no one party is able to form an executive with an outright majority of members, so executives based on a coalition of parties must be formed. There is an argument that such diversity of parties in the legislature allows for a wide range of political views to be represented in the government, in contrast to two-party systems where minority opinions can easily be lost. Against this, the reality is often that a minority party is often able to hold power which is disproportionate to its size, by threatening to withhold its membership of a coalition. Coalition governments also have a tendency to be very unstable and withdrawal of one party may bring down an executive. Radical change which occurred with the strong single party governments of the Conservative party in the 1980s may be much more difficult where a coalition government has to broker a compromise between all parties.

Social exclusion

Political parties have often based their principal ideology on a desire to see a more equitable distribution of wealth and life chances within society. Some great revolutions in history have been brought about by the socially excluded using force to overturn the power of an élite. The New Labour government of 1997 set about reducing social exclusion in a more low key manner, but nevertheless as an important part of its election promise.

Social exclusion is a shorthand term for what can happen when people or areas suffer from a combination of linked problems such as unemployment, poor skills, low incomes, poor housing, high-crime environments, bad health and family breakdown. In the past, governments have had policies that tried to deal with each of these problems individually, but there has been little success at tackling the complicated links between them, or preventing them from arising in the first place.

In response to these problems, the UK government created the Social Exclusion Unit in December 1997. Its remit has been to help improve government action to reduce social exclusion by producing 'joined-up solutions to joined-up problems'. Most of its work is based on specific projects, which the Prime Minister chooses following consultation with other ministers and suggestions from interested groups. The unit is staffed by a combination of civil servants and external secondees. They come from a number of government departments and from organizations with experience of tackling social exclusion – the probation service, housing, police, local authorities, the voluntary sector and business.

One of the unit's early reports focused on problems caused by housing estates which had become 'sink areas'. Numerous government agencies had tackled the problems, but more concerted collective action was needed if significant results were to be achieved. The unit's report on neighbourhood renewal was published in September 1998. It gave a detailed picture of the concentration in poor neighbourhoods of a range of interlocking problems such as high levels of unemployment, crime and ill health, and poor education. It showed how the gap with the rest of the country had widened, and analysed why previous initiatives to deal with the problems had failed. The report set out a range of issues on which urgent policy work was needed with the aim of bridging the gap between the poorest neighbourhoods and the rest. The Social Exclusion Unit set up 18 Policy Action Teams (PATs) to work on solutions, bringing together civil servants and outside experts to develop a National Strategy for Neighbourhood Renewal. Alongside the publication of the report, the £800 million 'New Deal for Communities' programme was announced, providing intensive support to some of the poorest neighbourhoods, beginning with 17 Pathfinder areas.

Redistribution of wealth

Left to market forces, numerous studies have suggested that the wealthier members of a society would continue to get richer, while the poor would find it difficult to escape from their relative poverty. Karl Marx's analysis predicted the end of capitalism on the basis that without the spending power of the poor, the wealthy owners of resources would have no markets for the products from which they made profits. In reality, Marx's thesis was weakened by new overseas opportunities to recirculate capital owners' wealth. During the twentieth century, progress towards a more egalitarian distribution of the wealth has been slow and has required intervention by governments.

Governments with socialist leanings have recognized that there is nothing inherently just in the pattern of market rewards that reflects the accidents of heredity and the labour skills that happen to be in demand at the time. A distinguishing feature of the left in politics is often its belief in a positive role for government. However, redistribution has acquired a bad name because it has been associated with the politics of envy. It has also sometimes been carried out in such a way as to interfere unnecessarily with incentives.

Under previous Labour governments, taxation on marginal income has exceeded 90 per cent. This has invariably entrenched the position of those who already own wealth or who can take their rewards in the form of professional perks, while discouraging those who want to better themselves without the aid of tax advisers.

Actually getting benefits to lower income groups can pose a challenge for policy makers. Minimum wage legislation, introduced in the United Kingdom in 1999, may provide guaranteed levels of income for the poorest members of society, but higher earning individuals invariably seek to maintain differentials, leaving minimum wage employees in a position of relative poverty, and possibly putting an employer at a competitive disadvantage compared to companies located in low-wage economies. An alternative approach to redistribution has been to increase the benefits paid to individuals who are not in work. But this has often led to a 'poverty trap' whereby it is not financially advantageous for an individual to enter employment, because the benefits that they are giving up are greater than the wages that they will earn. There are a number of structural issues that governments have sought to tackle in order to improve the relative economic standing of disadvantaged groups. As an example, many single parents have found it uneconomic to enter the labour market because the loss of benefits and costs of childcare are greater than their earnings.

Pursuing full employment may be an admirable goal as a means of reducing poverty. But public perceptions of government programmes to get people off of benefits and into employment can very easily change from enlightenment to harassment once pressure is put on people, whether they be the well-meaning unmarried mother or the work shy who would rather claim benefit than work.

LOCAL GOVERNMENT

Local authorities in the United Kingdom are responsible for a wide range of services, from social services and education to refuse collection and street cleaning. The structure of local government which was implemented in 1974 divided the largely rural areas of England into counties ('shire counties'), each with a County Council. The chief responsibilities of these County Councils included education, social services, emergency services, highways and refuse disposal. Shire counties were further subdivided into District Councils (sometimes designated as Borough or City Councils) which had responsibilities for housing, leisure services and refuse collection. Districts in rural areas were usually further divided into parishes with a Parish Council (sometimes designated as a Town Council) responsible for local matters such as the maintenance of playing fields.

In the larger conurbations, Metropolitan District Councils had greater functions than their shire county counterparts, for example they were additionally responsible for education and social services. Following the abolition of Metropolitan County Councils in 1986, responsibility for conurbation-wide services (such as public transport and emergency services) passed to a series of joint boards governed by the District Councils. In London, the pattern of government has been broadly similar to that of Metropolitan areas, although there is now an Assembly for the capital (see below). In Scotland, the structure of local government has been based on a two-tier system of Regional and District Councils.

From the mid-1990s, the basic structure of local government set up by the 1974 Act has been changed further by the appointment of commissions to study the needs of local government in individual areas. This has led to the emergence of 'unitary' authorities that combine functions of District and County Councils. Many large urban areas, such as Leicester, Nottingham and Bristol have gained their own unitary authorities, in the hope that previous duplication of facilities provided by District and County Councils can be avoided. As an example, the new 'unitary' authority for Leicester combines previous City Council functions of housing, refuse collection and car parking (among others) with responsibilities transferred from Leicestershire County Council for education, social services and highways.

Arguments for large County Councils based on economies of scale and centralized provision have given way to a philosophy based on small, locally responsive units acting as an enabler for services provided by subcontracted suppliers. Even a small, recreated county such as Rutland, it is argued, can provide many services previously considered too complex for such a small unit, by buying them in from outside suppliers, or by acting in partnership with other local authorities.

8.4.1   **The relationship between central and local government**

It has been argued that local government in Britain is losing its independence from central government, despite claims by successive governments that they support a philosophy of less government and a decentralization of powers. There is a lot of evidence of this erosion of local autonomy:

- Over half of local government income now comes in the form of grants from the Department of Environment, Transport and Regions

- Local authorities have had the ability to set rates on business premises taken away from them altogether and these are now determined by central government

■ Furthermore, central government has the power to set a maximum permitted total expenditure for a local authority and to set a maximum amount for its council tax due from householders.

In addition, legislation setting performance standards in education and social services (among others) has limited the independence of local government to set locally determined standards. Local authorities now have less local discretion in determining what is an acceptable standard for services in its area and in deciding between competing priorities. They have had increasing numbers of functions removed from their responsibility and placed with non-departmental public bodies (NDPBs) which are no longer answerable to the local authority (for example, colleges of further education now have their own governing bodies).

8.4.2   **Obtaining best value in local government**

Given that local authorities account for a high proportion of total public expenditure, central government has been increasingly determined in its efforts to ensure that authorities spend their money wisely and do not exceed total public sector spending limits. During the 1980s the UK government introduced Compulsory Competitive Tendering (CCT) for a range of services provided by local authorities. This required an ever-widening range of services which had been provided internally by an authority to be given to a private or public sector organization that could provide the service at the lowest cost. From relatively straightforward services such as refuse collection, the scope of CCT eventually extended to many professionals services provided by local authorities, including accountancy and legal services. By the 1990s it had become apparent that CCT's emphasis on cost reduction had done little to improve the quality of services provided by local authorities. Moreover, the process of competitive tendering consumed large amounts of staff time and the financial savings resulting from tendering were becoming more illusory.

An alternative approach was adopted by the Local Government Act 1999, which introduced the concept of 'best value' in specified local authorities. The Act places on authorities a duty to seek continuous improvement in the way in which they exercise their functions. At the heart of best value is a statutory performance management framework. This provides for a set of national performance indicators and standards set by the government. In order to ensure that the best-value performance indicators give a balanced view of performance the government has adopted five 'dimensions' of performance. These are:

■ Strategic objectives: why the service exists and what it seeks to achieve

■ Cost/efficiency: the resources committed to a service and the efficiency with which they are turned into outputs

■ Service delivery outcomes: how well the service is being operated in order to achieve the strategic objectives

■ Quality: the quality of the services delivered, explicitly reflecting users' experience of services

■ Fair access: ease and equality of access to services.

A series of best value performance indicators have been set by the government. The Best Value Corporate Health indicators provide a snapshot of how well the authority is performing overall. These indicators are designed to reflect the underlying capacity and performance of local authorities and other public bodies responsible for managing a significant share of public expenditure. Best Value Service Delivery indicators are designed to enable comparisons to be made between the performances of different authorities, including different types of authorities, and within an authority over time. Authorities need to set targets for all indicators which are relevant to the services they provide.

8.5   REGIONAL GOVERNMENT

The end of the 1990s saw a potentially fundamental change in the structure of government in the United Kingdom with the emergence of regional elected government. Although many European countries such as Germany and France have had some degree of regional government, this has been largely absent in the UK. The electorates of Scotland and Wales voted for new elected Assemblies from 1999. The Scottish Assembly has powers to raise up to 2p in the pound to spend as it wishes and is likely to become a significant element in the marketing environment of firms operating in Scotland. The impact of the Welsh Assembly is likely to be relatively less, as it has no tax-raising powers. Northern Ireland reinstated an elected assembly for the Province during 1998. London gained a regional Assembly in 1999, nearly two decades after the abolition of the Greater London Council. Advocates of regional Assemblies argue that they will allow legislation and economic policy to be developed that is better suited to the needs of their area. Critics would argue that they create more bureaucracy which will cost businesses time and money. Delays in implementing policies may occur where the aims of national and regional governments differ, but co-operation between the two is essential if a regional policy is to be successfully implemented. Legal challenges by the London Assembly against the Department of Transport, Environment and Regions over privatization of the London Underground demonstrated that interdependencies between regional and national governments are likely to remain strong.

The likely effects of regional governments on business organizations is ambiguous. On the one hand it can be argued that increasing amounts of UK legislation are merely enactments of EU directives which would need to be enacted regardless of whether it is the UK parliament or national assembly which assumes the responsibility. On the other hand there are many areas of discretion, which can lead to differences between regions. Where they have tax-raising revenues, regional assembly funds can be directed towards what are considered to be regionally important social goals. As an example of differences which can emerge, the Scottish Assembly voted in 2001 to fund long-term care for elderly people, something which was not available in England, and thereby opening up business opportunities in Scotland which were not available in England.

NON-DEPARTMENTAL PUBLIC BODIES (NDPBs)

The 1990s saw significant developments in the delegation of powers from government organizations to 'arm's length' executive agencies, often referred to collectively as quasi-autonomous non-governmental organizations (QUANGOs), or more correctly, Non-Departmental Public Bodies (NDPBs). In Britain, quasi-governmental bodies exist because direct involvement by a government department in an activity is considered to be inefficient or undesirable, while leaving the activity to the private sector may be inappropriate where issues of public policy are concerned. The quasi-government body therefore represents a compromise between the constitutional needs of government control and the organizational needs of independence and flexibility associated with private sector organizations.

There is nothing new in arm's length organizations being created by governments, for example the Arts Council has existed since before the Second World War. As the size of the state increased in the early post-Second-World-War period, there was concern that government departments were becoming overloaded. In 1968 the Fulton Committee came out in favour of hiving off some government activities and NDPBs were one means of doing this.

A flood of NDPBs created during the 1970s (e.g. the Equal Opportunities Board, Regional Tourist Boards and the Civil Aviation Authority) led to Conservative calls for a cut in their number. However, the incoming Conservative government of 1979 soon began adding to their number, after a token culling of a few unpopular bodies. In particular, the privatization programme led to the creation of regulators for the utilities. These are non-ministerial government departments, but with built-in independence from ministerial control. The Conservative governments from the 1980s onwards were responsible for a significant increase in the numbers of NDPBs, which had reached 5500 by 1994. In that year they accounted for £46.4 billion of expenditure, equivalent to about one-third of total government expenditure.

Many aspects of government have been devolved to NDPBs. These are some examples:

- Regulatory bodies (e.g. Oftel, Ofwat and Ofgem)

- Regional development agencies

- The Driver and Vehicle Licensing Agency.

NDPBs enjoy considerable autonomy from their parent department and the sponsoring Minister has no direct control over the activities of the body, other than making the appointment of the chairman. The Minister therefore ceases to be answerable to Parliament for the day-to-day activities of the body, unlike the responsibility that a Minister has in respect of a government department. The responsibilities of NDPBs vary from being purely advisory to making important policy decisions and allocating large amounts of expenditure. Their income can come from a combination of government grant, precepts from local authorities and charges to customers.

The main advantage of delegation to NDPBs is that action can generally be taken much more quickly than may have been the case with a government department, where it would probably have been necessary to receive ministerial approval before action was taken. Ministers may have less time to devote to the details of policy application with which many NDPBs are often involved, and may also be constrained to a much greater extent by broader considerations of political policy. Being relatively free of day-to-day political interference, NDPBs are in a better position to maintain a long-term plan free of short-term diversions which may be the result of direct control by a Minister who is subject to the need for short-term political popularity.

Against the advantages, NDPBs have a number of potential disadvantages over government departments. It is often argued that NDPBs are not sufficiently accountable to elected representatives for their actions. This can become an important issue where an NDPB is responsible for developing policy or is a monopoly provider of an essential service. Many have also questioned the actual independence of NDPBs from government, as many are still dependent on government funding for block grants. An NDPB can easily become unpopular with the public, especially where senior managers are seen paying themselves high salaries as they take 'business-like' decisions to cut back on services that they provide to the public.

THINKING AROUND THE SUBJECT

During the 1990s governments have sought to transform the United Kingdom's National Health Service from a slumbering, inwardly looking organization to one that is more focused on meeting patients' needs. In its attempts to become more professionally managed, governments have increasingly set NHS managers performance targets. By publishing many of these targets in the Patients' Charter, users of the NHS should be able to expect a minimum level of service as specified. The idea of introducing targets which mainly relate to customer handling rather than clinical issues has been dismissed by many as mere window dressing. But even the meaning of these non-clinical statistics is open to doubt, as hospitals find ways of making their performance look good on paper, if not in practice.

Accident and Emergency departments use triage nurses to assess new patients upon arrival, thereby keeping within their Patients' Charter target for the time taken to first see a new patient. However, Accident and Emergency departments may be slower to provide actual treatment, given the subsequent waiting time was not included as a Patients' Charter performance indicator.

Even the whole value of publishing performance indicators for hospitals has been questioned by many. What does it mean if a consultant or a department has a long waiting time for appointments? Rather than being an indicator of inefficiency, could it be that a long waiting list is an indicator of a consultant who is very popular with patients?

A major objective of delegation to NDPBs has been to ensure that services are provided more in line with users' requirements rather than political or operational expediency. High-level appointments to NDPBs have been made from the private sector with a view to bringing about a cultural change that develops a customer-focused ethos. For the marketing services industry, the development of NDPBs has resulted in many opportunities as they increasingly use the services of market research firms, advertising agencies and public relations consultants.

8.6.1 Public private partnerships (PPPs)

Public private partnership (PPP) is a term used to cover a wide range of activities in which the public and private sectors work together to improve services. One form of PPP is a project under the Private Finance Initiative (PFI), but PPP could also extend to other forms of partnership, for example, joint ventures. Traditionally, government has procured facilities and services which the private sector has supplied under contract to the public sector. Under partnership arrangements, the two sectors work together. For example, under the traditional route, a private sector contractor would build a new school to the Local Education Authority's (LEA's) specification, with associated maintenance and services then being provided by a range of private companies and the LEA. With PPP, one contractor provides the school and then operates a range of specific services such as maintenance, heating and school meals on behalf of the LEA through a longer term contract. This new way of working allows the private sector to contribute its expertise to the process and for both sectors to harness their energies, so as to find innovative solutions and secure better value for money.

The most significant benefits to government of PPP come through transferring risk to the private sector. This means that should a project under the PPP overrun its budget, the government and taxpayers would not be left to pick up the bill. Contrast this with a major project taken forward under direct contract to the public sector, such as London Transport's Jubilee Line Extension. This overran its planned budget by around £1.4 billion and opened nearly two years late, forcing the government to use taxpayers' money and grant additional funds to get the project completed. Under a proposed PPP for London Underground, the private sector would bear the risk of additional costs and the government would not have to fund any shortfalls. PPP is based on a belief that the private sector is more efficient at managing large engineering projects (such as modernization of the London Underground). In principle, a PPP will result in a lower level of government borrowing and it should also achieve best value. A public sector comparator is developed in order to establish whether the PPP represents better value. It will show the overall cost of raising the finance and actually doing the work under a wholly public sector arrangement.

However, critics of PPPs argue that the price of involvement by the private sector inevitably includes a high premium to cover the risk of a budget overrun which could come about for a variety of extraneous reasons. Although the government is saved the initial capital expenditure, over the longer term, it has to pay rental charges for the use of facilities, which could work out more expensive than undertaking the whole task itself. Where there is ambiguity over the PPP, disputes may arise over the parties' liability for costs.

THE EUROPEAN UNION

The European Union (EU), formerly known as the European Community (EC), has its origins in the European Coal and Steel Community. The EC was founded by the Treaty of Rome, signed in 1957 by the original six members of the ECSC: France, West Germany, Italy, Belgium, The Netherlands and Luxembourg. Britain joined the EC in 1972, together with Ireland and Denmark, to be joined by Greece in 1981, Spain and Portugal in 1986 and Austria, Finland and Sweden in 1995. The combined population of EU countries in 1998 was 374.5 million. Further expansion is expected, with the possibility of a number of Eastern and Central European states joining, although such an expansion raises issues about the nature of an enlarged EU.

On 1 January 1994 the EC linked with five of the seven members of the European Free Trade Association (EFTA) to create the 'European Economic Area' ('EEA'). Three of these members subsequently became full members of the EU. The EEA agreement extended the four basic freedoms of the EC to EEA members, that is, freedom of movement of services, freedom of movement of capital, freedom of movement of goods and freedom of movement of workers. Details of EU and EEA member states are shown in Table 8.2.

Table 8.2 Member states of the EU and EEA at 2001	
EU	EEA
Belgium	Iceland
Denmark	Norway
Finland	
France	
Germany	
Greece	
Ireland	
Italy	
Luxemburg	
Portugal	
Spain	
Sweden	
The Netherlands	
United Kingdom	

Aims of the EU

The Treaty of Rome initially created a Customs Union and a Common Market. The creation of a Customs Union has involved the introduction of a common external tariff on trade with the rest of the world and the abolition of tariffs between member states. When the United Kingdom joined the EC, tariffs tended to encourage trade with Commonwealth countries at the expense of European countries. In particular, the United Kingdom had been able to obtain a source of relatively cheap agricultural produce from Commonwealth countries, but on joining the EC was forced to phase in a common tariff for agricultural products imported from outside the EC.

An important aim of the Treaty of Rome was the creation of a common market in which trade could take place between member states as if they were one country. The implication of a common market is the free movement of trade, labour and capital between member states. So far, it is in agriculture that the most genuinely common market has been created, with a system of common pricing and support payments between all countries and free movement of produce between member states. Further development of a common market has been impeded by a range of non-tariff trade barriers, such as national legislation specifying design standards, the cost and risk of currency exchange and the underlying desire of public authorities to back their own national industries. In principle, the creation of the Single European Market in January 1993 should have removed many of these barriers, but many practical barriers to trade still remain, of which differences in language and cultural traditions are probably the most intractable.

There is considerable debate about the form that future development of the EU should take and in particular, the extent to which there should be political as well as economic union. Debate continues about the future of the EU and in recent times has focused on the following issues:

1 The creation of a common unit of currency has been seen by many as crucial to the development of a single European market, avoiding the cost and uncertainty for business and travellers of having to change currencies for cross-border transactions. The launch of the single European currency (the 'euro') in 1999 has reduced transaction costs for trade between member states and has allowed member states' central banks to reduce their holdings of foreign currency. Within the UK, opposition to monetary union has been based on economic and political arguments. Economically, a common currency would deny to countries the opportunity to revalue or devalue their currency to suit the needs of their domestic economy. This lack of flexibility implies a political sacrifice, as control of currency is central to government management of the economy (although it should be noted that the UK government has handed over control of monetary policy to the Bank of England in an attempt to depoliticize financial policy). During 2001 eurosceptics seized on guidance given by the European Central Bank (ECB) to the Irish government. Irish inflation was approaching upper limits set by the ECB, and in asking the Irish government to take fiscal measures to reduce inflation, this was seen as interfering in what was perceived as a very successful national economy.

Regardless of whether the UK government formally adopts the euro, businesses may start using the currency, in much the same way as non-US companies often trade in US dollars. It will gain acceptability if businesses perceive the currency as being stable and widely accepted.

2   Argument continues about the amount of influence the EU should have in nation states' social and economic policy. For example, previous UK governments have shown reluctance to agree to EU proposals designed to protect the employment conditions of workers, arguing that this would reduce the competitiveness of UK businesses. The UK government has supported the idea of 'subsidiarity' whereby decisions are taken at the most localized level of government that is compatible with achieving EU objectives. Cynics, however, have pointed out that the UK government has not always been willing to practise this principle at home, as witnessed by the gradual erosion of the powers of local authorities in favour of central government.

3   Many additional countries have now formally or informally applied to join the EU. There is concern that the arrival of less developed economies of Central and Eastern Europe could put strains on EU budgets. Many have argued that enlargement should allow the EU to become a loose federation of states, rather than a centralizing bureaucracy which many critics claim it has become.

4   The principle of free movement of people across borders remains controversial, in view of the possibility of large numbers of refugees or economic migrants being admitted by one state and then being automatically allowed to migrate to other member states.

5   Member states still have difficulty formulating a coherent foreign policy for the EU as a whole, as has been seen in the fragmented approach taken towards conflict in former Yugoslavia.

6   There remains widespread concern about the lack of democratic accountability of EU institutions, not helped by allegations of excessive bureaucracy and corruption.

8.7.2   The structure of the EU

The Treaty of Rome (as modified by the Treaty of Maastricht) developed a structure of government whose elements reflect in part the structure of the UK government. The executive (or Cabinet) is provided by the Council of Ministers; the secretariat (or Civil Service) is provided by the European Commission; while the legislature is provided by the European Parliament. The judiciary is represented by the European Court of Justice.

   The Treaty of Rome places constraints upon the policies that the institutions of the EU can adopt. The European Court of Justice is able to rule that an action or decision is not in accordance with the Treaty. In some cases, such as competition policy, the Treaty is quite specific, for example Articles 85 and 86 which define the basic approach to be adopted in dealing with cartels and monopoly power. On the other hand, the Treaty says little more on transport policy than that there should

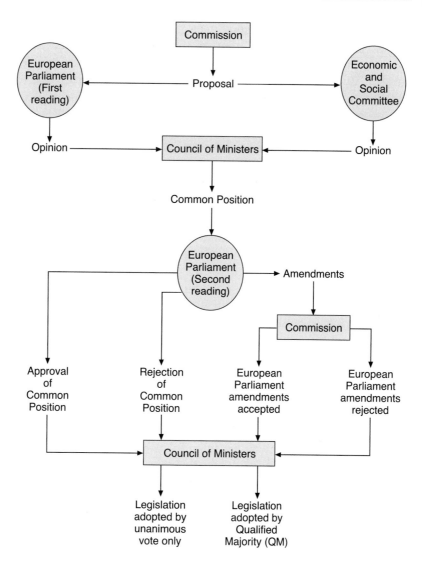

Figure 8.4
The process of co-operation in passing new European legislation

be a common policy, giving the community institutions considerable power to develop policies.

The activities of the EU are now directly funded from income received from customs duties and other levies on goods entering the EU from non-member countries. In addition, a value added tax collected by member states on purchases by consumers includes an element of up to 1.45 per cent which is automatically transferred to the EU budget. More recently, a new resource transfer payment between member states and the EU has been introduced which is based on the gross domestic product of each member state. The United Kingdom remains a net contributor to the EU budget.

New legislation is increasingly the result of co-operation between the various institutions of the EU. The process of co-operation is shown in Figure 8.4 and the role of the principal institutions described below.

The Council of Ministers

The Council of Ministers represents the governments of member states and can be regarded as the principal lawmaker of the EU, although it can only act on proposals submitted by the Commission. It has powers to:

- Adopt legislation
- Ratify treaties after consultation with the European parliament
- Ask the commission to undertake studies and to submit legislation
- Delegate executive and legislative powers to the Commission.

Each member state sends one Minister to the European Council of Ministers. Which Minister attends will depend on the subject being discussed – for example agriculture Ministers would be sent if the Common Agricultural Policy was being discussed. The Ministers of foreign affairs, of agriculture, and those with budgetary responsibilities meet more frequently, making a senior body within the Council, sometimes called the General Council. The chairmanship or presidency of the Council of Ministers rotates between countries in alphabetical order, with each period of presidency lasting for six months.

The Council of Ministers adopts new legislation either by simple majority, qualified majority or unanimity:

- Simple majority gives each Minister one vote and is used for proposals such as procedural rules for the convening of intergovernmental conferences. Qualified majority voting is based on a weighted voting system where member states' votes are roughly proportional to their size and economic strength (see Table 8.3). Qualified majority voting prevents smaller states being consistently outvoted and eliminates the risk of two of the larger member states constituting a blocking majority. A qualified majority is 62 votes out of a total of 87. A blocking minority is 26 votes. Examples of applications of this method of voting include legislation on completion of the internal market; the freedom to provide professional services across national borders; and measures to free-up the movement of capital within the EU.
- Unanimity is required on issues that are fundamental to individual member states' interests, such as enlargement of the EU, harmonization of taxation and extension of EU powers.

In 2000 an intergovernmental conference of ministers agreed to reduce the number of areas in which unanimity was required. With the prospect of enlargement, achieving unanimity between all member states was likely to become increasingly difficult.

The Council of Ministers can generally pass laws even if the European Parliament disagrees with them, unlike the practice within the UK system where Ministers must obtain approval of a majority of Members of Parliament. There are two main exceptions to this authority of the Council. Firstly, the European Parliament has power to approve or reject the EU budget (see below). Secondly, the Single European Act introduced a system of legislative co-operation between the

Table 8.3 Voting rights within European Union institutions

Country	Qualified voting rights of EU Council of Ministers	Number of MEPs returned to European Parliament
Germany	10	99
Italy	10	87
UK	10	87
France	10	87
Spain	8	64
The Netherlands	5	31
Belgium	5	25
Greece	5	25
Portugal	5	25
Austria	4	21
Sweden	4	22
Denmark	3	16
Finland	3	16
Ireland	3	15
Luxembourg	2	6
Total	87	626

Council and Parliament, obliging the Council and the Commission to take Parliament's amendments to proposals into consideration, although a unanimous vote by the Council of Ministers retains ultimate authority.

The Committee of Permanent Representatives (Coreper) complements the work of the Council of Ministers. Because Ministers have responsibilities to their own national governments as well as to the European Union, they cannot give a continuing presence. To make up for this, each member state sends one ambassador to the Committee, which is based in Brussels. Proposals are discussed in Coreper and its subcommittees before they reach Ministers. If Coreper reaches full agreement on the matter, it is empowered to pass it through the Council without further debate, but where disagreement occurs it is left for Ministers to discuss.

8.7.4

The European Commission

Each member state sends one Commissioner to the Commission (the larger members send two), each appointed by the member government for a renewable term of four years. They are supported in their work by a staff of about 14 000 civil servants, divided between 23 directorates-general and mainly based at the Commission's headquarters in Brussels. The Commission is headed by a President. Each Commissioner is given responsibility for a portfolio which could be for a policy area such as transport, or for administrative matters, such as the

Commission's relations with the Parliament, while others are given a combination of responsibilities in their portfolio. Unlike the Council of Ministers, all members of the Commission are supposed to act primarily for the benefit of the EU as a whole, rather than the country that they represent. This is spelt out in Article 157 of the Treaty of Rome which states that Commissioners 'shall neither seek nor take instruction from any other body'.

The Commission has an initiation, mediation and implementation role. As an initiator, it is the task of the Commission to draft proposals for legislation which the Council of Ministers has to consider. If the Council does not accept a proposal, it can only alter the draft by a unanimous vote. If unanimity cannot be achieved, the proposal has to go back to the Commission for it to draft a revised proposal which will be acceptable to the Council of Ministers.

As a mediator, the Commission can intervene in disputes between member states to try to find a solution through negotiation. The Commission has frequently acted as mediator in trade disputes between members, avoiding recourse to the European Court of Justice. As an implementer, the Commission undertakes the day-to-day administration of the EU. This involves monitoring the activities of member states to ensure that they do not conflict with community policy. In addition, the Commission implements community policies such as the Regional Development Fund and Common Agricultural Policy.

8.7.5   The European Parliament

Unlike the UK parliament, the European Parliament is primarily consultative and has relatively little power. Its main function is to monitor the activities of other EU institutions. It can give an opinion on Commission proposals, but only has powers to amend, adopt or reject legislation, especially the EU budget. It also has the theoretical power to dismiss the entire Commission, for which a censure motion must be passed by a two-thirds majority of Members. Although it can dismiss the entire Commission, the Parliament has no control over the selection of new Commissioners to replace those who have been dismissed. It does not yet have the power to initiate and enact legislation.

Members of the European Parliament are now directly elected by the constituents of each country. Parliament has a total of 626 members (MEPs), of which 87 represent United Kingdom constituencies, with other countries returning members roughly in proportion to their populations. The European Parliament generally meets in Strasbourg, but Parliamentary Committee meetings are held in Brussels and in Luxembourg, where the Parliament's Secretariat is mainly based. Members of the European Parliament increasingly belong to political rather than national groupings (e.g. the British Conservative MEPs sit in the European People's Party).

8.7.6   The European Court of Justice

The supreme legislative body of the EU is provided by the Court of Justice. Article 164 of the Treaty of Rome gave the Court the task of 'ensuring that the law is observed in the interpretation and implementation of the Treaty'. It is the final arbiter in all matters of interpreting EU treaties and rules on disputes between member states, between member states and the Commission and between the Commission and business organizations, individuals or EU officials. Although the Court can condemn violations of the Treaty by member governments, it has no sanctions against them except goodwill. The European Court of Justice can investigate complaints that the Commission has acted beyond its powers and, if upheld, can annul decisions of the Commission.

The European Court of Justice is composed of 15 judges, assisted by nine advocates-general. Each is appointed by common agreement between the 15 member states on the basis of their qualifications and impartiality, for a renewable six-year term of office. Members of the Court must put European interests before national interests. The Court can be called upon to settle disputes where the persuasion and negotiations of the Commission have failed to yield results. For example, in the area of competition policy, the Commission may by decision forbid an anticompetitive practice or impose a fine. The companies concerned can appeal to the European Court of Justice for the decision to be set aside. In one case, several dye producers appealed to the European Court of Justice against the fines imposed on them for an alleged price cartel. Before the days of Sunday shopping in the United Kingdom, the Court was called upon to give its judgement on whether retailers seeking to open on Sundays could claim that the UK's Shops Act 1950 was in conflict with the Treaty of Rome by restricting trade.

8.7.7 **Relationship between EU and UK government**

A distinction needs to be drawn between primary and secondary legislation of the EU. Primary legislation is contained in the Treaty of Rome (and subsequent treaties agreed by an intergovernmental conference) and takes precedence over national legislation, although national legislation may be required to implement it. Primary legislation can only be altered by an intergovernmental conference of all members. Secondary legislation is made by the Council of Ministers and the Commission under authority delegated to them by the treaties. Secondary legislation affects member states in several forms.

- *Regulations* automatically form part of the law of member states and apply directly to every individual in the EU. They give rights and duties to individuals that national courts must recognize.

- *Directives* are mandatory instructions to member states who must take steps to implement them through national legislation. For example, national laws concerning vehicle safety vary from state to state and as a result trade across frontiers may be impeded. One solution has been to harmonize standards between all member states by means of a directive. The directive will require member states to amend their national legislation governing the design of cars. Individuals will then have to obey the modified national law.

- *Decisions* of the EU are directly binding on the specific individuals or organizations to whom they are addressed, as where the Commission intervenes in a proposed merger between organizations.

Effects of EU membership on UK business organizations

The EU is having an increasingly important effect on business organizations in the United Kingdom. The relationship between a company and its customers is more and more being influenced by EU regulations and directives, for example in the provision of safety features in cars and the labelling of foods. The influence extends to the relationship between the firm and the public at large, as where the EU passes directives affecting advertising standards and pollution controls. Business organizations must monitor proposed EU legislation not only to spot possible changes in legislation which will eventually be implemented through national legislation, but also to lobby to bring about a desired change in EU law. To an increasing extent, lobbying of the UK parliamentary process is becoming less effective as the United Kingdom is bound to implement legislation emanating from the EU.

The extent to which the Single European market legislation will further affect business organizations is open to debate. The EU has already had the effect of removing tariff barriers within the Community and great progress has been made on EU legislation specifying common product design standards. Firms are increasingly seeing Europe as one market and designing standardized products which appeal to consumers in a number of EU states. Many would argue that overseas investors, especially American firms, have always regarded Europe as one market and developed products as varied as soft drinks and cars to satisfy the whole European market. However, no amount of legislation is likely to overcome the hidden barriers to trade provided by language and by ingrained market characteristics such as the UK practice of driving on the left and using electrical plugs that are not used elsewhere in Continental Europe.

The United Kingdom was not among the initial group of countries that

---

THINKING AROUND THE SUBJECT

Tobacco advertising is a very emotive issue, and while some countries have banned such advertising, the UK has managed with compromises based on voluntary codes of conduct. In 1998, the flexibility of such agreements seemed threatened by an EU directive that would effectively end tobacco advertising throughout the EU. The tobacco industry realized that the directive must be stopped at Brussels before it was incorporated into member states' legislation. Through its industry group, the Tobacco Manufacturers Association, it had failed through its previous lobbying to stop the directive, so now moved to challenge the directive in the European Court of Justice. The

Association claimed that the EU legislation is a public health matter dressed up as an internal single market measure. It argued that Brussels has no authority to make a public health directive under its powers to harmonize the internal market. It may sound like last minute desperate measures, but the industry had seen its sales declining sharply and a big increase in 'bootleg' sales of illegally imported cigarettes. Would the lobbying give up? The Tobacco Manufacturers Association seemed determined to do everything it could to stop the directive, even to the point of saying that it would be happy to plead freedom of speech under the European Convention on Human Rights.

launched the single European currency. Shortly after launch, the value of the euro fell sharply against sterling, making exports from the United Kingdom to the rest of the EU more expensive (and competitors' imports to the United Kingdom cheaper). The high value of sterling was blamed by many manufacturing companies for decisions to move operations to within the euro area, or to not make further investments in the United Kingdom. However, there was little evidence of actual amounts of inward investment falling during the period that the value of sterling remained high. Many firms benefited from the high value of sterling, as imported components became less expensive. The subject of the impact of the euro on business is considered further in Chapter 10.

8.7.9

The EU and the development of e-business

At the 2000 summit of EU leaders held in Nice, leaders stated their intention for Europe 'to become the most competitive and dynamic knowledge-based economy in the world'. A programme of action included: the creation of a fully integrated and liberalized telecoms market by the end of 2001; a single market for financial services by 2005; making all EU public services, including tenders, available on the Internet; an EU regulatory framework and common security standards for e-commerce; connecting all schools and training centres to the Internet; and creating an IT 'passport' of specific skills.

Since the summit, there has been a flurry of activity: an accelerated effort to boost national programmes for promoting e-business and getting schools online; and new laws and directives governing e-business. However, although the pace of change may be more brisk than before, those used to the rapid speed of developments in the Internet world still find EU processes very slow. Business is particularly frustrated by EU-wide government inaction in terms of creating a better environment for e-commerce to flourish in.

Can the EU rhetoric be matched by reality? A report by the UK research and consultancy group Gartner, identified a number of pressing challenges for the EU in its attempts to create an e-commerce friendly environment:

■ Antitrust authorities will have to resolve, more rapidly than at present, complex competition issues raised by mergers in the media and telecoms sectors, electronic marketplaces, wireless portals and public service providers.

■ Enterprises will need more flexible employment schemes and laws to cope with skills shortages in the information technology sector. Employers need the ability to import and outsource skills as required and a clearer legislative framework for teleworking.

■ Tax regulations need to be brought up to date to recognize the presence of Internet transactions. The Gartner study predicted that by 2003, the difference between European and US Internet tax schemes will become a major source of friction in international trade.

■ In order to boost consumers' trust in e-commerce and reduce legal uncertainty for enterprises, governments need to develop privacy laws which are relevant to the Internet.

The report painted a picture of national governments throwing money at the microenvironment of e-commerce, such as grants for computer training, often displacing money that could readily be provided by the private sector. Developing the macroenvironment for e-commerce throughout the EU is a much bigger challenge.

If the e-commerce-friendly business environment is achieved, the savings to the EU administration are likely to be considerable, with one estimate that the EU will save €700 billion (£500 billion) each year by moving more government transactions on to the Internet. In Berlin, for example, city officials have predicted savings of €7.8 billion (£5 billion) if only 50 per cent of administrative procedures could be transacted online by 2005.

The question remains as to just what it is possible for governments to do to create an e-commerce-friendly environment. Is responsibility for achieving it best left to the EU rather than national governments? Or is even the EU too small a unit for making decisions, when the Internet is progressively breaking down national boundaries?

8.7.10 Future developments of the EU

The European Union is in flux. Its main institutions of the Commission, the Council of Ministers and the European Parliament remain widely unloved and vulnerable to charges of inefficiency and lack of transparency. But, paradoxically, the EU is in many respects more active than ever before. The euro, introduced as a virtual currency in 1999, has spurred a continent-wide restructuring of business and financial markets.

The EU is committed to an ambitious enlargement that will nearly double its present membership from 15 to 27 by embracing the former Communist countries of Eastern and Central Europe plus Malta and Cyprus. Turkey, a candidate for membership later, has been offered a partnership agreement to help it to the stage where it can begin entry negotiations. Further ahead, the western Balkan countries of the former Yugoslavia are regarded as potential candidates for the EU.

The administration of the EU has subtly changed as it has matured. The initiative for many new proposals has been the European Council – summits of EU leaders held three or four times a year. By contrast, the European Commission has tended to become more of an administrator of programmes rather than the bold innovator that launched the single market in the 1980s. It was badly demoralized in March 1999 when the 20-strong Commissioners headed by Jacques Santer resigned after a critical report alleging nepotism, fraud and mismanagement. At the Nice summit in 2000, the leaders of member states identified the urgent task of defining how powers would be divided between Brussels and national governments and aimed to achieve this at an intergovernmental conference in 2004.

8.8 SUPRANATIONAL GOVERNMENTAL ORGANIZATIONS

National governments' freedom of action is further constrained by international agreements and membership of international organizations. In general, although the treaties of the EU impose duties on the UK government which it is obliged to follow, membership of other supranational organizations is voluntary and does not have binding authority on the UK government.

Probably the most important organization which affects UK government policy is the United Nations (UN). Its General and Security Councils are designed as fora in which differences between countries can be resolved through negotiation rather than force. In the field of international trade, the UN has sought to encourage freedom of trade through the United Nations Conference on Trade and Development (UNCTAD). In matters of national security, the United Kingdom is a member of the North Atlantic Treaty Organization (NATO) whose role is changing following the end of the 'Cold War'.

Because the importance to the United Kingdom of international treaties and organizations lies to such a great extent in their benefits for international trade, they are considered in more detail in Chapter 10.

8.9 INFLUENCES ON GOVERNMENT POLICY FORMATION

Political parties were described earlier as organizations that people belong to in order to influence government policy, generally over a range of issues. Political parties aim to work within the political system, for example by having members elected as MPs or local councillors. A distinction can be drawn between political parties and pressure groups or interest groups. These last two groups seek to change policy in accordance with members' interests, generally advancing a relatively narrow cause. Unlike members of political parties, members of pressure groups generally work from outside the political system and do not become part of the political establishment.

8.9.1 Pressure groups

Pressure groups can be divided into a number of categories. In the first place there is a division between those which are permanently fighting for a general cause; and those which are set up to achieve a specific objective and are dissolved when this objective is met – or there no longer seems any prospect of changing the situation. Pressure groups set up to fight specific new road building proposals fit into this category.

Pressure groups can also be classified according to their functions. *Sectional* groups exist to promote the common interests of their members over a wide range of issues. Trade unions and employers associations fall into this category. They represent their members' views to government on diverse issues such as proposed employment legislation, import controls and vocational training. This type of pressure group frequently offers other benefits to members such as legal representation for individual members and the dissemination of information to members. *Promotional* groups, on the other hand, are established to fight for specific causes, such as nuclear disarmament which is represented by CND.

Not all pressure groups represent a widespread body of grass-roots public opinion. Businesses also frequently join pressure groups as a means of influencing government legislative proposals that will affect their industry sector. An example of a powerful commercial pressure group is the British Road Federation, which represents companies with interests in road construction and lobbies government to increase expenditure on new road building.

Pressure groups can influence government policy using three main approaches.

1   The first, propaganda, can be used to create awareness of the group and its cause. This can be aimed directly at policy formers, or indirectly by appealing to the constituents of policy formers to apply direct pressure themselves. This is essentially an impersonal form of mass communication.

2   A second option is to try to represent the views of the group directly to policy formers on a one-to-one basis. Policy formers frequently welcome representations that they may see as preventing bigger problems or confrontations arising in the future. Links between pressure groups and government often become institutionalized, such as where the Department of Transport routinely seeks the views of the Automobile Association and RAC Foundation on proposals to change road traffic legislation. Where no regular contacts exist, pressure groups can be represented by giving evidence before a government appointed inquiry or by approaching sympathetic MPs, or by hiring the services of a professional lobbyist.

3   A third approach used by pressure groups is to carry out research and to supply information. This has the effect of increasing public awareness of the organization and usually has a valuable propaganda function. The British Road Federation frequently supplies MPs with comparative road statistics purporting to show reasons why the government should be spending more money on road building.

Pressure groups are most effective where they apply pressure in a low-key manner, for example where they are routinely consulted for their views. Lobbying of MPs – which combines elements of all three methods described above – has become increasingly important in recent years.

Sometimes pressure groups, or sectional interests within them, recognize that they are unlikely to achieve their aims using the channels described above. Recent years have seen an increase in 'direct action' by pressure groups, or breakaway sections of mainstream groups, against their target. Campaigners for animal rights, or those opposed to the use of genetically modified crops, have on occasions given up on trying to change the law and instead sought to disrupt the activities of organizations giving rise to their concerns. Organizations targeted in this way may initially put a brave face on such activities by dismissing them as inconsequential, but often the result has been to change the organization's behaviour, especially where the prospect of large profits is uncertain. Action by animal rights protesters contributed to the near collapse of Huntingdon Life Sciences (an animal testing laboratory), and many farmers were discouraged from taking part in GM crops trials by the prospects of direct action against their farms.

It is not only national governments to which pressure groups apply their attention – local authorities are frequently the target of pressure groups over issues of planning policy or the provision of welfare services. Increasingly, pressure is also being applied at the EU level. Again, the European Commission regularly consults some groups while other groups apply direct pressure to members of the Commission.

Business organizations have achieved numerous triumphs in attempting to influence the political environment in which they operate. The pressure group representing the tobacco industry – the Tobacco Advisory Council – has had a significant effect in countering the pressure applied by the anti-tobacco lobby, represented by Action on Smoking Health. Anti-smoking action by governments has been considerably watered down as a result.

Pressure groups themselves are increasingly crossing national boundaries to reflect the influence of international governmental institutions such as the EU and the growing influence of multinational business organizations. Both industrial and consumer pressure groups have been formed at a multinational level to counter these influences – a good example of the latter is Greenpeace.

| 8.9.2 | **Role of the media** |

The media – press, radio and television and increasingly the Internet – not only spreads awareness of political issues but also influences policy and decision making by setting the political agenda and influencing public opinion. The broadcast media in the United Kingdom must by law show balance in their coverage of political events, but the press is often more openly partisan. Campaigns undertaken by the press frequently reflect the background of their owners – the *Daily Telegraph* is more likely to support the causes of deregulation in an industry while the *Guardian* will be more likely to put forward the case for government spending on essential public services. It is often said that *The Times* and the BBC Radio 4 *Today* programme set the political agenda for the day ahead.

CASE STUDY

BUS INDUSTRY RESPONDS TO SHIFTS IN POLITICAL ENVIRONMENT

The provision of bus services in Britain has been significantly influenced by the nature of the political environment, both at a central and local government level. The bus industry can be used to illustrate many of the issues raised in this chapter, especially the changing attitude at central government level towards regulation of economic activity and at a local level to the changing role of local government.

In this changing political environment, the task of managing businesses within the sector has been transformed. The political environment has turned full circle, from reliance on free market forces until the 1920s, strict regulation until the 1980s, followed by a return to a political obsession with competitive markets. More recently, the cycle has appeared to be starting all over again, with calls for increased regulation of the sector.

The early 1920s saw large numbers of small entrepreneurs operating in competition with each other, resulting in sometimes wasteful and dangerous competitive practices. The dominant political attitude shifted during the 1920s away from a pure *laissez-faire* approach to one where state intervention in the economy was becoming more acceptable. Against this changing background, government was able to recognize that public transport was an important public service by passing the Road Traffic Act 1930. This required all bus routes to be licensed. Route licences gave the holder substantial monopoly power and large bus operating companies emerged during the 1930s by acquiring the licences of their smaller competitors. The companies thus acquired territorial monopolies which made it even more difficult for a small company to prove the need for a new service and thereby acquire a route licence. In these conditions, bus companies tended to be production rather than marketing led. A further recognition that public transport was an essential public service came when a large section of the bus industry was nationalized by the Labour government in 1948.

By the 1960s bus operation had ceased to be profitable outside the main corridors of movement, mainly due to increasing levels of car ownership. Faced with a deterioration in the quantity and quality of bus services, the Labour government of the late 1960s again intervened with the acquisition of the largest private sector group of companies, and the subsequent formation of the National Bus Company and Scottish Bus Group. These were given responsibility for running most of the large bus operators outside the major cities. The two companies were given strict financial rather than social objectives, although government did later intervene in a manner which appeared to make the companies an instrument of wider government policy. For example, they had been asked to keep fare increases down to help the government's anti-inflation policy.

Local authorities in a number of areas had for many years operated their own bus fleets for various reasons. Making profits to help keep the level of rates charged to ratepayers was one objective, but in addition, local authorities provided bus services out of civic pride and to ensure that a high standard of public service was provided. By the 1960s, local authority bus operations had also become generally unprofitable. They were often allowed to lose money if councillors decided that the service being provided justified being subsidized out of rates income.

By the 1970s, a highly regulated system of route licensing and companies having large territorial monopolies resulted in the business environment being very production rather than marketing oriented. Promotion was aimed almost entirely at existing users – providing basic information rather than trying to create a favourable image among potential users. Faced with an inelastic demand bus companies would set fares as high as politically possible with the regulatory Traffic Commissioners. Innovation in new products was nearly always reactive rather than proactive. Most innovation was aimed at cutting production costs – such as reducing the need to employ conductors through one person operation – rather than meeting the needs of consumers, such as providing faster journey times or a reliable service.

At the same time as the market for scheduled bus services appeared to be going into decline, the market for contract hire by schools, factories and private groups remained buoyant. In this market there were no quantity restrictions on operator licences, only the quality controls which applied equally to operators of scheduled bus services. The market was dominated by a large number of small firms aggressively competing against each other on price and the quality of service provided. It would be difficult for a production oriented company to survive in this environment for long.

By the 1980s, the question was being asked whether the unregulated environment which had encouraged a marketing orientation in the contract service sector could also be applied to the scheduled services sector to achieve the same effect. The traditional argument against deregulation was that licence holders who had a territorial monopoly provided some element of social service – they used profits generated on one route or at one time of day to cross-subsidize loss-making routes or less profitable evening and weekend Sunday services. The National Bus Company used this argument to defend itself, even though it had been given clearly defined profit rather than social goals by the government.

The political environment for bus operators changed significantly during the 1980s. The first change was brought about by the Conservative government's ideological belief that free and unregu-lated markets were inherently better than regulation, which was presumed to stifle innovation. The gov-ernment therefore abolished the need for route licences in most parts of the country. Any company could now operate a bus service subject to satisfying safety criteria. In addition, subsidies from local authorities to provide socially necessary, but unprofitable, bus services were put out to competitive tendering, rather than being allocated to the existing licence holder.

The second major change brought about was the restructuring and gradual dismantling of public sector bus operations. The ideology of the time considered that the state was bad at providing market-able goods and services compared to the private sector. Where a social service was considered desirable, this should be explicitly identified by policy makers in government and satisfied by market mechanisms. The first step was the breaking up of the National Bus Company and sale to the private sector. Many of the individual companies which it comprised were sold on favourable terms to their management and employees, fulfilling another wish of the Conservative government of the late 1980s – widespread capitalism. Local authorities – which had frequently operated their bus fleets as a quasi-social service were forced to restructure their operations by forming limited companies to which a board of directors was appointed with a view to eventual sale to the private sector.

Changes in the political environment had totally transformed the market for bus services during the 1980s. Marketing tools which had been used by the fast-moving consumer goods sector for many years, but ignored by this section of the bus industry, became widely used. Tactical pricing was used aggressively to gain market share, particularly by new entrants to a route who frequently made no charge to attract initial custom. Market-led new service developments occurred, such as high-frequency minibus services. Much more attention was paid to product quality, including reliability, availability of service information, training of staff and the appearance of vehicles. Corporate identity increasingly took as its starting point the values of the target customers rather than those of management.

Local monopolies of bus services had until the 1980s been seen as beneficial by the government, recognizing the implicit public service obligations of licence holders. However, in a sudden about-turn, bus operators were now subject to the same vetting for anticompetitive practices as most other industries. The Office of Fair Trading was constantly investigating claims that companies were trying to drive their competitors off the road using practices that were reminiscent of the 1920s. The powers of the OFT were weak and investigations often took a long time, allowing competitors to be driven out of a market in the meantime.

The early years of deregulation were characterized by a lot of competition between small- and medium-sized firms. However, by the mid-1990s, consolidation of the industry was beginning to create large companies, such as Stagecoach and the First Group, who had significant local monopoly power. As numbers of passengers continued to fall and fares continued to rise, cynics argued that a publicly regulated monopoly had effectively been replaced by private, unregulated monopolies, which the incoming Labour government of 1997 sought to address with tighter regulation. The government was reluctant to legislate for greater control, and besides did not want to commit government money to buying back the privatized bus companies. However, it has encouraged local authorities to work together with bus operators to create Quality Partnerships and increased funding available for innovative services.

CASE STUDY Review questions

1 Summarize the arguments for and against greater regulation of the bus industry.

2 To what extent has government policy towards the bus industry reflected the dominant political ideology of the time?

3 Briefly summarize the main marketing implications of a change from regulation to free competition for bus services.

CHAPTER Summary and links to other chapters

This chapter has explored the basis of government in the United Kingdom and the respective roles of local, national and European government. A two-way interaction occurs between government and business, in which business organizations monitor changes in the political environment, but also seek to influence the environment through lobbying. Pressure groups represent an increasingly important element of the political environment, working from outside the formal political system.

It should be quite apparent that the political environment impinges on a number of other aspects of a firm's marketing environment. Politicians have a significant impact on the national economic environment (Chapter 7) and indeed respond to changes in it. The level of competition within any market can be influenced by government policies on anticompetitive practices (Chapter 6). Government policy is translated into legislation (Chapter 9) and influences standards of behaviour expected from business (Chapter 5).

CHAPTER Review questions

1 Against the background of a worldwide trend towards privatization and deregulation, prepare a report for an Industry Association of your choice, assessing the potential threats and opportunities arising for your sector.

(Based on CIM Marketing Environment examination question)

2 Prepare arguments, for and against, greater control being exercised over business and marketing practices by government.

(Based on CIM Marketing Environment examination question)

3 Briefly identify the main areas of attention which the marketing manager of a UK bicycle manufacturer is likely to give to his or her political environment.

4 For a newspaper lobbying against government proposals to impose value added tax on newspaper sales, identify the key points within the government system at which lobbying could be applied.

5 For a British manufacturing company, briefly summarize the principal problems and opportunities presented by the development of closer economic and political union within the EU.

6 What measures can a large multinational business take to monitor the political environment in its various operating areas?

Selected further reading

For an overview of how government is managed in the United Kingdom, the following provide a useful insight:

Kester, I. (ed.) (1997) *Management in the Public Sector*, 2nd edn, ITP, London.
Lawton, A. (ed.) (1996) *Case Studies in Public Services Management*, Oxford, Blackwell.

The following provide a more specific focus on local government:

Keen, L. and R. Scase (1998) *Local Government Management*, Open University Press, Basingstoke.
Midwinter, A. and C. Monaghan (1995) 'The new centralism: local government finance in the 1990's', *Financial Accountability and Management*, vol. 11, no. 2, pp. 141–151.
Stoker, G. (1999) *The New Management of British Local Governance – Government Beyond the Centre*, Palgrave, Basingstoke.
Wilson, D. and Game, C. (1998) *Local Government in the United Kingdom*, Macmillan, Basingstoke.

The following explore the relationship between government and business:

Graham, P. (1995) 'Are public sector organisations becoming more customer centred?', *Marketing Intelligence and Planning*, vol. 13, no. 1, pp. 35–47.
McKenzie, S. and T. Rosewell (1997) 'Party time', *Marketing Business*, September, pp. 18–22.
Steiner, G. and J. Steiner, (1999) *Business, Government and Society*, McGraw-Hill, New York.

To many, the workings of the European Union are extremely complex and the following references provide a general overview:

Dinan, D. (1998) *Ever Closer Union: An Introduction to the European Union*, Macmillan, Basingstoke.
El-agraa, A. (2000) *The European Union: Economics and Policies*, Prentice-Hall, Hemel Hempstead.
Goodman, S.F. (1996) *The European Union*, 3rd edn, Macmillan, Basingstoke.
Swann, D. (2000) *The Economics of Europe: From Common Market to European Union*, Penguin Business, Harmondsworth.

The following official publications of the EU are also useful for monitoring current developments:

Basic Statistics of the Community
Bulletin of the European Commission of the European Communities

Finally, there is extensive coverage of the functions of pressure groups. The following references are useful for highlighting their relationship to business organizations:

Coxall, B. (2001) *Pressure Groups in British Politics*, Longman, Harlow.
Grant, W. (2000) *Pressure Groups and British Politics*, Palgrave, Basingstoke.

Useful websites

UK Government Gateway   This is an important access point to UK government websites. Links are provided to many local and national government sites.   **http://www.open.gov.uk/**

UK Parliament   Provides information about the House of Commons and House of Lords including details of Committees, Acts, Bills, Elections, Members of Parliament and Publications.   **http://www.parliament.uk/**

UK political parties   Websites of the main UK political parties can be found at the following addresses:
Labour: **http://www.labour.org.uk**
Conservative: **http://www.conservative-party.org.uk**
Liberal Democrat: **http://www.libdems.org.uk**

Best Value in Local Government   A forum for the UK local government (including police and fire) best value initiative. It will allow researchers and practitioners working with both pilot and non-pilot authorities to discuss how best value - economic, efficient and effective delivery of services – can be achieved.
http://www.jiscmail.ac.uk/lists/best-value-uk-local-government.html

EUsceptic.org   A website providing links to various organizations sceptical of the European Union.
http://www.eusceptic.orgl

European Union online   A useful entry point for information about the European Union. Provides information on the Parliament, the Council, the Commission, the Court of Justice, the Court of Auditors and other bodies of the European Union.   **http://europa.eu.int/index.en.htm**

Fact Sheets on the European Union   A comprehensive guide to how the European Community works, the Single Market, common policies, economic and monetary union and EU external relations.
http://www.europarl.eu.int/factsheets/default.en.htm

Key terms

Act of Parliament	Judiciary
Best value	Legislature
Cabinet	Lobbying
Charter Mark	Local government
Civil service	Non-departmental public bodies (NDPBs)
Directives	Parliamentary life cycle
European Commission	Political parties
European Council of Ministers	Pressure groups
European Court of Justice	Public private partnerships (PPs)
European Economic Area (EEA)	QUANGOs
European Union (EU)	Regional government
Executive	Regulation
Ideology	Social exclusion
Judicial review	Task forces

9

The legal environment

CHAPTER OBJECTIVES

The law of a country reflects the political and social attitudes of the country. It is quite common to talk about society becoming more litigious and business organizations can ill afford to ignore the legal implications of their actions. The aim of this chapter is to identify the key legal challenges and opportunities facing business organizations, in respect of the relationships with customers, suppliers, employees and intermediaries. The law also recognizes that business organizations owe a duty of care to society as a whole, for example through legislation to protect the ecological environment. The aim of this chapter is to create an awareness of the legal issues that impinge on business decisions. In addition to the law, this chapter discusses a range of quasi-law based on voluntary codes of conduct. After reading this chapter, you should be aware of the key elements of a business organization's legal environment, but the chapter cannot hope to provide definitive guidance on the law as it affects specific business organizations.

INTRODUCTION

In previous chapters we have considered the relationship between elements of an organization's micro- and macroenvironments at a fairly abstract level. In reality, these relationships are governed by a legal framework which presents opportunities and constraints for the manner in which these relationships can be developed.

We can identify a number of important areas in which the legal environment impinges on the activities of business organizations:

■ The nature of the relationship between the organization and its customers, suppliers and intermediaries is influenced by the prevailing law. Over time, there has been a tendency for the law to give additional rights to buyers of goods and additional duties to the seller, especially in the case of transactions between businesses and private individuals. Whereas the nineteenth-century entrepreneur in Britain would have had almost complete freedom to dictate the terms of the relationship with its customers, developments in statute law and common law now require, for example, the supplier to ensure that the goods are of satisfactory quality and that no misleading description of them is made. Furthermore, the expectations of an organization's customers have changed over time. Whereas previous generations may have resigned themselves to suffering injustice in their dealings with a business, today the expectation is increasingly for perfection every time. Greater awareness of the law on the part of consumers has produced an increasingly litigious society.

■ In addition to the direct relationship that a company has with its customers, the law also influences the relationship that it has with other members of the general public. The law may, for example, prevent a firm having business relationships with certain sectors of the market, as where children are prohibited by law from buying cigarettes or drinking in public houses. Also, the messages that a company sends out in its advertising are likely to be picked up by members of the general public, and the law has intervened to protect the public interest where these messages could cause offence (advertisements that are racially prejudicial, for example).

■ Employment relationships are covered by increasingly complex legislation which recognizes that employees have a proprietary interest in their job. Legislation seeks to make up for inequalities in the power of each party.

■ The legal environment influences the relationship between business enterprises themselves, not only in terms of contracts for transactions between them, but also in the way they relate to each other in a competitive environment. The law has increasingly prevented companies from joining together in anticompetitive practices, whether covertly or overtly.

■ Companies need to develop new products, yet the rewards of undertaking new product development are influenced by the law. The laws of copyright and patent protect a firm's investment in fruitful research.

■ The legal environment influences the production possibilities of an enterprise and hence the products that can be offered to consumers. These can have a direct effect – as in the case of regulations stipulating car safety design requirements – or an indirect effect – as where legislation to reduce pollution increases the manufacturing costs of a product, or prevents its manufacture completely.

The legal environment is very closely related to the political environment. Law derives from two sources: common law and statute law

■ The common law develops on the basis of judgements in the courts – a case may set a precedent for all subsequent cases to follow. The judiciary is independent of government and the general direction of precedents tends gradually to reflect changing attitudes in society.

■ Statute law, on the other hand, is passed by Parliament and to a much greater extent reflects the prevailing political ideology of the government.

The law is a very complex area of the business environment. Most businesses would call upon expert members of the legal profession to interpret and act upon some of the more complex elements of the law. The purpose of this chapter is not to give definitive answers on aspects of the law as it affects business organizations – this would be impossible and dangerous in such a short space. Instead, the aim is to raise awareness of legal issues in order to recognize in general terms the opportunities and restrictions that the law poses, and the areas in which business organizations may need to seek the specialized advice of a legal professional.

We begin by looking at some general principles of law – the law of contract, the law relating to negligence and the processes of the legal system in England. We will then consider the following specific areas of applications of the law, which are of particular relevance to businesses:

- Dealings between organizations and their customers for the supply of goods and services

- Contracts of employment

- Protection of intellectual property rights

- Legislation relating to production processes

- Legislation to prevent anticompetitive practices.

9.2	THE LAW OF CONTRACT

A contract is an agreement between two parties where one party agrees to do something (e.g. supply goods, provide a service, offer employment) in return for which the other party provides some form of payment (in money or some other form of value). A typical organization would have contracts with a wide range of other parties, including customers, suppliers, employees and intermediaries.

There can be no direct legal relationship between a company and any of these groups unless it can be proved that a contract exists. An advertisement on its own only very rarely creates a legal relationship. The elements of a contract comprise: offer, acceptance, intention to create legal relations, consideration and capacity.We will consider these in turn. We will also consider the case of misrepresentation, which may render a contract void, despite the apparent presence of these elements of contract.

9.2.1	Offer

An offer is a declaration by which the offeror indicates that they intend to be legally bound on the terms stated in the offer if it is accepted by the offeree. The offer may be oral, in writing or by conduct between the parties, and must be clear and unambiguous. It may be made to a particular person or to the whole world. It is extremely important that it be distinguished from an 'invitation to treat', which can be defined as an invitation to make offers. Normally, all advertisements are regarded as invitations to treat, as is illustrated in a case in which a man was charged with offering for sale live birds, bramble finches (*Partridge* v. *Crittendon* [1968] 1 WLR 286). A person reading the advertisement wrote, enclosing the money for the bird which was duly sent. The advertiser was charged with the offence of offering wild birds for sale, but it was held that the advertisement was not an offer but an invitation to treat and therefore he escaped the charge.

In the context of sales to customers it is important to note that priced goods on display in supermarkets and shops are not offers, but invitations to treat. Therefore, if a leather jacket is priced at £20 (through error) in the shop widow, it is not possible to demand the garment at that price. As the display is an invitation to treat, it is the consumer who is making the offer which the shopkeeper may accept or reject as he wishes.

9.2.2   Acceptance

Acceptance may be made only by the person(s) to whom the offer was made, and it must be absolute and unqualified – i.e. it must not add any new terms or conditions, for to do so would have the effect of revoking the original offer. Acceptance must be communicated to the offeror unless it can be implied by conduct. In the case of *Carlill* v. *Carbolic Smoke Ball Co.* ([1893] 1 QB 256 CA), the defendants were the makers of a smoke ball which was purported to prevent influenza. The advertisement stated that £100 would be given to any person catching influenza after having sniffed their smoke ball in accordance with the instructions given. The manufacturers deposited £1000 at a bank to show that their claim was sincere. Mrs Carlill bought a smoke ball in response to the advertisement, complied with the instructions but still caught influenza.

In Mrs Carlill's case, her purchase implied her acceptance, for this was an offer to the world at large and it was not therefore necessary to communicate her acceptance in person to the offeror. She sued for the £100 and was successful. It was argued by the defence that the advertisement was an invitation to treat, but in this rare instance it was held to be an offer.

9.2.3   Intention to create legal relations

The above case turned on the third element of a contract – the intention to create legal relations. It was held that, because the company had deposited the £1000 in the bank, this was evidence of its intention to be legally bound and therefore the advertisement constituted an offer. Generally, in all commercial agreements it is accepted that both parties intend to make a legally binding contract and therefore it is unnecessary to include terms to this effect.

9.2.4   Consideration

This factor is essential in all contracts unless they are made 'under seal'. Consideration has been defined as some right, interest, profit or benefit accruing to one party or some forebearance, detriment, loss or responsibility given, suffered or undertaken by the other – i.e. some benefit accruing to one party or a detriment suffered by the other. In commercial contracts generally, the consideration takes the form of a cash payment. However, in contracts of barter, which are common in some countries, goods are often exchanged for goods.

9.2.5   Capacity

Generally, any person or organization may enter into an agreement which may be enforced against them. Exceptions include minors, drunks and mental patients; for this reason, companies usually exclude people under 18 from offers of goods to be supplied on credit. Limited companies must have the capacity to make a contract identified in their Objects clause within their Articles and Memorandum of Association.

An offer may be revoked at any time prior to acceptance. However, if postal acceptance is an acceptable means of communication between the parties, then acceptance is effective as soon as it is posted, provided it is correctly addressed and stamped.

9.2.6   Misrepresentation

Generally it is assumed that statements which are made at the formation of a contract are terms of that contract, but many statements made during the course of negotiations are mere representations. If the statement is a term, the injured party may sue for breach of contract and will normally obtain damages that are deemed to put him or her in the position they would have been in if the statement had been true. If the statement is a mere representation, it may be possible to avoid the contract by obtaining an order – known as *rescission* – which puts the parties back in the position they were in prior to the formation of the contract. Even though the essential elements of a contract described above are present, the contract may still fail to be given full effect.

9.3   NON-CONTRACTUAL LIABILITY

Consider now the situation where a consumer discovers that goods are defective in some way but is unable to sue the retailer from which they were supplied because the consumer is not a party to the contract (which may occur where the goods were brought as a gift by a friend). The product may also injure a completely unconnected third party. The only possible course of action here has been to sue the manufacturer. This situation was illustrated in 1932 in the case of *Donaghue* v. *Stevenson*, where a man bought a bottle of ginger beer manufactured by the defendant. The man gave the bottle to his female companion, who became ill from drinking the contents as the bottle (which was opaque) contained the decomposing remains of a snail. The consumer sued the manufacturer and won. The House of Lords held that on the facts outlined there was remedy in the tort of negligence.

To prove negligence, there are three elements that must be shown:

1   That the defendant was under a duty of care to the plaintiff.
2   That there had been a breach of that duty.
3   That there is damage to the plaintiff as a result of the breach which is not too remote a consequence.

In the case, Lord Atkin defined a duty of care thus:

> A manufacturer of products, which he sells in such a form as to show that he intends them to reach the ultimate consumer in the form in which they left him with no reasonable possibility of intermediate examination, and with the knowledge that the absence of reasonable care in the preparation or putting up of the products will result in an injury to the consumer's life or property, owes a duty to the consumer to take reasonable care. You must take reasonable care

to avoid acts or omissions which you can reasonably foresee would be likely to injure your neighbour. Who then is my neighbour? The answer seems to be persons who are so closely and directly affected by my act that I ought reasonably to have them in contemplation as being so affected when I am directing my mind to the acts or omissions which are called in question.

The law of negligence is founded almost entirely on decided cases, and the approach adopted by the courts is one that affords flexibility in response to the changing patterns of practical problems. Unfortunately, it is unavoidable that with flexibility comes an element of uncertainty. Whether or not liability will arise in a particular set of circumstances appears to be heavily governed by public policy, and it is not clear exactly when a duty of care will arise. At present, the principles, or alternatively the questions to be asked in attempting to determine whether a duty exists are:

- Is there foreseeability of harm, and if so,

- Is there proximity – a close and direct relationship – and if so,

- Is it fair and reasonable for there to be a duty in these circumstances?

Having established in certain circumstances that a duty of care exists, defendants will be in breach of that duty if they have not acted reasonably. The question is: What standard of care does the law require? The standard of care required is that of an ordinary prudent man in the circumstances pertaining to the case. For example, in one case it was held that an employee owed a higher standard of care to a one-eyed motor mechanic and was therefore obliged to provide protective goggles – not because the likelihood of damage was greater, but because the consequences of an eye injury were more serious (*Paris* v. *Stepney BC* [1951]). Similarly, a higher standard of care would be expected from a drug manufacturer than from a greetings cards manufacturer because the consequences of defective products would be far more serious in the former case.

Where a person is regarded as a professional – i.e. where people set themselves up as possessing a particular skill, such as a plumber, solicitor, surgeon – then they must display the type of skill required in carrying out that particular profession or trade.

With a liability based on fault, the defendant can only be liable for damages caused by him or her. The test adopted is whether the damage is of a type or kind that ought reasonably to have been foreseen even though the extent need not have been envisaged. The main duty is that of the manufacturer, but cases have shown that almost any party who is responsible for the supply of goods may be held liable. The onus of proving negligence is on the plaintiff. Of importance in this area is s. 2(1) of the Unfair Contract Terms Act 1977, which states: 'a person cannot by reference to any contract term or notice exclude or restrict his liability for death or personal injury resulting from negligence', and s. 2(2): 'in the case of other loss or damage, a person cannot so exclude or restrict his liability for negligence except in so far as the contract term or notice satisfies the test of reasonableness'. Thus, all clauses that purport to exclude liability in respect of negligence resulting in death or personal injuries are void, and other clauses, e.g. 'goods accepted at owner's risk', must satisfy the test of reasonableness.

LEGAL PROCESSES

It has frequently been suggested that as a society develops economically, its citizens have a tendency to become increasingly litigious. Whereas less developed societies may rely to a large extent on a moral code to govern relationships between members of the society, those that are more developed tend to rely increasingly on a codification of morals expressed in legal rights and responsibilities. Moral governance can work effectively where moral values are shared widely and social pressures alone can often keep a sense of order between individuals. Governance on the basis of law, on the other hand, requires a more formal system of justice to resolve disputes. It is not only changes in the law itself that should be of concern to businesses, but also the ease of access to legal processes.

In England, a number of courts of law operate with distinct functional and hierarchical roles:

■ The Magistrates' Court deals primarily with criminal matters, where it handles approximately 97 per cent of the workload. It is responsible for handling prosecutions of companies for breaches of legislation under the Trade Descriptions and the Consumer Protection Acts. More serious criminal matters are 'committed' up to the Crown Court for trial.

■ The Crown Court handles the more serious cases that have been committed to it

THINKING AROUND THE SUBJECT

Consumers in the UK are rapidly learning the rights they have against firms who supply defective goods and services. Spurred on by numerous consumer programmes on television, the United Kingdom is following the example of the United States in becoming increasingly litigious. The fact that consumers know that they have rights against a supplier has increased the confidence with which they complain. One consequence of this has been the development of a breed of professional complainers who sometimes push their luck in seeking compensation from a company. Companies face a dilemma here, because there is a lot of evidence that if minor complaints are resolved early on, a customer can be converted to an enthusiastic advocate of the company. For this reason, many companies have gone out of their way to invite complaints and feedback about their goods and services. Supermarkets, rail operators and hotels have found themselves handing out thousands of pounds in vouchers and compensation to bogus complainants who are exploiting firms' fear of losing their loyal customers.

Often, companies have called the bluff of bogus complainants and defended their case in court, sometimes even gaining public sympathy where professional complainers have been exposed for fabricating their complaints and even inciting fellow customers to join them. But defending such cases costs time and money, which can only be added to the cost of the products a company sells. How can a company encourage constructive feedback while stemming the tide of opportunistic litigation?

for trial on 'indictment'. In addition, it also hears defendants' appeals as to sentence or conviction from the Magistrates' Court.

■ The High Court is responsible for hearing appeals by way of 'case stated' from the Magistrates' Court or occasionally the Crown Court. The lower court whose decision is being challenged prepares papers (the case) and seeks the opinion of the High Court.

■ The Court of Appeal deals primarily with appeals from trials on indictment in the Crown Court. It may review either sentence or conviction.

■ County Courts are for almost all purposes the courts of first instance in civil matters (contract and tort). Generally, where the amount claimed is less than £25 000, this court will have instant jurisdiction, but between £25 000 and £50 000, the case may be heard here, or be directed to the High Court, depending on its complexity.

■ When larger amounts are being litigated, the High Court will have jurisdiction at first instance. There is a commercial court within the structure which is designed to be a quicker and generally more suitable court for commercial matters. Only bankruptcy appeals from the County Court are heard here.

■ Cases worth less than £3000 are referred by the County Court to its 'Small Claims' division, where the case will be heard informally under arbitration, and costs normally limited to the value of the issue of the summons. The object of the Small Claims Court is to remove the disincentive to litigate due to the fear of High Court costs.

■ The Court of Appeals' Civil Division hears civil appeals from the County Court and the High Court.

■ The House of Lords is the ultimate appeal court for both criminal and domestic matters. However, where there is a European Issue, the European Court of Justice will give a ruling on the point at issue, after which the case is referred back to the UK court.

Figure 9.1
The structure of courts in England

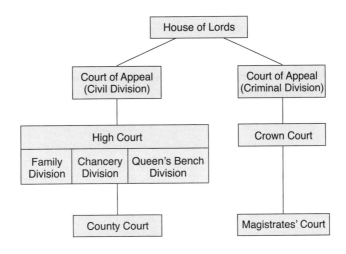

In addition to the court structure, there are numerous quasi-judicial tribunals which exist to reconcile disagreeing parties. Examples include Rent Tribunals (for agreeing property rents), Valuation Tribunals (for agreeing property values) and Employment Tribunals (for bringing claims covered by employment legislation).

Despite the existence of legal rights, the cost to an individual or a firm of enforcing its rights can be prohibitive, especially where there is no certainty that a party taking action will be able to recover its legal costs. For a typical intercompany dispute over a debt of £50 000, the party suing the debtor can easily incur legal expenses of several thousand pounds, not counting the cost of its employees' time. Where a case goes to the Court of Appeal, a company could be involved in inestimable costs. The legal process can also be very slow. In the case of an inter-company debt claim, a case may take up to 10 years between the first issue of a writ and compensation being finally received.

Numerous attempts have been made to make the legal system more widely accessible, such as the small claims section of County Courts which handle claims of up to £3000 in a less formal and costly manner than a normal County Court claim. There have also been attempts to reduce the risks by allowing, in certain circumstances, solicitors to charge their clients by results obtained in Court. There is a strong feeling that costs of running the courts system could be greatly reduced by reducing many bureaucratic and restrictive practices within the legal profession.

Despite moves to make legal remedies more widely available, access to the law remains unequal. Among commercial organizations, a small underresourced firm may be unable to put money up-front to pursue a case against a larger company which could defend itself with an army of retained lawyers. Similarly, private consumers are unequal in their access to the law. It has often been suggested that easy access to the law is afforded to the very rich (who can afford it) and the very poor (who may be eligible to receive legal aid). An apparent paradox of attempts to make the law more accessible is that these attempts may themselves overwhelm courts with cases with which they are unable to cope. Recent restrictions on funding for legal aid reflect the fact that there can be almost unlimited demand for legal remedies, but finite judicial capacity.

Central and local government is increasingly being given power to act as a consumer champion and to bring cases before the courts which are in the interest of consumers in general. Bodies that pursue actions in this way include:

- Trading Standards Departments which are operated by County Councils (by Borough Councils in Metropolitan areas). They have powers to investigate complaints about false or misleading descriptions of prices, inaccurate weights and measures, consumer credit and the safety of consumer legislation. Consumers' knowledge of their rights has often stretched the resources of Trading Standards Departments so that, at best, they can only selectively take action against bad practice.

- Environmental Health Departments of local authorities deal with health matters such as unfit food and dirty shops and restaurants. Consumers who suspect that they have suffered food poisoning as a result of eating unfit food at a restaurant may lodge a complaint with the local Environmental Health Department, which may collate similar complaints and use this evidence to prosecute the offending restaurant, or take steps to have it closed down.

■ Utility regulators have powers to bring action against companies that are in breach of their licence conditions.

9.5	LEGISLATION AFFECTING THE SUPPLY OF GOODS AND SERVICES

Prior to 1968, there was very little statutory intervention in the contractual relationship between business organizations and their customers, with a few exceptions such as those that came within the scope of the Food and Drugs Act 1955. Since the 1960s, there has been an increasing amount of legislation designed to protect the interests of private consumers who legislators have seen as unequal parties to a contract. In recent years, EU directives have been incorporated into UK legislation to provide additional duties for suppliers of goods and services. It should be noted that much of the legislation only applies to business to consumer contracts, and not business-to-business relationships. In the latter case, legislation has often presumed that parties have equal bargaining power and therefore do not need additional legislative protection.

In the following section, we will consider the following important pieces of statute law which have an impact on the relationship between an organization and its customers:

■ The Trade Descriptions Act 1968

■ The Sale of Goods Act 1979

■ The Misrepresentation Act 1967

■ The Consumer Protection Act 1987

■ The Consumer Credit Act 1974.

In addition, this section will review a number of quasi-legal codes of conduct operated by industry bodies.

9.5.1 Trade Descriptions Act 1968

The Trade Descriptions Act 1968 makes it an offence for a person to make a false or misleading trade description and creates three principal offences.

A false trade description to goods Under s. 1, this states that 'a person who, in the course of business, applies false trade descriptions to goods or suppliers or offers to supply goods to which a false description has been applied is guilty of an offence'. Section 2 defines a false trade description as including 'any indication of any physical characteristics such as quantity, size, method of manufacture, composition and fitness for purpose'.

A description is regarded as false when it is false or, by s. 3(2), misleading to a material degree. In one case it was held that to describe as 'new' a car that had sustained damage while in the manufacturer's compound was not an offence because of the excellent repair work carried out on the car which rendered the vehicle 'good as new' (R. v. *Ford Motor Co. Ltd* [1947] 3 All ER 489).

In some cases consumers are misled by advertisements that are economical with the truth. A car was advertised as having one previous 'owner'. Strictly this was true, but it had been owned by a leasing company who had leased it to five different buyers. The divisional court held this was misleading and was caught by s. 3(2) of the Trade Descriptions Act (R. v. *South Western Justices* ex parte *London Borough of Wandsworth, The Times* [20 January, 1983]).

A false statement of price   Section 11 makes a false statement as to the price an offence. If a trader claims that his prices are reduced, he is guilty of an offence unless he can show that the goods have been on sale at the higher price during the preceding six months for a consecutive period of 28 days.

A false trade description of services   Section 14 states that it is an offence to make false or misleading statements as to services. An example of this is illustrated in the case of a store that advertised 'folding doors and folding door gear – carriage free'. This statement was intended to convey to the consumer that only the folding door gear would be sent carriage-free on purchase of the folding doors. It was held that the advert was misleading and that it was irrelevant that it was not intended to be misleading (*MFI Warehouses Ltd*. v. *Nattrass* [1973] 1 All ER 762).

Defences under the Trade Descriptions Act are set out in s. 24(i):

a   that the commission of the offence was due to a mistake or to reliance on information supplied to him or to the act or default of another person, an accident or some other cause beyond his control; and

b   that he took all reasonable precautions and exercised all due diligence to avoid the commission of such an offence by himself or any person under his control.

For the defence to succeed, it is necessary to show that both subsections apply. In a case concerning a leading supermarket, a brand of washing powder was advertised as being 5p less than the price marked in the store. The defendants said that it was the fault of the store manager who had failed to go through the system laid down for checking shelves. The court held that the defence applied; the store manager was another person (s. 24(i)(a)) and the store had taken reasonable precautions to prevent commission of the offence (*Tesco Supermarkets Ltd* v. *Nattrass* [1971] 2 All ER 127).

9.5.2   **Sale of Goods Act 1979**

What rights has the consumer if on purchase he discovers that the goods are faulty or are different from those ordered? The Sale of Goods Act (SOGA) contains implied terms specifically to protect the consumer. A party deals as a consumer according to s. 12 of the Unfair Contract Terms Act 1977 if:

a he neither makes the contract in the course of a business nor holds himself out as doing so; and

b the other party does make the contract in the course of a business; and

c in the case of a contract governed by the law of sale of goods or hire purchase, the goods passing under the contract are of a type ordinarily supplied for private use or consumption.

The definition of consumer is extended by s. 20 (6) of the Consumer Protection Act 1987 which states:

a in relation to any goods, [consumer] means any person who might wish to be supplied with the goods for his own private use or consumption;

b in relation to any service or facilities, [consumer]means any person who might wish to be provided with the service or facilities otherwise than for the purposes of any business of his; and

c in relation to any accommodation, [consumer] means any person who might wish to occupy the accommodation otherwise than for the purposes of any business of his.

Section 13 of the Sale of Goods Act 1979 states that 'Where there is a contract for the sale of goods by description there is an implied condition that the goods will correspond with the description'. The sale is not prevented from being a sale by description even if the goods are on display and selected by the buyer. It is important to note that s. 13 applies to sales by private individuals and businesses.

In a case concerning a 1961 Triumph Herald, advertised for sale in the paper, it was discovered that the car was made up of two halves of different Triumph Heralds, only one of which was a 1961 model, and in the Court of Appeal the plaintiff's claim for damages was upheld (*Beale* v. *Taylor* [1967] 1 WLR 1993).

The goods must, for example, be as described on the package. If a customer purchases a blue long-sleeved shirt and on opening the box discovers that it is a red short-sleeved shirt, then he is entitled to a return of the price for breach of an implied condition of the contract.

An example that illustrates the operation of s. 13 is a case concerning the sale by one art dealer to another of a painting that both assumed genuine. It later transpired that the painting was a forgery. The buyer brought an action relying on a breach of s. 13(1) and s. 14(2) of SOGA. It was, however, held that the contract was not one for the sale of goods by description within s. 13(1) because the description of the painting as regards its author did not become a term of the contract. It was clearly fit for the purpose for which art is commonly bought and therefore of merchantable quality. In this case, 'by description [it] was held to imply that the description must have been so important a factor in the sale to become a condition of the contract' (*Harlingdon & Leinster Enterprises Ltd* v. *Christopher Hull/Fine Art Ltd* [1990] 1 All ER 737).

Section 14(2) as amended by the Sale and Supply of Goods Act 1994 states:

> Where the seller sells goods in the course of a business, there is an implied term that the goods supplied under the contract are of satisfactory quality.

Section 14(2A) gives a definition of satisfactory quality which now replaces the term 'merchantable quality':

> For the purposes of this Act goods are of satisfactory quality if they meet the standard that a reasonable person would regard as satisfactory, taking account of any description of the goods, the price (if relevant) and all other relevant circumstances.

This definition is further expanded by s. 14(2B) as follows:

> For the purposes of this Act, the quality of goods includes their state and condition and the following (among others) are in appropriate cases aspects of the quality of the goods:
>
> a   fitness for all the purposes for which goods of the kind in question are commonly supplied,
> b   appearance and finish,
> c   freedom from minor defects,
> d   safety, and
> e   durability.

Section 14(2C) states:

> The term implied by subsection (2) above does not extend to any matter making the quality of goods unsatisfactory:
>
> a   which is specifically drawn to the buyer's attention before the contract is made,
> b   where the buyer examines the goods before the contract is made, which that examination ought to reveal, or
> c   in the case of a sale by sample, which would have been apparent on a reasonable examination of the sample.

The moral for the consumer is therefore: examine thoroughly or not at all.

The implied term of unsatisfactory quality applies to sale goods and secondhand goods, but clearly the consumer would not have such high expectations of secondhand goods. For example, a clutch fault in a new car would make it unsatisfactory, but not so if the car were secondhand. In a secondhand car – again, depending on all the circumstances – a fault would have to be major to render the car unsatisfactory. Thus, the question to be asked is: 'Are the goods satisfactory in the light of the contract description and all the circumstances of the case?'

It is often asked for how long the goods should remain merchantable. It is perhaps implicit that the goods remain merchantable for a length of time reasonable in the circumstances of the case and the nature of the goods. If a good becomes defective within a very short time, this is evidence that there was possibly a latent defect at the time of the sale.

In one case, a new car which on delivery had a minor defect that was likely to, and subsequently did, cause the engine to seize up while the car was being driven was neither of merchantable quality nor reasonably fit for its purpose under s. 14. The purchaser could not, however, rescind the contract and recover the price because it was held that he had retained the car 'after the lapse of a reasonable time' without intimating to the seller that he had rejected it even though the defect had not at that time become obvious (*Berstein* v. *Pampson Motors (Golders Green) Ltd*

[1987] 2 All ER 220 N3). It was held that s. 35(1) of SOGA did not refer to a reasonable time to discover a particular defect: rather, it meant a reasonable time to inspect the goods and try them out generally. Thus, the owner, having been deemed to have accepted the car, was entitled to damages to compensate him for the cost of getting home, the loss of a tank of petrol and the inconvenience of being without a car while it was being repaired. Had there been any evidence that the car's value had been reduced as a result of the defect, he would obviously have been entitled to damages for that, too. The moral here is to examine thoroughly immediately on purchase.

Under s. 14(3), there is an implied condition that goods are fit for a particular purpose:

> Where the seller sells goods in the course of a business and the buyer, expressly or by implication, makes known to the seller ... any particular purpose for which the goods ... are being bought, there is an implied condition that the goods are reasonably fit for that purpose, whether or not it is a purpose for which goods are commonly supplied, except where the circumstances show that the buyer does not rely, or that it is unreasonable for him to rely, on the skill or judgement of the seller.

Thus, if a seller, on request, confirms suitability for a particular purpose and the product proves unsuitable, there would be a breach of s. 14(3); if the product is also unsuitable for its normal purposes, then s. 14(2) would also be breached. If the seller disclaims any knowledge of the product's suitability for the particular purpose and the consumer takes a chance and purchases it, then if it proves unsuitable for its particular purpose there is no breach of s. 14(3). The only circumstance in which a breach may occur is, again, if it were unsuitable for its normal purposes under s. 14(2).

In business contracts, implied terms in ss. 13–15 of the Sale of Goods Act 1979 can be excluded. Such exclusion clauses, purporting, for example, to exclude a term for reasonable fitness for goods (s. 14), are valid subject to the test of reasonableness provided that the term is incorporated into the contract (i.e. that the buyer is or ought reasonably to be aware of the term).

Where consumer contracts are concerned, then such clauses that purport to limit or exclude liability are void under s. 6(2) of the Unfair Contract Terms Act 1977. Obviously, the goods purchased must come within the scope of consumer goods, and thus items such as lorries or machinery would take the transaction outside the scope of a consumer sale.

The case of *R & B Customs Brokers Co Ltd* v. *United Dominions Trust Ltd* ([1988] I All ER 847) is of some importance to the business world. Here, a company operating as shipping broker and freight forwarding agent purchased a car for use by a director in the business. The sale was held to be a consumer sale within the meaning of s. 12 of the Unfair Contract Terms Act 1977 (UCTA); therefore a term for reasonable fitness for purposes under s. 14 of SOGA 1979 could not be excluded from the contract of sale (s. 6(2) of UCTA). The Court of Appeal followed the decision in a Trade Descriptions Act case in which a self-employed courier traded in his old car in part-exchange for a new car. The mileometer registered 18 100 miles, but it was evident that the true mileage was 118 000 miles. The owner was therefore prosecuted for having applied a false trade description to the car and was convicted by the magistrates' court. The Division Court allowed the appeal on the grounds that the vehicle was not disposed of in the course of a business – the point on which the prosecution turned. Lord Keith held that the expression 'in the course of a trade or business' in the context of an Act having consumer protection as its primary purpose conveys the concept of some degree of regularity. He said that the requisite degree of regularity had not been established here because a normal practice of buying and disposing of cars had not been established at the time of the alleged offence in the case. From this it follows that, had R & B Custom Brokers been dealing in cars, then the purchase of a director's car would not have been a consumer purchase. It is clear then that the self-employed – the sole traders – who no doubt assume that they are dealing in the course of a business are extremely well protected under the Sale of Goods Act and the Trade Descriptions Act. How anomalous it is when one considers that R & B Customs Brokers would no doubt be horrified if the Inland Revenue held that they were not operating in the course of a business and refused capital allowances on the director's car.

Where the buyer is dealing otherwise than as a consumer, any exclusion or limitation clause will be valid subject to the tests of reasonableness contained in s. 11 and schedule II of the Unfair Contract Terms Act 1977.

The Supply of Goods and Services Act 1982 (SGSA) offers almost identical protection where goods are passed under a Supply of Goods and Services contract in s. 3 (which corresponds to s. 13 of SOGA) and s. 4 (which corresponds to s. 14 of SOGA). Where exclusion clauses are incorporated that relate to the supply of goods, then s. 7 of the Unfair Contract Terms Act replaces s. 6, previously discussed.

Section 13 of SGSA provides that, where the supplier of a service under a contract is acting in the course of a business, there is an implied term that the supplier will carry out the service with reasonable care and skill. Reasonable care and skill may be defined as 'the ordinary skill of an ordinary competent man exercising that particular act'. Much will depend on the circumstances of the case and the nature of the trade or profession.

9.5.3   Misrepresentation Act 1967

The Misrepresentation Act 1967 provides remedies for victims of misrepresentation. For the purpose of the Act, an actionable misrepresentation may be defined as 'a false statement of existing or past fact made by one party to the other before or at the time of making the contract, which is intended to, and does, induce the other party to enter into the contract'.

Since the 1967 Act, it has been necessary to maintain a clear distinction between negligent misrepresentation and wholly innocent misrepresentation.

Section 2(1) states:

> Where a person has entered into a contract after a misrepresentation has been made to him by another party and as a result has suffered loss, then, if the person making the representation would be liable to damages in respect thereof had the misrepresentation been made

fraudulently, that person shall be so liable not withstanding that the misrepresentation was not made fraudulently, unless he pleads that he had reasonable grounds to believe and did believe up to the time the contract was made that the facts represented were true.

Section 2(2) states:

Where a person has entered into a contract after a misrepresentation has been made to him otherwise than fraudulently, and he would be entitled, by reason of the misrepresentation, to rescind the contract, then if it is claimed, in any proceedings arising out of the contract, that the contract ought to be or has been rescinded, the court or arbitrator may declare the contract subsisting and award damages in lieu of rescission, if of the opinion that it would be equitable to do so having regard to the nature of the misrepresentation and the loss that would be caused by it if the contract were upheld, as well as to the loss that rescission would cause to the other party.

The 1967 Act introduced a different type of misrepresentation (negligence under s. 2(i)), but this is misleading because negligence does not have to be proved, as Bridge LJ held in *Howard Marine and Dredging Co Ltd* v. *Ogden and Sons (Excavations) Ltd*:

The liability of the representor does not depend on his being under a duty of care, the extent of which may vary according to the circumstances in which the representation is made. In the course of negotiations leading to a contract the 1967 Act imposes an absolute obligation not to state facts which he cannot prove he had reasonable grounds to believe.

Section 2(2) empowers the court to refuse rescission or to reconstitute a rescinded contract and award damages in lieu.

To sum up, rescission is a remedy for all three types of misrepresentation. In addition to rescission for fraudulent misrepresentation, damages may be awarded under the tort of fraud, and in respect of negligent misrepresentation damages may be awarded under s. 2(1) of the 1967 Act. Under s. 2(2) damages may also be awarded at the discretion of the court, but, if so, these are in lieu of rescission.

The Property Misdescriptions Act 1991 built on the Misrepresentation Act and created a strict liability criminal offence of making, in the course of an estate agency or property development business, a false or misleading statement about a prescribed matter (s. 1(1)) to be specified in an order by the Secretary of State (s. 1(5)). The most common complaints from estate agents' (mis)descriptions include incorrect room sizes, misleading photographs and deceptive descriptions of local amenities. In one case, the agents blocked out in the photograph an ugly gasworks which overshadowed a house they were trying to sell.

9.5.4 The Consumer Protection Act 1987

The Consumer Protection Act 1987 came into force in March 1988 as a result of the government's obligation to implement an EU directive and provides a remedy in damages for anyone who suffers personal injury or damage to property as a result of a defective product. The effect is to impose a strict (i.e. whereby it is unnecessary to prove negligence) tortious liability on producers of defective goods. The Act supplements the existing law; thus, a consumer may well have a remedy in contract, in the tort of negligence or under the Act if he or she has suffered loss caused by a defective product.

A product is defined in s. 12 as 'any goods or electricity'; s. 45(1) defines goods as including substances (natural or artificial, in solid, liquid or gaseous form), growing crops, things compressed in land by virtue of being attached to it, ships, aircraft and vehicles.

The producer will be liable if the consumer can establish that the product is defective and that it caused a loss. There is a defect if the safety of the goods does not conform to general expectations with reference to the risk of damage to property or risk of death or personal injury. The general expectations will differ depending on the particular circumstances, but points to be taken into account include the product's instructions, warnings and the time elapsed since supply, the latter point to determine the possibility of the defect being due to wear and tear.

The onus is on the plaintiff to prove that loss was caused by the defect. A claim may be made by anyone, whether death, personal injury or damage to property has occurred. However, where damage to property is concerned, the damage is confined to property ordinarily intended for private use or consumption and acquired by the person mainly for his or her own use or consumption, thus excluding commercial goods and property. Damage caused to private property must exceed £275 for claims to be considered. It is not possible to exclude liability under the Consumer Protection Act.

The Act is intended to place liability on the producer of defective goods. In some cases the company may not manufacture the goods, but may still be liable, as follows:

1 Anyone carrying out an 'industrial or other process' to goods that have been manufactured by someone else will be treated as the producer where 'essential characteristics' are attributable to that process. Essential characteristics are nowhere defined in the Act, but processes that modify the goods may well be within the scope. It is important to note there that defects in the goods are not limited to those caused by the modifications, but encompass any defects in the product.

2 If a company puts its own brand name on goods that have been manufactured on its behalf, thus holding itself out to be the producer, that company will be liable for any defects in the branded goods.

3 Any importer who imports goods from outside EU countries will likewise be liable for defects in the imported goods. This is an extremely beneficial move for the consumer.

The Act is also instrumental in providing a remedy against suppliers who are unable to identify the importee or the previous supplier to him. If the supplier fails or cannot identify the manufacturer's importee or previous supplier, then the supplier is liable. It should be noted that if the product itself is defective the remedy lies in contract (usually SOGA 1979).

9.5.5   **Consumer Credit Act 1974**

This is a consumer protection measure to protect the public from, among other things, extortionate credit agreements and high-pressure selling off trade premises. The Act became fully operational in May 1985, and much of the protection afforded to hire purchase transactions is extended to those obtaining goods and services through consumer credit transactions. It is important to note that contract law governs the formation of agreements coming within the scope of the Consumer Credit Act. Also, the Act is applicable only to credit agreements not exceeding £25 000 or where the debtor is not a corporate body.

Section 8(1) states: 'A personal credit agreement is an agreement between an individual ('the debtor') and any other person ('the creditor') by which the creditor provides the debtor with credit of any amount.'

Section 8(2) defines a consumer credit agreement as a personal credit providing the debtor with credit not exceeding £25 000. Section 9 defines credit as a cash loan and any form of financial accommodation.

There are two types of credit. The first is a running account credit (s. 10(a)), whereby the debtor is enabled to receive from time to time, from the creditor or a third party, cash, goods and services to an amount or value such that, taking into account payments made by or to the credit of the debtor, the credit limit (if any) is not at any time exceeded. Thus, running account credit is revolving credit, where the debtor can keep taking credit when he or she wants it subject to a credit limit. An example of this would be a Visa or Mastercard.

The second type is fixed-sum credit, defined in s. 10(b) as any other facility under a personal credit agreement whereby the debtor is enabled to receive credit. An example here would be a bank loan. The Act then covers hire purchase agreements (s. 189), which are agreements under which goods are bailed or hired in return for periodical payments by the person to whom they are bailed or hired and where the property in the goods will pass to that person if the terms of the agreement are complied with and one or more of the following occurs:

- The exercise of an option to purchase by that person
- The doing of any other specified act by any party to the agreement
- The happening of any other specified event.

In simple terms, a hire purchase agreement is a contract of hire which gives the hirer the option to purchase the goods. The hirer does not own the goods until the option is exercised.

In addition to hire purchase agreements, also within the scope of the Act are conditional sale agreements for the sale of goods or land, in respect of which the price is payable by instalments and the property (i.e. ownership) remains with the seller until any conditions set out in the contract are fulfilled, and credit sale agreements, where the property (ownership) passes to the buyer when the sale is effected.

Unrestricted use credit is where the money is paid to the debtor direct and the debtor is left free to use the money as he or she wishes. Restricted use credit is where the money is paid direct to a third party (usually the seller), e.g. via Barclaycard or Access.

Debtor–creditor supplier agreements relate to the situation where there is a business connection between creditor and supplier, i.e. a pre-existing arrangement, or where the creditor and the supplier are the same person. Section 55 and ss. 60–65 deal with formalities of the contract, their aim being that the debtor be made fully aware of the nature and the cost of the transaction and his or her rights and liabilities under it. The Act requires that certain information must be disclosed to the debtor before the contract is made. This includes total charge for credit, and the annual rate of the total charge for credit which the debtor will have to pay expressed as a percentage. All regulated agreements must comply with the formality procedures and must contain:

- Names and addresses of the parties to the agreement
- Amount of payments due and to whom payable
- Total charge for credit
- Annual rate of charge expressed as a percentage
- Debtor's right to pay off early
- All the terms of the agreement
- The debtor's right to cancel (if applicable).

If a consumer credit agreement is drawn up off business premises, then it is a cancellable agreement designed to counteract high-pressure doorstep salesmen. If an agreement is cancellable, the debtor is entitled to a cooling-off period, i.e. to the close of the fifth day following the date the second copy of the agreement is received. If the debtor then cancels in writing, the agreement and any linked transaction is cancelled. Any sums paid are recoverable, and the debtor has a lien on any goods in his or her possession until repayment is made.

9.5.6   Codes of practice

Codes of practice do not in themselves have the force of law. They can, however, be of great importance to businesses. In the first place, they can help to raise the standards of an industry by imposing a discipline on their members not to indulge in dubious marketing practices, which – although legal – act against the long-term interests of the industry and its customers. Secondly, voluntary codes of practice can offer a cheaper and quicker means of resolving grievances between the two parties compared with more formal legal channels. For example, the holiday industry has its own arbitration facilities which avoid the cost of taking many cases through to the courts. Thirdly, business organizations are often happy to accept restrictions imposed by codes of practice as these are seen as preferable to restrictions being imposed by laws. The tobacco industry has more influence over restrictions on tobacco advertising if they are based on a voluntary code rather than imposed by law.

The post of Director General of the Office of Fair Trading is instrumental in encouraging trade associations to adopt codes of practice. An early example of a voluntary code is provided by the Motor Trade Association. On advertising, the code prohibits misleading comparisons of models and fuel consumption. Any statement must be substantiated by reference to the methods of testing and statements as to price must show clearly what is or is not incorporated in the figure. The code insists that unexpired warranties must be transferable and repair work must be capable of being carried out by any franchised dealer – not solely the dealer from whom the car was purchased. Similar criteria apply to used cars. Here the code states that mileage must be verified or the customer made aware. In the event of a dispute between a customer and a member of the Association, a conciliation service is available which reduces the need to resort to legal remedies.

Useful leaflets published by the Office of Fair Trading giving information regarding codes of practice can be obtained free of charge from local Consumer Advice Bureaux.

9.5.7 Controls on advertising

There are a number of laws that influence the content of advertisements in Britain. For example, the Trade Descriptions Act makes false statements in an advertisement an offence, while the Consumer Credit Act lays down quite precise rules about the way in which credit can be advertised. However, the content of advertisements is influenced just as much by voluntary codes as by legislation. Contrary to popular belief, there has been no law stating that cigarettes should not be advertised on television or that health warnings should be printed on all newspaper advertisements for cigarettes. Both of these have been examples of restrictions imposed on advertisers by a voluntary code.

For printed media, the Advertising Standards Authority (ASA) oversees the British Code of Advertising Practice which states that all advertisements appearing in members' publications should be legal, honest, decent and truthful. Thus, an advertisement by a building society offering 'free' weekend breaks was deemed to have broken the code by not stating in the advertisement that a compulsory charge was made for meals during the weekend. An advertisement by the fashion retailer H & M Hennes depicting a reclining female model dressed in underwear with the caption, 'Last time we ran an ad for Swedish lingerie 78 women complained – no men' was held to be offensive, inaccurate and sexist. The penalty for breaching the ASA code is the adverse publicity that follows, and ultimately the Authority could ban a business from advertising in all members' publications.

A stronger voluntary code is provided by the Independent Television Commission (ITC), which governs all terrestrial television broadcasting. Although the ITC is a statutory body, the Broadcasting Acts have devolved to the Commission the task of developing a code for advertisers. Like the ASA code, it, too, is continually evolving to meet the changing attitudes and expectations of the public. Thus, on some products restrictions have been tightened up – cigarette advertising is now completely banned on television, and loopholes have been closed which allowed tobacco brand names to be used to promote non-tobacco

Contrary to popular belief, advertising in the UK is constrained not primarily by the law. A much greater influence is exerted by quasi-legal codes of conduct (although the EU is acting to strengthen the role of legislation). While failure to comply with such codes of conduct does not bring with it the threat of punishment by the courts, non-compliance can nevertheless cause problems for a business.

The ASA, the industry body which regulates print and non-broadcast advertisements completed a major review in 1995 of its code of advertising practice. The revised code built on the previous requirement for all advertisements to be legal, decent, honest and truthful, but reflected changing public attitudes. The following are some of the changes that were deemed to be necessary:

■ To reduce problems of under-age drinking, the code banned alcohol advertisements in publications or on poster sites where more than 25 per cent of the potential audience is aged under 18. Advertisements should include a warning on the dangers of drinking and driving.

■ Advertising for slimming products aimed at children or adolescents were banned by the code, as is any suggestion that it is desirable to be underweight.

■ To further protect children's health, the code requires that no advertisement should encourage them to eat or drink near bedtime, to eat frequently throughout the day or to replace main meals with confectionery or snack foods.

■ Claims such as 'environmentally friendly' would not be allowed without convincing proof that a product causes no environmental damage.

■ Car manufactures were no longer to be allowed to make speed or acceleration the predominant message in their advertisement.

The ASA code is subscribed to by most organizations involved in advertising, including the Advertising Association, the Institute of Practitioners in Advertising and the associations representing publishers of newspapers and magazines, the outdoor advertising industry and direct marketing. Although the main role of the ASA is advisory, it does have a number of sanctions available against individual advertisers who break the code, ultimately leading to the ASA requesting its media members to refuse to publish the advertisements of an offending company. More often, the ASA relies on publicizing its rulings to shame advertisers into responding.

In general, the system of voluntary regulation of advertising has worked well in the United Kingdom. For advertisers, voluntary codes can allow more flexibility and opportunities to have an input to the code. For the public, a code can be updated in a less bureaucratic manner than may be necessary with new legislation or statutory regulations. However, the question remains as to how much responsibility for the social and cultural content of advertising should be given to industry-led voluntary bodies rather than being decided by government. Do voluntary codes unduly reflect the narrow financial interests of advertisers rather than the broader interests of the public at large? Doubtless, advertisers realize that if they do not develop a code which is socially acceptable, the task will be taken away from them and carried out by government in a process where they will have less influence.

products offered by the manufacturers, such as sportswear and overseas holidays. Restrictions on alcohol advertising have also been tightened up, for example by insisting that young actors are not portrayed in advertisements and by not showing them when children are likely to be watching. On the other hand, advertising restrictions for some products have been relaxed in response to changing public attitudes. Advertisements for condoms have moved from being completely banned to being allowed, but only in very abstract form, to the present situation where the product itself can be mentioned using actors in life-like situations. Similarly, restrictions on advertisements for women's sanitary products have been relaxed, although, as for condoms, the ITC code stipulates that advertisements should not be shown when children are likely to be viewing.

Numerous other forms of voluntary controls exist. As mentioned previously, many trade associations have codes which impose restrictions on how they can advertise. Solicitors, for example, were previously not allowed to advertise at all, but can now do so within limits defined by the Law Society. The health warnings that appear on packets of cigarettes are the result of a voluntary agreement between the government and the tobacco industry. The latter illustrates an important reason for the existence of many voluntary codes – namely, that an industry would prefer a code over which it has some influence rather than a law over which it has none. Government is saved the task of passing legislation and policing the law, while knowing that if the voluntary code fails to work it could still step in to pass legislation. In the field of advertising, the EU is currently proposing directives that will ultimately have the effect of giving legal effect to many of the voluntary codes that currently exist.

9.6 STATUTORY LEGISLATION ON EMPLOYMENT

Employment law is essentially based on the principles of law previously discussed. The relationship between an employer and its employees is governed by the law of contract, while the employer owes a duty of care to its employees and can be sued for negligence where this duty of care is broken. Employers are vicariously liable for the actions of their employees, so if an employee is negligent and harms a member of the public during the course of their employment, the injured party has a claim against the employer as well as the employee who was the immediate cause of the injury.

The common law principles of contract and negligence have for a long time been supplemented with statutory intervention. Society has recognized that a contract of employment is quite different from a contract to buy consumer goods, because the personal investment of the employee in their job can be very considerable. Losing a job without good cause can have a much more profound effect than suffering loss as a result of losing money on a purchase of goods. Governments have recognized that individuals should have a proprietary interest in their jobs and have therefore passed legislation to protect employees against the actions of unscrupulous employers who abuse their dominant power over employees. Legislation has also recognized that employment practices can have a much wider effect on society through organizations' recruitment policies.

In this section we will consider some of the areas in which statutory intervention has affected the environment in which organizations recruit, reward and dismiss employees. The information here cannot hope to go into any depth on particular legislative requirements, but aims instead to identify issues of concern. This chapter should also be read in conjunction with Chapter 4 on the internal environment. In that chapter we looked in general terms at issues such as the need for flexibility in the workforce. This chapter identifies particular legal opportunities and constraints, which help to define an organization's internal environment.

9.6.1 When does an employment contract occur?

It is not always obvious whether a contract of employment exists between an organization and individuals providing services for it. Many individuals working for organizations in fact provide their services as a self-employed subcontractor, rather than as an employee. The distinction between the two is important, because a self-employed contractor does not benefit from the legislation which only protects employees. There can be many advantages in classifying an individual as self-employed rather than as an employee. For the self-employed, tax advantages result from being able to claim as legitimate, business expense items that in many circumstances are denied to the employee. The method of assessing National Insurance and income tax liability in arrears can favour a self-employed subcontractor. For the employer, designation as self-employed could relieve the employer of many duties that are imposed in respect of employees but not subcontractors, such as entitlement to sick pay, notice periods and maternity leave.

There has been a great trend towards self-employment during the 1990s, and not surprisingly the UK government has sought to recoup lost tax revenue and to protect unwitting self-employed individuals, by examining closely the terms on which an individual is engaged. The courts have decided the matter on the basis of, among other things, the degree of control that the organization buying a person's services has over the person providing them, the level of integration between the individual and the organization, and who bears the business risk. If the organization is able to specify the manner in which a task is to be carried out, then an employment relationship generally exists. If, however, the required end result is specified, but the manner in which it is achieved is left up to the individual, then a contract for services will exist, in other words, self-employment. There is still ambiguity in the distinction between employment and self-employment, which has, for example, resulted in numerous appeals by individuals against classification decisions made by the Inland Revenue.

9.6.2 Flexibility of contract

Organizations are increasingly seeking a more flexible workforce to help them respond more rapidly to changes in their external environment. In Chapter 4 we

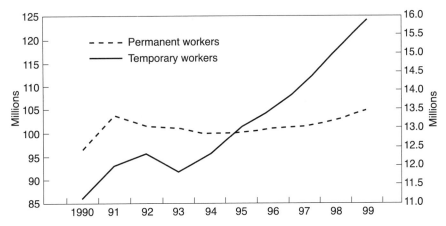

Figure 9.2
Trends in employment contracts within the EU

Note: Figures exclude Austria, Finland and Sweden, which joined the EU in 1995.
Source: Based on Eurostat.

saw some of the benefits to an organization of developing flexible employment practices.

Fixed-term employment contracts are increasing significantly in a number of European countries, partly due to the existence of tight labour market regulations that make it difficult for employers to recruit and dismiss permanent staff. Within Europe, there has been a tendency for national legislation to reflect EU directives by imposing additional burdens on employers of full-time, permanent employees. This can affect the ease with which staff can be laid off or dismissed should demand fall – for example in Germany, the Dismissals Protection Law (Kundigungsschutzgesetz) gives considerable protection to salaried staff who have been in their job for more than six months, allowing dismissal only for a 'socially justified' reason.

The move towards short-term contracts would appear to be a Europe-wide phenomenon. In Spain a third of the workforce is now employed on short-term contracts that last up to three years compared with less than 16 per cent 15 years ago, while in France the proportion of short-term contracts climbed from 6.7 per cent in 1985 to more than 13 per cent by 2000 (see Figure 9.2). But even in European countries with less restrictive employment laws, such as The Netherlands, short-term contracts have become more popular. The spread of short-term contracts is most apparent among young workers employed in insecure and highly mobile areas of the labour market such as retail and distribution. However, short-term contracts are also popular within the communication and information technology sectors, where entrepreneurial individuals may relish the freedom and opportunities in employment that rewards individual initiative and expertise.

The European Commission and most member state governments have been keen to ensure that part-time/short-term contract workers enjoy the same legal rights as those in full-time, permanent employment. In the UK, the Employment Relations Act 1999 requires the trade and industry secretary to make regulations to ensure that part-time/short-term contract workers are treated no less favourably than full-time/permanent workers. These regulations include provisions to implement the EU-level social partners' agreement and the subsequent Council Directive on part-time work (97/81/EC). In the United Kingdom, a worker must generally be employed for at least 12 months on a contract to secure such rights.

Despite imposing additional burdens, many European governments have encouraged the greater use of short-term contracts as a way of improving the flexibility of their national economies, for example through changes in welfare benefits which do not penalize short-term working.

9.6.3   Terms of the contract of employment

Under the Employment Rights Act 1996 it is required that an employer must issue its employees within 13 weeks of the date they start work, the written terms and conditions of their employment in detail. The details can, however, be placed on a staff notice board at a point where every member of the workforce it concerns can read it. In the statement there should be references to the following:

1   The job title
2   Which individuals or groups the document is addressed to
3   The starting date of the employment
4   The scale of wages and the calculations used to work this out
5   The periods in which wages are made
6   Hours of work and the terms and conditions
7   Holidays and holiday pay
8   Sickness and sickness pay
9   Pensions and pension schemes
10 How much notice the employee must give upon leaving and how much notice the company has to give the employee when terminating employment
11 Rules for discipline procedures
12 To whom any grievances are to be made and procedures

The terms of contract cannot be altered until both parties have discussed and agreed the new conditions.

9.6.4   Minimum acceptable contract terms

Legislators have recognized that employee and employer possess unequal bargaining power in the process of forming a contract of employment. Legislation therefore protects the interests of the weaker party – the employee – against the use of their power by unscrupulous employers. The following are examples of statutory intervention that protect employees' rights. Some would argue that intervention of this type has the effect of increasing the costs of businesses, thereby reducing their competitive advantage. However, as we saw in Chapter 4, a lot of statutory intervention is merely spreading current best practice to all employees.

Health and Safety legislation There is a wide range of regulations governing employers' duty to provide a safe working environment. There are not many Acts of Parliament principally devoted to health and safety. Most health and safety legislation is based on The Health & Safety at Work Act 1974 which provides a general duty to provide a safe working environment. The Act makes provision for specific regulations to be issued by government Ministers and these detailed regulations can have significant impacts on businesses. The following are some recent examples of regulations:

- The Control of Major Accident Hazards Regulations 1999
- The Control of Substances Hazardous to Health Regulations 1999
- The Lifts Regulations 1997
- The Railway Safety (Miscellaneous Provisions) Regulations 1997

The Health and Safety Executive oversees enforcement of these regulations.

Minimum wage legislation The national minimum wage came into force in the United Kingdom in 1999, implementing an earlier EU directive. The rate was introduced at £3.60 for workers aged 22 and over and £3 an hour for 18–21 year olds and there is provision for annual revision. Most adult workers in the UK must be paid at least the national minimum wage. This includes part-time workers, temporary or short-term workers, homeworkers, agency workers and casual labourers. An employee cannot be forced by an employer to accept a wage that is below the minimum wage and can claim compensation if they are sacked or victimized because they sought to enforce their right to the national minimum wage.

Working Hours: The EU's Working Time Directive of 1993 was implemented in the UK by the Working Time Regulations of 2000. By these regulations, workers cannot be forced to work for more than 48 hours a week on average. However, there are various exclusions to this time and workers can cancel any opt-out agreement whenever they want, although they must give their employer at least seven days' notice, or longer (up to three months) if this has been agreed.

9.6.5

Discrimination at work

Companies sometimes find themselves being required to recruit their second choice of staff in order to comply with legislation against racial and sexual discrimination. For example, one UK airline found through its research that the majority of its customers preferred its cabin crew to be female and subsequently recruited predominantly female staff for this role. The airline was fined for unlawful discrimination against men, even though it had been innovative in appointing women to the traditional male job of pilot. Legislation seeks to protect disadvantaged groups who may be discriminated against simply out of employers' ignorance. The Sex Discrimination Act 1975 (SDA) prohibits discrimination against women, and men, on the grounds of sex or of being married. The SDA makes the distinction between the concepts of direct and indirect discrimination. Direct sex discrimination occurs when an employee is treated less favourably because of her, or his, sex. Indirect discrimination occurs when a requirement or condition – which may seem 'neutral' in terms of how it impacts upon men and women – in fact has an adverse effect on women, or men, in general. The Equal Pay Act 1970 requires that a woman is entitled to the same pay (and other contractual conditions) as a man working for the same employer, provided they are doing similar work or work of equal value.

The legislation dealing with race discrimination derives from the Race Relations Act 1976 (RRA). By this Act, a person is guilty of race discrimination if '... on racial grounds he treats [a] person less favourably than he treats or would treat other persons'. Like the SDA, the RRA makes it illegal to discriminate directly or indirectly against a person on racial grounds. Research and official statistics demonstrate that people from ethnic minorities continue to experience severe discrimination in the field of employment. In the period from Spring 1989–91, the male unemployment rate for people from ethnic minorities was 13 per cent, compared to 7 per cent for white people. The respective figures for female unemployment were 12 per cent and 7 per cent (House of Commons, *Hansard* 21 May 1992). An analysis of the Department of Employment's Labour Force Survey, published in 1992 by the Policy Studies Institute, found that even when factors such as educational qualifications are excluded, unemployment rates among people from ethnic minorities are significantly higher than among white people.

9.6.6   Termination of contract

The proprietary interest of employees in their jobs is recognized by legislation which restricts the ability of an employer to terminate an employee's contract of employment.

Termination may come about because an individual's position is no longer required and the individual is declared redundant. The Employment Rights Act 1996 defines the circumstances in which redundancy takes effect and a sliding scale of payments which employees are entitled to if they are made redundant by their employer.

In circumstances other than redundancy, employers may not terminate a contract in a way which constitutes unfair dismissal. Under the Employment Rights Act, employees are not entitled to claim unfair dismissal until they have accumulated two years' service (to be reduced to one year by the Employment Relations Act 1999). Dismissal may be considered fair where an employee has not acted in good faith and/or has failed to observe previous warnings about poor conduct. Employment Tribunals judge whether a dismissal is fair or not, and judgement frequently centres on procedural issues. A finding of unfair dismissal may lead to an order for compensation and a request for reinstatement.

9.6.7   Rights to workers' representation

The political environment and the dominant political ideology have had a very close bearing on legislation regulating the activities of trade unions. Traditionally,

Labour governments have sought to advance the cause of organized labour, while Conservative governments have taken a more individualist approach to relationships between employers and employees. The incoming Conservative government of 1979 dismantled much of the legislation which had been passed by the previous Labour government to give greater rights for trade unions and greater duties for employers. The incoming Labour government of 1997 has gone some way to restoring trade union rights. This government inherited the 1993 Trade Union Reform and Employment Rights Act and the Trade Union and Labour Relations (Consolidation) Act 1992. The essence of this legislation was to make trade unions more accountable to their members and to reduce the risks to employers of loss resulting from politically inspired disputes. The following were key features covered by the legislation:

- Individuals affected by industrial action are able to seek an injunction to prevent unlawful industrial action taking place
- Seven days' notice must be given by trade unions of ballots and of industrial action
- Individuals have a right to challenge collective agreements
- Employers may refuse to recognize a trade union in specified circumstances
- All industrial action ballots must be postal and subject to independent scrutiny.

The Employment Relations Act 1999 amends a number of provisions of the previous legislation. For trade unions, the key element of the Act is a statutory procedure through which independent unions will be able to seek recognition for collective bargaining from employers with more than 20 employees. The Act amends previous legislation to enable employees dismissed for taking part in lawfully organized official industrial action to take cases of unfair dismissal to an employment tribunal where the dismissal occurs within eight weeks of the start of the action.

The Transnational Information and Consultation of Employees Regulations 1999 came into force in the UK in January 2000, implementing the EU Directive on European Works Councils. The directive covers undertakings which have more than 1000 employees in member states and more than 150 employees in each of two member states and sets out procedures for giving employees a statutory right to be consulted about a range of activities affecting the organization.

9.7   THE HUMAN RIGHTS ACT

The Human Rights Act came into force in the UK in 2000 and has presented a number of new legal challenges for business organizations. The Act incorporates the European Convention on Human Rights into domestic law. The Convention is a 50-year-old code of basic rights drawn up in the aftermath of the Second World War and covers such rights as that to a family life, to privacy and a fair trial. Prior to 2000, although UK courts could take note of the rights identified by the convention, they could not be directly enforced. So aggrieved parties often had to take cases to the European Court of Human Rights for a remedy, a lengthy and costly process.

The Act only incorporates part of the European Convention and does not incorporate any of the procedural rights of the Convention. However, it does include all of the following substantive rights:

- To life

- To freedom from torture or inhuman or degrading punishment

- To freedom from slavery, servitude, enforced or compulsory labour

- To liberty and security of the person

- To a fair trial

- To respect for private and family life

- To freedom of thought, conscience and religion

- To freedom of expression

- To freedom of assembly and association

- To marry and found a family

- To education in conformity with parents' religious and philosophical convictions

- To freedom from unfair discrimination in the enjoyment of these rights.

Many of the wider rights enshrined in the Human Rights Act are already protected by the United Kingdom's domestic legislation, e.g. Sex Discrimination Act 1975. From 2000, courts in the United Kingdom have been able to issue injunctions to prevent violations of rights, award damages and quash unlawful decisions. Individuals are now able to use the Act to defend themselves in criminal proceedings. The Act will not make Convention rights directly enforceable in proceedings against a private litigant; nor against a 'quasi-public' body unless that body was acting in a public capacity. However, private individuals and companies will have to take the Convention into account because the courts will be obliged to interpret the law so as to conform to it wherever possible.

In the early days of the Act a number of examples illustrated its possible impact on business organizations, including challenges about the legitimacy of local authority planning procedures and privacy of personal information. Despite early fears that the Human Rights Act would add significantly to business organizations' costs, it would appear that more recent cases have taken a balanced view on what is reasonable and in the public interest.

9.8   PROTECTION OF A COMPANY'S INTANGIBLE ASSETS

The value of a business enterprise can be measured not only by the value of its physical assets such as land and building: increasingly, the value of a business reflects its investment in new product development and strong brand images. To protect a company from imitators reaping the benefits of this investment but bearing none of its cost, a number of legal protections are available.

9.8.1 Patents

A patent is a right given to an inventor which allows him or her exclusively to reap the benefits from the invention over a specified period. To obtain a patent, application must be made to the Patent Office in accordance with the procedure set out in the Patents Act 1977. To qualify for a patent, the invention must have certain characteristics laid down – it must be covered by the Act, it must be novel and it must include an inventive step.

Nowhere does the Act define what is patentable, but under s. 1 it does specify what is not:

- S. 1(2)(a) discoveries, scientific theories or mathematical methods
- S. 1(2)(b) literacy, dramatic, musical or artistic works or any other aesthetic creations (obviously, works such as these are protected by copyright)
- S. 1(2)(c) schemes, rules or methods for performing a mental act, playing a game, doing business; or a program for a computer
- S. 1(2)(d) the presentation of information.

Of course, to qualify for a patent the invention must be novel in that it does not form part of the state of the art at the priority date (i.e. the date of filing for a patent, not the date of invention).

State of the art (s. 2(2)) comprises all matter that has at any time before that date been made available to the public anywhere in the world by written or oral description, by use or in any other way.

An inventive step (s. 3) is apparent if it is not obvious to a person skilled in the art having regard to the prior art other than co-pending patent applications which are deemed to be prior art for the purpose of testing for novelty only.

The effect of the Patents Act 1977 has only been to bring UK patent law more into line with that of the EU in accordance with the provisions of the European Patent Convention. As a result of the implementation of the Convention, there are almost uniform criteria in the establishment of a patent in Austria, Belgium, Switzerland, Germany, France, the United Kingdom, Italy, Liechtenstein, Luxembourg, The Netherlands and Sweden. A European Patent Office has been set up in Munich which provides a cheaper method to obtain a patent in three or more countries, but it should be noted that, if the patent fails as a result of an application to the European Patent Office, the rejection applies to all member states unless there is contrary domestic legislation which covers this part.

9.8.2 Trade marks

The Trade Marks Act 1994 which replaced the 1938 Act implemented the Trade Marks Harmonization Directive No. 89/104/EEC provides protection for trade marks (they are also protected under the common law of passing off). A trade mark is defined as any sign capable of being represented graphically which is capable of distinguishing goods or services of one undertaking from those of other undertakings (s. 1(1)).

Any trademark satisfying these criteria is registrable unless prohibited by s. 3(1) which prevents registration if:

a The signs do not satisfy the requirements of s. 1(1)

b Trade marks are devoid of any distinctive character

c Trade marks consist exclusively of signs or indications which may serve, in trade, to designate the kind, quality, quantity, intended purpose, value, geographical origin, the time of production of the goods or of rendering of services, or other characteristics of goods or services

d Trade marks consist exclusively of signs or indications which have become customary in the current language or in the *bona fide* and established practices in the trade.

Provided that, a trade mark shall not be refused registration by virtue of paragraph (b), (c) or (d) above if before the date of application for registration it has in fact acquired a distinctive character as a result of the use made of it.

A sign shall not be registered as a trade mark if it consists exclusively of (s. 3(2)):

a The shape which results from the nature of the goods themselves

b The shape of goods which is necessary to obtain a technical result

c The shape which gives substantial value to the goods.

In addition, a trade mark shall not be registered if:

a It is contrary to public policy or accepted principles of morality (s. 3(3))

b It is of such a nature as to deceive the public (for instance as to the nature, quality, geographical origin of the goods or service) (s. 3(3))

c Its use is prohibited in the UK by any enactment or rule of law (s. 3(4))

d It is defined as a specially protected emblem (s. 3(5))

e An application to register is made in bad faith (s. 3(6)).

If a trade mark is infringed in any way, a successful plaintiff will be entitled to an injunction and to damages.

9.8.3 Law and the Internet

The development of the Internet does not change the basic principles of law, but the law has on occasions become ambiguous in the light of technological developments.

Unlawful copying of material downloaded from the Internet (images, documents and particularly music) has focused attention on issues of ownership of intellectual property. Section 17 Copyright, Designs and Patents Act 1988 provides that:

(2) Copying in relation to a literary, dramatic, musical or artistic work means reproducing the work in any material form. This includes storing the work in any medium by electronic means.

Copying will, therefore, include downloading files from the Internet or copying text into or attaching it to an e-mail. Given the ability to copy material virtually instantaneously to potentially huge numbers, e-mail presents a serious risk of copyright infringement liability. Just what constitutes 'public domain' information and therefore lawfully copied has been raised in a number of cases.

In addition to copyright issues, the international nature of communications on the Internet makes it essential not to overlook questions such as where is the contract concluded, when is it concluded, what law governs it and where will any subsequent dispute be decided? Unexpected additional obligations may arise as a result of statements made during contract negotiations, for example by a salesperson to a customer. Even where the final written contract expressly excludes such representations, courts may be prepared to find that a collateral contract came into existence through the exchange of e-mail messages.

European Union countries have begun to introduce into national legislation a 1999 EU directive on electronic signatures. The directive comprises two major advances: the legal recognition of electronic signatures, which provide reliable identification of the parties engaged in an online transaction; and encryption, which enables companies to electronically protect documents liable to be intercepted during transmission, by wire or over the air. These measures will help companies doing business over the Internet to verify with accuracy the identity of their contracting partners and to improve online security standards for international business.

9.9 THE LAW AND PRODUCTION PROCESSES

As economies develop, there is a tendency for societies to raise their expectations about firms' behaviour, particularly where they are responsible for significant external costs (see Chapter 5). The result has been increasing levels of legislation, which constrain the activities of firms in meeting buyers' needs. Some of the more important constraints that affect business decisions are described below:

- Pollution of the natural environment is an external cost which governments seek to limit through legislation such as the Environmental Protection Act 1995, the Environment Act 1990 and the Water Resources Act 1991. Examples of impacts on firms include requirements for additional noise insulation and investment in equipment to purify discharges into watercourses and the atmosphere. These have often added to a firm's total production costs, thereby putting it at a competitive disadvantage, or made plans to increase production capacity uneconomic when faced with competition from companies in countries that have less demanding requirements for environmental protection.

- The rights of employees to enjoy safe working conditions has become increasingly enshrined in law as a country develops. In the United Kingdom, the Health and Safety at Work Act 1974 provides for large fines and, in extreme cases, imprisonment of company directors for failing to provide a safe working environment. Definitions of what constitutes an acceptable level of risk for employees to face change over time. As well as obvious serious physical injury, the courts in England now recognize a responsibility of firms to protect their employees against more subtle dangers such as repetitive strain injury. There has also been debate in cases brought before courts as to whether a firm should be responsible for mental illness caused by excessive stress in a job, and the courts have held that companies should be liable if the employee has suffered stress in the past which the company was aware of.

■ In many cases it is not sufficient to rely on law to protect customers from faulty outcomes of a firm's production. It is also necessary to legislate in respect of the quality of the *processes* of production. This is important where buyers are unable to fully evaluate a product without a guarantee that the method of producing it has been in accordance with acceptable criteria. An example of this is the Food Safety Act 1990 which imposes requirements on all firms who manufacture or handle food products to ensure that they cannot become contaminated (e.g. by being kept at too high a temperature during transport). Many small- to medium-sized food manufacturers have closed down, claiming that they cannot justify the cost of upgrading premises. Laws governing production processes are also important in the case of intangible services where customers may have little opportunity for evaluating the credentials of one service against another. For example, to protect the public against unethical behaviour by unscrupulous salespersonnel, the Financial Services Act 1986 lays down procedures for regulating business practices within the sector.

The traditional view of legislation on production is that the mounting weight of legislation puts domestic firms at a cost disadvantage to those operating in relatively unregulated environments overseas. Critics of overregulation point to the United Kingdom and the United States as two economies that have priced themselves out of many international markets.

Against this, it is argued that as the economy of a country develops, economic gains should be enjoyed by all stakeholders of business, including employees and the local communities in which a business operates. There are also many persuasive arguments why increasing regulation of production processes may not be incompatible with greater business prosperity:

1 Attempts to deregulate conditions of employment may allow firms to be more flexible in their production methods and thereby reduce their costs. However, there is evidence that a casualized workforce becomes increasingly reluctant to make major purchases, thereby reducing the level of activity in the domestic economy. In the United Kingdom, moves during the 1990s to free employers of many of their responsibilities to employees resulted in a large number of casual workers who were reluctant or unable to buy houses, resulting in a knock-on effect on supplies of home-related goods and services.

2 There is similarly much evidence that a healthy and safe working environment is likely to be associated with high levels of commitment by employees and a

high standard of output quality. The law should represent no more than a codification of good practice by firms.

3 Environmental protection and cost reduction may not be mutually incompatible, as the case study in Chapter 5 demonstrated.

9.10   LEGISLATION TO PROTECT THE COMPETITIVENESS OF MARKETS

Finally, we should recall our discussion in Chapter 6 about the presumed benefits of having markets which are competitive and free of harmful monopolistic or collusive tendencies. Because of the presumed superiority of competitive markets, the law of most developed countries has been used to try to remove market imperfections where these are deemed to be against the public interest. It was noted in Chapter 6 that the common law of England has developed the principle of restraint of trade through which anticompetitive practices have been curbed.

As the economy has become more complex, common law has proved inadequate on its own to preserve the competitiveness of markets. Common law has therefore been supplemented by statutory legislation. One outcome of statutory intervention has been the creation of a regulatory infrastructure, which in the United Kingdom includes the Office of Fair Trading, the Competition Commission and regulatory bodies to control specific industries. Much of the current regulatory framework in the United Kingdom is based on the requirements of Articles 85 and 86 of the Treaty of Rome.

In the United Kingdom, the 1998 Competition Act reformed and strengthened competition law by prohibiting anticompetitive behaviour. The Act introduced two basic prohibitions: a prohibition of anticompetitive agreements, based closely on Article 85 of the Treaty of Rome; and a prohibition of abuse of a dominant position in a market, based closely on Article 86 of the Treaty. The Act prohibits agreements which have the aim or effect of preventing, restricting or distorting competition in the United Kingdom. Since anticompetitive behaviour between companies may occur without a clearly defined agreement, the prohibition covers not only agreements by associations of companies, but also covert practices.

For further discussion of the application of legislation concerning anticompetitive practices and the task of defining the public interest, refer back to Chapter 6.

CASE STUDY

LEGISLATION STRENGTHENED IN A BID TO END 'NIGHTMARE' HOLIDAYS

Tour operators have probably felt more keenly than most businesses the effects of new legislation to protect consumers. Because holidays are essentially intangible, it is very difficult for a potential customer to check out claims made by tour operators' advertising until their holiday is underway, when it may be too late to do anything to prevent a ruined holiday. Traditional attitudes of 'let the buyer beware' can be of little use to holidaymakers who have little tangible evidence to base their decision on when they book a holiday.

Consumers have traditionally had very little comeback against tour operators who fail to provide a holiday which is in line with the expectations held out in their brochure. Their brochures have frequently been accused of misleading customers, for example by showing pictures of hotels which conveniently omit the adjacent airport runway or sewerage works. The freedom of tour operators to produce fanciful brochures was limited by the Consumer Protection Act 1987. Part III of the Act holds that any person, who, in the course of a business of his, gives (by any means whatsoever) to any consumers an indication which is misleading as to the price at which any goods, services, accommodation or facilities are available shall be guilty of an offence. These provisions of the Act forced tour operators to end such practices as promoting very low-priced holidays which in reality were never available when customers enquired about them – only higher priced holidays were offered. Supplements for additional items such as regional airport departures could no longer be hidden away in small print.

Tour operators see themselves as arrangers of holidays who buy in services from hotels, airlines and bus companies, among others, over whom they have no effective management control. It was therefore quite usual for tour operators to include in their booking conditions an exclusion clause absolving themselves of any liability arising from the faults of its subcontractors. If a passenger was injured by a faulty lift in a Spanish hotel, a tour operator would deny any responsibility for the injury and could only advise the holidaymaker to sue the Spanish hotel themselves. For some time, the courts in England recognized that it would be unreasonable to expect UK tour operators to be liable for actions which were effectively beyond their management control. However, an EU directive of 1993 (implemented in England by the Unfair Terms in Consumer Contracts Regulations 1994) sought to redress the balance by providing greater protection for customers of tour operators. The directive, when implemented in national legislation throughout the EU, makes all tour operators liable for the actions of their subcontractors. In cases which have been brought before courts in England, tour operators have been held liable for illness caused by food poisoning at a hotel and loss of enjoyment caused by noisy building work. To emphasize the effects of the directive, one British tour operator was even ordered to compensate a holidaymaker in respect of claims that she had been harassed by a waiter at a hotel which had been contracted by the tour operator.

Before the Unfair Terms in Consumer Contracts Regulations 1994 had been enacted, anyone who had felt unfairly treated by a tour operator had to take the offending company to court personally, often at great expense and inconvenience to themselves. The new regulation allows anyone to ask the Office of Fair Trading to take up a case on their behalf. In the case of unfair contract terms, the OFT can persuade the company voluntarily to remove the offending clause or to obtain an injunction removing the words from all future booking conditions. In principle, this move should be more proactive in preventing complaints by customers being brought in the first place, although doubts have been raised about the ability or willingness of the OFT to act as a consumer champion, given its reluctance in the past to bring prosecutions against traders.

In the space of less than a decade, the UK tour operating industry has been transformed from relying on exclusion clauses and seeking to rely on voluntary codes of conduct, especially the code of the Association of British Travel Agents (ABTA), in providing fair treatment for consumers. Many would argue that voluntary regulation had failed to protect consumers in accordance with their rising expectations. Legislation, while it was initially resisted by tour operators, has undoubtedly increased consumers' confidence in buying package holidays and lessened the chances of them buying a holiday from a rogue company, and thereby harming the reputation of the industry as a whole.

CASE STUDY Review Questions

1 What factors could explain the increasing amount of legislation which now faces tour operators?

2 Summarize the main consequences of the EU directive referred to above on the marketing of package holidays in the UK.

3 Is there still a role for voluntary codes of conduct in preference to legislation as a means of regulating the relationship between a tour operator and its customers?

CHAPTER Summary and links to other chapters

This chapter has noted the increasing effects that legislation is having on businesses. The principal sources of law have been identified. Statute law is becoming increasingly important, with more influence being felt from the EU. Legal processes and the remedies available to a firm's customers have been discussed. Voluntary codes of conduct are often seen as an alternative to law and offer firms lower cost and greater flexibility.

The discussion of business ethics in Chapter 5 relates closely to the legal environment. To many people, law is essentially a formalization of ethics, with statute law enacted by government (Chapter 8). The competition environment (Chapter 6) is increasingly influenced by legislation governing anticompetitive practices. We will see in Chapter 12 that legal protection for innovative new technologies is vital if expenditure on research and development is to be sustained. In addition to the aspects of law discussed in this chapter, legislation affects the status of organizations (Chapter 3), for example in the protection that is given to limited liability companies.

CHAPTER Review questions

1 Briefly identify the main ways in which the legal environment impacts on the activities of the sales and marketing functions of business organizations.

(Based on CIM Marketing Environment Examination)

2 Giving examples, evaluate the criticism that government legislation primarily impacts on those firms who can least afford to pay for it, mainly the small and the competitively vulnerable.

3 In the light of recent legislation in your own country, assess the extent to which the position of consumers compared to business has improved.

Provide a checklist for your brand manager to ensure that a new product complies with the main consumer legislation in force.

(Based on CIM Marketing Environment Examination)

4 Using an appropriate example, evaluate the virtues and drawbacks of using voluntary codes of practice to regulate business activity. (Based on CIM Marketing Environment Examination)

5 Philip, shopping at a large department store, sees a colourful spinning top which he buys for his grandson Harry. While purchasing the toy, he sees a prominent notice in the store which states: 'This store will not be held responsible for any defects in the toys sold.' The box containing the spinning top carries the description 'Ideal for children over 12 months, safe and non-toxic.' (Harry is 15 months old.) Within four weeks the spinning top has split into two parts, each with a jagged edge, and Harry has suffered an illness as a result of sucking the paint. Philip has complained vociferously to the store, which merely pointed to the prominent notice disclaiming liability. Philip has now informed the store that he intends to take legal action against it.

Draft a report to the Managing Director setting out the legal liability of the store.

6 Zak runs his own painting and decorating business and has been engaged to decorate Rebecca's lounge. While burning off layers of paint from the door with his blowtorch, Zak's attention is diverted by the barking of Camilla's Yorkshire terrier and as he turned round, the flame catches a cushion on the settee. Within seconds the room is filled with acrid smoke. Both the carpet and settee are damaged beyond repair and the dog, terrified, rushes into the road, where it is run over by a car. Consider Zak's legal liability.

Selected further reading

The following books provide a general overview of law as it affects commercial organizations:

Bradgate, J.R. (2000) *Commercial Law*, 3rd edn, Butterworth, London.
Lawson, R. (1998) *Business Law*, Pitman Publishing, London.
Oughton, D. and J. Lowry (2000) *Textbook on Consumer Law*, 2nd edn, Blackstone, London.

This chapter has discussed the basics of the law of contract and the following references provide useful further reading:

Davies, F.R. (1999) *Davies on Contract*, 8th edn, Sweet and Maxwell, London.
Oughton, D. and M. Davis (2000) *Sourcebook on Contract, Cavendish*, 2nd edn, London.
Treitel, G.H. (1999) *The Law of Contract*, 10th edn, Sweet and Maxwell, London.

Trade marks and patent laws are discussed in the following reference:

Phillips, J. and A. Firth (2000) *Introduction to Intellectual Property*, 4rd edn, Butterworths, London.

A valuable overview of employment law is provided in the following:

Lockton, D. (1999) *Employment Law*, 3rd edn, Macmillan, Basingstoke.

Finally, for a discussion of the legal and ethical basis to marketing relationships, the following is interesting:

Gundlach, G.T. and P.E. Murphy (1993) 'Ethical and legal foundations of relational marketing exchange', *Journal of Marketing*, October, vol. 57, pp. 35–46.

Useful websites

Business Bureau   A commercial site offering an overview of the legislation with particular relevance to small businesses.   **http://www.businessbureau-uk.co.uk/law/law.htm**

Commission for Racial Equality   **http://www.cre.gov.uk**

Disability Rights Commission   **http://www.disability.gov.uk/**

DTI   The Department of Trade and Industry's website gives the latest employment relations guidance.   **http://www.dti.gov.uk/er/regs.htm**

Equal Opportunities Commission   **http://www.eoc.org.uk**

Health and Safety Executive   **http://www.hse.gov.uk/pubns/hazards.htm**

HMSO   Provides full text of recent Acts of Parliament.   **http://www.legislation.hmso.gov.uk/**

International Labour Organization (ILO)   This website provides information on international work standards and national laws on labour and human rights.   **http://www.ilo.org**

Lex Mercatoria   A free site which provides information relevant to international law, and the implications of e-commerce.   **http://lexmercatoria.org**

National Association of Citizens Advice Bureaux   Offers advice on many legal issues.   **http://www.nacab.org.uk/**

University of Kent Law School links   A useful page providing links to numerous law related resources.   **http://library.ukc.ac.uk/library/lawlinks/**

Key terms

Codes of practice	Misrepresentation
Common law	Negligence
Contract	Patents
Discrimination	Statute law
Dismissal	Tort
Duty of care	Trade marks
Intellectual property rights	

10

The international business environment

CHAPTER OBJECTIVES

Business is increasingly being conducted globally rather than within the confines of national boundaries. The first aim of this chapter is to explore the underlying reasons for the globalization of trade, and the benefits to countries and individual firms from engaging in international trade. Barriers to international trade, including the problems presented by fluctuating national currencies are discussed. For individual firms, overseas ventures often end in failure and adequate exploratory research of the overseas business environment is essential to reduce risks. Methods of undertaking such research are discussed, together with strategies for successfully developing an overseas market.

THE TREND TOWARDS A GLOBAL BUSINESS ENVIRONMENT

At some point, many business organizations recognize that their growth can only continue if they exploit overseas markets. However, entering overseas markets can be extremely risky, as evidenced by examples of recent failures where companies failed to foresee all of the problems involved:

■ British Airways failed in its attempts to enter the North American market through its investment in the ailing airline USAir. British Airways had difficulties in overcoming trade union objections to changes in working practices among other things, which led the company to eventually pull out of its involvement with USAir.

■ The British retailer Laura Ashley failed to adapt its US stores to meet local conditions and in 1999 effectively abandoned the investment it had made in the US market.

■ Even the fast-food retailer McDonald's initially failed to make profits when it entered the UK market in the 1970s and had to rapidly adjust its service offer in order to achieve viability.

Nevertheless, a company which has successfully developed its business strategy should be well placed to extend this development into overseas markets. There are many examples of companies who have successfully done this, including the following:

■ The retailer Tesco successfully reduced its dependence on the saturated UK grocery market by developing outlets in the Far East and Eastern Europe.

- The UK bus and coach builder Henley diversified into the American market with its acquisition of the Bluebird company and now the majority of its sales and profits derive from the United States

- The Irish airline Ryanair started life with a route network which focused on Ireland. With successful expansion of that network, most of its services now do not call at its Irish base.

Many of the fundamental principles of environmental analysis which have been applied to a firm's domestic market will be of relevance in an international setting. The processes of identifying market opportunities and threats, developing strategies, implementing those strategies and monitoring performance involve fundamentally similar principles as those which apply within the domestic market. The major challenge to companies seeking to expand overseas lies in sensitively adapting business strategies which have worked at home to the needs of overseas markets whose environments may be totally different to anything previously experienced.

Globalization of the business environment has occurred because of a number of developments:

- There has been a tendency for barriers to international trade to be removed, facilitated by the efforts of the World Trade Organization.

- A tendency towards cultural convergence has reduced the differences between national market characteristics, thereby reducing the cost of adapting products to those specific markets.

- Improved communications (e.g. the telephone, air travel and the Internet) have reduced the cost of dealing with far-away places.

- The emergence of large multinational corporations (MNCs) has facilitated the process of seeing the world as one global market.

At a macroenvironmental level, success in international trade can help to explain the emergence and growth of many of the countries that have achieved economic pre-eminence in the world, during both modern and ancient times. The Venetians, Spaniards and later the British, Americans and Japanese all saw periods of rapid domestic growth coincide with the growth of their trade with the rest of the world.

International trade is becoming increasingly important, representing not only opportunities for domestic producers to earn revenue from overseas but also threats to domestic producers from overseas competition. The international trade of a nation is made up of the sum total of the efforts of its individual producers and consumers who decide to buy or sell abroad rather than at home. To gain a general overview of the reasons why trade between countries takes place, explanations can be found at two levels:

- At a microlevel, individual firms are motivated to trade overseas.

- At a macrolevel, the structure of an economy and the world trading system can either inhibit or encourage international trade.

We will consider first the microenvironmental reasons which lead firms to enter international trade, and then the aggregate macroenvironmental reasons why international trade takes place.

| 10.1.1 | **FIRMS' REASONS FOR ENTERING INTERNATIONAL TRADE** |

For an individual company, exporting to overseas markets can be attractive for a number of reasons. These can be analysed in terms of 'pull' factors, which derive from the attractiveness of a potential overseas market and 'push' factors that make an organization's domestic market appear less attractive.

1 For organizations seeking growth, overseas markets represent new market segments, which they may be able to serve with their existing range of products. In this way, a company can stick to producing products that it is good at. Finding new overseas markets for existing or slightly modified products does not expose a company to the risks of expanding both its product range and its market coverage simultaneously.

2 Saturation of its domestic market can force an organization to seek overseas markets. Saturation can come about where a product reaches the maturity stage of its life cycle in the domestic market, while being at a much earlier stage of the cycle in less developed overseas markets. While the market for fast-food restaurants may be approaching saturation in a number of Western markets – especially the United States – they represent a new opportunity in the early stages of development in many Eastern European countries.

3 As part of its portfolio management, an organization may wish to reduce its dependence upon one geographical market. The attractiveness of individual national markets can change in a manner that is unrelated to other national markets. For example, costly competition can develop in one national market but not others, world economic cycles show lagged effects between different economies, and government policies – through specific regulation or general economic management – can have counterbalancing effects on market prospects.

4 The nature of a firm's product may require an organization to become active in an overseas market. This particularly affects transport-related services such as scheduled airline services and courier services. For example, a UK scheduled airline flying between London and Paris would most likely try to exploit the non-domestic market at the Paris end of its route.

5 Commercial buyers of products operating in a number of overseas countries may require their suppliers to be able to cater for their needs across national boundaries. As an example, a company may wish to engage accountants who are able to provide auditing and management accounting services in its overseas subsidiaries. For this, the firm of accountants would probably need to have created an operational base overseas. Similarly, firms selling in a

number of overseas markets may wish to engage an advertising agency which can organize a global campaign in a number of overseas markets.

6 Similarly, there are many cases where private consumers demand goods and services that are internationally available. An example is the car hire business where customers frequently need to be able to book a hire car in one country for collection and use in another. To succeed in attracting these customers, car hire companies need to operate internationally.

7 Some goods and services are highly specialized and the domestic market is too small to allow economies of scale to be exploited. Overseas markets must be exploited in order to achieve a critical mass, which allows a competitive price to be reached. Specialized aircraft engineering services and oil exploration services fall into this category.

8 Economies of scale also result from extending the use of brands in overseas markets. Expenditure by a fast-food company on promoting its brand to UK residents is wasted when those citizens travel abroad and cannot find the brand that they have come to value. Newly created overseas outlets will enjoy the benefit of promotion to overseas visitors at little additional cost.

In addition to gaining access to new markets, individual firms may enter international trade to secure resource inputs. The benefits of buying overseas can include lower prices, greater consistency of supply, higher quality, or taking advantage of export subsidies available to overseas suppliers. In the case of raw materials that are not available in the domestic market, a firm may have little choice in its decision to buy from overseas.

10.1.2   **Macroenvironmental reasons for international trade**

From the perspective of national economies, a number of reasons can be identified for the increasing importance of international trade:

1 Goods and services are traded between economies in order to exploit the concept of comparative cost advantage. This holds that an economy will export those goods and services that it is particularly well suited to producing and import those where another country has an advantage. The principles of comparative cost advantage are discussed more fully in Section 10.2.1.

2 The removal of many restrictions on international trade (such as the creation of the Single European Market) has allowed countries to exploit their comparative cost advantages. Nevertheless, restrictions on trade remain, especially for trade in services.

3 Increasing household disposable incomes results in greater consumption of many categories of luxuries, such as overseas travel, which can only be provided by overseas suppliers. Against this, economic development within an economy can result in many specialized goods and services which were previously bought in from overseas being provided by local suppliers. Many developing countries, for example, seek to reduce their dependence on overseas banking and insurance organizations by encouraging the development of a domestic banking sector.

4   Cultural convergence which has resulted from improved communications and increasing levels of overseas travel has led to a homogenization of international market segments. Combined with the decline in trade barriers, convergence of cultural attitude allows many organizations to regard parts of their overseas markets as though they are part of their domestic market.

10.2   THEORY OF INTERNATIONAL TRADE

Today, the United Kingdom, like most industrialized countries, is dependent on international trade to maintain its standard of living. Some products that buyers have become accustomed to, such as tropical fruits and gold, would be almost impossible to produce at home. For products such as these the UK economy could overcome this lack of availability in three possible ways:

1   By using alternative products (which can be produced at home) in place of those that cannot be produced domestically. For example, faced with a domestic shortage of aluminium, many users could switch to domestically produced steel.

2   The domestic economy could try to produce the product at home. This is often impossible where key elements of production are missing (e.g. uranium cannot be produced in the United Kingdom because it is not a naturally occurring substance). In other cases, such as the production of tropical fruits, domestic production can be achieved, but only at a very high cost.

3   The third alternative is to import the goods from a country which is able to produce it.

A similar analysis could be made of the options facing all other countries, not just the United Kingdom. Rather than producers in the United Kingdom growing bananas at great expense for domestic consumption, while a producer in a tropical country attempted to grow temperate fruits, both could benefit by specializing in what they are good at and exchanging their output. This is the basis for the theory of comparative cost advantage.

10.2.1   Comparative cost advantage

The theory of comparative cost advantage can be traced back to the work of Adam Smith in the late eighteenth century and broadly states that the world economy – and hence the economies of individual nations – will benefit if all countries:

■   Concentrate on producing what they are good at and export the surplus

■   Import from other countries those goods that other countries are better able to produce than themselves.

Table 10.1 Production possibility table: food and coal			
	Food	or	Coal
Britain	40	or	40
Rest of world	160	or	40
World production total	200	or	80

The principles of comparative cost advantage can be illustrated with an example. For simplicity, the following example will assume that there are only two countries in the world – Britain and the 'rest of the world'. A second assumption is that only two products are made in the world – food and coal.

It is possible to draw up a table showing the hypothetical food and coal production possibilities of the two countries:

1   If Britain used all of its natural resources to produce coal, then it could produce 40 tons per year, but no food. It could, on the other hand, use all of its resources to produce 40 tons of food per year, but no coal.

2   By contrast, the rest of the world could produce 160 tons of food a year or 40 tons of coal. The different ratios reflect the fact that Britain and the rest of the world possess different combinations of resources.

3   The maximum possible world output of food is therefore 200 tons or of coal 80 tons.

This can be summarized in a production possibility table (Table 10.1).

Neither country is likely to produce solely coal or food. For Britain to give up 1 ton of coal production will result in an increase in food production of 1 ton. However, if the rest of the world gives up 1 ton of coal production, it can increase food production by 4 tons. In this example, Britain should continue to produce coal, because the comparative cost of giving up land for food is lower than the rest of the world. For Britain, the cost of 1 ton of food is 1 ton of coal. For the rest of the world, the cost of 1 ton of coal is 4 tons of food forgone. The rest of the world has a comparative cost advantage in the production of food (because the 'opportunity cost' of the resources used is lower than in Britain).

The next stage of analysing comparative cost advantages is to consider how production of coal and food may actually be divided between Britain and the rest of the world, and, from this, the pattern of trade that could take place. It is again assumed that there are only two countries in the world, that these are the only two goods traded and that total world production equals total consumption (i.e. stocks are not allowed to accumulate). An additional assumption will be made here that coal is more valuable than food. For the moment, it is assumed that 1 ton of coal is worth 5 tons of food.

Table 10.2 shows two situations:

■   Where both countries divide their resources equally between food and coal production, without engaging in trade, and

Table 10.2   Effects on a national economy of specialization based on comparative cost advantage

	Original production pattern – no trade		Revised production pattern – specialization	
	Food	Coal	Food	Coal
Britain	20	20	0	40
Rest of world	80	20	160	0
World production total	100	40	160	40
Value of 1 ton of food = 1 unit 1 ton of coal = 5 units	100	200	160	200
Total wealth	300 units		360 units	

■ A revised trade pattern where each country specializes in the product for which it has a comparative cost advantage.

On the basis of the assumptions made, Table 10.2 indicates that the world as a whole is better off as a result of the two countries specializing in doing what they are good at. Total wealth has gone up from 300 units to 360 units. This pattern would hold so long as the relative costs of production and the terms of trade remained the same. Of course, both of these could, in practice, change. Increased costs in Britain could change its comparative cost in producing food compared to the rest of the world. The pattern would also change if the value of coal went down in relation to the value of food, for example if 1 ton of coal was worth only half a ton of food, and not 5 as in this example.

It is clear that this has been a very simple example using quite unrealistic assumptions. However, it does show how international trade can benefit all nations. In reality, substitutions take place between large numbers of countries and an almost infinite range of products. Nevertheless, the underlying principles of exporting what a country is good at and importing those products that can be made more cheaply elsewhere still hold true. To give modern examples of what this actually means for the UK economy, Britain is good at producing pharmaceuticals which are sold abroad in large volume. It is not so good at producing labour-intensive textiles which are imported in large amounts from the relatively low-wage countries of the Far East.

Although the concept of comparative cost advantage was developed to explain the benefits to total world wealth resulting from each country exploiting its comparative cost advantages with regard to access to raw materials and energy supplies, it can also have application to the services sector. In this way, a favourable climate or outstanding scenery can give a country an advantage in selling tourism services to overseas customers, a point that has not been lost to tourism operators in the Canary Islands and Switzerland respectively. Another basis for comparative cost advantage for services can be found in the availability of low cost or highly trained personnel (cheap labour for the shipping industry and trained computer software experts for computer consultancy respectively). Sometimes the government of a country can itself directly create comparative cost advantages for a service sector, as where it reduces regulations and controls on an industry, allowing that industry to produce services for export at a lower cost than its more regulated competitors (e.g. many 'offshore' financial services centres impose lower standards of regulation and taxation than their mainstream competitors).

10.2.2 ### Limitations to the principle of comparative cost advantage

Unfortunately, the principles of comparative cost advantage may sound fine in theory, but it can be difficult to achieve the benefits in practice. In reality, the global ideals described above can become obscured by narrower national interests. Consequently, the full benefits of comparative cost advantage may not be achieved:

1 Imports can be seen as a threat to established domestic firms. Short-term political pressure to preserve jobs may restrict the ability of firms and individuals to import from the country that is best placed to produce specific products.

2 Governments seek to pursue a portfolio of activities within their economies in order to maintain a balanced economy. Also, governments may protect industries in order to create greater employment opportunities for particular social or regional groups of the population.

3 Governments may seek to temporarily protect fledgling new industries during their development stage in the hope that they will eventually be able to become strong enough to compete effectively in world markets. Competition early on could kill such infant industries before they are able to develop.

4 Trade may not take place in some products – or may be made more difficult – because the requirements of different markets vary. National regulations on matters such as food purity and electrical safety may make it uneconomic to produce special versions of a product for an overseas market.

5 Transport costs act as a deterrent to international trade. Although it may be cheaper to produce building materials in southern Europe than in the United Kingdom, the very high transport costs of getting them to the UK market will limit the amount that actually enters international trade.

6 National governments often artificially stimulate exports by giving export subsidies, allowing domestic producers to compete in world markets against more efficient producers. The EU, for example, has frequently been accused of subsidizing the export of agricultural products such as grain and meat to protect European farmers against competition from more efficient and less subsidized American and Australian farmers.

7 International politics may severely limit the trade that a country has with the rest of the world. Although the trade barriers that existed within Europe are now disappearing, there is increasing concern that the creation of the EU and

other trading blocs, such as the North American Free Trade Area, will have the effect of reducing trade between Europe and the rest of the world.

8 Sometimes governments have defence considerations in mind in restricting international trade (for example by restricting arms sales to hostile nations).

9 Imports may represent a threat to the culture of a country and governments seek to prevent their import. This particularly affects films and publications (e.g. the governments of many Muslim countries make it difficult for films made in the West to be imported).

Despite a plethora of international agreements to facilitate trade between nations, minor, and sometimes major, trade disputes occur between them. The countries involved may agree that the benefits of open markets and comparative cost advantage leading to benefits to all are fine in theory, but the actual short-term implications for them are too harmful. It could be that the government in one country is facing an election and restrictions on imports could gain rapid approval for the government. However, if one country is tempted to introduce some sort of control on imports from another country, it will almost inevitably result in retaliation by the other country. This can spiral, resulting in progressively declining world trade levels. The precise methods by which trade is restricted can take a number of forms:

■ The extreme form of import control is for a country to ban imports of a product or class of products from one or more countries.

■ A tariff can be imposed on goods of a specified type. Governments have imposed tariffs on imports where they believed the product was being 'dumped' by the exporting country at below its production cost, thereby threatening domestic producers with unfair competition. As an example, this was the reason given by the EU in 1995 for the imposition of tariffs ranging from 13 per cent to 48 per cent on bicycles imported from Indonesia, Malaysia and Thailand.

■ A quota on the volume of imports of a particular product can be imposed – imports of cars to the United Kingdom from Japan were restrained for a long time on the basis of a voluntarily agreed quota.

■ Governments sometimes impose covert controls as an alternative to more formal controls, in order to try to diffuse attention and avoid retaliation. A country may unreasonably claim that an exporting country's products do not meet quality or safety standards imposed by the former. This type of argument was used by many countries – many would argue unjustifiably – to ban imports of British beef, claiming that outbreaks of the cattle disease BSE made meat from the United Kingdom potentially unsafe. Sometimes, import documentation and procedures are made so complex that they act to increase the costs of importers relative to domestic producers.

10.2.3 | **Exchange rates**

Nation states generally have their own currency system which is quite distinct from the currency of their international trading partners. It follows therefore that the

Market mechanism and exchange rate determination: the interaction of the supply of, and demand for, a currency determines the exchange rate

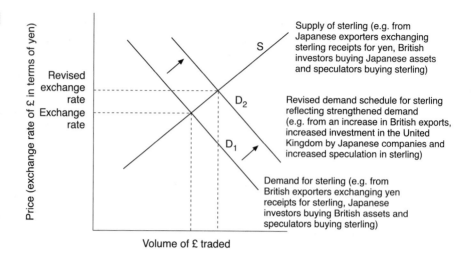

currency which a buyer wants to use as payment may not be the currency that a seller wants to receive as payment for goods or services. If a British customer buys a Japanese built car, they would expect to pay for their car in pounds sterling, and not Japanese yen. So the Japanese manufacturer must become involved in foreign exchange transactions by converting the sterling which it has received back into yen which it will need in order to buy components and to pay its workforce. The fact that different countries have their own currencies makes life for an exporter more complex and risky than for a company that just serves its domestic market.

The biggest problem arising from the use of multiple currencies for trade is that their value in relation to each other fluctuates through time. The value of one currency in terms of another currency is known as its exchange rate. The exchange rate of the yen to sterling will determine how many yen the Japanese car maker will receive for the sterling that it has received from its customers.

Currencies are just like any other commodity that is traded in a market. If the demand for a currency is great relative to its supply, then its 'price' (or exchange rate) will rise. The opposite will happen if there is excess supply of that currency. The principles of exchange rate determination are illustrated in Figure 10.1.

Changes in the supply of, or demand for, a currency can come about for a number of reasons:

1 Changes in demand for a nation's currency can result from a significant change in exports from that country. If UK exports to Japan suddenly increase, UK firms would be left holding large volumes of yen from their Japanese customers. When the UK exporting company went to the currency markets to exchange its yen for sterling, its demand for sterling would have the effect of pushing up the price of sterling in terms of yen.

2 An increase in imports by UK firms from Japan would have an opposite effect. Japanese firms would seek to change the sterling payments they have received into yen. Their supply of sterling will increase relative to demand for it and its price will fall. Of course, in this and the previous example, the actual

transactions would normally be handled routinely by the companies' bankers and most trading firms' transactions would be too small on their own to significantly affect exchange rates. Large overseas orders or the collective effects of many buyers and sellers however, could have a significant effect on exchange rates.

3 Demand for foreign currencies can similarly arise from transactions involving the purchase of assets overseas and the remission of profits and dividends overseas.

4 As in many commodity markets, demand for a currency at any given time is influenced by individuals' expectations about future price levels for a currency. Traders in currencies may use their reserves to buy currencies that they consider are likely to rise and sell those that they expect to fall. Expectations about changes in currency values can be based on factors such as the inflation rate in a country (which has the effect of reducing the purchasing power of its currency); growing imbalances between a country's imports and exports; and general government macroeconomic policy.

5 Intervention by government can affect the supply of, and demand for, its currency. For example, if a government seeks to raise the value of its currency in terms of other currencies (or at least prevent it falling), it can use its gold and foreign currency reserves to buy up its own currency, thereby raising its exchange rate.

From an importer's or exporter's point of view, fluctuations in exchange rates cause considerable uncertainty. Companies selling goods or services abroad may not be certain what revenue they will actually receive if they invoice in a foreign currency, since a change in the exchange rate – between agreeing the price and receiving payment – can earn them more or less than anticipated. Where imports are priced in a producer's currency, importers of goods or services may be uncertain about the final price of their purchases.

From a national government's perspective, a falling exchange rate creates inflationary pressures, since imports become relatively expensive (i.e. it takes more pounds to buy any given yen's worth of imported products). A falling exchange rate helps exporters to achieve overseas sales, because their products effectively become cheaper overseas. It also has the effect of making imports more expensive. Through both of these effects, employment opportunities in the domestic economy are enhanced by a relatively low exchange rate. Governments must balance the stimulus to companies that a low exchange rate brings with the inflationary pressure that it generally entails.

Individual companies can minimize their exposure to risks arising from exchange rate fluctuation in a number of ways:

1 Where it is important for a firm to be certain of the future cost of materials imported from overseas, it can buy contracts which provide it with a specified amount of foreign currency at an agreed time in the future, at an agreed exchange rate. So even if the value of a currency changes in the meantime,

a company can buy its materials from overseas at its budgeted price, using an overseas currency whose value was fixed during its budgeting process.

2   Where the buyer's or seller's currency has a history of volatility, they may decide to use a third currency which is regarded as a relatively stable or 'hard' currency. Many sectors of international trade, such as oil and civil aviation, are routinely priced in US dollars, regardless of the nationality of the buyer and seller.

3   The impact of currency fluctuations on large multinational companies can be reduced by trying to plan for expenditure (on components, etc.) in one currency to roughly equal the revenue it expects to earn in that currency. Any change in exchange rates therefore has an overall broadly neutral effect on the organization.

4   Fluctuating exchange rates can become an opportunity to companies who can rapidly shift their resources to take advantage of imports from countries that have suddenly become advantageous. Commodity traders operating in 'spot' markets may be able to switch supply sources according to changes in exchange rates.

10.2.4   Fixed exchange rates

An alternative to market-based fluctuating exchange rates is a fixed exchange rate system. Here, countries agree to maintain the value of each other's currency, or at least to keep fluctuations within a very narrow range. Where necessary, governments take action to maintain the agreed rates of exchange.

Prior to the full launch of the euro in 1999, the Exchange Rate Mechanism (ERM) of the EU's European Monetary System (EMS) sought to fix member states' exchange rates relative to other participating members' currencies (the 'parity' rate). Countries achieved this by a variety of policy measures. If a country sought to increase its exchange rate to bring it back up to parity, it could: increase interest rates (which in the short term can attract 'hot money' into a currency, thereby pushing up its value); carry out open market operations where the government uses gold and foreign currency reserves to buy up its own currency; and generally increasing speculators' confidence in its economy (e.g. by reducing inflation or a balance of payments deficit). The United Kingdom entered the ERM in October 1990, but left two years later when the short-term cost to the economy of maintaining its fixed parity with other European countries became too great. The high fixed value of sterling had caused interest rates to rise to very high levels (to support the strength of sterling in the marketplace) and had made exporters uncompetitive in overseas markets. At the same time, consumers enjoyed low prices for imports, exacerbating unemployment problems in the domestic economy.

10.2.5   European Monetary Union (EMU)

The launch of the euro in 1999 as a common currency for EU member states overcomes problems of fluctuating exchange rates between traders in countries that have adopted it. Its use will reduce the costs of trade between EU member states and should allow for the development of a 'hard' currency backed by substantial reserves, which is able to match the US dollar as a world currency. The UK did not join in the launch of the euro, arguing that a single currency reduces the scope for national governments to manage their economies. For a common currency to be stable over the longer term, it is important that all economies converge in terms of such factors as inflation rates and government spending. Without being able to adjust exchange rates and interest rates, national economic policy may be unable to tackle economic problems that are specific to a nation state. Despite the UK's reservations about joining the single European currency, it is likely that UK companies trading with other EU companies may nevertheless adopt the currency. For some, this may be a requirement of their EU trading partners, while others will see benefits in using a strong currency, in much the same way as the US dollar is used. The first two years of the euro saw its value gradually fall against major world currencies, suggesting that traders lacked confidence in the currency and/or the strength of the European economy. However, the value of most currencies is cyclical and the strength of the euro could in due course increase against other world currencies.

It was noted in Chapter 8 that control over currency amounts to control over the economy and one reason for Britain's less than enthusiastic embrace of the euro has been the recognition that the country's powers to take independent economic decisions will be greatly reduced. This has already been seen in the case of Ireland, where in 2000 it appeared that a low centrally determined interest rate was inappropriate for the national economy, which was showing signs of overheating with a rising rate of inflation and which could have been lessened by a high interest rate.

Opinion has been divided about the effects of the euro on UK business organizations. Advocates of the euro point to the greatly reduced transaction costs involved in trading with other EU countries and the greatly reduced risk of adverse currency movements between agreeing a price and actually completing a transaction. In the early days of the euro, many UK exporters were keen to join the euro area, as sterling was perceived as being overvalued relative to the euro, putting their exports at a competitive disadvantage. Against these arguments, many businesses in the UK were initially disappointed by the failure of the euro to become a strong and stable reserve currency and for many businesses the US dollar retained this role. Many businesses also recognized that a large currency area does not in itself guarantee a strong and stable currency and critics of the euro have pointed out that the world's largest currency areas such as Russia, China, India and Indonesia (but with the exception of the United States) are among the weakest economies, while some of the smallest currency areas, such as Singapore and Switzerland are among the most dynamic. Had the euro appreciated in value against sterling in its early days, instead of depreciating, the reaction of UK exporting businesses may have been that an independent currency had given new opportunities to gain competitive advantage against relatively high price euro area competitors.

Will the development of the single European currency eventually lead to uniform prices for a product throughout Europe? Advocates of the euro claim that this will be one of the currency's benefits, as price discrepancies become blatantly obvious and consumers shop around in the cheapest market. But what about price discrepancies that exist between different regions of the United Kingdom? The going rate for petrol in one town can be between 5 and 10 per cent different compared to a town just 20 or 30 miles away. This may seem remarkable considering the mobility of buyers and the ease of shopping around for petrol. Similarly, there is no immediately obvious reason why the price of used cars should vary between different regions of the United Kingdom. Similar price variations are present in the United States, which has much longer experience of a single currency. There, prices of most consumer goods tend to reach a high in the affluent north-east and are lowest in the relatively poor areas of the deep south. Why should this be? And what hope is there of the single European market harmonizing prices when there are such discrepancies of commodity type products within a single country?

10.3 OVERSEAS TRADE PATTERNS

The existence of comparative cost advantages and variations between countries in the types of goods and services demanded results in each country having its own distinctive pattern of overseas trade. The nature of a country's overseas trade can be described with respect to:

- The items that it imports and exports and
- The countries it trades with.

Trade patterns throughout the world change in response to changes in the economic, political, technological and social environments. For example, during the mid-1990s, the rising GDP per capita of many Far Eastern 'tiger economy' countries resulted in members of those countries purchasing increasing numbers of overseas holidays. At the same time, growing environmental protection legislation has resulted in many production processes being transferred from Western developed countries to less developed ones where regulations are relatively lax, leading to new export trade.

10.3.1 Measuring overseas trade

The difference between what a country receives from overseas and the amount it spends overseas is referred to as a country's balance of payments. Countries differ in the way in which they break down their overall balance of payments, but these can be broadly divided into:

- The purchase and sale of goods and services (usually described as current account transactions) and

Figure 10.2
Components of a
country's balance
of payments

Current account:	Credits	Debits
Visible trade	Exports	Imports
Invisible trade (including services, interest, profits and dividends)	Payments received from foreign countries	Payments made to foreign countries
Capital account	Inflow of capital	Outflow of capital

■ The acquisition and disposal of assets and liabilities abroad (referred to as capital account transactions).

Although it is common to talk about a country's overall balance of payments being in surplus or deficit, they must technically be balanced (Figure 10.2). If, for example, a country has a deficit in its current account, this has to be made up by running down one of its assets (e.g. by using holdings of foreign currencies to reduce a capital asset or borrowing from overseas and thereby increasing a capital liability). The opposite would be true if a country produced a current account surplus (holdings of foreign assets would increase or foreign liabilities would reduce).

Media headlines which describe a 'trade deficit' or 'surplus' generally refer to the current account element of the balance of payments. The components of the current and capital account elements are described below:

■ The *current account* is generally further divided into two components: a visible trade balance and an invisible trade balance. Visible trade includes transactions in manufactured goods, raw materials and fuel products. Invisibles comprise intangible sales and purchases overseas. Invisible trade is made up of services (e.g. tourism, insurance and shipping), including government services (e.g. payments to overseas armed forces and diplomatic missions), and interest, profit and dividends receivable from or payable abroad.

■ The *capital account* records outward and inward flows of capital for investment purposes (i.e. it excludes routine trading transactions). It includes payments made for long-term investment in tangible assets (e.g. new factories and equipment) and intangible assets (such as the purchase of shares in an overseas company). It also includes short-term movements of money between traders in the money markets (sometimes referred to as 'hot money').

10.3.2   **Measuring overseas transactions**

Traditionally, the value of manufactured goods has been measured as they pass through Customs, and from this information, the total value of imports and exports has been calculated. In the case of capital transactions, governments generally make provisions for large transactions to be reported (e.g. many

Table 10.3   UK overseas current account (£000 000)

Year	Visible trade Exports	Imports	Balance	Services balance	Current account surplus/deficit
1984	70 265	75 601	−5 336	4 205	−1 482
1986	72 627	82 186	−9 559	6 223	−864
1988	80 346	101 826	−21 480	3 957	−16 475
1990	101 718	120 527	−18 809	3 689	−19 293
1992	107 343	120 447	−13 104	5 051	−9 468
1994	134 465	145 059	−10 594	3 790	−1 684
1996	166 340	178 938	−12 598	7 142	−435
1999	165 667	192 434	−26 767	11 538	−12 106

Source: Based on *Annual Abstracts of Statistics.*

countries restrict the free movement of capital to a specified maximum amount per transaction). However, it is becoming increasingly difficult to measure the value and volume of overseas trade.

■ It is very difficult to accurately measure trade in services, which are transacted through a variety of means (e.g. the sale of insurance and banking services using postal and telecommunication methods). In the case of earnings and expenditure on tourism, it can be difficult to measure the total expenditure of tourists whose spending can be dispersed through a variety of business sectors. Governments estimate such figures using various survey techniques. However, initial estimates frequently have to be subsequently revised.

■ With the advent of the Single European Market, border controls on trade within the EU have been largely removed, so it is very difficult to get an accurate indication of the volume of imports and exports between EU member states. Again, overseas trade within the EU is measured using various survey techniques.

Having made these caveats, recent trends in the UK overseas current account are shown in Table 10.3. The years for which data are shown correspond roughly to turning points in worldwide business cycles.

10.3.3   Trends in UK overseas trade

A number of immediate observations can be made about the changing pattern of UK overseas trade:

1 During the recent past, the United Kingdom has run a deficit in its visible balance, but partly made up for this by having a surplus in invisibles. Although the visible trade balance has deteriorated in recent years, growth in the invisible balance has not been sufficient to counteract the decline in visible exports.

2   Overall, the UK current account has tended to be in deficit in recent years (i.e. although there has been a surplus in invisibles, these have not been sufficient to counteract a deficit in the visible balance).

3   The development of North Sea oil has made the visible balance of trade very dependent on world oil prices. The high visible trade surpluses of the early 1980s can be partly explained by the very high level of world oil prices, which benefited the United Kingdom as a net oil exporter. The world oil price had fallen by the end of the 1990s, accounting for some of the deterioration in the visible trade balance.

The overseas trade balance of a nation is very much influenced by the structure of its domestic economy. For the UK economy, the deterioration of the visible balance is symptomatic of the declining competitiveness of its manufacturing industries. Indices of competitiveness reached a low point during the late 1980s as many industry sectors became dominated by products from low-cost producers, especially those in the Far Fast, which had more flexible labour markets and had invested in new productive capacity. More recently, however, there are signs that the United Kingdom has regained some of its competitiveness. This is manifested in the growing number of foreign manufacturers who have located factories in the United Kingdom. While part of the reason for their UK investment is the avoidance of EU external tariff barriers, their decisions also reflect the attractiveness of an increasingly flexible UK labour market and government support for inward investment. However, doubts have been expressed about the sustainability of this inward investment if the United Kingdom remains outside the single European currency area.

Some indication of the importance of international trade in services for the United Kingdom can be seen by examining trade statistics. In 1999, the United Kingdom earned a surplus of £11.5 billion from international trade in services, compared to a deficit of £26.7 billion in goods and raw materials. A closer examination of trade statistics indicates the relative importance of the main service sectors. The most important in terms of overseas sales continues to be insurance and financial services, with credits ('exports') of £11.1 billion, set against debits of £0.7 billion. Travel-related sectors were the next most significant group recorded by national statistics, although in this area the United Kingdom is now a net importer of services (£22.6 billions of imports in 1999, compared with £14.3 billions of exports).

The year-to-year pattern of overseas trade is influenced by business cycles at a national and international level. The downward phase of the world business cycle has the effect of reducing the total value of world trade (or at least slowing down its rate of growth). The business cycles of individual countries may lead or lag the general cycle, or various local reasons may mean that a country is not significantly affected by the worldwide business cycle. A consumer boom in a domestic economy often has the effect of sucking in manufactured imports. The economic boom in the United Kingdom during the mid- to late 1980s, coupled with a high exchange rate, resulted in a very large increase in manufactured imports. At the same time, the domestic manufacturing sector was becoming increasingly uncompetitive, leading to a capacity reduction which limited its opportunities for exports. This contributed to the record visible trade deficits of the early 1990s, which were only corrected as the economic recession caused a reduction in consumer goods imports and falling production costs once more stimulated exports of manufactured goods. During the mid-1990s, UK consumer expenditure remained fairly depressed, but exporters were able to seize opportunities in overseas markets which emerged from their recessionary cycle ahead of the United Kingdom.

An indication of the changing relative competitiveness of UK business sectors can be found by examining ratios of:

■ Imports as a proportion of home demand and

■ Exports as a proportion of manufacturers' sales.

Department of Trade and Industry statistics indicate varying industrial perform-ance. In the case of the imports, the most recent figures indicate a particular weakness in office machinery and data processing equipment and instrument engi-neering and relatively limited penetration by imports in the case of food, drink and mineral products. For exports, transport equipment and chemicals performed strongly, while furniture, timber and paper products achieved low proportions of exports.

Trade patterns can also be analysed in terms of the origin and destination of a country's transactions. Recent years have witnessed a number of changes in the pattern of the United Kingdom's trading partners:

1 UK trade has become increasingly focused on the EU, accounting for 54 per cent of all imports to the United Kingdom in 1999 and 58 per cent of exports.

2 An increasing proportion of the United Kingdom's international trade is with developed economies, accounting in 1999 for over 80 per cent of total trade. The share of trade with developing economies has fallen, reflecting a growing self-sufficiency on the part of the latter.

3 Trade with the United States has gradually become a smaller proportion of the United Kingdom's international trade, accounting for about 12.8 per cent of imports and 14.5 per cent of exports in 1999.

4 The share of imports accounted for by oil-exporting countries has fallen with the development of North Sea oil reserves.

10.3.4   **Prospects for UK international trade**

The postwar years have been generally disappointing for the United Kingdom's balance of trade, with a worsening deficit in visible trade being only partly offset by surpluses in services and North Sea oil. In view of its extensive ownership of overseas assets, the United Kingdom can afford to continue running a moderate trade deficit, but governments have sought to keep deficits within tolerable limits. Very high deficits would probably lead to a fall in the value of sterling, which itself would be inflationary and may lead to an increase in interest rates. Governments would prefer to avoid the social, economic and political consequences of a large trade deficit.

Table 10.4	Ranking of most competitive countries for business		
Country	2000 ranking	1999 ranking	1998 ranking
United States	1	2	3
Singapore	2	1	1
Luxembourg	3	7	10
The Netherlands	4	9	7
Ireland	5	10	11
Finland	6	11	15
Canada	7	5	5
Hong Kong	8	3	2
United Kingdom	9	8	4
Switzerland	10	6	8
Taiwan	11	4	6

Source: Based on data presented to World Economic Forum, Davos, 2001.

League tables of international competitiveness have shown the United Kingdom slipping. For example, an OECD report in 1998 showed that an index of output per head in the United Kingdom was just 69, compared with 100 for the United States, 82 for Germany and 81 for Japan. The World Economic Forum regularly produces league tables of competitiveness, based on such factors as resource costs, flexibility of resources and taxation. The top ten list of most competitive countries (Table 10.4) shows the recent supremacy of the USA and a gradual deterioration in the UK's position.

Prescriptions for the United Kingdom's future prosperity in international trade have focused on a number of issues, including the following:

1 Continuing to improve the cost structure of UK industry, particularly through deregulation of the economy and improvements in the flexibility of labour.

2 Exploiting service sector competitive advantages, especially within the fields of banking and insurance. However, although the United Kingdom has histori-cally achieved surpluses in these fields, competition from newly developed countries has intensified. Many commentators have predicted that if it does not join the single European currency area, its role as a financial centre of Europe will be further weakened. Similarly, the United Kingdom should exploit opportunities in new and emerging sectors when they arise, for example bio-technology.

3 Many have pointed to the valuable role played by governments, such as the Japanese, in promoting a country's exports. In the United Kingdom, the emphasis of government policy has tended to lie in improving supply side efficiency rather than promoting specific sectors overseas.

4 It is argued that many UK companies have failed to invest in new capacity during periods of recession in order to meet an upturn in the world economy.

The consumer boom of the 1980s resulted in imports of goods such as agricultural equipment for which domestic production capacity had been cut during the previous recession and not subsequently replaced.

5   The proportion of GDP spent by the United Kingdom on research and development is low by international standards, placing doubts on the ability of its manufacturers to become world leaders in new product fields (this is discussed further in Chapter 12).

6   Finally, many commentators have pointed to the poor training in marketing and management skills of UK managers, which leaves them badly placed to tackle overseas markets aggressively, or even to protect their domestic markets from import competition. Worse still, many people suspect an anti-industry culture in which the best talent finds its way to the professions such as law and consultancy rather than management.

Many commentators have suggested that the United Kingdom is well positioned to take advantage of developments in the Internet. A study undertaken by Merrill Lynch in 2000 suggested that it was the second best-placed country to benefit from the 'new' Internet-based economy, just behind the United States, and ahead of Sweden, Switzerland, Finland, Ireland and The Netherlands.

It must not be forgotten that market mechanisms in themselves have a tendency to correct trade imbalances. A country with long-term trade deficits based on structural weaknesses in its economy will experience a weakening in the value of its currency, which will have the effect of making exports cheaper and imports dearer. Through a substitution effect in its domestic markets, domestic manufacturers will gain competitive advantage over importers, thereby reducing a trade deficit. Similarly, exports will become cheaper in overseas markets, again reducing a trade deficit. For countries which run continuing trade surpluses, market forces will tend to reduce the surplus. Continuing surpluses will cause a rise in the value of a country's currency, making exports more expensive and imports cheaper. Eventually, exports may become so expensive (when priced in buyers' currencies) that the country's exporters will establish factories overseas, and may even find it cheaper to assemble products overseas for import to its domestic market.

10.4   INTERNATIONAL TRADE INSTITUTIONS AND AGREEMENTS

The exploitation of comparative cost advantages through free trade may sound fine in theory, but is often difficult to achieve in practice, for the reasons described earlier in this chapter. There have therefore been many attempts to develop international agreements for the free movement of trade. At their simplest, international trade agreements comprise bilateral agreements between two countries to open up trade between the two. Sometimes, groups of countries join together to form trading blocs in which trade between member states is encouraged at the expense of trade with non-bloc members. There are also multilateral agreements between nations to develop free trade. Some of the more important are described below.

10.4.1   **The Single European Market**

A principal aim of the European Union has been the removal of barriers to trade between member states. The most significant step towards this was achieved through the EU's Single European Market programme and the development of the European Economic Area, which extended the principles of the single market to include members of the European Free Trade Area (EFTA). Since 1993 there has been a progressive easing of trade within the European Economic Area and the following are some of the benefits achieved:

■ The removal or reduction of institutional barriers to trade (e.g. reduced import/export documentation), thereby reducing travel times.

■ The technical harmonization of product standards, allowing for greater economies of scale and competition using a standardized product which is able to compete in multiple domestic markets.

■ The ability of companies with licences to operate in their home market to be able to extend these rights to other EU markets.

■ The liberalization of capital movements.

■ The removal of discriminatory public purchasing policies.

It has been estimated that the effects of the Single Market after five years of operation would have been to increase EU output as a whole by 7 per cent, for prices to fall by up to 6 per cent in real terms and for EU-wide employment to increase by 1.8 millions. These benefits will be achieved through a combination of reduced costs and increased competition which will have the effect of reducing local national monopoly power enjoyed by some suppliers. A number of UK sectors have been identified as likely beneficiaries of more open markets, able to exploit their comparative cost advantages. These include pharmaceuticals, the food and drink industry, insurance and civil aviation.

Despite the efforts of the Single European Market programme, a number of barriers to trade within the EU remain:

■ There is debate about the extent to which cultural variations within Europe will eventually be homogenized. Some of these variations are based on geographical factors (e.g. lifestyles and attitudes of the hot southern climates differ markedly from those of northern countries) and may be difficult to change.

■ Although harmonization of product standards has proceeded a long way, some problems remain. For example, the United Kingdom's non-standard design of electrical plugs or its practice of driving on the left may never be harmonized to a European standard.

■ It is still often necessary for individuals or firms to obtain licences before they can operate in another member state. Although removal of such barriers is on the EU agenda for reform, free trade in services has generally been harder to open up to cross-border trade than dealings in manufactured goods.

Nevertheless, the Single European Market has become a major trading bloc

THINKING AROUND THE SUBJECT

When does a requirement for rigorous staff training amount to a restrictive international trade practice? The French authorities have insisted that all guides accompanying groups on its ski slopes should take a test which is one of the toughest in Europe, citing the increased safety of groups which results. British tour operators have in the past provided ski guides who are generally assessed by companies for their basic mountain awareness abilities. They have assumed more of a social role than that of an expert guide in difficult terrain. British tour operators claim that their customers prefer the social informality of their guides rather than the formality of the French ski instructors. Is this an example of a covert restriction on international trade by the French authorities, keen to give preference to their own politically important local guides? Or does their action represent a genuine concern for safety (if not consumers' preferences) which is neutral in terms of its effects on foreign tour operators?

which has made trade within the bloc easier, while creating common policies with respect to trade with the rest of the world.

10.4.2 Other regional trading blocs

A number of other trading blocs exist in the world with aims which are similar to those of the EU. These include the North America Free Trade Area (NAFTA), the Gulf Co-operation Council (GCC) and the Association of South East Asian Nations (ASEAN). In the case of NAFTA, the United States, Canada and Mexico have sought to reduce barriers to trade between their countries so that each can exploit its comparative cost advantage. Some measures are already in place, but the creation of the single market will have increasing effect in the future. Inevitably, while trade is made easier within the free trade area, there is a danger of other outside countries being disadvantaged.

10.4.3 Organization for Economic Co-operation and Development (OECD)

The OECD was originally set up in 1947 to administer America's Marshall Aid programme in Europe, but subsequently turned increasing attention to the developing world. The OECD now has 21 members, including most European countries, the United States, Canada and Japan. It works by trying to co-ordinate the economic policies of members, to co-ordinate programmes of economic aid and by providing specialized services, especially information.

10.4.4 The World Bank

The World Bank (officially known as the International Bank for Reconstruction and Development) acts as an adviser to governments in the provision of international finance. The main role of the World Bank is to provide capital on favourable terms to aid the economic reconstruction of countries. In cases where it advances loans to overseas governments, it may require its advice to be incorporated into government policy as a condition of its loan.

10.4.5 The International Monetary Fund (IMF)

The IMF shared its origins with the OECD and World Bank in that all three institutions were created in the immediate postwar period and were seen as a means towards world economic regeneration. The IMF is essentially a world forum for international negotiations on governments' fiscal policies. Its original aims of regulating and stabilizing exchange rates have been somewhat undermined by the ability of traders and multinational companies to influence exchange rates, often having a bigger impact on markets than policies agreed by the IMF.

10.4.6 The World Trade Organization (WTO)

The WTO has its origins in the General Agreement on Tariffs and Trade (GATT) of the early post-war period. The signatories to the agreement sought to achieve greater international economic prosperity by exploiting fully the comparative cost advantages of nations by reducing the barriers that inhibited international trade. All the signatories agreed not to increase tariffs on imported goods beyond their existing levels and to work towards the abolition of quotas which restricted the volume of imports. The WTO has proceeded to reduce tariffs and quotas through several negotiating 'rounds'. It has also tried to redress the distortion to world trade and the unfair competitive advantage given to subsidized exporters of agricultural products. In recent years, the WTO has been accused of representing a Western agenda for economic development, allegedly to the disadvantage of less developed countries.

10.4.7 Other international agreements and institutions

A wide range of other agreements and institutions affect international trading companies. Some of these will be very general in nature and affect a wide range of businesses. An example in this category is the agreement to set up a European Bank for Reconstruction and Development, aimed at helping the restructuring of the emerging East European economies. Improved access to loans may help a wide range of exporters of capital equipment. There are many examples of bilateral agreements between countries which can influence the operations of business organizations. Agreements between countries on how the taxation of multinational companies should be handled can have serious implications for businesses, leading to the possibility of double claims for taxation where this possibility is not specifically excluded by a bilateral government agreement.

There are also very many agreements and institutions covering specific industries. An example of an institution that has a direct effect on an industry is the International Civil Aviation Organization (ICAO) to which most countries belong and which has agreed international safety standards for civil aviation. In other cases, agreements between countries can have a more indirect effect on a market, as with an international agreement signed to restrict international trade in ivory.

10.5 EVALUATING OVERSEAS BUSINESS OPPORTUNITIES

Overseas markets can represent very different opportunities and threats compared to those that an organization has been used to in its domestic market. Before a detailed environmental analysis is undertaken, an organization should consider in general terms whether the environment is likely to be attractive. By considering in this way such matters as political stability or cultural attitudes, an organization may screen out potential markets for which it considers further analysis cannot be justified by the likelihood of success. Where an exploratory analysis of an overseas environment appears to indicate some opportunities, a more thorough analysis might suggest important modifications to a product format which would need to be made before it could be successfully offered to the market.

This section firstly identifies some general questions which need to be asked in assessing the business environment of overseas countries and then considers specific aspects of researching such environments.

10.5.1 Macrolevel analysis of a foreign business environment

The combination of environmental factors that contributed to success within an organization's domestic market may be absent in a foreign country, resulting in the failure of export attempts. In this section, questions to be asked in analysing an overseas business environment are examined under the overlapping headings of the political, economic, social and technological environments.

The political environment At a national level, individual governments can influence attractiveness to business in a number of ways:

1 At the most general level, the stability of the political system affects the attractiveness of a particular national market. While radical change rarely results from political upheaval in most Western countries, the instability of many Eastern European governments can lead to uncertainty about the economic and legislative framework in which goods and services will be traded.

2 Licensing systems may be applied by governments in an attempt to protect domestic producers. Licences can be used to restrict individuals practising a particular profession (e.g. licensing requirements for accountants or solicitors may not recognize experience and licences obtained overseas) or they can be used to restrict foreign owners setting up an overseas operation.

3 Regulations governing product standards may require an organization to expensively reconfigure its products offer to meet local regulations, or may prohibit their sale completely.

4 Controls can be used to restrict the import of manufactured goods, requiring a company to create a local source of supply, leading to possible problems in maintaining consistent quality standards and also possibly losing economies of scale.

5 Production possibilities can be influenced by government policies. Minimum wage levels and conditions of service can be important in determining the viability of an overseas operation. For example, many countries restrict the manner in which temporary or seasonal staff can be employed. This could make the operation of a seasonal holiday hotel inflexible and uneconomic.

6 Restrictions on currency movements may make it difficult to repatriate profits earned from an overseas operation.

7 Governments are major procurers of goods and services and may formally or informally give preference in awarding contracts to locally owned organizations.

8 Legislation protecting trademarks varies between countries. In some countries, such as Russia and Thailand, the owner may find it relatively hard to legally protect itself from imitators.

The economic environment A generally accepted measure of the economic attractiveness of an overseas market is the level of GDP per capita. The demand for most products increases as this figure increases. However, organizations seeking to sell goods and services overseas should also consider the distribution of income within a country which may identify valuable niche markets. For example, the relatively low GDP per head of South Korea still allows a small and relatively affluent group to create a market for high-value overseas holidays.

An organization assessing an overseas business environment should place great emphasis on future economic performance and the stage that a country has reached in its economic development. While many Western developed economies face saturated markets for a number of products, less developed economies may be just moving on to that part of their growth curve where a product begins to appeal to large groups of people.

A crucial part of the analysis of an overseas business environment focuses on the level of competition within that market. This can be related to the level of economic development achieved within a country. In general, as an economy develops, its markets become more saturated. This is true, for example, of the market for household insurance which is mature and highly competitive in North America and most Western European countries, but is relatively new and less competitive in many developing economies of the Pacific Rim, allowing better margins to be achieved. In addition to competition for customers, a mature economy is also likely to experience stronger competition for labour resources, leading to higher wage costs.

The social and cultural environment An understanding of cultural differences between markets is very important for businesses contemplating entering foreign

Many Western companies have set their eyes on the potential of China, the world's most populous country and one which can bewilder westerners. But is it good enough to simply lump all of China together as one homogeneous business environment? With 22 provinces (23 if Taiwan is included), three municipalities and five autonomous regions, there is tremendous diversity in business environments. Exporters seeking success in China must analyse the country carefully and choose the most promising area as their point of entry.

There is a significant income difference between urban and rural areas and between coastal and inland areas, with cities (especially the coastal cities) generally being much richer than rural areas. Examples of cities at the top of this purchasing power list are Shenzhen, Guangzhou, Shanghai, Beijing, Tianjin, Hangzhou and Dalian.

Exporters are particularly interested in the distribution of 'trigger' levels of income, above which an individual's need for necessities are satisfied and they can become purchasers of imported Western luxury goods. The McKinsey management consulting firm estimated that in 1992 there were 60 million Chinese, mostly in the coastal provinces and urban areas, who had a per capita purchasing power of over US$1000, the critical figure above which

Chinese people typically start buying colour TVs, washing machines and imported clothing. It has been estimated that by 2001, the numbers above this $1000 threshold will be 200 million. However, care needs to be taken in interpreting official figures about wealth in China. The actual purchasing power of a dollar in China compared to the West is higher because many Chinese do not report all their income. There are also distortions caused by hidden savings and allowances received from family members living abroad. Furthermore, the Chinese typically pay very low or no rent, spend little on healthcare and education due to subsidies and are only allowed to have one or two children. There is also a booming black market in labour, goods, services and foreign exchange which further distort official statistics of wealth.

For exporters to China, getting their product to the market, at the right time and at the right place, can be very difficult, given the limitations of the communications infrastructure. This is especially true of the inland provinces and emphasizes the need for exporters to focus their marketing and distribution efforts on just a few of the richest areas. It has been observed that not even the largest multinational companies have attempted to take on the whole Chinese market at once.

markets. Individuals from different cultures not only buy different products, but may also respond in different ways to similar products. Attitudes towards work can affect production efficiency. Examples of differing cultural attitudes and their effects on international trade in goods and services include the following:

- Buying processes vary between different cultures. For example, the role of women in selecting a product may differ in an overseas market compared to the domestic market, thereby possibly requiring a different approach to product design and promotion.

- Some categories of goods and services may be rendered obsolete by certain types of social structure. For example, extended family structures common in some

Hilton International, owner of many of the world's most prestigious hotels, has joined the race to build the first hotel on the moon. Called the Lunar Hilton, the complex would have 5000 rooms. It would be powered by two huge solar panels and have its own beach and sea as well as a working farm. Experts disagree on the practicalities of life on the moon, but barriers seem to be diminishing as new discoveries are made. Hilton is not alone in its proposed development. Three Japanese companies have already spent £25 million on development work for their own moon projects. Compared to this, Hilton's expenditure to date of £100000 looks quite modest. Is the company mad in believing that people will want to visit the moon? Or is this just the kind of long-term strategic thinking that so many businesses lack? With the world becoming smaller and increasingly saturated with goods and services, does the moon offer a unique opportunity for expansion?

countries have the ability to produce a wide range of services within the family unit, including caring for children and elderly members.

■ A product that is taken for granted in the domestic market may be seen as socially unacceptable in an overseas market. Frequently encountered examples include pork products in Muslim countries and beef in Hindu countries.

■ Attitudes towards promotional programmes differ between cultures. The choice of colours in advertising or sales outlets needs to be made with care because of symbolic associations (e.g. the colour associated with bereavement varies between cultures).

■ What is deemed to be acceptable activity in procuring sales varies between cultures. In Middle Eastern markets, for example, a bribe to a public official may be considered essential, whereas it is unacceptable in most Western countries.

■ Attitudes to work differ between cultures, for example with respect to the role of women and deference to authority.

The technological environment An analysis of the technological environment of an overseas market is important for organizations who require the use of a well-developed technical infrastructure and a workforce that is able to use technology. Communications are an important element of the technological infrastructure – poorly developed telephone and postal communications may inhibit attempts to make credit cards more widely available, for instance.

10.6 SOURCES OF INFORMATION ON OVERSEAS MARKETS

The methods used to research a potential overseas market are in principle similar to those that would be used to research a domestic market. Companies would

Table 10.5   Sources of secondary information on overseas markets

Government agencies
   Department of Trade and Industry market reports
   Overseas governments – e.g. US Department of Commerce
   Overseas national and local development agencies

International agencies
   European Union (Eurostat, etc.)
   Organization for Economic Co-operation and Development (OECD)
   World Trade Organization (WTO)

United Nations (UN)
   International Monetary Fund (IMF)
   Universal Postal Union
   World Health Organization (WHO)

Research organizations
   Economic Intelligence Unit
   Dun and Bradstreet International
   Market research firms

Publications
   Financial Times country surveys
   Business International
   International Trade Reporter
   Banks' expert reviews

Trade associations
   Chambers of commerce
   Industry-specific association – e.g. ICAO

Online resources
   Eurostat
   Mintel Online
   FT Online

normally begin by using secondary data about a potential overseas market which is available to them at home. Sources that are readily available through specialized libraries, government organizations and specialist research organizations include Department of Trade and Industry information for exporters, reports of international agencies such as the OECD, chambers of commerce and private sources of information such as that provided by banks. Details of some specific sources are shown in Table 10.5.

Initial desk research at home will identify those markets that show greatest potential for development. An organization will then often follow this up with further desk research of materials available locally within the short-listed markets, often carried out by appointing a local research agency. This may include a review of reports published by the target market's own government and specialist locally based market research agencies.

Just as in home markets, secondary data have limitations in assessing market attractiveness. Problems in overseas markets are compounded by the greater difficulty in gaining access to data, possible language differences and problems of definition which may differ from those with which an organization is familiar. In the case of products that are a new concept in an overseas market, information on current usage and attitudes to the product may be completely lacking. For this reason, it would be difficult to use secondary data to try to assess the likely response from consumers to large out-of-town superstores in many Eastern European countries.

Primary research is used to overcome shortcomings in secondary data. Its most important use is to identify cultural factors which may require a product format to be modified or abandoned altogether. A company seeking to undertake primary research in a new proposed overseas market would almost certainly use a local specialist research agency. Apart from overcoming possible language barriers, a local agency would better understand attitudes towards privacy and the level of literacy that might affect response rates for different forms of research. However, the problem of comparability between markets remains. For example, when a Japanese respondent claims to 'like' a product, the result may be comparable to a German consumer who claims to 'quite like' it. It would be wrong to assume on the basis of this research that the product is better liked by Japanese consumers than German consumers.

Primary research is generally undertaken overseas when a company has become happy about the general potential of a market, but is unsure of a number of factors that would be critical for success, for example whether intermediaries would be willing and able to handle their product or whether traditional cultural attitudes will present an insurmountable obstacle for a product not previously available in that market. Prior to commissioning its own specific research, a company may go for the lower cost but less specific route of undertaking research through an omnibus survey. These are surveys regularly undertaken among a panel of consumers in overseas markets (e.g. the Gallup European Omnibus) which carry questions on behalf of a number of organizations.

10.7 MARKET ENTRY STRATEGIES

A new foreign market represents both a potential opportunity and a risk to an organization. A company's market entry strategy should aim to balance these two elements.

The least risky method of developing a foreign market is to supply that market from a domestic base. This is often not a cost-effective method of serving a market, and may not be possible in the case of some inseparable services where producer and consumer must interact. Where an exporter needs to set up production facilities overseas, risk can be minimized by gradually committing more resources to a market, based on experience to date. Temporary facilities could be established that have low start-up and close-down costs and where the principal physical and human assets can be transferred to another location. A good example of risk reduction through the use of temporary facilities is found in the pattern of retail development in East Germany following reunification. West German retailers who initially entered East Germany in large numbers were reluctant to commit themselves to building stores in specific locations in a part of the country that was still economically unstable and where patterns of land use were rapidly changing. The solution adopted by many companies was to offer branches of their chain in temporary marquees or from mobile vehicles – these could move in response to the changing pattern of demand. While the location of retail outlets remained risky, this did not prevent retailers from establishing their networks of distribution warehouses which were considered to be more flexible in the manner in which they could respond to changing consumer spending patterns.

Market entry risk reduction strategies also have a time dimension. While there may be long-term benefits arising from being the first company to develop a new product field in a foreign market, there are also risks. If development is hurried and launched before consistent quality can be guaranteed to live up to an organization's international standards, the company's long-term image can be damaged, both in the new foreign market and in its wider world market. In the turbulent business environment of Eastern Europe in the late 1980s, two of the world's principal fast-food retailers – McDonald's and Burger King – pursued quite different strategies.

THINKING AROUND THE SUBJECT

In the parcels business, firms need to operate globally in order to achieve economies of scale and to offer comprehensive facilities to customers. United Parcel Service of America (UPS) realized during the 1990s that it had been slipping behind competitors such as Federal Express in its global coverage, so sought expansion of its operating base in Europe. It spent over $1 billion buying 16 delivery businesses, with the result that in a very short period of time, it had put its brown uniforms on 25 000 Europeans and sprayed its brown paint on 10 000 delivery trucks. Virtually overnight, 'Big Brown' had become the largest parcel delivery company in Europe.

Expansion into Europe was not without its surprises for UPS. It encountered indignation in France, when drivers were told they couldn't have wine with lunch; protests in Britain, when drivers' dogs were banned from delivery trucks; dismay in Spain, when it was found that the brown UPS trucks resembled the local hearses; and shock in Germany, when brown shirts were required for the first time since 1945. UPS also had trouble integrating its European businesses and imposing its American ways on local managers, several of whom soon left the company. Labour laws were a major obstacle and challenged UPS's tendency in its home market to rely on many part-time workers and to use temporary layoffs if business is slow. Many European countries forbid temporary layoffs. The company also had problems with its methods of pricing. After realizing that its traditional method of charging by weight was causing it to get lumbered with carrying bulky guitars and hoola-hoops, UPS quickly switched to European methods of charging by volume.

What could UPS have done to avoid the problems that it encountered? Certainly it could have made a greater effort to study cultural differences and to adapt to local conditions. But wasn't one of the points of UPS's intended competitive advantage that it was bringing to Europe a new way of delivering parcels?

The former waited until political, economic, social and technological conditions were capable of allowing it to launch a restaurant that met its global standards. In the case of Burger King, its desire to be first in the market led it to offer a sub-standard service, giving it an image from which it was difficult to recover.

An assessment of risk is required in deciding whether an organization should enter a foreign market on its own or in association with another organization. The former maximizes the strategic and operational control that the organization has over its overseas operations, but it exposes it to the greatest risk where the overseas market is relatively poorly understood. A range of entry possibilities are considered in Sections 10.7.1–10.7.6.

10.7.1   **Exporting**

It is often possible for a company to gain a feel for a foreign market by exporting to it from its home base. Where economies of scale in production are high and transport costs are low, this is often a very cost-effective solution. To minimize risks associated with an unknown market, an exporter would often employ an export agent at home or an import agent in the overseas target market. The use of an agent may also be more cost-effective for the company than creating its own overseas salesforce. If initial export attempts succeed, a company may then consider setting up its own production base overseas. As an example of this strategy of gradual commitment, the Müller yoghurt company initially exported its premium yoghurts from Germany to the United Kingdom, until its market had grown to such an extent that it felt confident about committing resources to a new UK production centre.

Exporting is likely to be the less satisfactory option for manufacturers who produce high-volume, low-value products for which transport costs could put them at a competitive disadvantage in overseas markets. Exporting is generally not possible in the case of services that demand a high level of interaction between a company and its customers at the latter's home base (e.g. high contact services such as street cleaning subcontracting cannot be very easily exported without creating a base in the customer's home country).

Although the use of export/import agents may initially minimize risks for an exporter, their use also brings potential problems. Where an import agent acquires exclusive rights to market a product in a country, conflict can occur between the agent and exporter on marketing policy issues (e.g. in the early 1990s there was an acrimonious disagreement on policy between Nissan and its UK sole importer AFG).

10.7.2   **Direct investment in a foreign subsidiary**

This option gives an organization maximum control over its foreign operations, but can expose it to a high level of risk on account of the poor understanding that it may have of the overseas market. A company can either set up its own overseas subsidiary from scratch (as many UK hotel companies have done to develop hotels in overseas markets), or it can acquire control of a company that is already trading (such as the acquisition by the UK company Stagecoach of the US bus operator Coach USA).

Where the nature of the product offer differs relatively little between national markets or where it appeals to an international market (e.g. hotels), the risks from creating a new subsidiary are reduced. Where there are barriers to entry and the product is aimed at an essentially local market with a different culture to the domestic market, the acquisition of an established subsidiary may be the preferred course of action, although even this is not risk free.

10.7.3   ### Global e-commerce

The development of the Internet has offered new opportunities for organizations to enter foreign markets. The services sector in particular has benefited, because, compared with the manufactured goods sector, services generally have fewer problems of handling tangible goods that have acted as a constraint on the development of e-commerce for many goods manufacturers. At the business-to-business level, a lot of back-room service processing, such as invoicing, data entry and software development, can now be carried out in parts of the world where there is a plentiful supply of low-cost, skilled workers, and the results sent back to the customer by a data link (see Case Study). At the business-to-consumer level, many service providers now promote themselves to global audiences through the Internet. A consumer in the United Kingdom, for example, can find a hotel in Australia and book a room on line without the hotel needing to use an intermediary. The costs to service providers of reaching global audiences in this way can be very low.

The service sector has been at the leading edge of developments in e-commerce, helped by the absence of a tangible content which must be physically delivered. Travel-related services and financial services have seen major developments in e-commerce. However, the limitations of the Internet in gaining access to foreign markets should be recognized. For private consumers, purchasing through the Internet is often perceived as being very risky, and this riskiness is likely to increase when the supplier is based in a foreign country. In the case of Internet banking services offered in the UK from overseas, customers may find themselves not protected by legislation which protects customers of UK-based banks. Some services providers are reluctant to make their services available globally through the Internet in order to preserve price discrimination. Providers of inseparable services are often able to charge different groups different prices, without the fear of a low-price segment selling on the service to high-price segments. For this reason, airlines often restrict sales of tickets through the Internet to local national markets, to prevent customers buying in the cheapest global market.

Finally, it should be remembered that the Internet is becoming increasingly cluttered with websites, and it is not sufficient for an exporter to simply have a website. It must also ensure that the site is brought to the attention of a global audience. Many small businesses realize that the most cost-effective means of doing this is by paying various types of information intermediaries (such as online hotel booking agencies) to do this for them.

The recruitment sector was quick to recognize the value of the Internet as a tool for global expansion. Recruitment consultants earn a fee from finding and selecting a suitable individual for a vacant job which a client company seeks to fill. Recruitment using the Internet seemed to fit neatly with the growing recognition that the workforce was becoming more mobile and a global recruitment market existed for many types of employment. So transferring the traditional medium of printed job adverts on to the Web seemed to make perfect sense. But have the promises of global recruiting via the Internet been met?

The arrival of the Internet seemed to provoke a frenzy of activity in the recruitment industry. Viewed at its most simple, the Web offered a global notice board that allowed recruiters to pull in CVs and resumés from a massively expanded base of skilled workers. If a company in Guildford, UK, was having difficulty recruiting IT specialists in its home area, why not use the Internet to trawl for experts who may be living in Bulgaria or Greece, and unaware of the opportunities in the United Kingdom? There was also much excited talk about a global market in chief executive officers who could take their worldwide skills from one country to another.

Many entrepreneurs set up websites to use the medium of the Internet as a means of matching job hunters with vacancies. Many of these, lacking much experience in the world of recruitment consultancy soon went out of business. In other cases, established recruitment consultants set up their own online recruitment companies, for example Norman Broadbent set up a separate online division called myOyster and Harvey Nash set up FirstPersonGlobal (FPG).

The demise of many new Internet-based recruitment consultants stressed the point that the Internet is only a medium for communication and that if the company has very little worth communicating, it will offer no competitive advantage. Online recruiters soon realized that informal networks of employers and job seekers were crucial, or as one observer put it, the traditional headhunter's method of approaching people and tapping them on the shoulder would continue. Recruitment consultants sell their services on the back of discreet personal contact with a network of key executives. This was apparently not the world of the new and youthful dot.com outfits. Traditional headhunters cultivate an image of exclusivity, often with exclusive sounding addresses, such as London's Mayfair. Could a WWW address on its own carry much credibility? Could the Internet be used to extend the global reach of the consultants' traditional 'tap on the shoulder'?

It seemed that early hopes of using the Internet to create a global jobs market have been tempered by the reality that senior executives are unlikely to be willing to abandon trusted face-to-face contacts in favour of the perceived impersonality and insecurity of the Internet. Many people began to realize that in global markets, the Internet would only ever be a support medium and would never replace personal contacts which established recruitment agencies had built up. There may be more hope with lower salaried individuals, especially IT professionals.

Even for established recruitment agencies, the Internet posed problems in their bid for global expansion. Speed and global reach are certainly two factors in the Internet's favour, but what happens when this results in tens of thousands of applications being received for one job? How can a recruitment consultant operate with so many applications? How are they going to be able to discriminate between so many? Established companies also faced the problem of cannibalization, where their new online venture simply took business away from their established business, incurring additional costs, but resulting in no additional business.

10.7.4   Licensing/franchising

Rather than setting up its own operations in an overseas market, a company can license a local company to manufacture and sell a product in the local market. This is commonly used, for example, by soft drinks manufacturers who sell the right to companies to market a branded product in a foreign market. The licensee must usually agree to follow a product formulation closely and to maintain consistent standards of quality and brand image.

While exporters of manufactured goods frequently license a foreign producer to manufacture and sell their products, a company developing a service overseas is more likely to establish a franchise relationship with its overseas producers, which gives it greater control over the whole service production process. As with the development of a domestic franchise service network, franchising can allow an organization to expand rapidly overseas with relatively low capital requirements. While a clearly defined business format and method of conducting business is critical to the success of a foreign franchise operation, things can still go wrong for a number of reasons. The service format could be poorly proven in the home market, making overseas expansion particularly difficult. Unrealistic expectations may be held about the amount of human and financial resources that need to be devoted to the operation of a foreign franchise. Problems in interpreting the spirit and letter of contractual agreements between the franchisee and franchisor can result in acrimonious misunderstanding. In 1997, for example, the Body Shop took back control of its French franchises, claiming that they had been poorly performing in the hands of its local franchisees.

10.7.5   Joint ventures

An international joint venture is a partnership between a domestic company and a foreign company or government. A joint venture can take a number of forms and is particularly attractive to a domestic firm seeking entry to an overseas market where:

- The initial capital requirement threshold is high, resulting in a high level of risk.

- Overseas governments restrict the rights of foreign companies to set up business on their account, making a partnership with a local company – possibly involving a minority shareholding – the only means of entering the market.

- There may be significant barriers to entry which a company already based in the foreign market could help to overcome (for example, access to local intermediaries).

Table 10.6 Recent examples of international joint ventures

Venture partners	Holding (%)	Subsidiary/purpose
Equity joint ventures		
British Telecom	50	Development of Telfort telephone service
NS Dutch Railways	50	in The Netherlands
Prudential	50	Creation of Prudential Assicurazione to
Inholding (Italy)	50	provide insurance services in Italy
Abbey National	92	Creation of Abbey National Mutui to offer
Diners Club (Italy	0	mortgages in Italy
Winterthur (Switzerland)	8	
British Energy	50	Creation of new company Amergen to
PECO Energy	50	acquire nuclear power stations in the
		United States
Non-equity joint ventures		
Commercial Union		Agreement for CI to sell and distribute
Credito Italiano (Italy)		CU's life and non-life insurance policies
		in Italy
Hambros Merchant Bank		Co-operation agreement in cross-frontier
Bayerische Vereinsbank		merger and acquisition finance
(West Germany)		
Barclays Bank		Agreement gave Barclays Bank a
Tokyo Trust (Japan)		banking licence to operate in Japan to
		provide trust management and securities
		handling in collaboration with its partner

■ There may be reluctance of consumers to deal with what appears to be a foreign company. A joint venture can allow the operation to be fronted by a domestic producer with whom customers can be familiar, while allowing the overseas partner to provide capital and management expertise.

■ A good understanding of local market conditions is essential for success in an overseas market. It was noted above that the task of obtaining marketing research information can be significantly more difficult abroad as compared to an organization's domestic market. A joint venture with an organization already based in the proposed overseas market makes the task of collecting information about a market, and responding sensitively to it, relatively easy.

■ Taxation of company profits may favour a joint venture rather than owning an overseas subsidiary outright.

Some recent examples of joint ventures are shown in Table 10.6.

Strategic alliances These are agreements between two or more organizations where each partner seeks to add to its competencies by combining its resources with those of a partner. A strategic alliance generally involves co-operation between

An introduction to **one**world
The alliance that revolves around you

AmericanAirlines

BRITISH AIRWAYS

Canadian Airlines

CATHAY PACIFIC

QANTAS

Figure 10.3
With the globalization of markets, strategic alliances are becoming increasingly crucial in order to facilitate overseas growth. In the airline sector, an alliance such as the One World Alliance allows one airline's services to be marketed by all other alliance members. For customers, British Airways is able to offer 'seamless' travel around the globe on services of fellow alliance members. For the company, there are opportunities to rationalize its operations in foreign countries
(*Source*: Reproduced with permission of One World Alliance)

partners rather than joint ownership of a subsidiary set up for a specific purpose, although it may include agreement for collaborators to purchase shares in the businesses of other members of the alliance.

Strategic alliances are frequently used to allow individual companies to build upon the relationship that they have developed with their clients by allowing them to sell on services that they do not produce themselves, but are produced by another member of the alliance. This arrangement is reciprocated between members of the alliance. Strategic alliances have become important within the airline industry, where a domestic operator and an international operator can join together to offer new travel possibilities for their respective customers.

International strategic alliances can involve one organization nominating a supplier in related product fields as a preferred supplier at its outlets worldwide. This strategy has been used by car rental companies to secure a link-up with other transport principals, to offer what the latter sees as a value-added service. An example is the agreement between Hertz Car Rental and Eurotunnel to provide a new facility for customers of each company called 'Le Swap'. By the agreement, customers are able to rent a right-hand-drive car in the United Kingdom, travel through the tunnel by train and swap to a left-hand-drive car at the other end, and vice versa.

10.7.6   Management contracting

Rather than setting up its own operations overseas, a company with a proven track record in a product area may pursue the option of running other companies' businesses for them. This is particularly important for services-based organizations. For a fee, an overseas organization which seeks to develop a new service would contract a team to set up and run the facility. In some cases, the intention may be that the management team should get the project started and gradually hand over the running of the facility to local management. This type of arrangement is useful for an expanding overseas organization where the required management and technical skills are difficult to obtain locally. In countries where the educational infrastructure offers less opportunity for management and technical training, a company (or in many cases, overseas governments) can buy in state-of-the-art management skills. Developments in Eastern Europe have resulted in many opportunities for UK-based service companies, including the management of hotels, airlines and educational establishments (e.g. the former hotel group Forte was contracted to set up and operate a number of hotels in Eastern Europe and the University of Strathclyde was contracted to set up and run a Business School in Poland).

10.8   ADAPTING TO FOREIGN BUSINESS ENVIRONMENTS

Having analysed an overseas market and decided to enter it, an organization must make decisions that will allow it to successfully enter and develop that market. Decisions focus on the extent to which the organization should adapt its products to the needs of the local market, as opposed to the development of a uniform product that is globally applicable in all of its markets. In this section we will consider firstly decisions relating to product configuration, and then decisions about its pricing and promotion and finally decisions in respect of production methods.

10.8.1   Product decisions

Sometimes, products can be exported to a foreign market with little need for adaptation to local needs. Improved communications and greater opportunities for travel have helped create much more uniform worldwide demand for products. McDonald's and Coca-Cola, for example, now appeal to people from Boston to Beijing and from Manchester to Moscow (although in both of these examples, the company's products have been subtly adapted to local markets). Products often need to be adapted for a number of reasons:

- The law of an overseas country may set differing product standards. For example, regulations specifying vehicle lighting standards means that cars

How does a large American hotel chain adapt to the Japanese market? Hotels operated by Hilton International in the United States have bedrooms which to many visitors from overseas are surprisingly large. But what would an American think of a typical Japanese hotel? Land prices in America are generally fairly low outside of the main metropolitan areas, hence the relatively spacious facilities offered. But in Japan, space is at a premium and has given rise to all sorts of miniaturized hotel formats, aimed at keeping prices at an affordable level. How could Hilton International remain afford-able yet retain its generic brand values? Following extensive research, the company developed a hotel format which was appropri-ate to the Japanese market. To avoid the problem of visitors from America being shocked by the relatively cramped hotels, Hilton International developed a separate brand format *Wa No Kutsurog*, providing comfort and service the Japanese way.

often have to be respecified for foreign markets. Within the EU, harmonization of product standards is making this task much simpler for traders.

- Despite convergence of cultural values, inertia often results from centuries of tradition. It has taken time, for example, for the idea of fast food to take hold in France where the culture stresses eating as a pleasurable social experience. Tastes may take time to change, which helps to explain why McDonald's restaurants offer different menus in many of the markets that it serves.

- There are often good geographical reasons why products would need to be adapted. The hotter climates of Southern Europe result in different patterns of demand for ice cream, car design and clothing, for example.

- Socio-economic factors may call for product reformulation. For example, high incomes and low petrol prices combine with long travel distances to boost demand in the United States for large, well-specified cars, at the expense of small hatchbacks which are popular in the United Kingdom.

Against the tendency towards local adaptation, the development of a globally uniform product can also have its advantages. The use of a common brand name in overseas markets yields benefits from economies of scale in promotion. Standardization of the product can also yield economies of scale in market research and large-scale, centralized production methods.

10.8.2   Promotion decisions

A promotional programme that has worked at home may fail miserably in a foreign market. Usually, this is a result of the target country's differing cultural values, although legislation can additionally call for a reformulation of promotion. These are a few of the reasons why promotion reformulation may be needed:

- The law on promoting goods and services that are considered socially harmful varies between countries. For this reason, television advertising is not available in some countries for promoting some medicines, alcohol and children's products.

- The availability of promotional media varies between countries. While television advertising is widely used in the United Kingdom, the low levels of television ownership in some less developed countries may limit the potential for this form of communication.

- Different cultures respond to promotional messages in different ways, reflecting different attitudes towards hard-sell, brash and seductive approaches, for example.

- Certain objects and symbols used to promote a product might have the opposite effect to that which might be expected at home (e.g. animals that are successfully used to promote a product at home may be viewed with disgust in some markets).

- Sometimes, the brand name to be promoted will not work in the overseas market, so it may be changed. There are many examples of brand names that fail overseas. The Spanish brand of 'Bum' snacks would probably not sell well in English-speaking countries, for example.

- There can also be problems where legislation prevents an international slogan being used. In France, for example, law no. 75-1349 of 1975 makes the use of the French language compulsory in all advertising for goods and services – this also applies to associated packaging and instructions, etc.

In practice, a combination of product and promotion modification is needed in order to meet differing local needs and differences in local sensitivity to advertising.

10.8.3 Pricing decisions

A common global pricing policy will help to project a company as a global brand. However, the reality is that a variety of factors cause global organizations to charge different prices in the different markets in which they operate. There is usually no reason to assume that the pricing policies adopted in the domestic market will prove to be equally effective in an overseas market. Furthermore, it may be of no great importance to customers that comparability between different markets is maintained.

There are a number of factors which affect price decisions overseas:

- Competitive pressure varies between markets, reflecting the stage of market development that a service has reached and the impact of regulations against anticompetitive practices.

- The cost of making a product may be significantly different in foreign markets. For services that employ people-intensive production methods, variations in wage levels between countries will have a significant effect on total costs. Personnel costs may also be affected by differences in welfare provisions that employers are required to pay for. Other significant cost elements which often vary between markets include the level of property prices or rental costs. The cost of acquiring space for a retail outlet in Britain, for example, is usually significantly more than in Southern or Eastern Europe.

■ Taxes vary between different markets. For example, the rate of value added tax (or its equivalent sales tax) can be as high as 38 per cent in Italy compared to $17\frac{1}{2}$ per cent in the United Kingdom. There are also differences between markets in the manner in which sales taxes are expressed. In most markets, these are fully incorporated into price schedules, although on other occasions (such as in Singapore) it is more usual to price a service exclusive of taxes.

■ Local customs influence customers' expectations of the way in which they are charged for a product. While customers in the domestic market might expect to pay for bundles of goods and services, in an overseas market consumers might expect to pay a separate price for each component of the bundle. For example, UK buyers of new cars expect features such as audio equipment to be included in the basic price of a car, whereas buyers in many continental European countries expect to buy these as separate items.

■ For some service industries, it is customary in many countries to expect customers to pay a tip to the front-line person providing a service, as part of the overall price of the service.

■ Formal price lists for a service may be expected in some markets, but in others the prevalence of bartering may put an operator who sticks to a fixed price list at a competitive disadvantage.

■ Government regulations can limit price freedom in overseas markets. In addition to controls over prices charged by public utilities, many governments require 'fair' prices to be charged in certain sectors and for the prices charged to be clearly publicized.

■ A product that is considered quite ordinary in its domestic market may be perceived as exclusive in an overseas market and therefore it will adopt a higher price position. For example, the price position of the retailer Marks and Spencer is middle market in its domestic UK base, but the company has positioned its stores in Indonesia as up-market with a high price position relative to local competitors. By contrast, a company with a strong brand in its home market may have to adopt (initially at least) a lower price position when it launches into a competitive overseas market.

10.8.4   **Distribution decisions**

Market entry strategies were discussed earlier at a strategic level. It is also crucial to consider more operational issues of how a company is going to get its products through to the final consumer. The following factors should be taken into account:

■ Consumers' attitudes towards intermediaries may differ significantly in overseas markets. What is a widely accepted outlet in one country may be regarded with

Figure 10.4

National Car Rental has sought to simplify its pricing structure and strengthen its brand position by offering one price throughout Europe. Inevitably there is some risk inherent in this approach, as taxes and competitive pressures differ throughout Europe. In non-euro countries, there is also the potential problem of currency fluctuations. To try and limit these risks, the company has restricted the single price offer according to the type of car and type of customer

(*Source*: Reproduced with permission of National Car Rental)

suspicion in another. For example, the idea of buying cosmetics from a grocery store may be viewed with suspicion in many countries, although it is now accepted in most Western European countries.

■ The extensiveness of outlet networks will be influenced by customers' expectations about ease of access, which in turn may be based on social, economic and technological factors. The proliferation of many small-scale distributors in less developed economies, for example, can be partly explained by the lack of domestic refrigeration, which may favour frequent replenishment of household supplies from a local store rather than less frequent bulk buying from a large centralized store.

■ Differences in the social, economic and technological environments of a market can be manifested in the existence of different patterns of intermediaries. As an example, the interrelatedness of wholesalers and retailers in Japan can make it much more difficult for an overseas retailer to get into that market compared to other overseas opportunities. In some markets, there may be no direct equivalent of a type of intermediary found in the domestic market – estate agents on the UK model are often not found in many markets where the work of transferring property is handled entirely by a solicitor.

■ The technological environment can also affect distribution decisions. The relatively underdeveloped postal and telecommunications services of many Eastern European countries makes direct availability of goods and services to consumers relatively difficult.

■ What is a legal method of distributing goods and services in the domestic market may be against the law of an overseas country. Countries may restrict the sale of financial services, holidays and gambling services – among others – to a much narrower set of possible intermediaries than is the case in the domestic market.

10.8.5   People and production decisions

Where a company is planning to manufacture its products in a foreign market, it will need to ensure that its production methods comply with local regulations. Adaptation to local regulations governing employment is particularly important for labour-intensive service industries. Where goods or services produced overseas involve direct producer–consumer interaction, a decision must be made on whether to employ local or expatriate staff. The latter may be preferable where a service is highly specialized and may be useful in adding to the global uniformity of the service offering. In some circumstances, the presence of front-line expatriate serving staff can add to the appeal of a service. For example, a chain of traditional Irish bars established in continental Europe may add to their appeal by employing authentic Irish staff.

For relatively straightforward goods and services, a large proportion of staff would be recruited locally, leaving just senior management posts filled by expatriates. Sometimes, an extensive staff development programme may be required to ensure that locally recruited staff perform in a manner that is consistent with the company's global image. This can in some circumstances be quite a difficult task – a fast-food operator may have difficulty developing values of speed and efficiency among its staff in countries where the pace of life is relatively slow.

PHILIPPINES GETS A SHARE OF EMERGING WORLD TRADE IN DATA

Improvements in technology, changes in users' needs and the emerging information age illustrate how whole new categories of industries can appear very quickly with subsequent major effects on national economies and international trade.

Data processing was just such a service industry which emerged almost from nowhere during the 1980s and 1990s as organizations of all kinds found increasing need to enter data into computerized databases – records of customer sales, services performed, details of rolling stock movements, to name but a few. Many organizations were just beginning to appreciate the huge amount of data they were letting slip by, instead of analysing it to build up customer databases, or analyse performance levels, etc. In the early days, most firms regarded this as a back-room function that they could perform most cost effectively by using their own staff on their own premises. With time, an increasing volume of data to be processed and the growing sophistication of data analysis systems, many service companies emerged to take the burden of data processing off client companies.

At first, most data-processing companies operated close to their clients – closeness was demanded by the limitations of data communication channels. However, by the late 1980s, the rapid pace of development in the telecommunications industry – especially the development of satellites and fibre optic links – allowed large volumes of data to be transmitted over long distances much more cheaply and reliably than ever before. This opened the door to an international trade in data processing, and operators around the world soon stepped in to exploit their comparative cost advantages. In particular, the development of telecommunications allowed companies to operate in foreign countries where labour costs were low, working regulations relaxed and trade unions virtually non existent.

Data processing has established itself as a significant new sector of economies in the Caribbean, the Philippines and the Irish Republic. Each of these countries is characterized by relatively low wage rates with skills which are at least as good as those of workers in more developed countries.

The development of the Saztec company, based in Kansas in the United States, illustrates the way in which new service sectors emerge and can create new service sectors in developing economies. Saztec won contracts to process the data of many major organizations throughout the world, including a number of federal government agencies in the United States and the Home Office in the United Kingdom. Yet these services are generally produced far away from either the company's or the client's base. The company employs over 800 people in the Philippines, who earn an average of $50 per month – one-fifth of the salary paid to its staff at Kansas. Staff turnover, at less than 1% is much lower than the 35 per cent annual rate in Kansas. Furthermore, the company is able to obtain a higher quality of output by the military style organization and control of its staff – something that would not be accepted in the United States.

The Philippines has become an important exporter of data-processing services by exploiting its comparative cost advantage in labour inputs, something that is useful in capturing high volume, basic data input where accuracy and cost are paramount. Another country which has developed this service sector in a big way is Jamaica, which in addition to exploiting its low labour costs offers the advantages of a sophisticated infrastructure – such as satellite links – and generous tax incentives. Ireland by contrast has exploited the fact that it has a relatively highly educated and English speaking workforce who earn less than what their counterparts would earn in the United States or United Kingdom. A number of firms – such as Wright Investor Services – have been set up in Ireland to do more sophisticated financial analysis on behalf of the big London-based banks and insurance companies.

CASE STUDY Review questions

1 Why has data processing emerged as a major new service sector within the Philippines economy?

2 What other service sectors have emerged in international trade during the past two decades? What factors explain their emergence?

3 What are the advantages to the Philippines economy of developing its data-processing industry? Are there any disadvantages?

CHAPTER Summary and links to other chapters

This chapter began by discussing the reasons why international trade takes place. Despite the theoretical benefits of free movement of goods and services between countries, barriers to achieving such benefits remain. Currency fluctuations remain a major risk for international traders, although the single European currency alleviates that risk within the EU. The overseas business environment is likely to be very different to that experienced at home, and therefore it is essential that appropriate exploratory research is carried out. This chapter also discussed methods of overseas market entry that balance the need for risk reduction against the need to maintain control over an overseas venture.

This chapter has brought together many of the issues discussed in previous chapters and applied them specifically to the needs of an overseas market. For any market, it is important to study its competitiveness (Chapter 6); the state of its national economy (Chapter 7); its political system (Chapter 8); its social and cultural values (Chapter 11); and attitudes towards social responsibility (Chapter 5). Good information becomes particularly important for planning and controlling an overseas operation (Chapter 12).

CHAPTER Review questions

1 What are the nature of the gains arising from trade liberalization and why is it such a painful process?

(Based on CIM Marketing Environment Examination)

2 Explain who will be the winners and losers of trade liberalization in your own country. Summarize what advice you would give any company to ensure it ends up on the winning side.

(Based on CIM Marketing Environment Examination)

3 Your consultancy firm has decided to produce a brief booklet, in bullet point format, to provide advice to marketing clients who are considering establishing overseas operations.

Using relevant headings and points, produce an outline draft for this booklet, including a bibliography and useful sources of information.

(Based on CIM Marketing Environment Examination)

4 Summarize the advantages and disadvantages to a British capital goods manufacturer resulting from full European Monetary Union.

5 Suggest how the UK insurance industry can avoid going the same way as the motorcycle industry and losing out to overseas competition.

6 What cultural differences might cause problems for a hotel chain developing a location in India?

Selected further reading

For a general overview of trends in international business, consult the following:

Czinkota, M.R. and M. Kotabe (1997) *Trends in International Business*, Blackwell, Oxford.
Overseas Trade, a DTI-FCO magazine for exporters published 10 times per year by Brass Tacks Publishing, London.
World Trade Organization, *Annual Report*, published annually.
World Trade Organization, *Trade Policy Review* (serial).

For statistics on the changing pattern of UK trade, the following regularly updated publications of the Office for National Statistics provide good coverage:

Economic Trends: A monthly publication which includes statistics relating to international trade performance.
Overseas Direct Investment: Detailed breakdown of UK overseas direct investment activity, outward and inward, by component, country and industry.

For a general overview of international marketing management, the following texts provide a more detailed analysis of many of the points discussed in this chapter.

Bennett, R. (1998) *International Marketing*, Kogan Page. (Strategy, planning, market entry and implementation.)
Chee, H. and R. Harris (1998) *Global Marketing Strategy*, Pitman, London.
Cottrill, K. (1998) 'Strategies for world domination', *Journal of Business Strategy*, May–June, vol. 19, no. 3, pp. 36–40.
Douglas, S. and S. Craig (1999) *International Marketing Research*, John Wiley, Chichester.

Keegan, W.J. (1999) *Global Marketing*, Prentice-Hall, Hemel Hempstead.
Paliwoda, S.J. (1998) *International Marketing*, 3rd edn, Butterworth-Heinemann, Oxford.

The homogenization of world markets and the development of global brands is discussed in the following:
Ritzer, G. (1995) *The MacDonaldization of Society*, Pine Forge Press, Thousand Oaks, CA.

For a review of the development of the European Economic Area, the following are useful sources:
European Commission sources:
  Bulletin of the European Commission.
  Bulletin of Economic Trends in Europe (published by Eurostat).
Crossick, S. (1999) 'The European Union: integration or disintegration?' *European Business Journal*, Winter, vol. 11, no. 4, pp. 161–165.
Kahal, S. (1998) *Business in Europe*, McGraw-Hill, Maidenhead.
Krempel, M. (1999) 'The pan-European company: restructuring for a new Europe', *European Business Journal*, Autumn, vol. 11, pp. 119–127.
McDonald, F. and Dearden, S. (1998) *European Economic Integration*, Longman, Harlow.

Strategic alliances are becoming increasingly important and the following references provide greater insight into their operation:
Beamish, P.W. (1998) *Strategic Alliances: The Globalization of the World Economy*, Edward Elgar, Cheltenham.
Meyer, H. (1998) 'My enemy, my friend', *Journal of Business Strategy*, vol. 19, no. 5, pp. 42–46.
Mockler, R.J. (2000) *Multinational Strategic Alliances*, Wiley, Chichester.
Ohmae, K. (1989) 'The global logic of strategic alliances', *Harvard Business Review*, March–April, pp. 143–154.

Useful websites

Annual Barclays Country Reports   Country reports contain data on market analysis, economic policy, the political environment, recent trends and outlooks.
http://www.corporate.barclays.com/go/cms.nsf/lookup/188151117A7375FB8025690D004C0021

CIA World Publications   The World Fact Book published by CIA World Publications, this website gives access facts and statistics on more than 250 countries and other entities.
http://www.odci.gov/cia/publications/factbook/index.html

Country Risk Analysis   A rich source of historical data about world trading markets. Discusses economic, financial and political events which impact on international trade.
http://www.duke.edu/~charvey/Country_risk/couindex.htm

Economist Intelligence Unit   Selected free access is provided to global business intelligence reports.   http://www.eiu.com/

EU Euro website   The official EU website on the euro includes documents, legislation, links to other websites, and a search engine. It provides access to basic information and documentation on the euro.   http://europa.eu.int/euro/html/entry.html

Financial Times   The newspaper's archive includes country reports.   http://www.ft.com

Infonation   An interactive statistical database for the member states of the United Nations.
http://www.un.org/Pubs/CyberSchoolBus/infonation/e_infonation.htm

International Business Resources on the WWW   Michigan State University's site provides many useful links to statistical data and information resources.
http://www.ciber.msu.edu/busres/Static/Statistical-Data-Sources.htm

International Monetary Fund   Site contains IMF news, publications and international economic information.   http://www.imf.org/

Organization for Economic Co-operation and Development (OECD) International Trade   The OECD's database on international trade shows the value of each member country's exports and imports of goods and services by type.   **http://www.oecd.org/std/serint.htm**

Trade Partners UK   Advice and information from the Department of Trade and Industry for exporters. Provides information on overseas markets by region.   **http://www.tradepartners.gov.uk/**

UK overseas trade statistics   The site includes a summary of recent trade statistics.   **http://www.statistics.gov.uk**

US International Trade Statistics   US oriented, but contains a lot of data on world markets.   **http://www.census.gov/ftp/pub/foreign-trade/www/**

World Link   The online magazine of the World Economic Forum with a searchable archive.   **http://www.worldlink.co.uk/**

World Trade Organization   This site provides information on international trade developments, statistics, WTO documents and policies.   **http://www.wto.org/**

Key terms

Balance of payments	International trade
Barriers to trade	Joint ventures
Comparative cost advantage	Strategic alliances
Cultural convergence	Trading blocs
Exchange rates	Visible/invisible trade
Foreign direct investment	World Trade Organization
Globalization	

11

The social and demographic environment

CHAPTER OBJECTIVES

Society is changing at an increasingly rapid rate. Changes in lifestyles and attitudes can have profound implications for business organizations, both in terms of the goods and services which are supplied by organizations and the availability of employees to work in them. The relationship between society and business is a two-way one and change in the social environment is often a result of changes in business activities. The car, telephone and Internet are all examples of new products which have had profound social consequences. In Chapter 5 we looked at society's increasingly high expectations of business organizations. The aim of this chapter is to gain a greater understanding of changing attitudes and lifestyles and the effects of these changes on business organizations. The composition of society is also changing, as most Western countries see an increasing proportion of elderly people and more single person households. After reading this chapter you should be able to identify key demographic trends and their implications for business organizations.

Consider the following recent social changes that have occurred in the United Kingdom and many other Western countries:

- An increasing ethnic diversity, which is manifested in Asian and Indian communities in many towns of the United Kingdom.

- A rising divorce rate, which is manifested in a rising number of single person households and single parent families.

- A desire for instant gratification, manifested in individuals' desire to obtain goods and services 24 hours a day.

These are typical of changes that have concentrated the minds of business organizations as they attempt to supply goods and services which are of continuing relevance to the population. Companies that continue to base their efforts on the assumption of a typical white family unit which is prepared to wait for a long time before a product is delivered may find themselves targeting an increasingly small market segment.

As a result of social change, we have seen many goods and services become redundant, as they no longer satisfy a population whose needs, attitudes, values and behaviour have changed. The following are typical of goods and services which have disappeared or been greatly reduced in sales as a result of social change.

- Traditional drinking pubs have reduced in number as patterns of social relationships change and individuals seek more family-friendly pubs which serve food in a pleasant environment.

- The number of butchers' shops has been sharply reduced as consumers opt for a healthier lifestyle, based on foods which do not contain meat.

- Rural bus services have gone into decline as they fail to cater for a lifestyle in which an individual's community comprises not just their immediate neighbours, but people who may live many miles away.

On the other hand social change has resulted in a tremendous growth in the following goods and services:

- Microwave cookers and portable televisions have benefited from a move towards a 'cellular' household in which each member of the family operates in a much more independent manner than has traditionally been the case.

- Gyms and leisure facilities have benefited from individuals' increasing concern for health and personal fitness.

- The sale and use of cars has expanded in response to individuals' desire for a lifestyle in which their friends, workplace and leisure activities may be geographically dispersed.

It is very easy for individuals to take quite for granted the way they live. Furthermore, young people may imagine that people have always lived their lives that way. Taking one year with the next, social change may seem quite imperceptible, but when life today is compared with what it was like 10 years ago, noticeable changes begin to appear. If comparisons are made with 20 or 50 years ago, it may seem as if two entirely different societies are being compared. Simply by looking at an old movie, big differences become apparent, such as attitudes to the family, leisure activities and the items commonly purchased by consumers.

Change in society is also brought about by changes in its composition. Much recent attention has been given in many Western European countries to the effects of an ageing population on society. Taken to an extreme, some commentators have seen major problems ahead as an increasingly large dependent population has to be kept by a proportionately smaller economically active group in society. Some see this as challenging basic attitudes that individuals have towards the community and the family. At the very least, business organizations should be concerned about the effects of demographic change on patterns of demand for goods and services and the availability of a workforce to produce those goods and services.

It is bad enough not to recognize social change that has happened in the past. It is much worse to fail to read the signs of social change that is happening now and to understand the profound effects this could have on the goods and services that people will buy in the future.

This chapter begins by examining what can loosely be described as a society's social and cultural values. These are what make people in the United Kingdom different from what they were 20 years ago, or different from what people in Algeria or Indonesia are today. Social and cultural differences between countries focus on differences in attitudes, family structures and the pattern of interaction between individuals. Business organizations should understand the consequences of what may appear nebulous social changes for the types of things that consumers are likely to buy in the future.

New evidence of changing lifestyles sometimes emerges from the most unlikely sources. One interesting insight comes from the regular updating of the United Kingdom's retail prices index (RPI), which is used by many organizations as a benchmark for inflation in the national economy.

In principle, it is quite easy to take a typical shopping basket of consumers' purchases and to monitor what happens to the price of this basket from one year to the next. A problem occurs, however, because the contents of the basket are constantly changing as consumers' preferences change and products with low prices are substituted for more expensive products.

In 2001, the Office for National Statistics (ONS), which records the RPI, took a periodic look at the contents of its average shopping basket of 650 goods and services to reflect changes in national spending habits. The ONS takes advice from retail analysts, consults the diaries of families participating in regular shopping surveys and scrutinizes trade figures. The basket was amended to include for the first time organic food, salmon fillets, energy drinks, herbal teabags, cereal snacks and sunscreen lotion. Out went salad cream, rainbow trout, leeks, sterilized milk, doorstep-delivered milk – a victim of the steady increase in supermarket sales of milk from the shelves – and the household bread bin. The disappearance of the bread bin may reflect a change in habits away from buying standard loaves of bread in favour of a desire to experiment with specialist bread such as baguettes.

In an increasingly service-oriented culture, the RPI reflects the growing importance of services in a typical individual's spending pattern. From 2001, the shopping basket was amended to include health club membership, catering costs and bank overdraft charges.

Some items of fashion enter the shopping basket but may soon disappear. Cardigans have been entering and leaving the RPI as fashions change. In 2001, alcopops, baseball caps and laminate flooring joined, but are just as likely to go the way of women's ski pants and leave again if fashions change.

11.1.1   Social influences on behaviour

The way individuals behave as consumers is a result of their unique physical and psychological make-up on the one hand and a process of learning from experience on the other. The debate about the relative importance of nature and nurture is familiar to social psychologists. This chapter is concerned with the effects of learned behaviour on individuals' buying behaviour.

An individual learns norms of behaviour from a number of sources (Figure 11.1):

1   The dominant cultural values of the society in which they live.
2   The social class to which they belong.
3   Important reference groups, in particular the family.

Culture can be seen as an umbrella within which social class systems exist and reference groups exert influence on individuals or groups of individuals. The following sections consider the effects of each of these influences.

Figure 11.1
**Factors affecting
the socialization
process**

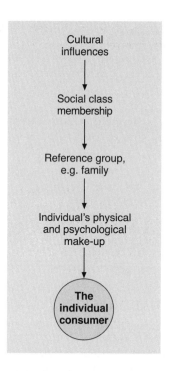

11.2   THE CULTURAL ENVIRONMENT

The Oxford English Dictionary defines culture as a '... trained and refined state of understanding, manners and tastes'. Central to culture is the concept of learning and passing down of values from one generation to the next. A culture's values are expressed in a complex set of beliefs, customs and symbols which help to identify individuals as members of one particular culture rather than another. The following are typical manifestations of cultural identity:

- Shared attitudes, for example towards the role of women or children in society.

- Abstract symbols and rituals, which can be seen in historic cultures by such events as harvest festivals and maypole dancing, and in more modern times by support for local football teams.

- Material manifestations, for example the literature and art of a culture or the style of decorations used in private houses.

It is common to distinguish between 'core' and 'secondary' cultural values:

- *Core cultural values* tend to be very enduring over time. In Britain, for example, the acceptance of monogamy represents a core belief and one that very few people would disagree with.

- *Secondary cultural values* are more susceptible to change over time. While there may be a core belief in the family, this does not prevent changes in attitudes towards the form that families should take, as is evident from the growing incidence of divorce and the increasing number of single parent families. It is shifts in these secondary cultural values that are particularly important for business organizations to monitor.

<table>
<tr><td>11.2.1</td></tr>
</table>

Subcultures

It is difficult to talk about a uniform culture for a society, because most cultures contain distinctive subcultures. The most obvious manifestations of subcultures are based on religious and ethnic differences, so in Britain it is common to talk about distinctive subcultures associated with people from Asia and Ireland, for example.

The United Kingdom is increasingly becoming a culturally diverse society. This is partly related to increasing levels of wealth which allows individuals greater freedom to choose their own lifestyle and means of self-expression. However, more importantly, cultural diversity arises from the growing numbers of people from overseas cultures who have settled in the country. Immigrants bring with them a distinctive set of cultural values and adapting to the values of the host country can be a difficult task for some. A lack of understanding from members of the host country may cause them to be seen as lazy, industrious or lacking in humour by the standards of the host culture, but they may nevertheless be perfectly normal by the standards of their home culture. Where members of ethnic minorities are concentrated into distinct areas (such as certain suburbs of London, Leicester and Bradford), their traditional cultural values may be strengthened and prolonged by mutual support and the presence of an infrastructure (such as places of worship and specialized shops) to support the values of the culture.

The presence of concentrations of ethnic subcultures in a town presents opportunities for businesses who cater for distinctive cultural preferences such as Halal butchers, bureaux for arranged marriages or travel agents specializing in travel to India.

Members of ethnic minorities have contributed to the diversity of goods and services available to consumers in the host country. The large number of Indian restaurants in Britain, for example, can be attributed to the entrepreneurial skills of immigrants, while many food products (such as kebabs and Chinese food) have followed the immigrants.

<table>
<tr><td>11.2.2</td></tr>
</table>

Effects of culture on business organizations

It is crucial for business organizations to fully appreciate the cultural values of a society, especially where an organization is seeking to do business in a country that is quite different from its own. The possible consequences of failing to do this can be illustrated by the following examples:

- When McDonald's entered the UK market, it initially found hostility from the British, who did not appreciate the brash, scripted 'Have a nice day' mentality of its staff. The company subsequently adapted its style of business to cater for British preferences.

- When Sock Shop opened stores in New York, it failed to appreciate the violent nature of an important subculture in the city and lost large amounts of money in armed raids.

■ Many UK businesses have set up operations overseas and gone about business in an open and above-board manner, only to find that corruption and the use of bribes is endemic in the local culture and essential for business success.

Cultural sensitivity affects many aspects of business planning and operations, for example:

■ Understanding processes of buyer behaviour (for example, the role of men in buying routine household goods varies between countries, leading sellers to adjust their product specification and promotional efforts to meet the needs of the most influential members of the buying unit).

■ Some products may be unacceptable in a culture and must be adapted to be culturally acceptable (e.g. the original formulation for McDonald's 'Big Mac' is unacceptable in Muslim cultures).

■ Symbols associated with products, such as the design and colour of packaging, may be unacceptable in some cultures (e.g. the colour white is associated with pureness in most Western European cultures, but in others it is associated with bereavement).

■ Distribution channel decisions are partly a reflection of cultural attitudes and not just economics and land use. Retailers and wholesalers may be seen as a vital part of a culture's social infrastructure and individuals may feel a sense of loyalty to their suppliers. Although it may appear economically rational for shoppers to buy in bulk, small local shops opening long hours may be seen by consumers as an extension of their pantry.

■ Advertising messages do not always translate easily between different cultures, reflecting culturally influenced standards of what is considered decent and appropriate.

■ Methods of procuring resources can vary between cultures. In some Far Eastern countries, it is essential to establish a trusting relationship with a buyer before the buyer will even consider placing an order. Sometimes it is essential to personally know the key decision maker or to offer a bribe, which is considered routine business practice in some cultures.

■ Obtaining employees is very much influenced by cultural factors. The notion of speedy service and commitment to the employer is often an unfamiliar set of values in cultures where commitment to the family comes very strongly first and timekeeping has little meaning.

Even in home markets, business organizations should understand the processes of gradual cultural change and be prepared to satisfy the changing needs of consumers. The following are examples of contemporary cultural change in Western Europe and the possible business responses:

■ Women are increasingly being seen as equal to men in terms of employment expectations and household responsibilities. This is reflected in the observation

Until a few years ago, the shelves of most newsagents would have been loaded with many general interest women's magazines (such as *Women's Own*, *Women's Weekly*, *Cosmopolitan*), but very few general interest magazines aimed at men. Why? Some cynics might have argued that women were more likely to have spare time at home and could sit around reading, while 'busy' men were out at work, in the pub or watching sport and did not have time to read magazines. There may just have been a bit of truth in this, but the main reason has been that women's magazines have been popular with advertisers. In the traditional household, it has been women who have made decisions on a wide range of consumer goods purchases. Advertising the benefits of toothpaste, yoghurt or jam would have been lost on most men who had little interest in what was put in front of them, and played little part in the buying process.

Take a look at the newsstand now and it will carry a wide range of men's general interest magazines, such as *FHM*, *Loaded*, *Maxim* and *Esquire*. Why have they suddenly mushroomed in number and in readership? Again, the answer lies in their attractiveness to advertisers. Talk of a male identity crisis may have spurred some sales, and it is evident that men are involved in a wider range of purchasing decisions than ever before. While some 'new men' may be taking a more active interest in the household shopping, many more are marrying later and indulging themselves in personal luxuries, an option which is less readily available to their married counterparts. With support from advertisers, the leading men's magazine in the United Kingdom, *FHM* was selling over 750 000 copies per issue in 1999, overtaking the leading women's magazine, *Cosmopolitan* which sold just under 500 000. The magazine racks provide an interesting commentary on the social structure of the country, and businesses' response to this change.

that women made up 47 per cent of the UK paid workforce in 1996, compared with 37 per cent in 1971. Examples of business responses include variants of cars designed to meet women's needs and ready prepared meals which relieve working women of their traditional role in preparing household meals.

- Greater life expectancy is leading to an ageing of the population and a shift to an increasingly 'elderly' culture. This is reflected in product design which reflects durability rather than fashionability.

- Leisure is becoming an increasingly important part of many peoples' lives and businesses have responded with a wide range of leisure-related goods and services.

- Increasing concern for the environment is reflected in a variety of 'green' consumer products.

There has been much recent discussion about the concept of 'cultural convergence', referring to an apparent decline in differences between cultures. It has been argued that basic human needs are universal in nature and, in principle, capable of satisfaction with universally similar solutions. Companies have been keen to pursue this possibility in order to achieve economies of scale in producing homogeneous products for global markets. There is some evidence of firms achieving this, for example the worldwide success of Coca-Cola and McDonald's. In the case of fast food, many Western chains have capitalized on deep-seated habits in some Far Eastern countries of eating from small hawkers' facilities by offering the same basic facility in a clean and hygienic environment.

The desire of a subculture in one country to imitate the values of those in another culture has also contributed to cultural convergence. This is nothing new. During the Second World War, many individuals in Western Europe sought to follow the American lifestyle, and nylon stockings from the United States became highly sought-after cultural icons by some groups. The same process is at work today in many developing countries where some groups seek to identify with Western cultural values through the purchases they make. Today, however, improved media communications allow messages about cultural values to be disseminated much more rapidly. The development of satellite television and the Internet hastens the process of creating shared worldwide values.

It can be argued that business organizations are not only responding to cultural convergence, they are also significant contributors to that convergence. The development of global brands backed up by global advertising campaigns has contributed to an increasing uniformity in goods and services offered throughout the world. Many commentators have described an 'MTV' generation which views global satellite television channels and who converge in their attitudes to consumption. The Internet is contributing to this process of apparent global homogenization. In some countries, cultural convergence has been seen as a threat to the sense of local identity that culture represents. Governments have therefore taken measures in an attempt to slow down this process of cultural homogenization. This has achieved significance in France where legislation requires the use of the French language – an important means of creating identity for any culture – in packaging and advertising for products. Attempts by firms to homogenize cultural values can meet with more widespread public resistance. One of the aims of Islamic Fundamentalism is to preserve traditional values against domination by Western cultural values.

<table>
<tr><td>11.2.3</td><td>**Social class**</td></tr>
</table>

In most societies, divisions exist between groups of people in terms of their access to privileges and status within that society. In some social systems, such as the Hindu caste system, the group that an individual belongs to exerts influence from birth, and it is very difficult for the individual to change between groups. Western societies have class systems in which individuals are divided into one of a number of classes. Although the possibilities for individuals to move between social classes in Western countries is generally greater than the possibilities of movement open to a member of a caste system, class values tend to be passed down through families.

While some may have visions of a 'classless' society which is devoid of divisions in status and privileges, the reality is that divisions exist in most societies and are likely to persist. It is common in Western societies to attribute individuals with belonging to groups that have been given labels such as 'working class' or 'middle class'. This emotional language of class is not particularly helpful to businesses who need a more measurable basis for describing differences within society.

Why do business organizations need to know about which social grouping an individual belongs? The basic idea of a classification system is to identify groups who share common attitudes and behaviour patterns and access to resources. This can translate into similar spending patterns. There are, for example, many goods and services that are most heavily bought by people who can be described as 'working class', such as the *Daily Star* newspaper and betting services, while others are more often associated with 'upper class' purchasers, such as Jaguar cars, the *Financial Times* and investment management services.

Businesses also need to take note of the class structure of society. As the size of each class changes, so market segments, which are made up of people who are similar in some important respects, also change. In the United Kingdom during the 1960s and 1970s it has been observed that a lot of people were moving into the 'middle classes'. The effects of taxation, the welfare state and access to education had flattened the class structure of society. For car manufacturers, this translated into a very large demand for mainstream middle-of-the-road cars. However, during the 1980s and 1990s, both the upper and lower classes tended to grow in what had become a more polarized society. In terms of car sales, there was a growing demand for luxury cars such as Jaguars and BMWs at one end of the market and cheaper cars such as Ladas at the other.

It is also useful to study the extent to which individuals are able to move from one class to another. In some societies, such as those with a caste system, it is almost impossible for individuals to change their class in society. In Western European countries, there is a belief by many that people can move around the class system on the basis of their efforts. The very fact that it is seen as possible to move classes may encourage people to see the world in a different way from that which has been induced in them during their years of socialization.

11.3 THE FAMILY

The family represents a further layer in the socialization process. It is important that business organizations understand changes in family structures and values because change in this area can impact on them in a number of ways. Consider the following impacts of families on business organizations:

1. Many household goods and services are typically bought by family units, for example food and package holidays. When family structures and values change, consumption patterns may change significantly.

2. The family is crucial in giving individuals a distinctive personality. Many of the differences in attitude and behaviour between individuals can be attributed to the values that were instilled in them by their family during childhood. These differences may persist well into adult life.

3   The family has a central role as a transmitter of cultural values and norms, and can exercise a strong influence on an individual's buying behaviour.

11.3.1   Family composition

Many people still live with the idea that the typical family comprises two parents, and an average of 2.4 children. In many Western European countries, this is increasingly becoming a myth with single person and single parent households becoming increasingly common. The following factors have contributed to changes in family composition:

- An increasing divorce rate, with about one-third of all marriages in the United Kingdom now ending in divorce.

- The age at which individuals first get married is becoming later (for females, this has risen from 23 in 1971 to 26 in 1996 and for males from 25 to 27).

- More people are living on their own outside a family unit, either out of choice or through circumstances (e.g. divorce, widowhood).

- Family role expectations have changed with an increasing number of career-oriented wives.

Changes in family composition have led firms to develop new goods and services that meet the changing needs of families, such as crèche facilities for working mothers and holidays for single parents. Advertising has increasingly moved away from portraying the traditional family group with which many individuals may have difficulty in identifying. Recent examples that have portrayed the new reality include an advertisement for McDonald's in which a boy takes his separated father to one of the company's restaurants and one for Volkswagen in which a career-minded woman puts her car before her husband.

11.3.2   Family roles

As well as changing in composition, there is evidence of change in the way that families operate as a unit. Many household products have been traditionally considered to be dominated by either the male or female partner, but these distinctions are becoming increasingly blurred as family roles change. In the United Kingdom, a report 'Social Focus on Women' published in 1998 by the Office of National Statistics highlighted some of the changes in family roles that have been occurring. For example:

- Although men may say they believe household tasks should be shared, only 1 per cent say they always do the washing and ironing. Household cleaning is carried out mainly by women in nearly two-thirds of households, and this proportion has been falling gradually over the last two decades.

- Just over a quarter of all men and a fifth of women agreed with the view that 'a husband's job is to earn money; a wife's job is to look after the family and home'. This is about half the level of agreement noted in 1987.

Is the role model family of husband, wife and two children becoming a myth? With a higher divorce rate, later marriage and smaller families, many have argued that the typical household unit is being radically reshaped. Yet this ideal type family still appears to be the format to strive for and is depicted in many advertisements for household goods and services. But can the increasing number of single parent households associate themselves with the message of traditional advertisements? McDonald's is one company that realized its advertising might need to be refocused if it is to address the growing number of 'non-typical' household units. One advert has shown a boy arranging a meeting between his separated parents in a branch of McDonald's. Another showed a boy giving his father advice about saving for the future. Behind the departure from the happy-families norm in fast-food marketing is the realization that the number of families in the United Kingdom with single parents has risen from 8 per cent in 1971 to nearly a quarter in 1997. McDonald's claimed that it could not credibly position itself as a family restaurant and show only pictures of mum and dad and two kids without the risk of alienating parents and children from different households.

- The number of women stating that the home and children are more important than a job fell from 15 per cent in 1987 to 7 per cent in 1997.

- The main evening meal is made mainly by women in just over a third of households, having halved in two decades.

There has been much debate about the fragmentation of families into 'cellular households' in which family members essentially do their own activities independently of other members. This is reflected in individually consumed meals rather than family meals and leisure interests that are increasingly with a family member's peer groups rather than other family members. Businesses have responded to the needs of the cellular household with products such as microwave cookers and portable televisions which allow family units to function in this way. It can also be argued, however, that new product developments are actually responsible for the fragmentation of family activities. The microwave cooker and portable television may have lessened the need for families to operate as a collective unit, although these possible consequences were not immediately obvious when they were launched. The family unit can expect to come under further pressures as new products, such as online entertainment and information services, allow individual members to consume in accordance with their own preferences rather than the collective preferences of the family.

11.4   **REFERENCE GROUPS**

The family is not the only influence on an individual as they develop a view of the world. Just as individuals learn from and mimic the values of parents and close

What role do children play in the purchase of goods which they ultimately consume? There has been considerable debate about the extent of 'pester power' where parents give in to the demands of children. Increasingly, advertisers are aiming their promotional messages over the heads of adults and straight at children. The ethics of doing this have been questioned by many, and some countries have imposed restrictions on television advertising of children's products. However, even with advertising restrictions, companies have managed to get through to children in more subtle ways, for example by sponsoring educational materials used in schools and paying celebrities to endorse their products. When it comes to such items as confectionery and toys, just what influence do children exert on the purchase decision? And when football clubs deliberately change their strip every season, is it unethical for the clubs to expect fanatical children to pester their parents to buy a new one so that they can keep up with their peer group?

relations, so too they also learn from and mimic other people outside their immediate family. Groups that influence individuals in this way are often referred to as reference groups. These can be one of two types:

1   *Primary* reference groups exist where an individual has direct face-to-face contact with members of the group.

2   *Secondary* reference groups describe the influence of groups where there is no direct relationship, but an individual is nevertheless influenced by its values.

11.4.1   Primary reference groups

These comprise people with whom an individual has direct two-way contact, such as those with whom an individual works, plays football or goes to church. In effect, the group acts as a frame of reference for the individual. Small groups of trusted colleagues have great power in passing on recommendations about goods and services, especially those where a buyer has very little other evidence on which to base a decision. For many personal services, such as hairdressing, word of mouth recommendation from a member of a peer group may be a vital method by which a company gains new business. If an individual needs to hire a builder, the first thing he or she is likely to do is ask friends if they can recommend a good one on the basis of their previous experience. For many items of conspicuous consumption, individuals often select specific brands in accordance with which brand carries most prestige with its primary reference group.

11.4.2   Secondary reference groups

These are groups with whom an individual has no direct contact, but which can nevertheless influence a person's attitudes, values, opinions and behaviour. Sometimes, individuals may be members of the group and this will have a direct influence on their behaviour patterns, with the group serving as a frame of

In 1998, the footwear company Nike reported its first loss for 13 years. It seemed that a fashion icon of the 1990s had suddenly become uncool with young people throughout the world. Parents were doubtless relieved as they were no longer pestered by their children to pay £50 for a pair of Nike branded trainers which to all intents and purposes were functionally similar to an unbranded pair of trainers selling for around £15. Amazingly, it is reported that a typical pair of Nike trainers costs only 46p to make in factories in China where human rights campaigners have questioned employment practices. The rise and fall of the company's products indicates the enormous pressure exerted by reference groups.

From the late 1950s, training shoes were essentially worn only by athletes. It was only in 1983 that trainers made their debut as a fashion item, following in the footsteps of Bob Marley who appeared on stage in football gear and tracksuits. With promotion by the basketball star Michael Jordan, Nike trainers were quickly adopted by urban youth and taken up by both sexes. Parents were driven to distraction by children who couldn't face the rejection of their peer group because they were wearing the 'wrong' brand of trainers.

By 1998, Nike shoes were falling out of favour as teenagers turned to Timberlands, Hush Puppies and Caterpillar brands. The style magazine *I-D* wrote that flashy trainers were being overlooked in favour of rugged, subtly shaded action shoes. Nike had suffered by becoming seen as old fashioned. These new brands had taken on the mantle of coolness. But how can companies spot changes in teenagers' fashions when many marketing managers are quite far removed from the thought processes of children? Tapping into their rapidly changing passions can be very tricky. One approach used by advertising agency Leo Burnett is to quiz school children about their likes and dislikes using the Internet.

Would a price cut have helped Nike to boost its sales? This is unlikely, as part of the appeal of Nike trainers has been the cachet that goes with their high price. If the price were made too low, they would become everyday items of footwear, and very uncool in the eyes of teenage followers of fashion. Price did not seem to be a factor in the switch to Timberlands and Caterpillar brands which generally cost at least £60 a pair.

reference for the individual member. Individuals typically belong to several groups which can influence attitudes and behaviour in this way, for example university groups, trade unions and religious organizations. A member of a trade union may have little active involvement with the organization, but may nevertheless adopt the values of the union such as solidarity.

At other times, an individual may not actually be a member of a group, but may aspire to be a member of it. Aspirational groups can be general descriptions of the characteristics of groups of people who share attitudes and behaviour. They range from teenage 'wannabees' who idolize pop stars through to businessmen who want to surround themselves with the trappings of their successful business heroes. It can be difficult to identify just which aspirational groups are highly sought at any one time. In the 1980s, the 'yuppie' was considered an aspirational group by many, but

THINKING AROUND THE SUBJECT

Football runs deep in the psyche of many British males (and, increasingly, females). Individuals show sometimes incredible loyalty to a football team and would spend considerable time and money travelling with fellow supporters to watch their team play. The importance of this team mentality has not been lost on marketers who have devised a number of ways of capitalizing on fans' loyalty. Children (and also adults) seek out the latest football strip for fear of looking out of place among their peer group. This has led many football clubs to make frequent changes to their team colours, knowing that there will be a loyal market which is not very price sensitive. Mobile phone companies also recognized the importance of latching on to football club loyalties. Cellnet and One-2-One launched schemes in 1998 to supply mobile phones branded with football strips. Special adaptations to the service allow text results to be provided on the phone at the push of a button.

Will supporting a team-branded phone provide an individual with respect among his or her peer group for being a true team supporter? Will fans be as loyal to their team-branded phone as they are to the team itself? Or will this be seen as another cynical attempt to exploit the goodwill that many fans have towards their club?

then largely disappeared in the recessionary period of the early 1990s. Middle-aged marketers marketing youth products may find it difficult to keep up with which pop stars and fashion models are currently in favour with teenagers.

Although a person may not be influenced by all the attitudes or behaviour patterns of a particular reference group, the fact that such influence occurs at all makes it important for businesses to try to identify the reference groups of the target markets they are selling to. The importance of secondary group influences tends to vary between products and brands. In the case of products that are consumed or used in public, group influence is likely to affect not only the choice of product but also the choice of brand. (For example, training shoes are often sold using a 'brand spokesperson' to create an image for the shoe. There are some people who are so influenced by the images developed by famous athletes wearing a particular brand that they would not want to be seen wearing anything else.) For mass-market goods which are consumed less publicly (e.g. many grocery items), the effects of reference groups are usually fewer.

11.5   **LIFESTYLES AND ATTITUDES**

Many organizations have recognized that traditional indicators of social class are of little relevance in understanding buyer behaviour. Instead of monitoring changes in such indicators, an analysis of changing attitudes is considered to be more useful. Changes in attitudes may be behaviourally manifested by changes in lifestyles.

11.5.1   **Lifestyles**

Lifestyle analysis seeks to identify groups within the population based on distinctive patterns of behaviour. It is possible for two people from the same social class carrying out an identical occupation to have very different lifestyles that would not be apparent if businesses segmented markets solely on the basis of easily identifiable criteria such as occupation. Consequently, product development and marketing communications have often been designed to appeal to specific lifestyle groups. This type of analysis can be very subjective and quantification of numbers in each category within a population at best can only be achieved through a small sample survey.

Studies have indicated a number of trends in lifestyles which have impacts on business organizations:

■ A growing number of individuals are becoming money rich, but time poor. Such individuals quite commonly seek additional convenience from their purchases, even if this means paying a premium price. Businesses have responded with such products as gourmet ready-prepared meals.

■ As individuals become financially more secure, their motivation to buy products typically changes from a need for necessities to a desire for the unusual and challenging. Businesses have responded with ranges of designer clothes, adventure holidays and personalized interior design services.

■ With the increase in numbers of single person households, the symbolic meaning of the home has changed for many people. Businesses have responded with a range of home-related products such as wide-screen televisions and gas-fired barbecues.

Gaining knowledge of the current composition and geographical distribution of lifestyle segments is much more difficult than monitoring occupation-based segments, for which data are regularly collected by government and private sector organizations. This is discussed again later in this chapter.

11.5.2   **Attitudes**

Attitudes should be distinguished from the behaviour that may be manifested in a particular lifestyle. An individual may have an attitude about a subject, but keep their thoughts to themselves, possibly in fear of the consequences if behaviour does not conform with generally accepted norms. A man may believe that it should be acceptable for men to use facial cosmetics, but be unwilling to be the first to actually change behaviour by using them.

It is important for businesses to study changes in social attitudes, because these will most likely eventually be translated into changes in buying behaviour. The change may begin with a small group of social pioneers, followed by more traditional groups who may be slow to change their attitudes and more reluctant to change their behaviour. They may be prepared to change only when something has become the norm in their society.

Figure 11.2
The growing number of money-rich, time-poor households presents new opportunities for businesses to provide convenient solutions for this group at a premium price. Somerfield Stores was an early retailer to identify this opportunity and in 1998 developed a home delivery service which delivers customers' shopping to their home or place of work. Since the service was launched, many competitors have copied and further developed this service proposition, most notably by allowing shoppers to do their shopping using the Internet from the convenience of their home or office

(*Source*: Reproduced with permission of Somerfield Stores Ltd)

Businesses have monitored a number of significant changes in individuals' attitudes in Western Europe, for example:

- Healthy living is considered to be increasingly important.
- Consumers have a tendency to want instant results, rather than having to wait for things.
- Attitudes are increasingly based on secular rather than religious values.

Business organizations have been able to respond to these attitude changes creatively, for example:

- Demand for healthy foods and gymnasium services has increased significantly. At first, it was only a small group of people whose attitude towards health led them to buy specialist products – now it is a mainstream purchase.

- The desire for instant gratification has been translated into strategies to make stock always available, next day delivery for mail-order purchases, instant credit approval and instant lottery tickets. Many people's attitudes have changed so that if an item is not instantly available, they will go elsewhere.

- Supermarkets in England have capitalized on the secularization of Sunday by opening stores and doing increasing levels of business on Sundays.

11.6 IDENTIFYING AND MEASURING SOCIAL GROUPS

So far we have discussed the changing composition of society in general terms, but now we need to turn our attention to possible methods by which organizations can identify specific groups within society. This is important if businesses are to be able to target differentiated goods and services at groups who have quite distinctive sets of attitudes and lifestyles.

The aim of any system of social classification is to provide a measure that encapsulates differences between individuals in terms of their type of occupation, income level, educational background and attitudes to life, among other factors. There are three theoretical approaches to measuring social groupings:

1 *By self-measurement* Researchers could ask individuals which of a number of possible groups they belong to. This approach has a number of theoretical advantages for organizations, because how an individual actually sees him- or herself is often a more important determinant of behaviour than some objective measure. If people see themselves as working class, they are probably proud of the fact and will choose products and brands that accord with their own self-image. The danger of this approach is that many people tend to self-select themselves for 'middle of the road' categories. In one self-assessment study, over two-thirds of the sample described themselves as 'middle class'.

2 *By objective approaches* These involve the use of measurable indicators about a person, such as their occupation, education and spending habits, as a basis for class determination. A number of these are discussed below.

3 *By asking third parties* This combines the objective approach of indicators described above with a subjective assessment of an individual's behaviour and attitudes.

Social scientists have traditionally used the second of these approaches as a basis for defining social groupings, largely on account of its objectivity and relative ease of measurement. However, organizations have also recognized that an individual's

Table 11.1	IPA basis for social classification
Class category	Occupation
A	Higher managerial, administrative or professional
B	Intermediate managerial, administrative or professional
C1	Supervisory or clerical, and junior managerial, administrative or professional
C2	Skilled manual workers
D	Semi- and unskilled manual workers
E	State pensioners or widows (no other earners), casual or lower grade workers, or long-term unemployed

attitudes can be crucial in determining buying behaviour, and have therefore been keen to introduce more subjective and self-assessed bases for classification. In the following sections we will review some bases commonly used by businesses for identifying social groups.

11.6.1 IPA classification system

One of the most long-standing and still widely used bases for social classification is the system adopted by the Institute of Practitioners in Advertising (IPA). It uses an individual's occupation as a basis for classification, on the ground that occupation is closely associated with many aspects of a person's attitudes and behaviour. The classes defined range from A to E and Table 11.1 indicates the allocation of selected occupation to groups.

Such an attempt to reduce the multidimensional concept of social grouping to a single measure is bound to be an oversimplification which leads to limited usefulness of the measure for business organizations. A person's occupation is not necessarily a good indicator of their buying behaviour, which was the reason for the classification system being created in the first place. For example, the owner of a large scrap metal business and a bishop would probably be put in the same occupational classification, but there are likely to be very significant differences in their spending patterns and the way they pass their leisure time. Nevertheless, the classification system described above is widely used. Newspapers regularly analyse their readership in terms of membership of these groups and go out of their way to show how many of the highly prized A/B readers they have.

11.6.2 Classification used for the UK Census

The data sets used by many organizations import data collected by the United Kingdom's Census of Population. Since 1921, government statisticians have divided the population into six classes, based on their occupation. But the expansion of workers in traditionally middle-class jobs such as finance and management led the government to increase the number of classes and to look more critically at an occupational title in terms of the life opportunities that it offers.

Table 11.2   Major occupational groups used in UK census data collection

1   Managers and senior officials

2   Professional occupations

3   Associate professional and technical occupations

4   Administrative and secretarial occupations

5   Skilled trades occupations

6   Personal service occupations

7   Sales and customer service occupations

8   Process, plant and machine operatives

9   Elementary occupations

The Standard Occupational Classification used for the Census was first published in 1990 and updated in 2000. It uses two main concepts for classifying individuals:

■ The kind of work performed (the job description), and

■ The competent performance of the tasks and duties (the required skills for the job).

Changes introduced in 2000 reflected the need to improve comparability with the International Standard Classification of Occupations and the changing needs of users of census data who were becoming increasingly dubious about the existing bases of classification. Revisions were influenced by innovations associated with technological developments and the redefinition of work, reflecting the educational attainment of those entering the labour market. The main features of the revision included:

■ A tighter definition of managerial occupations

■ A thorough overhaul of computing and related occupations

■ The introduction of specific occupations associated with the environment and conservation

■ Changes linked to the upgrading of skills, but the deskilling of manufacturing processes

■ The recognition of the development of customer service occupations and the emergence of remote service provision through the operation of call centres.

The major occupational groups defined by the census are shown in Table 11.2.

Each of these nine groups is broken down into further subgroups, so for example major group 2 (professional occupations) has a submajor group (21) of science and technology professionals which is broken down into a minor group (211) of science professionals, from which a unit (2111) of scientists can be identified.

In this revised system of classification there have been risers and fallers. Teachers, librarians, nurses and police officers were among the risers, based on the skills and security of their job. Workers in call centres fell according to this system of classification

11.6.3   Geodemographic classification systems

An alternative approach which is being adopted by many businesses is to redefine the idea of class by basing it on where an individual lives. A lot of research has shown a correlation between where a person lives and their buying behaviour. The type of house and its location says much more about an individual than occupation alone can. Income, the size of the family unit, attitudes towards city life/country living as well as occupation are closely related to residence. The classification of individuals in this way has come to be known as *geodemographic* analysis. A number of firms offer a geodemographic segmentation analysis which allows a classification of small geographical pockets of households according to a combination of demographic characteristics and buying behaviour.

A widely used classification system is ACORN (ACORN is an acronym of A Classification Of Residential Neighbourhoods). ACORN is a geodemographic segmentation method, using census data to classify consumers according to the type of residential area in which they live. Each postcode in the country can therefore be allocated an ACORN category. This classification has been found to be a more powerful differentiator of consumer behaviour than traditional socio-economic and demographic indicators. The ACORN categories, and their components, are described in Table 11.3.

Another widely used system is MOSAIC, offered by Experian Ltd. By analysing a lot of sales data from people in each postcode area, it is possible to build up a good picture of the lifestyle and spending patterns associated with each classification. It is also possible to see how the distribution of the population between different classifications changes over time (Figure 11.3).

11.6.4   Lifestyle bases of classification

Geodemographic classification systems tell business a lot more about individuals than their occupation alone can, but this still misses much detail about the lifestyle of particular individuals, or the size of groups who share a similar lifestyle. One widely used method is to base classification on an individual's stage in the family life cycle. The research company Mintel, for example, has for some time used family life cycle in its analysis of markets (Table 11.4). However, the company has advanced from the traditional family life cycle model by identifying a number of special categories which typify consumer habits in the early 2000s. Unlike the life stage groups, these groups represent only sections of the population and do not account for all adults. The groups are shown in Table 11.4.

Many research companies have developed much more subjective bases for defining lifestyle groups which rely on a verbal description of the groups. Obtaining information to support the validity of these groups is hard to come by and generally relies on small sample surveys of the population. For this reason,

Table 11.3   ACORN classifications

Group A – Thriving (approx 20% of population)	Wealthy achievers, suburban areas Affluent greys, rural communities' prosperous pensioners, retirement areas
Group B – Expanding (approx 11% of population)	Affluent executives, family areas Well-off workers, family areas
Group C – Rising (approx 8% of population)	Affluent urbanites, town and city areas Prosperous professionals, metropolitan areas better-off executives, inner city areas
Group D – Settling (approx 25% of population)	Comfortable middle-agers, mature home-owning areas Skilled workers, home-owning areas
Group E – Aspiring (approx 13% of population	New homeowners, mature communities White-collar workers, better-off multiethnic areas
Group F – Striving (approx 21% of population)	Older people, less prosperous areas Council estate residents, better-off homes Council estate residents, high unemployment Council estate residents, greatest hardships People in multiethnic, low income areas.

Figure 11.3 MOSAIC is a widely used geodemographic classification system

(*Source*: Reproduced with permission of Experian Ltd)

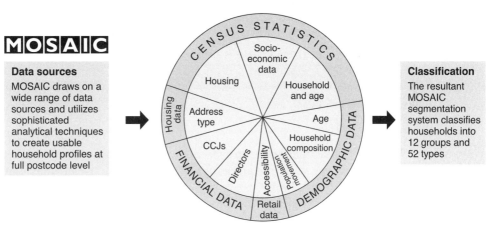

Data sources

MOSAIC draws on a wide range of data sources and utilizes sophisticated analytical techniques to create usable household profiles at full postcode level

Classification

The resultant MOSAIC segmentation system classifies households into 12 groups and 52 types

such ideal type classification systems are less well suited to monitoring social change than more objective systems based on quantifiable data.

Because of their subjectivity, there is a wide variety of lifestyle segmentation models which tend to reflect the needs of the companies that created them. For example, one model developed by Young and Rubicom described four lifestyle groups to which members of a population could be allocated:

1 *Conformers*, comprising the bulk of the population who typically may live in a suburban semi-detached house, drive a Vauxhall Astra, shop at Sainsbury's and book a Thomsons package holiday.

Table 11.4   Consumer lifestage and special categories as identified by Mintel

Lifestage groups	
Pre-family	Those aged under 35 who are not parents
Family	Those aged 15–54 with at least one child aged under 16 still at home
Empty-nesters	No family/empty-nesters aged 35–54 with no children (aged under 16)
Post-family	Post-family/retired, those aged over 55/not working
Special category groups	
Benefit dependents	Category Es aged 35+: those who are reliant solely on state benefits (around 10% of the adult population)
Families on a tight budget	Working C2Ds with at least one child aged under 16 in the household – the majority have limited incomes which must be spent on a relatively large household (around 10% of the adult population)
Better-off families	Working ABC1s with at least one child aged under 16 in the household (around 9% of the population)
Better-off empty nesters	ABC1s aged 35–64 who are working with no children (aged under 16) living at home. They are, therefore, the classic no family/empty-nesters with probably a high income that can be spent on themselves rather than on family (around 8% of the adult population
Working managers	Working ABs (around 9% of the population)
Working women	Women in part- or full-time employment (around 21% of the adult population)

2   *Aspirers*, a smaller group who are ambitious, innovative and keen to surround themselves with the trappings of success. This group may typically live in a trendy mews house, drive a GTI car, shop for brand-name clothes and take adventure holidays.

3   *Controllers*, by contrast, are comfortable in the knowledge that they have made it in life and do not feel the need to flaunt their success. They are more likely to live in a comfortable detached house, drive a Volvo, shop at Marks and Spencer and book their holiday through the local travel agent they trust.

4   *Reformers* have a vision of how life could be improved for everybody in society. At home, they may be enthusiastic about DIY and energy conservation. They may see their car more as a means of transport than a status symbol and buy own-label brands at Sainsbury's.

Of course, these are ideal types, and very few people will precisely meet these descriptions. However, they are a useful starting point for trying to understand who

What does an individual's choice of sandwich say about them? In 1998, the retailer Tesco undertook research that showed how complex the market for ready-made sandwiches had become, with clear segments emerging who sought quite different types of sandwiches. In an attempt to define and target its lunch customers more precisely, the company found that well-paid executives invariably insisted on 'designer' sandwiches made from ciabatta and focaccia with sun-dried tomatoes and costing about £2.50. Salespeople and middle-ranking executives were more inclined to opt for meaty triple-deckers. Upwardly mobile women aged 25–40 chose low-calorie sandwiches costing around £1.49. Busy manual workers tended to grab a sandwich that looked affordable, simple and quick to eat, such as the ploughman's sandwich that Tesco sold for £1.15. Tesco's research claimed that sandwiches have become an important statement made by individuals and need to be targeted appropriately. What do your snack meals say about you?

it is that a company is targeting. The numbers in each category have undoubtedly risen and fallen in the recent past. Aspirers seem to appear in great numbers during periods of economic boom, but become less conspicuous at the onset of a recession.

Many more informal, almost tongue-in-cheek bases for segmenting lifestyle groups are commonly used. It is common, for example, to talk about lifestyles that have been labelled Yuppies (young, upwardly mobile professionals), Dinkys (dual income, no kids yet) and Bobos (burnt out, but opulent), to name but a few. New descriptions emerge to describe new lifestyles. Again, these classifications are not at all scientific, but they give market researchers a chance to describe a target market.

11.7   DEMOGRAPHY

Demography is the study of populations in terms of their size and characteristics. Among the topics of interest to demographers are the age structure of a country, the geographic distribution of its population, the balance between male and females and the likely future size of the population and its characteristics.

11.7.1   The importance of demographic analysis to business organizations

A number of reasons can be identified why business organizations should study changing demographic structures.

1. On the demand side, demography helps to predict the size of the market that a product is likely to face. For example, demographers can predict an increase in elderly people living in the United Kingdom and the numbers living in the south-western region of the country. Businesses can use this information as a basis for predicting, for example, the size of the market for retirement homes in the south-west.

2 Demographic trends have supply-side implications. An important aim of business organizations is to match the opportunities facing an organization with the resource strengths that it possesses. In many businesses, labour is a key resource and a study of demographics will indicate the human resources that an organization can expect to have available to it in future years. Thus a business that has relied on relatively low wage, young labour, such as retailing, would need to have regard to the availability of this type of worker when developing its product strategy. A retailer might decide to invest in more automated methods of processing transactions and handling customer enquiries rather than relying on a traditional but diminishing source of relatively low-cost labour.

3 The study of demographics also has implications for public sector services which are themselves becoming more marketing oriented. Changing population structures influence the community facilities which need to be provided by the government. For example, fluctuations in the number of children has affected the number of schools and teachers required, while the increasing number of elderly people will require the provision of more specialized housing and hospital facilities suitable for this group.

4 In an even wider sense, demographic change can influence the nature of family life and communities and ultimately affects the social and economic system in which organizations operate. The imbalance that is developing between a growing dependent elderly population and a diminishing population of working age could affect government fiscal policy and the way in which we care for the elderly, with major implications for business organizations.

Although the study of demographics has assumed great importance in Western Europe in recent years, study of the consequences of population change dates back a considerable time. T.R. Malthus studied the effects of population changes in a paper published in 1798. He predicted that the population would continue to grow exponentially, while world food resources would grow at a slower linear rate of growth. Population growth would only be held back by 'war, pestilence and famine' until an equilibrium point was again reached at which population was just equal to the food resources available.

Malthus's model of population growth failed to predict the future accurately and this only serves to highlight the difficulty of predicting population levels, when the underlying assumptions on which predictions are based are themselves changing. Malthus failed to predict, on the one hand, the tremendous improvement in agricultural efficiency which would allow a larger population to be sustained, while, on the other hand, overlooking changes in social and cultural attitudes that were to limit family size.

11.7.2 **Global population changes**

Globally, population is expanding at an increasing rate. The world population level at AD 1000 has been estimated at about 300 million. Over the next 750 years, it rose

**Figure 11.4
Growth in world
population**

(*Source*: Based on
UN estimates, 1985)

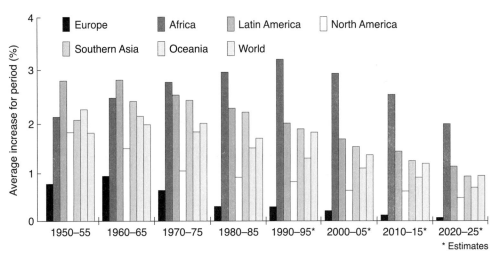

at a steady rate to 728 million in 1750. Thereafter, the rate of increase became progressively more rapid, doubling in the following 150 years to 1550 million in 1900 and almost doubling again to 3000 million in the 62 years to 1962. World population in 1996 was estimated at 5.8 billion in 1996 and is projected to reach 8.3 billion by 2025. The growth of world population has not been uniform, with recent growth being focused on Far East countries, especially Korea and China, as well as South America. By contrast, the total population levels of most Western developed countries are stable, or in some cases actually declining. An indication of the variation in population growth rates is given in Figure 11.4. It should, however, be noted that there is still considerable debate about the future world population levels, with many predictions being revised downwards.

A growth in the population of a country does not necessarily mean a growth in business opportunities, for the countries with the highest population growth rates also tend to be those with the lowest GDP per head. Indeed, in many countries of Africa, total GDP is not keeping up with the growth in population levels, resulting in a lower GDP per head. On the other hand, the growth in population results in a large and low-cost labour force, which can help to explain the tendency for many European-based organizations to base their design capacity in Europe but relatively labour-intensive assembly operations in the Far East.

11.7.3 **Changes in UK population level**

The first British census was carried out in 1801 and the subsequent 10-yearly census provides the basis for studying changes in the size of the British population. A summary of British population growth is shown in Table 11.5.

The fluctuation in the rate of population growth can be attributed to three main factors: the birth rate, the death rate and the difference between inward and outward migration. The fluctuation in these rates is illustrated in Figure 11.5. These three components of population change are described in more detail below.

Table 11.5   Population growth 1801–2003

Year	Population of England, Wales and Scotland (000s)	Average increase per decade (%)
1801	10 501	13.9
1871	26 072	9.4
1911	40 891	4.5
1941	46 605	5.8
1971	54 369	0.8
1981	54 814	2.4
1995	56 957	3.4
2011	58 794	1.7 (estimated)
2031	58 970	−0.5 (estimated)

Source: Based on *Annual Abstract of Statistics*; Government Actuary's Department and Population Censuses.

Figure 11.5
Changes in the UK birth rate, death rate and level of net migration, 1901–2011
(*Source*: Office of Population Censuses and Surveys, Government Actuary's Department. © Crown Copyright)

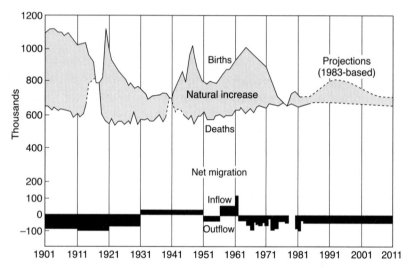

11.7.4   The birth rate

The birth rate is usually expressed in terms of the number of live births per 1000 population. Since the Second World War, the birth rate has shown a number of distinct cyclical tendencies. The immediate post-war years are associated with a 'baby boom', followed by a steady decrease in the number of births until 1956. Following this, the rate rose again until the mid-1960s during a second, but lesser, baby boom. The birth rate then fell until the mid-1970s, rising again in recent years.

In order to explain these trends, it is necessary to examine two key factors:

1 The number of women in the population who are of child-bearing age and
2 The proportion of these women who actually give birth (this is referred to as the *fertility* rate).

Table 11.6	General fertility rate – total births per 1000 women aged 15–44, United Kingdom	
Year	Fertility rate
1900	115.0
1933	81.0
1951	73.0
1961	90.6
1971	84.3
1981	62.1
1991	64.0
1993	62.0

Source: Office of Population Censuses and Surveys.

The peak in the birth rate of the early 1960s could be partly explained by the 'baby boom' children of the immediate post-war period working through to child-bearing age. Similarly, the children of this group are themselves now at child-bearing age, accounting for some of the recent increase in the birth rate. Greater doubt lies over reasons for changes in the fertility rate, usually expressed in terms of the number of births per 1000 women aged between 16 and 44. This has varied from a peak of 115 at the beginning of the century to a low point of 56.8 in 1983 (Table 11.6).

There are many possible explanations for changes in fertility rates and it is our difficulty in understanding the precise nature of these changes that makes popula-tion forecasting a difficult task. Some of the more frequently suggested causes of the declining fertility rate are listed below:

1   A large family is no longer seen as an insurance policy for future parental security. The extended family has declined in importance and state institutions have taken over many of the welfare functions towards elderly members of the family which were previously expected of children. Furthermore, infant and child mortality has declined and consequently the need for large numbers of births has declined. Alongside this falling need for large numbers of children has come a greater ability to control the number of births.

2   Children use household resources that could otherwise be used for consump-tion. The cost of bringing up children has been increasing as a result of increased expectations of children and the raising of the school leaving age. Although in many Western countries this is offset by financial incentives for having children, the cost of child rearing has increased relative to consumer purchases in general.

3   In addition to diverting household resources from the consumption of other goods and services, caring for children also has the effect of reducing the earning capacity of the household. Women may also seek additional status

and career progression by having fewer children or spacing them over a shorter period of time.

4   Birth rates tend to be related to current economic conditions, falling significantly in response to temporary economic recession and rising in response to a period of economic boom.

The death rate

Death rates are normally expressed as the number of people in the country that die in a year per 1000 of the population. This is sometimes called the crude death rate; the age-specific death rate takes account of the age of death and is expressed as the number of people per 1000 of a particular age group that die in a year.

In contrast to the volatility of the birth rate during the postwar period, the death rate has been relatively stable and has played a relatively small part in changing the total population level. The main feature of mortality in the United Kingdom has been a small decline in age-specific death rates, having the effect of increasing the survival chances of relatively old people. The age-specific death rate of women has fallen more significantly than men. The main reasons for the decline in age-specific death rates are improved standards of living, a better environment and better health services. While age-specific death rates have been falling in most advanced industrial countries, the United Kingdom has generally experienced a slower fall than most other EU member states.

Migration

If immigration is compared with emigration, a figure for net migration is obtained. During most periods of this century, the United Kingdom has experienced a net outflow of population, the main exceptions being the 1930s, caused by emigrants to the Commonwealth returning home during the depression, the 1940s when a large number of refugees entered the United Kingdom from Nazi Europe, and the late 1950s/early 1960s when the prosperity of the British economy attracted large numbers of immigrants from the new Commonwealth. Emigration has tended to peak at times of economic depression in the United Kingdom.

While migration has had only a marginal effect upon the total population level, it has had a more significant effect on the population structure. On the demand side, many immigrants have come from different cultural backgrounds and pose new opportunities and problems for segmenting markets for goods and services. Furthermore, immigrants themselves need to be segmented into various ethnic minorities, each with differing needs. Table 11.7 indicates the extent of the main ethnic minorities in the United Kingdom.

In some cases, completely new markets have emerged specifically for ethnic minorities, such as the market for black sticking plasters. It has sometimes proved difficult for established businesses to gain access to immigrant segments. Many established companies have not adequately researched the attitudes and buying processes of these groups, with the result that in markets as diverse as

Table 11.7   Great Britain population by ethnic group, 1996–97

	Number	Percentage of population
Black Caribbean	477 000	0.8
African	281 000	0.5
Other black	117 000	0.2
Indian	877 000	1.5
Pakistani	579 000	1.0
Bangladeshi	183 000	0.3
Chinese	126 000	0.2
Other ethnic groups	667 000	1.2

Source: Based on Social Trends, Office for National Statistics.

vegetables, clothing and travel, ethnic minorities have supported businesses run by fellow members of their minority group. On the supply side, immigrants have tended to be of working age and have filled a vital role in providing labour for the economy. Moreover, some Asian minorities have brought vital entrepreneurial skills to the economy. Balanced against this is the fact that the emigrants that Britain has lost have tended to be highly trained and represent a loss to the economy.

It must be noted that there are great differences between ethnic subgroups. Entrepreneurship is much greater among the Chinese group, where 22 per cent were classified as self-employed in 1996–97, compared to 19 per cent for Pakistanis and Bangladeshis, but only 7 per cent for black groups. The comparable figure was 12.5 per cent for whites. The age structure of ethnic minority groups gives rise to differences in the proportion who are dependent. Within the Bangladeshi group, for example, 42 per cent are under 16 (compared to a comparable figure of 20 per cent for whites), while only 20 per cent are in the economically most active group of 35–64 years (compared with 37 per cent for whites). These figures are reversed for the Chinese community where only 17 per cent are under 16 and 38 per cent between 35 and 64.

11.7.7

The age structure of the population

It was noted earlier that the total population of the United Kingdom – and indeed most countries of the EU – is fairly stable. Within this stable total, there has been a more noted change in the composition of particular age groups. The changes that have affected the size of a number of young and elderly age segments over time are illustrated in Figure 11.6.

A number of bulges in the distribution are evident and these can have important implications for business organizations. The reduction in teenagers has resulted in diminishing markets for companies who targeted these groups and also limits a traditional source of relatively low-cost labour. The increasing proportion of elderly people may alter many of the values of our youth-oriented culture. For

Figure 11.6
Size of selected age cohorts in United Kingdom, 1931–2001
(*Source*: Based on Population Censuses and Office of Population Censuses and Surveys estimates)

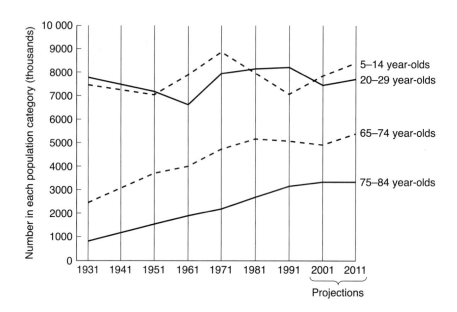

example, the emphasis on fashion and short-life products may give way to an emphasis on quality and durability as the growing numbers in the older age groups increasingly dominate cultural values. Another major issue that may affect the cultural environment of businesses is the growing imbalance between the size of the working population and an increasingly large dependent population. Government statistics show that between 1961 and 1996, the number of people of working age available to support the retired population decreased from 4.1 per pensioner to 3.3. This figure is expected to fall again slightly to 2020 but then fall again sharply as the baby boom generation starts to become eligible for their pensions. The ratio of those contributing to the pensions that sustain the retired population is smaller still, to take account of the fact that although many people of working age are available to work, many are either unemployed or pay no taxes. By 2020, each pensioner will be supported by the contributions of two tax-paying workers. This is expected to fall to 1.6 by 2040.

11.7.8 **Household structure**

Reference was made earlier in this chapter to the changing role and functions of family units, and this is reflected in an analysis of household structure statistics. A number of important trends can be noted:

1 There has been a trend for women to have fewer children. From a high point in the 1870s, the average number of children for each woman born in 1930 was 2.35, 2.2 for those born in 1945 and it is projected to be 1.97 for those born in 1965. There has also been a tendency for women to have children later in life. In the United Kingdom, the average age at which women have their first child has moved from 24 years in 1961 to 28 in 1996. There has also been

Figure 11.7
Ageing of the population is a major opportunity for many organizations. This manufacturer of stair lifts has targeted a segment of the population which is expected to grow rapidly in most Western countries
(*Source:* Reproduced with permission of Stannah Stair Lifts)

an increase in the number of women having no children. According to the Office of Population Census and Surveys, more than one-fifth of women born in 1967 are expected to be childless when they reach the age of 40, compared with 13 per cent of those born in 1947.

2 Alongside a declining number of children has been a decline in the average household size. This has fallen continuously from an average of 3.1 people in 1961 to 2.4 in 1997. There has been a particular fall in the number of very large households with six or more people (down from 7 per cent of all households in 1961 to under 2 per cent in 1997) and a significant increase in the number of one-person households (up from 14 per cent to 27 per cent over the same period). A number of factors have contributed to the increase in one-person households, including the increase in solitary survivors, later marriage and an increased divorce rate. The business implications of the growth of this group are numerous, ranging from an increased demand for smaller units of housing to the types and size of groceries purchased. A single person household buying for him- or herself is likely to use different types of retail outlets compared to the household buying as a unit – the single person may be more likely to use a niche retailer than the (typically) housewife buying for the whole family whose needs may be better met by a department store. A Mintel report showed a number of ways in which the spending patterns of single person households deviates from the average. For example, compared to the

British average, a person living in a single person household spends 49 per cent more on tobacco, 26 per cent more on household services and 23 per cent less on meat (Mintel, 1996).

3 Along with the rise in single person households has been a fall in other household types. Family households comprising one to three dependent children have fallen from 38 per cent of all households in 1961 to 25 per cent in 1996–97. Lone parents with children have increased during the same period from 6 to 10 per cent of all households.

The role of women in household structures has been changing, with a rising proportion having some form of employment (59 per cent in 1997). Along with this has been the emergence of a large segment of career-minded women who are cash rich but time poor. This has created new opportunities for labour-saving consumer durables in the home and for convenience foods. It has also resulted in women becoming important target markets for products that were previously considered to be male preserves, such as new cars.

11.7.9 Geographical distribution of population

The population density of the United Kingdom of 231 people per km^2 is one of the highest in the world. However, this figure hides the fact that the population is dispersed very unevenly between regions and between urban and rural areas. The distribution of population is not static.

Regional distribution   The major feature of the regional distribution of the United Kingdom population is the dominance of the south-east of England with 30 per cent of the population, and the industrial regions of the West Midlands, Lancashire and Yorkshire. By contrast, the populations of Scotland, Wales and Northern Ireland account in total for only 17 per cent of the UK population.

Movement between the regions tends to be a very gradual process. In an average year, about 10 per cent of the population will change address, but only about one-eighth of these will move to another region. Nevertheless, there have been a number of noticeable trends. Firstly, throughout the twentieth century there has been a general drift of population from the north to the Midlands and south. More recently, there has been a trend for population to move away from the relatively congested south-east to East Anglia, the south-west and home counties. This can be partly explained by the increased cost of industrial and residential location in the south-east, the greater locational flexibility of modern industry and the desire of people for a pleasanter environment in which to live. The drift of population is illustrated in Figure 11.8.

Urban concentration   Another trend has been a shift in the proportion of the population living in urban areas. Throughout most of Western Europe, the nineteenth and twentieth centuries have been associated with a drift from rural areas to towns. In the United Kingdom, this has resulted in the urban areas of Greater London, Greater Manchester, Merseyside, Greater Glasgow, West Midlands, West

Figure 11.8
Percentage population change by region, 1981–93

(*Source*: Based on information published by the Office of Population Censuses and Surveys, General Register Office (Scotland) and General Register Office (Northern Ireland))

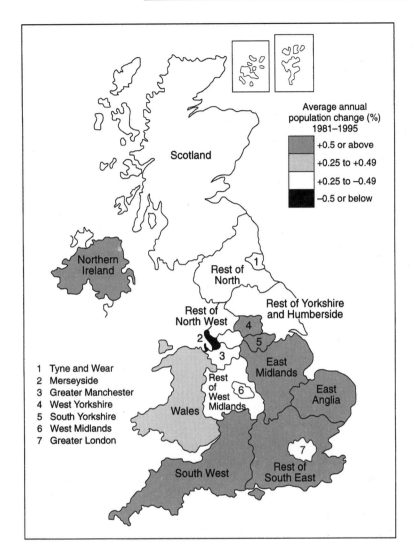

Yorkshire and Tyneside having just one-thirtieth of the United Kingdom's surface area, but nearly one-third of the total population. From the 1960s, the trend towards urbanization was partly reversed, with many of the larger conurbations experiencing a decline in population, combined with a deterioration in many inner city areas. Those moving out have tended to be the most economically active, leaving behind a relatively elderly and poor population. Much of the movement from the conurbations has been towards the rural areas just beyond the urban fringe. For example, London has lost population to the home counties of Berkshire, Buckinghamshire, Hertfordshire and Essex. The increasingly large dormitory population of these areas remains dependent on the neighbouring conurbation. Movement from urban to rural areas has brought about a change in lifestyle which has implications for businesses. Higher car ownership in rural areas has led more households to make fewer shopping trips for household

Is the United Kingdom's so called 'North–South divide' a myth or a reality? The government's annual publication 'Social Trends' highlights a number of stark contrasts, and points to an apparently widening gap. The most comprehensive indicator, based on GDP, shows that in 1999, people in London and the south-east were 59 per cent better off than those in the north-east – the poorest region. This gap has been growing, as comparable figures show the difference to have been 43 per cent 10 years earlier in 1989. The gap with the north-west increased from 31 per cent to 41 per cent, and with Yorkshire and Humberside from 34 per cent to 40 per cent. Indicators for a range of consumer durables show similar discrepancies in ownership between the regions. The proportion of all British jobs located in London and the south-east has risen from 27.7 per cent in 1989 to 29.1 per cent in 1999, while the combined share of the north-east, north-west and Yorkshire and Humberside has fallen from 24.1 to 22.9 per cent.

Despite growing disparities in economic wealth, evidence of quality of life has been more mixed in its implications for a north–south divide. With lower costs of housing, less traffic congestion and access to pleasant countryside, many northern cities, such as Leeds have witnessed a renaissance. Many organizations have relocated part of their operations out of the south-east area, as witnessed by the large number of call centres which have been located in the north-east.

Can businesses afford to see the country simply in terms of a north–south divide? Are there also important differences *within* regions, which allows the deprivation of Manchester's Moss Side to co-exist with prosperous Cheadle Hulme? Do regional imbalances in wealth present opportunities for businesses, not only in the prosperous south-east, but also the relatively less affluent northern regions?

goods, to travel further to the shop that best suits their lifestyle and to spend more on each trip. In this changed shopping pattern, the decision-making unit may comprise more members of the household than in an urban area where the (typically) wife may have made more frequent trips to the local supermarket by herself.

More recently, there has been a trend for young professional people to move back into town centres. For this group, having the facilities of a town centre close at hand without the need for increasingly expensive and time-consuming commuting has proved attractive. Town centres which were once deserted in the evening have often been brought back to life, helped by this group's patronage of wine bars, restaurants and all-night convenience stores.

11.7.10   **EU comparisons**

Although the population of most EU countries is stable, a number of structural differences can be noted between member states. From Table 11.8, it can be seen that an exporter to the Irish Republic will face a much younger age structure than

Table 11.8   A comparison of the population structure of EU member countries

Country	Total Population (1997)	Growth 1977–97 (%)	Aged 0–14 (%)	Aged 35–64 (%)	Aged 65+ (%)
Austria	8 068	6.6	17.5	67.2	15.3
Belgium	10 170	3.5	17.8	67.5	14.7
Denmark	5 275	3.8	17.5	67.3	15.2
Finland	5 132	8.5	18.9	66.5	14.6
France	58 494	10.3	19.2	65.1	15.7
Germany	82 028	4.9	16.2	68.1	15.7
Greece	10 485	12.6	16.1	67.7	16.2
Ireland	3 643	11.7	23.4	65.0	11.6
Italy	57 464	2.9	14.5	68.2	17.3
Luxembourg	418	15.9	18.6	67.2	14.2
The Netherlands	15 562	12.7	18.4	68.1	13.5
Portugal	9 935	5.7	17.0	68.3	14.7
Spain	39 299	8.7	15.7	68.2	16.1
Sweden	8 845	7.4	18.9	66.5	14.6
UK	58 873	4.8	19.4	64.8	15.8

Source: Compiled from National Statistical Office sources.

in the domestic UK market, and many more young people than in the former West Germany. The total population of the Irish Republic is also likely to grow the most rapidly, in contrast to Belgium and Germany, which are expected to fall.

It can be seen that population growth rates have varied considerably throughout the EU, ranging from the very modest growth of 2.9 per cent in Italy to the much higher 15.9 per cent in Luxembourg and 12.7 per cent in The Netherlands. It must be remembered that for any given increase in a country's GDP, the effect on individuals' spending power will be greater where the population growth is slower

Within these population totals, there are significant differences within the EU in the proportion of the population that is either young or elderly, with consequent implications for demand for age-related products. As an example, in 1997 the proportion of the population aged 65 and above ranged from 11.6 per cent in Ireland to 17.3 per cent in Italy. By contrast, Ireland has the greatest proportion of under 15s (23.4 per cent), compared to Spain which has the lowest (15.7 per cent).

In addition, the geographical distribution of the population and structure of household units differs between EU member states. For example, EU statistics show a number of interesting contrasts in geodemographic characteristics between member states which could have implications for the marketing of goods and services:

1 Very significant differences occur in home ownership patterns, with implications for demand for a wide range of home-related services. The proportion of households living in rented accommodation ranges from 21 per cent in Spain to 53 per cent in West Germany, while the proportion with a mortgage ranges from 8 per cent in Spain to 44 per cent in the United Kingdom.

2 The proportion of the population living within metropolitan areas varies from 13 per cent in Italy to 44 per cent in France. The resulting differences in lifestyles can have implications for goods and services as diverse as car repairs, entertainment and retailing.

3 The proportion of self-employed people ranges from 45 per cent in The Netherlands to 17 per cent in Italy, with implications for the sale of personal pension schemes, etc.

CASE STUDY

SUPERMARKETS GET READY FOR A NEW GENERATION OF 'YABs'

The grocery retail industry in the United Kingdom is dominated by a small number of very large supermarket chains operating from large superstores, with the names of Tesco, Sainsbury's, Safeway and ASDA being familiar to most shoppers. The high degree of concentration within the trade has not, however, influenced competition in any negative way as far as customers are concerned. The range of food and household items on sale has never been so varied and prices are very keen as the major players strive to capture further market share. However, consumer loyalty can never be guaranteed and an insight into the service requirements of shoppers may help the retailers retain their relationship with customers.

A study undertaken by the Henley Centre for Forecasting on behalf of one of the large multiples illustrates how research on the future of the market can form a basis for strategic change. In this instance the research was concerned with predicting patterns of shopping behaviour in the mid-1990s and particularly with establishing a set of market segments based on behaviour patterns.

The outcome of the Henley Centre's investigation was the identification of a number of different types of shopper based on a multivariable approach which took account of demographic factors such as age, sex and income as well as lifestyle, personality and finally attitude to the shopping experience. As with so many of these studies the resultant new breeds of shopper have been labelled with glib titles.

The Harried Hurrier will be the most important type of new shopper. They are typically burdened with squabbling children and crippled by a severe lack of time. Hurriers are averse to anything that eats into their precious minutes such as having too much choice, which makes them impatient. Another large group, but spending less money, will be the middle-aged Young-at-Heart who in contrast to the first group have time on their hands and like to try new products. An important and growing species of grocery shopper is the Young, Affluent and Busy (or 'YABs') for whom money is not a major constraint in their quest for convenience and more interesting products, but they do have a low boredom threshold. Two other types who are expected to grow in importance are the

Fastidious who are attracted by in-store hygiene and tidiness and the mainly male Begrudgers who only shop out of obligation to others. At the same time the Perfect Wife and Mother who is concerned with the balanced diet would appear to be on her way out. She is likely to be more than compensated for by the Obsessive Fad-Followers whose choice of food tends to be dominated by brand image and current trends.

It is expected that the new breeds will act as a catalyst for a shopping revolution. Although the already established need for convenience will still predominate, retail analysts anticipate some significant changes such as in store traffic-routing systems, one-way layouts, and themed food centres by nationality. There would appear to be a considerable amount to be gained from transforming the sometimes stressful encounter with the superstore into a pleasurable leisure activity.

However, balancing the needs of all these groups may prove to be a difficult task which may lead to greater specialization within the sector. For example, it is not impossible to imagine chains of speciality food retailers that act as menu stores offering the YABs the alternative of buying different dinner party food on different days, switching the emphasis from French to Italian to Indian recipes.

(Adapted from 'Keeping 'em Rolling in the Aisles', *Marketing Week*, 11 August 1989)

CASE STUDY Review questions

1 To what extent are segment descriptions such as those used for YABs and Harried Hurriers useful to supermarkets in supermarket planning?

2 Analyse some of the implications for a supermarket of the ageing of the population.

3 How can you explain differences between countries in grocery shoppers' behaviour?

CHAPTER Summary and links to other chapters

Societies are not homogeneous, and this chapter has explored the processes by which individuals develop distinct social and cultural values. The concepts of social class, lifestyles, reference groups, family structure and culture are important reference points for businesses and change in these must be monitored and addressed. Population totals and structures change and this chapter has reviewed the impact of demographic change on the marketing of goods and services. A changing population structure also has implications for the availability of employees.

There is a close link between this chapter and Chapter 5 where we looked at the social responsibility of businesses. As attitudes change, there has been a trend for the public to expect business organizations to act in a socially more acceptable manner. There are close links between the social environment and the political environment (Chapter 8), with the latter reflecting changes in the former. It has also been noted that technology can have a two-way effect with the social environment and understanding the complexity of society's changing needs calls for an information system that is comprehensive and speedy (Chapter 12). When a company enters an overseas market, it is likely to face a quite different set of cultural values (Chapter 10).

Review questions

1 (a) Discuss the likely impact of ageing on the labour market.

   (b) What recommendations would you make to a business currently reliant on recruiting large numbers of school leavers to meet its labour needs?

   (Based on CIM Marketing Environment Examination)

2 'Businesses will have to cope with changes in demand patterns as older consumers become more significant in their markets and younger people less so.' Explain, with examples, some of the opportunities provided by these changing demand patterns and how the marketer should address this buyer segment.

   (Based on CIM Marketing Environment Examination)

3. 'Ageing is one of the few trends that can be forecast with confidence.' Briefly explain why this is so, and suggest two forecasting approaches, showing how they might enable the marketer to forecast the future with greater confidence.

   (Based on CIM Marketing Environment Examination)

4 In what ways do you think the different culture of a less developed country may affect the marketing of confectionery that has previously been successfully marketed in the United Kingdom?

5 In what ways are the buying habits of a household with two adults and two children likely to change when the children leave home?

6 Critically assess some of the implications of an increasingly aged population on the demand for hotel accommodation in the United Kingdom.

References

Mintel (1996) *Single Person Households: Getting Younger, Richer and Happier*, Mintel, London.
Office for National Statistics (1998) *Social Focus on Women*, The Stationery Office, London.

Selected further reading

Social classification has been discussed widely and the following references are useful in a marketing context:

Grusky, D. (2001) *Social Stratification*, Westview Press, Boulder, CO.
Savage, M. (2000) *Class Analysis and Social Transformation: Sociology and Social Change*, Open University Press, Buckingham.
Sivados, E., G. Matthews and D. Curry (1997) 'A preliminary examination of the continuing significance of social class for marketing: a geodemographic replication', *Journal of Consumer Marketing*, November–December 1997, vol. 14, no. 6, pp. 463–477.
Worsthorne, P. (1998) 'Chain of being', *New Statesman*, 16 October, vol. 127, no. 4407, pp. 54–55. (Article about UK social class hierarchy.)

Distinctive aspects of business within ethnic minority groups is discussed in the following:

Light, I.H. and S.J. Gold (2000) *Ethnic Economies*, Academic Press, New York.

For further discussion of market segmentation methods, the following references build on the previous references:

Green, P. and A. Kreiger (1995) 'Alternative approaches to cluster based market segmentation', *Journal of the Marketing Research Society*, July, vol. 37, no. 3, pp. 221(119).

Mitchell, A. (1997) 'Segmentation: finding a niche', *Marketing Business*, November, pp. 16–21.

Weinstein, A. (1994) *Market Segmentation, Using Demographics, Psychographics and Other Niche Marketing Techniques to Predict and Model Customer Behaviour*, Probus, Chicago, IL.

For statistics on the changing structure of UK society and its habits, the following regularly updated publications of the Office for National Statistics provide good coverage:

Family Expenditure Survey: A sample survey of consumer spending habits, providing a snapshot of household spending. Published annually.

Population Trends: Statistics on population, including population change, births and deaths, life expectancy and migration.

Regional Trends: A comprehensive source of statistics about the regions of the United Kingdom allowing regional comparisons.

Social Trends: Statistics combined with text, tables and charts which present a narrative of life and lifestyles in the United Kingdom. Published annually.

Useful websites

ESRC Archive   A data archive of social sciences and humanities, providing links to many social sciences resources.   **http://dawww.essex.ac.uk**

Organization for Economic Co-operation and Development (OECD)   This site provides a summary of member states' population statistics.   **http://www.oecd.org/publications/figures/2000/english/Demography.pdf**

Social Science   A listing of social sciences resources, listed by subject headings.   **http://www.sosig.ac.uk**

Statbase   UK National Statistics' website, with summaries of numerous surveys of population characteristics, lifestyles and attitudes.   **http://www.statistics.gov.uk/statbase/mainmenu.asp**

Up My Street   An interactive site which highlights differences between areas in terms of social structures. Enter a postcode or a name of a town and a page will appear that displays data on that area. Data includes unemployment statistics, house prices, council rates and local community services.   **http://upmystreet.com**

World Population   World population data from the US census.   **http://www.census.gov/ipc/www/world.html**

Key terms

Age structure	Geodemographic analysis
Attitudes	Household structure
Birth rate	Life stages
Cellular household	Lifestyle
Census of population	Migration
Cultural convergence	Reference groups
Culture	Roles
Demography	Social class
Ethnic minorities	Subcultures
Family roles	Values

12

The technological and information environment

CHAPTER OBJECTIVES

The aim of this chapter is to explain how changes in the technological environment influence business decisions. The business environment is at present moving through a dynamic and turbulent phase driven by technological change, globalization, and increasingly competitive markets. No organization, whether in the public or private sector, large or small, new or old, can relax. In the last five years the pace of technological change affecting sales, marketing, customer service, and supply chain management, has continued to accelerate, particularly with the Internet, Web, and communications technology. The forces of technological change mean that enterprises now need to reevaluate many business activities and processes. Direct response marketing, telemarketing, database marketing, customer service, research and development, management information systems, channel management, supply chain management, procurement, Internet marketing, and electronic commerce are some emerging issues which are discussed in this chapter. Trying to predict future developments in technology is important, but can be costly. Investing in research and development, and responding to buyers' changing expectations is crucial if a company is to keep ahead in the technological race. After reading this chapter, you should have a good understanding of the diversity of technological impacts on business. As well as understanding the impacts of technology on business decisions, you should understand the interaction between technology and society. Technology not only emerges as a response to changing social values, but it also helps to shape those values.

WHAT IS TECHNOLOGY?

The word 'technology' can be easily misunderstood as simply being about computers and hi-tech industries such as aerospace. In fact, technology has a much broader meaning and influences our everyday lives. It impacts on the frying pan (Teflon-coated for non-stick), the programmable central heating timer, cavity wall insulation, the television, video, washing machine, car – in fact, just about everything in the home. The impact at work can be even greater, as technology changes the nature of people's jobs, creating new jobs and making others redundant. It influences the way we shop, our entertainment, leisure, the way we work, how we communicate and the treatment we receive in hospital.

Technology is defined in the *Longman Modern English Dictionary*, as 'the science of technical processes in a wide, though related, field of knowledge'. Dibb *et al.* (1997), define technology 'as the knowledge of how to accomplish tasks and goals'. Technology therefore embraces mechanics, electrics, electronics, physics, chemistry and biology and all the derivatives and combinations of them. The technological fusion and interaction of these sciences is what drives the frontiers of achievement forward. It is the continuing development, combination and application of these disciplines that give rise to new processes, materials, manufacturing systems, products and ways of storing, processing and communicating data. The fusion and interaction of knowledge and experience from different sciences is what sustains the 'Technological Revolution' (see Figure 12.1).

Kotler (1997) uses the term 'demand-technology life cycle' to help explain the relevance to businesses of technological advances. Products are produced and marketed to meet some basic underlying need of individuals. An individual product or group of products may be only one way of meeting this need, however, and indeed is likely to be only a temporary means of meeting this

Figure 12.1
Technological
fusion and
interaction

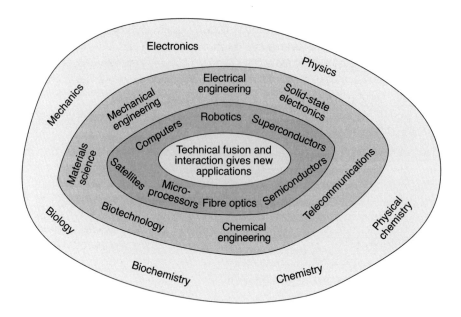

Figure 12.2
The demand-
technology life
cycle

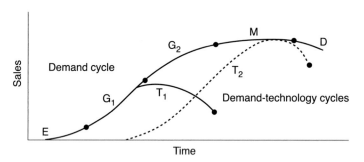

need. The way in which the need is met at any period is dependent on the level of technology prevailing at that time. Kotler cites the need of the human race for calculating power. The need has grown over the centuries with the growth of trade and the increasing complexity of life. This is depicted by the 'demand life cycle' in Figure 12.2, which runs through the stages of emergence (E), accelerating growth (G_1), decelerating growth (G_2), maturity (M) and decline (D).

Over the centuries, the need for calculating power has been met by finger-counting, abacuses, ready-reckoners, slide rules, mechanical adding machines (as big as an office desk), electrical adding machines (half the size of an office desk), electric calculators (half the size of a typewriter), battery-powered hand calculators and now pocket-sized computers. Kotler suggests that 'each new technology normally satisfies the need in a superior way'. Each technology has its own 'demand-technology life cycle', shown in Figure 12.2 as T_1 and T_2, which serves the demand cycle for a period of time. Each demand-technology life cycle will have a history of emergence, rapid growth, slower growth, maturity and decline, but over a shorter period than the more sustainable longer term demand cycle.

Business organizations should watch closely not only their immediate competitors, but also emerging technologies. Should the demand technology on which their product is based be undermined by a new demand technology, the consequences may be dire. If the emerging demand technology is not recognized until the new and superior products are on the market, there may be insufficient time and money available for the firm to develop its own products using the competing technology. Companies making mechanical typewriters, slide rules, gas lights and radio valves all had to adjust rapidly or go out of business. One way executives can scan the technological environment in order to spot changes and future trends is to study technology transfer.

The term 'technology transfer' can be used in a number of contexts. It is used to refer to the transfer of technology from research establishments and universities to commercial applications. It may also be used in the context of transfers from one country to another, usually from advanced to less advanced economies. Transfers also occur from one industry to another; technology then permeates through the international economy from research into commercial applications in industries that can sustain the initially high development and production costs. As the costs of the new technology fall, new applications become possible. Thus, the technology permeates through different industries and countries. Applications of technology first developed for the US space programme, for example, may now be found in many domestic and industrial situations. The National Aeronautics and Space Administration (NASA) established nine application centres in the United States to help in transferring the technology that was developed for space exploration to other applications (Kotler and Armstrong, 1996).

12.2   TECHNOLOGY AND SOCIETY

The rate at which technology is being enhanced and the rate at which it permeates through the world economy is of importance to business organizations. Product life cycles are typically becoming shorter. Expertise in a particular technology may no longer be a barrier preventing competitors from entering an industry. New entrants into an industry may benefit from the falling costs of technology or may be able to bypass the traditional technology by using some new and alternative technology.

The business manager should be interested in the degree to which technology influences his or her business. As we have learned, the environment is always changing and throwing up new challenges. Consider some historical antecedents: Bic produces a disposable plastic razor to challenge Wilkinson and Gillette; Imperial Typewriters is no longer in business, but Olivetti, once a typewriter manufacturer, now produces computers; the fountain pen is challenged by the ball-point, and in turn the ball-point is challenged by the fibre-tip. Failure to identify changes in technology soon enough may cause severe and sometimes terminal problems for companies. Although there can be sudden changes in technology that impact on an industry, it is the gradual changes that creep through the industry that may be harder to detect. Companies that anticipate, identify and successfully invest in emerging technologies should be able to develop a strategic advantage over the competition. As the demand-technology life cycle goes through the stage of rapid growth, they will grow with it. As growth slows and the cycle matures, competitors will find it increasingly hard to gain a foothold in the new and by now dominant technology.

Our lives are affected by the interaction between technological changes and the social, economic and political systems within which we live and work. Over the last half century the life of a mother has changed dramatically. With washing machines, dryers, dish washers, fridge freezers, and microwave cookers, modern textiles which are easier to wash and iron, convenience foods, and possibly the use of a car, the time devoted to household chores is much reduced. Partly as a result of these innovations, women are better educated and more likely to be in paid employment and thus contributing to an increased disposable income. Also flowing from these developments, shopping patterns change from daily shopping in small local shops, limited to what can be carried and with transport via the bus; to weekly shopping (perhaps even on a Sunday or in the middle of the night) using the car. The lives of school children also change with even the youngest being introduced to the computer. In 1999 the UK government announced a plan to link every school to the Internet. Business people now have a truly mobile office with a notebook computer and personal phone. They may be working from the car,

THINKING AROUND THE SUBJECT

The soap powder companies are popularly attributed with having invented modern marketing and have continuously been at the forefront of new sales and marketing techniques. But could their progress be undone by recent developments in technology? A South Korean company, Kyungwon Enterprise Company, has spent more than £2 billion developing a washing machine which does not use detergent to clean clothes.

According to the company, a device inserted into a washing machine is able to transform water into electrically charged liquid that cleans with the same results as a conventional synthetic detergent. Water is transformed inside the machine by forcing it through layers of special catalysts planted between electrodes. The system utilizes the natural tendency of water to return to a stable state and harnesses it for laundering, deodorizing and killing viruses. The system also promises to cut water consumption and to reduce the growing problem of water pollution by detergents. The developers of the system have applied for patents in over 60 countries. How are existing washing machine and detergent manufacturers likely to react? The washing machine manufacturer Hotpoint has certainly been monitoring developments closely and would doubtless seek a licence to use the technology, or develop an alternative technology not covered by patent. But what about the detergent manufacturers? Their market is unlikely to disappear overnight. The new system has still to be proven and even if it is shown to be effective, important segments for detergent could remain out of inertia or simply because the new technology does not cope with all tasks as well as traditional methods. The detergent companies may also embrace the new technology by developing ranges of complementary products, such as fragrant conditioners.

from home, or even from a client's office. We are experiencing the casualization of communications with people using personal phones, faxes, e-mail and SMS text messages expecting immediate responses, but of a less formal nature. Within the family, life can become more dysfunctional as individual members pursue their own lives and activities. With more TV channels and choice, so the greater need for additional TVs, at least one of which is likely to be linked to a games machine. Space will also need to be found for at least one computer. There will be more phones around the home and not just line extensions; additional numbers and personal phones will be the norm.

12.3   EXPENDITURE ON RESEARCH AND DEVELOPMENT

According to the Organization for Economic Co-operation and Development (OECD) the United Kingdom's expenditure on research and development (R&D) between 1981 and 1997 declined from 2.4 per cent of GDP to 1.87 per cent (Young, 1993; OECD, 2000). The United Kingdom's ranking against other major industrial nations (Group of Seven or G7 nations) has now slipped to fifth (Figure 12.3).

In real terms the United Kingdom's R&D expenditure declined in mechanical engineering, electronics, electrical engineering, motor vehicles and aerospace. Increases in expenditure were only recorded in chemicals, other manufactured products and non-manufactured products, thus reflecting the serious decline of UK manufacturing industry. The proportion of government expenditure within the total R&D expenditure is still falling. However, for some countries the

Figure 12.3
Gross domestic expenditure on R&D as a percentage of GDP
(*Source*: Based on OECD Observer, No. 183, August–September 1993, modified to include 1997 figures from OECD in Figures 2000 edition, **www.oecd.org/ publications/ebook**)

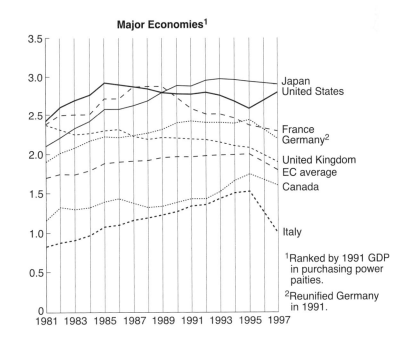

proportion of government R&D expenditure directed at defence remains high (Table 12.1), the United States, the United Kingdom and France being by far the biggest spenders with 54 per cent, 39.5 per cent and 24.8 per cent, respectively, of the governments R&D budget going to defence.

Research and development expenditure is often classified into three major types: basic, applied and experimental.

1   Basic or fundamental research is work undertaken primarily for the advancement of scientific knowledge without a specific application in view.

2   Applied research is work undertaken with either a general or specific application in mind.

3   Experimental development is the development of fundamental or applied research with a view to introduction of new, or the improvement of existing, materials, processes, products, devices and systems.

Classification is also often carried out on a sectoral basis, e.g. public or private, and by type of industry. The International Standard Industrial Classification Code (ISIC) is used. International comparisons of R&D expenditure should be used with caution. According to Young (1993) these difficulties in comparing statistics stem from:

■   Differences in the basic definitions of R&D and the boundaries between R&D and education, training, related scientific expenditure and administration costs.

■   Differences in counting numbers employed in R&D, e.g. definitions of full-time/part-time, directly or indirectly employed, qualifications and occupation.

■   Discrepancies in the sources and destination of funds, e.g. private and commercial organizations receive some public funds, but public bodies also receive some funding from private sources. This makes it difficult to calculate the proportion of R&D expenditure financed by governments as compared to that financed by the private sector. University expenditure is typically a mix of the two, for instance.

■   Difficulties in distinguishing the R&D element of large-scale defence programmes. According to Young the UK government has revised downwards the R&D expenditure in defence establishments.

■   Difficulties in assessing R&D funds flowing between countries, 'particularly between the components of multinational firms' (Young, 1993). The consolidated accounts of a multinational may show R&D expenditure, but in which country was it spent?

■   When to include expenditure on software development as R&D. Again according to Young (1993), in Canada 'software R&D is roughly a quarter of all industrial R&D and is spread across a wide range of industries'.

■   R&D expenditure undertaken by small firms is not usually recorded by government agencies (Lopez-Bassols, 1998).

In order to overcome these difficulties, economists at the OECD issue guidelines in the form of the *Frascati Manual* for use by government statisticians. This helps to

Table 12.1   Research and development[1], 1997 (Table 1) and patent applications

| | Gross Domestic Expenditure on R&D (GERD) | | | | Government budget appropriations for R&D | | Patent applications | | | |
| | % of GDP | % financed by | | Per capita at current USD[2] | % of GDP | of which Defence R&D % | Total in country | of which from abroad % | Applications abroad | Resident and abroad per 100 000 of total population |
		Government	Industry							
Canada	1.61[a]	31.9[a]	49.4[a]	380	0.37[c]	6.1[c]	53 648	93.7	92 681	317
France	2.24	40.2	50.3	476	0.99	24.8	107 413	87.5	183 814	337
Germany	2.32[a]	35.6[a]	61.7[a]	511	0.84	8.7	134 775	66.5	433 583	583
Italy	1.03[a]	51.1[a]	43.9[a]	213	0.59	2.6	79 094[a]	91.0[a]	85 874	149
Japan	2.91	18.1	74.0	715	0.61	4.8	415 698	16.0	380 510	578
UK	1.87	30.8	49.5	383	0.72	39.5	117 506	84.7	320 349	573
USA	2.77[a,b]	30.6[a,b]	65.7[a,b]	794[a,b]	0.89[a,c]	54.1[a,c]	230 336	48.1	1 583 862	638
G7	2.44	30.4	63.3	615	0.80	35.0				
EU-15	1.82	37.2	53.9	373	0.79	15.5				
OECD Total	2.21	31.3	62.4	453	0.72	30.9				

Notes:

Figures in italics are provisional.

1. Some national or OECD estimates.

2. Converted using Purchasing Power Parities; see note 1 on page 13.

a. 1998.

b. Excluding most or all capital expenditures.

c. Federal expenditure only.

Source: Based on OECD in figures 2000.

ensure that statistics are collected by each country on a similar basis, thereby aiding international comparison. The Frascati standards have now spread to most industrialized countries in the world, thus improving the reliability of comparable statistics. The manual is also updated regularly to take account of new issues, such as software R&D expenditure, for example. These internationally agreed definitions aid comparison between nations, although caution still needs to be exercised when using international statistics. The variations in the exchange rate, purchasing power of the currency in the domestic market and the reliability and comparability of the statistics all give grounds for caution.

The R&D figures do not make happy reading for UK industrialists and politicians. The figures for the United Kingdom's R&D expenditure in manufacturing are particularly bad with a decline in expenditure in almost every sector. The United Kingdom is well down the international league table on expenditure. Add to this the controversy surrounding cuts in academic research budgets affecting UK universities and the picture looks even worse. Research and development is the seed corn for the new technologies, processes, materials and products of the future. Failure in this area is likely to mean that UK companies are less competitive in the future.

Spending on R&D is not the only indicator, however, when looking for evidence of healthy innovative activity. The number of patents registered in a country is also a reflection of a healthy R&D culture and advanced economy. As might be expected Japan with 415 698 is ahead with the United States, 230 336, Germany, 134 775, and the United Kingdom, at 117 506 (OECD in Figures 2000). However, with multinationals conducting research in many countries and with multiple international registrations, it is becoming more difficult to track expenditure and patents by country. The OECD also collects data on the wider 'Investment in Knowledge' which includes public spending on education, and software development as well as the expenditure on R&D (Figure 12.4).

Having taken the broad macroview of technology thus far, the rest of this chapter looks more specifically at how technology impacts on a business and where it may be applied to improve business operations. The following areas of technology application will be discussed: product design, manufacturing and processing systems, storage and distribution, order and payment processing, materials handling, document handling, computerized information and communications, and office automation (see Figure 12.5).

12.4   PRODUCT DESIGN AND DEVELOPMENT

The design of a product is influenced by its components and materials, their price, and availability. Components and materials incorporating new technology may be more expensive than older components or traditional materials. They may also be in short supply. Using new components or materials may involve increased risks or delay the product launch because of more extensive testing. Products should be designed with a view to keeping material, manufacturing, handling and storage costs to a minimum. These issues should be considered at the outset of the

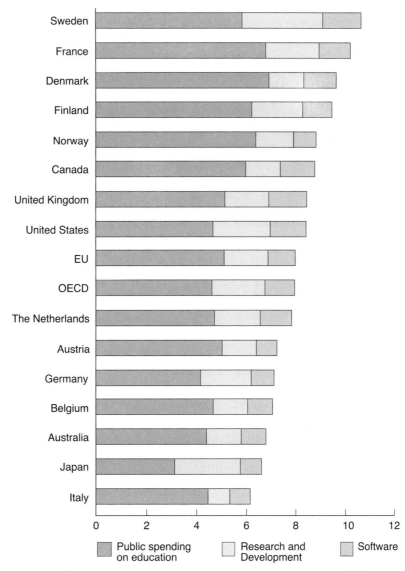

Figure 12.4
Investment in knowledge as a percentage of GDP for selected countries, 1995
(*Source*: Based on OECD in Figures 2000 Edition, **www.oecd.org/publications/ebook/**)

Note: The figures above exclude business training (typically 1 per cent of GDP) and some privately funded education and expenditure on market research.

design brief and not as an after-thought. Reducing product costs by 5 or 10 per cent can mean huge savings over the life of a product. In many industries computer-aided design (CAD) gives more flexibility and a speedier response to customer needs. As production methods may now give greater flexibility, it is possible to produce a wider variety of styles, colours and features based on a basic product. These planned variations should be designed in at the initial design stages, even though they may not be incorporated until much later.

It is argued that the life expectancy of products has generally tended to shorten as technology has advanced. The product life cycle (PLC) is a means of plotting

Figure 12.5
Impact of
technological
change on
company
operations

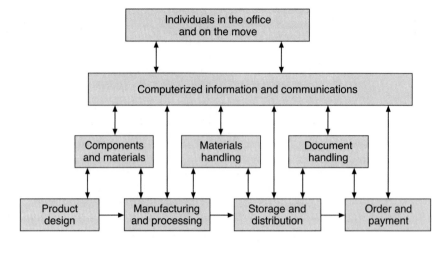

Figure 12.6
The product life
cycle

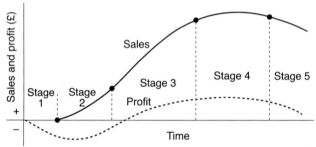

sales and profits over time (see Figure 12.6) in such a way that different stages in the life cycle can be identified and appropriate marketing strategies thus applied.

Five stages in the product life cycle can be identified:

1. *Product development prior to launch* At this point, sales are zero and development and investment costs are rising.

2. *Introduction of the product into the market* This means expensive launch costs and promotion. Profitable sales may take some time to develop.

3. *Growth stage* This is when the product is fully accepted into the market and healthy profits begin to materialize on the strength of increasing sales.

4. *Maturity* This refers to the period over which sales growth begins to slow and eventually stop. Profits may begin to decline as increasing competition puts pressure on prices and forces up promotional expenses to defend the market share.

5. *Decline* At this point sales begin to fall off and profits decline due to a lower volume of production.

Kotler (1997) makes a useful distinction between product category (say computers), product forms (e.g. Networked, desktop PC, laptop, notebook, and palm) and brands (individual product brands offered by particular manufacturers such as Dell, IBM and Apple). According to him, product categories tend to have

Figure 12.7
The new product development process

Idea generation → Evaluation and screening → Business analysis → Development → Testing → Commercializing

the longest life cycles and to stay in the mature stage for very long periods. They may begin to decline only with significant and fundamental changes in technology (as when typewriters come to be replaced by personal computers) or shifts in consumer preferences (away from smoking, for example). Product forms tend to show a more classical PLC, with each subsequent form showing a similar history to the previous one. For example, manual typewriters moved through the stages of introduction, growth and maturity, and entered decline as electronic typewriters were introduced. These then followed a similar history until they began to decline as personal computers were introduced. The old product category is now entering a decline stage as the new product category of personal computers has come well into the growth stage, and indeed into maturity. Individual brands follow the shortest PLC, as companies are constantly attempting to update their products to keep abreast of changes in technology, fashion, customer preferences and competitors' offerings. Rapid advances in technology may mean shortening PLCs in some industries. In consumer electronics, for example, advances in technology have allowed manufacturers to add more and more product features and to reduce prices as costs have fallen. Brands in this product category may have a life expectancy of only 18 months before they are withdrawn and replaced.

Managing the development of new products is a complex and risky business. While many textbooks will identify a linear process usually comprising about five stages, the reality involves a complex interaction between a number of forces. These external forces comprise technological developments, market demand, competitor activity, and possibly government influence. The internal organizational factors include management culture, R&D capabilities, engineering skills, production experience, management competence, access to finance and marketing ability.

The linear model of the new product development (NPD) process can be seen in Figure 12.7.

The process starts with *idea generation* which involves the search for new ideas. The next step is then *evaluation and screening* during which the ideas are assessed for potential. If the company has a short-term planning horizon and a conservative culture then revolutionary and innovative ideas may be dropped at this stage. As the company focuses on the short term and operates in its comfort zone it may reduce risks, but also it may be producing 'me too' products. In doing so, it may also miss innovative developments and technological shifts, and as a result jeopardize its long-term competitive position or even its own survival. The purpose of this stage is to reduce the number of ideas and to focus on further development of those with potential. Before engaging in expensive research and development an initial *business analysis* should be undertaken to assess the market potential of new ideas. For products aimed at an existing well-defined market, estimating total market potential should be reasonably straightforward. But what will be the share taken by the new product? How will consumers take to the new product? Will distributors like the product? How will competitors react? Will competitors launch a similar product? What price to charge? Is it likely to cost more, the same, or less, to produce? These are all questions that need to be considered when calculating the potential sales and profit. For innovative products that are new to the world or launched into emerging markets the calculations are more difficult.

For those products remaining the next stage is *development*. This is where the expenses, mainly associated with R&D, and/or engineering, are heaviest. Can the idea and new technology be developed into a workable product which can be produced in volume, at a reasonable cost, and which is practicable for the consumer. The *testing* stage may involve a number of activities. Testing the functional capabilities of the product may include technical tests, reliability tests, and performance tests. Market testing involves testing consumers' and dealers' attitudes to the product. The final decision as to whether to launch the product is made at this stage.

Commercializing is the last stage and involves the highest expenditure as the product is prepared for manufacture and launch into the market. Decisions on expected sales, what volume to manufacture, what to contract out and what to manufacture in house, are all critical. Product decisions such as the final form of the product, the number of variants to offer, features, size, colours, branding, and packaging all have to be made, as have decisions on pricing and dealer margins. Promotional strategies have to be finalized and the timing and logistics of the launch planned.

These stages are often presented as sequential linear activities with one stage being completed before the next commences. In reality not all the new product ideas come together and start the process at the same time. Ideas are generated at odd times and come from a wide variety of sources. The company needs to capture and evaluate these as and when they arise. From here on the company will have a number of products at different stages in the process at any one time. The development of some may be speeded up or slowed down as priorities are reassessed. Neither is the process completed in discrete stages as described above. Some new ideas may come from the company's blue-sky (speculative) research, so a certain amount of 'development' will have been done before the 'evaluation and screening' stage. 'Testing' is likely to begin before the 'development' stage is finished, and planning for 'commercialization' will commence before 'testing' is finished. The important point to note is that there should be formal reviews and reappraisal at regular intervals. Transition between the stages identified in the NPD process are appropriate times for such reviews.

There are, of course, internal barriers to the adoption of new technology. Individuals may be resistant to change in the organizational setting. They may have a fear of new technology itself, or for their job, or the disruption that change may bring. Change may disturb existing management structures, departmental power bases, individual authority, and working relationships.

12.5   FORECASTING NEW TECHNOLOGIES

Over the longer term one of the difficulties is forecasting technological developments. This is key for the health of a nation's economy. Those nations and companies who are first to develop a technological lead will grow, as the technology is embedded in new industries and products. Early developments in biotechnology in the United States and the United Kingdom, for example, in the mid 1980s have developed into a billion dollar global industry impacting on agriculture, pharmaceuticals, health and chemicals. Developments in the software industry transformed Silicon Valley in California in the 1980s and 1990s, just as the car industry transformed Detroit in the 1950s. The interaction between a favourable political and social climate, higher education and research, and entrepreneurial individuals, may transform a whole economy and have a global impact. For this reason governments are supporting partnerships between industry and academia in an attempt to predict future trends and developments.

The UK government has introduced the Foresight programme which was first announced in the 1993 White Paper 'Realizing our Potential'.

> The Foresight Programme brings together industry, academia, and Government to consider how the UK can take advantage of opportunities to promote wealth creation and enhance our quality of life.

There are 16 panels looking into different industrial sectors. The first findings were published in 1995 and it is claimed that government departments and research councils are 'reflecting Foresight findings in their development of policies and science, engineering, and technology spending decisions'. According to Pilat (1998) this approach is used throughout the OECD countries to help with policy design. Pilat suggests that there are 'a limited number of technologies which will occupy centre-stage'. In the future these are:

- Information and communication technologies, particularly high density components and new software.

- Health and science technologies, including biotechnology, genomics, combinatorial chemistry.

- Manufacturing technologies such as robotics, micro- and nanoscale fabrication.

- Advanced materials with characteristics including high temperature resistance, light weight and bio-compatible.

- Biotechnology applications facilitating clean industrial products and processes, and the recycling of waste and old products.

- Energy efficiency technologies.

- Interdisciplinary activities such as photonics, bionics and bioelectronics.

The successful countries and companies are already encouraging research into these areas, and targeting research funding.

12.6 MANUFACTURING AND PROCESSING

Technology impacts on manufacturing and processing systems, particularly in computerized numerical control (CNC) machine tools, computer-aided manufacturing

(CAM), integrated manufacturing (IMS) and just-in-time (JIT) systems. With CNC, the machine tool is directly linked to a microprocessor so that the instructions can be created and stored. This gives greater reliability and quicker changeover times. Previously, the machine would have been controlled by punch cards or cassette tapes. CAM involves linking computers to a number of machine tools and assembly robots that are interfaced with computer-controlled material handling systems. Sections of the manufacturing process are thus integrated into the same production control system. CAD/CAM (computer-aided design/computer-aided manufacturing) is where parts designed on the computer can be programmed directly into the machine tool via the same computer system. These systems can save hundreds of hours over previous methods involving the separate activities of design, building models and prototypes and then programming separate machines for production.

Integrated manufacturing systems (IMS) enable a number of CAM subsystems to be integrated together within a larger computer controlled system. A number of manufacturers are attempting to integrate the total manufacturing process. This, however, is very difficult to do in practice, as plant and equipment are often of different ages, were designed by different companies and use different control systems. While it is possible to design a total IMS from scratch, the investment costs are likely to be prohibitive for most companies.

Just-in-time systems are designed to limit stockholding and handling costs. A supplier is expected to deliver components to the right delivery bay, at a specific day and time. There may be heavy penalties for failing to deliver on time. Components can then be moved directly onto the production floor ready for use on the line. This requires close co-operation between the manufacturer and supplier and usually is made possible only by the use of computerized information systems and data links.

These developments in technology impact on small companies and large, and on traditional industries such as textiles and shoes as well as on new ones. Generally speaking, modern manufacturing systems allow production lines to be run with greater flexibility and higher quality, making it easier to produce product variations and allowing a speedier change-over between products thus minimizing down-time.

Such developments in production technology present companies with a number of opportunities for gaining a competitive advantage. Firstly, developments in these areas are likely to contribute to a reduction in costs. Aiming to be a low-cost manufacturer should help in achieving a higher return on investment by allowing a higher margin and/or a higher volume of sales at lower prices. Secondly, modern manufacturing techniques allow for greater flexibility in production; thus, a wider variety of product variations may be produced without incurring onerous cost penalties. Thirdly, lead times between orders and delivery can be improved. Finally, it is possible to ensure that the quality of the products is more consistent and of a higher standard. Recent advances in integrated manufacturing systems using computer-controlled industrial robots has meant that some car makers, for example, can produce totally different models on the same production line. Thus, low-volume/high-value cars can be produced more cheaply by utilizing an automated line previously set up for the high-volume output of another model. The company can take a higher profit margin or pass on lower prices to its customer, or a combination of both.

STORAGE AND DISTRIBUTION

The storage and distribution of goods has also benefited from advances in technology. In particular, the increased capacity and reliability of computerized data-processing and storage combined with improved data transmission and computer-controlled physical handling systems have led to reductions in costs and improvements in service. It is now possible to hold less stock at all stages in the distribution chain for a given product variety. From the retailer's perspective they can reduce the amount of stock on the sales floor and in the back room.

These developments would not have been possible, however, without a great deal of co-operation and the integration of other technologies. The systems developed depend on each individual product having a unique code number and the equipment at the point of sale being able to read that number. Manufacturers, retailers and other interested parties co-operated under the auspices of the Article Number Association (ANA) to devise a numbering system, to allocate numbers and set standards for the use of what have become known as 'barcodes'. 'The aim of the ANA is to improve inter-company logistics, increase efficiency of trade and add value to the companies involved and their customers' (ANA, 1998). Each product item is allocated a unique number, so that each product variation by size and colour can be identified by the manufacturer. In the words of the Article Number Association, a 430 g can of peas, for example, has a different number from a 300 g can. A tin of blue paint has a different number from the same size can of red paint. According to the ANA, nearly 100 per cent of grocery products now carry a barcode on the packaging, and over 50 per cent of general merchandise. Membership of the ANA now totals over 7000 firms, and the association has recently merged with the Electronic Commerce Association to form the Association of Standards and Practices in Electronic Trade which trades under the name of e-Centre UK.

At first, these barcodes were read by light pens and were only suitable for outlets with a medium volume of daily sales such as clothing retailers. Very high-volume outlets such as supermarkets had to wait for the development of the laser scanner, which can now be seen in most modern grocery stores in the United Kingdom. The product is simply passed over the scanner at the checkout so that the computerized till can read the barcode. It is these systems that provide itemized till receipts.

For a national clothing retailer, the improved service and reduction in costs are achieved by linking computerized tills to a central computer and stock control system which connects all stores and warehouses (Figure 12.8). In many cases large suppliers are linked directly into the system. Items purchased are read with a laser scanner at the till, which in addition to logging the price identifies the item. At the end of the day's trading, or periodically during the day, the central computer checks on the sales through each till. Replacement orders can then be placed with

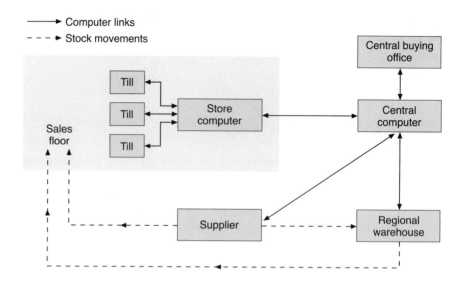

Figure 12.8

Systems linking the retail store, warehouse and head office

the nearest warehouse by the computer, and if necessary the warehouse stock will be replenished by calling off further orders from the supplier. In the warehouse, orders can be processed overnight or the next day and delivered the following evening or early the next morning. On delivery to the store, most of the items will be placed directly onto the rack on the sales floor, thus considerably reducing the need for back-room storage. This allows for a greater range of items to be stocked in a given floor space, as the stock on the rack for each item is reduced. The space previously given over to back-room storage (up to a third of the total space in a high street store) can now be opened up as part of the sales floor. Thus, the total selling space is increased, sales turnover per square metre is increased and the range of items carried is increased. There is less overstocking, fewer out-of-stock situations and less shrinkage. Immediate price changes can be introduced and there is generally tighter price control. The tighter financial control, higher sales turnover and increased profits may help pay for the investment in computers, new out-of-town warehousing, transport and physical handling systems. The systems that are dependent on these computerized tills are known as EPOS (electronic point of sale) and are discussed later in the chapter.

Other benefits of these systems are obtained from the sales information collected and stored by computer. Sales of individual product items can be analysed. For fast-moving fashion items, this is vital information. In the past, a whole season's estimated sales had to be ordered in advance from the supplier – a risky business in the fashion world. Now initial orders from the supplier may be kept relatively low. Fast-selling lines can be identified using the computerized information and projections of sales made; further orders can then be placed with the supplier. This may be based on the first few days of a line being placed on sale. The whole process of business is thus speeded up. The links between store, warehouse, buying office and supplier become much more dynamic. Stockholding by the individual store may be as low as two days' sales, compared with a week in the late 1970s. Barcode scanning systems are also used throughout the distribution

Figure 12.9
Article numbering
for traded units
(*Source*: Used with
permission of the Articel
Number Association)

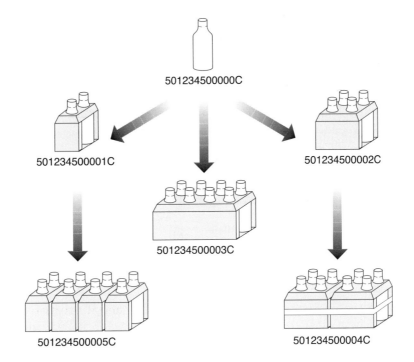

chain. Outer cases are referred to as 'traded units' and can include pallets. The ANA co-ordinates the allocation of numbers that are used for traded units as well as consumer units. These barcodes for the 'traded units' are also machine-readable, so the outer case can be controlled more effectively at every stage in the distribution channel, from the manufacturer to the retailer or customer. According to the ANA, every traded unit which differs by the nature or quantity of its contents must have a different number (Figure 12.9).

As companies come to rely very heavily on these systems, any problems in the system can have an adverse effect on logistical and financial operations. Hamley's, the famous London toy store, reported a fall in profits which was said to be due to problems with information systems, which prevented stores from managing their stock at the optimal level. Retail groups acquiring competitor companies now face a much more difficult task in integrating the newly acquired stores. Previously the take-over required rebranding with the new company's logo and house style, selling off old stock and replacement with new, and refurbishment of some stores. Now all tills and local computer systems are likely to need replacing; the newly acquired stores networked into the group computer, information, and communication systems; and staff trained in the new systems.

12.8   ORDER AND PAYMENT PROCESSING

This chapter continues to explore specific methods by which technology has been used to improve the efficiency and effectiveness of transactions within a supply

Table 12.2   Benefits of EPOS

Improved management information
   Store-by-store comparison of sale
   Direct product profitability analysis
   Sales-promotional effectiveness

Operational efficiency
   Better stock control
   Quicker stocktaking
   Reduced shrinkage
   No item pricing
   Faster price changes

Improved customer service
   Faster checkout throughput
   Fewer queues
   Itemized sales receipts
   Reduced operator error

Source: Adapted from Fletcher, 1995, p. 367.

chain. In particular, organizations must aim to cut the cost of stockholding, yet still be able to respond efficiently and effectively to customers' requests. In a previous section we considered the impact of computer systems and data links on storage and distribution. The combination of barcodes, laser scanners, computerized tills, data links and powerful computers with remote terminals has much improved the control of stock. Systems are constantly being improved, as is the reliability and speed with which the systems operate. These systems are also expensive to install and run. However, as the technology improves and competition increases between suppliers of systems, we can expect the costs to come down.

Electronic point of sale (EPOS) systems mean that each till will total the goods purchased by the individual and record the transaction in the normal way. In addition to the daily cash analysis, however, EPOS systems may provide stock reports and an analysis of sales figures, and improve control over each till and the staff using it. The retailer no longer has to price each individual item, as the price only needs to be displayed on the shelf or the rack. This saves labour and allows for easier price changes. The customer benefits from itemized till receipts, a faster checkout, greater choice and fewer items out of stock (Table 12.2).

Electronic funds transfer at point of sale (EFTPOS) has all the benefits of EPOS plus electronic funds transfer. This means that the computerized till is now fitted with a card reader, and data links into the banking system can transfer funds electronically. The customer's credit card such as Mastercard and Visa, or debit card such as Switch and Delta, is presented in the normal way, the cashier swipes this through the card reader, the till prints out the slip for signature and the customer retains the top copy. The customer's credit-card company or current account (depending on the card used) is debited with the sale and the retailer's account is credited. The convenience for customers and retailers is enhanced, the accuracy of transactions is increased, cash handling is reduced and the costs of

Table 12.3   Benefits of EFTPOS

Benefits to retailers
- Reduced paperwork
- Single system for all cards
- Reduction in volume and cost of cash handling
- Reduced security risk
- Reduction in fraud
- Faster checkout time
- Faster payment into retailer's account

Benefits to customers
- Less need to carry large amounts of cash
- More choice in methods of payment
- No £50 limit as with cheques
- Itemized receipts and statements easy to check
- Faster checkout time

Source: Adapted from Fletcher, 1995.

processing the sale are also significantly reduced (Table 12.3). These systems have now been applied to many types of retailing operations, including, for example, supermarkets, DIY superstores, clothing retailers, petrol stations, book shops and hotels. Changes are also impacting on business-to-business transactions in a similar way with electronic data interchange (EDI) and the development of 'extranets' (restricted access computer networks).

In business-to-business transactions the speed at which orders can be captured and processed by a company's systems denotes the speed at which orders and invoices can be dispatched and payment collected. Closely associated and inseparable from the system is the document handling, which includes orders, manufacturing dockets, picking notes, dispatch/delivery notes, invoices and statements. Advances in technology will continue to influence all of these aspects of the business.

Golden Wonder Crisps, a UK manufacturer of crisps and snacks, provides an example of how business-to-business transactions have been transformed in the 1990s. The van sales representative takes an order from the local shop and drops off the goods. The order is entered in the van sales representative's portable computer, which will then print out a delivery note to leave with the buyer. In the evening the sales representative connects the portable computer through to the head office mainframe computer via the telephone line. The mainframe draws out the sales data and passes back any messages. Next day the invoice is raised by the head office computer and posted so as to arrive the third day after delivery.

When these systems were first developed in the early 1980s, it would take up to 20 minutes to download this data. Today it takes only a few minutes with new portable computers, and the data transmission is much more of a two-way process. It is possible for the mainframe to input into the representative's portable the sales journey cycles for the coming weeks, relevant customer information, updates on products and prices, notes on special promotional deals and messages from the manager.

How do you sell highly specialized electronics components that range from a simple bag of clips through to sophisticated scanning equipment? Few retailers would have the capacity to handle such a big product range efficiently and effectively. But the UK-based company RS Components has used advanced order handling techniques to become the United Kingdom's largest distributor of electronic and electrical components. Its products are sold via a catalogue to industrial, educational, research and public sector organizations. Its particular unique selling proposition is the range of products stocked and the speed of delivery. This is how it works. Regular customers have their own customer number. The customer phones RS and the call should be answered instantaneously. With 20 phone lines and a computer-controlled exchange which places the call to one of the telesales staff, the call should not ring more than three times. The customer gives a customer number, order number, part numbers of products ordered and quantity ordered – that is all. This information is typed directly into the computer by the telesales person. The total call should not take more than a few seconds. The computerized telephone system handles 7500 calls per day. The computer prints out the invoice/order-picking document. The order-picking document starts its run through a computerized warehouse with its bin. A barcode is attached to the front of the bin that directs it along a conveyor system only to those bays holding stock for that order. The order is packed and shipped the same day, and the invoice, folded and placed in an envelope by document-handling equipment, is also posted the same day. Express delivery companies are used to ensure next-day delivery. The speed and efficiency of a system such as this, which can handle 10 000 separate orders per day with same-day despatch of goods and invoices is staggering. The service has now been extended to take orders through the Internet.

This system is now being used for the direct salesforce serving the larger retailers and cash-and-carries. Orders received one day are downloaded to the mainframe the same evening. Overnight or the next day (day 2), the mainframe raises the picking and despatch notes. On day 3 the order is despatched, and the invoice is printed and posted. In the late 1970s this whole process would have taken between seven and ten days.

12.9   ELECTRONIC BUSINESS

The huge volume of transactions taking place daily between businesses in modern economies has prompted a number of companies to encourage the development and use of electronic transactions. The ANA defines Electronic Data Interchange (EDI) as 'the computer to computer exchange of structured data, sent in a form that allows for automatic processing, with no manual interaction' (ANA, 1998). A number of systems are now in place. Previously the limitations of telecommunica-

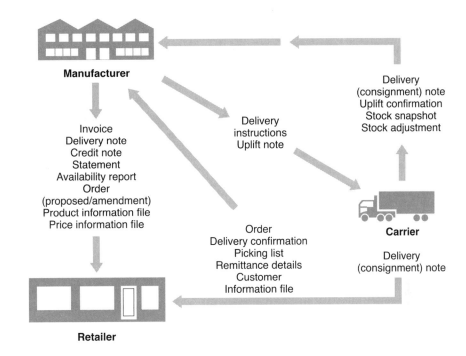

Figure 12.10
Electronic data transmission of trading documents

Manufacturer

Delivery
(consignment) note
Uplift confirmation
Stock snapshot
Stock adjustment

Delivery
instructions
Uplift note

Invoice
Delivery note
Credit note
Statement
Availability report
Order
(proposed/amendment)
Product information file
Price information file

Carrier

Order
Delivery confirmation
Picking list
Remittance details
Customer
Information file

Delivery
(consignment) note

Retailer

tions, the problems of incompatible computers and their software, and the lack of legal status for electronic documents prevented business-to-business communication via computers and electronic mail. These technical and legal problems are now behind us, and the ANA, along with the support of a number of leading organizations, has set standards for and promoted the use of electronic communication. TRADACOMS (Trading Data Communications) is the term used to cover the standards developed by the ANA.

Standards are set at two levels. Firstly, common standards are applied to all the paper documents in terms of layout, which ensure clarity and improved efficiency. Secondly, the way in which these paper documents are configured electronically into computerized documents is standardized. This allows EDI, which means that data can be transmitted directly between one company's computer system and another's for automatic processing. This computer-to-computer communication improves speed, accuracy and efficiency of document transmission between manufacturers and their customers and the carriers (Figure 12.10). The benefits are fewer pricing errors, reduced costs, lower stock holdings, and reduced working capital (ANA, 1998). Documents and data that can be transmitted directly from computer to computer include orders, packing instructions, invoices, credit notes, delivery notes, statements, general text, availability reports, remittance advice, stock adjustments, product information, prices and customer details.

Major computer and telecommunication companies are involved in providing the system interchange services. These allow direct computer-to-computer communications (even between different hardware and software) via the telecommunications system. TRADANET is one such system (Figure 12.11). Companies can transmit or collect data from this electronic mailbox at any time. Transmissions

Figure 12.11
How TRADANET
works

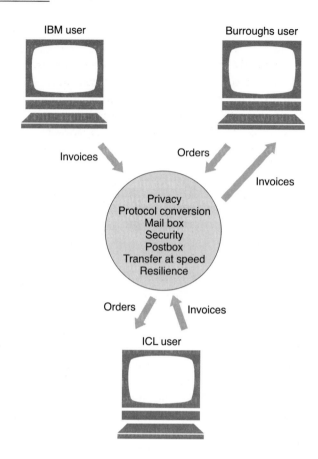

to any number of receivers need only be input into the system once, leaving the TRADANET service to route and distribute the data quickly and in security to each recipient's electronic mail box.

There are a number of such systems operating in the United Kingdom and throughout Europe and the rest of the world. In addition to the well-established TRADACOMS standard and the TRADANET network, which provide a general service, there is ODETTE (Organization for Data Exchange by Teletransmissions in Europe), which provides a European service. Various systems have been designed to serve specific industries such as motor manufacturing, pharmaceuticals, electronics and chemicals

Electronic data interchange is a closed commercial system for business-to-business transactions, which is controlled by the ANA and member companies. In many industries it has been very successful over the last 18 years. Ferne (1997) cites the findings of the OECD's Sacher Report that provides some examples of electronic commerce via EDI. Examples include banks with 70 per cent of transactions automated, a US retailer with 100 per cent of transactions with suppliers automated amounting to over $10 billion, a European car manufacturer with electronic links to 800 suppliers and electronic transactions of $7 billion etc.

Developments in these areas will influence manufacturing, processing, distribution, sales and order payment systems. The examples already discussed illustrate some of the links between computer systems used for processing and storing data and those used for communicating within and between different sites via telecommunications. The power of computers continues to increase and their size and price continues to reduce. Developments in satellites, optic fibre cable, exchanges and the miniaturizing of electronic components have given us satellite television, fax machines, the mobile phone and the notebook computer. Telecommunication networks have had to be increased in capacity to deal with huge volumes of electronic data generated by computers and transmission of electronic information via EDI and the Internet.

Electronic commerce is now developing very fast over the Internet. The Internet or World Wide Web (WWW) differs from EDI in that it is an open system that anyone can log-on to via a personal computer and a modem to link the computer to the telephone network. No one person, organization or government controls or owns the WWW. It developed as a means of transferring large volumes of information between academic and government research centres in the United States. Soon people were sending messages via electronic-mail (e-mail). More universities hooked up, commercial companies became involved, as did the telecommunication giants. As the personal computer developed so did the software, netware, browsers, search engines, etc., to interface between the user and the Internet. Messages and information are relayed quickly via servers and hubs to their final destination.

Initially the system was used by technical experts to send data, and text messages followed subsequently. Commercial companies began to post web pages on the Internet so those interested could browse through the information. Soon websites were developed which provided more information and eventually led to the development of interactive sites. With the development of protocols for encoding financial and other sensitive information the Internet can now be used to purchase services and products using a credit card. Latest developments mean that the screen can be integrated with a telephone call so that the web page can be viewed at the same time as using the phone to talk to the telesales operator. The system is now proving popular with business-to-business users and individual consumers. It is borderless and cheap to use, access being via the price of a local phone call.

The number of Internet hosts within an economy provides an indication of the speed of adoption. Figure 12.12 produced by the OECD shows the number of Internet hosts relative to the population. Although in the United Kingdom we may think of ourselves as an advanced economy, particularly with regard to computing and the Internet, we only meet the OECD average for the number of sites.

Such a deregulated system operating across international boundaries poses new challenges as it develops from an information service, to a promotional tool, and finally a sales and distribution channel facilitating transactions. Concerns have been expressed in four areas: confidentiality of individual information, consumer protection for those purchasing goods, under which legal system does the transaction take place, and concern over the difficulty of governments collecting sales taxes.

The OECD Sacher Report (Ferne, 1997) identified three priority areas for governments. The first is for governments to actively support the development of

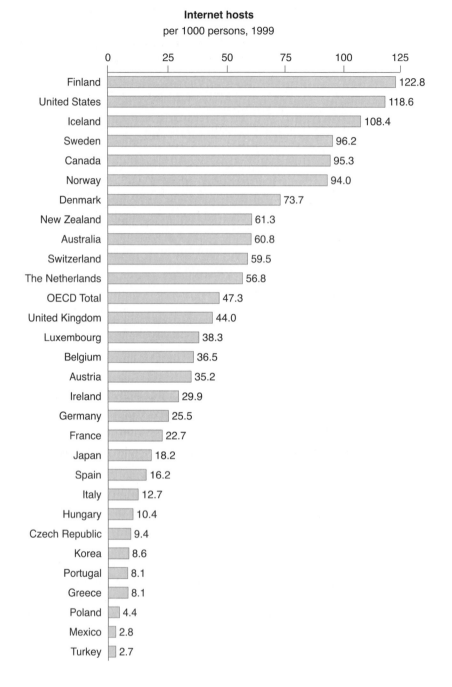

Internet hosts
per 1000 persons, 1999

Finland	122.8
United States	118.6
Iceland	108.4
Sweden	96.2
Canada	95.3
Norway	94.0
Denmark	73.7
New Zealand	61.3
Australia	60.8
Switzerland	59.5
The Netherlands	56.8
OECD Total	47.3
United Kingdom	44.0
Luxembourg	38.3
Belgium	36.5
Austria	35.2
Ireland	29.9
Germany	25.5
France	22.7
Japan	18.2
Spain	16.2
Italy	12.7
Hungary	10.4
Czech Republic	9.4
Korea	8.6
Portugal	8.1
Greece	8.1
Poland	4.4
Mexico	2.8
Turkey	2.7

electronic commerce by encouraging the development of the infrastructure. Governments have traditionally controlled telecommunications and television industries by either direct ownership or licensing. Technologies in computing, telecommunications, data networks and television are now converging rapidly. The report recommends that governments should encourage this by modifying regulatory regimes where necessary and by working to commonly agreed international protocols.

The second recommendation, according to Ferne, is that all governments should 'raise the visibility of electronic commerce and promote new partnerships with the private sector in order to co-ordinate technical, economic and political choices'. It is suggested that governments may seek to appoint a chief information officer to co-ordinate these activities.

The third recommendation is that governments themselves should acquire the skills to participate in the electronic information age. Regulatory issues need to be dealt with urgently and as they arise. Legal issues surrounding the 'definitions, practices and structures' of electronic commerce are now being addressed. International protocols need to be further developed for dealing with 'consumer protection to fraud and crime prevention and comprising intellectual property, electronic identity, definition of residence, liability, auditing, and the control, unauthorized use and protection of databases'. The issue of taxation is also of concern, particularly for taxes based on sales. Sales taxes are often refunded to exporters at despatch, but reapplied on receipt in the country of importation. These issues have not been fully resolved for Internet transactions.

E-business embraces many aspects of business that are moving closer together and which require integration. Terminology is constantly changing as the technology and concepts develop and managers and academics from differing functions interact. It is helpful to make a distinction between e-business and e-commerce. e-business may be defined as:

> ... the ability to integrate local and wide area networks through the use of Internet protocols to effectively remove the barriers between businesses, their customers and their suppliers in global markets. (National Computing Centre, 2001)

This is a broader definition than that usually attributed to the narrower function of e-commerce which has been defined as;

> ... transactions of goods or services for which payment occurs over the Internet or other wide area networks. (Chaffey et al. 1999)

Intranet systems are private internal systems (as opposed to open and public systems) constructed using Internet and Web technology. They are internal to an organization and can only be accessed and used with permission and passwords. These systems provide a similar function to the older EDI systems, but are more flexible and user friendly. A company's Intranet system can link together an organization that is geographically dispersed and facilitate links between an organization and its business partners such as suppliers and distributors. Such a system is often described as an 'extranet'.

12.10   SUPPLY CHAIN AND CHANNEL MANAGEMENT

A number of writers, consultants and software suppliers see the new technology simply as a new and alternative channel to market. E-commerce is seen as a low-cost and yet widespread channel with unlimited potential penetration. While there have been some new headline grabbing companies set up solely as e-commerce enterprises (the dot.com start-ups) the reality for most is a much more complex scenario.

Friedman and Goodrich (1998) published research by Oxford Associates into the transaction cost of differing channels for a US high-technology company which showed the cost of sales as follows; direct sales at $500, distributor sales at $246, telesales at $27 and e-commerce at $4.50. They argue that sales, marketing and administrative costs account for a substantial element in any organization. The research undertaken by Oxford Associates in a number of industries suggests that 'most companies achieve a 20 to 40 percent reduction in transaction costs when selling through distributors and partners, 40 to 45 percent when selling through call centres, and over 50 percent when selling over the Internet'. However, they warn against following a cost reduction strategy. They suggest 'begin with customer buyer behaviour, not cost objectives'. Customer preferences are what matter and these are not necessarily linked to customer size or order size. Some customers, both business and personal, call for low-involvement, low-cost transactional purchases. Others may wish for a more personal, high service level, and a longer term relationship or partnership. If customers are knowledgeable about costs and service levels then the choice is theirs. Friedman and Goodrich argue that the organization's channels should 'align with customers' buying preferences and behaviour.' However, low-cost channels such as call centres and Internet do provide new opportunities to reach small- and medium-sized customers direct who were previously uneconomic to service via a field salesforce.

E-procurement by businesses has become established and early adopters claim improved supply chain management and 50 per cent savings on purchasing costs (Whittle, 2001a). Research by Dynamic Markets Ltd reported in Whittle suggests that 76 per cent of respondents felt it was the way forward, 72 per cent thought it would bring significant benefits and 68 per cent thought that companies that do not use it will lose out.

Nestlé are not alone in building Intranet systems to link all parts of the organization together and to link the organization to its suppliers, service providers, distributors and retailers. Other companies with advanced systems include British American Tobacco with markets in 180 countries and manufacturing in 50, with over 320 brands, and Tesco, the UK grocery market leader which has set up a Trading and Information Exchange (TIF) to serve its suppliers. Over 600 suppliers use it most days, about 70 per cent of the total. The company expect to save £100 million in its first three years of operation (Gann, 2000).

Other writers, Whittle (2001c), Byrne (2000), Crockett (2000), for example, suggest that many companies are not going far enough and should consider, reengineering their whole business by integrating all the business processes into an Internet infrastructure. Linking Web enabled customized ordering to JIT manufacturing, with links back to component suppliers seems to be the ideal way to speed up business processes, improve customer satisfaction and reduce costs. Transparency of short-term forecasting, product availability, orders received, order status, shipments and other data means that the business partners from suppliers to distributors can reduce costs and improve service levels. From Dell (computers) to

Nestlé, the Swiss food giant, is reported to have budgeted an expenditure of $1.8 billion over the three years 2000–03 on Internet systems and applications. The company employs 230 000 people in 509 factories and 83 countries and produces 8000 products. The company intends to review all operations in the supply chain and 'use the Web to streamline purchasing' and 'tie together its disparate operations'. Nestlé buyers in different countries/divisions now help each other out by exchanging information over the group's Intranet. Group purchasing is helping to cut costs by an average of 10 per cent. In the United States small retailers are already able to order online and the intention is to substantially reduce the 100 000 phoned and faxed orders received each year, thus reducing order-processing costs. Larger customers such as the supermarket multiples are already linked electronically and the partners exchange sales reports and demand forecasts daily in addition to order processing and tracking. This has helped cut inventory by 15 per cent. Could Nestlé ever hope to sell its products direct to the end consumer? The company is not interested in retailing its generally low-value products direct to consumers. Instead the Web will be used as a marketing tool and will take an increasing share of the traditional advertising budget of $1.2 billion.

Source: Echilkson and Weintraub, 2000.

Pillsbury (food) to Herman Miller (furniture) and Cemex (cement), many differing companies are discovering the benefits of business process integration.

12.11 ELECTRONIC RETAIL

Earlier, e-business was distinguished from e-commerce and it was noted that definitions of e-commerce can differ between individuals and organizations. It is worth considering a few of the many definitions of e-commerce. Kalakota and Whinston (1997) describe e-commerce as 'the capability of buying and selling products on the Internet and other online services'. Similarly, Chaffey *et al.* (1999), define e-commerce as 'transactions of goods or services for which payment occurs over the Internet or other wide area networks'. The definition adopted by Treese and Stewart (1998) takes a more strategic and managerial perspective: 'Top line: the ability to reach new customers and create more intimate relationships with all customers. Bottom line: drastic cost reductions for distribution and customer service can he made.' It is clear from these definitions that e-commerce has opportunities in terms of improving the efficiency and effectiveness of the organization, but also a more strategic and competitive aspect: the need to attract customers, fulfil their expectations with good customer service and continue that relationship with them.

Recent texts on e-commerce (e.g. Kalakota and Whinston, 1997; Turban *et al.*, 2000) have suggested that using the Internet for conducting business activities generally offers the following benefits:

- Services of the company can be extended to add value for the customer.
- Shopper profiles can be established and exploited to develop better marketing and business strategies.
- New technology can be integrated with existing sales and inventory infrastructure, such as payment and distribution systems.
- Cross-selling of products can be generated via advertising and promotional activities.
- Sales can be safeguarded by identifying alternatives when a requested item is unavailable or would require time to deliver.
- Customers can be targeted with promotions based on the customers' individual interests and preferences.
- Red tape and administration can be reduced when systems are established.
- Efficiency can be increased in the company's operations.
- Retailers can be linked with other branches/suppliers thus improving the supply chain and reducing the amount of time to process transactions.

There are some limitations to e-commerce that can be summarized as follows:

- Systems often require high capital outlay, and there may be a slow return on investment.
- Many 'pure' e-commerce companies have failed in their first year.
- Perceived security risks regarding sensitive data have to be overcome, such as credit-card numbers.
- Compatibility within the technological architecture can be a limitation.
- Technological delays and failures continue to pose a risk.
- A poor online storefront can be a deterrent for potential customers.

Many of these limitations have been experienced by companies, particularly those 'dot.com' companies which do not have established 'high street' business operations. The most notable of these has been the much publicized demise of boo.com (Pitcher, 2000). The challenges of e-commerce differ for different business sectors, and we now look at some examples from services and business-to-consumer (B2C) products.

12.11.1   Services

The service sector has been at the leading edge of developments in electronic commerce, helped by the fact that there is often very little, if any tangible content which must be physically delivered to the customer. Travel-related services and financial services have seen major developments in electronic commerce. According to Forrester Research (in Flood, 2001), Internet airline ticket sales topped $7 billion in 2000 and US online hotel bookings were over $2 billion. Although research estimates and forecast sales vary widely most surveys agree that travel is the largest e-commerce sector.

The importance of e-commerce to the hotel industry is identified by Terry Macalister (2000) who reports that 'Bass, the brewer and world's second largest hotel operator, ... predicted it would hit its $1bn (£630m) annual target for Internet room booking revenues within four years'. The group owns Holiday Inns, Inter-Continental, Crown Plaza Hotels, Southern Pacific Hotels, and Bristol Hotels and Resorts, which amounts to 2800 hotels and 450000 rooms. Internet bookings are already running at $144 million per year equivalent to 3 per cent of revenue. Another example is the establishment of a joint e-commerce venture between Hilton, Forte and Accor hotel chains, which was announced on 15 May 2000 (BBC, 2000) to include 800000 rooms. Although these international chains are making great strides, smaller national chains seem to be struggling to keep up.

The characteristics of the hotel industry are that it receives a high average spend, a high proportion of corporate purchases, but also many individual customers. It may involve a complex buying decision requiring an information search, and making use of partners and third party agents. The purchase is also frequently in a location with which the buyer is unfamiliar. In other words, this is an industry for which the Internet should be ideal. Web pages can be used to provide information about particular hotels and their environs, enquire about vacancies and price and make a booking. The difficulties for the industry have been in matching the new Web technology with the old. The industry has been a heavy user of proprietary view data systems linking agents to tour companies, hoteliers and airlines. However, the difficulty for integrated package holiday companies or agencies is that their systems have to interface with different airline systems, reservation systems, accommodation providers, and so on, as well as with any new front end e-commerce retailing (Whittle, 2001b). Building these interfaces is a complex and time-consuming activity. Although 'bricks and mortar' travel companies were slow to enter e-commerce their powerful brands and multichannel approaches are expected to be very successful. Small specialist travel companies should also benefit from a Web presence.

12.11.2 Business-to-consumer (B2C) products

In business-to-consumer (B2C) products the main sectors to benefit form e-commerce are music/books/video, PCs/software, small electronic products, clothing and food. According to a survey by Ernst & Young covering 12 countries and 4000 consumers (Wheeler, 2001) the most frequently purchased product categories are CDs and books. In fact there are no surprises in their list (Table 12.4). The top five product categories have been served by direct marketing channels for years, initially by catalogue and mail, then by telephone, and now by the Internet.

Although 'bricks and mortar' companies may have been a little late into the fray they are now doing rather well compared to some dot.com start-ups. According to MMXI Europe 2000 survey (Wheeler, 2001) six of the Top Ten UK retail sites are traditional 'bricks and mortar' retailers. Many high street names are transforming themselves into 'click and mortar' companies including Argos (general household

Amidst the high expectations held by many about trade over the Internet, intangible services have rated highly in many assessments of what could be most profitably handled. The lack of tangibles reduces the problem of labour-intensive delivery systems and can allow the Internet to be used as both a promotional and distribution channel. Airlines, holiday companies and banks have been early developers of their own websites. A report published by the UK Consumers' Association in 1997 (Consumer Transactions On The Internet) high-lighted some of the pitfalls to consumers of buying through the Internet. Despite being theoretically the most capable of promotion and delivery through the Internet, intangible services are also the most risky for consumers. What comeback have buyers got against a company that doesn't deliver what it promised, when the company is based in a possibly unknown location? How can buyers ensure that advertisers of services are legitimate traders? Is a terrestrial promotion campaign essential to support a virtual company?

Table 12.4   Percentage of Internet buyers who have purchased selected products, 2000

Category	%
CDs and music	67
Books	65
PCs	53
Tickets	39
Videos and film	36
Small electronic	30
Clothing	28
Food and drink	23
Toys	15

Source: Ernst & Young, in Wheeler, 2001.

catalogue sales), Tesco (grocery supermarket), Dixons (household electrical), Comet (electrical appliances), PCWorld (computers), W H Smith (books and stationery).

The traditional problems of home shopping and delivery remain:

- Small orders
- High transport costs
- Goods not compatible with the letter/mail box
- Inability to offer a timed delivery window
- Most economical delivery times for companies are 9 am to 5 pm, Monday to Friday, when the customer is most likely to be out
- Difficulty of returning goods.

In addition customers' expectations of 'e-tailers' have risen (Bingham, 2001). When ordering online customers expect to have prices and stock confirmed as well as a delivery date and preferably the time. Customers also expect to be told of any delays particularly when they are waiting in for the delivery.

CORDLESS PHONE SERVICE LAUNCH ENDS IN A TANGLE

In 2000 the UK government held an auction for five new '3rd generation' mobile telephone licences. To the astonishment of observers, the auction raised a total of £22 billion, showing a huge act of faith by the phone companies in the new technology. To some observers, the price paid by the companies was excessive and would never be recouped, especially if another new technology came along which satisfied consumers' needs more cost effectively. Others saw the licence as the key to a whole new world of mobile telephony in which the mobile phone would be positioned not just as a device for voice communication, but a vital business and information tool. It may take some time to tell who was right, but lessons can be learnt from the launch of Telepoint services a decade earlier. The case illustrates that new technology itself cannot be guaranteed to provide a profitable business opportunity – a thorough understanding of the wider business environment is also essential.

Since the initial UK launch of cellular telephone networks in the early 1980s by Cellnet and Vodafone, the advantages of being able to make calls from any point had proved popular with the self-employed, travelling salespersonnel and business executives, among others. Beyond these segments, the service remained too expensive, and possibly over specified, for more casual users.

In January 1989, the UK government issued licences to four companies – Zonephone (owned by Ferranti), Callpoint (owned by a consortium of Mercury Telecommunications, Motorola and Shaye), Phonepoint (British Telecom, STC, France Telecom, Deutsche Bundespost and Nynex) and Hutchison Telecom – to operate a network of low-cost mobile phones aimed at the mass market (commonly referred to as 'Telepoint'). These would allow callers to use a compact handset to make outgoing calls only, when they were within 150 metres of a base station, these being located in public places such as railway stations, shops and petrol stations.

As in the case of many new markets which suddenly emerge, operators saw advantages of having an early market share lead. Customers who perceived that one network was more readily available than any other would – all other things being equal – be more likely to subscribe to that network. Thus operators saw that a bandwagon effect could be set up. To gain entry to the market at a later stage could become a much more expensive market challenger exercise. With relatively low costs involved in setting up a Telepoint network, three of the four licensed operators rushed into the market, signing up outlets for terminals as well as new customers.

Such was the speed of development that the concept was not rigorously test-marketed. To many, the development was too much product led, with insufficient understanding of buyer behaviour and competitive pressures. Each of the four companies forced through their own technologies, with little inclination or time available to discuss industry standard handsets which could eventually have caused the market to grow at a faster rate and allowed the operators to cut their costs.

Rather than thoroughly test out customer reaction to Telepoint in a small test market (as French Telecom had done with its Pointel system in Strasbourg prior to its full national launch) the operators sought to develop national coverage overnight. This inevitably led to very patchy results, with no outlets in some areas and heavy congestion in a few key sites. There were also the inevitable teething problems in getting the equipment to function correctly.

Worse still for the Telepoint operators, the nature of the competition had been poorly judged. Originally, a major benefit of Telepoint had been seen as removing the need to find a working telephone kiosk from which to make an outgoing call. In fact, the unreliability of public kiosks on which demand was based receded as British Telecom dramatically improved reliability, as well as increasing their availability at a number of key sites. Competition from Mercury had itself increased the number of kiosks available to users. At the top end of the Telepoint target market, the two established cellular operators had revised their pricing structure which made them more attractive for the occasional local user.

The final straw for Telepoint operators came with the announcement by the government of its proposal to issue licences for a new generation of personal communications networks – these would have the additional benefit of allowing both incoming and outgoing calls, and would not be tied to a limited base station range. While this in itself might not have put people off buying new Telepoint equipment, it did have the effect of bringing new investment in Telepoint networks to a halt, leaving the existing networks in a state of limbo.

Faced with the apparent failure of their new service development strategies, the Telepoint operators looked for ways of relaunching their services by refocusing their benefits to new target markets. Now that the initial target of street-based outgoing callers had all but disappeared, new ideas were developed. Hutchison Telecom, for instance, combined an outgoing handset with a paging device which would allow business and self-employed people to keep in touch with base – the service was in effect being positioned as a cheap alternative to the two cellular networks. Similarly, the relaunch of Phonepoint focused on meeting the needs of three key targets – small businesses, mobile professionals and commuters. Furthermore, the company aimed to achieve excellence within the London area – where a network of 2000 base stations was planned – rather than spreading its resources thinly throughout the country. Other targets had been identified for Telepoint technology – office networks for example offered the chance for employees within an organization to keep in touch, without the need to be near a wired phone.

Two years after its initial launch, it had been estimated that no more than 5000 subscribers in total had been signed up for Telepoint, or roughly one per base station, instead of the hundreds which were needed for viability. With hindsight, it could be argued that the launch might have been more successful had the service been more rigorously tested and developed before launch and if target markets had been more carefully selected. Moreover, many of the competitors might probably have wished that they had carried out a more rigorous environmental analysis, in which case they might have been less enthusiastic about launching in the first place.

Review questions

1 Review the launch of Telepoint in the context of the 'demand-technology life cycle'. Where would '3rd generation' mobile phones fit in this life cycle

2 Summarize the environmental factors that contributed to the demise of Telepoint services.

3 How would the launch of Telepoint services differ in a less developed country with a less sophisticated telecommunications infrastructure?

CHAPTER **Summary and links to other chapters**

This chapter has considered technological change from the macroperspective and examined the impact of technology on different aspects of the business at the microlevel. In both instances the relevance of technological change to business success has been stressed. At the macrolevel of technological change, the key points to remember concern the demand-technology life cycle. This will be influenced by the level of R&D expenditure, not only in a particular industry, but also in related and sometimes unrelated industries. The fusion and interaction of different technologies results in new applications and processes which eventually may give rise to whole new industries. Technology permeates through from academic and research institutions into industry, from one industry to another, and from one economy to another. However, if the UK manufacturing sector has become a follower rather than a leader, then it will have lost a much-needed competitive advantage in world markets. Managers should be just as concerned with the long-term prospects of their company as with yesterday's sales. Research and development is too important to be left to the technical experts. Production, finance and marketing people need to be involved in the R&D process along with the scientists and development engineers, and senior board members. The board of directors needs to show serious interest and should be seen to be giving R&D the priority it requires.

At the microlevel, the chapter has considered the impact of technology on the company's products and operations; product design and development, manufacturing and processing; storage and distribution; order and payment processing; and information and communication systems via electronic business. With regard to the specific areas of business operations referred to throughout the chapter, marketing managers and other executives may look to the medium-term horizon for planning purposes. The aim is not only to improve efficiency of business operations, but also to ensure that the benefits are passed on to the customer. These customer benefits may include better preorder services such as product availability and specification, information, faster quotations and quicker design customization. Improved postorder services may include shorter delivery times, delivery to JIT requirements, installation, training, EDI, the Internet and itemized till receipts.

The technological environment is constantly changing. In many industries during the 2000s and beyond, change will be the norm rather than the exception. Companies that focus on customer needs, competitor activity and technological developments, rather than simply aiming to sell what the factory makes, are more likely to succeed.

The dynamics of the information, communications and technology revolution is impacting on all organizations in the developed world: new and old, large and small, commercial and governmental.

The business environmental forces are pushing towards increased globalization and competition. Organizations are under pressure to reduce costs, increase profitability, enhance quality and improve customer service. Investment in IT and communications systems can be relatively inexpensive for small businesses. But for large, well-established organizations that have to reengineer all their business processes the costs and time involved are substantial. Customers, suppliers and internal departments demand real-time information and immediate response to queries. Increasingly customers expect an organization that trades under one corporate name to be a seamless organization.

The challenge for many organizations is to integrate their internal systems (discussed in Chapter 4) within a local area network/Intranet, and to patch these into the Internet via the Web. This will require careful strategic thought. For most established organizations implementation will take some time, have to be in stages, and will be expensive in the short term. Long-term benefits will accrue to the winners, no doubt, both to the organization and the customers. Information technology and communication systems are now of strategic importance and a means by which to establish a competitive advantage. They determine the cost base, and now influence how an organization is structured and run, and how it communicates to its suppliers and customers. More available information will result in increasing power for the customers who are interested in convenience, speed, control, choice and comparability, in addition to demanding world-class quality products and service.

The interrelationship between technology and society was stressed in Chapter 11 and this chapter has explored not only technology's response to changes in society, but also the effects of changing technology on social values.

Technology has opened up many opportunities for businesses to enter global markets, and these were discussed in more detail in Chapter 10.

Finally, issues of privacy and security surrounding new technologies have attracted the attention of the law (Chapter 9) and parliamentary legislators.

In the following chapter we will explore further how developments in information technology are helping businesses to better understand their complex environment and to respond more rapidly to change in it.

CHAPTER Review questions

1. Should the United Kingdom be concerned about its relatively poor showing (compared with its main competitor countries) in R&D?

2. Should marketing managers be involved in the R&D process, and if so what should their role be?

3. Can you identify any product class that has been recently affected by changes in the demand-technology life cycle and, if so, what has been the impact of the change?

4. Identify some recent technological developments and discuss the benefits these have brought to the consumer.

5. How have recent advances in technology helped companies improve their marketing operations?

6 What are the ingredients that led to the successful development and implementation of 'article numbering' in the United Kingdom?

7 Have governments a role to play in fostering an R&D culture and in encouraging technological development?

8 What are the main differences between EDI and the Internet?

9 How might the development of e-commerce via the Internet affect our future?

10 Discussion question

In the pub one Friday evening two men were overheard discussing electronic shopping. Both men worked in the computer industry, had lots of 'kit' at home, and had been connected to the World Wide Web for some time. They were exchanging views about the latest developments on the Internet and getting quite excited about the possibilities of buying their weekly groceries over the Net and having them delivered. This would take the drudgery out of supermarket shopping they agreed. Both men worked long hours and when asked the last time they had seen the inside of a supermarket, neither could remember. Both were married. One wife, although quite capable of holding a good job, did not work at all, had no need to work and was quite happy to look after the family (two children), and do the supermarket shopping. The other was in a very similar position, although she had taken up part-time work as the children were a little older. Neither woman was much taken with computers and thought that being tied to a computer all day, and half the evening, would be a life of drudgery.

Question:

Examine the situation from

a The point of view of the working men.

b The point of view of the housewives.

c Now examine the situation from a marketing perspective (target markets, cost factors, sales potential, etc.).

d Do you think that shopping for groceries via the Internet will become a mainstream activity, and if so by when?

e Discuss the advantages and limitations of setting up the system to operate from existing supermarket outlets in contrast to establishing new warehouses and home delivery system to cater for Internet shopping.

References

ANA (1988) Article Numbers Association, (online) **www. ana.co.uk**, accessed 11 November 1998.
BBC (2000) 'The Today Programme', BBC Radio 4, 8.45 a.m., 12 May.
Bingham, D (2001) 'Home delivery: sorting out the e-tail supply chain', *Connect*, vol. 6, no. 5, February, pp. 30–33.
Byrne, J. (2000) 'Make sure your business thrives in the 21st century', *Computing*, 31 August, pp. 3121–3123.

Chaffey, D., P. Bocij, A. Greasley and S. Hichie (eds) (1999) *Business Information Systems: Technology Development and Management*, FT-Pitman, London.

Crockett, R. (2001) 'Putting an 'e' in the production line', *Computing*, 4 May, pp. 35–38.

Dibb, S., L. Simkin, W.M. Pride and O.C. Ferrell (1997) *Marketing: Concepts and Strategies*, 3rd European edn, Houghton Mifflin Boston, MA.

Echilkson, W. and A. Weintraub (2000) 'Web gives Nestlé the sweetest feeling', *Computing*, 14 December, pp. 67–70.

Ferne, G. (1997) The Policy Implications of 'E-Commerce', *The OECD Observer*, October–November, no. 208, pp. 9–10.

Fletcher, K. (1995) *Marketing Management and Information Technology*, 2nd edn, Prentice-Hall International, Hemel Hempstead.

Flood, G. (2001) 'Online travel businesses fly high on the net', *Computing*, 8 March, pp. 48–49.

Foresight (1998) **www.foresight.gov.uk/itec**, accessed 10 November 1998.

Friedman, L.G. and G. Groodrich (1998) 'Sales strategy in a multiple channel environment', *Journal of Selling and Major Account Management*, vol. 1, no. 1, pp. 38–48.

Gann, R. (2000) 'Go with the flow of supply and demand', *Computing*, 20 April, pp. 35–38.

Kalakota, R. and A.B. Whinston (1997) *Electronic Commerce: A Managers Guide*, Addison Wesley Longman, New York.

Kotler, P. (1997) *Marketing Management: Analysis. Planning, Implementation, and Control*, 9th edn, Prentice-Hall, Englewood Cliffs, NJ.

Kotler, P. and G. Armstrong (1996) *Principles of Marketing*, 7th edn, Prentice-Hall, Englewood Cliffs, NJ.

Lopez-Bassols, V. (1998) *The OECD Observer*, August–September, no. 213, pp. 16–19.

Macalister, T. (2000) 'Bass predicts £1bn net bookings', *Guardian*, 28 March.

National Computing Centre (2001) 'The people implications of effective e-business', *Guidelines*, no. 257.

OECD in Figures 2000 Edition, **www.oecd.org/publications/ebook/**

Pilat, D. (1998) *The OECD Observer*, August–September, no. 213, pp. 5–8.

Pitcher, G. (2000) 'Content is king and Boo was guilty of high treason', *Marketing Week*, 25 May, p. 27.

Treese, G.W. and L.C. Stewart (1998) *Designing Systems for Internet Commerce*, Addison Wesley Longman, New York.

Turban, E., J. Lee, D. King and H.M. Chung (2000) 'Economic, Global and other issues in EC', in *Electronic Commerce: A Managerial Perspective*, Prentice-Hall, Upper Saddle River, NJ, pp. 425–62.

Wheeler, E. (2001) 'Online shopping is tough for the pure-players', *Computing*, 1 February, pp. 40–41.

Whittle, S. (2001a) 'Early adapters are sold on online purchasing', *Computing*, 1 February, p. 39.

Whittle, S. (2001b) 'Travel's come a long way on the net', *Computing*, 8 March, pp. 50–51.

Whittle, S. (2001c) 'E-Business leaders are afraid of change', *Computing*, 8 March, p. 47.

Young, A. (1993) 'What Goes into R&D?', *The OECD Observer*, August–September, no. 183.

Selected further reading

The following provide contemporary insights into the role of innovation in organizations and the relationship between business and research and development.

Dosi, G., D. Teece and J. Chytry (1997) *Technology, Organization and Competitiveness*, Oxford University Press.

Gander, P. (1997) 'Brief encounters', *Marketing Business*, March, pp. 30–34.

Murdoch, A. (1998) Survival of the Fittest, Marketing Business, July, pp. 16–20.

There are now dozens of books about marketing on the Internet ranging from textbooks to quick 'how to' books.

Chaffey, D. (2000) *Internet Marketing*, Prentice-Hall, London.

Chaston, I. (2000) *E-Marketing Strategy*, McGraw-Hill, Maidenhead.

Gabay, J.J. (2000) *Successful Cyberm@rketing in a week*, Hodder and Stoughton, London.

Useful websites

Confederation of British Industry Innovation Trends Survey   A review of the CBI's survey on companies' perceptions of innovation.   **http://www.cbi.org.uk/innovation/**

IBM E-Commerce Case Studies   Contains news and e-commerce case studies.
http://www2.software.ibm.com/casestudies/swcs.nsf/topstories

OECD Electronic Commerce site   Site maintained by the OECD on electronic commerce. Includes news releases, conference reports, policy analysis and statistical work.   **http://www.oecd.org/dsti/sti/it/ec/**

UK Foresight programme   Provides a review of the UK government's technology Foresight programme.
http://www.foresight.gov.uk

Vanderbilt University's eLab   eLab was founded by Vanderbilt University in 1994 to study the business implications of commercializing the World Wide Web. It has emerged as one of the premiere research centres in the world for the study of electronic commerce.   **http://ecommerce.vanderbilt.edu/**

Virtual Society Research Programme   An ESRC-funded programme at Oxford University into the sociology of electronic technologies. Useful social sciences links and research.   **http://www.virtualsociety.org.uk**

Keywords

Article numbering	Internet
Computer-aided-design (CAD)	Just-in-Time (JIT) systems
Computer-aided manufacturing (CAM)	New product development process
Demand-technology life cycle	Product life cycle
Electronic commerce	Research and development (R&D)
Electronic Data Interchange (EDI)	Technology fusion
Electronic Point of Sale (EPOS)	Technology transfer

Part 4

Bringing it together: environmental analysis

13

The dynamic business environment: analysis and response

CHAPTER OBJECTIVES

So far, this book has divided the business environment into a number of seemingly separate components. In reality, of course, all of these components are closely interrelated and it is the task of management to take a holistic view of the business environment and how it impacts on its operations. The aim of this chapter is to bring together the analysis of various elements of a company's business environment in a way that is actionable by managers. This chapter stresses the importance of looking forward to the future and various models used to try to forecast future environmental change are discussed, together with strategies by which companies can respond to such change.

Business organizations are increasingly surrounded by mountains of information. The best organizations make sure that they have the right information, collected at the right time, made available in the right place and given to the right people to act upon. Information processing is increasingly becoming a firm's source of competitive advantage. This chapter explores the role of information in allowing managers to understand their operating environment, and develop responses to changes in that environment.

THE IMPORTANCE OF ENVIRONMENTAL KNOWLEDGE

Information represents a bridge between the organization and its environment and is the means by which a picture of the changing environment is built up within the organization. Management is responsible for turning information-based knowledge into specific marketing plans.

In 1991, Ikujiro Nonaka began an article in the *Harvard Business Review* with a simple statement: 'In an economy where the only certainty is uncertainty, the one sure source of lasting competitive advantage is knowledge' (Nonaka, 1991). A firm's knowledge base is likely to include, among other things, an understanding of the precise needs of customers; how those needs are likely to change over time; how those needs are satisfied in terms of efficient and effective production systems and an understanding of competitors' activities. We are probably all familiar with organizations where knowledge seems to be very poor – the overoptimistic sales forecast which results in unsold stockpiles, the delivery which does not happen as specified, or junk mail which is of no interest at all. On the other hand, customers may revel in a company which delivers the right service at the right time and clearly demonstrates that it is knowledgeable about changes in consumers' preferences. The small business owner may have been able to achieve all of this in his or her head, but in large organizations the task of managing knowledge becomes much more complex. Where it is done well, it can be a significant contributor to a firm's sustainable competitive advantage.

Let us define the terms 'knowledge' and 'information'. Even though in some senses they may be used interchangeably, many writers have suggested that the two concepts are quite distinct. In fact, knowledge is a much more all-encompassing term which incorporates the concept of beliefs that are based on information (Dretske, 1981). It also depends on the commitment and understanding of the individual holding those beliefs, which are affected by interaction and the development of judgement, behaviour and attitude (Berger and Luckmann, 1966). Knowledge only has meaning in the context of a process or capacity to act. Drucker noted that 'There is no such thing as knowledge management, there are only knowledgeable people. Information only becomes knowledge in the hands of someone who knows what to do with it' (Drucker, 1999). Knowledge, then, is evidenced by its association with actions, and its source can be found in a combination of information, social interaction and contextual situations which affect the knowledge accumulation process at an individual level.

Here we need to distinguish between knowledge at the level of the individual and at the level of the organization. Organizational knowledge comprises shared understandings and is created within the company by means of information and social interaction and provides potential for development. It is this form of knowledge that is at the heart of knowledge management. Organizational progress is made when knowledge moves from the domain of the individual to that of the organization.

Two different types of knowledge about the environment can be identified. First, there is knowledge which is easily definable and is accessible, often referred to as 'explicit' knowledge. This type of knowledge can be readily quantified and passed between individuals in the form of words and numbers. Because it is easily communicated it is relatively easy to manage. Knowledge management is concerned with ensuring that the explicit knowledge of individuals becomes a part of the organizational knowledge base, and that it is used efficiently and contributes where necessary to changes in work practices, processes and products. This, however, is not the limit of knowledge management. The second type of knowledge comprises the accumulated knowledge of individuals which is not explicit, but which can still be important to the successful operation of an organization. This type of knowledge, often known as 'tacit' knowledge, is not easy to see or express, it is highly personal and is rooted in an individual's experiences, attitudes, values and behaviour patterns. This type of 'tacit knowledge' can be much more difficult to formalize and disseminate within an organization. If tacit knowledge can be captured, mobilized and turned into explicit knowledge, it would then be accessible to others in the organization and enable the organization to progress rather than have individuals within it having to continually relearn from the same point. The owner of a small business could have all this information readily available in his or her head. The challenge taken on by many large corporations is to emulate the knowledge management of the small business owner. One outcome of a knowledge-based organization has often been referred to as the 'learning organization' in which the challenge is to learn at the corporate level from what is known by individuals who make up the organization.

The transition from individuals' information about the business environment to corporate environmental knowledge requires sharing of knowledge by all concerned. The extent to which this is achieved is influenced by factors in internal environmental factors which were discussed in Chapter 4. A knowledge management programme is needed to break down a *lassez-faire* attitude, and would typically include the following elements:

Figure 13.1
A process model
of transforming
information about
the environment
into corporate
knowledge which
can be acted upon

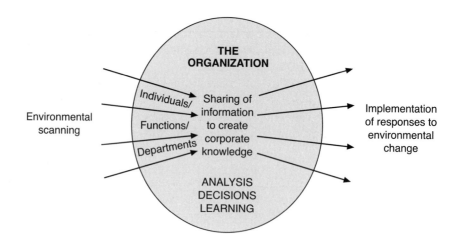

- A strong knowledge-sharing culture, which can only emerge over time with the development of trust.

- Measures to monitor that sharing, which may be reflected in individuals' performance reviews.

- Technology to facilitate knowledge transfer, which should be as user-friendly as possible.

- Established practices for the capture and sharing of knowledge – without clearly defined procedures, the technology is of only limited value.

- Leadership and senior management commitment to sharing information – if senior management doesn't share information, why should anybody else bother?

Information and knowledge have to be seen in the context of the interfunctional dynamics of an organization. A timely supply of appropriate information provides feedback on an organization's performance, allowing actual performance to be compared with target performance. On the basis of this information, control measures can be applied which seek – where necessary – to put the organization back on its original targets. Organizations also learn from the past, in order to better understand the future. For making longer term planning decisions, historical information is supplemented by a variety of continuous and *ad hoc* studies, all designed to allow better informed decisions to be made. Information cannot in itself produce decisions – it merely provides data which must be interpreted by managers. As an interfunctional integrator, a management information system draws data from all functional areas of an organization, and increasingly from other members of an organization's value chain.

As information collection, processing, transmission and storage technologies improve, information is becoming more accessible not just to one particular organization, but also to its competitors. Attention is therefore moving away from how information is collected to who is best able to make use of the information. It is too simple to say that managers commission data collection by technical experts and make decisions on the basis of this data. There has been research interest in the relationship between managers and market researchers, focusing on the role of trust between the two and how its presence helps to reduce risk (Moorman, Zaltman and Deshpande, 1992).

Recent technological innovations – for example electronic point of sale systems (EPOS) – have enabled companies to greatly enhance the quality of the service they provide in terms of speed, accuracy and consistency. In turn, the resulting increase in operational efficiency, combined with the additional information which it is now possible to generate, has allowed organizations to improve other areas of their product offer – such as the development of customer loyalty programmes – as a means of gaining competitive advantages. Organizations must also understand the effects of macroenvironmental factors such as the state of the local or national economy. Without this broader environmental information, routine pieces of market research information, such as the market share held by a company's brands over the past year, cannot be interpreted meaningfully.

THINKING AROUND THE SUBJECT

The knowledge-based firm is grounded on an assumption that it is able to obtain a ready supply of information about customers, actual and potential, so what happens when those customers tire of giving information about themselves? After all, if information has value in the hands of firms, consumers might reasonably think that it has value if they retain the information about themselves. As more and more organizations try to gather information about their customers' changing needs, there is a danger of 'survey fatigue' setting in. Just how many times can you ask customers questions about their preferences and attitudes, before the whole process of carrying out a survey spoils the enjoyment of a service itself? Do customers think that their comments will ever be taken notice of by management? A report prepared in 1998 by the Future Foundation found that only 50 per cent of consumers were happy to provide personal information to firms with which they deal, down from over 60 per cent in 1995. A core of people appear to be not interested in taking part in data collection exercises at all, and will not fill in questionnaires. Careful organization of surveys can improve response rates. Stopping people when they are in a hurry to get away will not make an interviewer popular, but catching them when they are captive with nothing else to do (e.g. waiting at the baggage carousel in an airport) may be more successful. Some companies have tried to make the whole process of carrying out a survey enjoyable. The airline Virgin Atlantic uses its seat-back entertainment system to provide an interactive electronic questionnaire which passengers can complete at their leisure. Many companies offer prize incentives in return for completion, but does this encourage people to skip through the questions without much thought, simply in order to qualify for the reward? If companies leave questionnaires for self-completion with no price incentive and no intervention by an interviewer, how can they be sure that they get a representative sample of respondents? It has often been noted that customers who are very happy or very dissatisfied are the most likely to volunteer information. But what about the mass of people who hold average views about a service? These are likely to be underrepresented and a challenge for marketers to learn about.

To summarize, information allows management to improve its strategic planning, tactical implementation of programmes and its monitoring and control. A practical problem is that information is typically much more difficult to obtain to meet strategic planning needs than it is to meet operational and control needs. There can be a danger of managers focusing too heavily on information which is easily available (typically internal information) at the expense of that which is needed (typically macroenvironmental information).

13.2   INFORMATION SYSTEMS

Many analyses of organizations' information collection and dissemination activities take a systems perspective. The collection of marketing information can be seen as one subsystem of a much larger management information system. Other systems typically include production, financial and human resource management systems. In a well-designed management information system, the barriers between these systems should be conceptual rather than real – for example, sales information is of value to all of these subsystems to a greater or lesser extent (see Figure 13.2).

For most organizations operating in a competitive environment, a crucial role is likely to be played by the marketing information system. This has been defined by Kotler as a system that:

> ... consists of people, equipment and procedures to gather, sort, analyze, evaluate and distribute needed, timely and accurate information to marketing decision-makers. (Kotler, 1997)

In so far as a marketing information subsystem can be identified, it can conceptually be seen as comprising four principal components, although in practice, they are operationally interrelated:

- Much information is generated internally within organizations, particularly in respect of operational and control functions. By carefully arranging its collection and dissemination, internal data can provide a constant and up-to-date flow of information at relatively little cost, useful for both planning and control functions.

- Marketing research is that part of the system concerned with the structured collection of marketing information. This can provide both routine information about marketing effectiveness, such as brand awareness levels or delivery performance, and one-off studies, such as changing attitudes towards diet or the pattern of income distribution.

- Marketing intelligence comprises the procedures and sources used by managers to obtain pertinent information about developments in their marketing environment, particularly competitor activity. It complements the marketing research system, for whereas the latter tends to focus on structured and largely quantifiable data collection procedures, intelligence gathering concentrates on picking up relatively intangible ideas and trends. Marketing management can gather this intelligence from a number of sources, such as newspapers, specialized cutting services, employees who are in regular contact with market

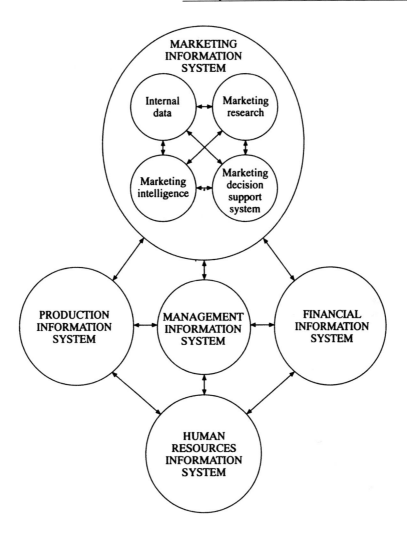

Figure 13.2
A marketing
information
system within the
context of a
management
information
system

developments, intermediaries and suppliers to the company, as well as special-ized consultants. Table 13.1 shows some commonly used secondary (i.e. pre-viously collected) sources of information which are used for environmental scanning.

■ Decision Support Systems comprise a set of models that allows forecasts to be made. Information is both an input to such models – in that data is needed to calibrate a model – and an output, in that models provide information on which decisions can be based. Models are frequently used by companies, when deciding on where to locate new distribution outlets. Historical data may, for example, have established a relationship between one variable (e.g. the level of sales achieved by a particular service outlet) and other variables (e.g. pedestrian traffic in a street). Predicting the sales level of a proposed new outlet then

---

Table 13.1   Secondary sources of information commonly used for scanning the marketing environment

National media – e.g. *Financial Times* industry surveys

Trade, technical and professional media – e.g. *Travel Trade Gazette, Marketing Week*

Government departments and official publications – e.g. *Annual General Household Survey,* transport statistics

Local chambers of trade and commerce

Professional and trade associations – e.g. Association of British Travel Agents, Law Society

Yearbooks and directories, e.g. *Dataquest*

Subscription services, providing periodic sector reports on market intelligence and financial analyses, such as Keynote, MEAL, Mintel, etc.

Subscription electronic databases, e.g. Mintel OnLine

Competitors' websites and publications

THINKING AROUND THE SUBJECT

The story is told of two representatives from a tour operator who were sent abroad to investigate the possibilities for offering package holidays in the format which had worked well at home. The main finding was that very few people in that market bought package holidays. But what did this mean? One representative sent back a message saying that the current level of sales indicated a lack of interest in the product, and the market should therefore be best avoided in favour of other possible markets. But to the other, this was the sign of huge potential – 'Just wait until these people discover the advantages of buying package holidays!' This simple example emphasizes that any analysis of overseas market potential can only be based on a combination of factual analysis and judgement.

---

becomes a matter of measuring pedestrian traffic at a proposed site, feeding this information into the model and calculating the predicted sales level.

For those organizations that have set up marketing information systems, a number of factors will determine their effectiveness:

■ *The accuracy with which the information needs of the organization have been defined* Needs can themselves be difficult to identify and it can be very difficult to draw the boundaries of the firm's environments and to separate relevance from irrelevance. This is a particular problem for large multiproduct firms. The mission statement of an organization may give some indication of the boundaries for its environmental search, for example, many banks have mission statements which talk about becoming a dominant provider of financial services in their domestic market. The information needs therefore include anything related to the broader environment of financial services rather than the narrower field of banking.

■ *The extensiveness of the search for information*   A balance has to be struck between the need for information and the cost of collecting it. The most critical elements of the marketing environment must be identified and the cost of collecting relevant information weighed against the cost that would result from an inaccurate forecast.

■ *The appropriateness of the sources of information* Information for decision making can typically be obtained from numerous sources. As an example, information on changes in social trends can be measured using a variety of quantitative and qualitative techniques. Companies often rely on the former when only the latter can give a depth of understanding that makes for better management decisions. Successful companies use a variety of appropriate sources of information.

■ *The speed of communication* The information system will only be effective if information is communicated quickly and to the people capable of acting on it. Deciding what information to withhold from an individual and the concise reporting of relevant information can be as important as deciding what information to include if information overload is to be avoided.

13.3	**FORWARD PLANNING WITH RESEARCH**

As a planning tool, marketing research provides management with market and product-specific information, which allows it to minimize the degree of uncertainty in planning its business activities. This risk minimization function can apply to the whole of the business operation, or to any of its constituent parts, such as advertising.

Information about the current state of a company's environment is one thing. It can be quite another to try to forecast the state of the environment in the future, and how this will impact on a company's sales. At a macroenvironmental level, simple extrapolation of trends often proves inadequate where major economic, social, political or technological change occurs. For example, extrapolation breaks down when events such as wars, new health scares and medical discoveries dramatically change the price and availability of a product or of competing products.

For some products, markets have historically shown very little turbulence and are unlikely to alter dramatically in the future. The market for undertakers' services will probably remain stable and simple demand forecasting techniques may be appropriate. However, many industries involving high technology are extremely turbulent, with rapid changes in technology occurring, sometimes overshadowing existing products. As an example, typesetting and telex bureaux saw steady growth during the 1980s, but then saw a rapid contraction following the widespread advance of low-cost personal computers. Historical trends could not be relied upon to predict the future.

Forecasting the future involves a combination of scientific analysis and artistic judgement. No element of the marketing environment can be seen in isolation, and forecasts can only be made by a holistic understanding of the environment.

THINKING AROUND THE SUBJECT

Research commissioned by the decision support software specialist Business Objects in 1997 painted a bleak picture of the way managers use information to make decisions. Of 100 senior managers selected from the list of *The Times* Top 1000 companies, more than three-quarters admitted to relying on gut instinct rather than hard facts when making decisions. Of managers, 60 per cent claimed not to receive the right quality or quantity of information to make a decision, even though 99 per cent had access to a computer. More worryingly, a majority of sales and marketing managers surveyed claimed that they relied on other people for information that they were dubious about, or which was out-of-date. The prospect emerged of an information underclass who relied on instinct based decision-making processes.

Nevertheless, a question remains about the extent to which information can actually provide answers. In a changing environment, it is the quality of interpretation of data that gives a firm a competitive advantage in its use of information. Will management ever be reduced to a scientific study of data, or will there always be scope for intuition?

13.4 FRAMEWORKS FOR ANALYSING THE BUSINESS ENVIRONMENT

There are two aspects to be considered when describing an analytic framework with which to analyse the business environment:

1 A definition of the elements that are to be included in the analysis and

2 The choice of methods by which these input elements are to be used in predicting outcomes.

The nature of the framework used bears a relation to the nature of the dominant business environment at the time. In the relatively stable environment that existed during the middle years of this century, management could control its destiny by controlling current performance. In the turbulent environment of the 1990s, control becomes dependent upon management's ability to predict the future and respond to change.

Diffenbach (1983) has argued that detailed environmental analysis became important only in the mid-1960s. Prior to that, the marketing environment was analysed primarily for the purpose of making short-term economic forecasts. The developments to include a longer term appreciation of the wider economic, technological, demographic and cultural elements of the environment came about in three stages:

1 An increased appreciation of environmental analysis was encouraged by the emergence of professional and academic interest in the subject.

2 Awareness of the concepts of environmental analysis led to academic analysis of the subject.

3 Eventually, the concepts that had been vindicated by subsequent academic

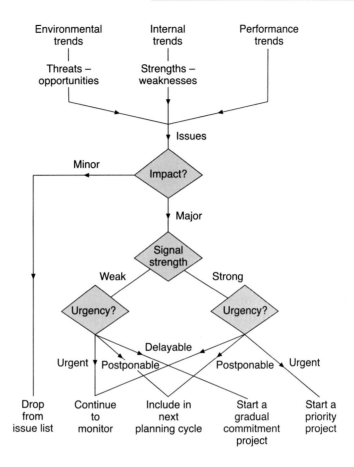

Figure 13.3
Ansoff's model of strategic issue analysis
[*Source:* Based on H.I. Ansoff (1985) *Marketing Strategy and Management.* Reproduced by permission of Macmillan Ltd. © H.I. Ansoff 1979]

analysis were taken on board by business organizations and used as a tool for strategic decision making.

As frameworks for analysis have developed in sophistication, so has the paradox that, by the time sufficient information has been gathered and analysed, it may be too late for the firm to do anything about the opportunities or threats with which it is faced. Ansoff (1984) has put forward a framework that helps to overcome this decision-making dilemma. His model allows the firm to respond rapidly to problems whose precise details are a surprise, but whose general nature could have been predicted. Ansoff's model of strategic issue analysis is shown in Figure 13.3. The central feature of the model is the continued monitoring of the firm's external and internal environments for indicators of the emergence of potentially strategic issues that may significantly influence the firm's operations in future. The focal point for Ansoff's analysis is the issue, such as the emergence of environment-alism, rather than the conventional headings of the economic, technological envir-onments, etc. The model allows for a graduated response: as soon as weak signals are picked up, steps are taken to allow for the possibility of these issues developing further. Responses become more precise as the signals become more amplified over time. In other words, Ansoff's model avoids the need for a firm to wait until it has sufficient information before taking a decision, it responds gradually as information emerges.

Choice of framework

A range of analytic frameworks is available for companies to use in analysing their marketing environment and making strategic marketing decisions. The choice of framework will depend upon four factors.

Firstly, the *level of turbulence* in the marketing environment will vary between firms operating in different markets. For example, the marketing environment of an undertaker has not been, and in future is even less likely to be, as turbulent as that of a brewery. An extrapolation of recent trends might be adequate for the former type of business, but the latter must seek to understand a diverse range of changing forces if it is to be able to accurately predict future demand for its products.

Secondly, the *cost* associated with an inaccurate forecast will reflect the capital commitment to a project. A clothing manufacturer can afford to trust his or her judgement in running off a small batch of jackets, the cost of making a mistake will probably be bearable, unlike the cost of building a chemical refinery on the basis of an inaccurate forecast. The latter situation calls for relatively sophisticated analytic techniques.

Thirdly, more sophisticated *analytic techniques* are needed for long-time-scale projects where there is a long time lag between the planning of the project and the time it comes into production. The problem of inaccurate forecasting will be even more acute where an asset has a long lifespan with few alternative uses.

Finally, *qualitative* and *quantitative techniques* may be used as appropriate. In looking at the future, facts are hard to come by. What matters, is that senior management must be in the position to make better informed judgements about the future in order to aid decision making and planning.

We will begin our analysis with two basic building blocks of environmental analysis – the marketing audit and SWOT analysis.

The marketing audit

It has been customary for business organizations to undertake financial audits to check on their financial health. Increasingly, the principles of the independent and objective audit are being applied to examine how effective an organization has been in addressing the markets which it serves. The tool used for this has often been referred to as a *marketing audit*, which has been defined by Kotler (1997) as:

> ... a comprehensive, systematic, independent and periodic examination of a company's or business unit's marketing environment, objectives, strategies and activities with a view to determining problem areas and opportunities and recommending a plan of action to improve the company's marketing performance.

The marketing audit is not itself a framework for decisions. It is essentially a set of procedures by which an organization explicitly asks questions, about the internal and external environments in which marketing operates, as well as the performance of the marketing functions themselves (such as the firm's distribution and pricing effectiveness). The process begins by the appointment of an independent person to undertake the audit. This could be a consultant from outside the organization, or somebody from another position within the firm, either sideways or above the function being audited. A self-audit could be undertaken, but at the risk of a loss of objectivity. However, a number of books containing checklists and questions are published which will aid objectivity.

A large part of the audit is devoted to an objective analysis of the micro- and macroenvironment. In the case of the macroenvironment the audit would independently verify or challenge any assumptions that the company had been making; for instance about the likely rate of economic growth or the speed of change in the technological environment. In the case of the microenvironment, the person undertaking an audit of the distribution environment could proceed by asking retailers themselves about how they perceive the company's products and future trends in retailing for that type of product.

The marketing audit would also look inwardly to examine the relationships within the marketing function and between it and other functional areas of the firm. Organizational structures and decision-making procedures would be objectively assessed for effectiveness.

The availability of good-quality, timely information is crucial to undertaking a marketing audit.

13.4.3 SWOT analysis

A method widely used in marketing audits is a grid used to plot internal strengths and weaknesses in one half of the grid and external opportunities and threats in the other half. The terms opportunities and threats should not be viewed as 'absolutes', for as Johnson and Scholes (1988: 77) point out, what might appear at first sight to be an opportunity may not be so when examined against an organization's resources and the feasibility of implementing a strategy.

A SWOT analysis summarizes the main environmental issues in the form of opportunities and threats (O&T) facing an organization. With this technique, these are specifically listed alongside its strengths and weaknesses (S&W). The strengths and weaknesses are internal to the organization and the technique is used to put realism into the opportunities and threats. In this way, the environment may be assessed as giving rise to a number of possible opportunities, but if the organization is not capable of exploiting these because of internal weaknesses then they should perhaps be left alone.

The principles of a SWOT analysis are illustrated in Figure 13.4 by examining how an airline which has an established reputation as a charter carrier could use the framework in assessing whether to enter the scheduled service market between London and Paris.

13.4.4 Trend extrapolation

At its simplest level, a firm identifies a historic and consistent long-term change in demand for a product over time. Demand forecasting takes the form of multiplying

Figure 13.4
SWOT analysis
for a hypothetical
airline
considering entry
to the scheduled
London–Paris air
travel market

Strengths
Strong financial position
Good reputation with existing customers
Has aircraft that can service the market

Weaknesses
Has no allocated take-off or landing 'slots'
    at main airport
Poor network of ticket agents
Aircraft are old and expensive to operate

Opportunities
Market for business and leisure travel is
    growing
Deregulation of air licensing allows new
    opportunities
Costs of operating aircraft are falling

Threats
Channel Tunnel may capture a large share
    of market
Deregulation will result in new competitors
    appearing
Growth in air travel will lead to more
    congestion

current sales by a historic growth factor. In most markets, this can at best work effectively only in predicting long-term sales growth at the expense of short-term variations.

Trend extrapolation methods can be refined to recognize a relationship between sales and one key environmental variable. An example might be an observed direct relationship between the sale of new cars to the private buyer sector and the level of disposable incomes. Forecasting the demand for new cars then becomes a problem of forecasting what will happen to disposable incomes during the planning period. In practice, the task of extrapolation cannot usually be reduced to a single dependent and independent variable. The car manufacturer would also have to consider the relationship between sales and consumer confidence, the level of competition in its environment and the varying rate of government taxation.

While multiple regression techniques can be used to identify the significance of historical relationships between a number of variables, extrapolation methods suffer from a number of shortcomings. Firstly, one variable is seldom adequate to predict future demand for a product, yet it can be difficult to identify the full set of variables that have an influence. Secondly, there can be no certainty that the trends identified from historic patterns are likely to continue in the future. Trend extrapolation takes no account of discontinuous environmental change, as was brought about by the sudden increase in oil prices in 1973. Thirdly, it can be difficult to gather information on which to base an analysis of trends, indeed, a large part of the problem in designing a marketing information system lies in identifying the type of information that may be of relevance at some time in the future. Fourthly, trend extrapolation is of diminishing value as the length of time used to forecast extends. The longer the time horizon, the more chance there is of historic relationships changing and new variables emerging.

Trend extrapolation as applied by most business organizations is a method of linking a simple cause with a simple effect. As such, it does nothing to try to understand or predict the underlying variables, unless extrapolation is applied to these variables too.

At best, trend extrapolation can be used where planning horizons are short, the number of variables relatively limited and the risk level relatively low. A retailer may use extrapolation to forecast how much ice cream will be demanded in summer. A historic relationship between the weather (quantified in terms of sunshine hours or average daily temperatures) may have been identified, onto which a long-term relationship between household disposable income and the domestic freezer population has been added. The level of demand for ice cream during the following month could be predicted with reasonable accuracy; with input from the Meteorological Office on the weather forecast, from the Treasury or *Economist's* forecast of household disposal incomes (relatively easy to obtain if the forecast period is only one month), and from statistics showing recent trends in household freezer ownership (available from the *Annual General Household Survey*).

13.4.5 ### Expert opinion

Trend analysis is commonly used to predict demand where the state of the causative variables is known. In practice, it can be very difficult to predict what will happen to those variables themselves. One solution is to consult expert opinion to obtain the best possible forecast of what will happen to them.

In Diffenbach's (1983) study of American corporations, 86 per cent of all firms said they used expert opinion as an input to their planning process. Expert opinion can vary in the level of speciality, from an economist being consulted for a general forecast about the state of the national economy to industry-specific experts. An example of the latter are the fashion consultants who study trends at the major international fashion shows and provide a valuable source of expert opinion to clothing manufacturers seeking to know which types of fabric to order, ahead of a fashion trend.

Expert opinion may be unstructured and come either from a few individuals inside the organization or from external advisers or consultants. The most senior managers in companies of reasonable size tend to keep in touch with developments by various means. Paid and unpaid advisers may be used to keep abreast of a whole range of issues such as technological developments, animal rights campaigners, environmental issues, government thinking and intended legislation. Large companies may employ MPs or MEPs (Members of the European Parliament) as well as retired civil servants as advisers. Consultancy firms may be employed to brief the company on specific issues or monitor the environment on a more general basis.

In today's modern economy, it is essential that businesses monitor not only the domestic environment, but also the European Union and the international environment. Today, as much legislation affecting companies comes from the EU as from the UK government. Legislation passed in the United States can have an indirect affect on UK companies, even though their products may not be intended for sale in America. What is happening in America today may be happening in Europe next year.

Relying on individuals may give an incomplete or distorted picture of the future. There are, however, more structured methods of gaining expert opinion. One of the best known is probably the Delphi method. This involves a number of experts, usually from outside the organization, who (preferably) do not know each other and who do not meet or confer while the process is in play. A scenario, or scenarios, about the future are drawn up by the company. These are then posted out to the experts. Comments are returned and the scenario(s) modified according to the comments received. The process is run through a number of times with the scenario being amended on each occasion. Eventually a consensus of the most likely scenario is arrived at. It is believed that this is more accurate than relying on any one individual, because it involves the collected wisdom of a number of experts who have not been influenced by dominant personalities.

<table>
<tr><td>13.4.6</td><td>**Scenario building**</td></tr>
</table>

Scenario building is an attempt to paint a picture of the future. It may be possible to build a small number of alternative scenarios based on differing assumptions. This qualitative approach is a means of handling environmental issues that are hard to quantify because they are less structured, more uncertain and may involve very complex relationships.

Often the most senior managers in a company may hold no common view about the future. The individuals themselves are likely to be scanning the environment in an informal way, through conversations with colleagues and subordinates within the organization and through business acquaintances and friends outside. The general media and business and technical publications will also shape a person's 'view' of the future. Individuals will vary in their sensitivity to the environment. Such views may never be harnessed in any formal way, but they may be influencing decisions taken by these individuals. Yet the views each person holds may never have been exposed to debate or challenge in a way that would allow the individual to moderate or change his or her view.

Scenario building among senior management will help individuals to confirm or moderate their views. A new perspective may be taken on issues or forthcoming events. A wider perspective may be taken by individuals who may become more sensitive to the environment and the impact it can have on business. A more cohesive view may be adopted by senior management which may help strategy formulation and planning. The scenarios may be built up over a number of meetings which may be either totally unstructured or semistructured, with each meeting focusing on different aspects of the environment. The approach may be used at different levels of management in a large organization; a multinational company may build scenarios at the global, regional and country level. For example, Johnson and Scholes (1988) cite the example of Shell UK Ltd which has used this approach on a number of occasions. In the early 1980s, it was used as part of the company's methodology for attempting to assess the demand for oil depending on a number of alternative scenarios (see the case study of the Shell Oil Company below). Chapter 12 discussed the UK government's Foresight programme that attempts to bring together experts from industry, academia and government in an attempt to identify and evaluate trends in technological developments.

How do you predict the future demand for oil products? Simple techniques based on extrapolation of previous trends have been found lacking by events such as wars in the Middle East. The traditional approach used by Shell, like most of the major oil companies, forecast the amount of refinery capacity which it would need to meet consumer demand for refined oil-based products by extrapolating recent patterns of demand. It assumed that recent trends would by and large continue and was caught largely unaware in 1973 by the actions of OPEC. OPEC, a cartel of Middle Eastern oil producers, had used its monopoly power to reduce the supply of crude oil and thus force up crude oil prices threefold. This represented a very severe discontinuity in recent trends, and left most oil companies facing much lower levels of demand than they had previously planned for. Most oil companies were not much better prepared for the second sudden OPEC price rise that occurred in 1983.

Today, Shell tries to manage its future by developing a range of possible scenarios of future business environments. From these scenarios, managers can develop plans of action to meet each eventuality that could be envisaged. Identifying the nature of scenarios can be a challenge to management's creativity.

One example quoted by Shell to justify its scenario-based approach to planning is the oil price collapse which occurred in 1986. In 1984, crude oil prices stood at $28 a barrel. Other oil companies using trend extrapolation predicted that oil prices would stabilize over the next two years at the $25–$30 a barrel level. The prospect of it falling to $15 may have seemed far fetched to many planners, yet in February 1986 the world market price of oil fell first to $17 a barrel, before drifting down to a low point of $10 two months later.

Shell claimed it was much better prepared for this price collapse as it had envisaged a scenario in which this occurred and developed a contingency plan of action in the event of it taking place. This covered, for example, alternative plans for investment in new energy sources and renewal plans for its shipping fleet. For most of its activities, Shell was trading in commodity markets in which product differentiation was either very difficult or impossible. The ability to learn and react rapidly to environmental change gave Shell its only major advantage over its competitors.

More recently, Shell's approach to scenario building demonstrated its values during the Gulf War. Although Shell had not foreseen the details of the conflict which followed the invasion of Kuwait by Iraq, it had envisaged a scenario in which there was a serious disruption to oil supplies in the Gulf region, whether this came by war, accident or another cause. Contingency plans allowed the company to rapidly replace oil supplies from alternative sources and to redeploy its tanker fleet. The speed with which the company could adjust the forecourt price of petrol to the consumer in response to volatile spot market prices had been increased with improved internal communications.

For the future, Shell feels that attitudes towards the environment represent an opportunity for alternative scenario building. The company has developed two scenarios. In the first scenario, the world moves towards sustainable growth, with a change in attitudes towards consumption among consumers throughout the world and increasing controls on pollution creating processes. The second scenario envisages a drop in environmentalism as an issue, with increasing emphasis on the need to generate economic wealth – at a national level. Governments may seek to stimulate employment even if this results in greater environmental damage, whilst concern for worldwide approaches to the control of pollution may give way to increasing trade barriers as countries struggle for short-term economic survival. The contingency plan for the former eventuality might include shifting resources to increase production of wind-generated electricity or biodegradable packaging.

The development of scenario building methods has seen the increasing importance attributed within Shell to the forecasting of business environments. It has attributed its high and stable level of profits to this approach. The first business environment planners at Shell were seen as eccentric mavericks whose conclusions were seen as relatively marginal to achieving the short-term aims of most managers. Today, the findings of the business environment planners at Shell are communicated within the organization more effectively and managers attach much more significance to the scenarios presented by drawing up their own response plans.

13.4.7   Influence diagrams and impact grids

A more applied approach is to assess the likely impact of specific aspects of environmental change on the business. One method is to construct influence diagrams (Narchal *et al.*, 1987), so that a better understanding of the relationships between environmental forces can be obtained. If the price a company has to pay for raw materials is a critical factor, then the forces that influence the price of raw materials will be of interest to it. By monitoring these it will have an earlier warning about price rises than if it were to wait until its supplier told it of the price increase. In the influence diagram (Figure 13.5), a positive relationship means that if the value of one force rises then the pressure on the dependent factor will be in the same direction. A negative relationship means that if the value of the environmental force rises then the pressure on the dependent factor is the opposite direction, downwards.

A number of specific influence diagrams may be used to improve the understanding of how forces in the environment may influence particular aspects of the business. To gain a broader view, impact grids can be constructed. Specific environmental forces or events are identified and their impact on particular aspects of the business are assessed (see Jenster, 1987). Weighting the assessment on a simple scale, say 1 equals no effect and 10 equals substantial or critical impact, will help decision making. A simple grid can then be constructed as in Figure 13.6.

For those companies that wish to structure the environmental analysis in a more detailed way, there are two different, but complementary, methods of impact analysis. The simplest is trend impact analysis (TIA), where the movements in a particular variable are plotted over time and the projected value is assessed (Figure 13.7).

A further development of trend impact analysis is cross-impact analysis (CIA), which is used in an attempt to assess the impact of changes in one variable on other variables. This is much more difficult to do but at the minimum it will help mangers to understand the possible relationships between forces in the

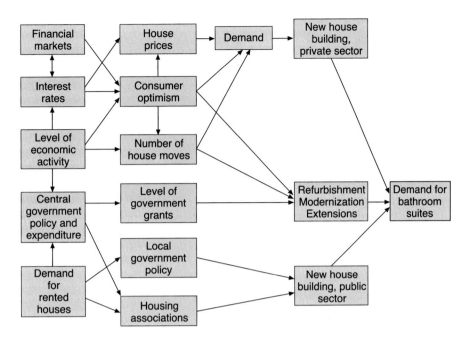

Figure 13.5
An example of an influence diagram

Figure 13.6
Environmental impact grid:
0 = no effect,
10 = substantial or critical impact

Environment change / Impact on UK car market	UK government raises VAT	EU directive to limit exhaust emissions	EU announces plans for single currency	Japanese car makers abandon voluntary limits on imports to Europe	Technological breakthrough for battery car
UK demand	8				
EU demand	0				
UK production levels	4				
Prices	8				
Production costs					
Marketing costs					

environment. At best, it will provide key information in order to aid strategic decision making (see Figure 13.8). It is reported that the General Electric Company (USA) uses these impact grids as an aid to writing scenarios.

A scenario for the early 2000s may be that the use of personal phones is set to grow very rapidly as the technology improves and prices continue to fall. Will young single professional people decide that they do not need a traditional fixed phone in their apartment? One mobile phone may be all they need. Newly married couples are likely to have his and her personal phones rather than install a fixed phone in the home. A cross-impact study undertaken by British Telecom may reveal

Figure 13.7
Trend impact
analysis

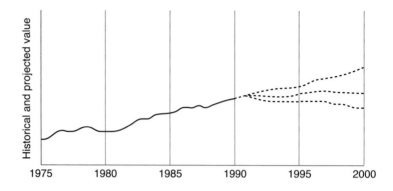

Figure 13.7
Trend impact
analysis

Wild cards \ Possible events	OPEC force price of oil to $30/barrel	OPEC fall out: oil drops to $12/barrel with oversupply	Economic downturn becomes recession and lasts 5 years	Government increases car and petrol taxes
Clean-burn petrol engine developed				
Japanese launch first mass-produced battery-powered car				
Environment deteriorates suddenly; car drivers in Western world limited to 30 miles per day				

Figure 13.8
Cross-impact
analysis

a serious threat to their traditional domestic fixed line business. What is more, it is likely that the high-income, high-use customers will be the first to desert traditional suppliers.

13.4.8   Environmental threat and opportunity profile (ETOP)

Kotler (1997) defines a marketing opportunity as 'an attractive arena for company marketing action in which the company would enjoy a competitive advantage'. He suggests that opportunities should be assessed for their attractiveness and success probability. Attractiveness can be assessed in terms of potential market size, growth rates, profit margins, competitiveness and distribution channels; other factors may be technological requirements, degree of government interference, environmental concerns and energy requirements. Set against the measure of attractiveness is the probability of success. This depends on the company's strengths and competitive advantage; such issues as access to cash, lines of credit or capital to finance new

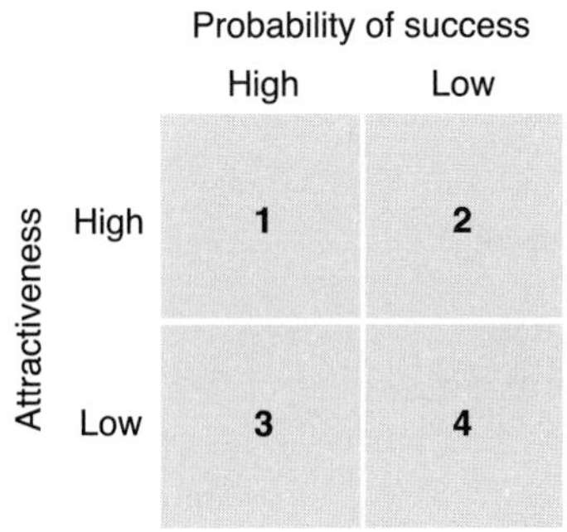

Probability of success

High   Low

Figure 13.9
Opportunity matrix: 1. Attractive opportunity which fits well with company's capabilities; 2. Attractive opportunity, but with low probability of success: poor fit with company's capabilities; 3. High probability of success if company takes this opportunity, but not an attractive market; 4. Let's forget this one

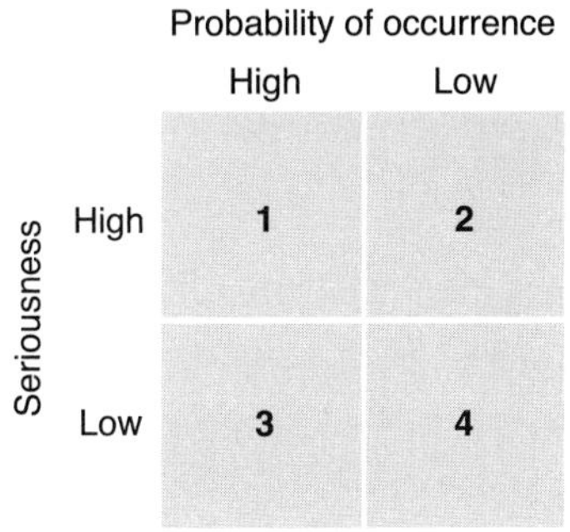

Probability of occurrence

High   Low

Figure 13.10
Threat matrix: 1. Competitor launches superior product; 2. Pound sterling rises to $3; 3. Higher costs of raw materials; 4. Legislation to cover 'environment friendly' claims on labels

developments. Technological and productive expertise, marketing skills, distribution channels and managerial competence will all need to be taken into account. A simple matrix (Figure 13.9) can be constructed to show the relationship between attractiveness and success probability.

Kotler describes an environmental threat as 'a challenge posed by an unfavourable trend or development in the environment that would lead, in the absence of purposeful marketing action, to the erosion of the company's or industry's position'. In this case the threats should be assessed according to their seriousness and the probability of occurrence. A threat matrix can then be constructed (Figure 13.10).

In order for the environmental analysis to have a useful input into the business planning process, a wide range of information and opinions needs to be summarized in a meaningful way. This is particularly so if a number of the techniques described in this chapter have been used in a wide-ranging analysis. The information collated from the detailed analysis needs to be simplified and summarized for planning purposes. The environmental threat and opportunity profile (ETOP) provides a summary of the environmental factors that are most critical to the company (Figure 13.11). These provide a useful report to stimulate debate among

Figure 13.11
Environmental
threat and
opportunity profile
(ETOP):
probability scale
from 0.1 (very
unlikely to
happen) to 0.9
(very likely to
happen)

Factor	Major opportunity	Minor opportunity	Neutral	Minor threat	Major threat	Probability
Economic Interest rates rise to 15%					✓	0.8
£ falls to $1.40	✓					0.4
Disposable incomes do not rise for 5 years				✓		0.3
Political Change of political party–more spending on education and public transport			✓			0.9
Legal EU bans flavouring additives in snacks				✓		0.1
Market Competitor launches major TV campaign				✓		0.5

senior management about the future of the business. Some authors suggest trying to weight these factors according to their importance and then rating them for their impact on the organization.

13.4.9   Porter's five forces model of industry competitiveness

Porter's (1985) model helps managers identify the factors that affect the intensity of competition within a particular industry. The model illustrates the relationship between different players and potential players in the industry. The five forces requiring evaluation are: the power of suppliers, the power of buyers, the threat of new entrants, the threat of substitute products and the intensity of rivalry between competing firms (Figure 13.12).

The power of suppliers   The power of suppliers is likely to be high if the number of suppliers are few and/or the materials, components and services are in short supply. The suppliers of microprocessor silicone chips and compact discs have held a powerful market position due to their dominance of technology and high demand for their products.

The power of buyers   Buyer power is likely to be high if there are relatively few buyers, if there are alternative sources of supply and if the buyer has low switching

How much should a company bid for a TV franchise? In 1991, a new opportunity arose in the United Kingdom for companies to bid for commercial television breakfast franchises issued periodically by the government. Since the last issue of franchises in 1981 the government had changed the regulations (Broadcasting Act) for commercial television and the criteria by which bidders for the franchise would be judged. In short, the government's intention was to create more competition in the bidding to raise revenue and to curtail broadcasting monopolies. The franchise would now go to the highest bidder subject to a minimum 'quality threshold'. According to the *Observer* (Twisk and Brooks, 1991), a number of new bidders were attempting to take the franchise away from TV AM. In particular, a consortium called Daybreak, whose partners included ITN, the *Daily Telegraph*, MAI (an advertising group), Carlton Communications, NBC (American TV network) and Taylor Woodrow (a construction company). With the experience held by consortium members, it saw an opportunity for which there was a high probability of success. Among other bidders were a consortium that included London Weekend

Television, STV (Southern Television) and Broadcast Communications (owned by the *Guardian* newspaper and Disney).

The Broadcasting Act meant that the next time the franchise came up for renewal the bidding would be much more competitive. This came at a difficult time for TV broadcasters due to adverse environmental conditions. Advertising revenues were under pressure because of stagnant advertising spending resulting from the recession of the late 1980s. The government had also awarded a franchise for another new channel, Channel 5 that was struggling to make headway in its early years. There was also pressure from some quarters for the BBC to be allowed to carry advertising so as to reduce its dependence on the public purse. Satellite TV and cable were well established by this time and gaining in popularity after aggressive marketing. Production costs also continued to rise and sponsorship of programmes had been slow to take off.

With so much uncertainty in the market it proved difficult for bidders to know how much they should bid for the franchise, with the result that bid prices are reported to have varied widely.

costs. During the 1980s and 1990s, Britain's grocery retailing has become increasingly dominated by five very large organizations. According to the Nielsen Grocery Service (Mintel, 1998) Asda, Safeway, Sainsbury's, Somerfield and Tesco held 77.8 per cent market share by turnover in 1997. Since the 1970s, the power in the marketplace has steadily shifted away from the manufacturers of grocery products to the grocery retailers.

The threat of new entrants   The threat of new entrants will be higher if there are low barriers to entry. New entrants may already be in the industry in another country, but decide to move into your geographic market. A number of South Korean car manufacturers, including Hyundai and Daewoo, moved into the UK and other European markets during the 1980s and 1990s. Some Indian motor

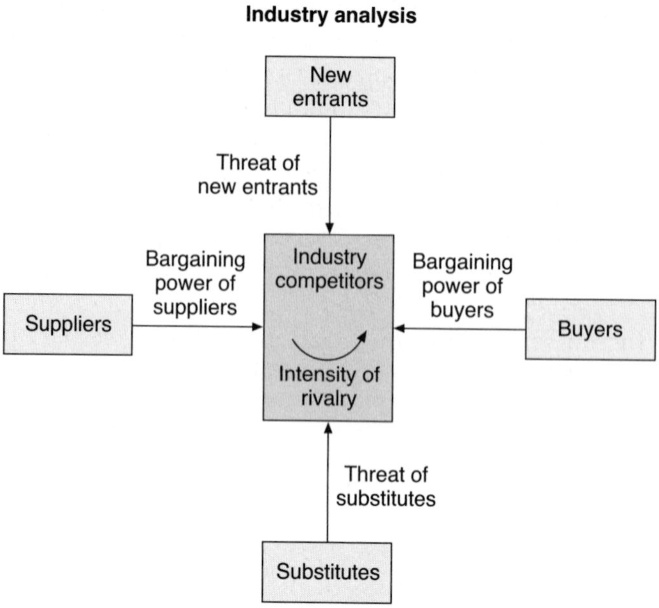

Figure 13.12
Industry
competitiveness
[*Source:* Based on M.E.
Porter (1985) *Competitive*
Advantage, Free Press,
New York]

Industry analysis

cycle and scooter manufacturers (who have a very strong home market and low costs of production) are beginning to show interest in European markets. Alternatively, new entrants may arrive from outside the industry. BIC, whose technology base was plastic moulding, made disposable ball-point pens. Some years ago they were able to successfully diversify into the wet shave razor market with plastic disposable razors, thus challenging established market leaders such as Gillette and Wilkinson in their core business.

The threat of substitute products Substitute products are likely to emerge from alternative technologies, particularly as the economics of production change. Initially the new technology may have high costs associated with it. However, as the technology and experience develops, the level of investment rises and production volumes increase, then costs of production will fall with economies of scale. Manufacturers will then look for more and more applications. Artificial sweeteners for sugar, lighters for matches, plastic containers for glass, polyester for cotton and personal computers for typewriters are obvious examples. These substitutes may change the whole economics of an industry and threaten the survival of the traditional product providers.

Intensity of rivalry between competing firms The intensity of rivalry may be high if two or more firms are fighting for dominance in a fast-growing market. For example, this occurred in the United Kingdom's personal phone market during the mid 1990s. Also in the fight to establish the dominant format for the domestic VCR player during the early 1980s between three competing technologies, VHS (the UK winner), Betamax and U-matic. The need is to become established as the dominant technology or brand before the industry matures. Companies are likely to engage heavily in promotional activity involving advertising and promotional incentives to buy. In a mature industry, particularly if it is characterized by high fixed costs and excess capacity, the intensity of competitive rivalry may be very high. This is because manufacturers (e.g. cars) or service providers (e.g. airlines) need to operate at near maximum capacity to cover overhead costs. As the industry matures, or at times of cyclical down-turn or when a number of companies have invested in new capacity, firms fight to maintain their maximum level of sales. Price cuts and discounting may become commonplace and profits will be eroded. Low-cost producers with high brand loyalty have the best chance of survival.

Porter's five forces model of industry competitiveness helps understanding of the microenvironment. Monitoring these forces will provide managers with some insight into the competitive rivalry that characterizes their industry.

| 13.5 | FORMING A VIEW OF ENVIRONMENTAL INFLUENCE |

The pace at which senior managers believe the environment is changing and the nature of that change is likely to influence their decision making and planning. Four broad patterns of environmental change may be considered, as shown in Figure 13.13. In part (a) of the figure, senior management believes that there is a stable environment with little change. In part (b), senior management believes that

Figure 13.13
Four patterns of environmental change: past trend, ... future trend

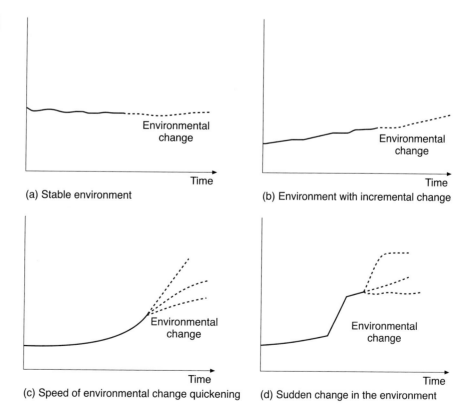

(a) Stable environment

(b) Environment with incremental change

(c) Speed of environmental change quickening

(d) Sudden change in the environment

Figure 13.14
Simple/complex
and stable/
dynamic
environments

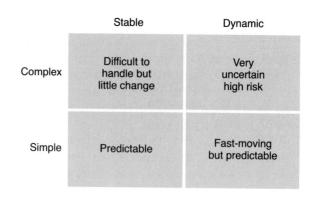

there is incremental change at a known and predictable pace. In part (c), the pace of change is quickening and becoming harder to anticipate. In part (d), the environment may be subject to sudden change as a major factor has a dramatic impact on other environmental forces, for example sudden steep increases in oil prices.

Other considerations for senior management are whether the environment is simple or complex and stable or dynamic (Figure 13.14). Here it is the relationship between the company and its environment that is in question and whether this is changing. Is the environment moving from being simple to becoming more complex, for example? Or is it moving from a period of stability into one of dynamism? The same environmental change may be seen as an opportunity by one company, and a threat by another. The view taken will be influenced by the analysis undertaken, the views of senior management, and the ability of the company to respond.

Chapter 1 introduced the three basic components of the marketing environment, which were the organization's internal environment and the external environment comprising the microenvironment and the macroenvironment. The organization's internal environment refers to the structure, processes and activities of the marketing department itself and its relationship to other business functions and activities. This is the controllable environment. The external environment is the uncontrollable element and has two components. The microenvironment is composed of all organizations and individuals who directly or indirectly affect the activities of the organization. This is sometimes referred to as the industry or task environment. It is thus necessary for the organization to track the behaviour of the market, its competitors, customers, channel members and suppliers. The macroenvironment is composed of those forces that influence the international and domestic economy and society as a whole. These forces are sometimes summarized as sociological, technological, economic and political and are often abbreviated to STEP, or PEST to aid memory.

Having completed an analysis of the business and marketing environment, ideally by means of a marketing audit, the information needs to be distilled into a SWOT summary (Figure 13.15). The strengths and weaknesses are in respect of the organization's internal environment and the opportunities and threats come from the external environment.

Figure 13.15
Links between environmental analysis and planning

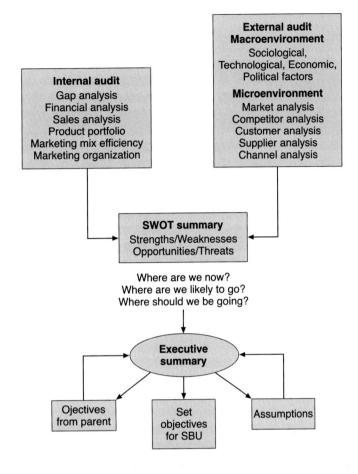

Figure 13.15
Links between environmental analysis and planning

Management needs to be able to answer the questions 'Where are we now?' and 'Where are we likely to go?' given the present performance and future environment. The SWOT summary, then, provides a key input to the planning process. If we assume that we are preparing a business plan for a strategic business unit (an SBU may be a subsidiary or division of a larger organization), then the chief executive officer (CEO) has to set the business objectives for the coming financial year. In arriving at a decision the CEO has to balance a number of conflicting demands. The parent organization and the board of directors will have expectations regarding the performance of the SBU. These will be expressed in financial terms such as return on capital employed (ROCE), sales revenue, profit as a percentage of sales and rate of growth, etc. The chief executive of the SBU is involved in negotiations during the setting of these objectives. During the process the CEO is conscious of the recent performance of the business (from the internal audit) and the threats and opportunities presented from the external audit. In accepting the financial objectives from the parent organization the CEO needs to ensure that they are realistic and achievable, given the current and future environment. This may seem obvious but remember that the parent organization may be a multinational with a head office in another country or continent. The environmental forces to which the head office managers and directors are exposed may be quite different from those influencing the local SBU.

In negotiating the objectives with the parent and in setting the SBU objectives it is beneficial to state explicitly the key assumptions made. Therefore, if the growth rate of the economy will directly influence your business it is necessary to state what level you have assumed over the planning period. Likewise for interest rates, levels of disposable income, business confidence indices and exchange rates. These would all be primary assumptions. If your business is dependent on others then some secondary or derived assumptions may need to be stated. If 80 per cent of your business is sales to the automotive industry then specifying the assumed level of car sales would be important. Likewise, if you manufacture bathroom suites and fittings your business is directly dependent on the sales of new housing and the refurbishment of existing housing stock, both of which are influenced by the level of interest rates.

Planning in larger businesses is a complex activity. Once the business operates over a number of product groups, industries and international markets, then an environmental analysis needs to be conducted at the local level as well as the SBU and corporate level. Forming a cohesive view about the environment becomes much more difficult. In managing a business senior executives have to balance the immediate requirements of existing operations against the longer-term require-ments of shaping and developing the future business. Where does the organization wish to be in 5 and 10 years' time? Because the organization cannot change the business environment, it would be wise to attempt to monitor and predict it and then to shape the business to maximize the opportunities and minimize the threats posed by the environment.

CASE STUDY

HC MOBILITY LTD

This UK manufacturer of mobility and other aids for the disabled was established 50 years ago by Harold Challenger, and is still in family hands today. Sales grew steadily until 1986 when Bill Challenger, soon after taking over the business, took the decision to enter the French market. Sales to EU countries have since grown rapidly and today 35 per cent of sales are exported. There was a steep learning curve on entry into Europe, says Bill; 'We decided to have a crack at the French market after meeting a French agent at the London trade show. He liked one or two of our products and our prices were sharp.' Other agents were added over the years and now they cover five markets: France, the Netherlands, Belgium, Denmark and Spain.

In the United Kingdom sales have been traditionally handled via the eight sales representatives who sell to stockist as well as direct to hospitals and nursing homes. Nursing homes are difficult to deal with as average order values are low and the sales reps spend too much time drinking coffee. More orders come in by phone these days than ever they used to, and Bill is concerned that the phone system is overloading. According to Bill it was the new catalogue which they introduced a few years ago that did it. Customers are now happy to phone in and quote the order number from the catalogue. If the product is in stock, it will be despatched the same day. His daughter Jenny, on her last visit home from university, suggested they set up a call centre or get wired up to the Internet!

Bill decided to review the ordering process and the associated problems of phone lines and computers as soon as he had cleared the paperwork in a day or two. The paper had been mounting up recently due to the amount of documentation being put out by government departments: the local council, UK government departments, and the EU. 'There is a never ending stream of new legislation or proposed changes', according to Jill, the company secretary: 'product liability, warranties, rights of distributors and sales agents, sales promotion, and a new data protection act in the last few months alone.' And now some of the European agents are asking if we will be pricing in euros?

Sales were still growing and it was a job to keep up with the service requirements of customers. From the database set up recently it was obvious that not all consumers were poor and frail. People were living longer and many were reasonably well off, and prepared to pay for the convenience of mobility and comfort in their old age. Mobility aids were no longer a utilitarian market with purely functional products being purchased and provided by the National Health Service. In fact Jenny had said, when she was last home, that a local distributor in her university town of Leicester had been advertising on local radio. Now that gave Bill an idea.

CASE STUDY Review questions

1. Discuss the relationship between changing demographics, disposable income, and market segmentation with reference to the case.

2. Identify the possible sources of the new regulations/legislation affecting medium sized business such as this. (Be specific, government is too general. Which governments and which departments?)

3. How will the introduction of the euro affect such a business as this?

4. How is technology impacting on this business? What options does Bill have in his review of the ordering process and associated problems of phone lines and computers? What, if any, will be the impact on the rest of the organization such as: office staff, sales representatives and European sales agents.

CHAPTER Summary and links to other chapters

Information is becoming increasingly important as a means by which organizations gain advantage in a competitive business environment. With recent advances in a firm's ability to collect data, greater attention is now placed on the effective use of information. 'Keeping in touch' drives a firm's information collection and it is important that methods of data collection, analysis and dissemination are appropriate to this task. As firms grow, their information management activities tend to become more complex. Numerous frameworks are available for analysing the business environment. The choice of framework will depend, among other things, on the complexity of the environment, the speed of change and the cost of inaccurately predicting change in the environment.

There are close linkages between this chapter and Chapter 6 where we discussed the nature of competition. In all but the most 'perfect' markets, understanding competitors is crucial to market success. An important consideration in predicting the future is the likely consequence of any change in the political and legal environments (Chapters 8 and 9), where change can occur quite suddenly. Change in the social and demographic environment (Chapter 11) tends to be more gradual. Finally, Chapter 12 discussed developments in information technology which are improving organizations' ability to gather and analyse information about their business environment.

CHAPTER Review questions

1 What factors make an organization's environment so complex?

Using an industry example, suggest relevant sources of information it might access to help it understand its complexity.

(Based on CIM Marketing Environment Examination)

2 Your government has approached an independent group of economic forecasters to undertake a SWOT analysis of the national economy. Prepare a short series of relevant slides to support the forthcoming presentation of this analysis.

(Based on CIM Marketing Environment Examination)

3 All the industries listed below experienced a turbulent business environment during the 1990s. Select one of these industries (or any other industry with which you are familiar) and identify the changes encountered.

Telephones, TV, hospitals, electricity, defence, computing, retailing.

4 Choose an industry and look ahead about three to five years and build a scenario for the future.

5 Construct an influence diagram for a product category of your choosing. Some ideas are:

(a) Retirement apartments (private sector for sale or rent)

(b) Children's bikes

(c) Conservatories

(d) Fabric material (used for curtaining and furniture coverings)

(e) Computer-controlled document handling machinery (for handling, collating and folding documents or leaflets and stuffing envelopes).

6 For those of you in work attempt to construct an 'environmental impact grid' for your business.

7 Group project

Genetically modified (GM) ingredients are now appearing in food sold in UK supermarkets. Agri-businesses and some food manufacturers believe there are substantial benefits to using genetically modified crops (and possibly animals in the future). Some food manufacturers claim NOT to use GE ingredients. Some pressure groups and customers believe they should be made illegal. Most customers are unsure and possibly confused. Supermarkets are treading cautiously. This is a complex business–environmental problem. Technology makes it possible. Government legislation appears not to cover the issue. Main players in the markets are unsure. There is potentially a new industry worth billions of pounds in an embryonic state. It potentially affects us all.

Conduct an environmental audit on this topic. Look at the issues from the point of view of different players: producers, manufacturers, retailers, consumers and government. (If there is more than one group each could take up the position of one of the players.)

8 Group project

Cars propelled by traditional fuels such as petrol and diesel are claimed to pollute our cities and damage the environment. Investigate the alternative fuels under development and evaluate their benefits and limitations? What environmental forces may speed up or slow down the introduction

References

Ansoff, H.I. (1984) *Implementing Strategic Management*, Prentice-Hall, Englewood Cliffs, NJ.

Berger, P.L. and T. Luckmann (1966) *The Social Construction of Reality*, Doubleday, Garden City, NY.

Christopher, M., M. McDonald and G. Wills (1980) *Introducing Marketing*, Pan, London.

Diffenbach, J. (1983) 'Corporate environmental analysis in US corporations', *Long Range Planning*, vol. 16, no. 3, pp. 107–116.

Dretske, F. (1981) *Knowledge and the Flow of Information*, MIT Press, Cambridge, MA.

Drucker, P.F. (1999) *Management Challenges for the 21st Century*, Harper and Row, New York.

Glueck, W.F. (1980) *Business Policy and Strategic Management*, 3rd edn, McGraw-Hill, New York.

Jenster, P.V. (1987) 'Using critical success factors in planning', *Long Range Planning*, vol. 20, no. 4, pp. 102–109.

Johnson, G. and K. Scholes (1988) *Exploring Corporate Strategy*, Prentice-Hall, Hemel Hempstead.

Kohili, A.K. and B.J. Jaworski (1990) 'Marketing orientation: the Construct report, propositions and management implications, *Journal of Marketing*, April, vol. 54, 1–18.

Kotler, P. (1997) *Marketing Management: Analysis, Planning, Implementation and Control*, 9th edn, Prentice-Hall International, Hemel Hempstead.

Mintel (1998) 'Food retailing, retail market shares, grocery market shares' (CD-ROM), Figure 47, 1993–97.

Moorman C., G. Zaltman and R. Deshpande (1992) 'Relationships between providers and users of market research: the dynamics of trust within and between organizations', *Journal of Marketing Research*, August, vol. 29, 314–328.

Narchal, R.M. *et al.* (1987) 'An environmental scanning system for business planning', *Long Range Planning*, vol. 20, no. 6, pp. 96–105.

Nonaka, I. (1991) 'The knowledge-creating company', *Harvard Business Review*, vol. 69, no. 6, pp. 96–104.

Piercy, N. (1985) *Marketing Organization: An Analysis of Information Processing, Power and Politics*, Allen and Unwin, London.

Porter, M.E. (1985) *Competitive Advantage*, Free Press, New York.

Twisk, R. and R. Brooks (1991) 'Ex-BBC chief spearheads breakfast bid with blast at "Terrible TV-am"', *The Observer*, 28 April, p. 1.

Selected further reading

There are many texts on the subject of marketing management which focus on how an organization can implement measures to respond to a changing external environment. The following are useful:

Fifield, P. (1998) *Marketing Strategy*, 2nd edn, Butterworth-Heinemann, Oxford.

Kotler, P. (1997) *Marketing Management: Analysis, Planning, Implementation and Control*, 9th edn, Prentice-Hall, Hemel Hempstead.

Piercy, N. (1997) *Market-led Strategic Change*, 2nd edn, Butterworth-Heinemann, Oxford.

For a review of classic articles which discuss the methods by which companies compete in changing market environments, the following are useful:

Diffenbach, J. (1983) 'Corporate Environmental Analysis in US Corporations', *Long Range Planning*, vol. 16, no. 3, pp. 107–116.

Porter, M.E. (1985) *Competitive Advantage*, Free Press, New York.

Competition within the Internet environment is discussed in the following:

Porter, M.E. (2001) 'Strategy and the Internet', *Harvard Business Review*, March, pp. 63–78.

For a general discussion of the principles of marketing research, the following texts are recommended:

Birn, R.J. (1999) *Effective Use of Marketing Research*, Kogan Page, London.

Chisnall, P. (1996) *Marketing Research*, 5th edn, McGraw-Hill, Maidenhead.

Proctor, T. (1997) *Essentials of Marketing Research*, Pitman, London.

Quee, W.T. (1998) *Marketing Research*, 3rd edn, Butterworth Heinemann, Oxford.

West, C. (1999) *Marketing Research*, Macmillan, Basingstoke.

The important role played by information in business planning is discussed in the following articles:

Collis, D.J. and Montgomery, C.A. (1998) 'Creating corporate advantage', *Harvard Business Review*, vol. 76, no. 3, pp. 71–83.

Czerniawska, F. and G. Potter (1998) *Business in a Virtual World: Exploiting Information for Competitive Advantage*, Macmillan, Basingstoke.

Greco, J. (1999) 'Knowledge is power', *Journal of Business Strategy*, March–April, vol. 20, pp. 176–89.

Nonaka, I. (1991) 'The knowledge-creating company', *Harvard Business Review*, vol. 69, no. 6, pp. 96–104.

The following references develop the above point by analysing the interpersonal dimension of information exchange within organizations

Deshpande, R. and G. Zaltman (1984) 'A comparison of factors affecting researcher and manager perceptions of market research use, *Journal of Marketing Research*, February, vol. 21, pp. 32–38.

Moorman C., G. Zaltman and R. Deshpande (1992) 'Relationships between providers and users of market research: the dynamics of trust within and between organizations', *Journal of Marketing Research*, vol. 29, August, pp. 314–328.

Useful websites

Business Information discussion site   Business-Information-All is a forum for teachers and researchers working in the area of business information management, business information systems or business information technology.   **http://www.jiscmail.ac.uk/lists/business-information-all.html**

Ernst and Young Center for Business   The Ernst and Young Center for Business Innovation website contains downloadable knowledge management publications, surveys, details of the 'Knowledge Advantage 1998', and a discussion on 'Managing the Knowledge Organization'.
http://www.businessinnovation.ey.com/

Impact Of E-Business On Office Work   A Canadian website offering useful overviews of how office support work processes are changing, and the skills and labour market knowledge that office workers are likely to need in the future.   **http://www.ont.hrdc-drhc.gc.ca/english/lmi/eaid/occ.info/ebusReport/full.e.html**

Managing Organizational Knowledge   This Ernst and Young site contains an online discussion forum on managing organizational knowledge.   **http://www.businessinnovation.ey.com/**

Shell   This site provides a useful description of the way the Shell oil company uses scenario building in its business planning.   **http://www.shell.com/royal-en/content/1,5028,25432-50913,00.html**

WWW Virtual Library on Knowledge Management   A comprehensive site containing links, online forums, articles, magazines, analyses and news.   **http://www.brint.com/km/**

Key terms

Audits	Knowledge management
Decision support systems	Learning organization
Environmental impact grids	Management information systems
Environmental scanning	Scenarios
Expert opinion	SWOT analysis
Five forces model	Trend analysis
Forecasting	

14

Case Studies

Five case studies are presented here which bring together a number of issues discussed in previous chapters. All the cases focus on organizations that have faced significant changes in their business environments. Their challenge has been first to identify the change that was occurring, to understand its impact on their business, and then to make decisions about how they could most effectively respond to the change. For each case study, a number of discussion questions are posed. The cases represent a range of different business environments:

1. **CD Marketing Services Ltd** was operating a low-tech door-to-door leaflet distribution service which was being challenged by companies offering sophisticated targeting services using computerized databases. Should the company capitalize on its strengths in its established sector? It knows this sector well, but did this sector face oblivion? What strengths did it have to take on its much larger rivals if it wished to move into the much more high-tech and growing customer profiling and database management sector?

2. **Bonar Teich Flexibles Ltd** specialized in vacuum coating materials under very high temperatures. It had a full order book, but was facing challenges from new methods of metalizing. Should it invest in the new technology which was expensive and risky, or keep with what was proven? This case study illustrates the opportunities presented by new technology and how a UK company evaluated the market potential.

3. **SRI Air-conditioning Appliances, India**, were constrained from developing their market by high sales taxes. Government changes to the level and method of taxation led to a fall in prices, an increase in demand, and new product development. However, these changes also caught the eye of foreign-owned multinational companies.

4. **Bass Brewers Ltd** entered the Czech Republic shortly after the end of the communist era, where it found a highly fragmented market for beer and a very different social environment. Bass saw opportunities to use its skills in brand development and distribution to bring about the profitable consolidation of the Czech beer market. But with very low beer prices, and a well financed Japanese competitor also seeking dominance of the market, how could Bass earn profits? Eventually, Bass pulled out of the Czech markets, having never made a profit.

5. **Project Keyhole** attempts to discover more about the attitudes, behaviour and lifestyle of consumers. Quantitative approaches to the study of individuals can miss a lot of detail and this approach seeks the whole truth by living with people as they make consumption choices. As a window on the world, is this approach more meaningful for businesses than traditional database driven profiling systems?

CD MARKETING SERVICES LTD

Few people would have imagined 50 years ago that large amounts of consumer profile data would be bought and sold by companies. But today the collection, analysis and dissemination of information has led to the emergence of a whole new service sector. Services organizations have been both major consumers of information services and producers of increasingly sophisticated services. Information has become ever more crucial to firms in their attempts to target new customers and to track existing ones. The 'information age' and firms' desire to target customers individually rather than *en masse* has given rise to new opportunities for services suppliers who have kept their eyes on social and technological change. A seemingly bewildering array of organizations have developed a previously unimaginable range of information services which help client companies to get their message to customers more cost effectively than their competitors.

One company that has ridden the crest of the information wave is Circular Distributors Ltd. It has been in business for over half a century as a supplier of targeted messages, acting on behalf of numerous goods and services suppliers. Like most companies in the services sector, it has found its business environment changing at an increasingly rapid rate. The company has been deeply affected by technological developments which affect the way it operates and by the expectations of its customers and the activities of its competitors. An analysis of its recent performance shows how business organizations must constantly monitor their environment and respond to change.

The company is essentially in the business of supplying direct marketing services. As a proportion of all firms' promotional expenditure, direct marketing has been increasing its share during the 1990s, giving rise to exciting opportunities with companies who had developed a sound knowledge of techniques for dealing with customers on a one-to-one basis. Some indication in the shift of promotional expenditure is shown in Figure 14.1. When the direct mail component of this expenditure is examined more closely, it is evident that the business-to-consumer element was expanding more rapidly during the 1990s than the business-to-business element (Figure 14.2).

Circular Distributors was founded over 50 years ago as a very low-tech distributor of leaflets from door to door. In its early years it delivered 10 million free samples for Lever Brothers in the first ever door-to-door distribution of its kind. From a scatter-gun approach to distribution, the company had gradually refined its techniques to deliver promotional leaflets and sample offers of products which typically included shampoo, tea bags and soap. Fifty years ago, many manufacturers of fast moving consumer goods would have been more than happy with the company's approach which by today's standards would be considered quite simplistic. It was essentially putting a fairly generic product into the hands of a fairly homogeneous market to encourage trial and hopefully a subsequent purchase. Over time, markets have become more fragmented as distinctive lifestyle groups have emerged. In response to this, companies have sought to differentiate their products to appeal to ever smaller niche segments. The fairly generic, low-value added service which Circular Distributors was selling had become too blunt an instrument for fast-moving consumer goods (fmcg), companies, who now had an exciting range of value-added marketing services available to them to target customers more cost effectively.

Circular Distributor's present management team headed by Nick Wells and three fellow directors

Figure 14.1
Advertising expenditure by medium
(*Source*: Adapted from Advertising Association data)

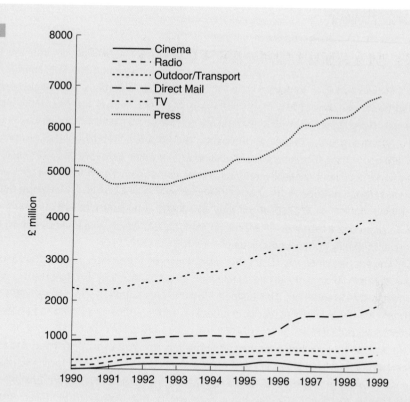

Figure 14.2
Composition of direct mail volume 1990–1999
(*Source*: Adapted from Royal Mail data)

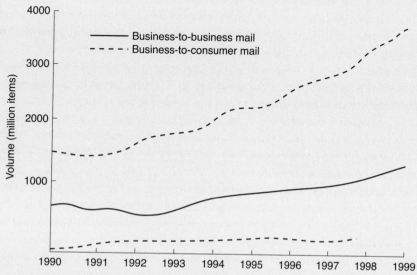

had taken control of the company in a £1.1 million management buyout in 1991. An important part of the new management's business development plan during the 1990s was based on a publication called *Emma's Diary*, launched in 1992 and produced in association with the Royal College of General Practitioners. The 132-page booklet is a week-by-week guide to pregnancy and is given out by GPs and midwives to women when their pregnancy is confirmed. Research has shown that it is read by 78 per cent of expectant mothers and 81 per cent of first-time mothers-to-be. This gives *Emma's Diary* higher readership than all the competing 13 parenting magazines combined.

Advertising in the bi-annual publication by producers of baby-related products has accounted for almost a third of *Emma's Diary's* revenue. A further third of revenue comes from companies paying for the distribution of product samples in the mother's gift pack, which is distributed free to readers through Superdrug shops. The mother's gift pack is an effective marketing medium, collected in 1999 by 400 000 of the total of 720 000 expectant mothers. The remaining one-third of revenue comes from sales of consumer information, which is gathered when expectant mothers register to qualify for the mother's pack.

The success of *Emma's Diary* prompted a spin-off publication in 1997. Operating under the same *Emma's Diary* brand name, the *One Step Ahead* publication is distributed by registrars when a baby's birth is registered. The editorial content concentrates on child-accident prevention. Some 84 per cent of new parents receive the booklet and more than half go on to collect a baby gift pack from Boots' stores.

By 1999 the company appeared to be moving along at a very pedestrian pace. In the information age, too much of its energies appeared to be directed at stuffing envelopes, and too little to the collection, analysis and sale of marketing information. The third of revenue for *Emma's Diary* which came from data sales had highlighted the possibilities for the company, but it seemed to be moving at a much slower pace than other companies such as Claritis and Experian who were growing rapidly through the sale of consumer information. In June 1999 the *Sunday Times* ran an article on the company and the expert commentators consulted were not over impressed. Ray Perry of the Chartered Institute of Marketing described Circular Distributors as 'a flat and stagnant company' that needed 'a new lease of life and a new identity'. John Eggleston of KPMG said its managers 'need to take action quickly, accept that growth demands some risk and develop firm and practical plans' to seize opportunities for growth. Managers were criticized for focusing too much on internal issues and lacking the drive to respond to market changes. The article concluded: 'If Circular Distributors is to maintain its profits, it needs to provide door-to-door services of a higher value. It must change its image from a letter-box-stuffing operation to a distributor of marketing materials and services. Ultimately it may need to change its name to attract the right clients'.

The criticism implicit in the *Sunday Times* article goaded the company into a more adventurous approach to its business. For a start, the company changed its name from Circular Distributors to CD Marketing Services and developed Lifestyle Marketing as a brand in its own right to distinguish it from the relatively low value letterbox distribution service. The Circular Distributors name was retained for the door to door distribution service. This part of the business was still very large and in 1999 delivered a total of more than one and a half billion items throughout the United Kingdom. Within its portfolio of services, the sale of consumer information may have been the star or growth service, but door-to-door distribution was in danger of going from being a cash cow to a dog.

During 1999 the company invested heavily in new technologies aimed at giving it a competitive advantage in the growing field of data analysis. The immediate effect of this investment was to reduce profits by about £400,000, but this expenditure contributed to an increase in sales to £33 million and profits to £2.4 million. CD invested heavily in developing more sophisticated services than stuffing promotional material and product samples through letterboxes.

Meanwhile, CD developed two further publications that followed a similar formula to the original *Emma's Diary*. In April 2000, CD began to publish *Emma's Diary Pre-School Guide*, aimed at mothers of children aged 3–5 and distributed through doctors' surgeries when youngsters are brought in for their MMR inoculation booster. A further publication called *Married Life ... The Small Print* was planned for launch in August 2000. This would contain relevant editorial material and sample packs, and would be distributed to couples when they visit vicars and registrars to make wedding arrangements. Both publications generate revenue through advertising and sample packs. However, even greater emphasis was placed on data collection for subsequent sale. Both publications included reader survey forms which generated a 21 per cent response rate during a pilot in November 1999 – high by market research industry standards.

In developing these more specifically targeted products, the company had subtly changed its core business. The emphasis was now as much on collecting information about consumers as on distributing product samples. The focus of the company's service offer had shifted from distribution to information management.

The most important role of the company's new publications was to collect data on consumers at key stages in their life cycles. By 1999 CD already had a database of 3.5 million families, with 1.1 million having been collected in the past two years. It was now collecting data on 600 000 families each year, with 100 000 being 'cleansed' to remove those that change address. The aim was to build Britain's largest database of families with young children.

What was the nature of the service being offered by the company's Lifecycle Marketing division? Segmented lists of consumers created by the company could be rented by organizations for one-off use. The company also sold licences by which other organizations could include CD's data in their own databases. As a further service, CD offered its clients the chance to include specific questions in its publications, for which the client would have exclusive rights to use the data generated. Given the growing difficulty of getting consumers to respond to questionnaires, and the high response rates achieved by CD's targeted publications, this service was highly valuable in its own right.

Who were the customers for CD's information services? The two most important groups of customers were financial services and home-shopping businesses, which each accounted for about 30 per cent of data sales. Remaining sales were spread between suppliers of baby products, children's book clubs and various other types of business. All these clients were attracted by the fact that readers of the company's publications were going through some form of life change, such as becoming a parent or getting married, or having a child starting at school. Each of these life changes is typically associated with new spending priorities and in the absence of previous knowledge about these new types of purchases, mailshots may be particularly welcomed by individuals. Client companies particularly valued the high coverage of the target segments and the low wastage rate within the lists.

In 1999, the company expected that within three years the revenue of its Lifecycle Marketing division would grow almost threefold, generating sales of £3 million from the publications and gift packs, and more significantly, £4 million from information sales. This was a much faster growth rate than that of the core door-to-door distribution business, which had continued to show modest growth. But did a dash into information services spell dangers as well as opportunities for the company?

The company knew the door-to-door business inside out and had carved a valuable niche for itself where it could offer unrivalled coverage, flexibility and economies of scale. But now that it was moving into the supply of information services it was competing on territory already staked out by much larger competitors. Companies such as Claritas, ICD and Experian had already built up massive databases of consumer information. ICD, for example, claimed to have an average of 72 pieces of information about every household in the country. They could also offer services in many of the overseas markets which their clients operated in. It was not good enough for CD to claim that it had superior knowledge of a small number of niche market segments, because its larger competitors had been steadily building up ever more sophisticated databases of consumer niches. The company saw a major problem in convincing clients to defect from its larger competitors to use its own information services. Would CD always be seen as a low-value letterbox stuffer? Or could it use its long standing relationships with many fmcg companies to add information services to its service offer? The company needed to build trust and confidence among clients that had never used its services or only perceived the company as a provider of lower value door-to-door distribution.

At the same time, the company was aware that it should not lose sight of its core letterbox market which was still profitable. A number of initiatives to raise the value of services offered to clients were attempted, for example offering a weekend distribution service. The company had previously only operated a weekday distribution service, but had identified that clients' messages could be more effective if they were delivered to a target customer on the day when they have most time to read it. New types of clients appeared for the door-to-door service, such as Internet Service Providers who sought distribution of free CD ROMs to targeted households. The company also extended its gift pack concept by delivering it door to door, without the need to collect it from a designated retail outlet. During 2000, a trial took place to distribute children's school packs door-to door. Each pack consisted of a plastic bag containing a back-to-school calendar (carrying advertising messages), a CD-ROM from an Internet service provider and samples of products aimed at children aged between 5 and 14. A response card sought to increase the volume of information that the company could sell on to its clients.

Circular Distributors also sought to expand into mainland Europe. It formed strategic alliances with a number of companies who are members of the European Letterbox Marketing Association, so that it is now able to offer its UK clients a 'one-stop shop' distribution service to 140 million homes in France, Germany, Spain and Italy. As evidence that it was taking European expansion seriously, it recruited three multilingual sales staff to handle European sales. By having the ability to offer Europe-wide distribution, the company hoped that it would be able to cater for clients such as L'Oreal, Kimberley-Clark and Gillette who have pan-European marketing operations. Europe-wide distribution was expected to generate £2.5 to £3 million in additional business during 2001.

The company has moved into areas of expertise which were previously unknown to it and has thereby taken big risks. But in the rapidly changing market for information services, it could not afford to stand still. New methods of distributing information to target customers are appearing all the time, with recent examples being the Internet, digital television and WAP mobile phones. How widely should CD spread its resources? Which new media are worth investing in, and which ones may disappear as quickly as they appeared? How far can the company's brand be stretched? There is a great danger that any investment in emerging media may be too little to be effective. It could simply end up having some representation with all media, but being effective in none. The company has made tentative steps into the Internet by setting up a website for *Emma's Diary*, and has gained some information about visitors to the site. It has also earned some revenue from 'click throughs' to advertisers on the site. But to be in this business seriously, the company needs to devote serious amounts of time and resources to it. With an ever-increasing number of Internet Service Providers offering portals which seek users and advertisers, CD is just one of many minnows in a crowded marketplace.

Circular Distributors has moved from providing a low-value service in a slowly growing market to providing higher value services in rapidly expanding markets. Although the information age has produced many opportunities, it has also produced many casualties among companies that have expanded too fast and failed to deliver a credible value proposition to their customers. During early 2000, 'Dot.com' fever appeared to reach a peak with large amounts of money being poured into new ventures seeking to gain more information about consumers. Should CD have taken a bolder approach or was caution more appropriate? And what about door-to-door distribution, the bread and butter of CD's business – shouldn't the company focus on what it knows best? For the future, one of the main problems facing the company is knowing just where the next threat to its business will come from. What, for instance will the effect of third generation mobile phones be on consumer information services? Which new technologies should the company invest in? What new services should it seek to offer? Where does the traditional service of door-to-door distribution fit into its portfolio?

Sources: based on the following:

Circular Distributors Ltd website (http: // www .cdltd.co.uk) and http: // www. Emmasdiary.co.uk) Direct Mail Information Service (http: // www . dmis/keystats/html) *Sunday Times* Enterprise Network 21 May 2000 p(3) 17

CASE STUDY   Review questions

1 What business is CD Marketing Services in? What business should it be in?

2 Draw a product/market expansion matrix identifying the growth options for CD Marketing Services. How would you assess the riskiness of each identified growth option?

3 On what bases can CD position itself relative to its competitors? What position would you recommend that it adopts? What do you consider to be the most important sources of sustainable competitive advantage for CD?

4 What methods should the company use to scan its environment for new opportunities/threats? How should they be assessed?

5 There is a view that information technology will increasingly allow CD's clients to do much of the data analysis that they currently buy in from CD. In such a scenario, how can CD add value to its service offer?

6 Critically assess CD's opportunities for overseas expansion. What factors should influence the company's overseas expansion strategy?

BONAR TEICH ELECTRON BEAM METALLIZING

Case prepared by Clive Fielding and Bob Hartley.
Information in this case has been adjusted to retain confidentiality.

This case study illustrates the opportunities presented by new technology and how a UK company evaluated the market potential.

What is metallizing?

Metallizing is the popular term for vacuum coating under very high temperatures, a process used to apply ultra-thin coatings (thinner than a human hair) to a variety of materials. The coating material, in this case metallic aluminium, is vaporized in a vacuum and condensed onto a film made from another material, in this case plastic film. Aluminium imparts a bright finish, but also gives plastic film a good barrier to light, oxygen, moisture and odours. Not only does packaging look good on the shelves, but it extends the shelf life of the product. In addition to the packaging industry uses include bottle tops, gift wrapping, car trims and insulation.

Packaging is the largest single market in tonnage. The required combinations of attractiveness and effectiveness means that the metallized film is of interest to firms, especially in the fast moving consumer goods (fmcg) industries, who are often looking for new ideas. Metallized packaging film has become more popular in recent years, particularly in the food industry where it is now used, for example, on biscuits, tea bags and crisps. These customers, though, are price sensitive as a small rise in packaging costs can have a significant impact on selling price.

Metallizing at Bonar Teich

Bonar Teich Flexibles, of Derby, part of the Low and Bonar Group has been producing metallized plastic films for packaging since 1983. In 1987, they were producing to capacity, their products were well established, and the company was considering further investment in metallizing. Market research was undertaken and the size and growth rates of the European market were established. Research from a number of sources showed:

Market size

- The overall market size for metallized plastic film in Western Europe in 1986 was 21–23 000 tonnes.
- Packaging accounted for approximately 50 per cent
- Growth was estimated to be 13 per cent per annum.
- Some products were expected to grow by up to 40 per cent per annum.

Table 14.1   Market share for metallized plaster film

Company	Market shares UK (%)	W. Europe (%)
Camvac (UK)	50	30
Convertec (UK)	20	10
Bonar Teich (UK)	10	3
MF&P (UK)	10	3
Others (European)	10	54

The company was aware that if it were to extend its applications into more price-sensitive sectors, such as packaging for grocery products, prices and therefore costs would have to be lower. Alternative technologies for metallizing were investigated. A new machine was available, but the technology was new and not in commercial production and thus presented some development risks. Close co-operation with the suppliers of the machine dependent on the new technology would be required. Teething problems could be expected. Development and commissioning trials using the new technology could be expected to take longer than with the proven technology. Once the new machine is in commercial production there is the risk that its performance may never quite match the initial expectations or claims of the manufacturer. The estimated performance of the new technology, then, has to be matched against the proven reliability and performance of the conventional machines. Financial projections have to be made on the basis of this technical judgement. A summary of the competing technologies follows.

Conventional technology v. new technology

All commercial metallizing is done on a batch process as rolls of material are loaded on to the machine for processing. However, there are some important differences between the conventional process and the new technology (see Figure 14.3). With the conventional method of 'resistance-heated evaporation' the roll of material is loaded into the processing chamber and the vacuum pumped down. The vacuum reduces the evaporation temperature of the coating material and prevents oxidation. The material is processed by unwinding the material in such a way that it passes over the aluminium which is vaporized at very high temperature. This process coats the plastic film with the aluminium and the now metallized material is received onto the rewind drum. The vacuum is then broken so that the finished product can be removed from within the machine. The efficiency of the process, actual running time of the machine to total time from start to finish of the operation, is 50 per cent. This is because of the time taken to load the machine and then pumpdown the vacuum at the start, and to allow cooling at the end before the roll of metallized material can be removed. The actual speed at which the machine can process the material is 450 metres per minute. The machine can only use aluminium as a coating material as the maximum temperature at the source of evaporation is 1500 °C. The consumable costs are 0.235 pence per square metre. The machine is mechanically complex, but of proven technology with a known reliability.

The new technology uses an 'electron beam evaporation' process. The principles by which the machine works are the same as with the conventional machine. The roll of material is unwound and passes over a heat source where the coating material is vaporized. The now metallized material is

Figure 14.3
Conventional versus new technology in metallizing: (a) Resistance heated evaporation (conventional); (b) Election beam evaporation (new technology)
(*Source*: Bonar Teich)

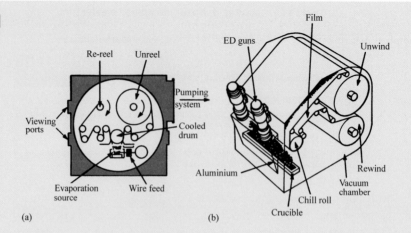

(a)   (b)

then received onto the rewind drum. There are a number of important differences, though. Firstly, the roll of material and the rewind drum are located outside the vacuum chamber, so that there is no need for waiting time to break the vacuum and allow for cooling. The evaporation energy is provided by two electron beams which can give a higher operating temperature, up to 2200°C. This means that other materials, in addition to aluminium, can be used in the metallizing process if desired. The machine can operate up to speeds of 600 metres per minute. Very thick coatings can be applied at full speed if desired.

Financial estimates

The parent company of Bonar Teich was prepared to invest in their packaging businesses if projects gave a worthwhile return. The financial estimates for the investment are shown below. No sales for years one and two were assumed and sales of £1.75 million was judged to be the Electron Beams maximum capacity on five-day working. The same figure was used for the conventional machine, but an element of overtime was assumed. The capital costs of the new technology was £1.60 million and of the conventional machine £1.45 million. Profit and return on capital employed (ROCE) was projected as shown in the table. For reasons of confidentiality the profit is shown as a percentage based on the conventional machine with year three being the base of 100 per cent.

Table 14.2   Financial projections for investment in new metallizing plant

	Year 3	Year 4	Year 5	Year 6
Sales £000s	820	1315	1750	1750
Profit %				
Electron beam	120	234	328	328
Conventional	100	200	283	283
ROCE %				
Electron beam	13.0	26.5	34.5	38.5
Conventional	12.0	25.5	32.5	36.5

Both machines showed a satisfactory return, with payback periods of less than four years of operation and an increase in manning of 10.

What would you do?

Would you invest in another conventional machine staying with the proven technology? Or risk investing in the new, but commercially untried, Electron Beam machine with its claimed superior performance? You will find it useful to assess the technology balance by summarizing the key characteristics of the competing technologies, before comparing the financial figures.

CASE STUDY 3

SRI AIR-CONDITIONING APPLIANCES, INDIA

Case prepared by Ciby James and Bob Hartley.
Information in this case has been adjusted to retain confidentiality.

Company information

Shriram Refrigeration Industries (SRI) is a division of SIEL Ltd, a large Indian conglomerate company. Shriram manufactures air-conditioning units, compressors and commercial refrigeration appliances such as drinking water coolers and bottle coolers. Its air-conditioning appliances are sold under the Shriram brand name.

Product information

Air conditioning is available in various forms. Central air-conditioning systems operate much as a central heating system does in colder climates. The compressor is located outside and cold air is distributed to the rooms via ducts built into the building. Packaged air-conditioning are similar systems, but only serve part of the building. With a split air-conditioning system a smaller compressor is also located outside and cool air is distributed to a limited number of vents serving a room. Air-conditioning appliances are complete self-contained electrical units, which are of two basic types. The compact type stands alone on the floor, which is wired into the room's electrical supply. The second is a window unit, which in a new building design will fit just below the window with the compressor protruding outside and in an old building the unit will replace a window.

Market background

Air-conditioning units are considered a luxury by the Indian government and have traditionally attracted a high level of excise duty. Up until 1993 a high-fixed excise duty (effectively 60 per cent and greater) applied on all units up to 1.5 tonnes. Manufacturers had little incentive therefore to make smaller units suitable for the domestic market, as the price differential was minimal due to the high fixed tax. Domestic consumers and small businesses that could afford to, bought large capacity units whether needed or not.

Due to the high duty, demand was stifled and this gave rise to an unorganized or informal sector. Households, small shops and businesses simply bought air-conditioners from local assemblers who would put together a unit from parts, and thus did not have to pay the high excise duties. However, quality suffered, as the assemblers often did not have suitable standard equipment. Shriram supplied compressors to this market.

By the end of 1993, the market was in the order of 150 000 units per annum, however, more than 50 per cent of sales were via the unorganized market. In the organized or formal sector the government was a major purchaser with some sales going to the private corporate sector. Prices and specifications for government organizations were dictated by the government through annual contract agreements. Quality was not important nor was product development. The standard size of unit available was 1.5 tonnes.

The result was a fragmented market, with low volumes, served by eight domestic manufacturers in the organized sector and around a thousand small assemblers in the unorganized sector. The maximum output of the market leader was between 30 000 and 40 000 units, the capacity of other major competitors being considerably lower. At this time, SRI were in fifth position in the market.

Change to duty

In 1994 and again in 1995, the government made adjustments to the excise duty after intense lobbying by the industry and also as part of the Indian government's plan for economic reforms and relaxation of state controls. In 1994, the duty was changed to an *ad valorem* tax so that duty was applied as a percentage of the basic selling price, and in 1995 the duty was lowered to 40 per cent. Prior to 1993 market growth rates were in the region of 6 per cent. In 1994 the market growth rate reached 45–50 per cent per annum. This rapid pace of growth was sustained for some years, as pent-up demand was unleashed.

This burst in growth is partly a result of the lower duty being passed on in lower prices (Table 14.1), but also the manufacturers have became much more sensitive to customer demands. Product development led to the introduction of smaller units suitable for the domestic market and the *ad valorem* tax meant that such units were available at a more realistic price.

Shriram took the lead in introducing these smaller compact air-conditioners, which were in the 0.5 and 0.75 tonne capacity range. These air-conditioning systems suitable for smaller rooms were affordably priced and economical in running. They helped create a new market segment particularly among middle-class first-time buyers. This introduction helped SRI improve its market share and position.

Table 14.3   Prices for air-conditioning units in Indian rupees (Rs)

Unit capacity tonnes	1993 price	1994 price	1995 price
1.5	28 000	27 000	26 000
1.0	n/a	21 000	20 000
0.5	n/a	17 000	15 000

Notes: Inflation approximately 8% pa. during this period.
Exchange rates: Rs30 = US$1
Rs50 = £1 sterling.

Table 14.4	Indian Consumer Preferences (1993)
1	Black and white TV
2	Fridge
3	Colour TV
4	Air-cooler
5	Washing machine
6	2-wheeler (scooter/motorbike)
7	VCR
8	Car
9	Air-conditioner

Overall, the industry saw new designs with enhanced features and improved quality introduced. Competition intensified as the consumers became more sophisticated and the manufacturers more sensitive to the market.

Total market sales in 1995 were expected to be in the order of 300 000 to 350 000 units. The role of the unorganized market is expected to decline in future years as excise duties are lowered further. Market research commissioned by SIEL Ltd in 1993 shows a potential of 900 000 units by 1998–99. Research also indicated that 50 per cent of this demand would be for the smaller capacity units. However, air-conditioners are still way down the 'wants list' of the average Indian consumer. The same research ranked air-conditioners last on a set of nine consumer durable items in terms of order of preference for purchase. The current household penetration for air-conditioners in urban households in India is less than 1 per cent (Table 14.2).

The future

The manufacturers are now meeting capacity restraints in the peak-selling season with three to four weeks becoming the normal delivery time.

With very high growth rates forecast to continue SRI feel they need to act in order to take advantage of the opportunity. Being part of the much larger Indian conglomerate SIEL, the division has access to the necessary financial resources. A modern production line for air-conditioners would have a capacity of 200 000 units compared to the current lines in India which produce a maximum of 40 000 units. The division felt that to build a plant of such capacity would require some form of technical collaboration with a foreign partner firm. Also component parts would need to be imported at least in the short term until local suppliers could scale up their output and improve quality.

The competition

The product portfolios of the six major players in the air-conditioning market show a differing profile reflecting the emerging market segments (Table 14.3).

Voltas

Voltas has been in the market since 1954 and the name is synonymous with air-conditioning. The company has the widest range of room air-conditioners. It is also established in central

Table 14.5   Major competitors: product portfolios for air-conditioners and related products

	Voltas	Carrier	Videocon	Shriram	Amtrex	BlueStar
Air-conditioning installed*						
central air-conditioning	✓					✓
packaged air-conditioning	✓					✓
split air-conditioning	✓	✓	✓	✓	✓	✓
Air-conditioning appliances*						
window air-conditioning	✓	✓	✓	✓	✓	✓
compact air-conditioning				✓		
Compressors*†		?	?		✓	
Drinking water coolers‡	✓			✓		✓
Refrigerators	✓		✓			
Washing machines	✓		✓			

Notes:

* Air-conditioners can be designed and built into buildings at the time of construction or refurbishment. Central air-conditioning serves the whole building, packaged air-conditioning serves part of a building, a split air-conditioning usually serves one room, but via a number of vents. All these have a separate compressor located outside or on top of the building. Air-conditioning appliances are complete self-contained units suitable for one room. Window air-conditioners are designed to fit in the place of a window or just below the window and vent directly to the outside. Compact air-conditioning units are self-contained appliances free-standing on the floor or fixed to a wall.

† SRI (Shriram) is a merchant manufacturer of air-conditioning and refrigeration compressors (i.e. it manufactures for other OEMs). Voltas and Carrier manufacture compressors, but it is believed largely for their own needs.

‡ Drinking water coolers are for use in offices and factories.

and packaged air-conditioning. Voltas is also a major player in the white goods business, with its refrigerators and washing machines. Voltas has decided to take on the threat from foreign multinationals by fast expanding in the white goods market through import of technology from major global companies. Market share in 1994–95 was 33 per cent and the company expects a 45 per cent growth in sales.

Carrier

Set up in India in 1987, the company did not start making profits until after 1993 when it recovered after the reduction in duties caused the boom in demand. Carrier has a range of room air-conditioners of state-of-the-art design. In 1994–95 its market share was 20 per cent. The company has not indicated any intention of entering into the sub 1 ton segment, but could soon enter the central air-conditioning segment. It also commands a market share of 45 per cent in the split air-conditioning segment.

Carrier's advertising budget is very high compared to other players and today the company enjoys a very high recall level among air-conditioner users which is second only to Voltas. The company is leveraging its association with the Carrier Corporation, world leader and pioneer in air-conditioning, in its advertising.

Videocon

Videocon, a very large Indian electronics manufacturer (turnover Rs2000 million), announced on 4 July 1995 (*Indian Telegraph*: 19) plans to build a new air-conditioning plant in Dubai. The company's

Indian air-conditioning plant has a capacity of 40 000 units. However, they see a market opportunity in the Gulf States where the market is estimated to be two million units; with only 1.4 million being produced locally in Saudi Arabia and the rest being imported. The Dubai plant is to have a capacity of 50 000 units and will be on stream within nine months.

A number of international players have also shown an interest in the Indian market. At various domestic exhibitions there have been displays by, among others, GE and Carrier, Sanyo, National Panasonic and Mitsubishi, Goldstar, Samsung and Whirlpool. Import duties on air-conditioners and air-conditioning components may go down further in the next few years making it viable to import air-conditioning units.

CASE STUDY Discussion questions

1. Identify the reasons contributing to the growth of the air-conditioning market in India.

2. What would be the advantages and limitations of SRI entering into collaboration with a foreign manufacturer?

3. If a partnership is established with a well-known and branded international company, should SRI be advised to continue with their own name, Shriram, or use the established international brand name?

4. What criteria should be used to determine the capacity of the plant to be built?

5. Comment on the alternative strategies being pursued by SRI and the main competitors.

CASE STUDY 4

THE CZECH BEER MARKET – A BITTER SWEET VENTURE FOR BASS

Why should one of the UK's leading brewers choose to develop the market for beer in a country which is already saturated with famous beers at rock bottom prices? To lovers of real ale, the Czech Republic is probably a heaven. But to Bass Breweries, the Czech market represented an opportunity waiting to be developed. However, a study of Bass's venture into the Czech Republic illustrates that understanding the environment of an emerging market can involve a lot of risks.

Eastern Europe, and the Czech Republic in particular, has one of the world's highest rates of per capita consumption of beer, which in 1997 stood at 160 litres per person, double the rate of most Western European countries. The Czech Republic has a long tradition of brewing, with some of the world's oldest and most respected beers, including the Staropramen, Ostravar and Vratislav brands. One of the reasons for the high consumption of beer has been its high quality and low price. The price of a litre of beer in 1997 was typically less than a quarter of what a comparable litre would have cost in the UK, the low price reflecting low taxes and low margins for producers.

So in a country of high-quality beers and low prices, what could Bass possibly hope to add to the market? When it first looked at the beer market in the Czech Republic, it saw a fragmented market where marketing was just emerging after decades of centralized planning. Beer drinkers had become used to a mentality of taking what was available, rather than seeking the best product to suit their needs. Bass saw that the fragmented market was ripe for consolidation. In 1997, the three largest breweries held only 55 per cent of the market, with another 25 per cent being made up of small regional brewers, none of whom had a national market share of over 3 per cent. Even Budwar, possibly the best known Czech beer in the UK, accounted for just 3 per cent of the domestic market. Many of the Czech Republic's near neighbours had similar structural problems and opportunities in their beer sector and, like other Western investors, Bass saw the country as a platform for expansion into the rest of Eastern Europe.

In addition to exploiting the Czech market, Bass also saw an opportunity to develop global markets for the high-quality beers which were currently confined to the domestic Czech market. Bass could use its global distribution network to exploit the brands in a way that would have been impossible to domestic companies.

Bass first invested in the Czech Republic in 1994, with a 34 per cent stake in Prague Breweries, later increasing this to 46 per cent. This brought Bass three Prague-based breweries which would have seemed quite small and unsophisticated by UK standards. In 1995, it bought 78 per cent of Vratislavice nad Nisou (with two breweries in north Bohemia) and 51 per cent of Ostravar, a brewery in north Moravia. In 1996 Bass acquired a controlling interest in Prague Breweries when it increased its stake to 51 per cent. In 1997, the three companies in which it had invested were merged under the name Prague Breweries, in which Bass has a 55 per cent stake. This made Prague Breweries the second-biggest brewer in the Czech Republic, but it still only had a 14 per cent market share. The market leader, Prazdroj, had 27 per cent. Bass had started the process of consolidation in the industry, but it still had a long way to go if it was to match progress in Western Europe.

The merger of the three breweries started the process of reducing competition in the sector. It also gave an opportunity to begin cutting costs, by disposing of three of its six breweries. It decided early on that its core business was brewing and subsequently sold on its acquired soft drinks businesses to Corona.

A further approach to making the Czech market profitable was the development of strong brands which could be sold at decent margins. By 1997 Bass had four national and three regional brands, but took a pragmatic approach to retaining the long-established regional brands – they would be retained as long as people continued to buy them. Doubtless Bass was mindful of the short-sightedness of UK brewers' attempts to suppress regional brands a couple of decades earlier, only to see them find a valuable role a few years later. Its first new product development in the country was a premium lager called Velvet, developed and brewed in the Czech Republic, but with the help of Bass in the UK. From the beginning, Bass sought to position Velvet as something quite different to commodity beers. It had a distinctive smooth, creamy head and Bass commissioned special glasses for it to be served in. To add to its differentiation, Bass provided training for bar staff on how to pour and serve it. Velvet was aimed at high-income consumers and promoted through bars and restaurants with targeted tastings. Promotional support was provided by advertising in *Elle*, *Harper's Bazaar* and *Esquire*, and by a dedicated sales team. Despite the conservatism of Czech drinkers, Bass had successfully found a niche market – the emerging middle classes in stylish bars. Bass's strategy has been to invest heavily in brands for the long term. In developing a brand, the company has started with a research programme among consumers to learn more about their beer needs, followed with research on respondents' perceptions of competing brands. It then undertook lifestyle segmentation, something previously unheard of.

Another strength of Bass in its home market is distribution and this represented another opportunity in the Czech market. By the end of 1997, a new sales, marketing and distribution structure was in place, making it possible to distribute national brands efficiently and effectively. The structure included national marketing, key account and business development teams, along with a unified salesforce and distribution network. In three years, one result of this reorganization had been to increase penetration of the company's products from 50 to 80 per cent of all retail outlets in the country.

Overcoming cultural barriers of the Czech people proved to be one of the biggest challenges for Bass. It seemed that many people found the change to a market-based system difficult to cope with, after 40 years of centralized planning. The whole idea of customer focus seemed to lack credibility among employees who had been used to customers having no choice. While Bass might have been expert at brewing, branding and distribution issues, it underestimated how much time it would have to spend on changing management issues and instilling Western values into staff. Problems were encountered in getting people to make decisions, motivating them to act on their decision and then having to check that agreed actions were actually being undertaken. Recruitment, appraisal and reward increasingly stressed a number of key attitudes of mind: being customer focused, results driven and innovative, behaving with integrity, treating people with respect, and showing respect for the community. As an example of the problems that had to be overcome, sales people had a pride that prevented them from listening to retailers, fostered by years of production orientation.

Bass had never managed to achieve profitability in the Czech market. Despite being an early mover in the consolidation of the Czech beer market, it was increasingly threatened by other international brewers who had gone through the same process of evaluating overseas markets and decided to enter the Czech market.

The biggest threat came from the Japanese investment bank Nomura International which was battling with Bass's Czech brands to dominate the country's beer market. Nomura had acquired Radegast and Pilsner, giving it 44 per cent of the Czech beer market and critics claimed that it was using its marketing muscle to win exclusive contracts with pubs and restaurants, keeping beer prices down. Bass, along with many of the smaller brewers, contended that Nomura was illegally abusing its dominant position and formally complained to the Czech government's Office for Economic Competition. The government regulator originally blocked the Radegast–Pilsner marketing merger to protect small brewers, but reversed its decision in 1999, citing a technicality. Bass had argued that in the Czech Republic, beer is a loss-making industry, and the current practices of Nomura would just give the market leader a chance to squeeze everyone else out in due course.

Back home, all the major UK breweries were undertaking reviews of what business they should be in, and Bass decided that its future should lie in the growing leisure sector (where it owned restaurants, hotels and fitness centres) rather than brewing. It came to an agreement for the Belgian brewer Interbrew SA to acquire all Bass's brewing operations. Although the takeover of Bass's UK operations was blocked by the Department of Trade and Industry on competition grounds, Interbrew's acquisition of Bass's non-UK businesses was cleared by the European Commission.

Interbrew already had a significant part of its business in Central and Eastern Europe, with operations in Russia, Ukraine, Hungary, Croatia, Romania, Bulgaria, Montenegro and the Czech Republic. It had a long-term vision for Bass's brands and following the acquisition of Bass's Czech assets, earmarked 3 billion Czech Koruna for development of Prazske Pivovary. Could it succeed where Bass had not been able to earn a profit?

Source: based on 'Brewing Up', *Marketing Business*, December 1998: 26–30.

CASE STUDY   Review questions

1 Review the alternative market entry strategies that were open to Bass in 1994 and assess each for its level of risk.

2 Identify the principal barriers Bass faced in developing a marketing culture in its Czech operations. How can it overcome these barriers?

3 Critically assess the problems and opportunities for Interbrew's investment in the Czech Republic arising from further integration of the country into the European Union.

CASE STUDY 5

PROJECT KEYHOLE SEEKS TO GET CLOSE TO UNDERSTANDING CONSUMERS' ATTITUDES, BEHAVIOUR AND LIFESTYLES

How can we actually tell what social change is going on? Do companies make too many assumptions about social habits? Structured questionnaire surveys may have a role for collecting large-scale factual data, but they have major weaknesses when it comes to understanding individuals' attitudes. Qualitative approaches, such as focus groups can get closer to the truth, but participants often still find themselves inhibited from telling the full story. Many marketing managers, especially those without large research budgets, inevitably end up relying on their own personal experiences to understand how consumers behave. This may be easy for target markets which are in the 20–40 age range (the age of typical marketers), but how do you understand the social environment in which teenagers or elderly people live?

A means of getting close to the truth has been devised by the advertising agency BMP DDB, and involves a company researcher living with a family for several days to record their every move. BMP hopes that Project Keyhole will be used by clients who are looking for more than the data gathered using traditional quantitative and qualitative research techniques. Participants record their views and actions on a digital video camera, in the presence of a researcher who stays with them from 8 a.m. until 10 p.m. for a few days. A normal project would last four or five days and the client company may be invited along for part of the time. Participants are paid £100 for their troubles. Who drinks the fresh orange juice in the house? How long do they spend cooking dinner? How do they actually cook the ready-prepared meals they bought earlier? Does the family eat together? What did they do with the direct mail when it came through the letter box? Did they use the coupon offer which it contained? These are examples of the vital information that sponsoring companies hope to get hold of in order to develop and target their products more effectively.

According to the company, the advantage of this method over conventional research is that it picks up inconsistencies between what people say they do and what they actually do. Following them throughout the day allows the researcher to see why a person's habits might change according to random factors like their mood, the time of day or the weather. Crucially it reveals the quirks in our behaviour that businesses are desperate to gain an insight into. For example, a person's store-card data might tell you that they buy butter and margarine, but it does not tell whether they eat the bread fresh, or toast it first before putting margarine on it.

In 1998, the magazine *Marketing* put this novel research method to the test with a family called the Joneses. It then compared the results of this approach with more traditional methods of profiling customers. In short, established quantitative profiling systems of companies such as CACI, Claritas and Experian might say one thing about the behaviour of a family, using lifestyle and electoral roll data, but did they bear any relation to reality?

The information that the researcher gathered in a short space of time told a lot about the Joneses. By contrast, the database information about the Joneses, although detailed and often accurate, could not capture the quirks and details that make up the personality of the family. For example, it transpired that the Joneses had a keener than average eye on value for money. Although information on them from the four database companies correctly suggested that they enjoy luxuries like good food and foreign holidays, it did not say anything about the real-life factors that influence their purchasing decisions. The most noticeable of these was that although they like good food, Mrs Jones mixed her shopping between the supermarket and a local discount store which sells cut-price brands. This means that she only bought at Tesco or Sainsbury's what she could not get cheaper elsewhere. She showed the researcher a can of branded plum tomatoes which she got for 10p at the discount store as an example, explaining that it would have cost 26p in the supermarket. Mrs Jones prided herself on being able to hunt down bargains like this and occasionally rewarded herself by buying 'something luxurious', such as smoked salmon from Marks and Spencer. The freezer had an important role to play as it allows Mrs Jones to buy things she sees on special offer even if she does not need them immediately.

Mrs Jones's eye for an offer made her a keen scrutinizer of direct mail. She checked mailings for 'catches' in the small print and for any special offers. She collected mailers worth chasing up on a clip on the fridge door, along with vouchers collected from magazines. Mrs Jones financial nous means that she managed the family's money.

Not surprisingly, these details did not come out in database information. Of the commercial databases, CACI's People UK and Lifecycle UK databases seemed to be most at variance with the reality of the Jones's life. They got their ages wrong, incorrectly surmised that they took business flights and incorrectly attributed Mr Jones with being computer literate. Nobody in the household read the *FT* or the *Independent* as predicted – they read the *Daily Mail* instead. Some of the other points made by CACI were right, but were felt to be very generalized and could apply to anybody.

Claritas seemed to be much closer to reality. The Jones's predicted jobs were about right and the database was correct in stating that they had credit and store cards. They managed to say that the Joneses liked antiques, perhaps learnt as a result of them occasionally buying *Homes and Antiques* magazine. They were similarly correct in stating that they liked gardening, DIY, foreign travel and eating out. The database had predicted that the family would be most likely to own a Ford or Renault car. In fact, Mrs Jones owned a Ford, while Mr Jones had a company Renault.

Source: based on 'Keeping up with the Joneses', *Marketing*, 19 November 1998: 28–29.

CASE STUDY Review questions

1 Why is it important to study the composition of the family buying unit? To what extent do you think this research approach will give a complete understanding of how family units make decisions?

2 What new possibilities, if any, for identifying distinctive lifestyle groups are opened up by this approach to the study of buyer behaviour?

3 Critically assess the scope for expanding this type of research as a means of learning more about changing consumer attitudes, beliefs and lifestyles.

Glossary

Accelerator effect   The idea that a small increase in consumer expenditure can lead to a very large increase in investment in capital equipment.

Aggregate demand   The total expenditure on goods and services in an economy.

Attitudes   An individual's consistently favourable or unfavourable feelings about an object, person or idea.

Balance of payments   A record of all transactions between domestic consumers and firms and those based overseas.

Branding   The process of creating a distinctive identity for a product which differentiates it from its competitors.

Business cycle   Fluctuations in the level of activity in an economy, commonly measured by employment levels and aggregate demand.

Cartel   An association of suppliers which seeks to restrict costly competition between its members.

Competitive advantage   A firm has a marketing mix that the target market sees as meeting its needs better than the mix of competing firms.

Consumer   The individual who uses up a good or service so that it has no further economic value.

Cost-push inflation   Price inflation that results from an increase in the cost of producing goods and services.

Cross-elasticity of demand   A measure of the responsiveness of demand for one good or service to changes in the price of another good or service.

Culture   The whole set of beliefs, attitudes and ways of behaving shared by a group of people.

Customers   People who buy a firm's products. (*Note*: customers may not be the actual *consumers* of the product.)

Decision support system Techniques and processes used to facilitate better decisions by managers.

Demand-pull inflation Price inflation which results from excessive demand for goods and services relative to their supply.

Demography The study of population characteristics.

Devaluation A reduction in the value of one currency in relation to other currencies.

Direct marketing Direct communication between a seller and individual customers using a promotion method other than face-to-face selling.

Discriminatory pricing Selling a product at two or more prices, where the difference in prices is not based on differences in costs.

Economics of scale Costs per unit fall as output rises.

Ecu The unit of currency used within member states of the EU which are full members of the European Monetary System.

Elasticity of demand The change in volume of demand for a product in response to a change in some parameter, e.g. the price of the product.

Electronic commerce Transactions of goods or services for which payment occurs over the Internet or other wide area networks.

Entrepreneur An individual who takes risks to profitably exploit business opportunities.

Environment Everything that exists outside the boundaries of a system.

Environmental set The elements within an organization's environment which are currently of major concern to it.

Ethics A culturally defined understanding of what is right and wrong.

EU The European Union, formerly known as the European Community (EC).

Exchange rate The price of one currency expressed in terms of another currency.

Exclusion clause A clause in a contract which excludes or restricts liability of one party to the other.

External benefits Product benefits for which the producer cannot appropriate from recipients.

External costs Production costs which are borne by individuals or firms who are not compensated for the costs they incur.

Factors of production The inputs to a value creation process, commonly defined as land, labour and capital (entrepreneurship is often included).

Fiscal policy Government policy on public borrowing, spending and taxation.

Five forces Porter's model of the competitive environment of any firm, which comprises the threat of new entrants and substitute products, the bargaining powers of customers and suppliers, and competition among current competitors.

Franchise An agreement where a franchisor develops a good service format and marketing strategy and sells the right for other individuals or organizations ('franchisees') to use that format.

Geodemographics The study of consumer behaviour based on an individual's area of residence.

Globalization A tendency to treat the world as though it was part of an organization's domestic market.

Gross domestic product (GDP)   A measure of the value of goods and services produced in an economy during a specified period.

Gross national product (GNP)   Similar to GDP, but with the addition of net income earned from overseas investments (after deducting investments remitted overseas).

Horizontal integration   Merging of firms' activities at a similar point in a value chain.

Human resource management   Management activity related to the effective and efficient recruitment, training, motivation, reward and control of an organization's employees.

Imperfect market   A market in which the assumptions of perfect competition are violated.

Implied term   A term in a contract which is understood by the parties, but not explicitly written into it.

Income elasticity of demand   A measure of the responsiveness of demand for a product to changes in household incomes.

Inflation   A rise in the general level of prices of goods and services.

Intermediaries   Individuals or organizations who are involved in transferring goods and services from the producer to the final consumer.

Internal marketing   The application of the principles and practices of marketing to an organization's dealings with its employees.

Investment   Expenditure on products which are not consumed immediately, but which will yield further economic benefits in the future.

Invisible trade   Overseas trade in services, as distinct from 'visible' goods.

Joint venture   An agreement between two or more firms to exploit a business opportunity, in which capital funding, profits, risk and core competencies are shared.

Just-in-time delivery   Reliably getting products to customers just before customers need them.

Knowledge   Information which incorporates the concept of beliefs that are based on information.

Learning organizaton   An organization that learns about its environment and adapts to change through effective information sharing and decision-making activities.

Lobbying   Seeking to influence decisions by other individuals/organizations.

Macroeconomics   The study of the working of large scale economic systems.

Marginal cost   The addition to total cost resulting from the production of one additional unit of output.

Market   A place (actual or virtual) where buyers and sellers meet to exchange things of value.

Market economy   An economy which distributes goods and services on the basis of consumers' decisions rather than centrally planned allocation.

Market failure   A situation where the assumptions underlying competitive markets break down, resulting in inefficient and ineffective distribution of goods and services.

Market segmentation A process identifying groups of customers with a broad product market who share similar needs and respond similarly to a given marketing mix formulation.

Marketing The management process which identifies, anticipates and supplies customer requirements efficiently and profitably (CIM definition).

Marketing audit A systematic review of a company's marketing activities and of its marketing environment.

Marketing mix The aspects of marketing strategy and tactics that marketing management use to gain a competitive advantage over its competitors. A conceptual framework which usually includes elements labelled product, price, promotion, place, people, physical evidence and processes.

Matrix organization An organization structure which relies on coordination of management functions, rather than a strict hierarchical functional control.

Merger The amalgamation of two or more organizations.

Microeconomics The study of the behaviour of individual economic units (e.g. consumers and firms).

Misrepresentation A false statement made by one party in a contract.

Mission statement A means of reminding everyone within an organization of the essential purpose of the organization.

Monetarism A view of the national economy which attributes instability in the economy to issues of money supply.

Money supply The amount of money in an economy.

Monopoly A market in which there is only one supplier. Rarely achieved in practice, as most products have some form of substitute.

Multiplier effect The addition to total income and expenditure within an economy resulting from an initial injection of expenditure.

Needs The underlying forces that drive an individual to make a purchase and thereby satisfy that individual's needs.

Oligopoly A market dominated by a few interdependent suppliers.

Perfect competition A market in which there are no barriers to entry, no one firm can dominate the market, there is full information available to all buyers and sellers, and all sellers sell an undifferentiated product.

Positioning Developing a marketing mix which gives an organization a competitive advantage within its chosen target market.

Pressure group A group which is formed to promote a particular cause.

Price elasticity of demand A measure of the responsiveness of demand for a product to change in the price of the product.

Privatization Government policy to transfer economic activity from the public to the private sector.

Product mix The total range of goods and services offered by an organization.

Productivity The efficiency with which inputs are turned into outputs.

Profit The excess of revenue over costs (although it can be difficult to calculate costs, and therefore profit).

Quality The standard of delivery of goods or services, often expressed in terms of the extent to which they meet customers' expectations.

Reference groups   Individuals or groups of individuals that a person seeks to associate their identity with.

Relationship marketing   A means by which organizations seek to maintain an ongoing relationship between itself and its customers, based on continuous patterns of service delivery, rather than isolated and discrete transactions.

Scenario   A hypothetical picture of an environment which may occur in the future.

Services   Essentially intangible product offers which do not result in the ownership of anything.

SMEs   Small and medium sized enterprises.

Social responsibility   Accepting corporate responsibilities to customers and non-customers which go beyond legal or contractual requirements.

Sole trader   A business the identity of which is indistinguishable from that of its owner.

Stakeholder   Any person with an interest in the activities of an organization (e.g. customers, employees, government agencies, and local communities).

SWOT   An organization's internal Strengths and Weaknesses, matched against its extrenal Opportunities and Threats.

Trading Bloc   An agreement between a group of nations to make trade between members easier than trade with other countries.

Value chain   The sequence of activities and organizations involved in transforming a product from one which is of low value to one that is of high value.

Vertical integration   The extension of a firm's activities to prior or subsequent points in a value chain.

Virtual organization   An organization which has no physical manifestation, but is made up of formal and informal networks of parties.

Visible trade   Overseas trade in manufactured goods.

Index of authors cited

Index of organizations and brands cited

Subject index